MW00768396

AFFORDABLE TO BUILD HOME DESIGNS

5th Edition

A collection of 300 of our finest affordable-to-build residential designs culled from the portfolios of award-winning architects and designers across the country.

the Garlinghouse company

the
Garlinghouse
company

Affordable to Build, 5th Edition

Printed and bound in the USA.

James D. McNair III, *CEO & Publisher*
Steve Culpepper, *Editorial Director*
Debbie Cochran, *Managing Editor*
Christopher Berrien, *Art Director*
Debra Novitch, *Assistant Art Director*
Andrew Russell and Melani Gonzalez, *Production Artists*

Color Section Design by Melani Gonzalez

The photographed homes may have been modified to suit individual tastes.

Submit all Canadian plan orders
to the following address:
Garlinghouse Company, 102 Ellis Street, Penticton, BC V2A 4L5

Library of Congress: 97-77625
ISBN: 1-893536-01-7

Table of Contents

Cover plan #24245, featured on page p.18, Photography by John Ehrenclou

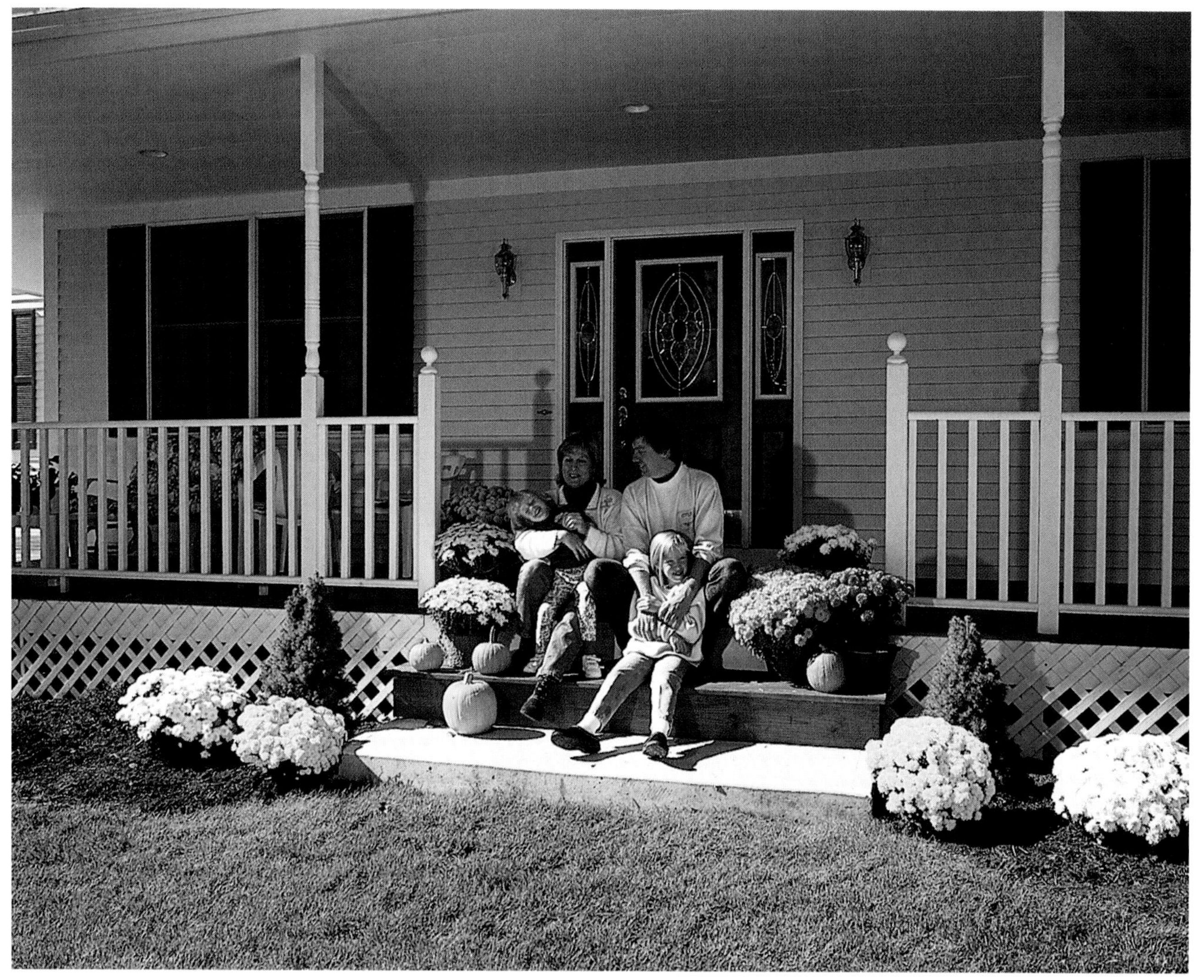

Efficiency with a Flair

Classic Styling Creates a Pleasingly Livable Home

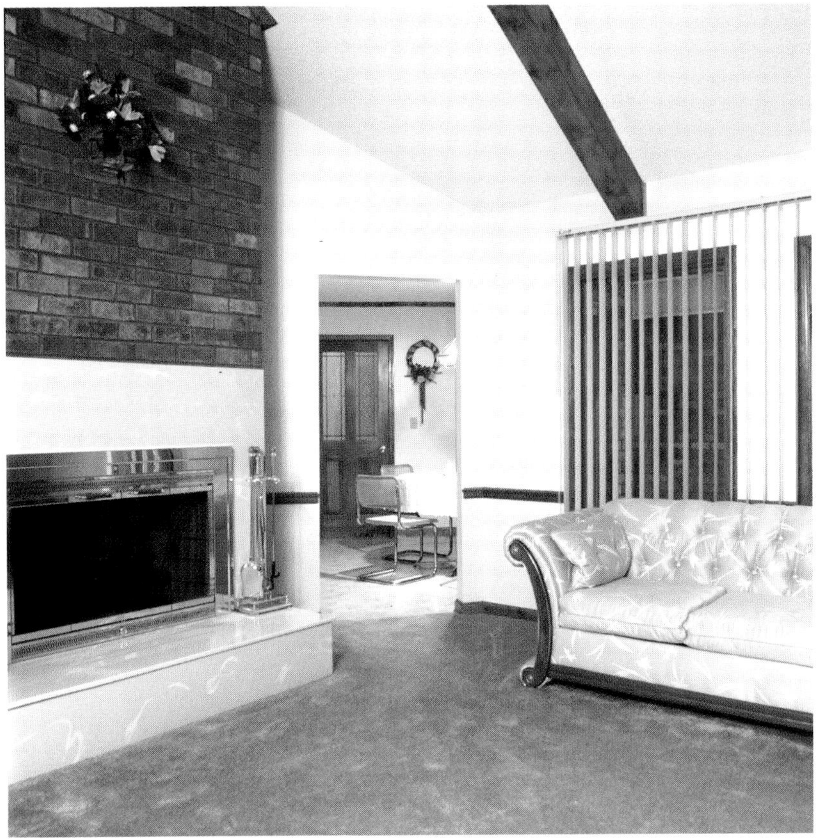

Every nook and cranny in this sophisticated brick bungalow is thoughtfully utilized, from the hidden two-car garage to the trapezoid-shaped kitchen with its sunny breakfast nook, pantry and adjoining utility room. And it is achieved with style and attention to detail.

For example, the family room, which features rustic ceiling beams, a built-in bar and floor-to-ceiling brick fireplace with raised hearth, is designed to capture the maximum in natural light and outdoor views. Three tall windows along the back wall lead the eye to the adjacent patio and backyard landscaping, and fill the room with sunshine. The family room is also centrally located, separating the main bedroom wing from a private bedroom that is ideally situated for an au pair or in-laws.

Additional amenities include a master bath with his and her closets, private lavatory, garden tub, roomy shower stall and separate vanities.

top left In the family room, stained wood chair railing and ceiling beams contrast nicely with the marble fireplace surround, providing an aesthetically pleasing mix of formal and informal.

left The raised cathedral cabinet doors and unusual transom window in the kitchen help set an updated Country tone, which is carried into the breakfast nook.

above Speckled brick and roof shingles complement curved windows and decorative quoining to create a cozy, inviting look for this attractive one-level home.

Design 22004

Price Code	D
Total Finished	2,070 sq. ft.
Main Finished	2,070 sq. ft.
Garage Unfinished	474 sq. ft.
Dimensions	52'x68'6"
Foundation	Slab
Bedrooms	4
Baths	2 full 1 three-quarter
Roof Framing	Stick
Exterior Walls	2x4

PHOTOGRAPHY BY
John Ehrenclou

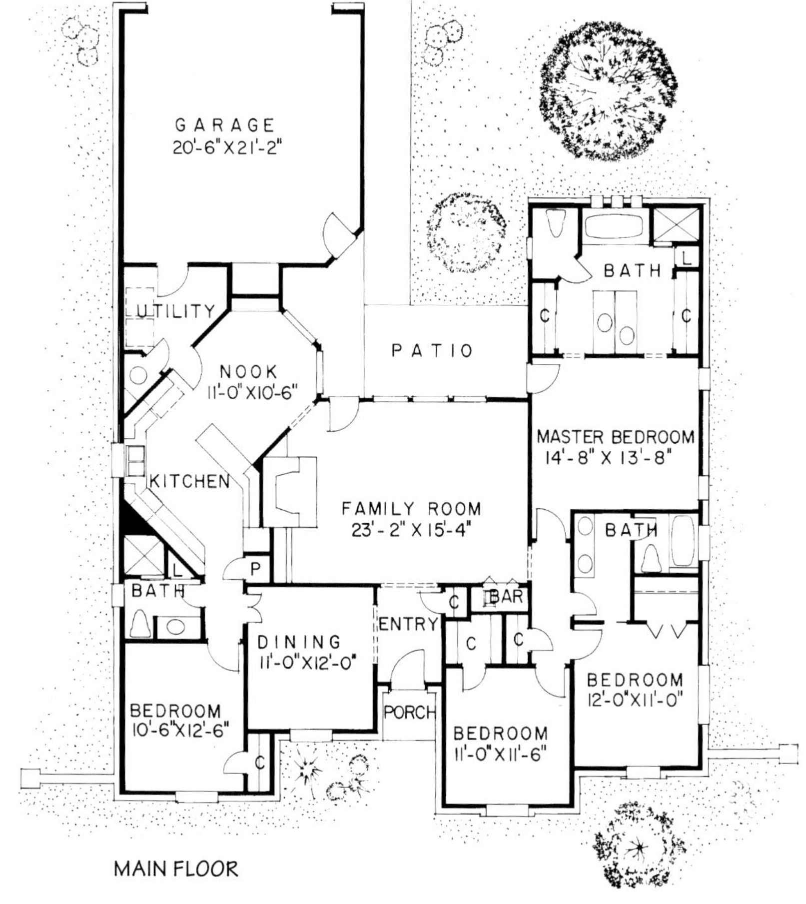
GARAGE
20'-6"X21'-2"
UTILITY
NOOK
11'-0"X10'-6"
PATIO
BATH
MASTER BEDROOM
14'-8" X 13'-8"
KITCHEN
FAMILY ROOM
23'-2" X 15'-4"
BATH
BATH
BAR
ENTRY
DINING
11'-0"X12'-0"
BEDROOM
10'-6"X12'-6"
PORCH
BEDROOM
11'-0"X11'-6"
BEDROOM
12'-0"X11'-0"

MAIN FLOOR

Brick Chic

Details Create Affordable Elegance

above Hidden at the back of the house lies a fabulous surprise: the soft sophistication of the dining room bay, wrapped in the embrace of a spacious patio with sturdy decked flooring.

Style is the name of the game in this elegant three-bedroom ranch. Featuring a focused floor plan strong on shared, informal spaces, it transforms those spaces into high-fashion statements with classic devices like Palladian windows and decorative pillars.

Take a look at the dining room. The spacious windowed bay forms an exquisite semicircle that extends onto the planked patio, flooding the eating and kitchen areas with warm, natural light. In the family room, striking arched openings mark the entrances from the foyer and kitchen, and extend along its entire rear portion. Each arch is delineated by stately columns.

These same architectural elements are carried outside to ensure design continuity and a smooth transition of form and function. The stepped exterior lines and long, low-slung roofline create instant curb appeal, while the low-maintenance brick facade assures time for pursuing things far more enjoyable than seasonal upkeep.

above A series of hipped-roof bumpouts, arresting window designs and use of ornamental brick lend a fresh yet refined look to this very attractive single-level home.

Design 22020

Price Code	C
Total Finished	1,772 sq. ft.
Main Finished	1,772 sq. ft.
Garage Unfinished	469 sq. ft.
Dimensions	77'8"x50'
Foundation	Slab
Bedrooms	3
Full Baths	2
Roof Framing	Stick
Exterior Walls	2x4

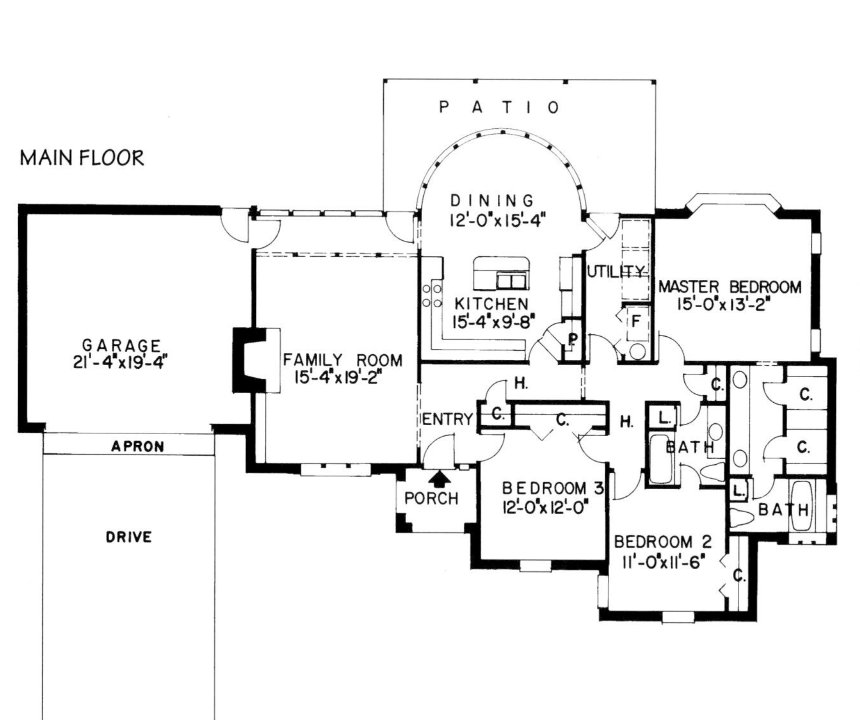
MAIN FLOOR
PATIO
DINING
12'-0"x15'-4"
KITCHEN
15'-4"x9'-8"
UTILITY
MASTER BEDROOM
15'-0"x13'-2"
GARAGE
21'-4"x19'-4"
FAMILY ROOM
15'-4"x19'-2"
P
F
H.
C.
ENTRY
C.
C.
H.
L.
BATH
C.
C.
APRON
PORCH
BEDROOM 3
12'-0"x12'-0"
L.
BATH
BEDROOM 2
11'-0"x11'-6"
C.
DRIVE

PHOTOGRAPHY BY
John Ehrenclou

Cozy Stone Cottage

The Ultimate in Single-Level Living

PHOTOGRAPHY BY
John Ehrenclou

A combination of hip and pitched roof lines cap this charming bungalow with style, while the recessed front door shelters all who enter from the weather.

Looking for a compact home with loads of light and character? You've found it. The uncluttered layout and abundant window in this floor plan complement imaginative use of decorative elements like sloped ceilings to create a sense of height and spaciousness you would not expect in a bungalow footprint.

Likewise, the sunken living room — delineated by a handsome wet bar, built-in bench seat flanked by boxed planters, and sophisticated wall angles — remains open to primary traffic and gathering areas. The patio (shown here as a sunroom with tiled floor and skylights) brings the outdoors inside and allows living space to spill outside.

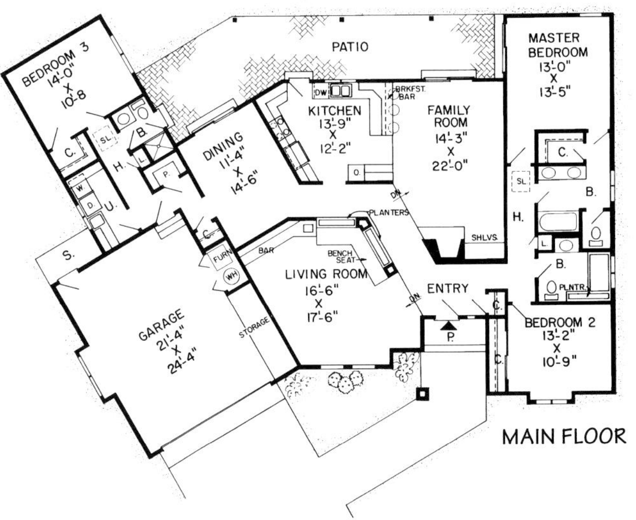

PATIO
BEDROOM 3
14'-0"
X
10'-8"
MASTER
BEDROOM
13'-0"
X
13'-5"
KITCHEN
13'-9"
X
12'-2"
BRKFST. BAR
FAMILY
ROOM
14'-3"
X
22'-0"
DINING
11'-4"
X
14'-6"
PLANTERS
BENCH SEAT
BAR
LIVING ROOM
16'-6"
X
17'-6"
SHLVS.
ENTRY
GARAGE
21'-4"
X
24'-4"
STORAGE
BEDROOM 2
13'-2"
X
10'-9"

MAIN FLOOR

The French doors, tiled flooring, skylights and a veritable wall of windows in this beautifully designed sunroom creates an instant outdoor environment while providing all the comforts of home.

Design 10508

Price Code	E
Total Finished	2,251 sq. ft.
Main Finished	2,251 sq. ft.
Garage Unfinished	533 sq. ft.
Dimensions	78'6"x55'4"
Foundation	Crawlspace
Bedrooms	3
Baths	2 full, 1 half
Roof Framing	Stick
Exterior Walls	2x6

Classic New England Country

The Charm of Yesteryear, the Amenities of Today

PHOTOGRAPHY COURTESY OF
Alan Mascord Design Associates

Brick and wood siding, raised-panel shutters and a spacious front porch combine to create this home's pleasing countrified façade.

Are you looking for a home that successfully melds areas for family fun and formal entertaining? A home with the architectural finesse of French doors and arched entry ways as well as the casual ambience of a fireplace and front porch swing? If so, this is the floor plan for you.

Elements that show for your taste for the finer things in life include elegant ceiling treatments in the dining room and two back bedrooms, a formal living room, and a master bedroom suite with every amenity: dramatic vaulted ceilings, his and her closets, a dressing area and double vanity.

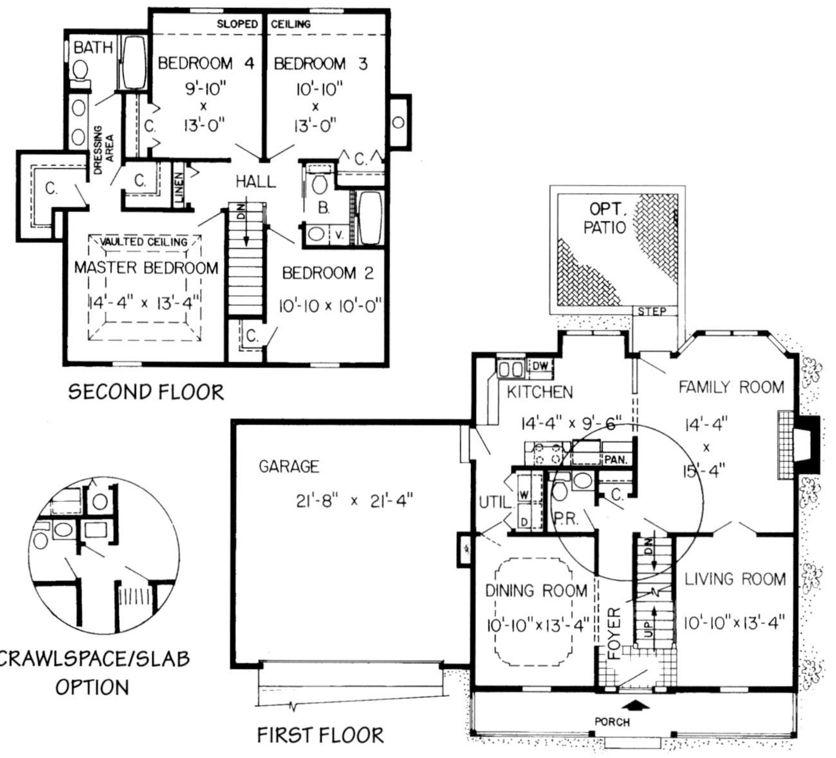
SLOPED CEILING
BATH
BEDROOM 4
9'-10" x 13'-0"
BEDROOM 3
10'-10" x 13'-0"
DRESSING AREA
C.
HALL
LINEN
B.
V.
VAULTED CEILING
MASTER BEDROOM
14'-4" x 13'-4"
BEDROOM 2
10'-10 x 10'-0"
DN
SECOND FLOOR
OPT. PATIO
STEP
DW
KITCHEN
14'-4" x 9'-6"
FAMILY ROOM
14'-4" x 15'-4"
GARAGE
21'-8" x 21'-4"
PAN.
UTIL
W
D
P.R.
DN
DINING ROOM
10'-10"x13'-4"
FOYER
UP
LIVING ROOM
10'-10"x13'-4"
PORCH
FIRST FLOOR
CRAWLSPACE/SLAB OPTION

Design 34027

Price Code	C
Total Finished	1,960 sq. ft.
First Finished	955 sq. ft.
Second Finished	1,005 sq. ft.
Basement Unfinished	930 sq. ft.
Garage Unfinished	484 sq. ft.
Dimensions	52'x31'
Foundation	Basement Crawlspace, Slab
Bedrooms	4
Baths	2 full, 1 half
Roof Framing	Stick
Exterior Walls	2x4, 2x6

Woodland Escape

The Perfect Plan to Create Serious Cabin Fever

If you've ever dreamed of building a cabin in the woods for weekend get-aways and relaxing vacations, this stunningly simple home may be just what the doctor ordered.

Outside, pitched gable ends with decorative barge-board, and natural clapboard and shingle siding complement the four-over-four double-hung windows, creating a rustic impression that is at once inviting and familiar. And the dual wing design, separated by the understated covered entrance, builds an expectation of summer camp quarters.

Inside, however, the scene changes dramatically to sophisticated angles and polished wood. Overhead paned windows, strategically placed on the exterior to look like your ordinary second floor variety, unexpectedly pour light into the living room and bedrooms. Since this floor plan is one level only, the interior impact of these seemingly standard windows is immediate and extraordinary.

Other features capture the eye and imagination, as well. A freestanding stone fireplace backed by double-sided contemporary shelving and built-ins adds to the countrified cosmopolitan ambience, and features a charming mantle beam for displaying dried floral arrange-ments or favorite collectibles.

Hardwood floors gleam throughout, adding to the warmth of natural materials underfoot. Above, knotty pine ceilings, soffits and cathedral slopes draw attention

above The homespun character of this picturesque cabin builds on the beauty of its natural surroundings with shingle siding and stark simplicity, all of which belie the wonders within.

opposite Imagine curling up by the magnificent mortared stone fireplace with a cup of hot chocolate and the latest best seller while rain beats on the roof or snow piles in soft drifts outside.

above Natural light streams into the front bedroom, where unadorned paned windows sandwiched between the planked ceiling and floor carry through the pleasing elements of the cabin's refined country interior theme.

right In the galley-shaped kitchen, cottage-style cabinetry open to the knotty pine boards overhead provides ample room for theme decorating, such as silk plants, tins or colorful bins.

to the soaring heights within, and instill the main gathering areas with an easy-going attitude.

The two bedrooms sit by themselves opposite the main living areas, both offering wonderful views of the surrounding woodsy environment, and share the cabin's single full bath.

Note how the French doors lead from the main entry hall directly onto the back deck, and again from the living room to the private porch.

The porch connects to the deck, which then steps down into the backyard — a perfect set up for outdoor entertaining. In fact, the porch can be used as an additional room in the summertime, extending the living room right out into the arms of nature.

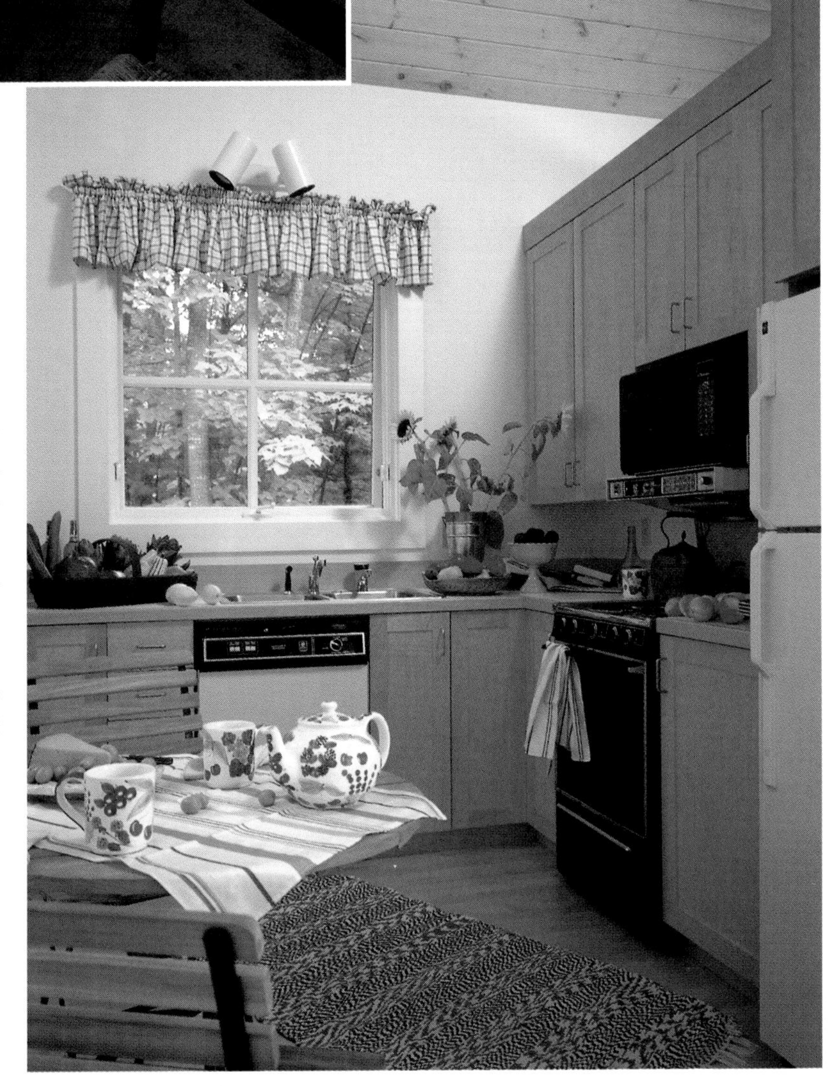

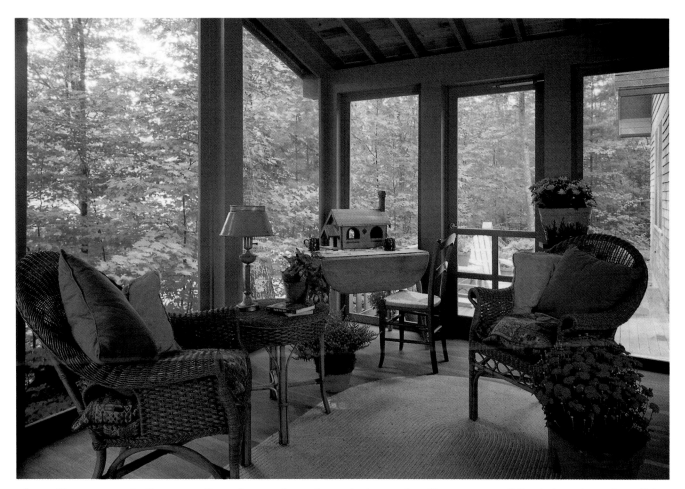

above The sunroom's floor-to-ceiling glass walls and sturdy beamed ceiling create a fully sheltered outdoor living environment where nature can be enjoyed in complete comfort.

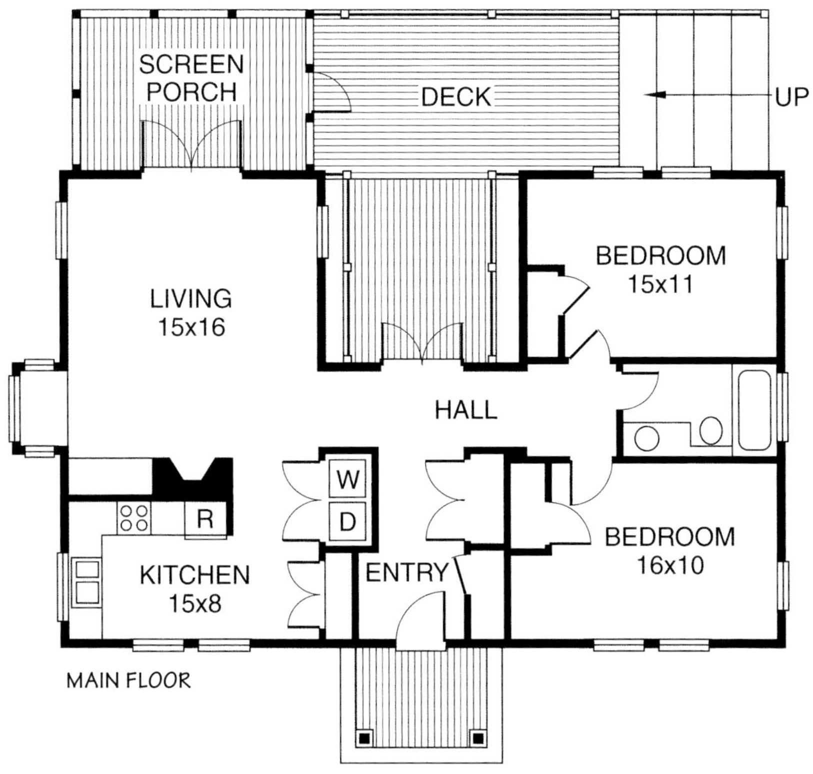

SCREEN PORCH
DECK
UP
LIVING 15x16
BEDROOM 15x11
HALL
W
D
R
KITCHEN 15x8
ENTRY
BEDROOM 16x10

MAIN FLOOR

Design 32122

Price Code	A
Total Finished	1,112 sq. ft.
Main Finished	1,112 sq. ft.
Basement Unfinished	484 sq. ft.
Porch Unfinished	152 sq. ft.
Dimensions	47'x45'6"
Foundation	Basement Crawlspace
Bedrooms	2
Full Baths	1
Main Ceiling	9'
Vaulted Ceiling	18'9"
Roof Framing	Stick
Exterior Walls	2x6

PHOTOGRAPHY COURTESY OF
The Meredith Corporation

Contemporary Colonial Allure

Unexpected Architectural Elements Adds Style and Personality

above Sidelights surrounding the formal front door and a right wing with an unexpected roofline peak set this house apart from traditional colonials.

Surprise is the operative word for this updated Colonial gem, designed to ingeniously shroud its soaring contemporary interior with a traditional exterior. From an asymmetrical clerestory stair balcony to the warmth of solid hardwood floors, there is much to appreciate in the home's artful fusion of old and new.

It all begins with the quaintly columned front porch that presents a charming face to the neighborhood and beckons you over the threshold. Once inside, you are greeted by vast, open spaces and the drama of sloped ceilings. In keeping with the combined architectural character of the unique floor plan, steps set off by customary painted rails and maple/oak banisters lead from the living room to the sunken dining room where hinged glass doors open onto a large rectangular deck.

A stone's throw away, in the U-shaped kitchen, a peninsula counter top provides extra space for food preparation and serves as a breakfast or snack bar.

The spacious family room is defined by a bank of windows and atrium doors, which fill the area with natural light and offer unobstructed views of the yard and deck. This gives the room an outdoor feeling, making it a handy back up when the weather doesn't allow entertaining outside. But its undisputed focal point it the stunningly simple bricked fireplace, stationed where its cheerful flames can be enjoyed by people gathered in the kitchen and dining room, as well as those in the room itself.

Upstairs, the stylistic synthesis continues with his and her closets and vanities, and opposing corner garden tub and shower in the master bedroom suite. Deliberately positioned across the back of the house, this area serves as the ultimate in private retreats.

Both secondary bedrooms front the upper level and lead into the hallway, which descends to the first floor via a double-balustraded staircase.

right Designed to bring the outdoors inside, the family room basks in natural light provided by valanced atrium doors, double windows and a thoughtfully placed skylight.

below The warm glow of wood resounds throughout this country kitchen with its burnished cathedral cabinet doors and clear maple floors. Above the sink, double windows overlook the deck and backyard – perfect for passing through delectable tidbits for outdoor grilling.

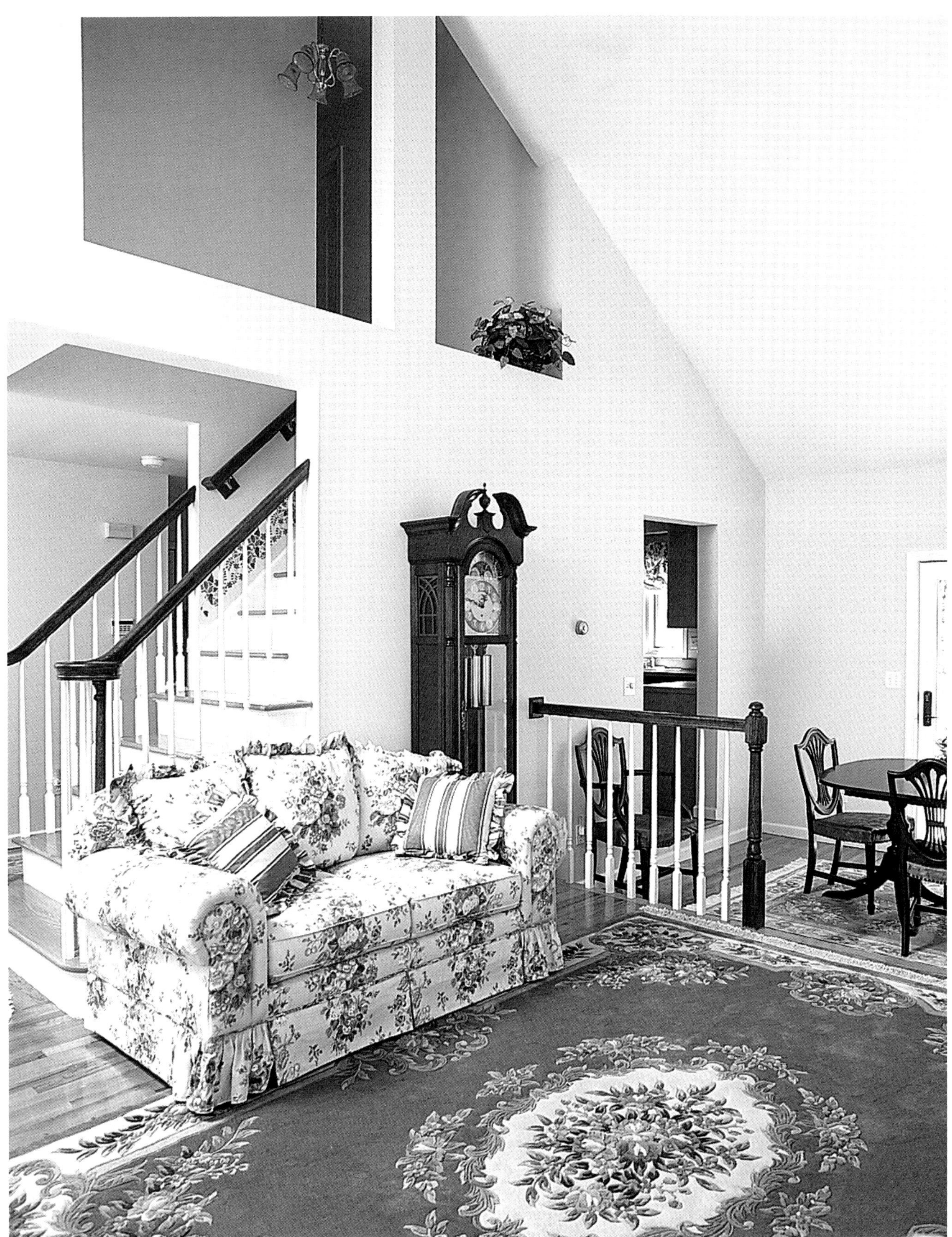

above Contemporary lines and traditional materials mesh beautifully in the inviting, yet formal, foyer/living room/dining room configuration, which offers an expansive view from the second-floor balcony.

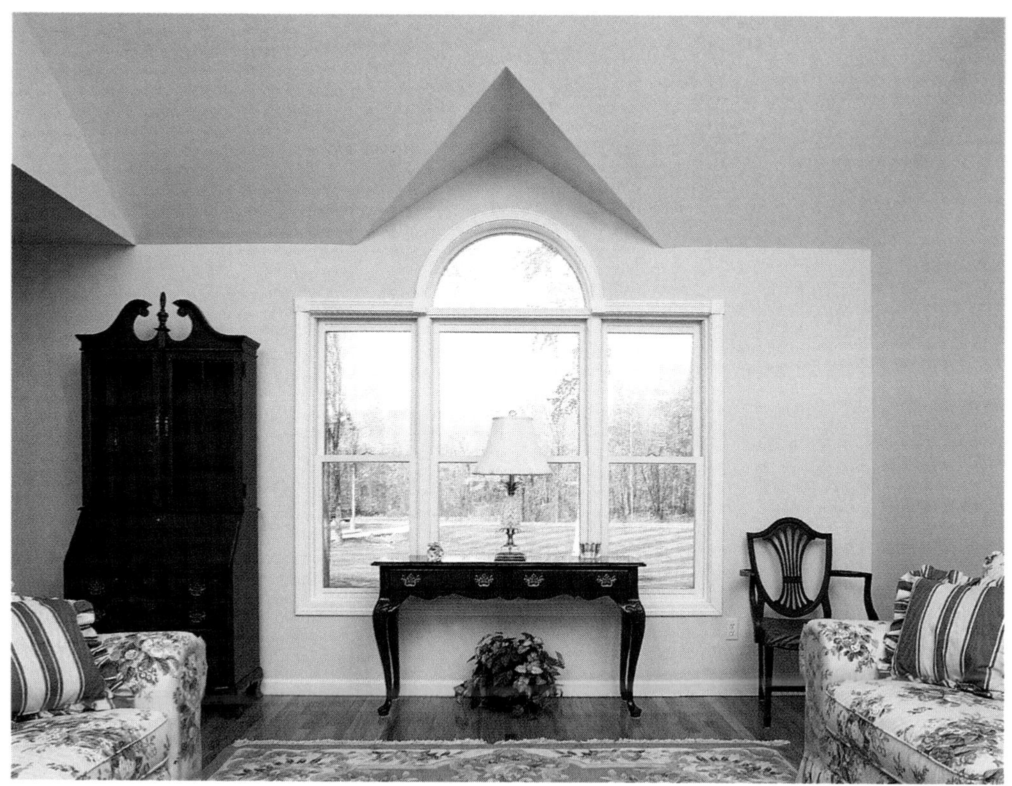

left In the formal living room, a unique triangular alcove just above the wall and ceiling junction draws the eye immediately to the elegant Palladian window, which works beautifully with the sloped ceiling to create extraordinary height and drama.

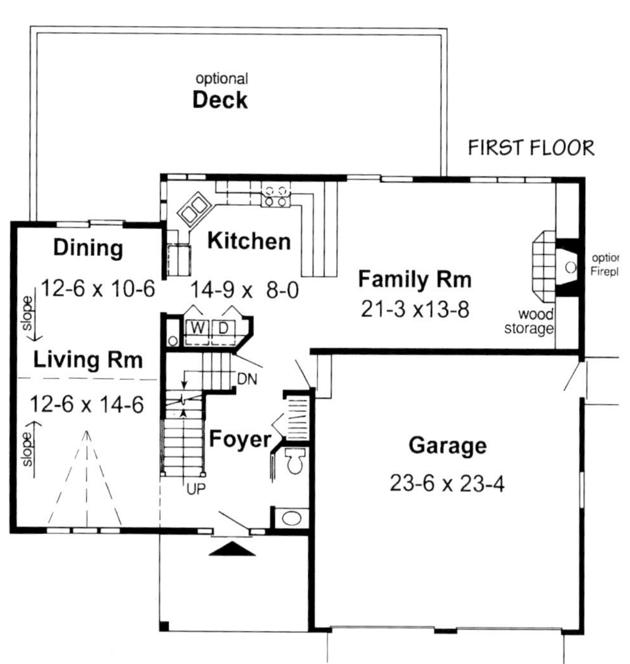
optional
Deck
FIRST FLOOR
Dining
12-6 x 10-6
Kitchen
14-9 x 8-0
Family Rm
21-3 x13-8
wood
storage
Living Rm
12-6 x 14-6
DN
Foyer
UP
Garage
23-6 x 23-4

Design 34878

Price Code	C
Total Finished	1,838 sq. ft.
First Finished	1,088 sq. ft.
Second Finished	750 sq. ft.
Basement Unfinished	750 sq. ft.
Garage Unfinished	517 sq. ft.
Dimensions	50'x36'8"
Foundation	Basement Crawlspace, Slab
Bedrooms	3
Baths	2 full, 1 half
Roof Framing	Stick
Exterior Walls	2x4, 2x6

PHOTOGRAPHY COURTESY OF
The Garlinghouse Company

D W

CRAWLSPACE/SLAB OPTION

SECOND FLOOR

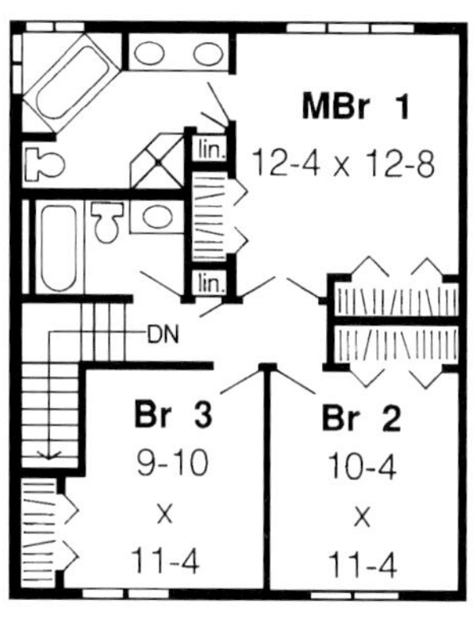
MBr 1
12-4 x 12-8
lin.
lin.
DN
Br 3
9-10
x
11-4
Br 2
10-4
x
11-4

A Bit of Victoriana

Simple, Elegant Lines Allow Gracious Living

This is a house designed for today's active lifestyles, with plenty of impressive touches for formal occasions and just the right amount of down-to-earth details to be totally practical.

The decorative columns and balustrades of the wrap-around porch create an initial sense of early Victorian, as do the gabled roofline, shutters and front door sidelights. Yet, because the basic lines are so simple, the overall effect is one of contemporary country charm. And that feeling is meticulously duplicated throughout the home's carefully designed interior.

From the moment you step into the spacious foyer, quiet gentility surrounds you. Hardwood floors gleam. The handsome stairway climbs to a second floor landing flooded with light from the Palladian window. Note the deep, elevated window seat tucked into its cushioned base. And don't overlook the built-in wooden shelving — the perfect place to showcase favorite knick-knacks, photos, artwork, books and memorabilia. There, too, a railed balcony opens over the entire entryway, offering exhilarating views into the living room and generous family room beyond.

That same balconied area provides a solid buffer between the two secondary bedrooms and master bedroom suite, which occupies one complete side of the upper level. Pocket doors lead into a master bath built to contain all the amenities — twin vanities, a corner shower stall and garden tub — in a comfortable, cozy space. The main bath also features twin vanities, so guests and/or children can move about without bumping elbows — an important consideration for those rush-around school mornings!

right The classic roofline with its steep gable pitches is complemented and softened by a Palladian-style transom window centered on the second floor.

above White painted cabinetry and mullioned windows contrast nicely with the natural warmth of hardwood floors, imbuing the kitchen with a clean, contemporary country look.

Downstairs, additional architectural treats, arresting half walls topped with columns lead into the living room where a fireplace welcomes guests, and provides intimacy for romantic interludes, executive entertaining, or holiday parties. At the same time, the half-wall design keeps the front section of the house open and airy, allowing light to flow through to the dining room on the opposite side of the foyer.

Behind the living room and dining room are the home's key gathering areas. Here, family time melds with the culinary arts and informal social activities. Mom or Dad can handle monthly bills at the built-in kitchen desk while the kids do their homework at the counter extension or in the adjoining family room. And the expansive deck, which borders the back perimeter of the house, adds plenty of outdoor living space.

right Who wouldn't want to snuggle up on this wonderful window seat? Add a few throw pillows, an afghan and an excellent book, and you've got a real Victorian hideaway!

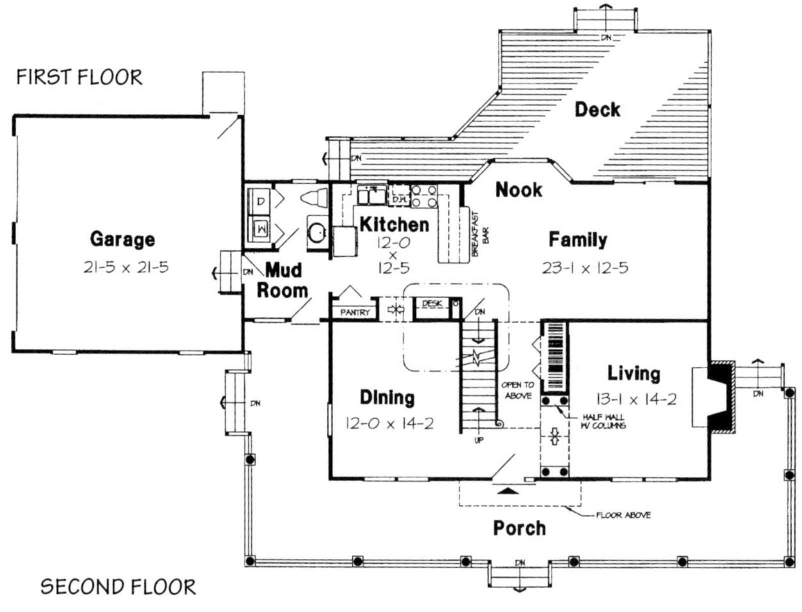

FIRST FLOOR
Deck
Nook
Kitchen
12-0 x 12-5
Family
23-1 x 12-5
Garage
21-5 x 21-5
Mud Room
PANTRY
DESK
Dining
12-0 x 14-2
Living
13-1 x 14-2
OPEN TO ABOVE
HALF WALL W/ COLUMNS
Porch
FLOOR ABOVE

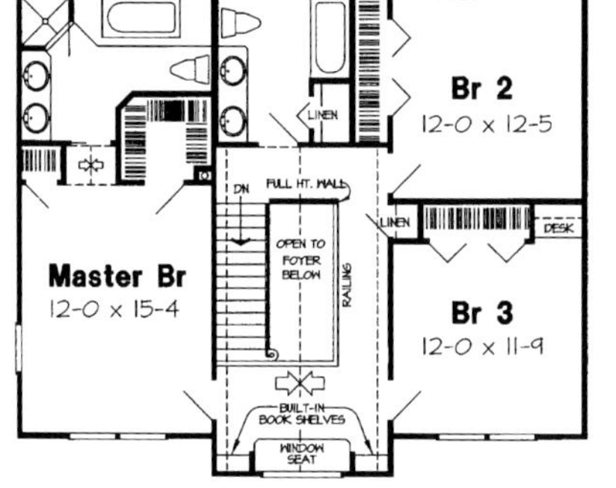

SECOND FLOOR
Br 2
12-0 x 12-5
LINEN
FULL HT. WALL
OPEN TO FOYER BELOW
RAILING
DESK
Master Br
12-0 x 15-4
Br 3
12-0 x 11-9
BUILT-IN BOOK SHELVES
WINDOW SEAT

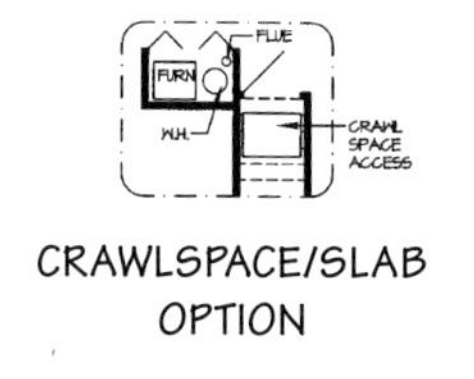

FLUE
FURN
W.H.
CRAWL SPACE ACCESS

CRAWLSPACE/SLAB OPTION

Design 24245

Price Code	D
Total Finished	2,083 sq. ft.
First Finished	1,113 sq. ft.
Second Finished	970 sq. ft.
Basement Unfinished	1,113 sq. ft.
Garage Unfinished	480 sq. ft.
Porch Unfinished	581 sq. ft.
Dimensions	74'x41'6"
Foundation	Basement Crawlspace, Slab
Bedrooms	3
Baths	2 full, 1 half
First Ceiling	8'
Second Ceiling	8'
Roof Framing	Stick
Exterior Walls	2x4, 2x6

PHOTOGRAPHY BY
John Ehrenclou

Updated Four-Square

The Perfect Plan for Any Lot

PHOTOGRAPHY COURTESY OF
Alan Mascord Design Associates

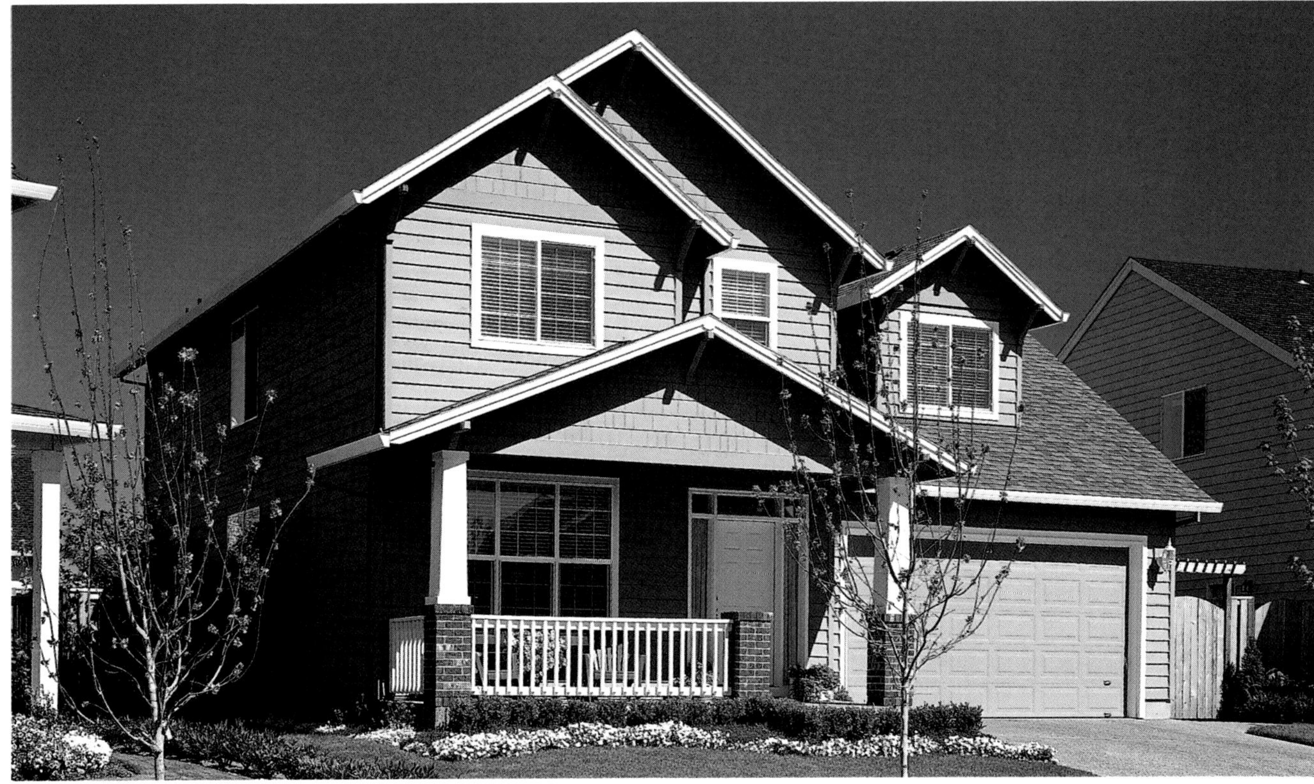

The period façade of this winsome home harkens back to the early 20th century when compact four-squares were favored over rambling Victorians and Colonials. Like its predecessors, this home packs lot of living into its stylized square footage.

Much of the first floor is unobstructed by walls, with arch-and-column configurations serving as the sole delineation for the dining area. The Great room and eat-in kitchen are backed by abundant windows, which allow light to stream in unhindered. The second floor features an expansive, windowed bonus room over the garage — perfect for games, exercise equipment or a home office.

Design 81033

Price Code	C
Total Finished	1,946 sq. ft.
First Finished	1,082 sq. ft.
Second Finished	864 sq. ft.
Bonus Unfinished	358 sq. ft.
Garage Unfinished	620 sq. ft.
Dimensions	40'x52'
Foundation	Crawlspace
Bedrooms	4
Baths	2 full, 1 half
First Ceiling	9'
Second Ceiling	8'
Roof Framing	Stick/Truss
Exterior Walls	2x6

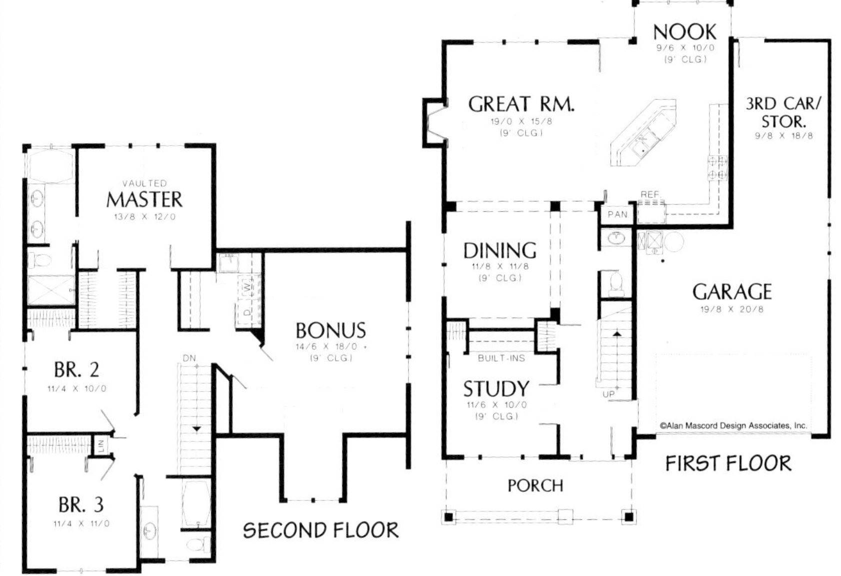
VAULTED
MASTER
13/8 X 12/0
BR. 2
11/4 X 10/0
BR. 3
11/4 X 11/0
DN
BONUS
14/6 X 18/0 +
(9' CLG)
SECOND FLOOR
NOOK
9/6 X 10/0
(9' CLG)
GREAT RM.
19/0 X 15/8
(9' CLG)
3RD CAR/
STOR.
9/8 X 18/8
REF
PAN
DINING
11/8 X 11/8
(9' CLG)
GARAGE
19/8 X 20/8
BUILT-INS
STUDY
11/6 X 10/0
(9' CLG)
UP
PORCH
FIRST FLOOR
©Alan Mascord Design Associates, Inc.

Enchanting Hillside Cottage

Period Touches Create a Home with Personality

PHOTOGRAPHY COURTESY OF
Jannis Vann & Associates, Inc.

Cozy and comfortable, this home welcomes you with a quaint front porch, lightly gingerbreaded to recall the decorative motifs of the Victorian era.

Adaptable to sloped lots, this floor plan is ideal for young executive families or retired couples.

The foyer opens into the combined living/dining and kitchen areas, which is designed for easy traffic flow to the roomy breakfast nook and adjoining sundeck. The master bedroom suite, located on the opposite side of the house, is spacious without being ostentatious, and contains all the amenities.

The secondary bedrooms — both with charming sloped ceilings — are upstairs, as is the second full bath, and connect to abundant under-eave storage.

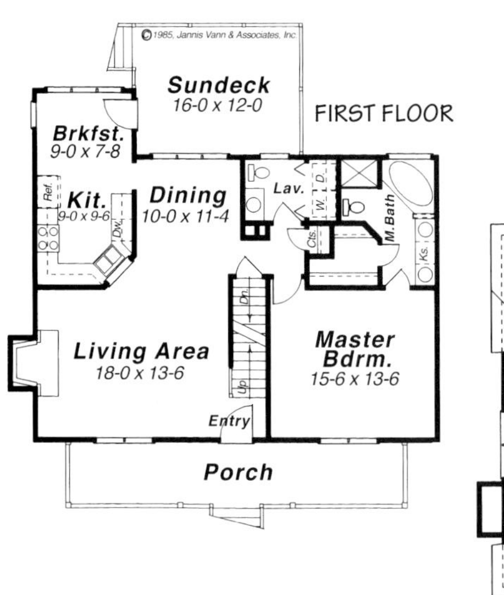

Sundeck
16-0 x 12-0
FIRST FLOOR
Brkfst.
9-0 x 7-8
Kit.
9-0 x 9-6
Dining
10-0 x 11-4
Lav.
M.Bath
Living Area
18-0 x 13-6
Master
Bdrm.
15-6 x 13-6
Entry
Porch

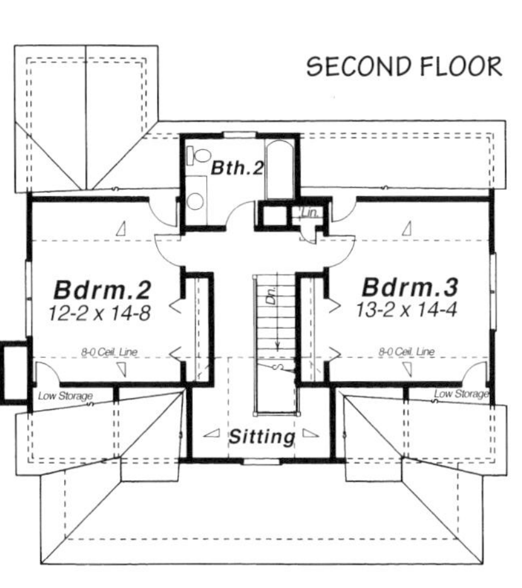

SECOND FLOOR
Bth.2
Bdrm.2
12-2 x 14-8
Bdrm.3
13-2 x 14-4
Sitting
Low Storage
Low Storage

Design 93269

Price Code	B
Total Finished	1,735 sq. ft.
First Finished	1,045 sq. ft.
Second Finished	690 sq. ft.
Basement Unfinished	465 sq. ft.
Garage Unfinished	580 sq. ft.
Dimensions	40'4"x44'
Foundation	Basement
Bedrooms	3
Baths	2 full, 1 half
First Ceiling	8'
Roof Framing	Stick
Exterior Walls	2x4

Carriage House Garage

A Plan That Proves Simple is Often Best

The garage becomes an important to this home's exterior appeal, with an updated carriage house hat lends character and space for two cars.

Inside, an open layout and various decorative elements immediately direct your eye to the left. There, an arched entryway bordered by striking columns frames the Great room with its tasteful fireplace and vaulted ceiling. Immediately behind lies the dining room, also with a vaulted ceiling and sliders that showcase backyard landscaping. The highly functional kitchen with its pantry, built-in desk and corner counter extension is situated across the hall from the den, which can serve as a third bedroom. The master bedroom suite is tucked behind the garage for maximum privacy.

Design 81036

Price Code	B
Total Finished	1,557 sq. ft.
Main Finished	1,557 sq. ft.
Garage Unfinished	434 sq. ft.
Dimensions	50'x50'
Foundation	Basement Crawlspace, Slab
Bedrooms	3
Full Baths	2
Main Ceiling	9'
Roof Framing	Truss
Exterior Walls	2x6

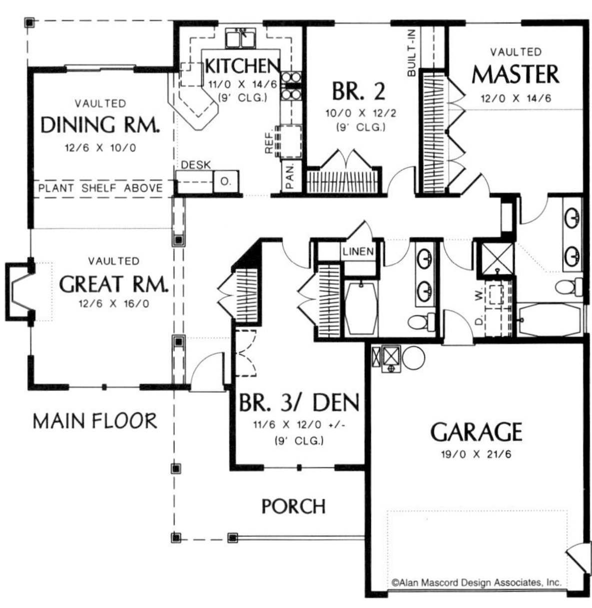
KITCHEN
11/0 X 14/6
(9' CLG.)
BR. 2
10/0 X 12/2
(9' CLG.)
BUILT-IN
VAULTED
MASTER
12/0 X 14/6
VAULTED
DINING RM.
12/6 X 10/0
DESK
REF.
PAN.
PLANT SHELF ABOVE
LINEN
VAULTED
GREAT RM.
12/6 X 16/0
BR. 3/ DEN
11/6 X 12/0 +/-
(9' CLG.)
MAIN FLOOR
GARAGE
19/0 X 21/6
PORCH
©Alan Mascord Design Associates, Inc.

Attractive and Efficient

A Lot of Living on a Single-Level

As you step through the front door, the foyer is flanked on one side by columns and arches opening into the formal dining and living rooms; French doors lead into the den on the other side. The family room and kitchen lie straightahead, complete with a generous brick fireplace and floor-to-ceiling built-ins, cheerful breakfast bay, and center island with plenty of space to accommodate conversation and food preparation.

Secondary hallways with pleasing angles lead to the laundry room and garage, and bedrooms. The master suite is stunning with a vaulted ceiling and skylights, double vanities, huge walk-in closet, garden tub and private lavatory.

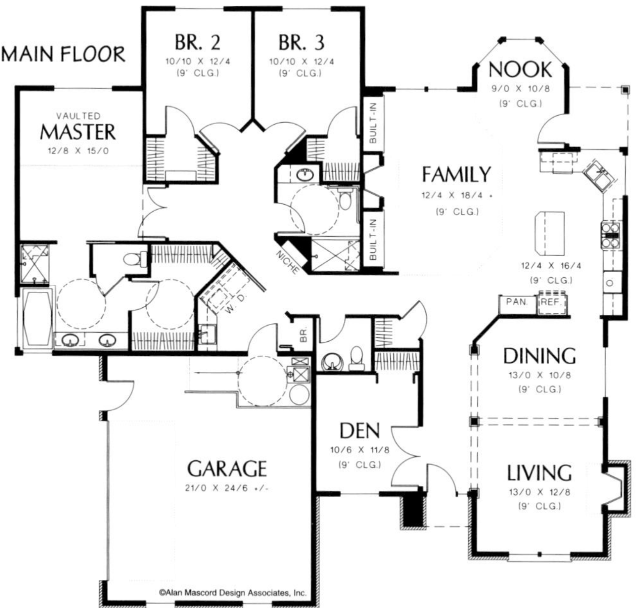
MAIN FLOOR
BR. 2
10/10 X 12/4
(9' CLG.)
BR. 3
10/10 X 12/4
(9' CLG.)
NOOK
9/0 X 10/8
(9' CLG.)
VAULTED
MASTER
12/8 X 15/0
BUILT-IN
FAMILY
12/4 X 18/4 +
(9' CLG.)
BUILT-IN
NICHE
W. D.
12/4 X 16/4
(9' CLG.)
PAN.
REF.
BR.
DINING
13/0 X 10/8
(9' CLG.)
DEN
10/6 X 11/8
(9' CLG.)
GARAGE
21/0 X 24/6 +/-
LIVING
13/0 X 12/8
(9' CLG.)
©Alan Mascord Design Associates, Inc.

Design 81038

Price Code	E
Total Finished	2,394 sq. ft.
Main Finished	2,394 sq. ft.
Garage Unfinished	543 sq. ft.
Dimensions	63'x60'
Foundation	Crawlspace
Bedrooms	4
Baths	2 full, 1 half
Main Ceiling	9'
Roof Framing	Truss
Exterior Walls	2x6

Dollhouse Delight

Victorian Detailing Sets this Home Apart

Reminiscent of the carriage house of old right down to the stone fireplace and foundation, this home contains everything you need for a cozy, comfortable lifestyle.

The sheltered front porch leads you right into the formal living room, set off by a dramatic vaulted ceiling and angled arched openings connected by columns. Just beyond is the shared kitchen/dining area, which is roomy enough for a large center island and pantry.

The home's left wing contains a full bath, two secondary bedrooms and a pleasing master bedroom suite.

Design 81037

Price Code	A
Total Finished	1,275 sq. ft.
Main Finished	1,275 sq. ft.
Garage Unfinished	440 sq. ft.
Dimensions	40'x58'
Foundation	Crawlspace
Bedrooms	3
Full Baths	2
Main Ceiling	9'
Roof Framing	Truss
Exterior Walls	2x6

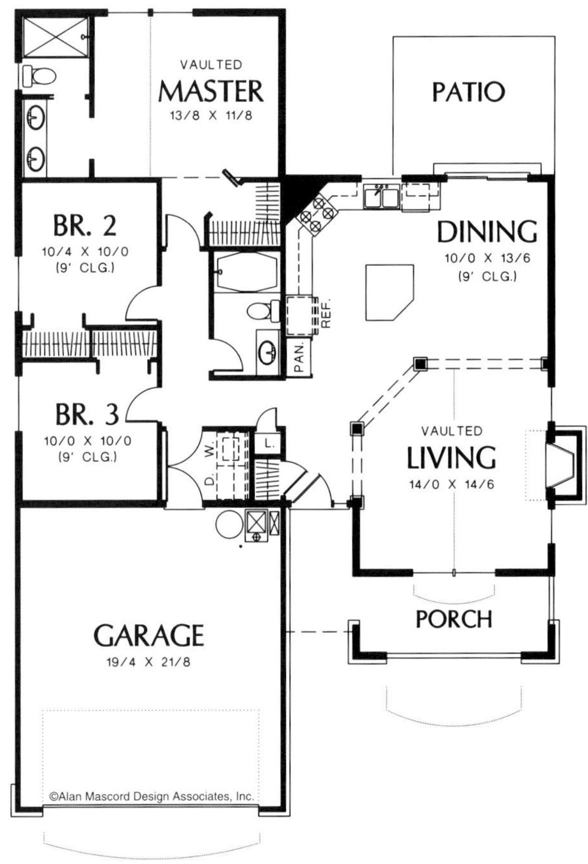
VAULTED
MASTER
13/8 X 11/8
PATIO
BR. 2
10/4 X 10/0
(9' CLG.)
DINING
10/0 X 13/6
(9' CLG.)
REF.
PAN.
BR. 3
10/0 X 10/0
(9' CLG.)
W.
D.
L.
VAULTED
LIVING
14/0 X 14/6
PORCH
GARAGE
19/4 X 21/8

MAIN FLOOR

Farmhouse Dream

Old and New Combine in Stunning Style

Enchanting elements from yesteryear make this home as delightful to look at as it is to live in. Doghouse Dormers, gable pitches, decorative bargeboard and spindled porch railings invite you inside, where the impressive two-story entryway sets the stage for interior drama. Amenities abound here: the living room with French doors and distinctive tray ceiling; the spacious kitchen with pantry, built-in desk and octagonal peninsula counter; the bright breakfast nook that leads out to a broad deck. At the top of the stairs, a custom seat beneath the lovely Palladian window beckons the weary, as does the luxurious whirlpool tub in the master bath. Note the generous closet space throughout and built-in desk in the front bedrooms.

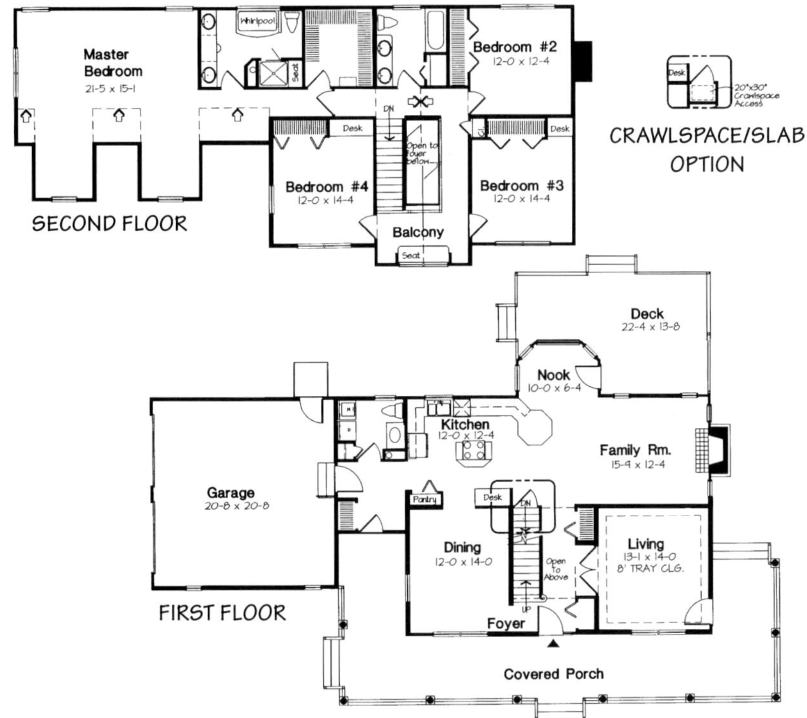

Master Bedroom 21-5 x 15-1
Whirlpool
Seat
Bedroom #2 12-0 x 12-4
DN
Desk
Open to Foyer Below
Desk
Bedroom #4 12-0 x 14-4
Bedroom #3 12-0 x 14-4
Balcony
Seat
SECOND FLOOR
Desk
20"x30" Crawlspace Access
CRAWLSPACE/SLAB OPTION
Deck 22-4 x 13-8
Nook 10-0 x 6-4
Kitchen 12-0 x 12-4
Family Rm. 15-4 x 12-4
Garage 20-8 x 20-8
Pantry
Desk
DN
Dining 12-0 x 14-0
Open To Above
Living 13-1 x 14-0 8' TRAY CLG.
UP
Foyer
FIRST FLOOR
Covered Porch

Design 24733

Price Code	F
Total Finished	2,673 sq. ft.
First Finished	1,148 sq. ft.
Second Finished	1,525 sq. ft.
Basement Unfinished	1,199 sq. ft.
Garage Unfinished	484 sq. ft.
Dimensions	74'x41'8"
Foundation	Basement Crawlspace Slab
Bedrooms	4
Baths	2 full, 1 half
First Ceiling	8'
Second Ceiling	8'
Roof Framing	Stick
Exterior Walls	2x4

Brick and Stone Sophistication

Keystones and Quoining Create Instant Curb Appeal

Beginning in the foyer, which spirals up two levels, the home's exterior grace is carried inside with dramatic use of arches and decorative pillars to delineate important gathering spaces. Note how the kitchen faces into the Great room, its boomerang-shaped counter angled to invite people to chat with the chef. And the sizeable breakfast nook allows ample room for informal dining. Also, don't overlook the seclusion of the first floor master bedroom suite.

The second floor, with its secondary bedrooms and sprawling bonus room, is open to the foyer below and frames the impressive view with attractive wood rails. Floor-to-ceiling bookshelves and a built-in computer desk border the front and side of the large landing.

Design 50004

Price Code	D
Total Finished	2,248 sq. ft.
First Finished	1,672 sq. ft.
Second Finished	576 sq. ft.
Bonus Unfinished	264 sq. ft.
Basement Unfinished	1,672 sq. ft.
Garage Unfinished	488 sq. ft.
Dimensions	60'x50'4"
Foundation	Basement
Bedrooms	3
Baths	2 full, 1 half
First Ceiling	8'
Second Ceiling	8'
Roof Framing	Truss
Exterior Walls	2x4

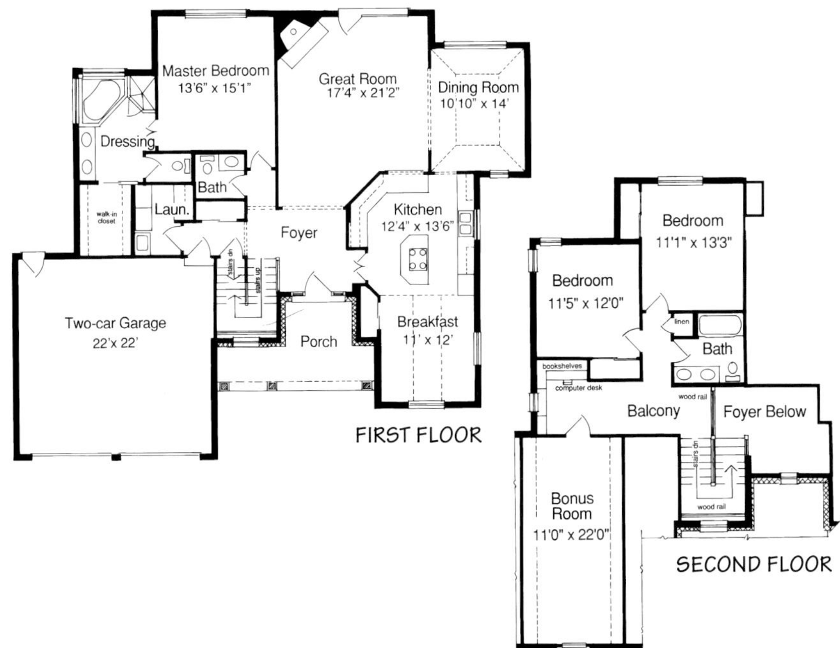
Master Bedroom
13'6" x 15'1"
Great Room
17'4" x 21'2"
Dining Room
10'10" x 14'
Dressing
Bath
Laun.
Foyer
Kitchen
12'4" x 13'6"
Two-car Garage
22'x 22'
Porch
Breakfast
11' x 12'
FIRST FLOOR
Bedroom
11'1" x 13'3"
Bedroom
11'5" x 12'0"
Bath
Balcony
Foyer Below
Bonus
Room
11'0" x 22'0"
SECOND FLOOR

Casually Cosmopolitan

The Ideal Look for a Heavily Wooded Lot

Natural wood shingles and mortared stone add warmth and texture to this unusual façade, which melds a variety of architectural elements to achieve a welcoming "lodge" look. Barn siding, cottage windows, and a six panel front door all work together to make a bold, yet charming, impression.

Such casual elegance characterizes this home's interior, as well. Imagine the entertaining possibilities of this floor plan! The expansive Great room, with its fireplace and imposing vaulted ceiling, sits wide open to the combined kitchen/dining area — with nothing to obstruct traffic flow. Beside it, the den also features the drama of a vaulted ceiling, as well as French doors leading to the soaring two-story foyer.

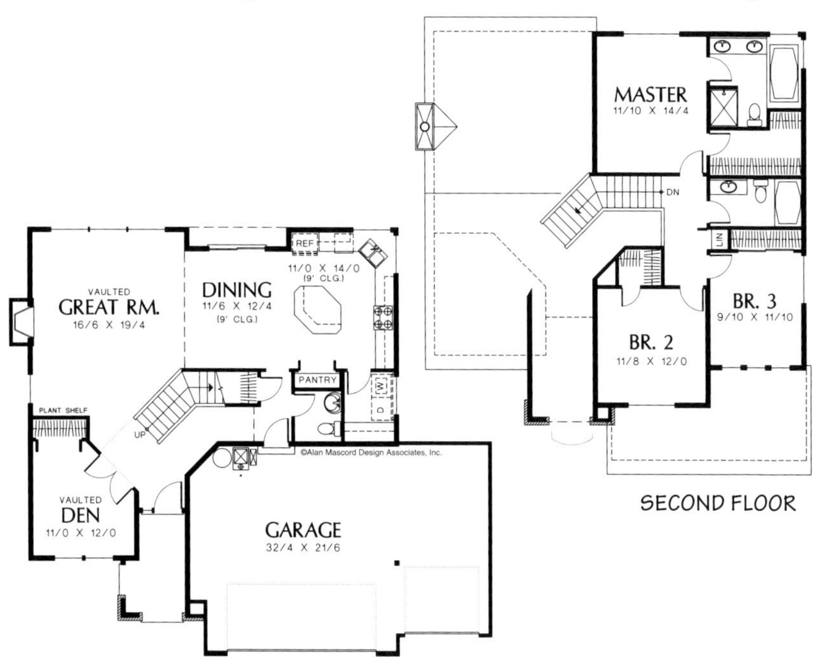

MASTER
11/10 X 14/4
DN
LIN
BR. 3
9/10 X 11/10
BR. 2
11/8 X 12/0
SECOND FLOOR
VAULTED
GREAT RM.
16/6 X 19/4
DINING
11/6 X 12/4
(9' CLG.)
REF
11/0 X 14/0
(9' CLG.)
PANTRY
W
D
PLANT SHELF
UP
VAULTED
DEN
11/0 X 12/0
GARAGE
32/4 X 21/6
©Alan Mascord Design Associates, Inc.
FIRST FLOOR

Design 81034

Price Code	C
Total Finished	1,893 sq. ft.
First Finished	1,087 sq. ft.
Second Finished	806 sq. ft.
Garage Unfinished	636 sq. ft.
Dimensions	40'x45'
Foundation	Crawlspace
Bedrooms	3
Baths	2 full, 1 half
First Ceiling	9'
Roof Framing	Stick
Exterior Walls	2x6

Stylish Ranch Retreat

Compact Comfort at an Affordable Price

Shake shingles, arched windows with decorative keystones, twin gables and a cozy, old-fashioned front porch turn this ranch into a real conversation piece. And the aesthetic delights don't stop at the double front doors.

Charming details, such as reveal ceilings in the dining room and master bedroom, create a sense of style — as does the decorative wood railing lining the left side of the dining room. Additionally, the living room is enhanced with ceiling beams and a fireplace that adds warmth and ambience to the main activity areas.

Design 24700

Price Code	A
Total Finished	1,312 sq. ft.
Main Finished	1,312 sq. ft.
Basement Unfinished	1,293 sq. ft.
Garage Unfinished	459 sq. ft.
Porch Unfinished	84 sq. ft.
Dimensions	50'x40'
Foundation	Basement Crawlspace, Slab
Bedrooms	3
Full Baths	2
Main Ceiling	8'
Roof Framing	Stick
Exterior Walls	2x6

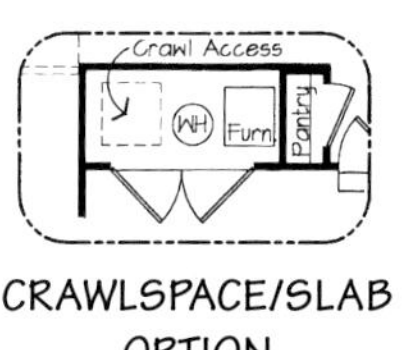
Crawl Access
WH
Furn.
Pantry

CRAWLSPACE/SLAB OPTION

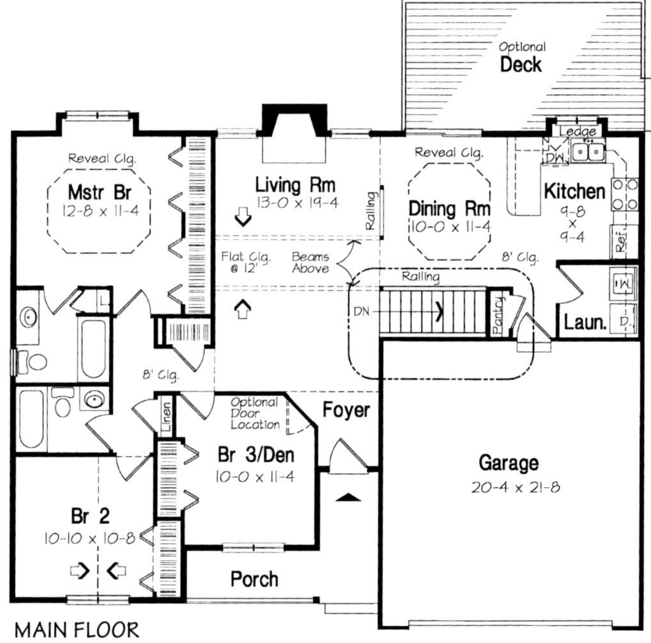
Optional
Deck
Reveal Clg.
Mstr Br
12-8 x 11-4
Living Rm
13-0 x 19-4
Reveal Clg.
Dining Rm
10-0 x 11-4
Kitchen
9-8 x 9-4
Ledge
DW
Ref.
Railing
Flat Clg. @ 12'
Beams Above
8' Clg.
Railing
DN
Pantry
W
D
Laun.
8' Clg.
Linen
Optional Door Location
Foyer
Br 3/Den
10-0 x 11-4
Garage
20-4 x 21-8
Br 2
10-10 x 10-8
Porch

MAIN FLOOR

Captivating Adirondack Cabin

Open Vistas and Room to Relax

Rustic doesn't get much better than this three-bedroom charmer. From the shed-roof porch to the mullioned windows and stone fireplace, every effort has been made to create the look and feel of amountain cabin.

The simplicity of the first-level all-purpose kitchen/ dining and living area is accentuated by 16-foot sloped ceilings, which lend light and loftiness to the space. The layout here is practical, with an L-shaped kitchen providing plenty of room for a center island. A stoop just outside the back door can be enclosed to house a washer and dryer or provide additional storage.

Upstairs — in a world of its own — the master bedroom also features sloped ceilings, plus plenty of corners and angles to achieve the cozy ambience of an attic room.

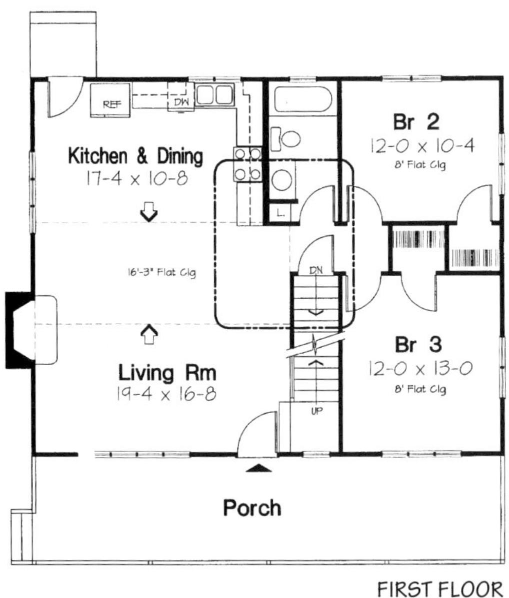
REF
DW
Kitchen & Dining
17-4 x 10-8
16'-3" Flat Clg
Living Rm
19-4 x 16-8
Br 2
12-0 x 10-4
8' Flat Clg
Br 3
12-0 x 13-0
8' Flat Clg
DN
UP
Porch

FIRST FLOOR

DN
Flat Clg @ 7'-6"
Master Br
12-0 x 13-4

SECOND FLOOR

FURN
WH
Crawl Space Access

CRAWLSPACE/SLAB OPTION

Design 34600

Price Code	A
Total Finished	1,328 sq. ft.
First Finished	1,013 sq. ft.
Second Finished	315 sq. ft.
Basement Unfinished	1,013 sq. ft.
Dimensions	36'x36'
Foundation	Basement, Slab Crawlspace
Bedrooms	3
Full Baths	2
First Ceiling	8'
Second Ceiling	7'6"
Roof Framing	Stick
Exterior Walls	2x4, 2x6

Outdoor Living at its Best

A Fun, and Efficient Home

This delightful woodland retreat brings the outdoor experience inside, mixing Alpine allure and ski lodge sensibility in a family-friendly floor plan designed for socializing. Here, you can relax amid Mother Nature, enjoying the views afforded by expansive decks and a front wall of windows, or retreat to the secluded master bedroom suite.

The open galley kitchen allows the cook to work while people pull up stools to chat or mingle in the family room and dining area. All these rooms are capped by a soaring cathedral ceiling that transitions into an airy loft and two bedrooms with full bath on the second level. A brick fireplace adds to the home's rustic feel. And don't overlook the attached playhouse/shed and greenhouse.

Design 10515

Price Code	D
Total Finished	2,015 sq. ft.
First Finished	1,280 sq. ft.
Second Finished	735 sq. ft.
Dimensions	32'x40'
Foundation	Crawlspace
Bedrooms	3
Baths	2 full, 1 half
First Ceiling	8'
Second Ceiling	8'
Roof Framing	Stick
Exterior Walls	2x6

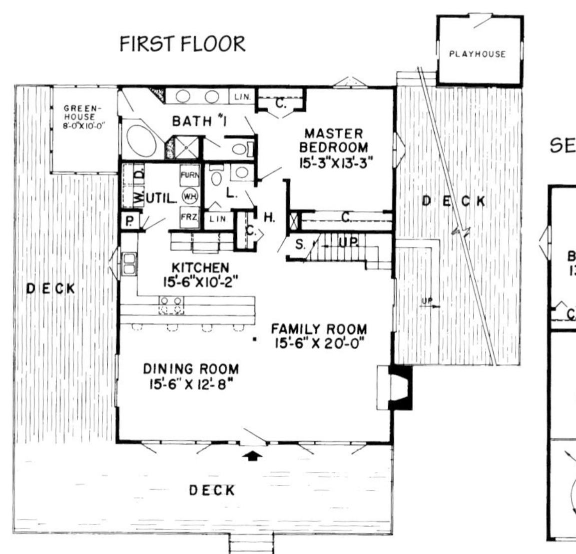
FIRST FLOOR
PLAYHOUSE
GREEN-HOUSE 8'-0"X10'-0"
BATH #1
LIN.
C.
MASTER BEDROOM 15'-3"X13'-3"
W.D.
UTIL.
FURN
WH
FRZ
LIN
L.
H.
C.
P.
S.
UP
DECK
KITCHEN 15'-6"X10'-2"
FAMILY ROOM 15'-6" X 20'-0"
DINING ROOM 15'-6" X 12'-8"
DECK
DECK
SECOND FLOOR
BEDROOM #2 13'-0"X 13'-3"
B#2
BEDROOM #3 11'-4" X 13'-3"
H.
C.
C.
C.
L
C.
C.
DN.
LOFT 15'-9" X 12'-0"
OPEN TO MAIN FLOOR

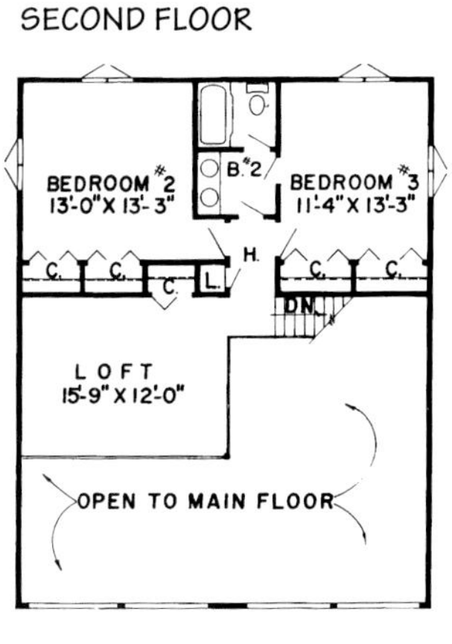

PLAN NO. 90288

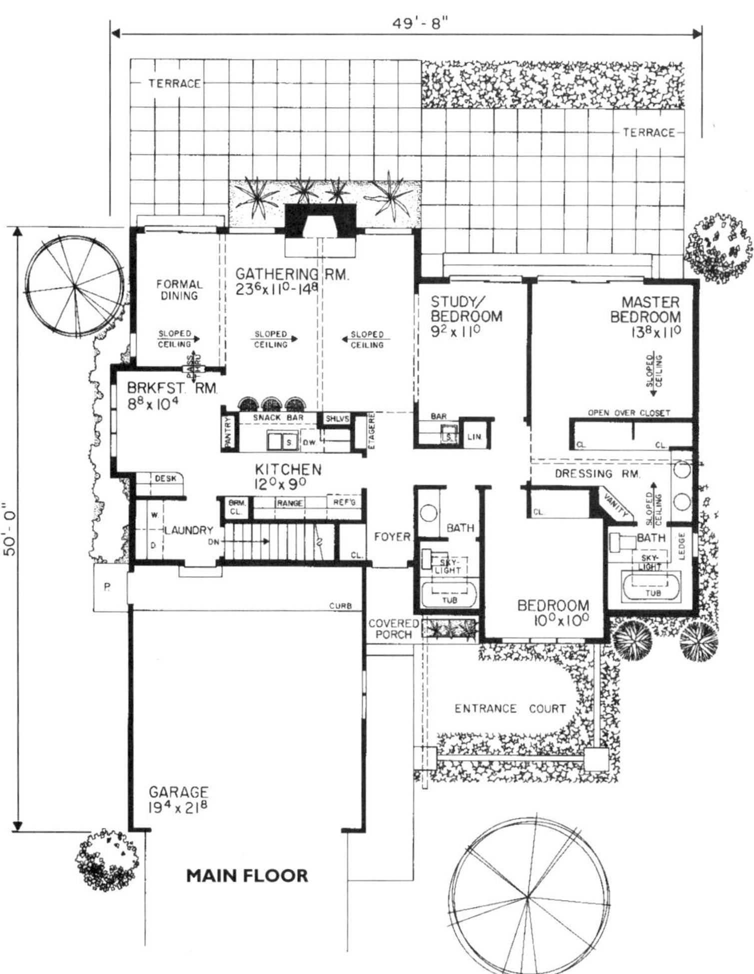
49'-8"
TERRACE
TERRACE
FORMAL DINING
GATHERING RM.
23⁶x11⁰-14⁸
SLOPED CEILING
SLOPED CEILING
SLOPED CEILING
STUDY/ BEDROOM
9² x 11⁰
MASTER BEDROOM
13⁸x11⁰
SLOPED CEILING
BRKFST. RM.
8⁸ x 10⁴
SNACK BAR
SHLVS
PANTRY
ETAGERE
BAR
LIN.
OPEN OVER CLOSET
CL.
CL.
KITCHEN
12⁰x 9⁰
DESK
DRESSING RM.
VANITY
SLOPED CEILING
RANGE
REF'G
CL.
LAUNDRY
DN
FOYER
CL.
BATH
SKY-LIGHT
TUB
BATH
SKY-LIGHT
TUB
LEDGE
50'-0"
P
CURB
COVERED PORCH
BEDROOM
10⁰x10⁰
ENTRANCE COURT
GARAGE
19⁴ x 21⁸
MAIN FLOOR

Soaring Ceilings Add Space and Drama

Price Code: A

- This plan features:
  - — Two bedrooms (with optional third bedroom)
  - — Two full baths
- A sunny Master Suite with a sloping ceiling, private terrace entry, and luxurious garden Bath with an adjoining Dressing Room
- A Gathering Room with fireplace a Study and formal Dining Room, flowing together for a more spacious feeling
- A convenient pass-through that adds to the efficiency of the galley Kitchen and adjoining Breakfast Room
- This home is designed with a basement foundation

MAIN FLOOR — 1,387 SQ. FT.
GARAGE — 440 SQ. FT.

Total living area: 1,387 sq. ft.

PLAN NO. 93279

Open Spaces

Price Code: A

- This plan features:
- — Three bedrooms
- — Two full baths
- A Living Area, Kitchen and Dining Room that connect to form a great space
- A central, double fireplace adding warmth and atmosphere to the Living Area, Kitchen and the Dining Room
- An efficient Kitchen that is highlighted by a peninsula counter that doubles as a breakfast bar
- A Patio that can be accessed from the Dining Area
- This home is designed with crawlspace and slab foundation options

MAIN FLOOR — 1,388 SQ. FT.
GARAGE — 400 SQ. FT.

Total living area:
1,388 sq. ft.

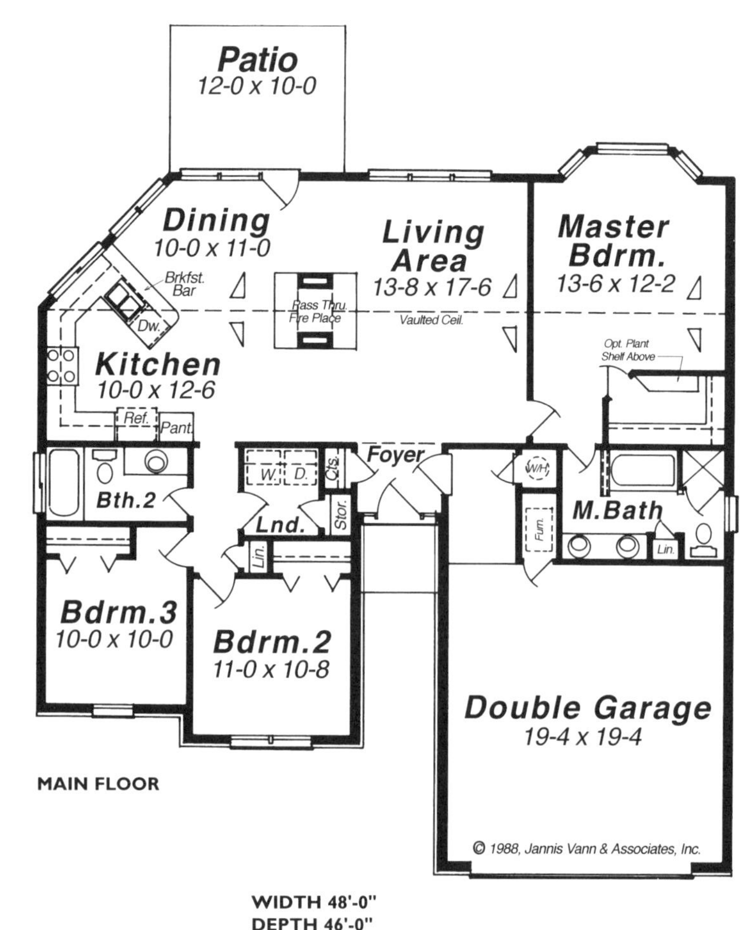

Patio
12-0 x 10-0
Dining
10-0 x 11-0
Living
Area
13-8 x 17-6
Master
Bdrm.
13-6 x 12-2
Brkfst.
Bar
Dw.
Pass Thru
Fire Place
Vaulted Ceil.
Opt. Plant
Shelf Above
Kitchen
10-0 x 12-6
Ref.
Pant.
Bth.2
W.
D.
Clo.
Foyer
W/H
Lnd.
Stor.
M.Bath
Furn.
Lin.
Lin.
Bdrm.3
10-0 x 10-0
Bdrm.2
11-0 x 10-8
Double Garage
19-4 x 19-4
MAIN FLOOR
© 1988, Jannis Vann & Associates, Inc.
WIDTH 48'-0"
DEPTH 46'-0"

PLAN NO.99208

Cozy Traditional with Style

Price Code: C

- This plan features:
  - Three bedrooms
  - Two full baths
- A convenient one-level design
- A galley-style Kitchen that shares a snack bar with the spacious Gathering Room
- Inviting focal point fireplace in Gathering Room
- An ample Master Suite with a luxury Bath which includes a whirlpool tub and separate Dressing Room
- Two additional Bedrooms, one that could double as a Study, located at the front of the house
- This home is designed with a basement foundation

MAIN FLOOR — 1,830 SQ. FT.
BASEMENT — 1,830 SQ. FT.

Total living area:
1,830 sq. ft.

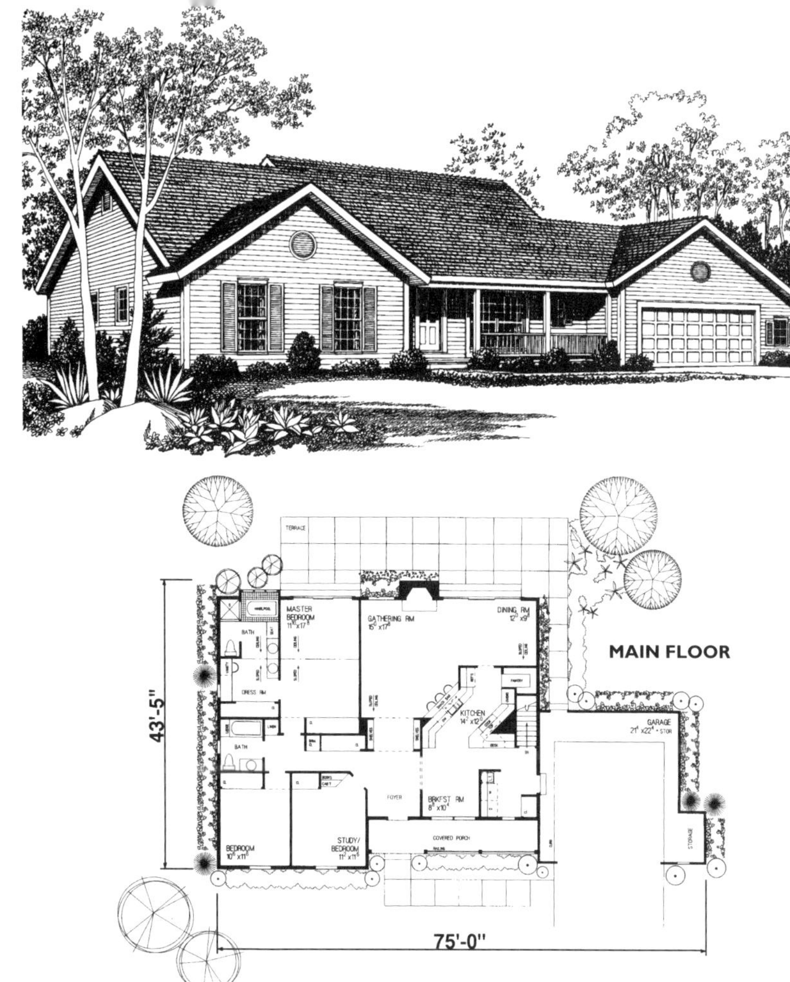

MAIN FLOOR
43'-5"
75'-0"

PLAN NO.10839

Perfect Compact Ranch

Price Code: B

- This plan features:
  - Two bedrooms
  - Two full baths
- A large, sunken Great Room, centralized with a cozy fireplace
- A Master Bedroom with an unforgettable Bathroom including a skylight
- A huge three-car Garage, including a work area for the family carpenter
- A Kitchen, including a Breakfast Nook for family gatherings
- This home is designed with basement, slab and crawlspace foundation options

MAIN FLOOR — 1,738 SQ. FT.
BASEMENT — 1,083 SQ. FT.
GARAGE — 796 SQ. FT.

Total living area:
1,738 sq. ft.

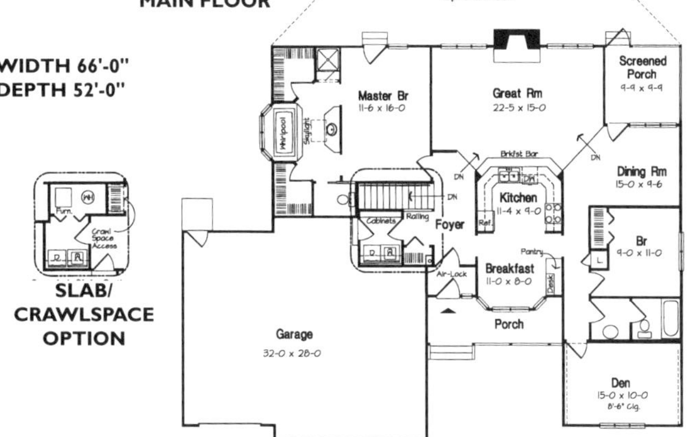

MAIN FLOOR
Optional Deck
WIDTH 66'-0"
DEPTH 52'-0"
Screened Porch
4-4 x 4-4
Master Br
11-6 x 16-0
Great Rm
22-5 x 15-0
Dining Rm
15-0 x 9-6
Kitchen
11-4 x 9-0
Foyer
Br
9-0 x 11-0
Breakfast
11-0 x 8-0
Porch
Garage
32-0 x 28-0
Den
15-0 x 10-0
SLAB/
CRAWLSPACE
OPTION

PLAN NO.20160

Streetside Appeal

Price Code: D

- This plan features:
  - — Three bedrooms
  - — Two full and one half baths
- An elegant Living and Dining Room combination that is divided by columns
- A Family/Hearth Room with a two-way firepla to the Breakfast room
- A well-appointed Kitchen with built-in Pantry, peninsula counter and double corner sink
- A Master Suite with decorative ceiling, walk-i closet and private Bath
- Two additional Bedrooms that share a full Bathroom
- This home is designed with basement, slab anc crawlspace foundation options

FIRST FLOOR — 1,590 SQ. FT.
SECOND FLOOR — 567 SQ. FT.
BASEMENT — 1,576 SQ. FT.
GARAGE — 456 SQ. FT.

Total living area: 2,157 sq. ft.

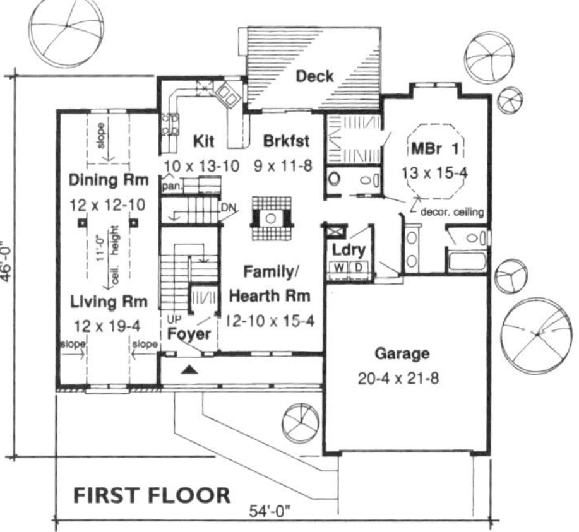
Deck
Kit
10 x 13-10
Brkfst
9 x 11-8
MBr 1
13 x 15-4
decor. ceiling
Dining Rm
12 x 12-10
slope
11'-0" ceil. height
Living Rm
12 x 19-4
Family/
Hearth Rm
12-10 x 15-4
Ldry
W D
Foyer
UP
DN
pan
Garage
20-4 x 21-8
46'-0"
54'-0"
FIRST FLOOR

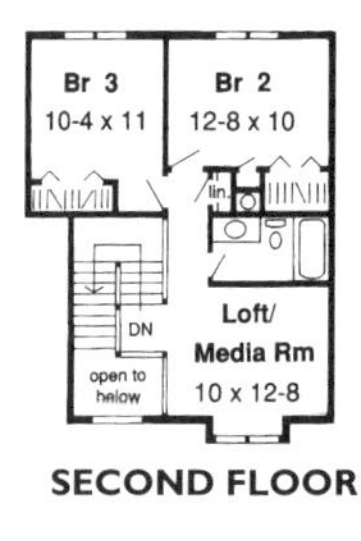
Br 3
10-4 x 11
Br 2
12-8 x 10
lin
DN
open to below
Loft/
Media Rm
10 x 12-8
SECOND FLOOR

PLAN NO.20198

Dramatic Ranch

Price Code: C

- This plan features:
  - — Three bedrooms
  - — Two full baths
- A large Living Room with a stone fireplace an decorative beamed ceiling
- A Kitchen/Dining Room arrangement which makes the rooms seem more spacious
- A Laundry with a large Pantry located close to the bedrooms and the Kitchen
- A Master Bedroom with a walk-in closet and a private Master Bath
- Two additional bedrooms, one with a walk-in closet, that share the full hall Bath
- This home is designed with a basement foundation

MAIN FLOOR — 1,792 SQ. FT.
BASEMENT — 818 SQ. FT.
GARAGE — 857 SQ. FT.

Total living area: 1,792 sq. ft.

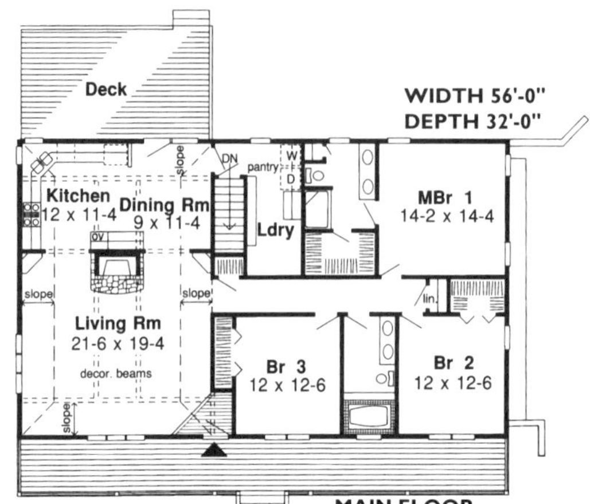
Deck
WIDTH 56'-0"
DEPTH 32'-0"
Kitchen
12 x 11-4
Dining Rm
9 x 11-4
DN
pantry
W D
Ldry
MBr 1
14-2 x 14-4
slope
Living Rm
21-6 x 19-4
decor. beams
lin
Br 3
12 x 12-6
Br 2
12 x 12-6
MAIN FLOOR

Rustic Retreat

Price Code: A

- This plan features:
  - Two bedrooms
  - One full bath
- A wrap-around deck equipped with a built-in barbecue for easy outdoor living
- An entry, in a wall of glass, opens the Living area to the outdoors
- A large fireplace in the Living area opens into an efficient Kitchen, with a built-in pantry that serves the Nook area
- Two Bedrooms share a centrally located full bath with a window tub
- A Loft area ready for multiple uses
- This home is designed with a crawlspace foundation

MAIN FLOOR — 789 SQ. FT.
LOFT — 108 SQ. FT.

Total living area:
897 sq. ft.

PLAN NO.24309

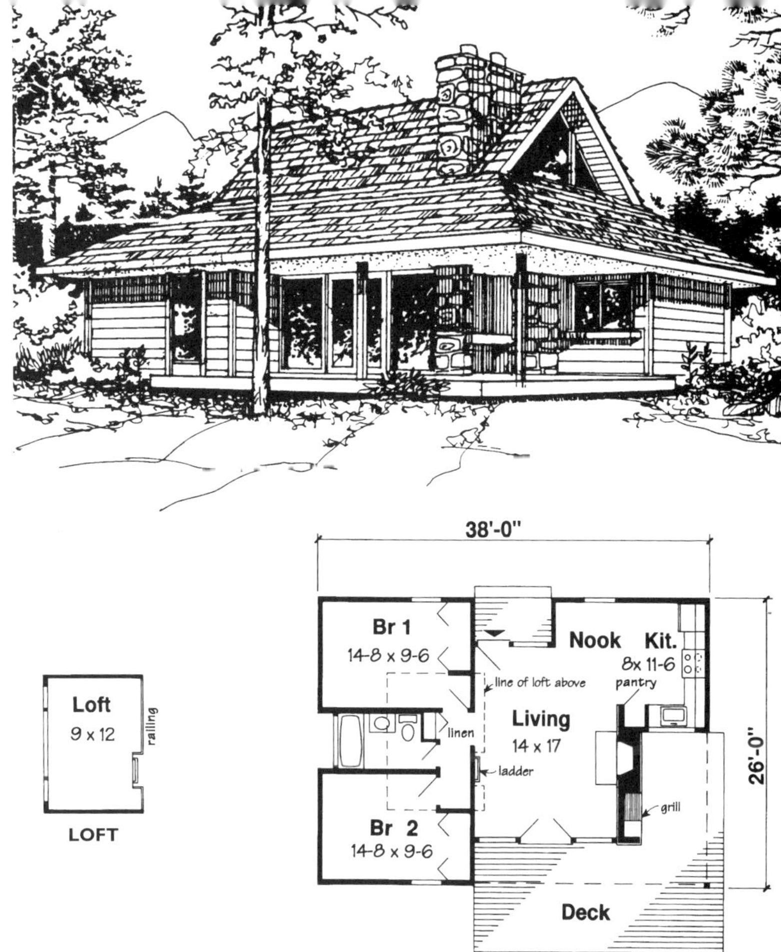

38'-0"
26'-0"
Br 1
14-8 x 9-6
Nook
Kit.
8x 11-6
line of loft above
pantry
Living
14 x 17
linen
ladder
grill
Br 2
14-8 x 9-6
Deck
MAIN FLOOR
Loft
9 x 12
railing
LOFT

Family Favorite

Price Code: A

- This plan features:
  - Three bedrooms
  - Two full baths
- An open arrangement with the Dining Room that combines with ten-foot ceilings to make the Living Room seem more spacious
- Glass on three sides of the Dining Room which overlooks the Deck
- An efficient, compact Kitchen with a built-in Pantry and peninsula counter
- A Master Suite with a romantic window seat, a compartmentalized private Bath and a walk-in closet
- Two additional Bedrooms that share a full Bath
- This home is designed with basement, slab and crawlspace foundation options

MAIN FLOOR — 1,359 SQ. FT.
BASEMENT — 1,359 SQ. FT.
GARAGE — 501 SQ. FT.

Total living area:
1,359 sq. ft.

PLAN NO.20156

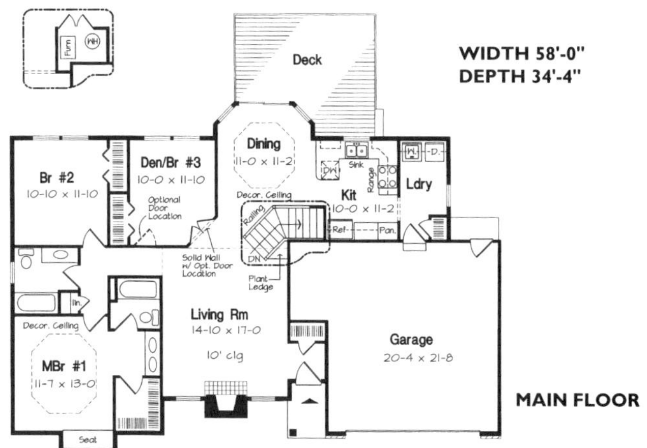

Deck
WIDTH 58'-0"
DEPTH 34'-4"
Dining
11-0 x 11-2
Den/Br #3
10-0 x 11-10
Optional Door Location
Br #2
10-10 x 11-10
Kit
10-0 x 11-2
Ldry
Sink
Range
Ref.
Pan.
Decor. Ceiling
DN
Plant Ledge
Solid Wall w/ Opt. Door Location
Living Rm
14-10 x 17-0
10' clg
Garage
20-4 x 21-8
Decor. Ceiling
MBr #1
11-7 x 13-0
Seat
MAIN FLOOR

PLAN NO. 91901

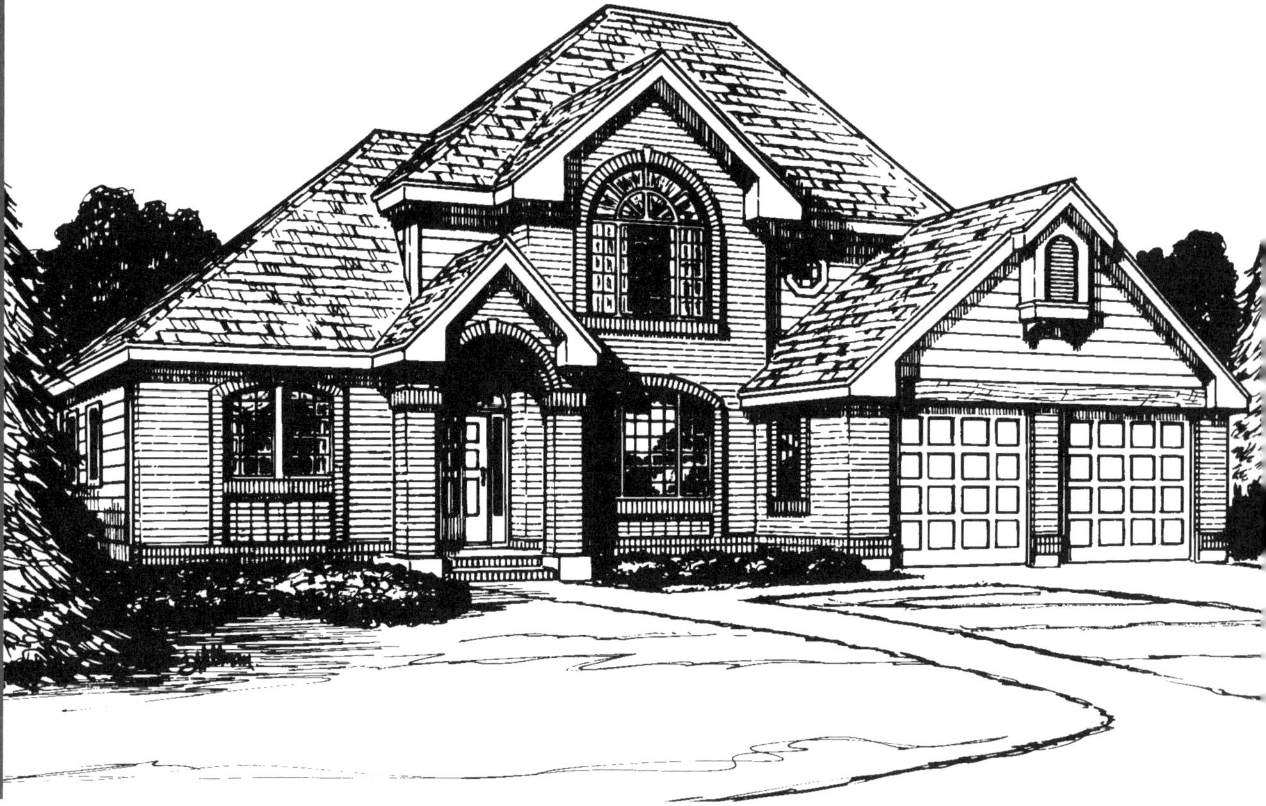

Rich Classic Lines

Price Code: D

- This plan features:
- — Four bedrooms
- — Three full and one half baths
- The two-story Foyer is flooded by light through a half-round transom
- The Great Room is accented by a two-sided fireplace, and provides access to the Patio
- A work island in the Kitchen adds to its efficiency along with a built-in desk and a Pantry
- This home is designed with a basement foundation

FIRST FLOOR — 1,496 SQ. FT.
SECOND FLOOR — 716 SQ. FT.
BASEMENT — 1,420 SQ. FT.
GARAGE — 460 SQ. FT.

Total living area:
2,212 sq. ft.

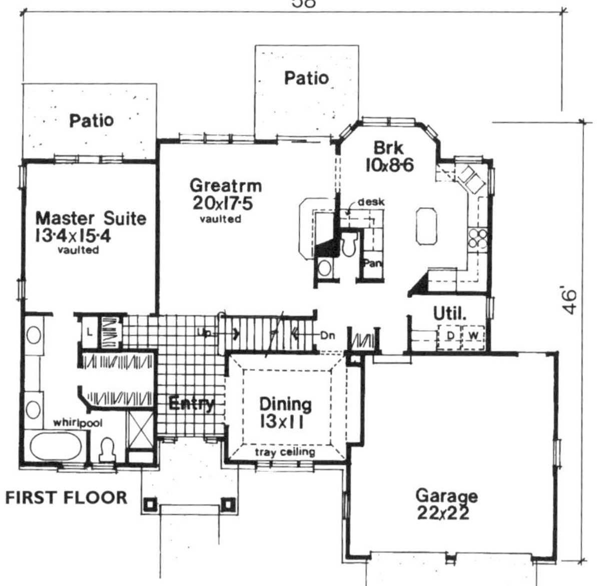

58'
Patio
Patio
Brk
10x8-6
Greatrm
20x17-5
vaulted
desk
Master Suite
13-4x15-4
vaulted
Pan
46'
Util.
D W
Up
Dn
L
whirlpool
Entry
Dining
13x11
tray ceiling
Garage
22x22
FIRST FLOOR

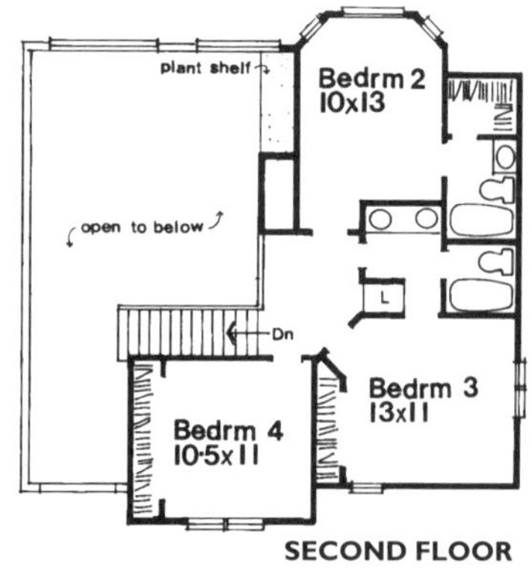

plant shelf
Bedrm 2
10x13
open to below
L
Dn
Bedrm 3
13x11
Bedrm 4
10-5x11
SECOND FLOOR

Spectacular Traditional

Price Code: A

This plan features:

- Three bedrooms
- Two full baths
- The use of gable roofs and the blend of stucco and brick to form a spectacular exterior
- A high vaulted ceiling and a cozy fireplace, with built-in cabinets in the Den
- An efficient, U-shaped Kitchen with an adjacent Dining Area
- A Master Bedroom, with a raised ceiling, that includes a private Bath and a walk-in closet
- Two family Bedrooms that share a full Bath
- This home is designed with crawlspace and slab foundation options

AIN FLOOR — 1,237 SQ. FT.
ARAGE — 436 SQ. FT.

Total living area:
1,237 sq. ft.

PLAN NO.92502

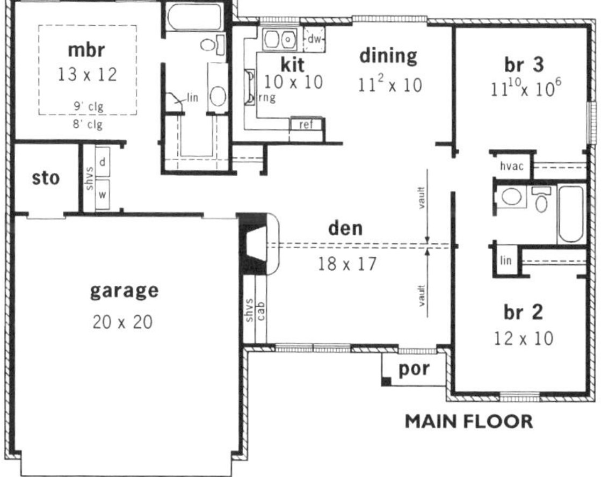
mbr
13 x 12
9' clg
8' clg
lin
kit
10 x 10
rng
dw
ref
dining
11² x 10
br 3
11¹⁰ x 10⁶
hvac
lin
sto
shvs
d
w
den
18 x 17
vault
vault
garage
20 x 20
shvs
cab
br 2
12 x 10
por
MAIN FLOOR

WIDTH 50'-0"
DEPTH 38'-0"

Nice Curb Appeal

Price Code: D

This plan features:

- Three bedrooms
- Two full and one half baths
- An exciting roofline and a textured exterior provide a rich, solid look to this home
- The lovely Foyer views the cozy fireplace and stylish French door in the Great Room
- The formal Dining Room has a tray ceiling and a wide entrance to the Great Room
- The roomy, well-equipped Kitchen includes a pass-through to the Great Room
- Large windows in the Breakfast Area flood the room with natural light, making it a bright and cheery place to start your day
- The private, first floor Master Bedroom has a luxurious Bath
- This home is designed with a basement foundation

IRST FLOOR — 1,524 SQ. FT.
ECOND FLOOR — 558 SQ. FT.
ONUS — 267 SQ. FT.
ASEMENT — 1,460 SQ. FT.

Total living area:
2,082 sq. ft.

PLAN NO.92642

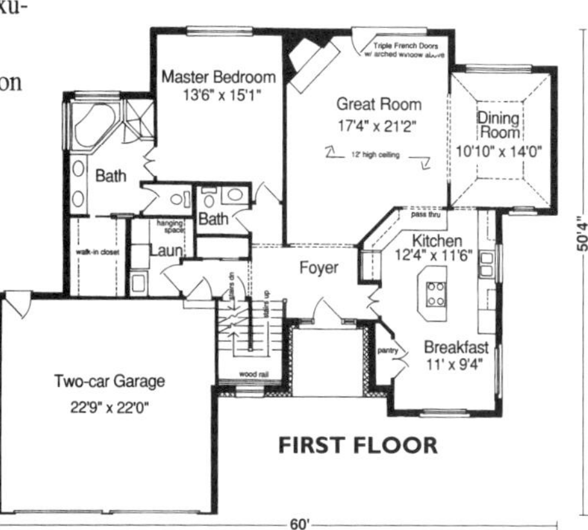
Master Bedroom
13'6" x 15'1"
Great Room
17'4" x 21'2"
Dining Room
10'10" x 14'0"
Bath
Bath
Laun
Foyer
Kitchen
12'4" x 11'6"
Breakfast
11' x 9'4"
Two-car Garage
22'9" x 22'0"
FIRST FLOOR
50'4"
60'

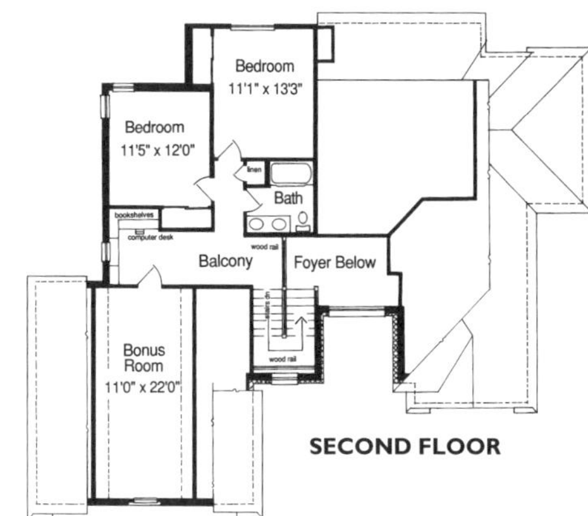
Bedroom
11'1" x 13'3"
Bedroom
11'5" x 12'0"
Bath
Balcony
Foyer Below
Bonus Room
11'0" x 22'0"
SECOND FLOOR

PLAN NO. 91021

Inviting Porch Has Dual Functi

Price Code: A

- This plan features:
  - — Three bedrooms
  - — Two full baths
- An inviting, wrap-around Porch Entry with slid glass doors leading right into a bayed Dining R
- A Living Room with a cozy feeling, enhanced b the fireplace
- An efficient Kitchen opening to both Dining an Living Rooms
- A Master Suite with a walk-in closet and privat Master Bath
- This home is designed with basement, slab and crawlspace foundation options

MAIN FLOOR — 1,295 SQ. FT.
GARAGE — 400 SQ. FT.

Total living area:
1,295 sq. ft.

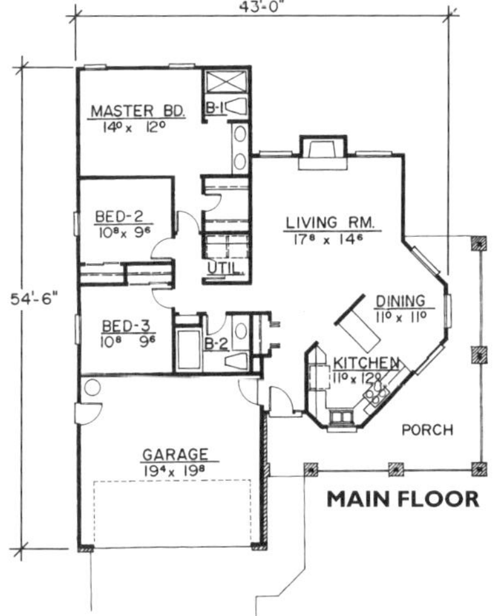

43'-0"
54'-6"
MASTER BD.
14⁰ x 12⁰
B-1
BED-2
10⁸ x 9⁶
LIVING RM.
17⁶ x 14⁶
UTIL.
BED-3
10⁸ 9⁶
B-2
DINING
11⁰ x 11⁰
KITCHEN
11⁰ x 12⁰
PORCH
GARAGE
19⁴ x 19⁸
MAIN FLOOR

PLAN NO. 92644

Distinctive Design

Price Code: C

- This plan features:
  - — Three bedrooms
  - — Two full and one half baths
- An impressive pilaster Entry opens into the Fo with a landing staircase highlighted by decorat windows
- The Great Room is accented by a hearth firepl and French doors with an arched window abov
- The formal Dining Room is enhanced by a furn ture alcove and a decorative window
- This home is designed with a basement founda

FIRST FLOOR — 1,036 SQ. FT.
SECOND FLOOR — 861 SQ. FT.
GARAGE — 420 SQ. FT.

Total living area:
1,897 sq. ft.

Laun. Bath Breakfast 10'8" x 11' 10'6" x 13'6" Kitchen pantry Great Room 14'10" x 17'1" French doors w/ arched window above high ceiling wood rail Foyer stairs up stairs dn furniture alcove Dining Room 11' x 13'7" Two-car Garage 20' x 21' 38' 48'

FIRST FLOOR

walk in closet Master Bedroom 12' x 14'11" Bedroom 10'6" x 11'2" Great Room Below computer desk Bath Bath Balcony Bedroom 11' x 12' stairs dn window seat

SECOND FLOOR

PLAN NO. 91343

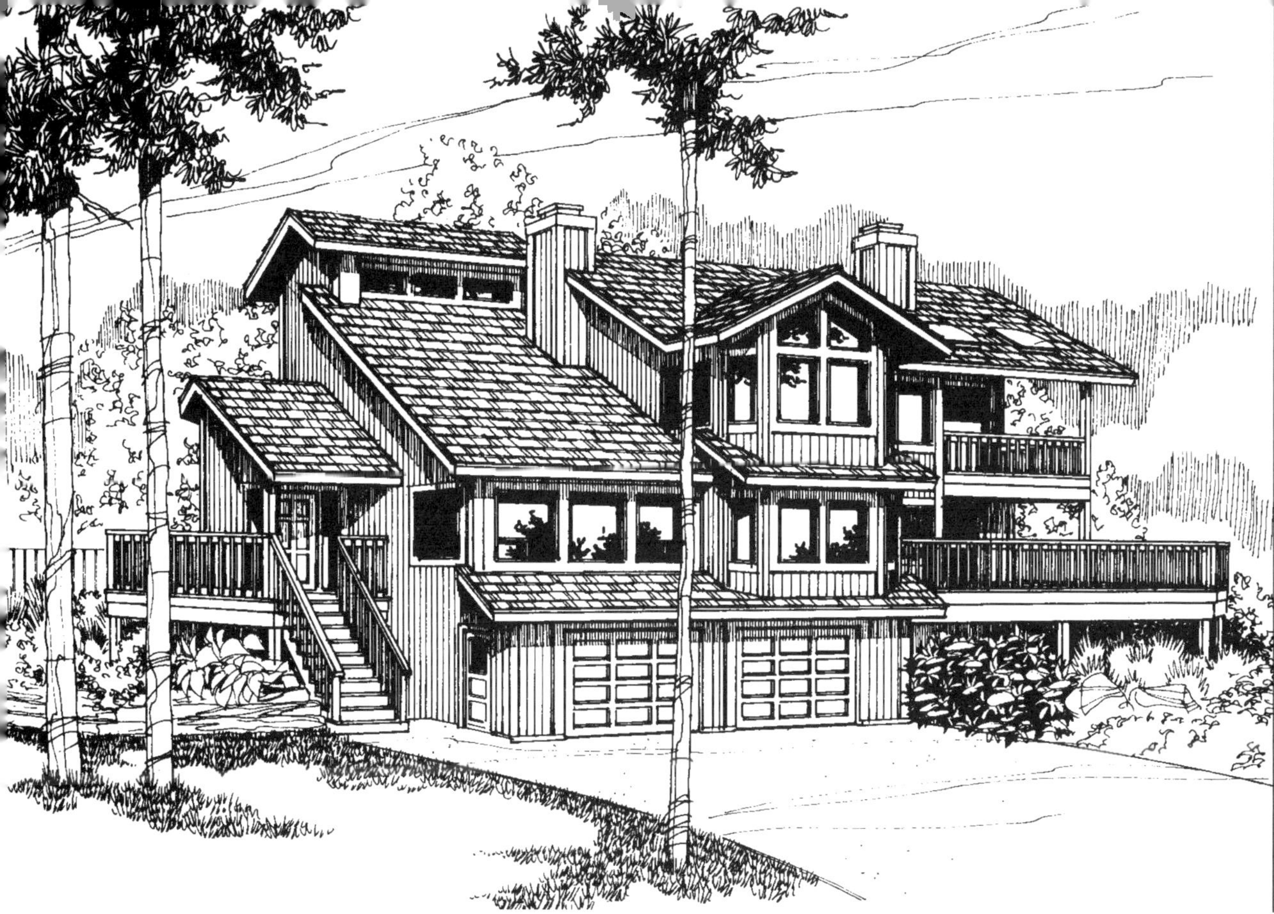

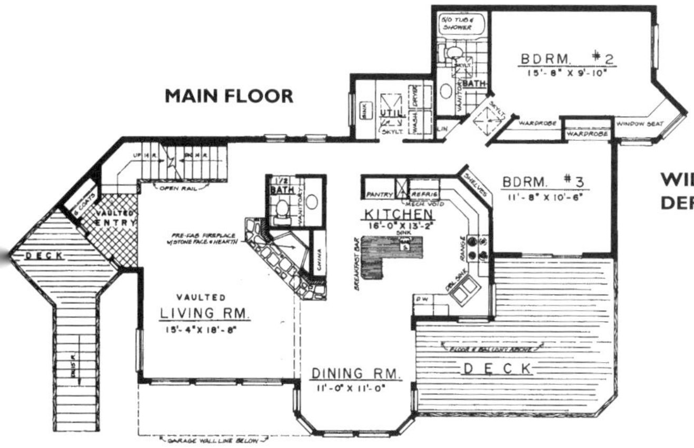

MAIN FLOOR

BDRM. #2 15'-8" X 9'-10"

BDRM. #3 11'-8" X 10'-6"

KITCHEN 16'-0" X 13'-2"

VAULTED LIVING RM. 15'-4" X 18'-8"

DINING RM. 11'-0" X 11'-0"

DECK

WIDTH 67'-0"
DEPTH 41'-0"

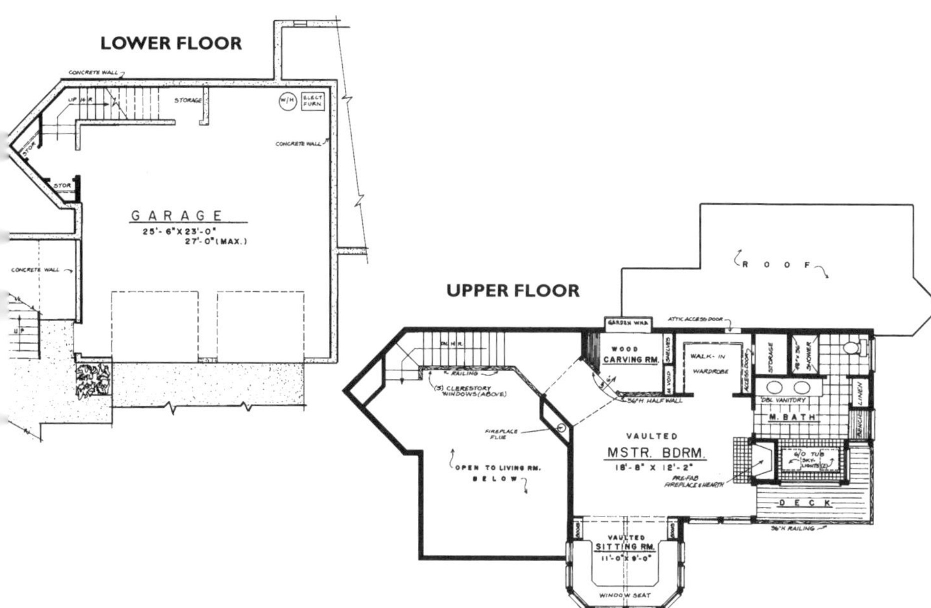
LOWER FLOOR
GARAGE
25'-6" X 23'-0"
27'-0" (MAX.)
UPPER FLOOR
ROOF
WOOD CARVING RM.
WALK-IN WARDROBE
M. BATH
VAULTED
MSTR. BDRM.
18'-8" X 12'-2"
OPEN TO LIVING RM. BELOW
DECK
VAULTED
SITTING RM.
11'-0" X 8'-0"
WINDOW SEAT

Ideal for Sloping View Site

Price Code: D

- This plan features:
- — Three bedrooms
- — Two full and one half baths
- A stone-faced fireplace and vaulted ceiling are located in the Living Room
- An island food preparation center with a sink and a Breakfast bar are featured in the Kitchen
- Sliding glass doors lead from the Dining Room to the Deck
- This home is designed with a combo basement and crawlspace foundation option

FIRST FLOOR — 1,338 SQ. FT.
SECOND FLOOR — 763 SQ. FT.
LOWER FLOOR — 61 SQ. FT.
GARAGE — 779 SQ. FT.

Total living area: 2,162 sq. ft.

PLAN NO. 98415

Split-Bedroom Plan

Price Code: A

- This plan features:
- —Three bedrooms
- —Two full baths
- A tray ceiling gives a decorative touch to the Master Bedroom and a vaulted ceiling tops the five-piece Master Bath
- A full Bath located between the secondary Bedrooms
- A corner fireplace and a vaulted ceiling highlights the heart of the home, the Family Room
- This home is designed with basement, slab and crawlspace foundation options

MAIN FLOOR — 1,429 SQ. FT.
BASEMENT — 1,472 SQ. FT.
GARAGE — 438 SQ. FT.

Total living area: 1,429 sq. ft.

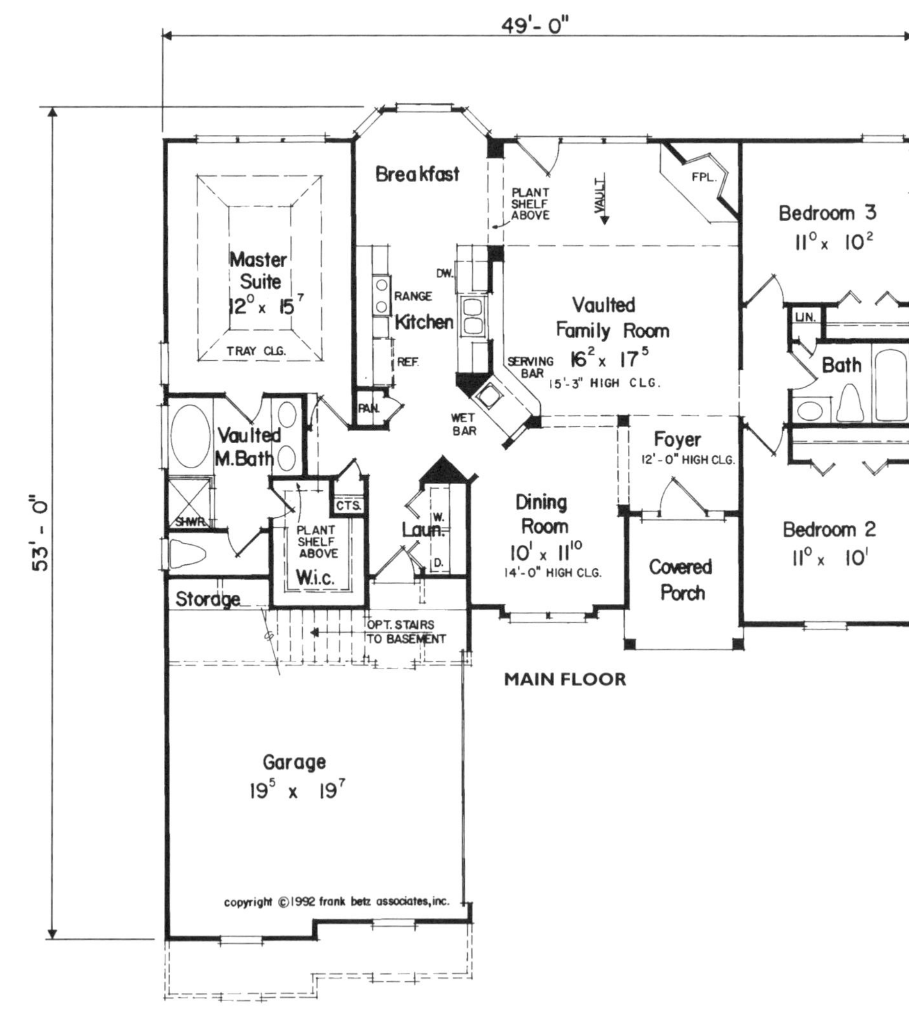

49'- 0"
53' - 0"
Breakfast
PLANT SHELF ABOVE
VAULT
FPL.
Bedroom 3
11⁰ x 10²
Master Suite
12⁰ x 15⁷
TRAY CLG.
DW.
RANGE
Kitchen
REF.
PAN.
Vaulted Family Room
16² x 17⁵
SERVING BAR
15'-3" HIGH CLG.
LIN.
Bath
WET BAR
Foyer
12'-0" HIGH CLG.
Vaulted M.Bath
SHWR.
CTS.
PLANT SHELF ABOVE
W.i.c.
Laun.
W.
D.
Dining Room
10¹ x 11¹⁰
14'-0" HIGH CLG.
Covered Porch
Bedroom 2
11⁰ x 10¹
Storage
OPT. STAIRS TO BASEMENT
MAIN FLOOR
Garage
19⁵ x 19⁷
copyright ©1992 frank betz associates, inc.

PLAN NO. 34049

Stone-Faced Façade

Price Code: D

- This plan features:
  - — Four bedrooms
  - — Three full baths
- Sloping ceilings and open spaces characterize this well-designed four-bedroom home
- The Dining Room just off the two-story Foyer adjoins the sunny Breakfast Room and the convenient U-shaped Kitchen with island work area
- This home is designed with a basement foundation

FIRST FLOOR — 1,496 SQ. FT.
SECOND FLOOR — 520 SQ. FT.
BASEMENT — 1,487 SQ. FT.
GARAGE — 424 SQ. FT.

Total living area: 2,016 sq. ft.

FIRST FLOOR

SECOND FLOOR

PLAN NO.82030

Old-Fashioned Appeal

Price Code: B

- This plan features:
  - — Three bedrooms
  - — Two full baths
- A Porch and dormers enhance the Country appeal
- A computer center on the second floor is a perfect place for children to study
- This home is designed with basement, crawlspace and slab foundation options

FIRST FLOOR — 990 SQ. FT.
SECOND FLOOR — 551 SQ. FT.
GARAGE — 367 SQ. FT.
PORCH — 367 SQ. FT.

Total living area:
1,575 sq. ft.

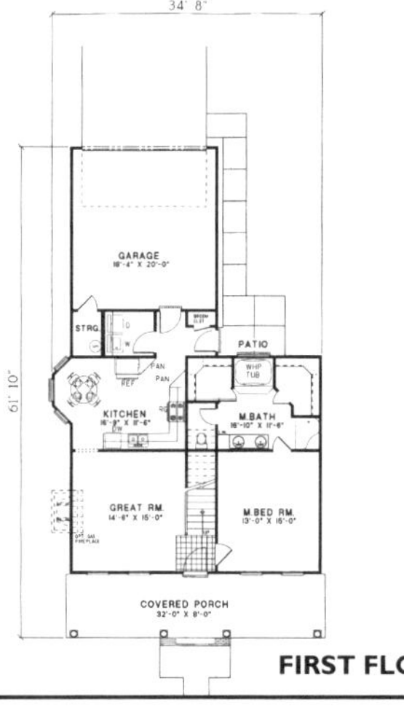

34' 8"
GARAGE
STRG.
PATIO
KITCHEN
M.BATH
GREAT RM
M BED RM
COVERED PORCH
61' 10"

FIRST FLOOR

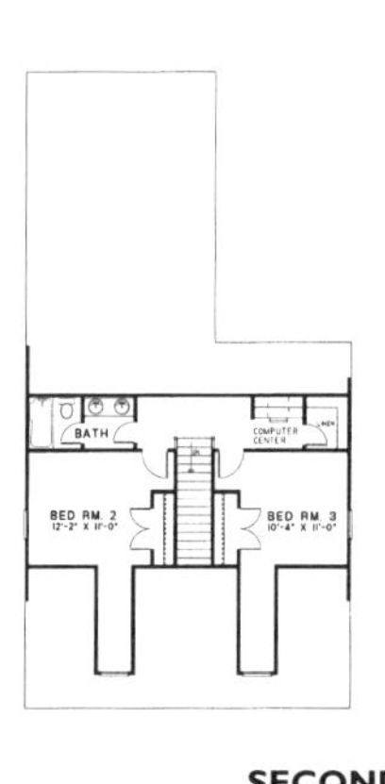

BATH
COMPUTER CENTER
BED RM. 2
BED RM. 3

SECOND FLOOR

PLAN NO.34054

Great Kitchen Area

Price Code: A

- This plan features:
  - — Three bedrooms
  - — Two full baths
- A Dining Room with sliding glass doors to the backyard
- Access to the Garage through the Laundry Roo
- A Master Bedroom with a private full Bath
- A two-car Garage
- This home is designed with basement, slab and crawlspace foundation options

MAIN FLOOR — 1,400 SQ. FT.
BASEMENT — 1,400 SQ. FT.
GARAGE — 528 SQ. FT.

Total living area:
1,400 sq. ft.

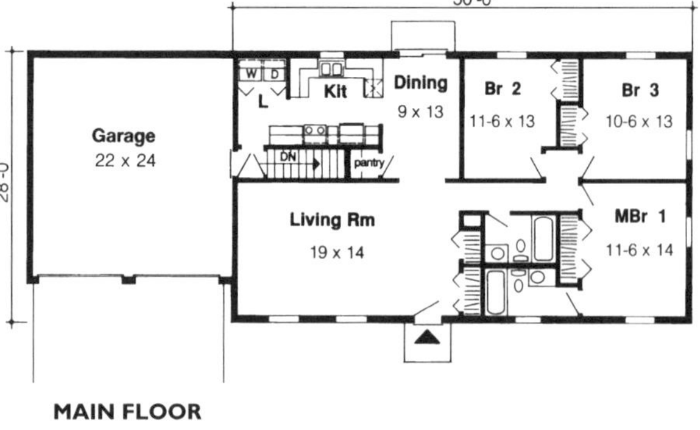

50'-0"
28'-0"
Garage
22 x 24
W D
L
Kit
Dining
9 x 13
DN
pantry
Br 2
11-6 x 13
Br 3
10-6 x 13
Living Rm
19 x 14
MBr 1
11-6 x 14

MAIN FLOOR

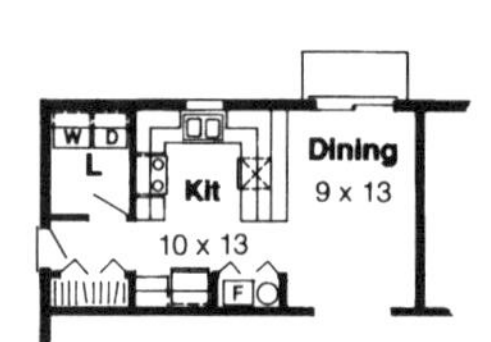

W D
L
Kit
10 x 13
Dining
9 x 13
F

ALTERNATE PLAN W/CRAWLSPACE

PLAN NO. 94683

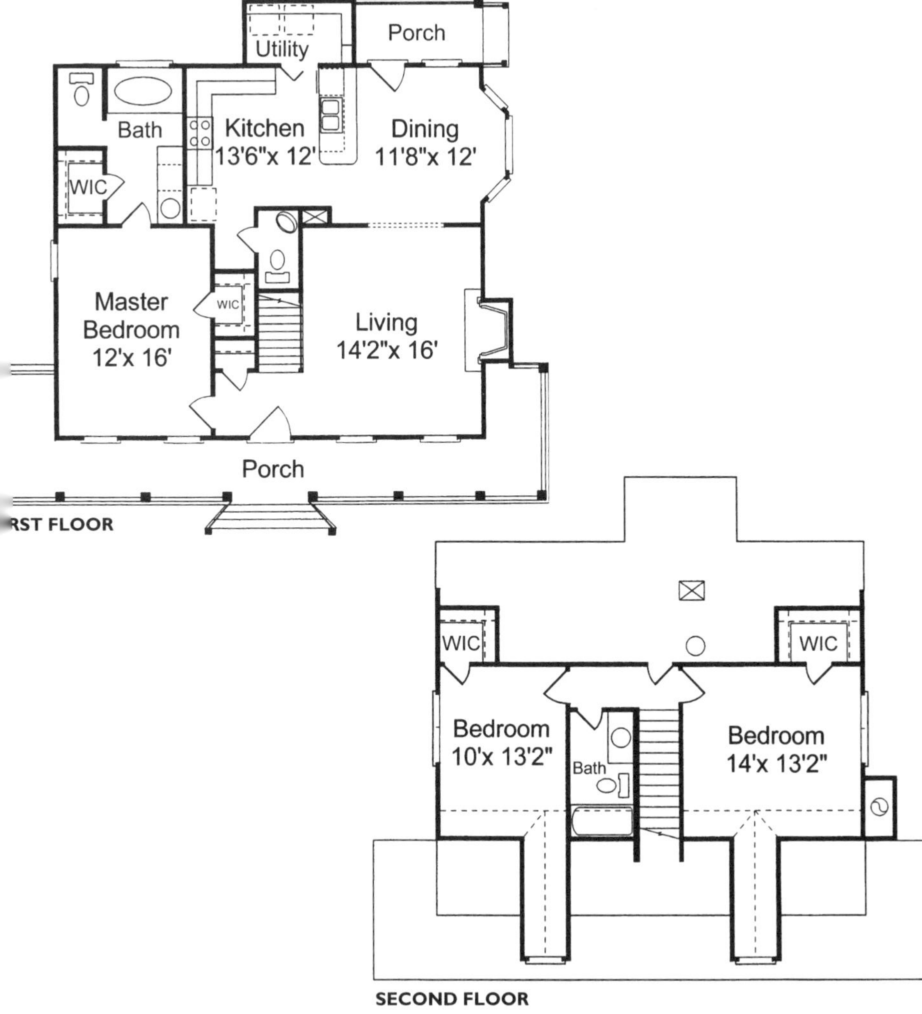

Utility
Porch
Bath
Kitchen 13'6"x 12'
Dining 11'8"x 12'
WIC
Master Bedroom 12'x 16'
WIC
Living 14'2"x 16'
Porch
RST FLOOR
WIC
WIC
Bedroom 10'x 13'2"
Bath
Bedroom 14'x 13'2"
SECOND FLOOR

Wrapping Front Porch

Price Code: C

- This plan features:
- — Three bedrooms
- — Two full baths
- A wrapping front Porch creates a country welcome at the entrance of this home
- The Living Room is accented by a fireplace and is open to the Dining Room creating an easy transition when entertaining
- The Kitchen includes a penisula snack bar and easy access to the Laundry/Utility Room
- The secondary bedrooms include walk-in closets and easy access to a full Bathroom
- This home is designed with crawlspace and slab foundation options.

FIRST FLOOR - 1,046 SQ. FT.
SECOND FLOOR - 572 SQ. FT.

Total living area:
1,618 sq. ft.

PLAN NO.91055

Perfect for First-Time Buyers

Price Code: C

- This plan features:
- — Three bedrooms
- — Two and a half baths
- A friendly, covered Porch sheltering the front entrance
- A comfortable Family Room with a sliding glass door to the backyard, a Utility Closet with washer and dryer and access to the Kitchen
- A cozy Master Bedroom with a recessed dormer window, an oversized, walk-in closet and a private Bath
- This home is designed with a crawl-space foundation

FIRST FLOOR — 805 SQ. FT.
SECOND FLOOR — 961 SQ. FT.
GARAGE — 540 SQ. FT.

Total living area:
1,766 sq. ft.

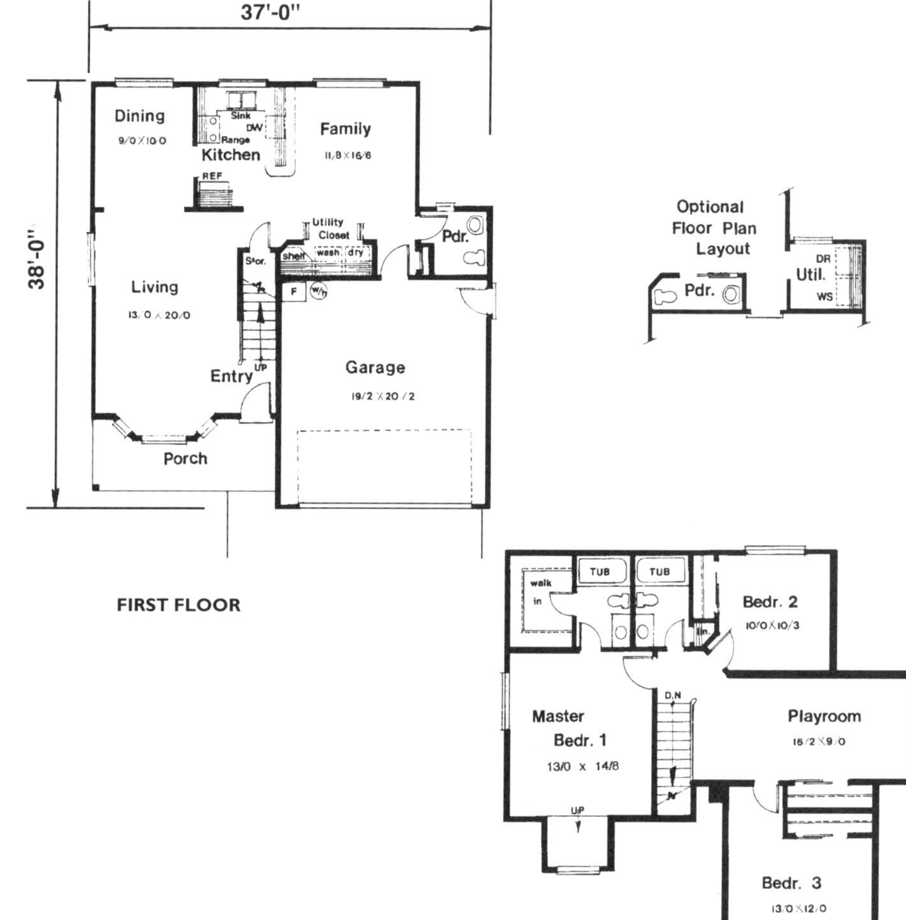

37'-0"
38'-0"
Dining
9/0 X 10/0
Sink
DW
Range
Kitchen
REF
Family
11/8 X 16/6
Utility Closet
shelf
wash
dry
Stor.
F
W/H
Pdr.
Living
13/0 X 20/0
Entry
UP
Garage
19/2 X 20/2
Porch
FIRST FLOOR
Optional Floor Plan Layout
Pdr.
Util.
DR
WS
walk in
TUB
TUB
lin.
Bedr. 2
10/0 X 10/3
Master Bedr. 1
13/0 x 14/8
DN
UP
Playroom
16/2 X 9/0
Bedr. 3
13/0 X 12/0
SECOND FLOOR

L-Shaped Front Porch

Price Code: A

This plan features:

- Three bedrooms
- Two full baths
- Attractive wood siding and a large L-shaped covered Porch
- Front entry leading to generous Living Room with a vaulted ceiling
- Large two-car Garage with access through Utility Room
- Roomy secondary Bedrooms share a full Bath
- Kitchen highlighted by a built-in pantry and a garden window
- Vaulted ceiling adds volume to the Dining Room
- Private Master Suite, enhanced by abundant closet space, separate vanity and linen storage
- This home is designed with a crawlspace foundation

MAIN FLOOR — 1,280 SQ. FT.

Total living area: 1,280 sq. ft.

PLAN NO.98747

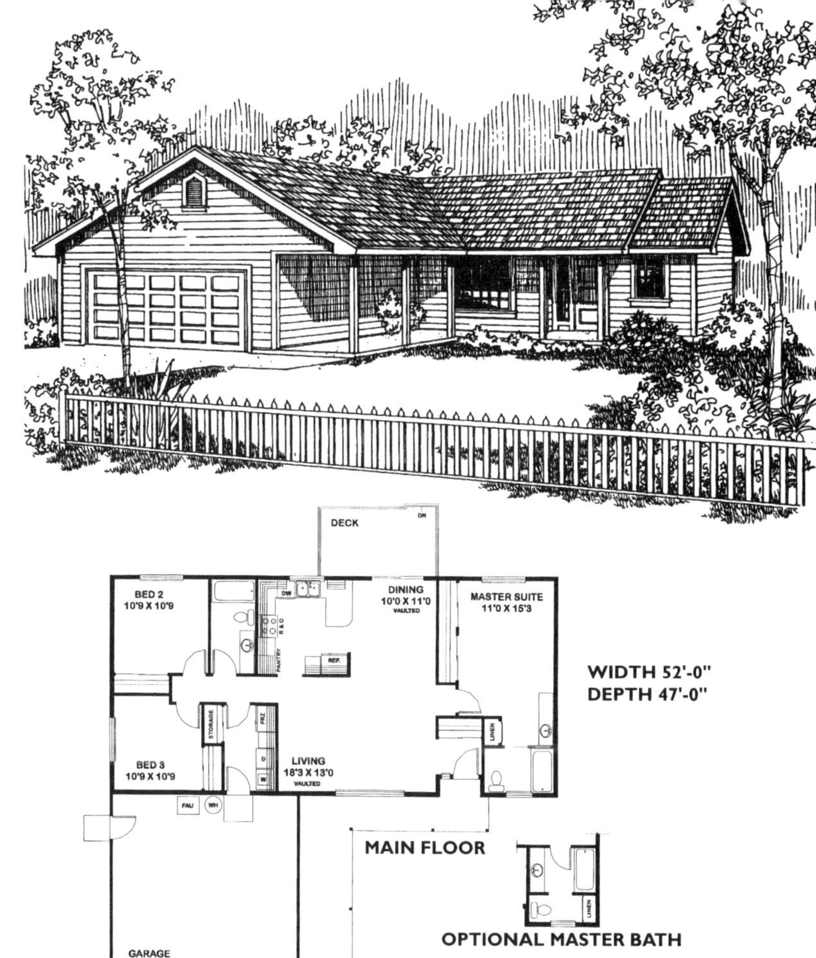
DECK
DN
BED 2
10'9 X 10'9
DW
PANTRY
DINING
10'0 X 11'0
VAULTED
MASTER SUITE
11'0 X 15'3
REF
STORAGE
FRZ
LINEN
BED 3
10'9 X 10'9
LIVING
18'3 X 13'0
VAULTED
FAU
WH
GARAGE
21'3 X 21'9

WIDTH 52'-0"
DEPTH 47'-0"

MAIN FLOOR

OPTIONAL MASTER BATH

Repeating Gables

Price Code: E

This plan features:

- Four bedrooms
- Two full and one half baths
- The impressive exterior features double gables and an arched window
- The spacious Foyer separates the formal Dining Room and Living Room
- The roomy Kitchen and Breakfast Area are adjacent to the large Family Room which has a fireplace and access to the rear Deck
- The Master Bedroom features a private Bath with dual vanity, shower stall and whirlpool tub
- The three additional Bedrooms share a full Bath
- This home is designed with a basement foundation

FIRST FLOOR — 1,207 SQ. FT.
SECOND FLOOR — 1,181 SQ. FT.
BASEMENT — 1,207 SQ. FT.
GARAGE — 484 SQ. FT.

Total living area: 2,388 sq. ft.

PLAN NO.92692

Deck
Breakfast
16'11" x 15'10"
Family Room
20'0" x 13'6"
Kitchen
pantry
butler's pantry
Laun.
Bath
Living Room /Library
11'6" x 15'4"
Two-car Garage
21' x 22'2"
Dining Room
13'2" x 12'0"
Foyer
Porch
37'4"
59'-10"

FIRST FLOOR

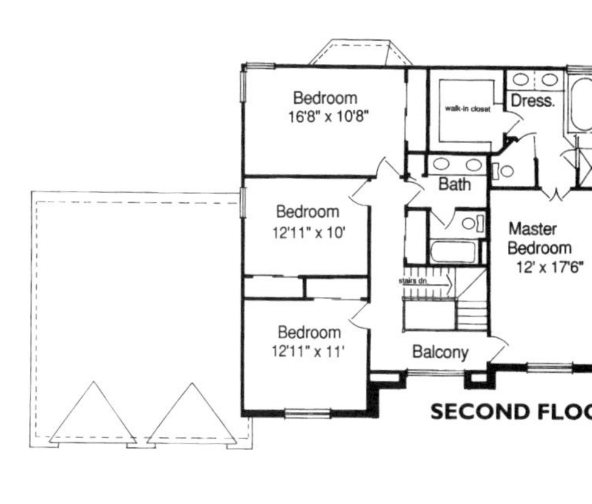
Bedroom
16'8" x 10'8"
walk-in closet
Dress.
Bath
Bedroom
12'11" x 10'
Master
Bedroom
12' x 17'6"
Bedroom
12'11" x 11'
Balcony

SECOND FLOOR

To order your Blueprints, call 1-800-235-5700

PLAN NO. 94986

Ten-Foot Entry

Price Code: B

- This plan features:
  - —Three bedrooms
  - —Two full baths
- Large volume Great Room highlighted by a fireplace flanked by windows
- Roomy Master Bedroom Suite has a volume ceiling and special amenities: a skylighted Dressing/Bath Area, plant shelf, a large walk-in closet, a double vanity and a whirlpool tub
- This home is designed with a basement foundation
- Alternate foundation options available at an additional charge. Please call 1-800-235-5700 for more information.

MAIN FLOOR — 1,604 SQ. FT.
GARAGE — 466 SQ. FT.

Total living area:
1,604 sq. ft.

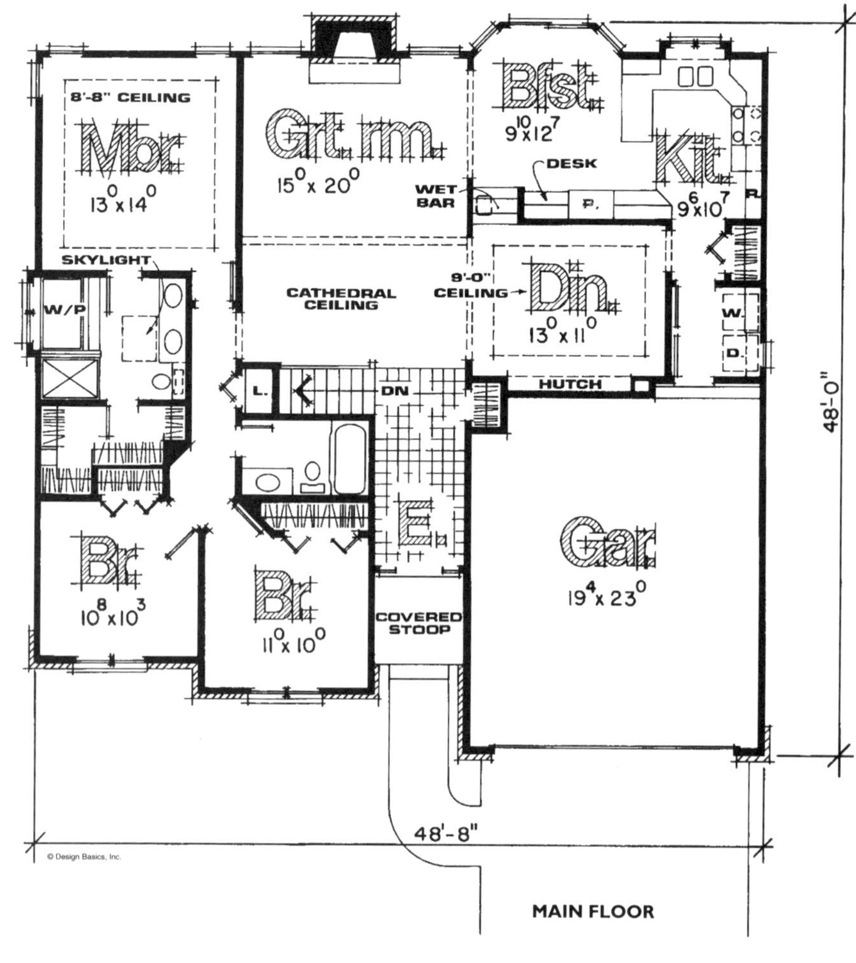

8'-8" CEILING
Mbr.
13⁰x14⁰
Grt. rm.
15⁰ x 20⁰
Bfst.
9¹⁰x12⁷
DESK
Kit.
9⁶x10⁷
WET BAR
P.
R.
SKYLIGHT
W/P
CATHEDRAL CEILING
9'-0" CEILING
Din.
13⁰ x 11⁰
W.
D.
L.
DN
HUTCH
48'-0"
Br.
10⁸x10³
Br.
11⁰x 10⁰
E.
Gar.
19⁴x 23⁰
COVERED STOOP
48'-8"
© Design Basics, Inc.

MAIN FLOOR

PLAN NO. 91053

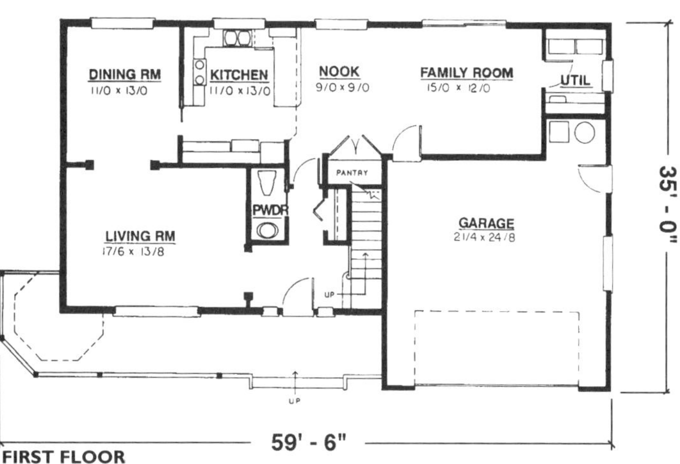
DINING RM
11/0 x 13/0
KITCHEN
11/0 x 13/0
NOOK
9/0 x 9/0
FAMILY ROOM
15/0 x 12/0
UTIL
PANTRY
PWDR
LIVING RM
17/6 x 13/8
GARAGE
21/4 x 24/8
UP
35' - 0"
59' - 6"
FIRST FLOOR

Updated Victorian

Price Code: D

- This plan features:
  - — Three bedrooms
  - — Two full and one half baths
- The classic Victorian exterior design of this home is accented by a wonderful Turret Room and second floor covered Porch
- The efficient, U-shaped Kitchen with loads of counterspace and a peninsula snack bar, opens to an eating Nook and Family Room for informal gatherings and activities
- This home is designed with a crawl-space foundation

FIRST FLOOR — 1,150 SQ. FT.
SECOND FLOOR — 949 SQ. FT.
GARAGE — 484 SQ. FT

Total living area:
2,099 sq. ft.

BEDRM • 2
13/10 x 10/0
BEDRM • 3
13/10 x 10/0
LINEN
DN
MASTER BEDROOM
15/0 x 14/0 AVG.
W•I•C
B • 3
M • B
SITTING
FRENCH
36" RAILING
SECOND FLOOR

PLAN NO.34150

Elegant Window Treatment

Price Code: A

- This plan features:
- — Two bedrooms (optional third)
- — Two full baths
- A huge, arched window that floods the Den with natural light
- Compact, efficient use of space
- An efficient Kitchen with easy access to the Dining Room
- A fireplaced Living Room with a sloping ceiling and a window wall
- This home is designed with basement, slab and crawlspace foundation options

MAIN FLOOR — 1,492 SQ. FT.
BASEMENT — 1,486 SQ. FT.
GARAGE — 462 SQ. FT.

Total living area:
1,492 sq. ft.

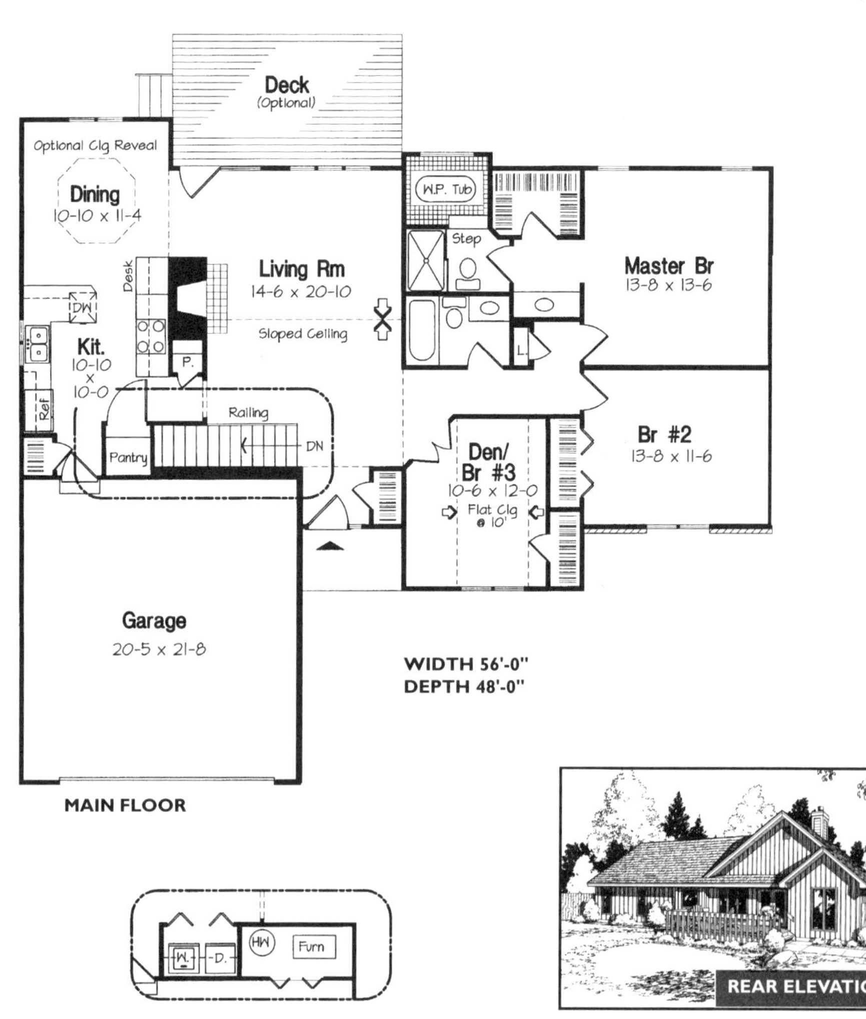

Deck
(Optional)
Optional Clg Reveal
Dining
10-10 x 11-4
Desk
DW
Kit.
10-10
x
10-0
Ref
P.
Pantry
Railing
DN
Living Rm
14-6 x 20-10
Sloped Ceiling
W.P. Tub
Step
L
Master Br
13-8 x 13-6
Br #2
13-8 x 11-6
Den/
Br #3
10-6 x 12-0
Flat Clg
@ 10'
Garage
20-5 x 21-8
WIDTH 56'-0"
DEPTH 48'-0"
MAIN FLOOR
W.
D.
HW
Furn
REAR ELEVATIO

PLAN NO. 99420

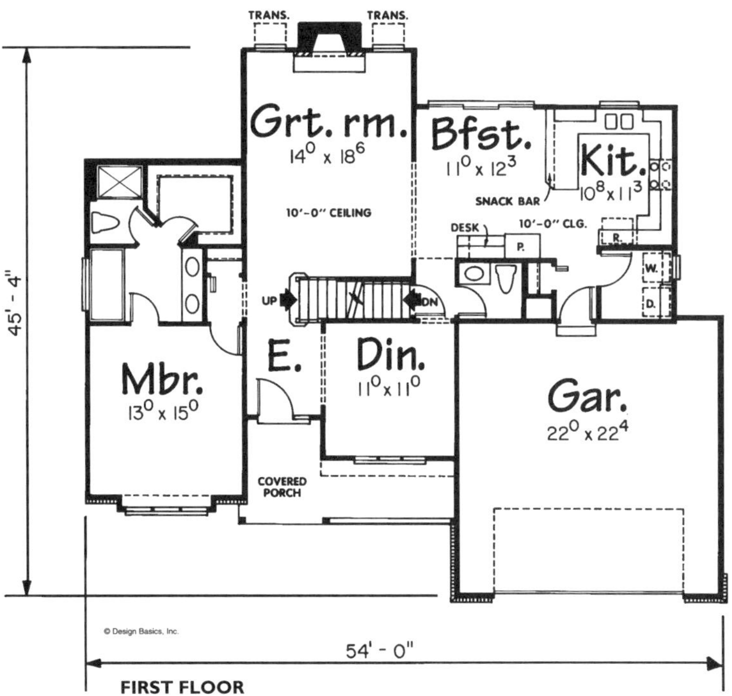

TRANS.
TRANS.
Grt. rm.
14^0 x 18^6
10'-0" CEILING
Bfst.
11^0 x 12^3
Kit.
10^8 x 11^3
SNACK BAR
DESK
10'-0" CLG.
P.
R.
W.
D.
UP
DN
Mbr.
13^0 x 15^0
E.
Din.
11^0 x 11^0
Gar.
22^0 x 22^4
COVERED PORCH
45' - 4"
54' - 0"
© Design Basics, Inc.
FIRST FLOOR

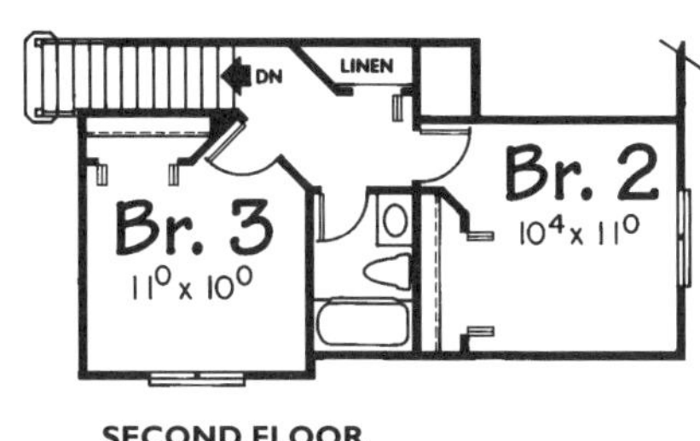

DN
LINEN
Br. 3
11^0 x 10^0
Br. 2
10^4 x 11^0
SECOND FLOOR

Simplicity at its Finest

Price Code: B

- This plan features:
  - — Three bedrooms
  - — Two full and one half baths
- A covered Porch gives the home a nostalgic feel
- The volume Great Room offers a fireplace with transom windows on either side
- The formal Dining Room overlooks the Porch, which has easy access to the Kitchen
- This home is designed with a basement foundation
- Alternate foundation options available at an additional charge. Please call 1-800-235-5700 for more information.

FIRST FLOOR — 1,298 SQ. FT.
SECOND FLOOR — 396 SQ. FT.
BASEMENT — 1,298 SQ. FT.
GARAGE — 513 SQ. FT.

Total living area:
1,694 sq. ft.

PLAN NO. 93432

Porch Awaits a Comfy Chair

Price Code: C

- This plan features:
- — Three bedrooms
- — Two full and one half baths
- The Country-style front Porch provides a warm welcome
- The Family Room is highlighted by a fireplace and front windows
- The Dining Room is separated from the U-shaped Kitchen by an extended counter
- This home is designed with slab and crawlspace foundation options

FIRST FLOOR — 1,288 SQ. FT.
SECOND FLOOR — 545 SQ. FT.
GARAGE — 540 SQ. FT.

Total living area: 1,833 sq. ft.

Storage
22 x 24
Garage
WIDTH 50'-8"
DEPTH 74'-0"
Dining
13 x11
Kitchen
12 x 11
9' Ceiling
D
W
L
Family Room
15 x 19
9' Ceiling
Stairs Up
Open Above
Foyer
Master
15 x 14
9' Ceiling
Porch
39/6 x 8
FIRST FLOOR
L
Br.#2
15 x 11
8' Ceiling
Br.#3
13 x 11
8' Ceiling
Stairs Down
Attic Storage
Attic Storage
SECOND FLOOR

PLAN NO.93909

Inviting Wrap-Around Porch

Price Code: B

This plan features:

- Three bedrooms
- Two full baths
- A warm and inviting welcome, achieved by a wrap-around porch
- A skylight illuminating the Entry
- A corner gas fireplace and two skylights highlighted in the Great Room
- Flowing from the Great Room, the Dining Room naturally lighted by the sliding glass doors to a rear Deck and a skylight above
- A well-appointed, U-shaped Kitchen separated from the Dining Room by a breakfast bar and including another skylight
- A luxurious Master Bedroom equipped with a plush Bath and access to a private Deck
- Two additional Bedrooms sharing the full Bath and receiving light from the dormers
- This home is designed with a basement foundation

IAIN FLOOR — 1,716 SQ. FT.

Total living area:
1,716 sq. ft.

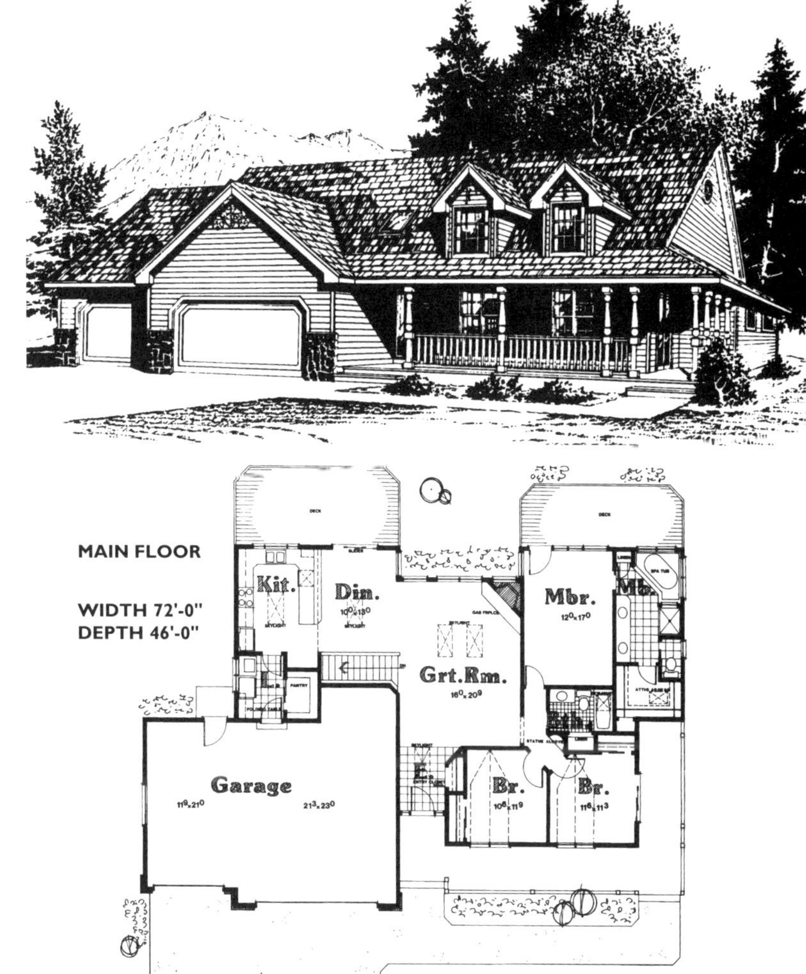

MAIN FLOOR
WIDTH 72'-0"
DEPTH 46'-0"
Kit.
Din.
Grt.Rm.
Mbr.
Mb.
Garage
Br.
Br.

PLAN NO.92610

Unique Turret Master Bedroom

Price Code: D

This plan features:

- Three bedrooms
- Two full and one half baths
- Graceful two-story Foyer with apron staircase
- Sunken Great Room with focal point fireplace and atrium door to Deck
- Efficient U-shaped Kitchen with work island, built-in Pantry, Breakfast Nook and adjoining Dining Room with bay window
- Sloped ceiling accents window alcove in Master Bedroom offering a plush Bath and walk-in closet
- Two second floor Bedrooms have private access to a double vanity Bath
- This home is designed with a basement foundation

IRST FLOOR — 1,625 SQ. FT.
ECOND FLOOR — 475 SQ. FT.
ARAGE — 437 SQ. FT.

Total living area:
2,101 sq. ft.

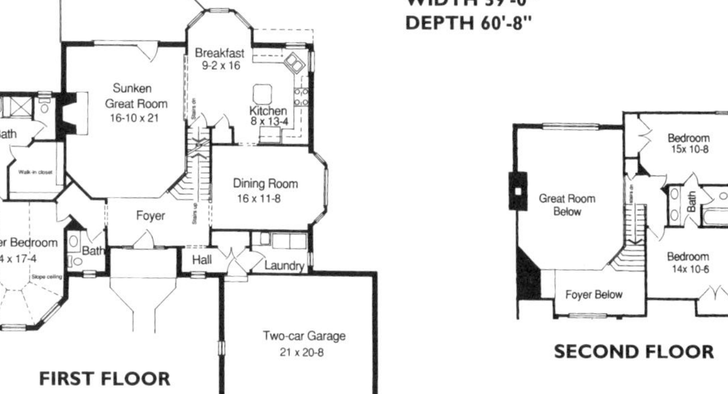

WIDTH 59'-0"
DEPTH 60'-8"
Deck
Breakfast
9-2 x 16
Sunken
Great Room
16-10 x 21
Kitchen
8 x 13-4
Bath
Dining Room
16 x 11-8
Foyer
Master Bedroom
14 x 17-4
Bath
Hall
Laundry
Two-car Garage
21 x 20-8
FIRST FLOOR
Bedroom
15x 10-8
Great Room
Below
Bath
Bedroom
14x 10-6
Foyer Below
SECOND FLOOR

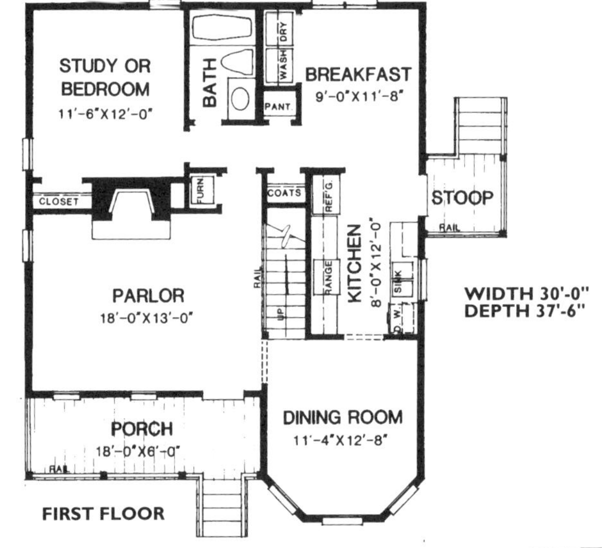
STUDY OR
BEDROOM
11'-6"X12'-0"
BATH
WASH
DRY
PANT
BREAKFAST
9'-0"X11'-8"
CLOSET
FURN
COATS
REF'G.
STOOP
RAIL
RANGE
KITCHEN
8'-0"X12'-0"
SINK
D.W.
PARLOR
18'-0"X13'-0"
UP
WIDTH 30'-0"
DEPTH 37'-6"
DINING ROOM
11'-4"X12'-8"
PORCH
18'-0"X6'-0"
RAIL
FIRST FLOOR

Compact Victorian

Price Code: B

- This plan features:
  - Three bedrooms
  - Three full baths
- The large front Parlor has a raised hearth fireplace
- The efficient galley Kitchen easily serves the formal Dining Room and informal Breakfast Room
- The beautiful Master Suite has two closets, an oversized tub and double vanity, plus a private Sitting Room with a bay window and vaulted ceiling
- This home is designed with basement, slab and crawlspace foundation options.

First floor — 954 sq. ft.
Second floor — 783 sq. ft.

Total living area:
1,737 sq. ft.

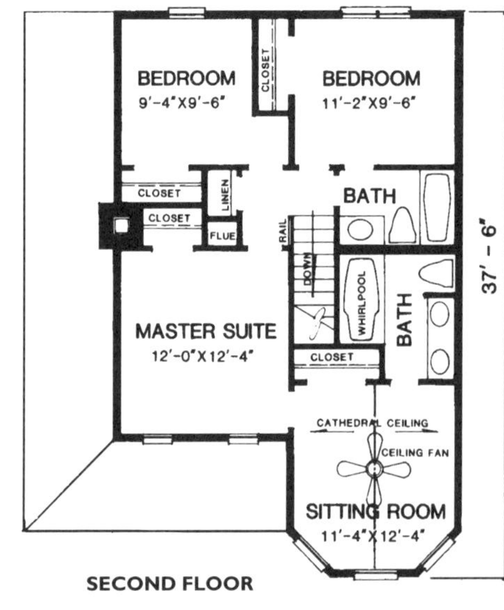
BEDROOM
9'-4"X9'-6"
CLOSET
BEDROOM
11'-2"X9'-6"
CLOSET
LINEN
CLOSET
FLUE
BATH
RAIL
DOWN
WHIRLPOOL
BATH
37' - 6"
MASTER SUITE
12'-0"X12'-4"
CLOSET
CATHEDRAL CEILING
CEILING FAN
SITTING ROOM
11'-4"X12'-4"
SECOND FLOOR

PLAN NO. 94608

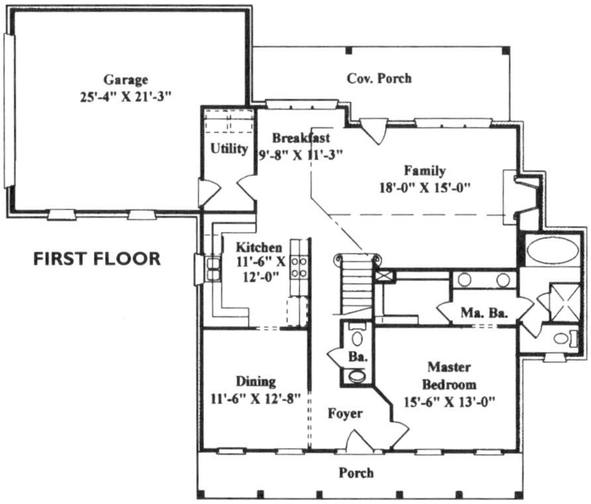

52' - 10"

FIRST FLOOR

Garage 25'-4" X 21'-3"

Cov. Porch

Utility

Breakfast 9'-8" X 11'-3"

Family 18'-0" X 15'-0"

Kitchen 11'-6" X 12'-0"

Ma. Ba.

Ba.

Dining 11'-6" X 12'-8"

Master Bedroom 15'-6" X 13'-0"

Foyer

Porch

63' - 10"

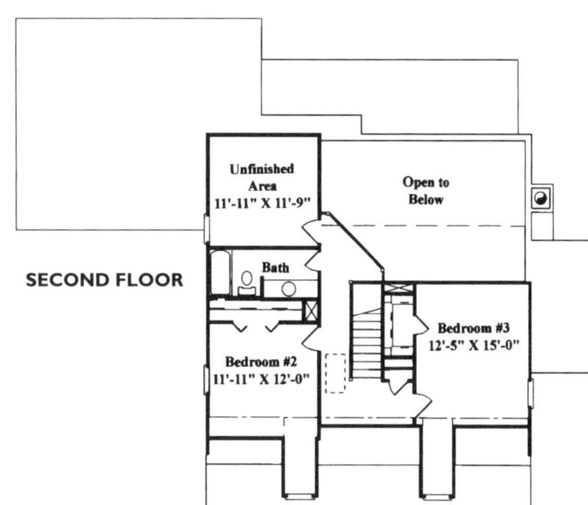
SECOND FLOOR
Unfinished Area
11'-11" X 11'-9"
Open to Below
Bath
Bedroom #3
12'-5" X 15'-0"
Bedroom #2
11'-11" X 12'-0"

Pillars Please the Eye

Price Code: D

- This plan features:
- — Three bedrooms
- — Two full and one half baths
- A welcoming front Porch leads into a two-story Foyer with banister staircase
- An expansive Family Room with a cozy fireplace, large windows and access to Covered Porch and Breakfast Area below vaulted ceiling
- A hub Kitchen efficiently serves formal Dining Room and bright Breakfast Area
- This home is designed with crawlspace and slab foundation options

FIRST FLOOR — 1,395 SQ. FT.
SECOND FLOOR — 676 SQ. FT.
GARAGE — 489 SQ. FT.

Total living area:
2,071 sq. ft.

PLAN NO. 34043

A Home for Today and Tomorrow

Price Code: B

- This plan features:
  - — Three bedrooms
  - — Two full baths
- An intriguing Breakfast Nook off the Kitchen
- A wide open, fireplaced Living Room with gla sliders to an optional Deck
- Step-saving arrangement of the Kitchen betwe the Breakfast Area and formal Dining Room
- A handsome Master Bedroom with sky-lit com partmentalized Bath
- This home is designed with basement, slab an crawlspace foundation options

MAIN FLOOR — 1,583 SQ. FT.
BASEMENT — 1,573 SQ. FT.
GARAGE — 484 SQ. FT.

Total living area:
1,583 sq. ft.

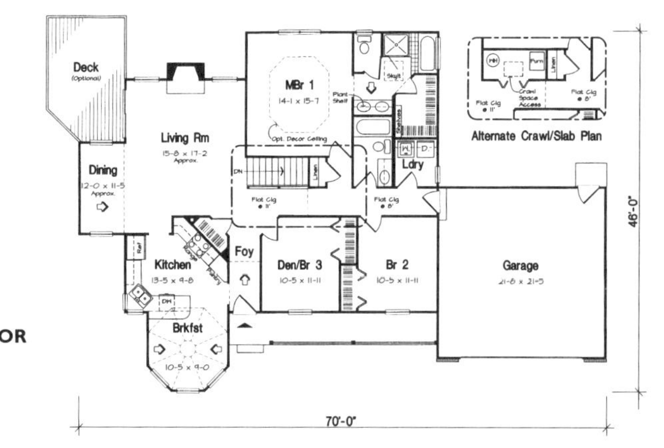

Deck
Living Rm
15-8 x 17-2
MBr 1
14-1 x 15-7
Dining
12-0 x 11-5
Kitchen
13-5 x 4-8
Foy
Den/Br 3
10-5 x 11-11
Br 2
10-5 x 11-11
Ldry
Garage
21-8 x 21-5
Brkfst
10-5 x 9-0
Alternate Crawl/Slab Plan
46'-0"
70'-0"

MAIN FLOOR

PLAN NO. 92609

A Little Drama

Price Code: C

- This plan features:
  - — Three bedrooms
  - — Two and one half baths
- A full twelve-foot-high Entry with transom an sidelights, multiple gables and a box window
- A sunken Great Room with a fireplace and access to a rear Porch
- A Breakfast Bay and Kitchen flowing into eac other and accessing a rear Porch
- A Master Bedroom with a tray ceiling, walk-in closet and a private Master Bath
- This home is designed with a basement foundation

FIRST FLOOR — 960 SQ. FT.
SECOND FLOOR — 808 SQ. FT.
BASEMENT — 922 SQ. FT.
GARAGE — 413 SQ. FT.

Total living area:
1,768 sq. ft.

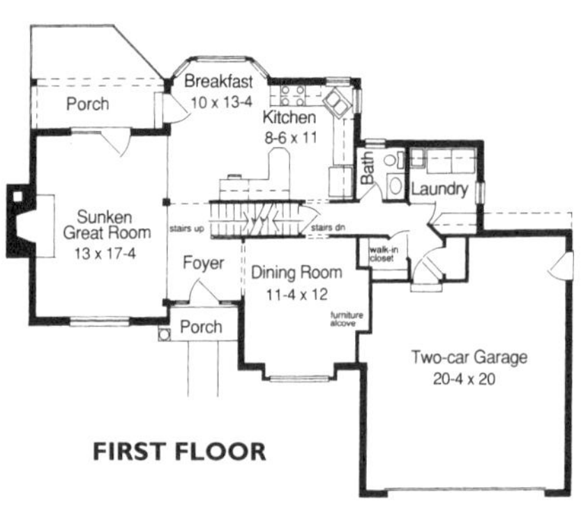

Porch
Breakfast
10 x 13-4
Kitchen
8-6 x 11
Bath
Laundry
Sunken
Great Room
13 x 17-4
Foyer
Dining Room
11-4 x 12
Porch
Two-car Garage
20-4 x 20
FIRST FLOOR

Bedroom
11-4 x 11-4
Bath
Hall
Great Room
Below
Foyer
Below
Master
Bedroom
12 x 16
Bath
Bedroom
11-4 x 9-6
SECOND FLOOR
WIDTH 55'-4"
DEPTH 40'-4"

PLAN NO.93212

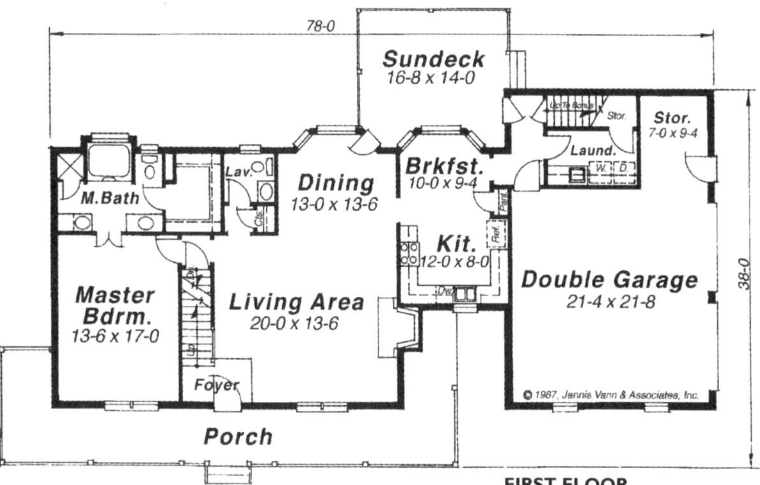

78-0
Sundeck
16-8 x 14-0
Stor.
7-0 x 9-4
Laund.
Brkfst.
10-0 x 9-4
Dining
13-0 x 13-6
Lav.
M.Bath
Kit.
12-0 x 8-0
Double Garage
21-4 x 21-8
38-0
Master
Bdrm.
13-6 x 17-0
Living Area
20-0 x 13-6
Foyer
Porch
© 1987, Jannis Vann & Associates, Inc.

FIRST FLOOR

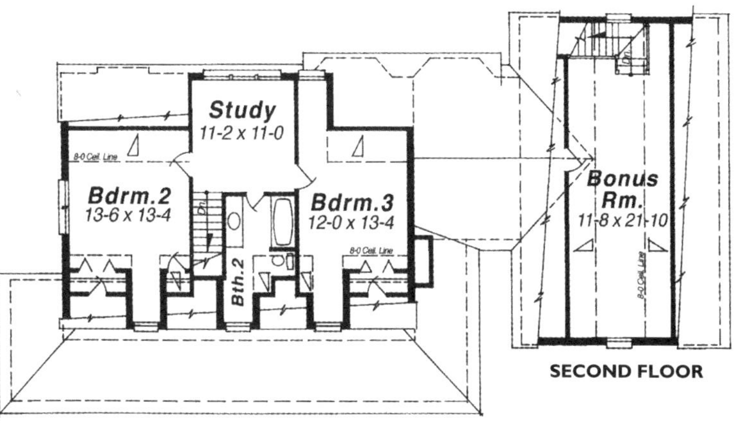

Study
11-2 x 11-0
Bdrm.2
13-6 x 13-4
Bdrm.3
12-0 x 13-4
Bth.2
Bonus
Rm.
11-8 x 21-10

SECOND FLOOR

Country Living

Price Code: D

- This plan features:
- — Three bedrooms
- — Two full and one half baths
- The Country-style Porch and dormers give this plan an old-fashioned feel
- The large Living Room with a cozy fireplace opens to the Dining Room for easy entertaining
- The first floor Master Suite has an elegant Bath
- This home is designed with basement, slab and crawlspace foundation options

FIRST FLOOR — 1,362 SQ. FT.
SECOND FLOOR — 729 SQ. FT.
BONUS — 384 SQ. FT.
BASEMENT — 988 SQ. FT.
GARAGE — 559 SQ. FT.

Total living area:
2,091 sq. ft.

PLAN NO. 94602

Arch Window Accents

Price Code: B

- This plan features:
  - — Three bedrooms
  - — Two full bathrooms
- Sheltered entry leads into pillared Foyer defining Living and Dining Room areas
- A cozy fireplace and access to covered Porch featured in Living Room
- Efficient Kitchen offers a work island, Utility and bright Breakfast Area
- Master Bedroom wing enhanced by a luxurious Bath with a walk-in closet, double vanity and Spa tub
- This home is designed with crawl-space and slab foundation options

MAIN FLOOR — 1,704 SQ. FT.

Total living area:
1,704 sq. ft.

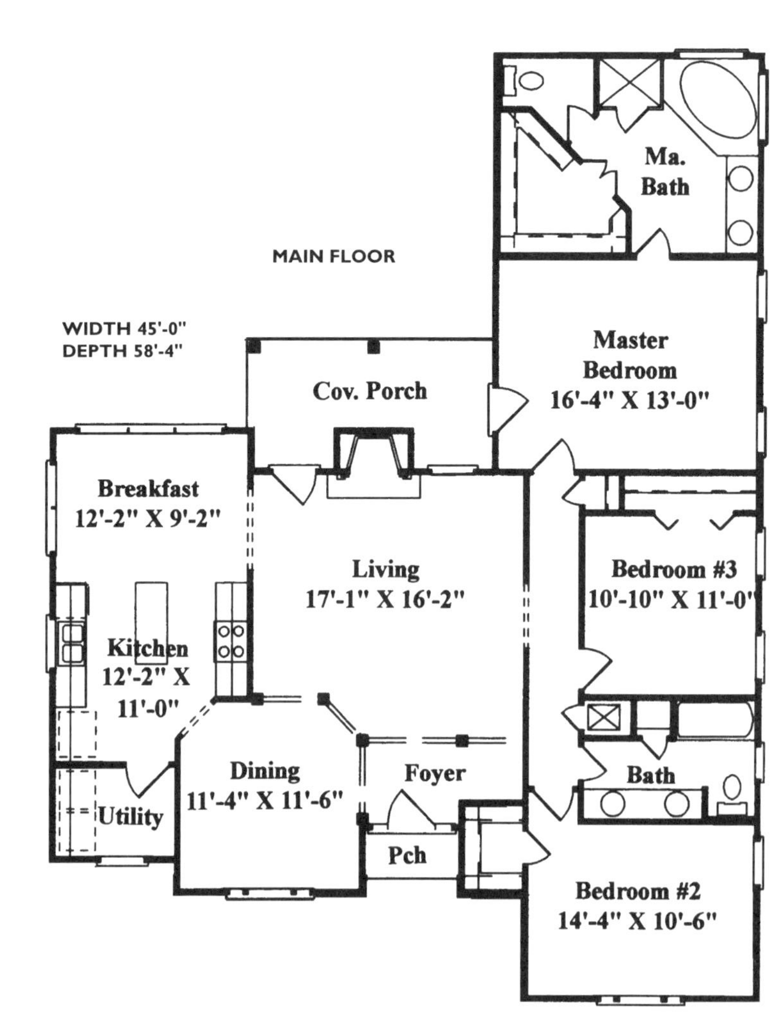
MAIN FLOOR
WIDTH 45'-0"
DEPTH 58'-4"
Ma. Bath
Master Bedroom 16'-4" X 13'-0"
Cov. Porch
Breakfast 12'-2" X 9'-2"
Living 17'-1" X 16'-2"
Bedroom #3 10'-10" X 11'-0"
Kitchen 12'-2" X 11'-0"
Dining 11'-4" X 11'-6"
Foyer
Bath
Utility
Pch
Bedroom #2 14'-4" X 10'-6"

Carefree Convenience

Price Code: B

This plan features:

- Three bedrooms
- Two full baths
- A galley Kitchen, centrally located between the Dining, Breakfast and Living Room areas
- A huge Family Room which exits onto the patio
- A Master Suite with double closets and vanities with two additional Bedrooms share a full Bathroom
- This home is designed with a slab foundation

AIN FLOOR — 1,600 SQ. FT.
ARAGE — 465 SQ. FT.

Total living area:
1,600 sq. ft.

PLAN NO.10674

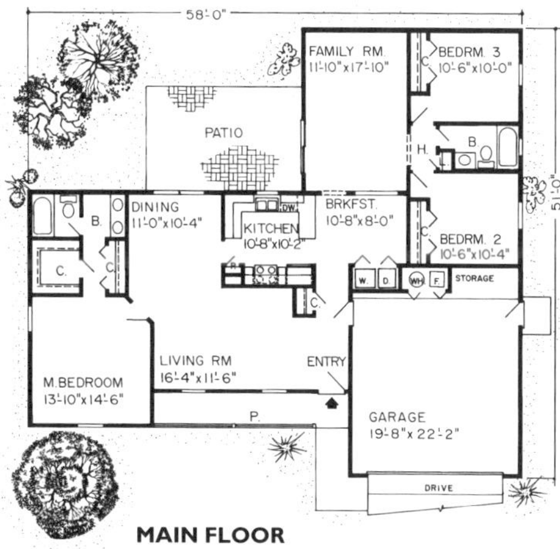
58'-0"
51'-0"
FAMILY RM.
11'-10"x17'-10"
BEDRM. 3
10'-6"x10'-0"
PATIO
B.
H.
DINING
11'-0"x10'-4"
KITCHEN
10'-8"x10'-2"
BRKFST.
10'-8"x8'-0"
BEDRM. 2
10'-6"x10'-4"
STORAGE
M.BEDROOM
13'-10"x14'-6"
LIVING RM
16'-4"x11'-6"
ENTRY
GARAGE
19'-8"x22'-2"
DRIVE
MAIN FLOOR

Arched Windows

Price Code: E

This plan features:

- Three bedrooms
- Two and one half baths
- A vaulted Foyer flanked by a soaring Living Room with huge palladian windows
- A Family Room with a massive two-way fireplace
- A Master Suite with garden spa, private Deck access, and a walk-in closet
- This home is designed with basement, slab and crawlspace foundation options

RST FLOOR — 1,752 SQ. FT.
COND FLOOR — 620 SQ. FT.
ASEMENT — 1,726 SQ. FT.
ARAGE — 714 SQ. FT.

Total living area:
2,372 sq. ft.

PLAN NO.20368

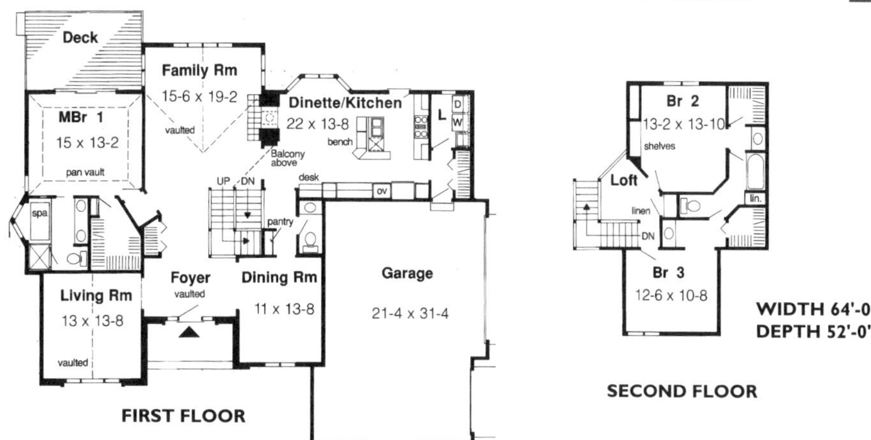
Deck
Family Rm
15-6 x 19-2
vaulted
MBr 1
15 x 13-2
pan vault
Dinette/Kitchen
22 x 13-8
bench
Balcony above
desk
UP DN
pantry
spa
Living Rm
13 x 13-8
vaulted
Foyer
vaulted
Dining Rm
11 x 13-8
Garage
21-4 x 31-4
Br 2
13-2 x 13-10
shelves
Loft
linen
DN
Br 3
12-6 x 10-8
WIDTH 64'-0"
DEPTH 52'-0"
FIRST FLOOR

SECOND FLOOR

PLAN NO. 93021

Open Concept Home

Price Code: A

- This plan features:
  - — Three bedrooms
  - — Two full baths
- An angled Entry creating the illusion of space
- Two square columns that flank the bar and separate the Kitchen from the Living Room
- A Dining Room that may service both formal and informal occasions
- A Master Bedroom with a large walk-in closet
- A large Master Bath with double vanities, linen closet and whirlpool tub/shower combination
- This home is designed with crawlspace and slab foundation options

MAIN FLOOR — 1,282 SQ. FT.
GARAGE — 501 SQ. FT.

Total living area: 1,282 sq. ft.

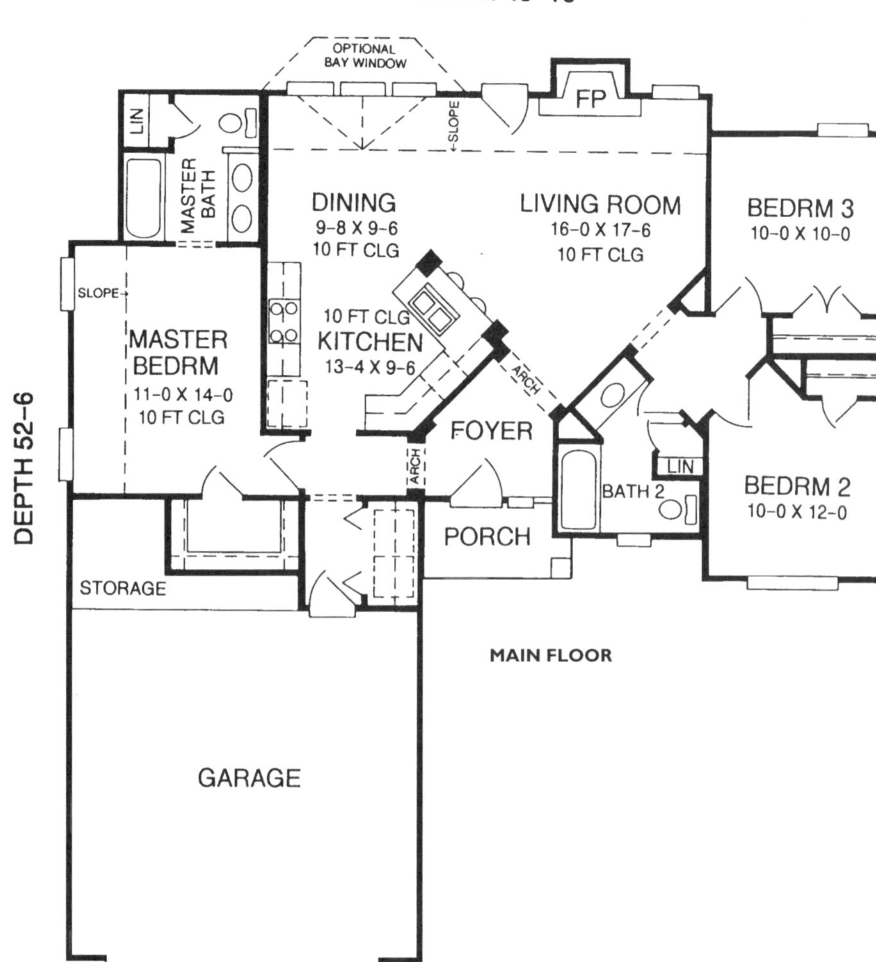

WIDTH 48–10
OPTIONAL BAY WINDOW
FP
SLOPE
LIN
MASTER BATH
DINING
9–8 X 9–6
10 FT CLG
LIVING ROOM
16–0 X 17–6
10 FT CLG
BEDRM 3
10–0 X 10–0
SLOPE
MASTER BEDRM
11–0 X 14–0
10 FT CLG
10 FT CLG
KITCHEN
13–4 X 9–6
ARCH
FOYER
ARCH
LIN
BATH 2
BEDRM 2
10–0 X 12–0
DEPTH 52–6
PORCH
STORAGE
MAIN FLOOR
GARAGE

PLAN NO. 92646

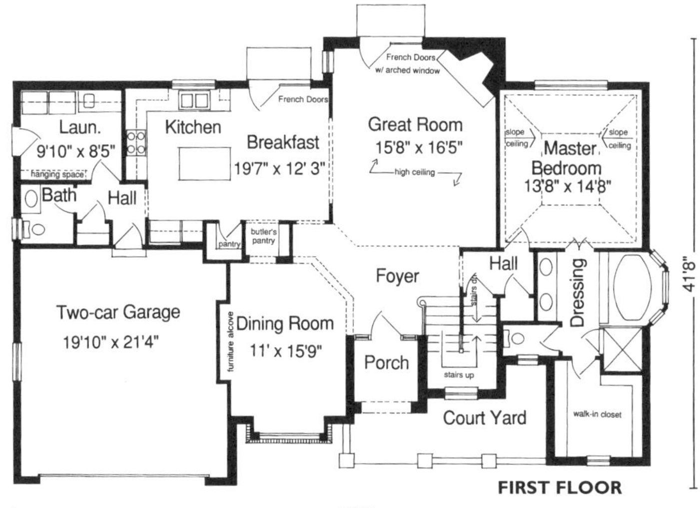
French Doors w/ arched window
Great Room
15'8" x 16'5"
high ceiling
Kitchen
Breakfast
19'7" x 12' 3"
French Doors
Laun.
9'10" x 8'5"
hanging space
Bath
Hall
pantry
butler's pantry
slope ceiling
Master Bedroom
13'8" x 14'8"
Two-car Garage
19'10" x 21'4"
Dining Room
11' x 15'9"
furniture alcove
Foyer
stairs dn
Hall
Dressing
Porch
stairs up
Court Yard
walk-in closet
41'8"
FIRST FLOOR
61'0"

slope ceiling
Bedroom
10'8" x 13'5"
Bedroom
10'9" x 10'
Great Room Below
linen
linen
Hall
Bath
Balcony
stairs dn
desk
bookshelves
Bedroom
11' x 11'2"
Porch
slope ceiling
slope ceiling
SECOND FLOOR

Old World Charm

Price Code: E

- This plan features:
- — Four bedrooms
- — Two full and one half baths
- Balustrade railings and a front Courtyard create an impressive facade
- The Great Room has a corner fire-place, high ceiling and French doors
- The Country Kitchen with a work island and two Pantries is adjacent to the Breakfast Area, Laundry Room and Garage Entry
- The Master Bedroom features a sloped ceiling, and plush Bath
- This home is designed with a base-ment foundation

FIRST FLOOR — 1,595 SQ. FT.
SECOND FLOOR — 725 SQ. FT.
BASEMENT — 1,471 SQ. FT.
GARAGE — 409 SQ. FT.

Total living area:
2,320 sq. ft.

PLAN NO. 90844

Country Influence

Price Code: B

- This plan features:
- — Three bedrooms
- — Two full and one half baths
- The wrap-around Deck provides outdoor living space, ideal for a sloping lot
- The Master Bedroom has a half Bath and ample closet space
- Another Bedroom on the first floor adjoins a full Bath
- The second floor Bedroom/Studio, with a private Deck, has a nearby full, Bath and a Loft Area
- This home is designed with a basement foundation

FIRST FLOOR — 1,086 SQ. FT.
SECOND FLOOR — 466 SQ. FT.
BASEMENT— 1,080 SQ. FT.

Total living area:
1,552 sq. ft.

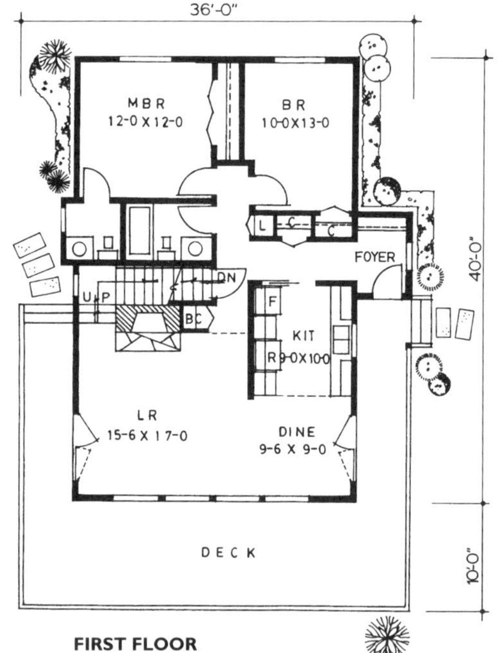
36'-0"
MBR
12-0 X 12-0
BR
10-0X13-0
L
C
C
FOYER
DN
UP
BC
F
KIT
R
9-0X10-0
LR
15-6 X 17-0
DINE
9-6 X 9-0
DECK
40'-0"
10'-0"

FIRST FLOOR

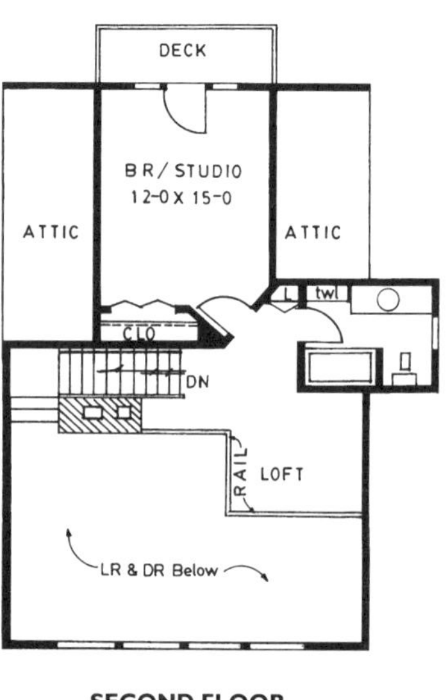
DECK
BR/STUDIO
12-0 X 15-0
ATTIC
ATTIC
L
twl
CLO
DN
RAIL
LOFT
LR & DR Below

SECOND FLOOR

PLAN NO. 99450

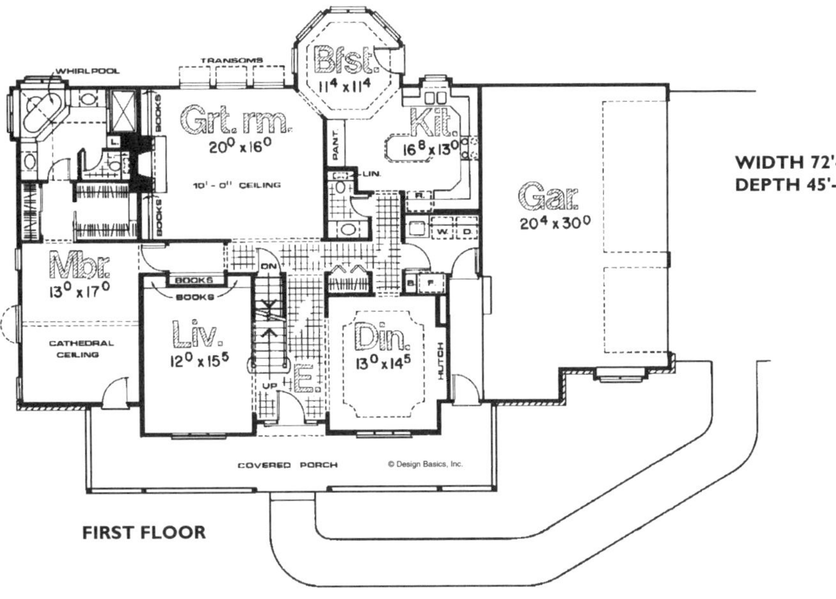
WHIRLPOOL
TRANSOMS
Bfst.
11⁴ x 11⁴
Grt. rm.
20⁰ x 16⁰
10'-0" CEILING
BOOKS
PANT
Kit.
16⁸ x 13⁰
LIN.
Gar.
20⁴ x 30⁰
Mbr.
13⁰ x 17⁰
CATHEDRAL CEILING
Liv.
12⁰ x 15⁵
Din.
13⁰ x 14⁵
HUTCH
DN
UP
E.
COVERED PORCH
© Design Basics, Inc.

WIDTH 72'-0"
DEPTH 45'-4"

FIRST FLOOR

SECOND FLOOR

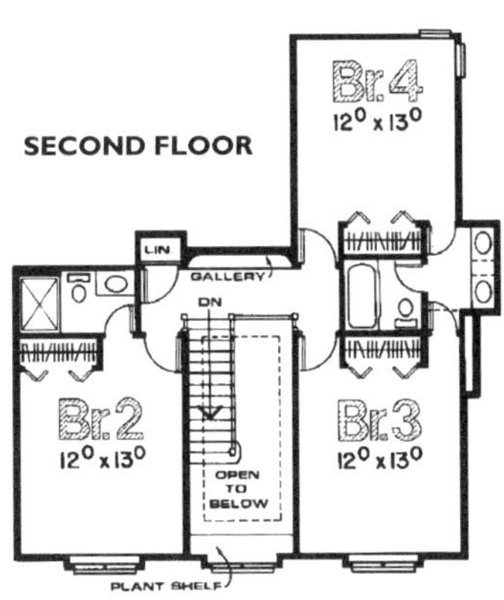
Br. 4
12⁰ x 13⁰
LIN
GALLERY
DN
Br. 2
12⁰ x 13⁰
OPEN TO BELOW
Br. 3
12⁰ x 13⁰
PLANT SHELF

Fashionable Country-Style

Price Code: F

- This plan features:
  - — Four bedrooms
  - — Two full, one three-quarter and one half baths
- The large, covered front Porch adds old-fashioned appeal to this modern floor plan
- The Kitchen has a center island and is adjacent to the gazebo-shaped Breakfast Area
- This home is designed with basement and slab foundation options
- Alternate foundation options available at an additional charge. Please call 1-800-235-5700 for more information.

FIRST FLOOR — 1,881 SQ. FT.
SECOND FLOOR — 814 SQ. FT.
BASEMENT — 1,881 SQ. FT.
GARAGE — 534 SQ. FT.

Total living area:
2,695 sq. ft.

PLAN NO. 91418

Carefree Comfort

Price Code: B

- This plan features:
- — Three bedrooms
- — Two full baths
- A dramatic vaulted Foyer
- A range-top island Kitchen with a sunny eating Nook surrounded by a built-in planter
- A vaulted ceiling in the Great Room with a built-in bar and corner fireplace
- A Master Bedroom with a private reading Nook, vaulted ceiling, walk-in closet, and a well-appointed private Bath
- This home is designed with basement, slab and crawlspace foundation options

MAIN FLOOR — 1,665 SQ. FT.

Total living area:
1,665 sq. ft.

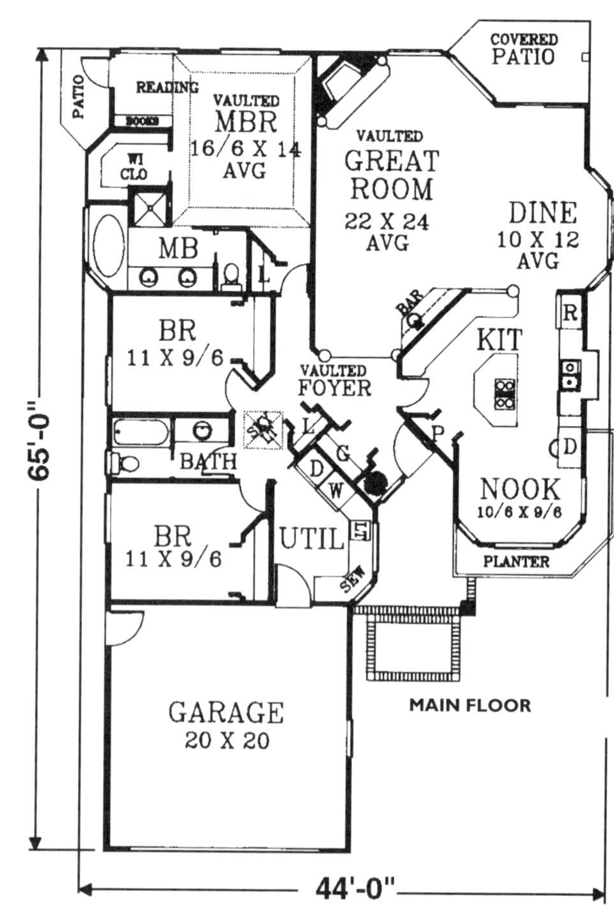

COVERED PATIO
PATIO
READING
BOOKS
VAULTED MBR 16/6 X 14 AVG
WI CLO
VAULTED GREAT ROOM 22 X 24 AVG
DINE 10 X 12 AVG
MB
BR 11 X 9/6
BAR
KIT
R
VAULTED FOYER
BATH
P
D
W
NOOK 10/6 X 9/6
BR 11 X 9/6
UTIL
SEW
PLANTER
65'-0"
GARAGE 20 X 20
MAIN FLOOR
44'-0"

UTIL
D
W

ALTERNATE BASEMENT PLAN

PLAN NO. 20164

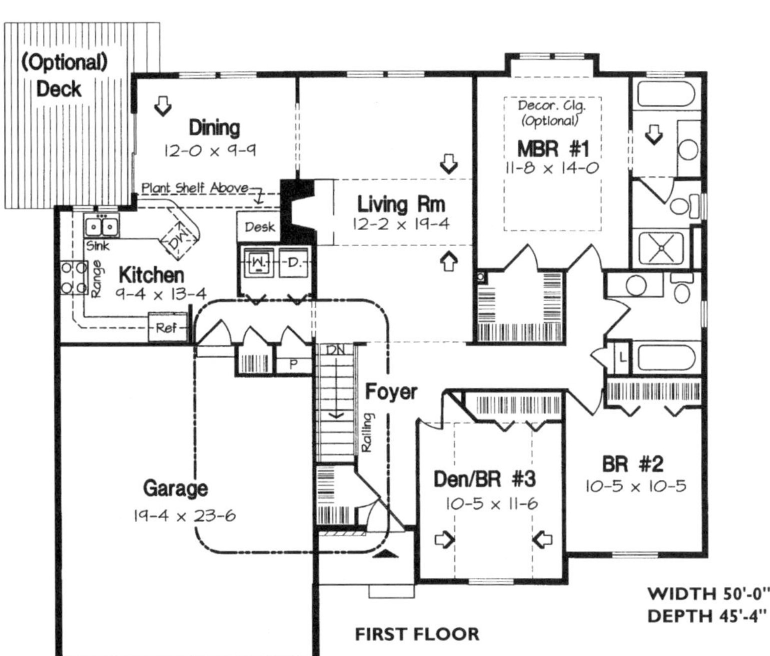
(Optional)
Deck
Dining
12-0 x 9-9
Plant Shelf Above
Sink
Range
Kitchen
9-4 x 13-4
Ref
Desk
W.
D.
Living Rm
12-2 x 19-4
Decor. Clg.
(Optional)
MBR #1
11-8 x 14-0
P
DN
Foyer
Railing
L
Garage
19-4 x 23-6
Den/BR #3
10-5 x 11-6
BR #2
10-5 x 10-5
WIDTH 50'-0"
DEPTH 45'-4"
FIRST FLOOR

Easy Living

Price Code: A

- This plan features:
  - Three bedrooms
  - Two full baths
- A dramatic sloped ceiling and a massive fireplace in the Living Room
- A Dining Room crowned by a sloping ceiling and a plant shelf also having sliding doors to the Deck
- A U-shaped Kitchen with abundant cabinets, a window over the sink and a walk-in Pantry
- This home is designed with basement, slab and crawlspace foundation options

FIRST FLOOR — 1,456 SQ. FT.
BASEMENT — 1,448 SQ. FT.
GARAGE — 452 SQ. FT.

Total living area:
1,456 sq. ft.

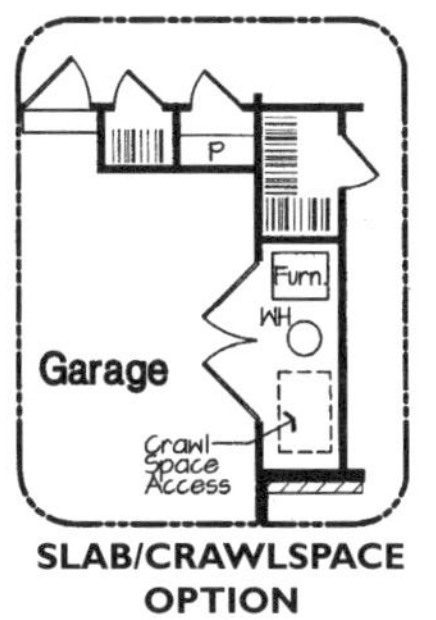
P
Furn.
WH
Garage
Crawl Space Access

SLAB/CRAWLSPACE OPTION

PLAN NO. 20083

One-Level with a Twist

Price Code: B

- This plan features:
- — Three bedrooms
- — Two full baths
- Wide-open active areas that are centrally located
- A spacious Dining, Living, and Kitchen area
- A Master Suite at the rear of the house with a full Bath
- Two additional Bedrooms that share a full Bath and the quiet atmosphere that results from an intelligent design
- This home is designed with basement, slab and crawlspace foundation options

MAIN FLOOR — 1,575 SQ. FT.
BASEMENT — 1,575 SQ. FT.
GARAGE — 475 SQ. FT.

Total living area:
1,575 sq. ft.

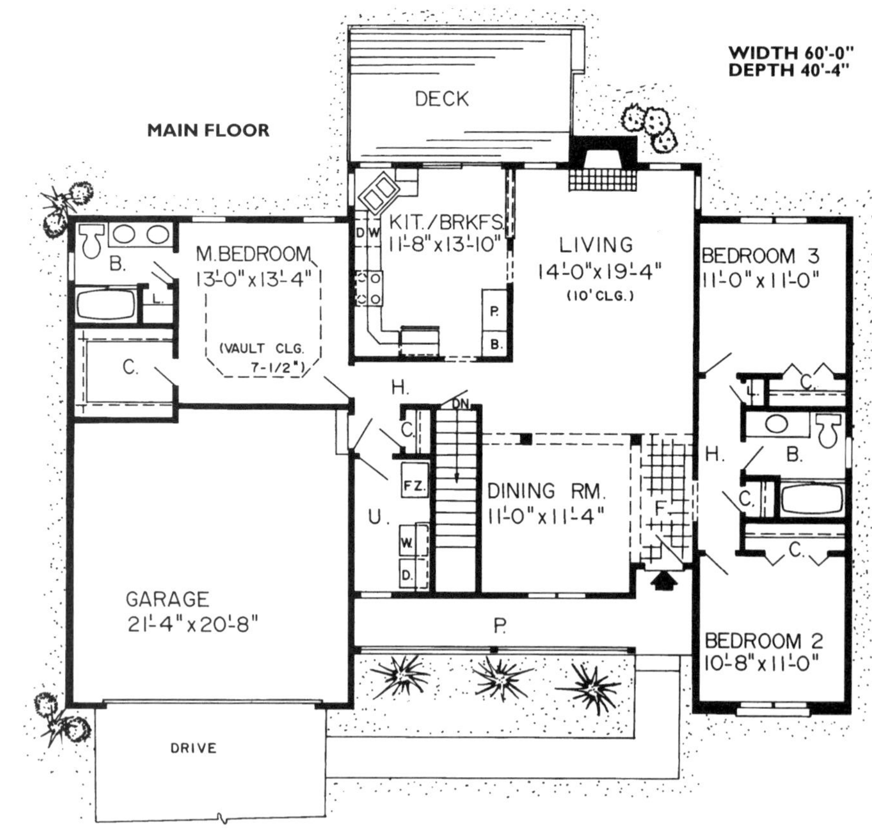

WIDTH 60'-0"
DEPTH 40'-4"
MAIN FLOOR
DECK
KIT./BRKFS.
11'-8"x13'-10"
LIVING
14'-0"x19'-4"
(10' CLG.)
BEDROOM 3
11'-0"x11'-0"
M.BEDROOM
13'-0"x13'-4"
(VAULT CLG. 7-1/2")
DW
P.
B.
L.
C.
H.
DN
F.Z.
DINING RM.
11'-0"x11'-4"
U.
W.
D.
F.
GARAGE
21'-4"x20'-8"
P.
BEDROOM 2
10'-8"x11'-0"
DRIVE

To order your Blueprints, call 1-800-235-5700

Cottage Charm

Price Code: A

This plan features:

- Two bedrooms
- One full baths
- Thoughtful use of space packs a lot of living into the charming design
- The Living Room features a volume ceiling, which helps define the space
- The second floor Master Bedroom has a large walk-in closet
- An upper-level Loft with open-rail balcony creates a private Sitting Area
- This home is designed with a crawlspace foundation

RST FLOOR — 593 SQ. FT.
ECOND FLOOR — 383 SQ. FT.

Total living area:
976 sq. ft.

PLAN NO.65003

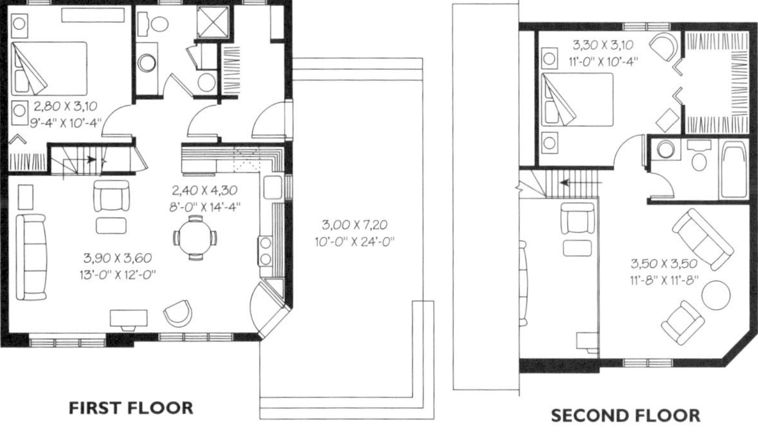

2,80 X 3,10
9'-4" X 10'-4"
2,40 X 4,30
8'-0" X 14'-4"
3,90 X 3,60
13'-0" X 12'-0"
3,00 X 7,20
10'-0" X 24'-0"
3,30 X 3,10
11'-0" X 10'-4"
3,50 X 3,50
11'-8" X 11'-8"
FIRST FLOOR
SECOND FLOOR

WIDTH 22'-8"
DEPTH 26'-8"

Cozy Cottage

Price Code: A

This plan features:

- Three bedrooms
- One full and one half baths
- The Living Room and Dining Room are open to each other and share a fireplace in this charming cottage
- The efficient L-shaped Kitchen is open to the Dining Room and is large enough for a table or the addition of a center island.
- The first floor Bedroom could be used as a Den and has a lovely corner bay window
- Two additional second floor Bedrooms each have large closets and share a Bath
- This home is designed with a basement foundation

RST FLOOR — 753 SQ. FT.
ECOND FLOOR — 505 SQ. FT.
ASEMENT — 753 SQ. FT.

Total living area:
1,258 sq. ft.

PLAN NO.65140

3,70 x 3,40
12'-4" x 11'-4"
3,20 x 2,60
10'-8" x 8'-8"
4,50 x 3,70
15'-0" x 12'-4"
3,00 x 2,70
10'-0" x 9'-0"

FIRST FLOOR

WIDTH 30'-0"
DEPTH 28'-0"

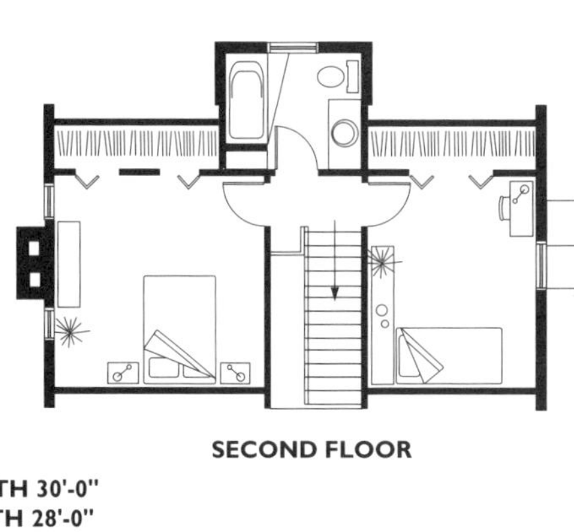

SECOND FLOOR

PLAN NO. 90444

Traditional Ranch

Price Code: E

- This plan features:
  - — Three bedrooms
  - — Three full baths
- The Great Room has skylights, a fireplace and a vaulted ceiling
- The double L-shaped Kitchen has an eating bar open to the bayed Breakfast Room
- The Master Suite has a walk-in closet, corner garden tub, dual vanity and a linen closet
- The two additional Bedrooms, each with a walk-in closet and built-in desk, share a full Bath
- This home is designed with basement and crawlspace foundation options

MAIN FLOOR — 1,996 SQ. FT.
LOFT — 305 SQ. FT.

Total living area:
2,301 sq. ft.

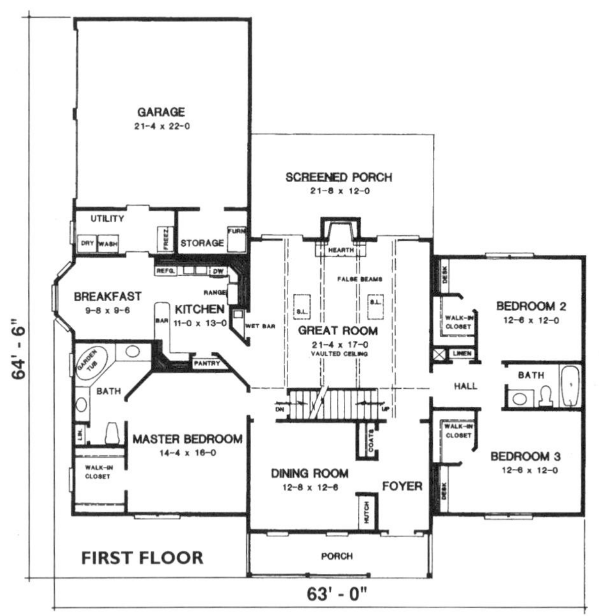
GARAGE
21-4 x 22-0
SCREENED PORCH
21-8 x 12-0
UTILITY
STORAGE
BREAKFAST
9-8 x 9-6
KITCHEN
11-0 x 13-0
GREAT ROOM
21-4 x 17-0
VAULTED CEILING
BEDROOM 2
12-6 x 12-0
BATH
HALL
MASTER BEDROOM
14-4 x 16-0
BEDROOM 3
12-6 x 12-0
DINING ROOM
12-8 x 12-8
FOYER
PORCH
FIRST FLOOR
64' - 6"
63' - 0"

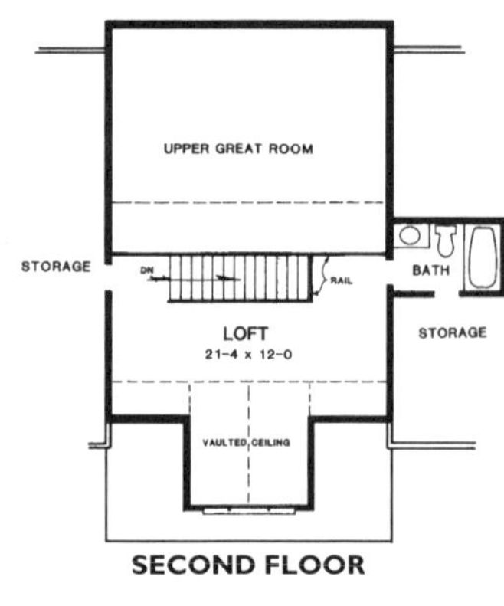
UPPER GREAT ROOM
STORAGE
BATH
LOFT
21-4 x 12-0
STORAGE
VAULTED CEILING
SECOND FLOOR

PLAN NO. 99641

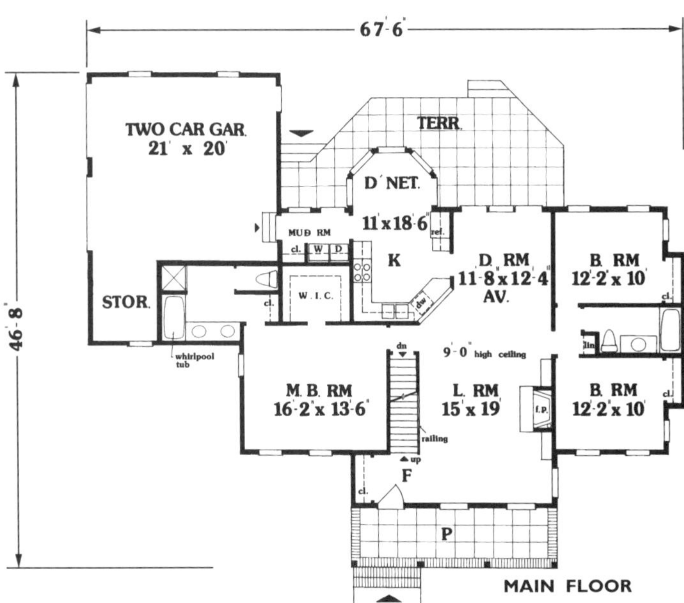

67'6"
TWO CAR GAR.
21' x 20'
TERR.
D'NET.
11'x18'6"
MUD RM
cl.
W
D
ref.
K
D. RM
11'8"x12'4"
AV.
B. RM
12'2"x10'
STOR.
W. I. C.
cl.
dw
46'8"
whirlpool tub
dn
9'-0" high ceiling
lin
M.B. RM
16'2"x13'6"
L. RM
15'x19'
F.P.
B. RM
12'2"x10'
railing
up
F
cl.
P
MAIN FLOOR

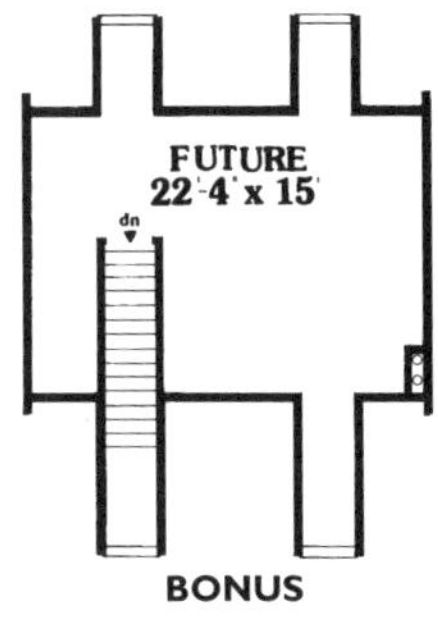

FUTURE
22'4"x15'
dn
BONUS

Southern Charm

Price Code: B

- This plan features:
  - Three bedrooms
  - Two full baths
- A varied roof line with dormers and a charming colonnaded front Porch sheltering the entrance
- An expansive Living Room enhanced by nine-foot ceilings and a bookcase-flanked fireplace, opening into the Dining Room
- A Master Suite with a large walk-in closet and a compartmented Bath with a separated stall shower, whirlpool tub, double-basin vanity and linen closet
- This home is designed with basement and slab foundation options

MAIN FLOOR — 1,567 SQ. FT.
BONUS FLOOR — 462 SQ. FT.
BASEMENT — 1,567 SQ. FT.
GARAGE — 504 SQ. FT.

**Total living area:
1,567 sq. ft.**

PLAN NO.10652

Two-Way Fireplace

Price Code: E

- This plan features:
  - — Three bedrooms
  - — Two full and one half baths
- A large Kitchen with cook-top island and a Breakfast Area opening to the Deck
- Built-in cedar closets and spacious Bedrooms
- A Master Suite loaded with a walk-in closet, sk light, double vanities and a sunken tub
- A vaulted formal Dining Room and ceiling fan the Kitchen and Living Room
- This home is designed with a basement founda

FIRST FLOOR — 1,789 SQ. FT.
SECOND FLOOR — 568 SQ. FT.
BASEMENT — 1,789 SQ. FT.
GARAGE — 529 SQ. FT.

Total living area:
2,357 sq. ft.

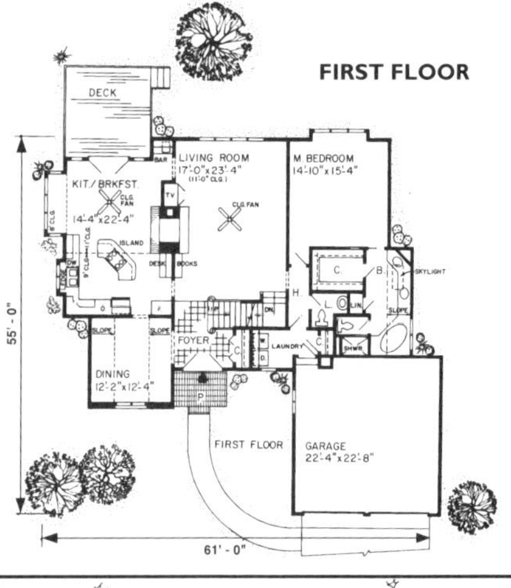

DECK
LIVING ROOM
17'-0"x23'-4"
M. BEDROOM
14'-10"x15'-4"
KIT./BRKFST.
14'-4"x22'-4"
FOYER
DINING
12'-2"x12'-4"
GARAGE
22'-4"x22'-8"
55'-0"
61'-0"

FIRST FLOOR

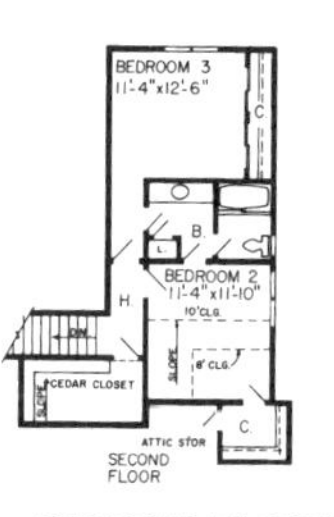

BEDROOM 3
11'-4"x12'-6"
BEDROOM 2
11'-4"x11'-10"
CEDAR CLOSET
SECOND FLOOR

SECOND FLOOR

PLAN NO.24701

Convenient Floor Plan

Price Code: B

- This plan features:
  - — Three bedrooms
  - — Two full baths
- Central Foyer leads to Den/Guest Room with arched window below vaulted ceiling and Liv Room accented by two-sided fireplace
- Efficient, U-shaped Kitchen with peninsula counter/breakfast bar serving Dining Room a adjacent Utility/Pantry
- Master Suite features large walk-in closet and private Bathroom with double vanity and whirlpool tub
- Two additional Bedrooms with ample closet space share full Bath
- This home is designed with basement, slab an crawlspace foundation options

MAIN FLOOR — 1,625 SQ. FT.
BASEMENT — 1,625 SQ. FT.
GARAGE — 455 SQ. FT.

Total living area:
1,625 sq. ft.

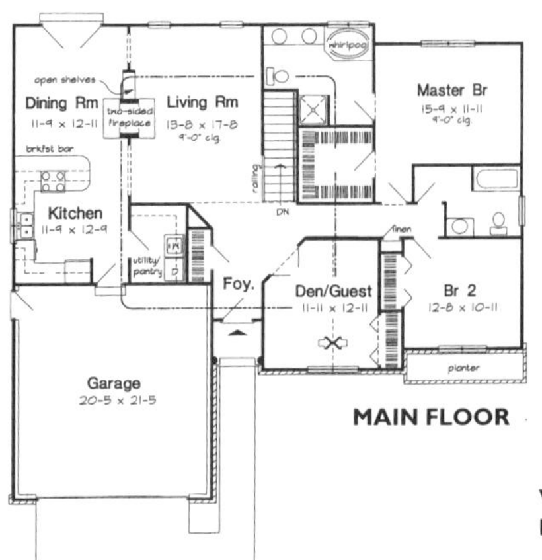

Dining Rm
11-9 x 12-11
Living Rm
13-8 x 17-8
Master Br
15-9 x 11-11
Kitchen
11-9 x 12-9
Foy.
Den/Guest
11-11 x 12-11
Br 2
12-8 x 10-11
Garage
20-5 x 21-5

MAIN FLOOR

Living Rm
13-8 x 17-8
Foy.

ALTERNATE FOUNDATION

WIDTH 54'-0"
DEPTH 48'-4"

PLAN NO. 91731

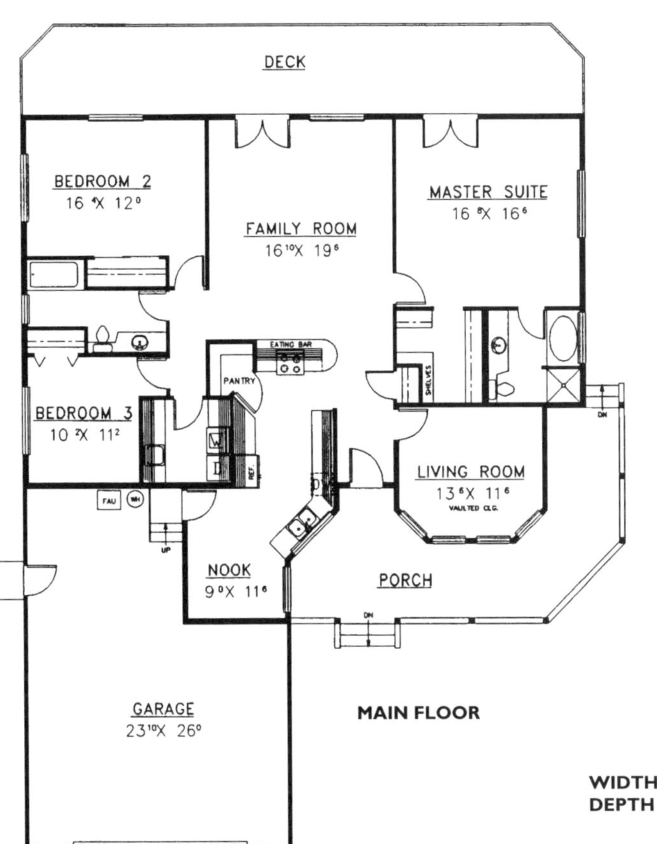
DECK
BEDROOM 2
16^4 X 12^0
FAMILY ROOM
16^{10} X 19^6
MASTER SUITE
16^8 X 16^6
EATING BAR
PANTRY
SHELVES
BEDROOM 3
10^2 X 11^2
LIVING ROOM
13^8 X 11^6
VAULTED CLG.
NOOK
9^0 X 11^6
PORCH
GARAGE
23^{10} X 26^0
MAIN FLOOR

WIDTH 51'-6"
DEPTH 65'-0"

Country-Style Charm

Price Code: C

- This plan features:
  - Three bedrooms
  - Two full baths
- Brick accents, front-facing gable, and railed wrap-around covered Porch
- A built-in range and oven in a L-shaped Kitchen
- A Nook with Garage access for convenient unloading of groceries and other supplies
- A bay window wrapping around the front of the formal Living Room
- A Master Suite with French doors opening to the Deck
- This home is designed with a crawlspace foundation

MAIN FLOOR — 1,857 SQ. FT.
GARAGE — 681 SQ. FT.

Total living area:
1,857 sq. ft.

PLAN NO. 90458

Two-Story Farmhouse

Price Code: E

- This plan features:
  - Three bedrooms
  - Two full and one half baths
- The wrap-around Porch adds nostalgic appeal to this home
- The Great Room with fireplace has direct access from the Foyer
- An island, double sink, plenty of counter/cabinet space and a built-in Pantry complete the Kitchen
- The second floor Master Suite has a five-piece private Bath and a walk-in closet
- This home is designed with basement and crawlspace foundation options.

FIRST FLOOR — 1,125 SQ. FT.
SECOND FLOOR — 1,138 SQ. FT.
BASEMENT — 1,125 SQ. FT.

Total living area: 2,263 sq. ft.

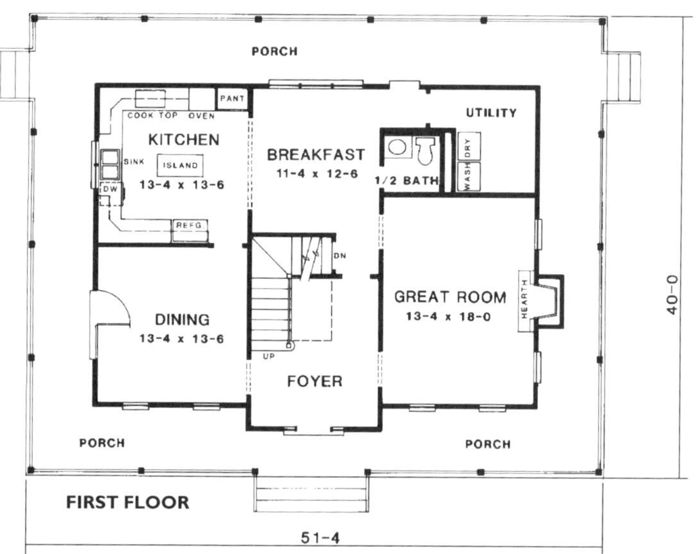

PORCH
PANT
COOK TOP OVEN
KITCHEN
SINK
ISLAND
13-4 x 13-6
DW
REFG
BREAKFAST
11-4 x 12-6
UTILITY
WASH DRY
1/2 BATH
DN
DINING
13-4 x 13-6
UP
FOYER
GREAT ROOM
13-4 x 18-0
HEARTH
40-0
PORCH
PORCH
FIRST FLOOR
51-4

W.I. CLOSET
SPA TUB
HIS
SHOWER
BATH
MASTER BATH
HERS
LINEN
BEDROOM 2
13-4 x 11-0
HALL
CLOSET
CLOSET
MASTER BEDROOM
13-4 x 18-0
BEDROOM 3
13-4 x 11-0
SITTING AREA
11-4 x 7-6
WINDOW SEAT
SECOND FLOOR

PLAN NO. 92640

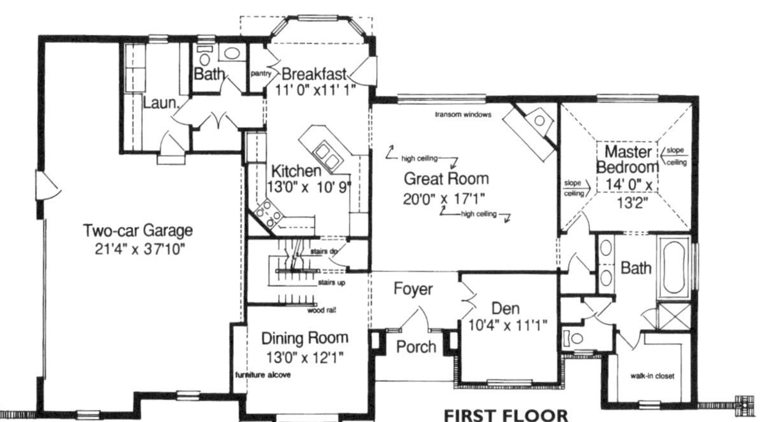
Bath
pantry
Breakfast
11' 0" x11' 1"
Laun.
transom windows
Kitchen
13'0" x 10'9"
high ceiling
Great Room
20'0" x 17'1"
high ceiling
Master
Bedroom
14' 0" x
13'2"
slope ceiling
slope ceiling
Two-car Garage
21'4" x 37'10"
stairs dn
stairs up
wood rail
Foyer
Den
10'4" x 11'1"
Bath
Dining Room
13'0" x 12'1"
furniture alcove
Porch
walk-in closet
FIRST FLOOR

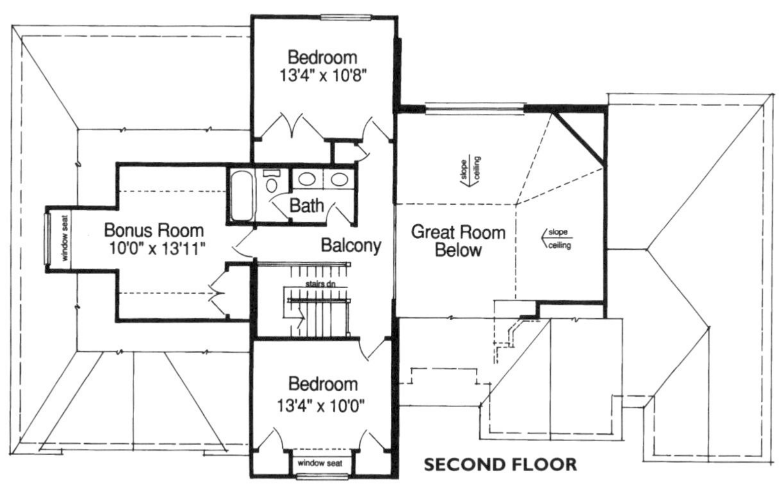
Bedroom
13'4" x 10'8"
slope ceiling
Bath
window seat
Bonus Room
10'0" x 13'11"
Balcony
Great Room
Below
slope ceiling
stairs dn
Bedroom
13'4" x 10'0"
window seat
SECOND FLOOR

Charm and Personality

Price Code: D

- This plan features:
  - Three bedrooms
  - Two full and one half baths
- The Great Room has a cathedral ceiling and a fireplace
- The efficient Kitchen offers plenty of angled counter space
- Secluded Master Bedroom with a slope ceiling, compartmentalized Bath and walk-in closet provides privacy
- This home is designed with a basement foundation
- Alternate foundation options available at an additional charge. Please call 1-800-235-5700 for more information.

FIRST FLOOR — 1,670 SQ. FT.
SECOND FLOOR — 580 SQ. FT.
BONUS — 222 SQ. FT.

Total living area: 2,250 sq. ft.

PLAN NO.91340

Wheelchair Acccessible

Price Code: A

- This plan features:
  - — Two bedrooms
  - — Two full baths
- A carport and wrap-around Veranda make this home ideal for warm climates
- Wheelchair-accessible features include an optional ramp, enlarged halls and doors, and turnaround space in a Bath and the Kitchen
- A Master Bath option includes two closets
- This home is designed with crawlspace and sl foundation options

MAIN FLOOR — 1,111 SQ. FT.

Total living area:
1,111 sq. ft.

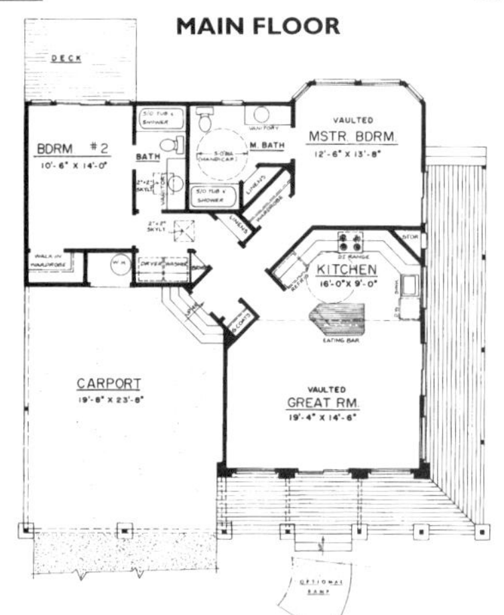
MAIN FLOOR
DECK
BDRM #2
10'-6" X 14'-0"
VAULTED
MSTR. BDRM
12'-6" X 13'-8"
M. BATH
BATH
KITCHEN
16'-0" X 9'-0"
CARPORT
19'-8" X 23'-8"
VAULTED
GREAT RM.
19'-4" X 14'-6"

WIDTH 46'-0"
DEPTH 44'-0"

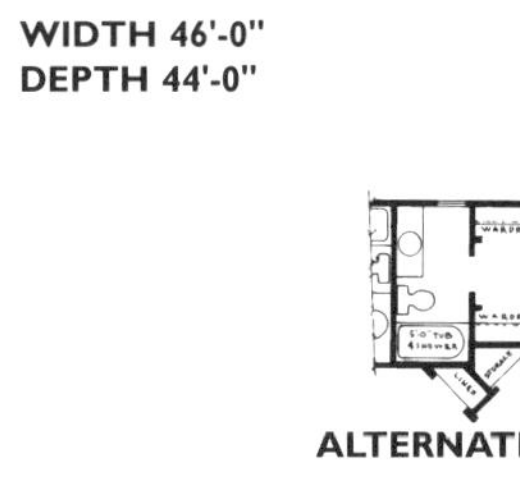

ALTERNATE BATH

PLAN NO.65001

Open And Airy

Price Code: A

- This plan features:
  - — Three bedrooms
  - — Two full baths
- The two-story Living Room features a woodstove and open staircase
- A cozy Lounge on the second floor affords privacy in this spacious plan
- This home is designed with a basement foundation

FIRST FLOOR — 1,024 SQ. FT.
SECOND FLOOR — 456 SQ. FT.
BASEMENT — 1,024 SQ. FT.

Total living area:
1,480 sq. ft.

WIDTH 32'-0"
DEPTH 40'-0"

4,40 X 3,60
14'-8" X 12'-0"
4,20 X 6,80
14'-0" X 22'-8"
4,40 X 3,60
14'-8" X 12'-0"

FIRST FLOOR

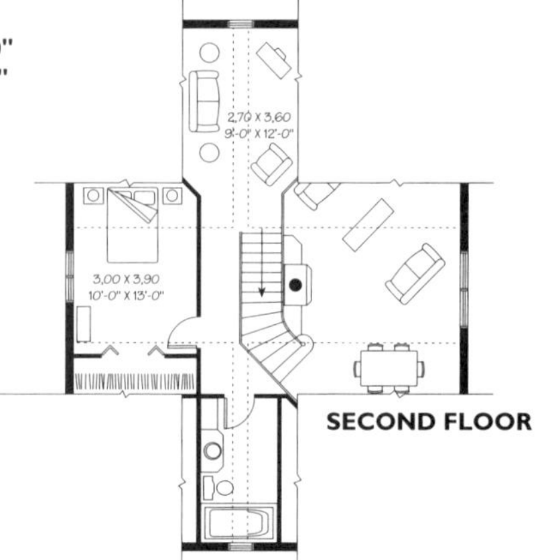
2,70 X 3,60
9'-0" X 12'-0"
3,00 X 3,90
10'-0" X 13'-0"

SECOND FLOOR

Expansive, Not Expensive

Price Code: C

This plan features:

- Three bedrooms
- Two full baths
- A Master Suite with his and her closets and a private Master Bath
- Two additional Bedrooms that share a full athroom
- A pleasant Dining Room that overlooks a rear arden
- A well-equipped Kitchen with a built-in planning orner and eating space
- This home is designed with basement, slab and rawlspace foundation options

AIN FLOOR — 1,773 SQ. FT.

Total living area:
1,773 sq. ft.

PLAN NO. 90423

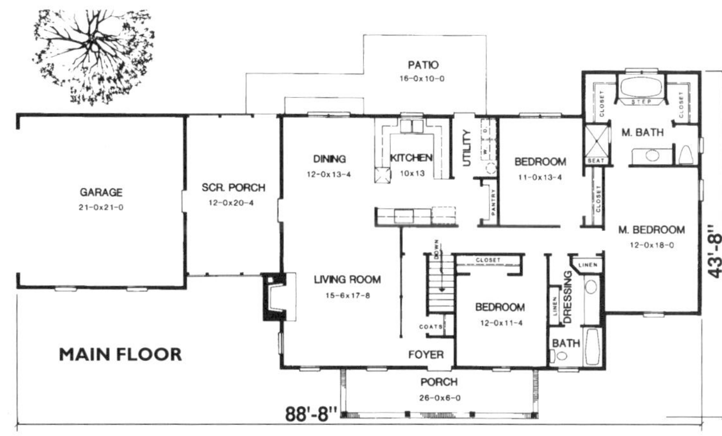
PATIO
16-0x10-0
GARAGE
21-0x21-0
SCR. PORCH
12-0x20-4
DINING
12-0x13-4
KITCHEN
10x13
UTILITY
BEDROOM
11-0x13-4
M. BATH
M. BEDROOM
12-0x18-0
LIVING ROOM
15-6x17-8
BEDROOM
12-0x11-4
DRESSING
BATH
FOYER
PORCH
26-0x6-0
MAIN FLOOR
43'-8"
88'-8"

Small and Stylish

Price Code: B

This plan features:

- Two bedrooms
- One full and one half baths
- The large Living Room has many tall windows and a delightful corner fireplace
- The pleasant U-shaped Kitchen is open to the Dining Room and has a breakfast bar for additional seating
- The Screened Porch off the Living Room adds a ovely retreat to this cozy home
- The first floor half Bath is combined with a laundry closet for space-saving efficiency
- The two second floor Bedrooms each have large losets and share a Bath
- This home is designed with a basement foundation

RST FLOOR — 895 SQ. FT.
ECOND FLOOR — 565 SQ. FT.
ASEMENT — 1,074 SQ. FT.

Total living area:
1,460 sq. ft.

PLAN NO. 65002

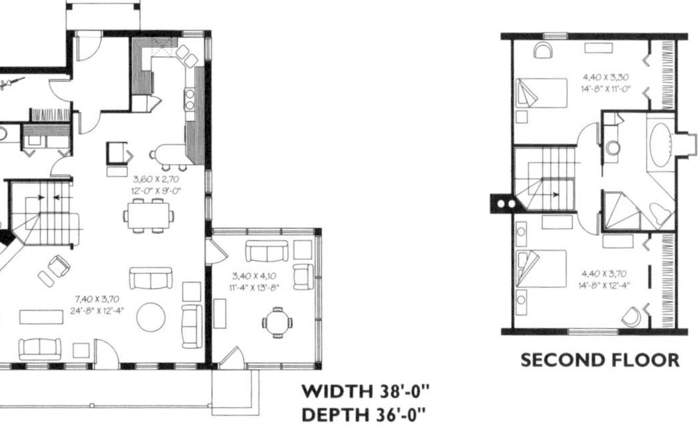
3,60 X 2,70
12'-0" X 9'-0"
7,40 X 3,70
24'-8" X 12'-4"
3,40 X 4,10
11'-4" X 13'-8"
4,40 X 3,30
14'-8" X 11'-0"
4,40 X 3,70
14'-8" X 12'-4"
SECOND FLOOR
WIDTH 38'-0"
DEPTH 36'-0"

FIRST FLOOR

PLAN NO. 65309

Turret Adds Interest

Price Code: D

- This plan features:
- — Three bedrooms
- — Two full and one half baths
- A turret adds to the curb appeal of this delightful home
- The Living Room includes a two-sided fireplace that is shared with the Dining Room
- The Kitchen features a center-island work station and breakfast bar and includes a Breakfast Area with access to a rear Deck
- The Bonus Area over the Garage offers possibilities for expansion
- This home is designed with a basement foundation

FIRST FLOOR — 874 SQ. FT.
SECOND FLOOR — 1,301 SQ. FT.
GARAGE — 528 SQ. FT.
BONUS — 425 SQ. FT.

Total living area: 2,175 sq. ft.

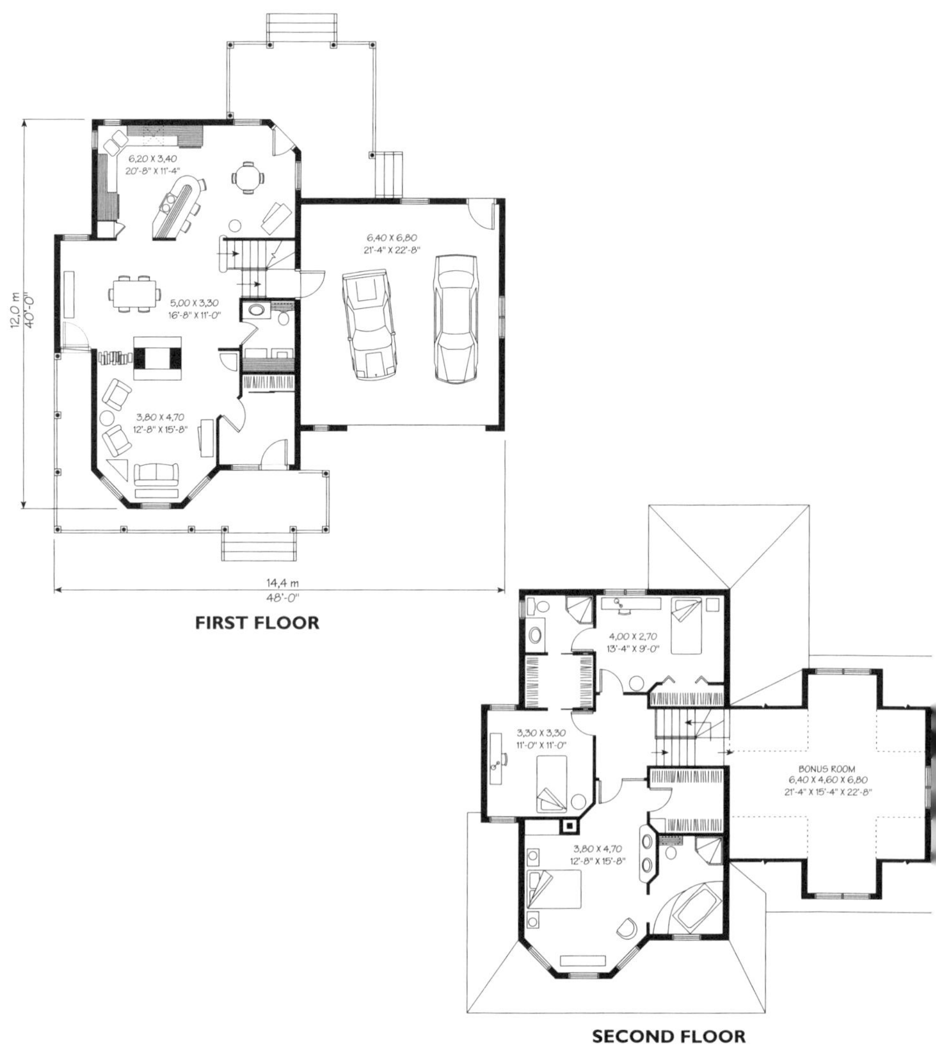
6,20 X 3,40
20'-8" X 11'-4"
6,40 X 6,80
21'-4" X 22'-8"
5,00 X 3,30
16'-8" X 11'-0"
3,80 X 4,70
12'-8" X 15'-8"
12,0 m
40'-0"
14,4 m
48'-0"
FIRST FLOOR
4,00 X 2,70
13'-4" X 9'-0"
3,30 X 3,30
11'-0" X 11'-0"
BONUS ROOM
6,40 X 4,60 X 6,80
21'-4" X 15'-4" X 22'-8"
3,80 X 4,70
12'-8" X 15'-8"
SECOND FLOOR

PLAN NO. 68121

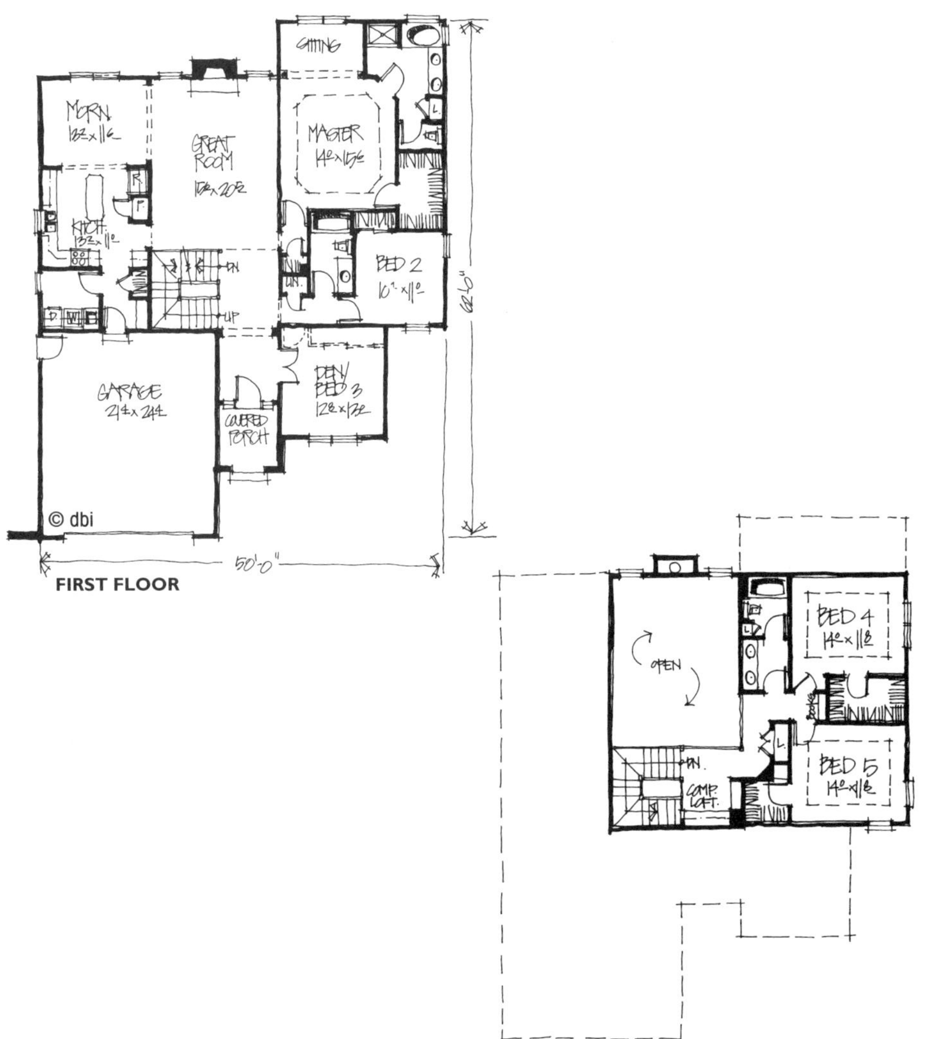

SITTING
MASTER
MORN.
GREAT ROOM
KITCH.
BED 2
DEN/ BED 3
GARAGE
COVERED PORCH
© dbi
50'-0"
FIRST FLOOR
OPEN
BED 4
BED 5
COMP. LOFT
SECOND FLOOR

Great Family Home

Price Code: F

- This plan features:
  - Five Bedrooms
  - Three full baths
- A covered entry protects all that enter from inclement weather
- The Great Room, highlighted by a fireplace, flows easily into the Morning Room
- The island Kitchen is located near the Garage entrance into the house offering ease in unloading groceries
- The Master Suite includes a sitting area, walk-in closet and a private Bathroom
- This home is designed with a basement foundation

FIRST FLOOR — 1,902 SQ. FT.
SECOND FLOOR — 691 SQ. FT.
BASEMENT — 1,902 SQ. FT.
GARAGE — 540 SQ. FT.

Total living area
2,593 sq. ft.

PLAN NO. 90378

Dynamic Angles

Price Code: A

- This plan features:
- — Two bedrooms with possible third bedroom or loft
- — Two full baths
- The Living Room has dynamic, soaring angles, a clerestory window and a fireplace
- The compact Kitchen has a corner sink and a peninsula counter to serve the Dining Area
- The first floor Master Suite has a full Bath and walk in-closet
- Walk-in closets are featured in all the Bedrooms
- This home is designed with a basement foundation

MAIN FLOOR — 878 SQ. FT.
UPPER FLOOR — 405 SQ. FT.

Total living area:
1,283 sq. ft.

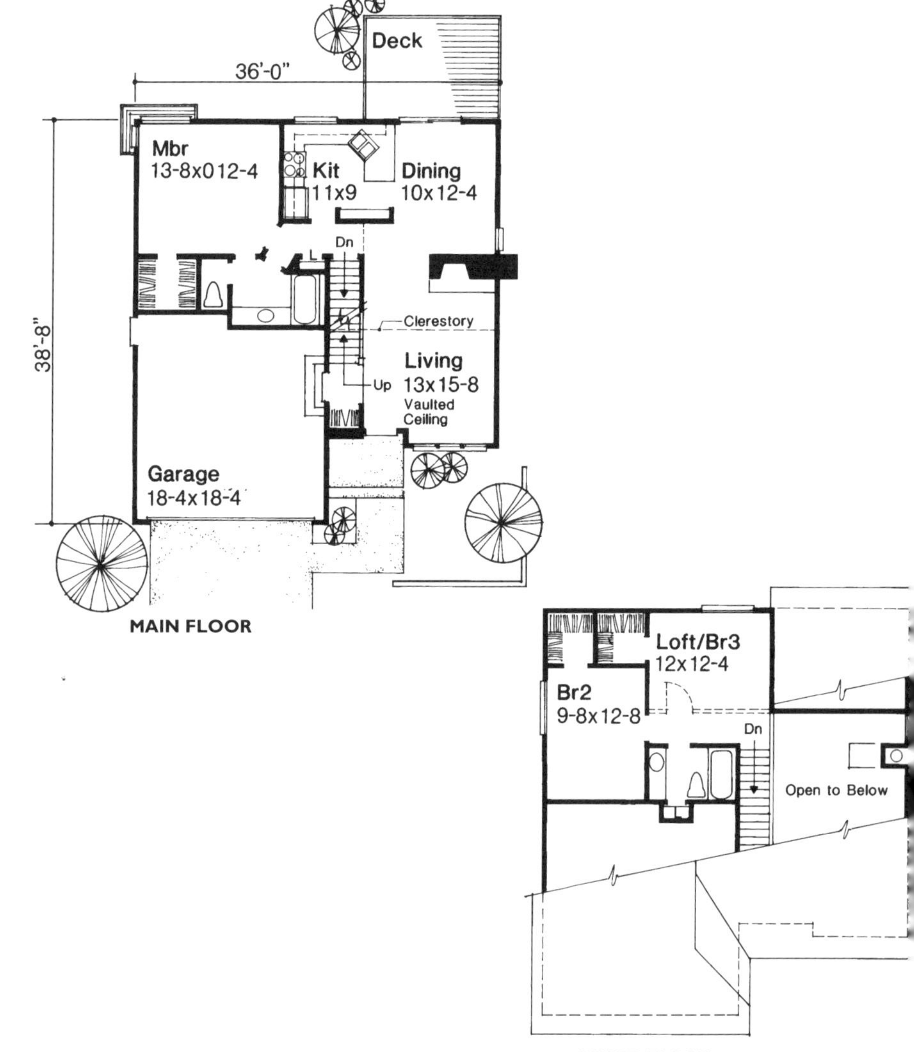

Deck
36'-0"
38'-8"
Mbr
13-8x012-4
Kit
11x9
Dining
10x12-4
Dn
Clerestory
Living
13x15-8
Vaulted Ceiling
Up
Garage
18-4x18-4
MAIN FLOOR
Loft/Br3
12x12-4
Br2
9-8x12-8
Dn
Open to Below
UPPER FLOOR

Private Master Suite

Price Code: A

This plan features:

- Three bedrooms
- Two full baths
- A spacious Great Room enhanced by a vaulted ceiling and fireplace
- A well-equipped Kitchen with windowed double sink
- A secluded Master Suite with decorative ceiling, private Master Bath, and walk-in closet
- Two additional Bedrooms sharing Bath
- This home is designed with crawlspace and slab foundation options

AIN FLOOR — 1,293 SQ. FT.
ARAGE — 433 SQ. FT.
RCH — 76 SQ. FT.

Total living area:
1,293 sq. ft.

PLAN NO.92523

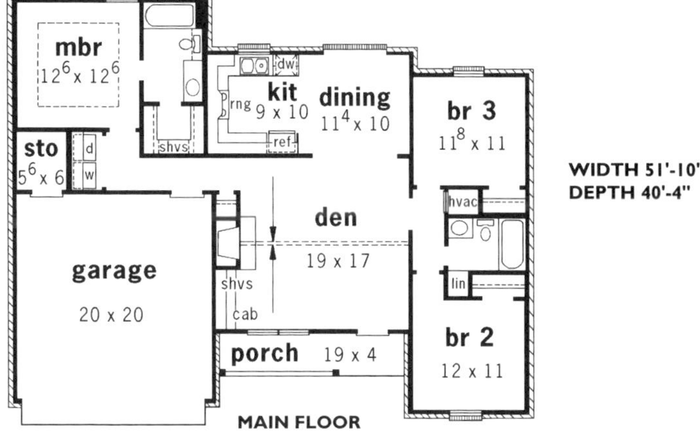

mbr
12⁶ x 12⁶
kit
9 x 10
dining
11⁴ x 10
br 3
11⁸ x 11
sto
5⁶ x 6
den
19 x 17
garage
20 x 20
porch
19 x 4
br 2
12 x 11
WIDTH 51'-10"
DEPTH 40'-4"
MAIN FLOOR

Small Elegant Touches

Price Code: B

This plan features:

- Three bedrooms
- Two full baths
- The Great Room is crowned in a decor ceiling treatment and includes a gas fireplace and columns at its entry from the Foyer
- The Dining Room entry is adorned by columns and has direct access to the Kitchen
- The efficient Kitchen includes a pantry and peninsula counter/snack bar for meals on the run
- The Breakfast Area accesses the Grilling Porch for summer cookouts
- The Master Suite includes a lavish bath and decor ceiling
- This home is designed with crawlspace and slab foundation options

AIN FLOOR — 1,627 SQ. FT.
ARAGE — 392 SQ. FT.

Total living area:
1,627 sq. ft.

PLAN NO.82012

52' 8"
60' 6"
MASTER SUITE
GRILLING PORCH
BRKFAST RM.
STORAGE
BED RM. 2
BED RM. 3
GARAGE
KITCHEN
FOYER
GREAT RM.
DINING RM.
ENTRY PORCH
MAIN FLOOR

PLAN NO. 98425

Lavishly Appointed

Price Code: C

- This plan features:
- — Three bedrooms
- — Two full and one half baths
- The Dining Room, Living Room, Foyer and Master Bath all topped by high ceilings
- Kitchen is enhanced by a serving bar and a Pantry is open to Breakfast Room
- Living Room with a large fireplace and a French door to the rear yard
- Master Suite located on opposite side from secondary Bedrooms, allowing for privacy
- This home is designed with basement and crawlspace foundation options

MAIN FLOOR — 1,845 SQ. FT.
BONUS — 409 SQ. FT.

Total living area:
1,845 sq. ft.

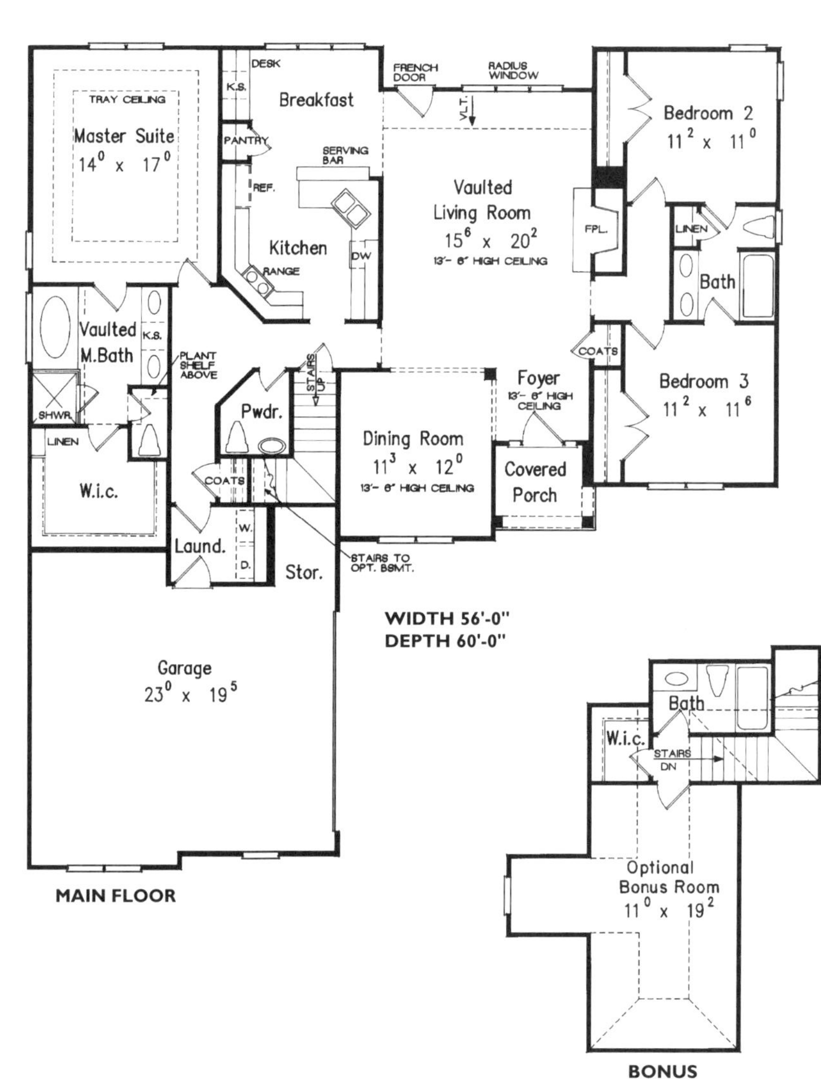

TRAY CEILING
Master Suite
14⁰ x 17⁰
DESK
K.S.
Breakfast
PANTRY
SERVING BAR
REF.
Kitchen
RANGE
DW
FRENCH DOOR
RADIUS WINDOW
V.T.
Vaulted Living Room
15⁶ x 20²
13'- 6" HIGH CEILING
FPL.
Bedroom 2
11² x 11⁰
LINEN
Bath
COATS
Bedroom 3
11² x 11⁶
Vaulted M.Bath
K.S.
PLANT SHELF ABOVE
SHWR.
LINEN
W.i.c.
Pwdr.
STAIRS UP
COATS
Laund.
W.
D.
Stor.
Dining Room
11³ x 12⁰
13'- 6" HIGH CEILING
Foyer
13'- 6" HIGH CEILING
Covered Porch
STAIRS TO OPT. BSMT.
WIDTH 56'-0"
DEPTH 60'-0"
Garage
23⁰ x 19⁵
MAIN FLOOR
Bath
W.i.c.
STAIRS DN
Optional Bonus Room
11⁰ x 19²
BONUS

To order your Blueprints, call 1-800-235-5700

PLAN NO. 65137

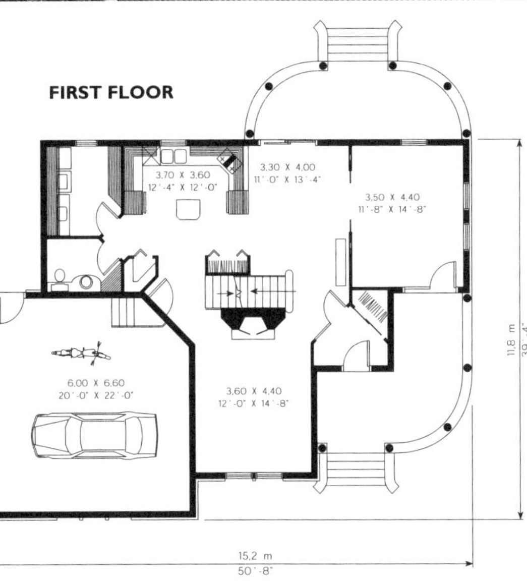

FIRST FLOOR
3,70 X 3,60
12'-4" X 12'-0"
3,30 X 4,00
11'-0" X 13'-4"
3,50 X 4,40
11'-8" X 14'-8"
6,00 X 6,60
20'-0" X 22'-0"
3,60 X 4,40
12'-0" X 14'-8"
11,8 m
39'-4"
15,2 m
50'-8"

Curved Porch

Price Code: D

- This plan features:
  - Four bedrooms
  - Two full and one half baths
- Pocket doors in the Solarium and an airlock Entry are energy-saving features of this home
- Built-in cabinets offers ample storage in the Laundry Room and Kitchen
- This home is designed with a basement foundation.

FIRST FLOOR — 1,085 SQ. FT.
SECOND FLOOR — 1,050 SQ. FT.
BASEMENT — 1,050 SQ. FT.
GARAGE — 440 SQ. FT.

Total living area:
2,135 sq. ft.

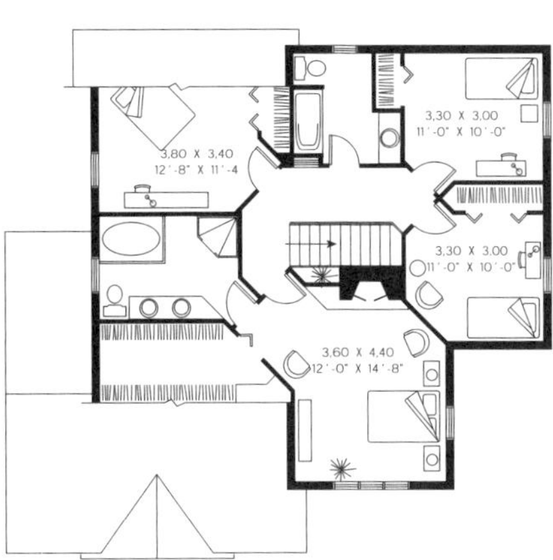

SECOND FLOOR
3,80 X 3,40
12'-8" X 11'-4
3,30 X 3,00
11'-0" X 10'-0"
3,30 X 3,00
11'-0" X 10'-0"
3,60 X 4,40
12'-0" X 14'-8"

PLAN NO. 10785

Farmhouse Flavor

Price Code: C

- This plan features:
- — Three bedrooms
- — Two full and one half baths
- A inviting wrap-around Porch adds old-fashioned charm
- Two-story Foyer
- A wood stove in the Living Room that warms the entire house
- A modern Kitchen flowing easily into the bayed Dining Room
- A first floor Master Bedroom with private Master Bath
- This home is designed with basement, slab and crawlspace foundation options

FIRST FLOOR — 1,269 SQ. FT.
SECOND FLOOR — 638 SQ. FT.
BASEMENT — 1,269 SQ. FT.

Total living area:
1,907 sq. ft.

WIDTH 47'-0"
DEPTH 39'-0"

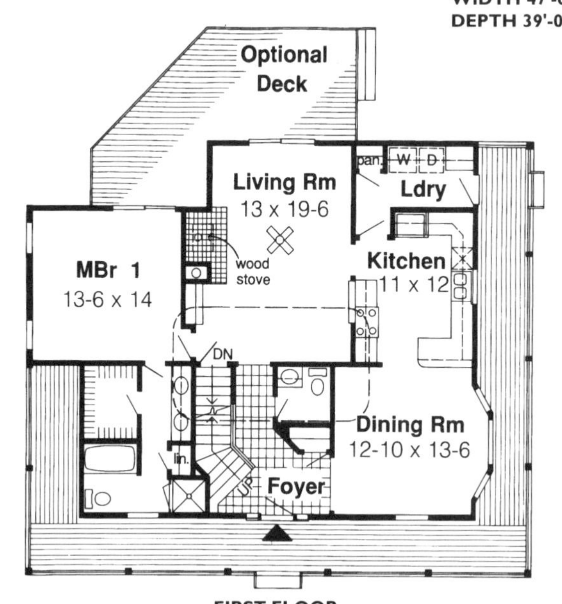

Optional Deck
Living Rm
13 x 19-6
pan
W D
Ldry
wood stove
MBr 1
13-6 x 14
Kitchen
11 x 12
DN
lin.
Dining Rm
12-10 x 13-6
Foyer

FIRST FLOOR

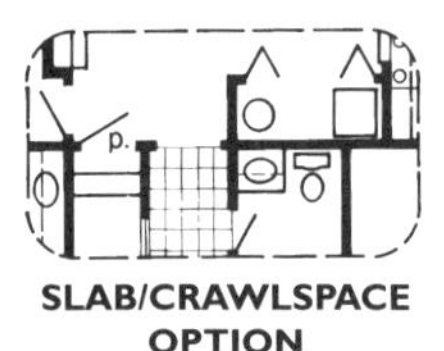

SLAB/CRAWLSPACE OPTION

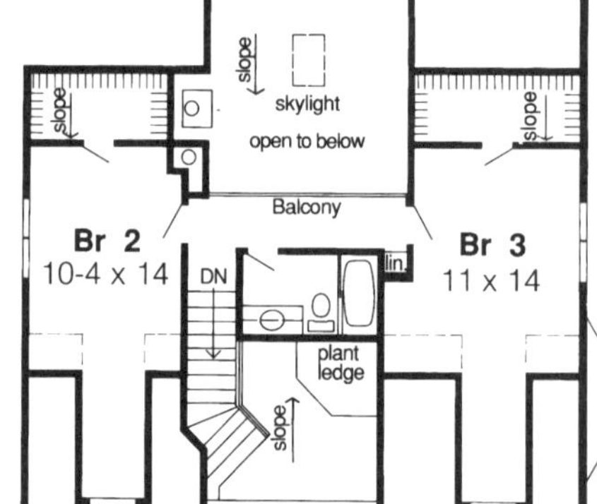

slope
skylight
open to below
slope
Balcony
Br 2
10-4 x 14
Br 3
11 x 14
DN
lin.
plant ledge
slope

SECOND FLOOR

PLAN NO. 24718

Gazebo Porch

Price Code: A

67'-0"

Master Br
14-5 x 12-0

Great Rm
14-0 x 16-7

Porch
11-5 x 7-0

FURN.
W.H.

Dining
11-5 x 9-3

2-SIDED F.P.

Garage
23-8 x 23-9

SH.
W.P. TUB

SERVING

Kitchen
11-7 x 10-1

P.
W.
D.
L.

Br 2
11-0 x 10-0

Brkfst
11-7 x 7-9

Br 3
10-2 x 10-0

SHLV.
LEDGE

Porch

MAIN FLOOR

- This plan features:
  - — Three bedrooms
  - — Two full baths
- A corner Gazebo provides space to relax on the front Porch
- The Dining Room and the Great-Room share a two-sided fireplace
- The Breakfast Area is defined by the Kitchen snack bar and a row of curved windows overlooking the front Porch
- This home is designed with crawlspace and slab foundation options

MAIN FLOOR — 1,452 SQ. FT.
GARAGE — 584 SQ. FT.

**Total living area:
1,452 sq. ft.**

PLAN NO. 93015

Great Room Heart of the Hom

Price Code: A

- This plan features:
- — Three bedrooms
- — Two full baths
- Sheltered Porch leads into the Entry with arches and a Great Room
- Spacious Great Room with a ten-foot ceiling above a wall of windows and rear yard access
- Efficient Kitchen with a built-in Pantry, a Laun closet and a Breakfast Area accented by a decorative window
- A bay of windows enhances the Master Bedroo which also contains a double vanity Bath and a walk-in closet
- Two additional Bedrooms with ample closets share a full Bath
- This home is designed with a slab foundation

MAIN FLOOR — 1,087 SQ. FT.

Total living area:
1,087 sq. ft.

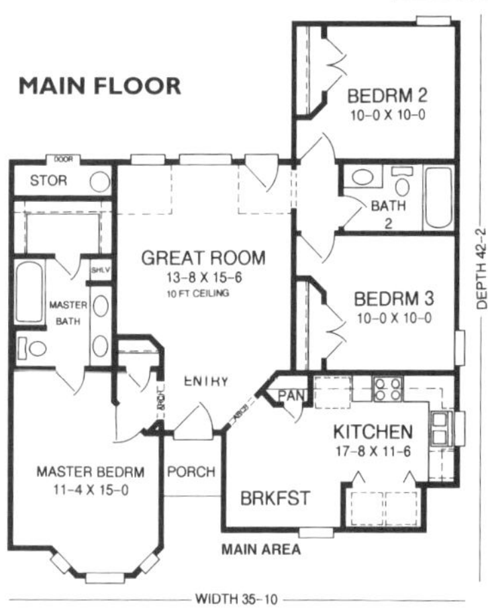
MAIN FLOOR
BEDRM 2
10-0 X 10-0
STOR
BATH
2
GREAT ROOM
13-8 X 15-6
10 FT CEILING
MASTER
BATH
BEDRM 3
10-0 X 10-0
ENTRY
PAN
KITCHEN
17-8 X 11-6
MASTER BEDRM
11-4 X 15-0
PORCH
BRKFST
MAIN AREA
DEPTH 42-2
WIDTH 35-10

PLAN NO. 65015

Three Season Porch

Price Code: A

- This plan features:
- — Three bedrooms
- — Two full baths
- A three-season porch offers expanded living space during the mild weather months
- A cozy fireplace in the Living Room creates a warm atmosphere
- The first floor bedroom has a full bath with bo shower and tub in close proximity
- The two secondary bedrooms are located on th second floor
- The home is designed with a basement founda tion

FIRST FLOOR — 858 SQ. FT.
SECOND FLOOR — 502 SQ. FT.

Total living area:
1,360 sq. ft.

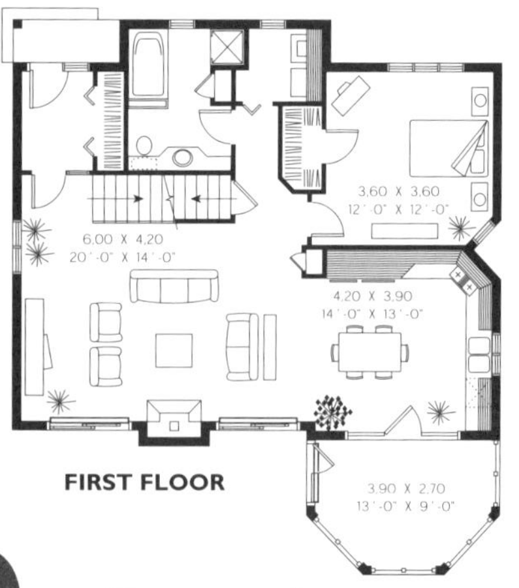
3,60 X 3,60
12'-0" X 12'-0"
6,00 X 4,20
20'-0" X 14'-0"
4,20 X 3,90
14'-0" X 13'-0"
3,90 X 2,70
13'-0" X 9'-0"

FIRST FLOOR

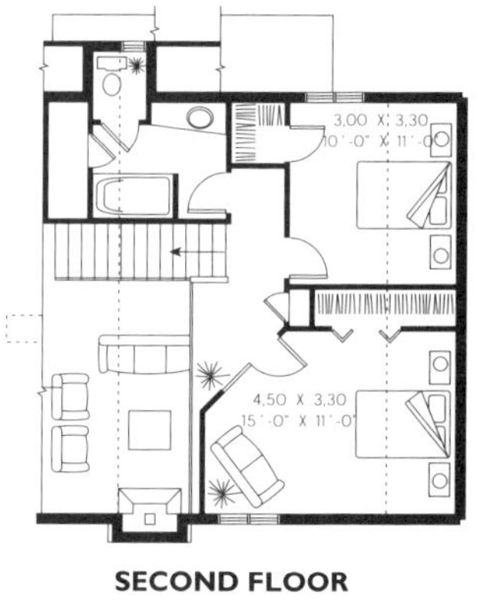
3,00 X 3,30
10'-0" X 11'-0"
4,50 X 3,30
15'-0" X 11'-0"

SECOND FLOOR

Distinctive Details

Price Code: D

'his plan features:

- Three bedrooms
- Two full and one half baths
- The distinctive mix of architectural details of the his home hint of Victorian roots
- The small tiled Foyer has a staircase to the sec-ond floor and the efficient Kitchen to the left
- A serving bar and open layout to the Dining Room highlight the Kitchen
- The expansive Living Room offers grand views of the outdoors
- This home is designed with a basement oundation

RST FLOOR — 1,291 SQ. FT.
COND FLOOR — 738 SQ. FT.

Total living area:
2,029 sq. ft.

PLAN NO. 32084

Photography supplied by the Meredith Corporation

WIDTH 55'-8"
DEPTH 37'-6"

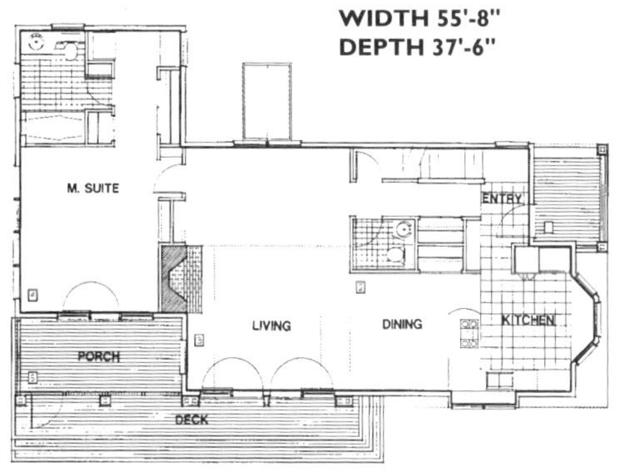
M. SUITE
ENTRY
LIVING
DINING
KITCHEN
PORCH
DECK

FIRST FLOOR

STUDY LOFT
BEDROOM
OPEN
BEDROOM

SECOND FLOOR

Inexpensive Ranch Design

Price Code: A

his plan features:

- Three bedrooms
- Two full baths
- large picture window brightening the Breakfast rea
- well-planned Kitchen
- Living Room which is accented by an open eam across the sloping ceiling and wood burn-ng fireplace
- Master Bedroom with an extremely large Bath rea
- his home is designed with basement, slab and rawlspace foundation options

AIN FLOOR — 1,500 SQ. FT.
SEMENT — 1,500 SQ. FT.
RAGE — 482 SQ. FT.

Total living area:
1,500 sq. ft.

PLAN NO. 20062

MAIN FLOOR

DECK
M. BEDROOM
15'-4" X 13'-4"
LIVING RM.
14'-0" X 20'-0"
DINING
10'-6" X 10'-0"
KIT.
12'-0" X 12'-0"
FOYER
BEDROOM 2
10'-0" X 11'-0"
BEDROOM 3
10'-0" X 11'-0"
GARAGE
19'-4" X 20'-4"
49'-8"
44'-4"

PLAN NO. 92643

Arched Accents Give Impact

Price Code: D

- This plan features:
- — Three bedrooms
- — Two full and one half baths
- Keystone arch accents entrance into open Foyer with lovely angled staircase and sloped ceiling
- Master Bedroom wing features a lavish Bath with two vanities, large walk-in closet and corner window tub
- This home is designed with a basement foundation

FIRST FLOOR — 1,542 SQ. FT.
SECOND FLOOR — 667 SQ. FT.
BASEMENT — 1,470 SQ. FT.
GARAGE — 420 SQ. FT.

Total living area:
2,209 sq. ft.

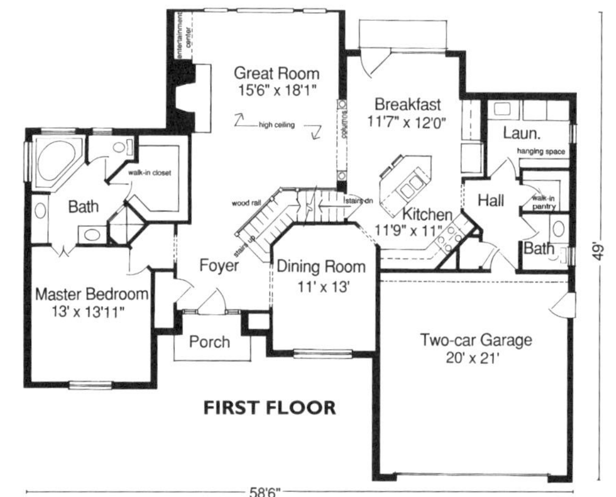

Great Room
15'6" x 18'1"
high ceiling
Breakfast
11'7" x 12'0"
Laun.
hanging space
walk-in closet
Bath
wood rail
stairs dn
Kitchen
11'9" x 11"
Hall
walk-in pantry
Bath
Foyer
Dining Room
11' x 13'
Master Bedroom
13' x 13'11"
Porch
Two-car Garage
20' x 21'
49'
58'6"
FIRST FLOOR

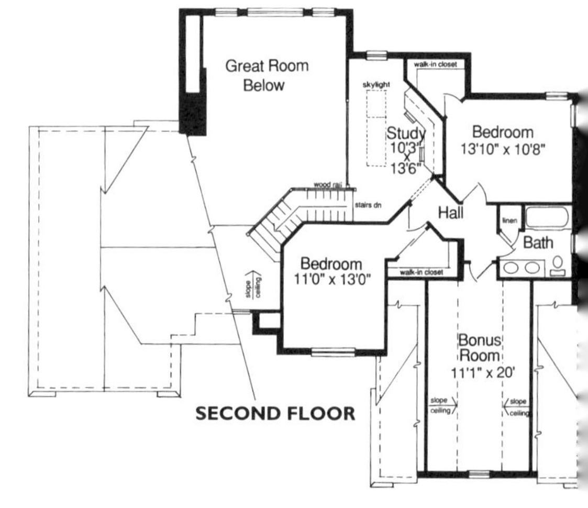

Great Room
Below
walk-in closet
skylight
Study
10'3" x 13'6"
Bedroom
13'10" x 10'8"
wood rail
stairs dn
Hall
linen
Bath
Bedroom
11'0" x 13'0"
walk-in closet
slope ceiling
Bonus Room
11'1" x 20'
slope ceiling
slope ceiling
SECOND FLOOR

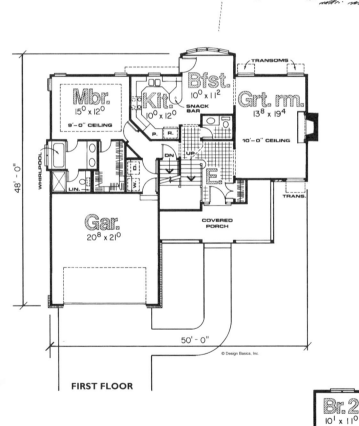

PLAN NO. 99404

Updated Farmhouse

Price Code: B

- This plan features:
  - — Three bedrooms
  - — Two full and one half baths
- The Great Room has a volume-ceiling and a fireplace
- Master Suite provides privacy, a walk-in closet and a Bath with all amenities
- This home is designed with a basement foundation
- Alternate foundation options available at an additional charge. Please call 1-800-235-5700 for more information.

FIRST FLOOR — 1,191 SQ. FT.
SECOND FLOOR — 405 SQ. FT.
GARAGE — 454 SQ. FT.
BASEMENT— 1,191 SQ. FT.

Total living area:
1,596 sq. ft.

FIRST FLOOR

SECOND FLOOR

PLAN NO. 91342

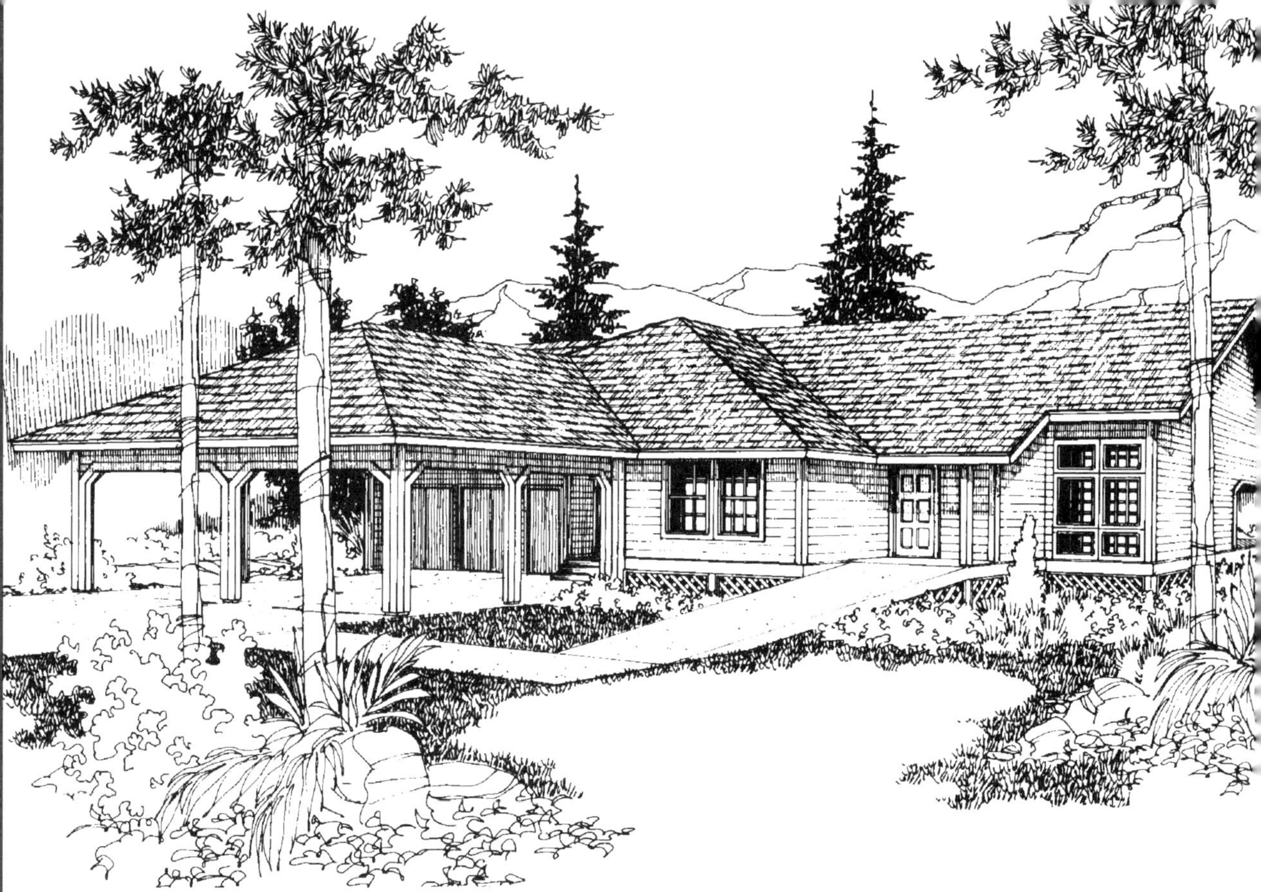

Easy-Living Design

Price Code: A

- This plan features:
  - — Three bedrooms
  - — Two full baths
- For handicapped individuals a Master Bath plan is available
- Vaulted Great Room, Dining Room and Kitchen areas
- A Kitchen accented with angles and an abundance of cabinets for storage
- A Master Bedroom with an ample sized wardrobe, large covered private deck, and private bath
- This home is designed with crawlspace and slab foundation options

MAIN FLOOR — 1,345 SQ. FT.

Total living area: 1,345 sq. ft.

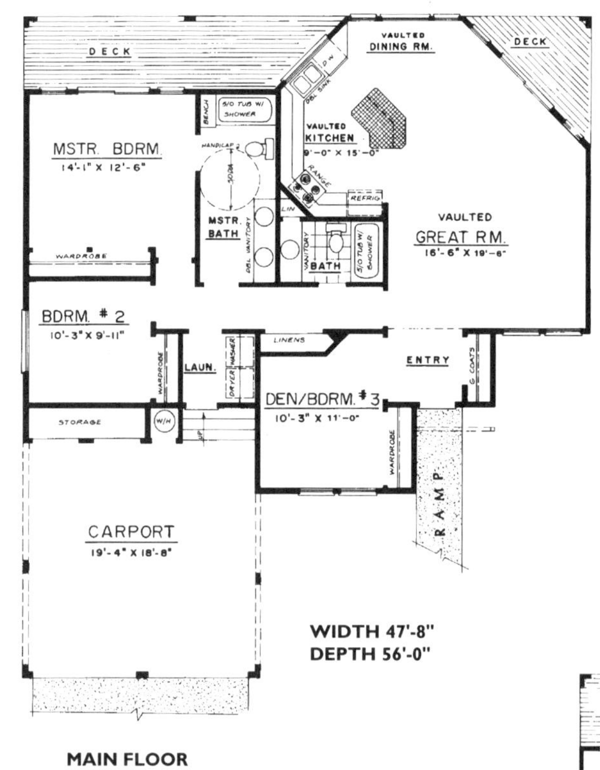
DECK
VAULTED DINING RM.
DECK
MSTR. BDRM. 14'-1" X 12'-6"
VAULTED KITCHEN 9'-0" X 15'-0"
VAULTED GREAT RM. 16'-6" X 19'-6"
MSTR BATH
BATH
WARDROBE
BDRM. # 2 10'-3" X 9'-11"
LAUN.
LINENS
ENTRY
DEN/BDRM. # 3 10'-3" X 11'-0"
STORAGE
CARPORT 19'-4" X 18'-8"
RAMP
WIDTH 47'-8"
DEPTH 56'-0"

MAIN FLOOR

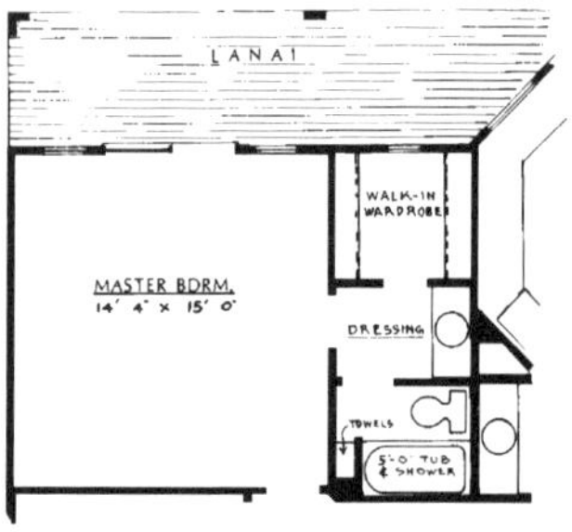

LANAI

MASTER BDRM. 14' 4" X 15' 0"

WALK-IN WARDROBE

DRESSING

ALTERNATE BATH

Comfortable Informal Design

Price Code: A

ʗhis plan features:

- Three bedrooms
- Two full baths
- Warm, country front Porch with wood details
- Spacious Activity Room enhanced by a pre-fab ireplace
- Open and efficient Kitchen/Dining Area high-ighted by bay window, adjacent to Laundry and Garage entry
- Corner Master Bedroom offers a pampering Bath vith a garden tub and double vanity topped by a vaulted ceiling
- Two additional Bedrooms with ample closets hare a full Bath
- This home is designed with crawlspace and slab oundation options

AIN FLOOR — 1,300 SQ. FT.
ARAGE — 576 SQ. FT.

Total living area:
1,300 sq. ft.

PLAN NO.94801

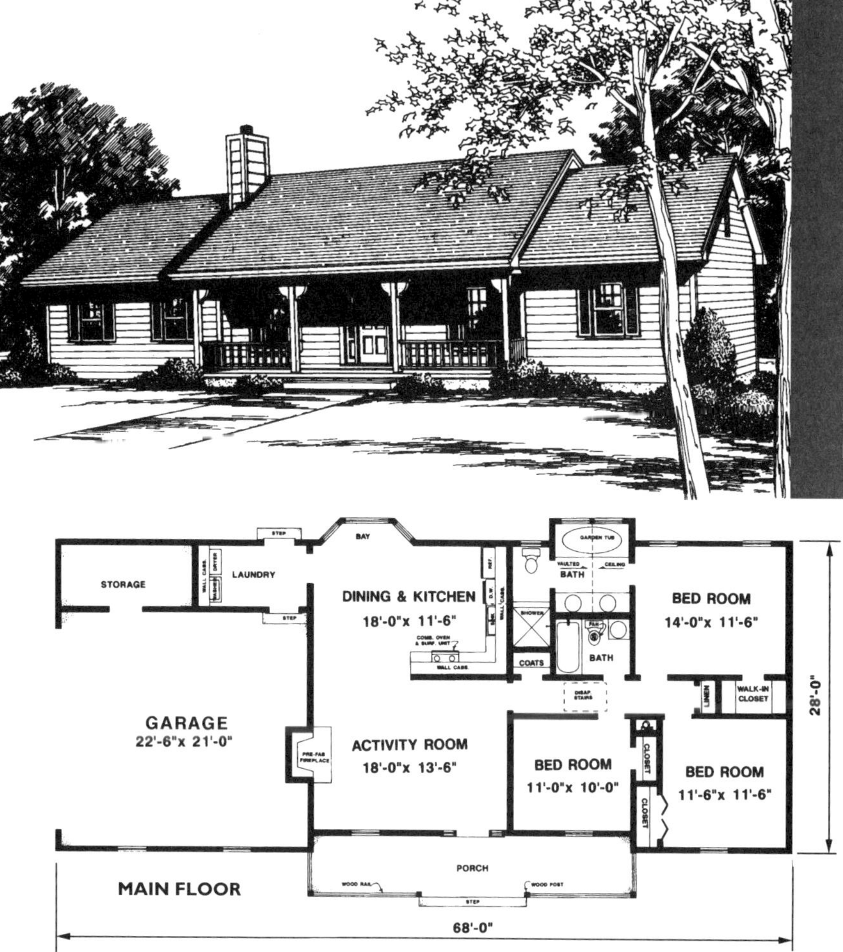

STORAGE
LAUNDRY
STEP
BAY
DINING & KITCHEN
18'-0"x 11'-6"
GARDEN TUB
VAULTED CEILING
BATH
BED ROOM
14'-0"x 11'-6"
COATS
BATH
WALK-IN CLOSET
LINEN
GARAGE
22'-6"x 21'-0"
ACTIVITY ROOM
18'-0"x 13'-6"
BED ROOM
11'-0"x 10'-0"
CLOSET
BED ROOM
11'-6"x 11'-6"
PORCH
WOOD RAIL
WOOD POST
MAIN FLOOR
68'-0"
28'-0"

Garage on an Angle

Price Code: C

ʗhis plan features:

- Three bedrooms
- Two full baths
- The Family Room includes three sets of French doors to the rear porch and a fireplace
- The efficient Kitchen features an octagonal Breakfast area and a cook top island
- The Master Suite includes a lavish whirlpool ath and a large walk-in closet
- The secondary bedrooms have easy access to a ull bath
- This home is designed with a basement, slab or rawlspace foundation

AIN FLOOR — 1,751 SQ. FT.
SEMENT — 1,751 SQ. FT.
ARAGE — 527 SQ. FT.

Total living area:
1,751 sq. ft.

PLAN NO.68130

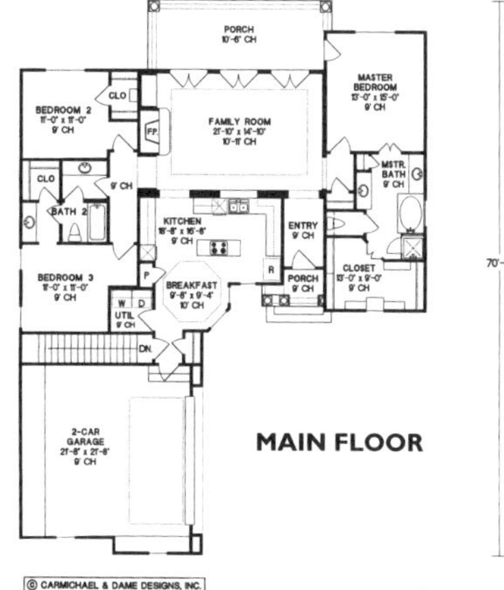

PORCH
MASTER BEDROOM
FAMILY ROOM
BEDROOM 2
CLO
BATH 2
KITCHEN
ENTRY
BEDROOM 3
BREAKFAST
UTIL
PORCH
CLOSET
2-CAR GARAGE
MAIN FLOOR
© CARMICHAEL & DAME DESIGNS, INC.

PLAN NO. 90476

Split-Bedroom Ranch

Price Code: C

- This plan features:
- — Three bedrooms
- — Two full baths
- The formal Foyer opens into the Great Room which features a vaulted ceiling and a hearth fireplace
- The covered front Porch and rear Deck provide additional space for entertaining
- This home is designed with basement, slab and crawlspace foundation options

MAIN FLOOR — 1,804 SQ. FT.
BASEMENT — 1,804 SQ. FT.
GARAGE — 506 SQ. FT.

Total living area:
1,804 sq. ft.

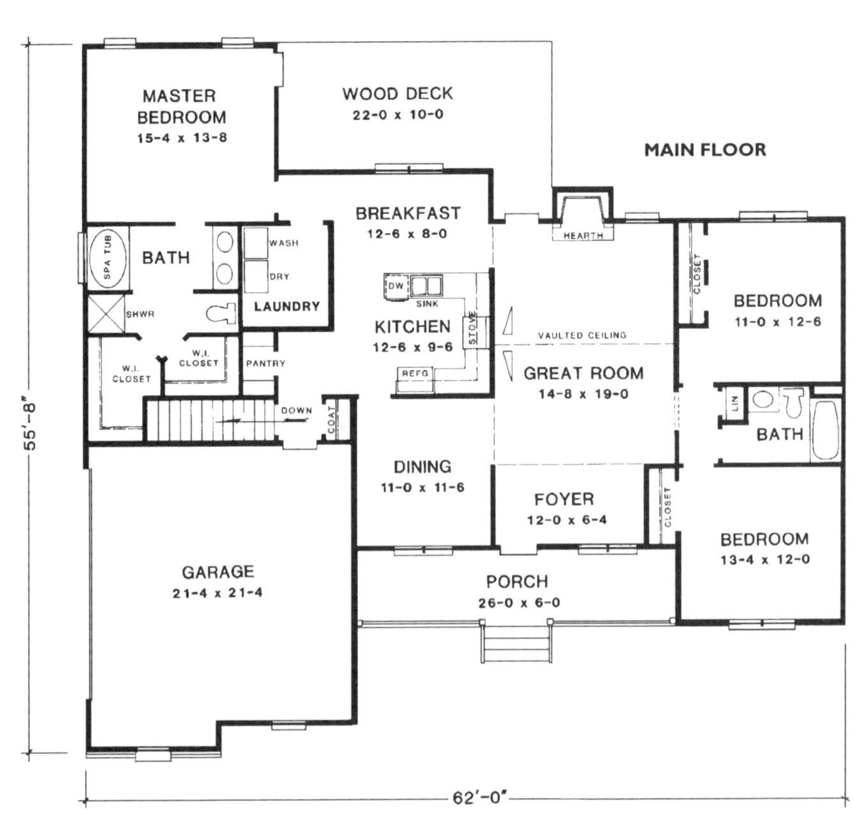
MAIN FLOOR
MASTER BEDROOM 15-4 x 13-8
WOOD DECK 22-0 x 10-0
BREAKFAST 12-6 x 8-0
HEARTH
BATH
SPA TUB
WASH
DRY
LAUNDRY
SHWR
W.I. CLOSET
W.I. CLOSET
PANTRY
DW
SINK
KITCHEN 12-6 x 9-6
STOVE
REFG
VAULTED CEILING
GREAT ROOM 14-8 x 19-0
CLOSET
BEDROOM 11-0 x 12-6
LIN
BATH
DOWN
COAT
DINING 11-0 x 11-6
FOYER 12-0 x 6-4
CLOSET
BEDROOM 13-4 x 12-0
GARAGE 21-4 x 21-4
PORCH 26-0 x 6-0
55'-8"
62'-0"

To order your Blueprints, call 1-800-235-5700

PLAN NO. 90450

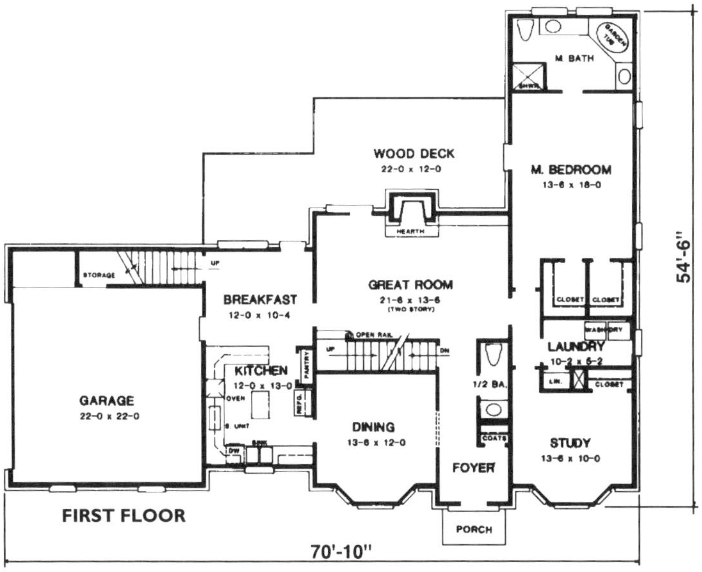

FIRST FLOOR

70'-10"

54'-6"

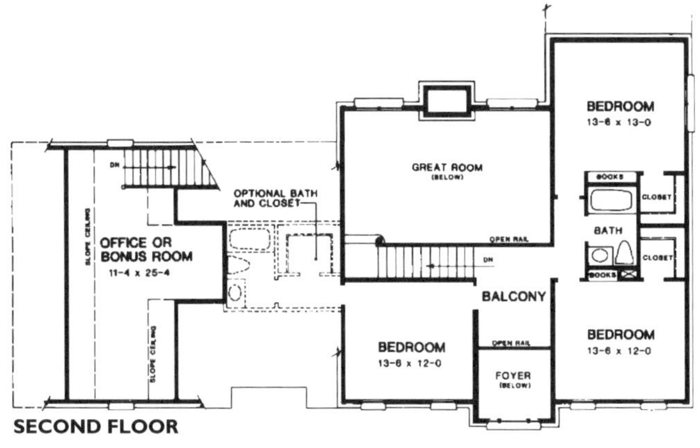

BEDROOM
13-6 x 13-0
GREAT ROOM
(BELOW)
OPTIONAL BATH
AND CLOSET
OFFICE OR
BONUS ROOM
11-4 x 25-4
SLOPE CEILING
OPEN RAIL
BATH
CLOSET
BOOKS
BALCONY
BEDROOM
13-6 x 12-0
FOYER
(BELOW)
BEDROOM
13-6 x 12-0
SECOND FLOOR

Proud and Prestigious

Price Code: E

- This plan features:
  - — Four bedrooms
  - — Two full and one half baths
- The Great Room has a two-story ceiling and a fireplace, and access to the Deck
- Master Suite provides privacy and includes his and her walk-in closets, plus Master Bath
- This home is designed with basement and crawlspace foundation options

MAIN FLOOR — 1,637 SQ. FT.
GARAGE — 434 SQ. FT.

Total living area:
2,398 sq. ft.

PLAN NO.93017

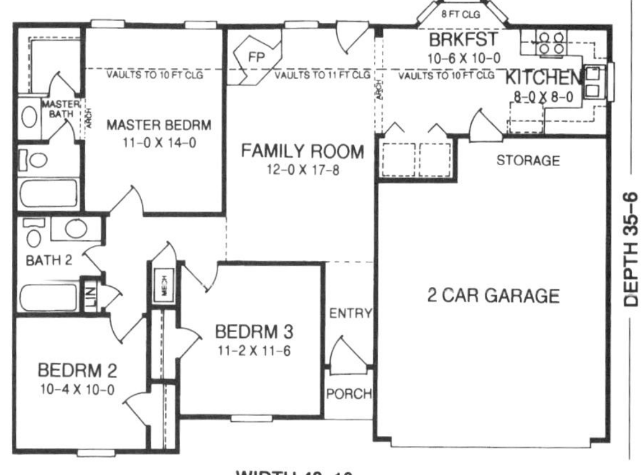
8 FT CLG
BRKFST
10-6 X 10-0
FP
VAULTS TO 10 FT CLG
VAULTS TO 11 FT CLG
VAULTS TO 10 FT CLG
KITCHEN
8-0 X 8-0
MASTER BATH
ARCH
MASTER BEDRM
11-0 X 14-0
FAMILY ROOM
12-0 X 17-8
STORAGE
BATH 2
LIN
BEDRM 3
11-2 X 11-6
ENTRY
2 CAR GARAGE
DEPTH 35-6
BEDRM 2
10-4 X 10-0
PORCH
WIDTH 48-10
MAIN FLOOR

Distinguished Plan

Price Code: A

- This plan features:
  - — Three bedrooms
  - — Two full baths
- A traditional brick elevation with quoin accent
- A large Family Room with a corner fireplace a direct access to the outside
- An arched opening leading to the Breakfast A
- A bay window illuminating the Breakfast Area with natural light
- An efficiently designed U-shaped Kitchen with ample cabinet and counter space
- A Master Suite with a private Master Bath
- Two additional Bedrooms that share a full Bathroom
- This home is designed with crawlspace and sl foundation options

MAIN FLOOR — 1,142 SQ. FT.
GARAGE — 428 SQ. FT.

Total living area:
1,142 sq. ft.

PLAN NO.82011

Garage Storage

Price Code: B

- This plan features:
  - — Three bedrooms
  - — Two full baths
- At the heart of the home, the Kitchen opens to Dining Room/Hearth Room with a fireplace
- A sloped ceiling and a fireplace enhance the Great Room, located next to the Foyer
- Glass block decorates the Master Bath
- This home is designed with basement, slab an crawlspace foundation options

MAIN FLOOR — 1,654 SQ. FT.
GARAGE — 400 SQ. FT.
PORCH — 203 SQ. FT.

Total living area:
1,654 sq. ft.

49' 0"
GLASS BLOCKS
M. BATH
BED RM. 3
COVERED PORCH
DINING RM. / HEARTH RM.
MASTER SUITE
STRG.
BED RM. 2
KITCHEN
GARAGE
FOYER
GREAT RM.
PRCH
58' 6"
MAIN FLOOR

PLAN NO. 91026

Home on a Hill

Price Code: A

his plan features:

- hree bedrooms
-)ne full and one three-quarter baths
- weeping panels of glass and a wood stove cre-
te atmosphere in the Great Room
- he Kitchen opens to the warmth of the
ireat Room
- he two main floor Bedrooms share a full Bath
- he huge Sleeping Loft has a three-quarter Bath
- his home is designed with basement foundation

RST FLOOR — 988 SQ. FT.
COND FLOOR — 366 SQ. FT.
SEMENT — 742 SQ. FT.
RAGE — 283 SQ. FT.

Total living area:
1,354 sq. ft.

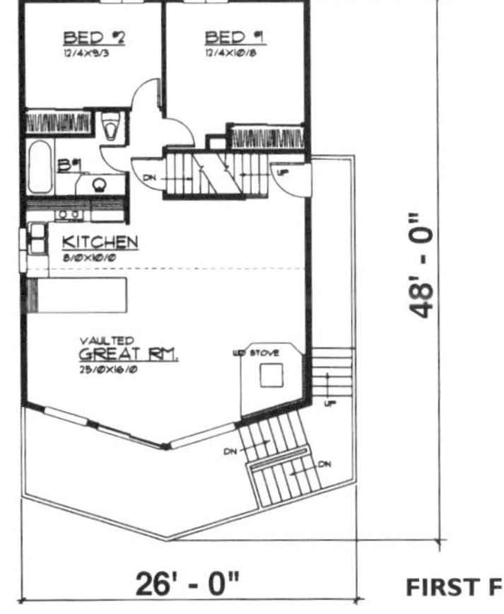

BED #2
12/4X9/3
BED #1
12/4X10/8
B#1
KITCHEN
8/0X10/10
VAULTED
GREAT RM.
25/0X16/0
48' - 0"
26' - 0"

FIRST FLOOR

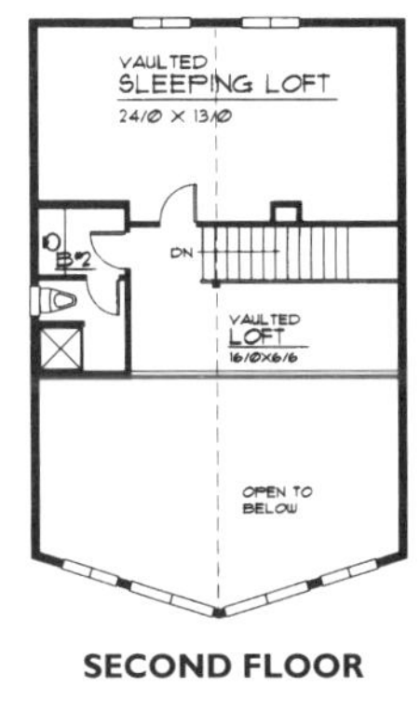

VAULTED
SLEEPING LOFT
24/0 X 13/0
B#2
VAULTED
LOFT
16/0X6/6
OPEN TO
BELOW

SECOND FLOOR

PLAN NO. 92649

Multiple Gables

Price Code: B

This plan features:

- Three bedrooms
- Two full baths
- A Foyer area that leads to a bright and cheery
Great Room capped by a sloped ceiling and
highlighted by a fireplace
- The Dining Area includes double-hung windows
and angles, adding light and dimension to
the room
- A functional Kitchen providing an abundance of
counter space with additional room provided by
a breakfast bar
- A rear Porch is accessed from the Dining Area
- A Master Bedroom Suite including a walk-in
closet and private Bath
- Two additional Bedrooms share a full Bath
- This home is designed with a basement
foundation

AIN FLOOR — 1,508 SQ. FT.
ASEMENT — 1,439 SQ. FT.
ARAGE — 440 SQ. FT.

Total living area:
1,508 sq. ft.

MAIN FLOOR

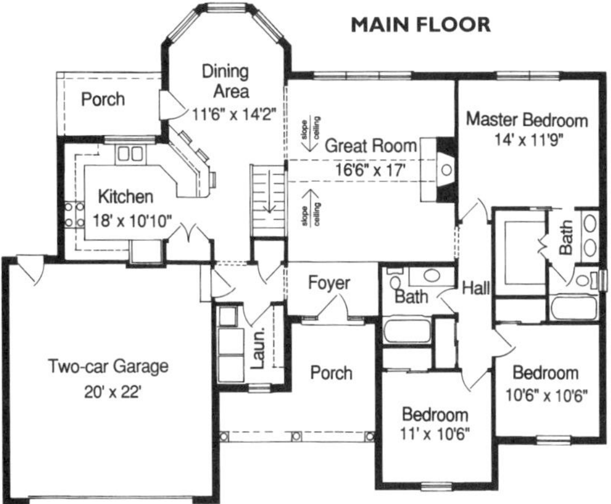

Porch
Dining
Area
11'6" x 14'2"
Great Room
16'6" x 17'
Master Bedroom
14' x 11'9"
Kitchen
18' x 10'10"
Bath
Foyer
Bath
Hall
Two-car Garage
20' x 22'
Laun.
Porch
Bedroom
10'6" x 10'6"
Bedroom
11' x 10'6"

PLAN NO.90966

Stately Manor

Price Code: E

- This plan features:
- — Three bedrooms
- — Two full and one half baths
- A Porch serving as a grand entrance
- A very spacious Foyer with an open staircase and lots of angles
- A beautiful Kitchen equipped with a cook-top island and a full bay window wall that includes a roomy Breakfast Nook
- A Living Room with a vaulted ceiling that flows into the formal Dining Room for ease in entertaining
- This home is designed with a basement foundation

FIRST FLOOR — 1,383 SQ. FT.
SECOND FLOOR — 997 SQ. FT.
BASEMENT — 1,374 SQ. FT.
GARAGE — 420 SQ. FT.

Total living area: 2,380 sq. ft.

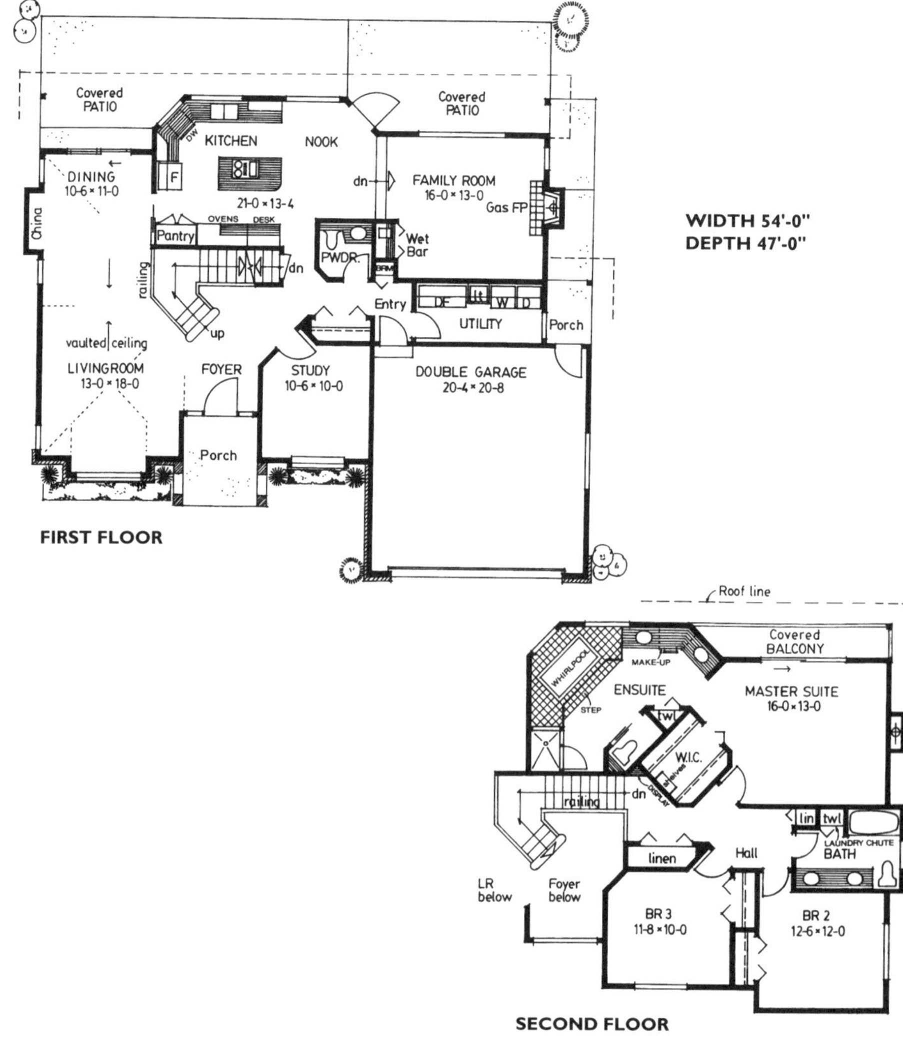

Covered PATIO
Covered PATIO
KITCHEN
NOOK
21-0 × 13-4
DINING
10-6 × 11-0
China
Pantry
OVENS
DESK
FAMILY ROOM
16-0 × 13-0
Gas FP
Wet Bar
PWDR.
Entry
UTILITY
Porch
vaulted ceiling
LIVINGROOM
13-0 × 18-0
FOYER
STUDY
10-6 × 10-0
DOUBLE GARAGE
20-4 × 20-8
Porch
FIRST FLOOR
WIDTH 54'-0"
DEPTH 47'-0"
Roof line
Covered BALCONY
WHIRLPOOL
MAKE-UP
ENSUITE
MASTER SUITE
16-0 × 13-0
STEP
twl
W.I.C.
railing
dn
lin
twl
LAUNDRY CHUTE
BATH
linen
Hall
LR below
Foyer below
BR 3
11-8 × 10-0
BR 2
12-6 × 12-0
SECOND FLOOR

PLAN NO. 90409

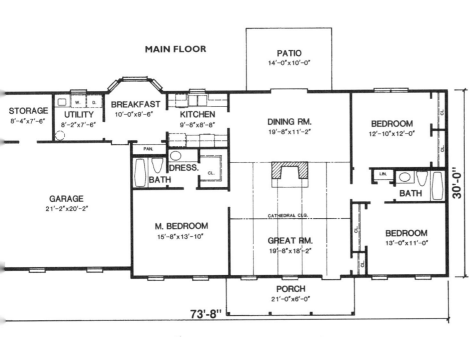

MAIN FLOOR

PATIO
14'-0"x10'-0"

STORAGE
8'-4"x7'-6"

UTILITY
8'-2"x7'-6"

W. D.

BREAKFAST
10'-0"x9'-6"

KITCHEN
9'-8"x8'-8"

DINING RM.
19'-8"x11'-2"

BEDROOM
12'-10"x12'-0"

CL. CL.

PAN.

DRESS.

CL.

BATH

LIN.

BATH

GARAGE
21'-2"x20'-2"

CATHEDRAL CLG.

M. BEDROOM
15'-8"x13'-10"

GREAT RM.
19'-8"x18'-2"

CL. CL.

BEDROOM
13'-0"x11'-0"

PORCH
21'-0"x6'-0"

30'-0"

73'-8"

Easy Living

Price Code: B

- This plan features:
- — Three bedrooms
- — Two full baths
- A massive fireplace separating Living and Dining Rooms
- An isolated Master Suite with a walk-in closet and compartmentalized Bath
- A galley-type Kitchen between the Breakfast Room and Dining Room
- This home is designed with basement, slab and crawlspace foundation options

MAIN FLOOR — 1,670 SQ. FT.
BASEMENT — 1,670 SQ. FT.
GARAGE— 427 SQ. FT.

Total living area:
1,670 sq. ft.

PLAN NO.94116

Small, But Not Lacking

Price Code: B

- This plan features:

—Three bedrooms

—Two full baths

- Great Room adjoining the Dining Room for e in entertaining
- Kitchen highlighted by a peninsula counter/sn bar extending work space and offering convenience in serving informal meals or snacks
- Split bedroom plan allowing for privacy for th Master Bedroom Suite with a private Bath an walk-in closet
- Two additional Bedrooms sharing the full bath room
- Garage entry convenient to the Kitchen
- This home is designed with a basement foundation

MAIN FLOOR — 1,530 SQ. FT.
GARAGE — 440 SQ. FT.

Total living area:
1,546 sq. ft.

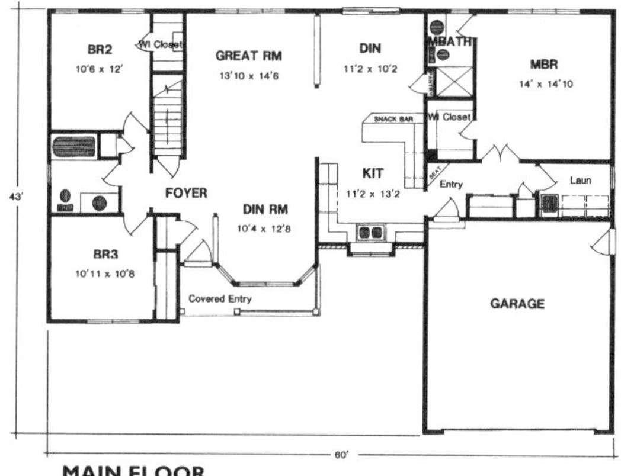

BR2
10'6 x 12'
WI Closet
GREAT RM
13'10 x 14'6
DIN
11'2 x 10'2
MBATH
MBR
14' x 14'10
SNACK BAR
WI Closet
KIT
11'2 x 13'2
Entry
Laun
FOYER
DIN RM
10'4 x 12'8
BR3
10'11 x 10'8
Covered Entry
GARAGE
43'
60'

MAIN FLOOR

PLAN NO.24708

Cozy Country Ranch

Price Code: B

- This plan features:

— Three bedrooms

— Two full baths

- Front Porch shelters outdoor visiting and entrance into Living Room
- Expansive Living Room highlighted by a box window and hearth fireplace between built-ins
- Columns frame entrance to Dining Room with access to back yard
- Efficient U-shaped Kitchen with direct access the Screened Porch and the Dining Room
- Master Bedroom wing enhanced by a large wa in closet and a double vanity Bath with a whirlpool tub
- Two additional Bedrooms with large closets, share a double vanity bath with Laundry Cent
- This home is designed with basement, slab an crawlspace foundation options

MAIN FLOOR — 1,576 SQ. FT.
BASEMENT — 1,454 SQ. FT.
GARAGE — 576 SQ. FT.
PORCH — 391 SQ. FT.

Total living area:
1,576 sq. ft.

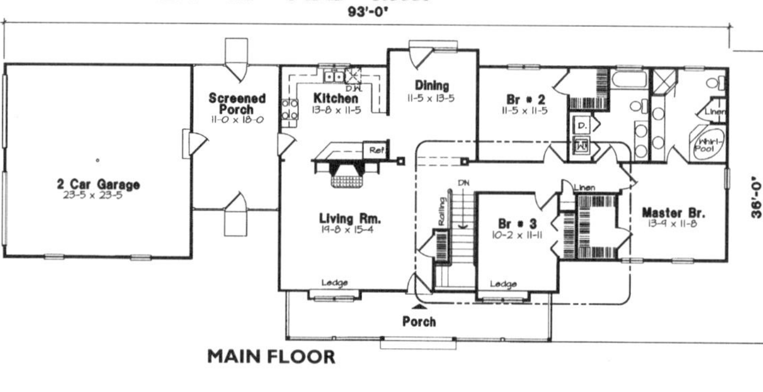

93'-0"
Screened Porch
11-0 x 18-0
Kitchen
13-8 x 11-5
Dining
11-5 x 13-5
Br # 2
11-5 x 11-5
2 Car Garage
23-5 x 23-5
Living Rm.
14-8 x 15-4
Br # 3
10-2 x 11-11
Master Br.
13-4 x 11-8
Linen
Whirl-Pool
Ledge
Porch
36'-0"

MAIN FLOOR

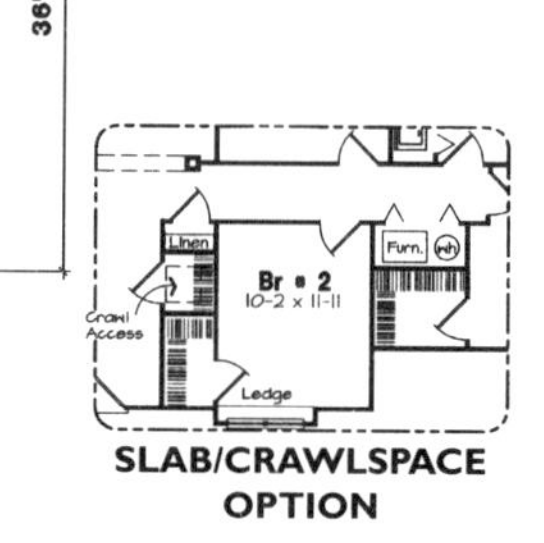

Linen
Br # 2
10-2 x 11-11
Furn.
Crawl Access
Ledge

SLAB/CRAWLSPACE OPTION

To order your Blueprints, call 1-800-235-5700

PLAN NO. 90440

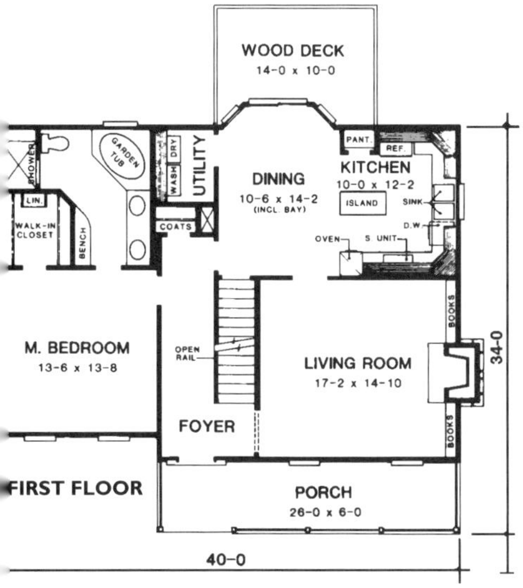

WOOD DECK
14-0 x 10-0
DINING
10-6 x 14-2
(INCL. BAY)
KITCHEN
10-0 x 12-2
PANT.
REF
ISLAND
SINK
D.W.
OVEN
S. UNIT
UTILITY
WASH
DRY
GARDEN TUB
SHOWER
LIN.
WALK-IN CLOSET
BENCH
COATS
M. BEDROOM
13-6 x 13-8
OPEN RAIL
LIVING ROOM
17-2 x 14-10
BOOKS
BOOKS
34-0
FOYER
FIRST FLOOR
PORCH
26-0 x 6-0
40-0

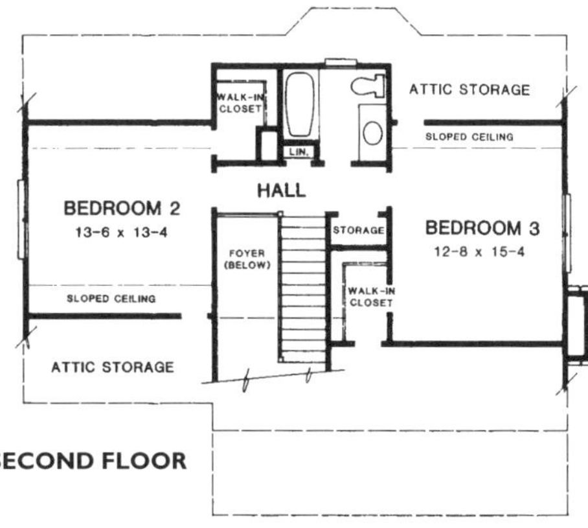

ATTIC STORAGE
SLOPED CEILING
WALK-IN CLOSET
LIN.
HALL
BEDROOM 2
13-6 x 13-4
STORAGE
BEDROOM 3
12-8 x 15-4
FOYER (BELOW)
WALK-IN CLOSET
SLOPED CEILING
ATTIC STORAGE
SECOND FLOOR

Rustic Warmth

Price Code: C

- This plan features:
- — Three bedrooms
- — Two full baths
- A fireplaced Living Room with built-in bookshelves
- A fully-equipped Kitchen with an island
- A sunny Dining Room with glass sliders to a wood Deck
- A first floor Master Suite with walk-in closet and lavish Master Bath
- This home is designed with basement and crawlspace foundation options

FIRST FLOOR — 1,100 SQ. FT.
SECOND FLOOR — 664 SQ. FT.
BASEMENT — 1,100 SQ. FT.

Total living area:
1,764 sq. ft.

PLAN NO. 65143

Victorian Details

Price Code: E

- This plan features:
- — Four bedrooms
- — Three full and one half baths
- Stone and clapboard siding and a gracious circular Porch create a beautiful facade
- This home is designed with a basement foundation

FIRST FLOOR — 1,358 SQ. FT.
SECOND FLOOR — 894 SQ. FT.
BASEMENT — 525 SQ. FT.
BONUS — 312 SQ. FT.

Total living area:
2,252 sq. ft.

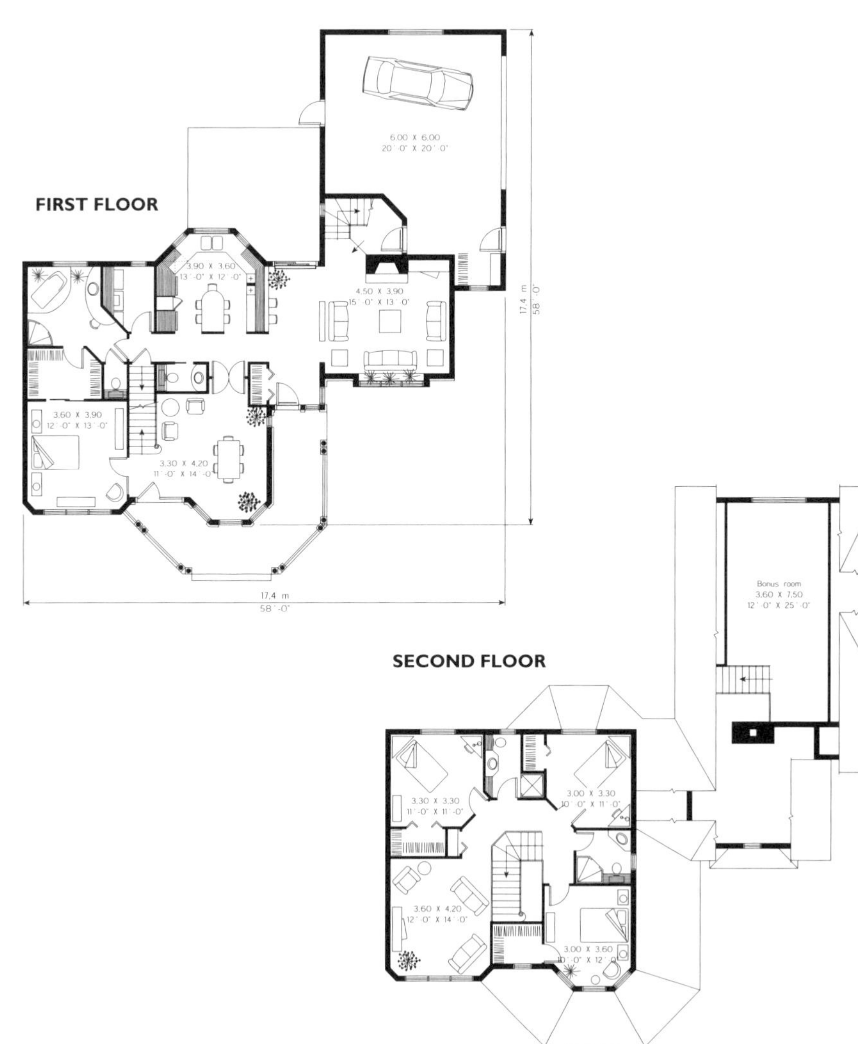
FIRST FLOOR
6.00 X 6.00
20'-0" X 20'-0"
4.50 X 3.90
15'-0" X 13'-0"
3.90 X 3.60
13'-0" X 12'-0"
3.60 X 3.90
12'-0" X 13'-0"
3.30 X 4.20
11'-0" X 14'-0"
17.4 m
58'-0"
SECOND FLOOR
Bonus room
3.60 X 7.50
12'-0" X 25'-0"
3.30 X 3.30
11'-0" X 11'-0"
3.00 X 3.30
10'-0" X 11'-0"
3.60 X 4.20
12'-0" X 14'-0"
3.00 X 3.60
10'-0" X 12'-0"

PLAN NO. 82013

48' 0"
GLASS BLOCKS
WHP TUB
SEAT
SHWR
M.BATH
KNEE SPACE
LIN
MASTER SUITE
15'-0" X 13'-3"
MEDIA CENTER
GREAT RM.
16'-2" X 18'-0"
STRG.
6'-0" X 4'-0"
WH
LAU.
REF
RG
KITCHEN
9'-10" X 11'-0"
DW
43' 0"
GARAGE
19'-0" X 20'-0"
PAN
FOYER
10' CLNG
8" COLUMNS
BRKFAST RM.
9'-10" X 8'-0"
DINING RM.
10' CLNG
11'-6" X 12'-6"
PRCH
FIRST FLOOR

Master Bath for Two

Price Code: C

- This plan features:
- — Three bedrooms
- — Two full and one half baths
- The Master Bath provides a two-person whirlpool tub and separate vanities
- A peninsula counter with a snack bar defines the Kitchen and the Breakfast Room
- This home is designed with basement, slab and crawlspace foundation options

FIRST FLOOR — 1,356 SQ. FT.
SECOND FLOOR— 441 SQ. FT.

Total living area: 1,797 sq. ft.

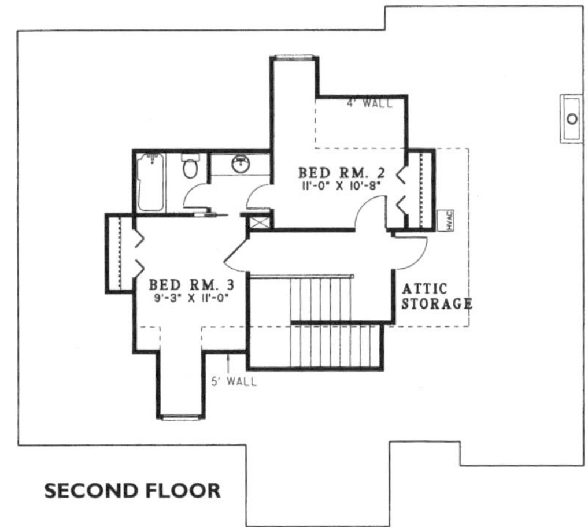
4' WALL
BED RM. 2
11'-0" X 10'-8"
BED RM. 3
9'-3" X 11'-0"
ATTIC STORAGE
5' WALL
SECOND FLOOR

PLAN NO.92625

Side-Load Garage

Price Code: B

- This plan features:
  - — Three bedrooms
  - — Two full baths
- A sloped ceiling tops the Dining Room and the Great Room
- The Great Room features an angled fireplace ar has access to a rear Patio
- The efficient U-shaped Kitchen takes in backya views through the bay-windowed Breakfast Bay
- The Master Bedroom includes a private Bath w garden tub and a deep walk-in closet
- Two additional Bedrooms at the front of the ho have ample closet and one features a slope ceili
- This home is designed with a basement founda

MAIN FLOOR — 1,746 SQ. FT.
BASEMENT — 1,560 SQ. FT.
GARAGE — 455 SQ. FT.

Total living area:
1,746 sq. ft.

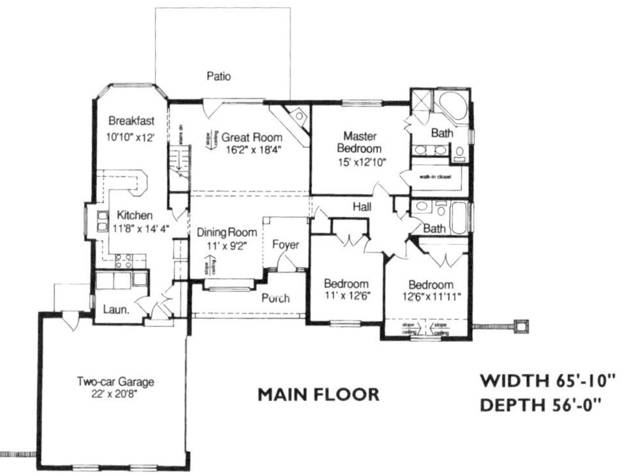
Patio
Breakfast
10'10" x12'
Great Room
16'2" x 18'4"
Master
Bedroom
15' x12'10"
Bath
Kitchen
11'8" x 14' 4"
Hall
Dining Room
11' x 9'2"
Foyer
Bath
Bedroom
11' x 12'6"
Bedroom
12'6"x11'11"
Porch
Laun.
Two-car Garage
22' x 20'8"
MAIN FLOOR
WIDTH 65'-10"
DEPTH 56'-0"

PLAN NO.68126

Secluded Master Suite

Price Code: C

- This plan features:
  - — Three bedrooms
  - — Two full and one half baths
- A fireplace and a front arched window accent Family Room
- The Kitchen and Breakfast Areas are open to each other with an angled peninsula snack ba from which there can be easy interaction from the Family Room
- The Master Bedroom Suite includes a lavish Master Bath and a walk-in closet
- The secondary Bedrooms have easy access to full Bath
- This home is designed with basement, slab ar crawlspace foundation options

FIRST FLOOR — 1,387 SQ. FT.
SECOND FLOOR — 471 SQ. FT.
BONUS — 243 SQ. FT.
GARAGE — 509 SQ. FT.

Total living area
1,858 sq. ft.

FIRST FLOOR
MASTER BATH
MASTER BEDROOM
CLO
UTIL
PWD
BRKFST
PORCH
CLO
FAMILY ROOM
KITCHEN
2-CAR GARAGE
© Carmichael & Dame
ENTRY
DINING ROOM
PORCH
CLO
52'-10"
52'-11"

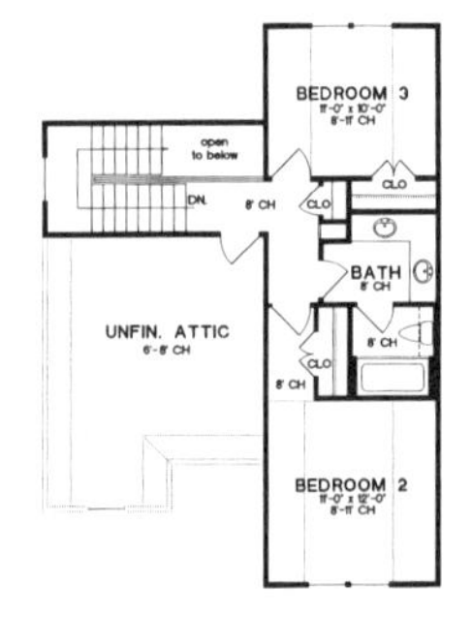
BEDROOM 3
open to below
UNFIN. ATTIC
BATH
BEDROOM 2
SECOND FLOOR

To order your Blueprints, call 1-800-235-5700

PLAN NO. 90353

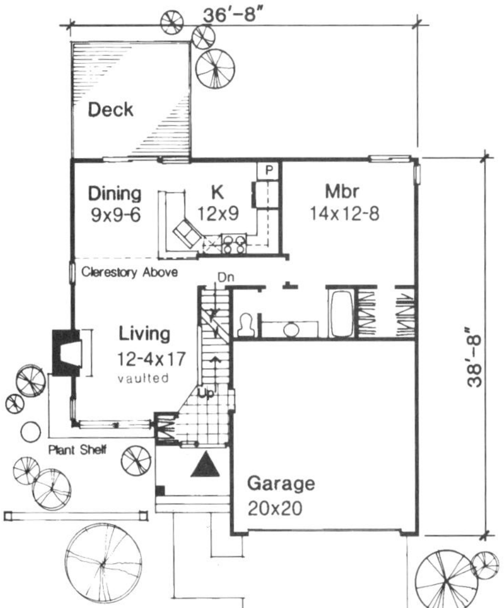

36'-8"
Deck
Dining
9x9-6
K
12x9
P
Mbr
14x12-8
Clerestory Above
Dn
Living
12-4x17
vaulted
Up
Plant Shelf
Garage
20x20
38'-8"

FIRST FLOOR

Vaulted Ceiling

Price Code: A

- This plan features:
  - — Three bedrooms
  - — Two full baths
- A vaulted ceiling in the Living Room and the Dining Room, with a clerestory window above
- The Master Bedroom has a walk-in closet and a private Bath
- The efficient Kitchen has a corner double sink and a peninsula counter
- The Dining Room has sliding glass doors to the Deck
- The Living Room has a fireplace and a great corner window
- This home is designed with a basement foundation

MAIN FLOOR — 846 SQ. FT.
UPPER FLOOR — 400 SQ. FT.

Total living area: 1,246 sq. ft.

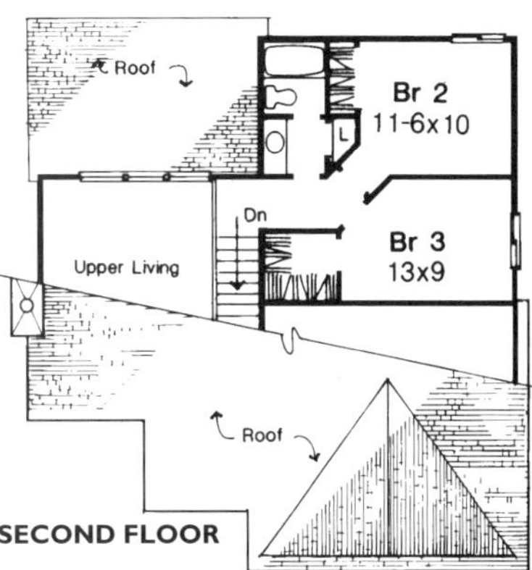
Roof
Br 2
11-6x10
L
Dn
Br 3
13x9
Upper Living
Roof

SECOND FLOOR

PLAN NO. 92629

Quality and Diversity

Price Code: D

- This plan features:
  - — Four bedrooms
  - — Two full and one half bath
- Elegant arched entrance from Porch into Foyer and Great Room beyond
- Corner fireplace and atrium door highlight Great Room
- Hub Kitchen with walk-in Pantry and peninsula counter easily accesses glass Breakfast Bay, backyard, Great Room, Dining Room, Laundry and Garage
- This home is designed with a basement foundation

FIRST FLOOR — 1,401 SQ. FT.
SECOND FLOOR — 621 SQ. FT.
BASEMENT — 1,269 SQ. FT.
GARAGE — 478 SQ. FT.

Total living area: 2,022 sq. ft.

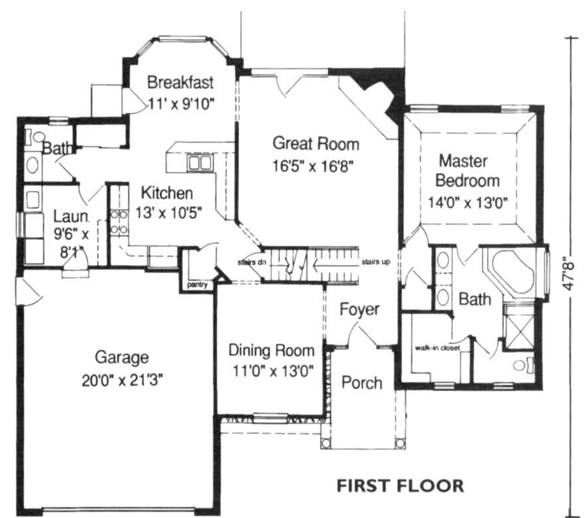
Breakfast
11' x 9'10"
Great Room
16'5" x 16'8"
Master Bedroom
14'0" x 13'0"
Bath
Kitchen
13' x 10'5"
Laun
9'6" x 8'1"
stairs dn
stairs up
pantry
Bath
Foyer
Garage
20'0" x 21'3"
Dining Room
11'0" x 13'0"
walk-in closet
Porch
47'8"
55'4"

FIRST FLOOR

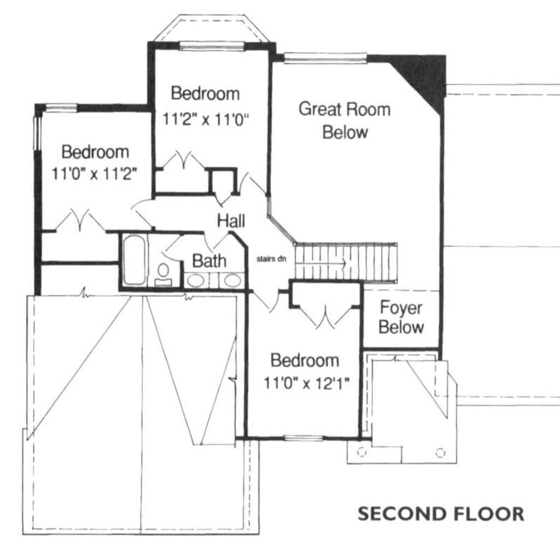
Bedroom
11'2" x 11'0"
Great Room
Below
Bedroom
11'0" x 11'2"
Hall
Bath
stairs dn
Foyer
Below
Bedroom
11'0" x 12'1"

SECOND FLOOR

Cabin In the Country

Price Code: A

his plan features:

- wo bedrooms
- ne full and one half baths
- large Screened Porch at the front of the house ffers a seasonal extra room
- he combination Living and Dining Area has a ozy fireplace for added warmth
- he efficiently laid out Kitchen has a built-in antry
- wo large Bedrooms, one with a private half ath, are located at the rear of the home
- his home is designed with crawlspace and slab oundation options

RST FLOOR — 928 SQ. FT.
REENED PORCH — 230 SQ. FT.
ORAGE — 14 SQ. FT.

Total living area:
928 sq. ft.

PLAN NO.90433

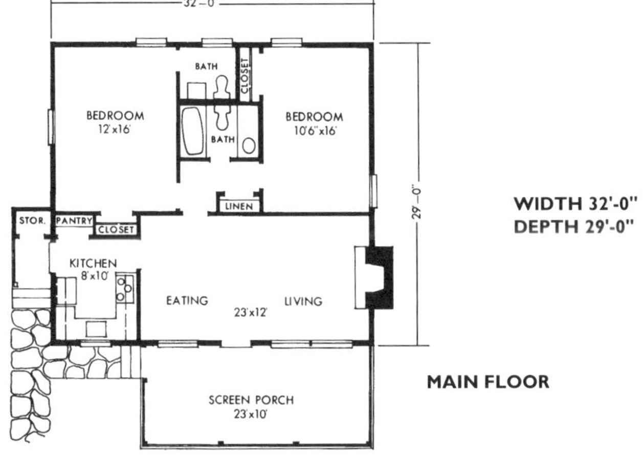

32'-0"
BATH
CLOSET
BEDROOM
12'x16'
BATH
BEDROOM
10'6"x16'
LINEN
STOR.
PANTRY
CLOSET
KITCHEN
8'x10'
EATING
23'x12'
LIVING
29'-0"
SCREEN PORCH
23'x10'

WIDTH 32'-0"
DEPTH 29'-0"

MAIN FLOOR

Let the Sunshine In

Price Code: B

This plan features:

- Three bedrooms
- Two full baths
- A wrap-around Deck allows for expanded living pace in the mild weather
- The highly windowed Living Room has an open ayout including the Dining Area
- The first floor Bedroom has private access to a full Bath
- Two secondary Bedrooms on the second floor hare a private Sitting Loft
- This home is designed with a basement foundation

RST FLOOR — 946 SQ. FT.
COND FLOOR — 604 SQ. FT.

Total living area:
1,551 sq. ft.

PLAN NO.65141

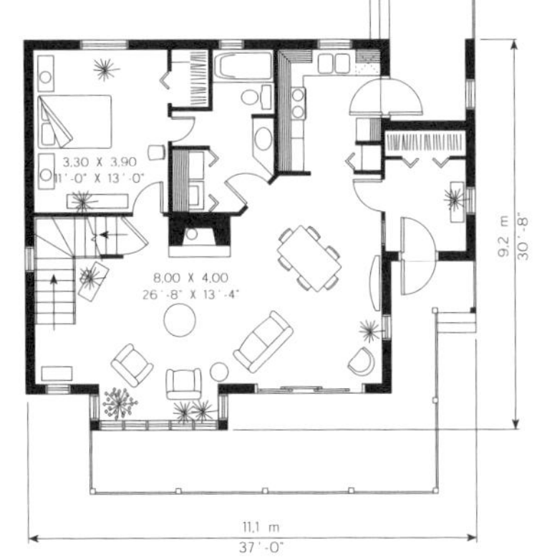

3.30 X 3.90
11'-0" X 13'-0"
8.00 X 4.00
26'-8" X 13'-4"
9.2 m
30'-8"

11,1 m
37'-0"

FIRST FLOOR

3.10 X 3.90
10'-4" X 13'-0"
3.10 X 3.90
10'-4" X 13'-0"
2.70 X 3.00
9'-0" X 10'-0"

SECOND FLOOR

PLAN NO. 91514

Large Front Window

Price Code: B

- This plan features:
  - — Three bedrooms
  - — Two full and one half baths
- An outstanding, two-story Great Room with an unusual floor-to-ceiling corner front window and cozy hearth fireplace
- An efficient Kitchen with a work island, pantry, a corner, double sink opening to the Great Room, and a bright bay window eating Nook
- A quiet Master Suite with a vaulted ceiling and a plush Bath with a double vanity, Spa tub and walk-in closet
- This home is designed with a crawlspace foundation

FIRST FLOOR — 1,230 SQ. FT.
SECOND FLOOR — 477 SQ. FT.

Total living area: 1,707 sq. ft.

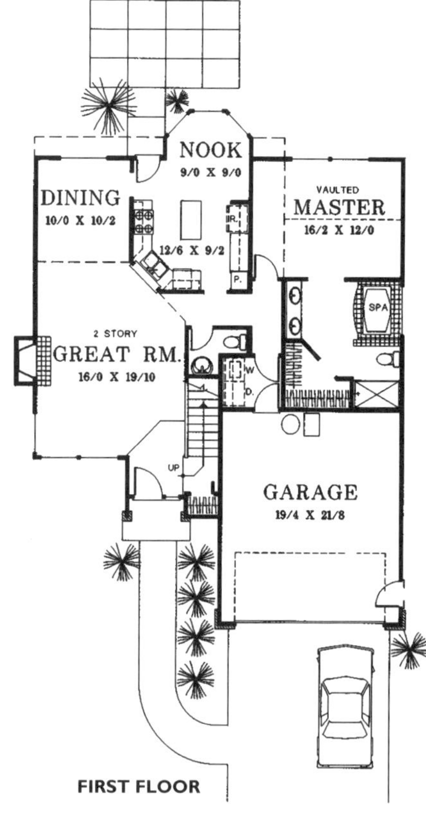
NOOK
9/0 X 9/0
DINING
10/0 X 10/2
VAULTED
MASTER
16/2 X 12/0
12/6 X 9/2
SPA
2 STORY
GREAT RM.
16/0 X 19/10
UP
GARAGE
19/4 X 21/8

FIRST FLOOR

WIDTH 40'-0
DEPTH 53'-0

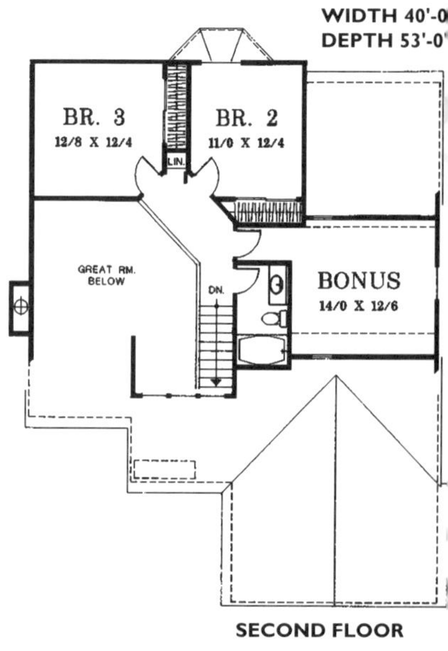
BR. 3
12/8 X 12/4
BR. 2
11/0 X 12/4
LIN.
GREAT RM.
BELOW
DN.
BONUS
14/0 X 12/6

SECOND FLOOR

PLAN NO. 92220

Southern Hospitality

Price Code: C

- This plan features:
  - — Three bedrooms
  - — Two full baths
- Welcoming covered Veranda catches breezes
- Easy-care tiled Entry leads into Great Room with fieldstone fireplace, cathedral ceiling and atrium door to another Covered Veranda
- A bright Kitchen/Dining Room includes a stovetop island/ snack bar, built-in pantry and desk and access to covered Veranda
- This home is designed with basement, slab and crawlspace foundation options

MAIN FLOOR — 1,830 SQ. FT.
GARAGE — 759 SQ. FT.

Total living area: 1,830 sq. ft.

COVERED VERANDA
KITCHEN/ DINING 21 X 15 9" CLGS.
DW
REF
PANTRY
O/MW
DESK
MSTR. BDRM. 14 X 16 VAULTED CLG. 9" TO 11"
SLOPED CLGS. 9" TO 11"
9" CLGS.
WALK-IN-CLOS.
H.W.
C/H
W. D.
LAUND.
HALL 9" CLGS.
3 CAR GARAGE 23 X 33
GREAT ROOM 22 X 16 CATHEDRAL CLGS.
ENT. 10" CLGS.
LIN.
BDRM #2 12 X 13 10" CLGS.
BDRM. #3 11 X 12 9" CLGS.
SERVICE PORCH
COVERED VERANDA

MAIN FLOOR

WIDTH 75'-0"
DEPTH 52'-3"

PLAN NO. 98423

Easy One-Floor Living

Price Code: B

- This plan features:
- — Three bedrooms
- — Two full baths
- A spacious Family Room topped by a vaulted ceiling and highlighted by a large fireplace and a French door to the rear yard
- A serving bar open to the Family Room and the Dining Room, a Pantry and a peninsula counter adding more efficiency to the Kitchen
- This home is designed with basement, slab and crawlspace foundation options

MAIN FLOOR — 1,617 SQ. FT.
BASEMENT — 1,685 SQ. FT.
GARAGE — 400 SQ. FT.

Total living area: 1,671 sq. ft.

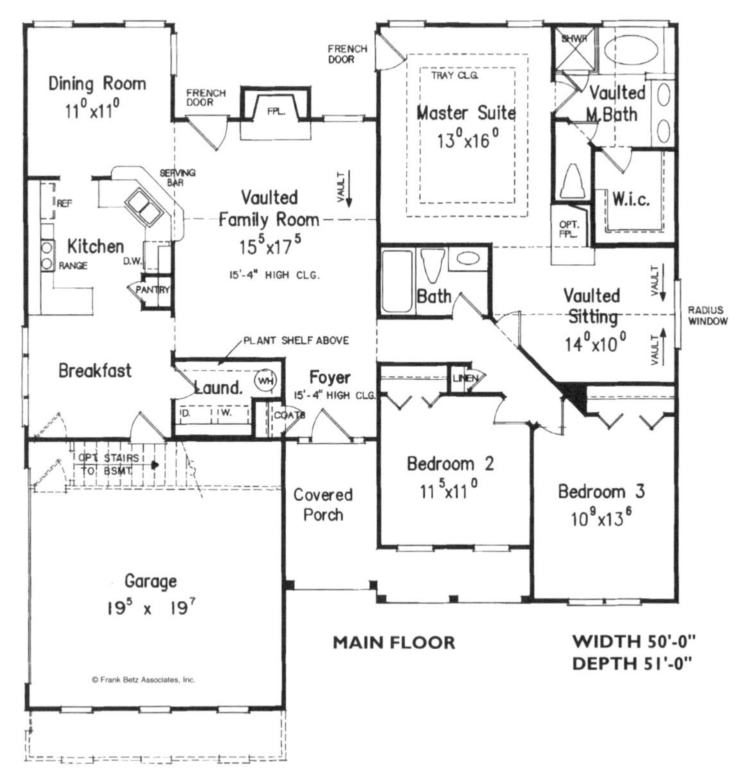

Dining Room
11⁰x11⁰
FRENCH DOOR
FPL.
FRENCH DOOR
TRAY CLG.
Master Suite
13⁰x16⁰
SHWR.
Vaulted
M.Bath
SERVING BAR
REF
Vaulted
Family Room
15⁵x17⁵
VAULT
Kitchen
RANGE
D.W.
PANTRY
15'-4" HIGH CLG.
W.i.c.
OPT. FPL.
Bath
Vaulted
Sitting
14⁰x10⁰
RADIUS WINDOW
PLANT SHELF ABOVE
Breakfast
Laund.
WH
Foyer
15'-4" HIGH CLG.
LINEN
COATS
OPT. STAIRS TO BSMT.
Bedroom 2
11⁵x11⁰
Bedroom 3
10⁹x13⁶
Covered
Porch
Garage
19⁵ x 19⁷
© Frank Betz Associates, Inc.
MAIN FLOOR
WIDTH 50'-0"
DEPTH 51'-0"

An Affordable Floor Plan

Price Code: A

This plan features:

- Three bedrooms
- Two full baths
- A covered Porch entry
- An old-fashioned hearth fireplace in the vaulted ceiling Living Room
- An efficient Kitchen with U-shaped counter that is accessible from the Dining Room
- A Master Bedroom with a large walk-in closet and private Bath
- This home is designed with crawlspace and slab foundation options

AIN FLOOR — 1,410 SQ. FT.
ARAGE — 484 SQ. FT.

Total living area: 1,410 sq. ft.

PLAN NO.91807

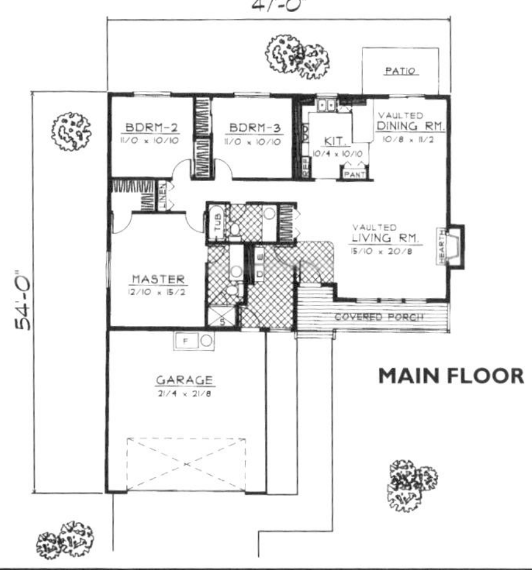
47'-0"
54'-0"
PATIO
BDRM-2 11/0 x 10/10
BDRM-3 11/0 x 10/10
KIT. 10/4 x 10/10
VAULTED DINING RM. 10/8 x 11/2
PANT
VAULTED LIVING RM. 15/10 x 20/8
MASTER 12/10 x 15/2
COVERED PORCH
GARAGE 21/4 x 21/8

MAIN FLOOR

Expansion Possiblities

Price Code: B

This plan features:

- Three bedrooms
- Two full and one half baths
- The Bonus area over the Garage offers opportunities for expansion, perhaps as a children's playroom
- The Great Room and the formal Dining Area adjoin creating the illusion of a much large space
- The Kitchen has an island/snack bar for meals on the go
- A convenient Grilling Porch is accessed from the Nook
- The Master Suite includes a five piece, luxurious bath and a U-shaped walk-in closet
- This home is designed with basement, slab and crawlspace foundation options

RST FLOOR — 1,155 SQ. FT.
COND FLOOR — 529 SQ. FT.
ONUS ROOM — 380 SQ. FT.
ARAGE — 400 SQ. FT.

Total living area: 1684 sq. ft.

PLAN NO.82010

47' 0"
50' 0"
WHP TUB
MASTER BATH
GRILLING PORCH 14'-0" X 6'-0"
KITCHEN 11'-0" X 10'-0"
NOOK 7'-0" X 9'-0"
LAU.
STORAGE 10'-0" X 6'-0"
MASTER SUITE 11'-6" X 14'-0"
ISLAND
GARAGE 19'-8" X 19'-4"
8" COLUMNS
GREAT RM. 15'-6" X 16'-0"
DINING 10'-2" X 14'-0"
FOYER
PRCH

FIRST FLOOR

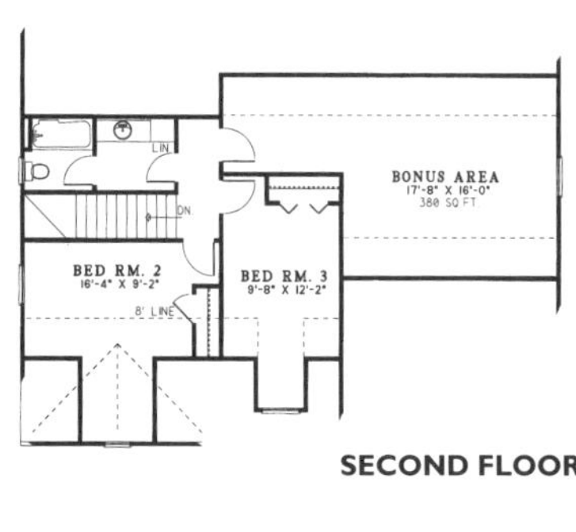
BONUS AREA 17'-8" X 16'-0" 380 SQ FT
BED RM. 2 16'-4" X 9'-2"
BED RM. 3 9'-8" X 12'-2"

SECOND FLOOR

PLAN NO. 99365

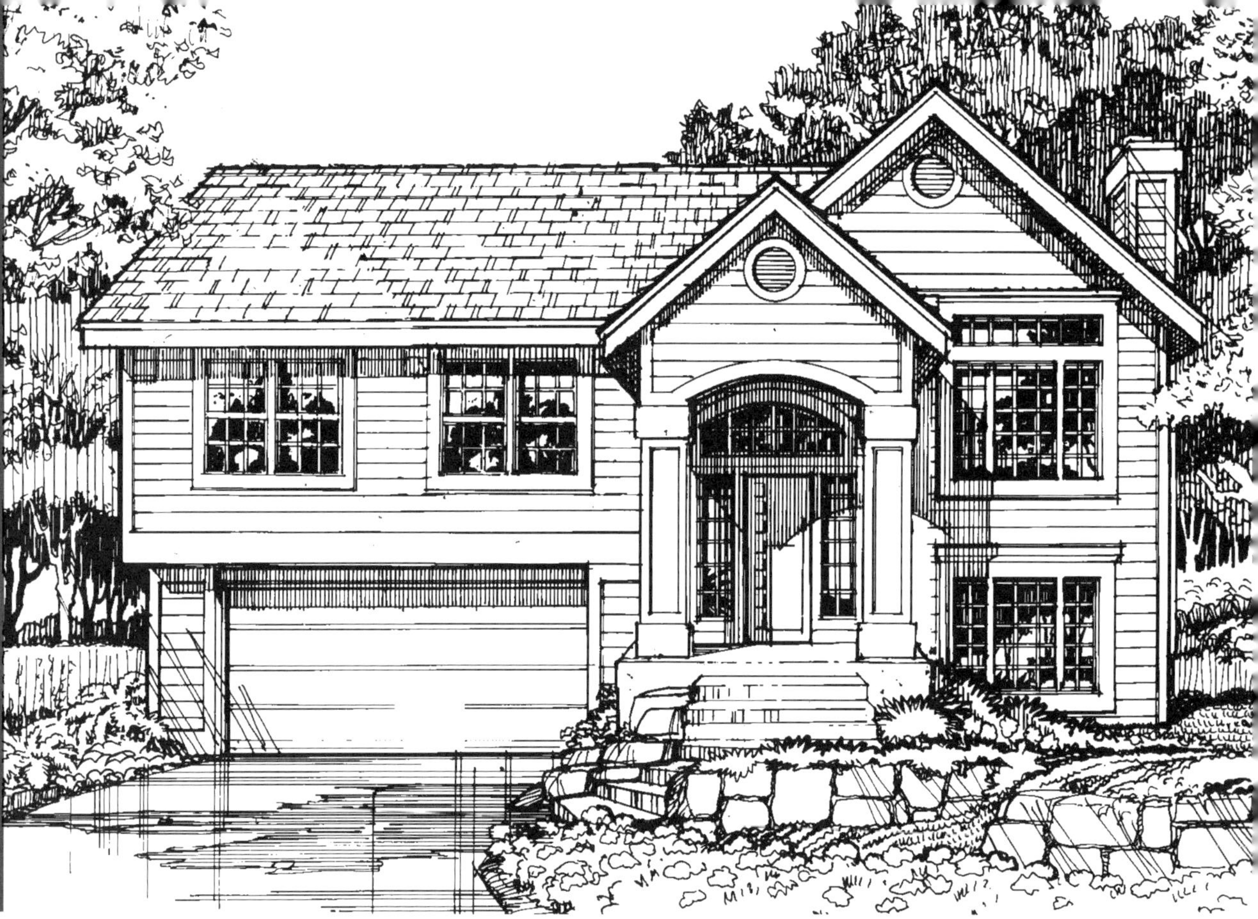

Country Charm

Price Code: A

- This plan features:
- — Three bedrooms
- — Two full baths and opt. half bath
- Ten-foot high ceilings in the Living Room, Family Room and Dinette area
- A heat-circulating fireplace
- A Master Bath with separate stall shower
- A two-car Garage with access through the Mudroom
- This home is designed with a basement foundation

MAIN FLOOR — 1,203 SQ. FT.
BASEMENT — 676 SQ. FT.
GARAGE — 509 SQ. FT.

Total living area:
1,203 sq. ft.

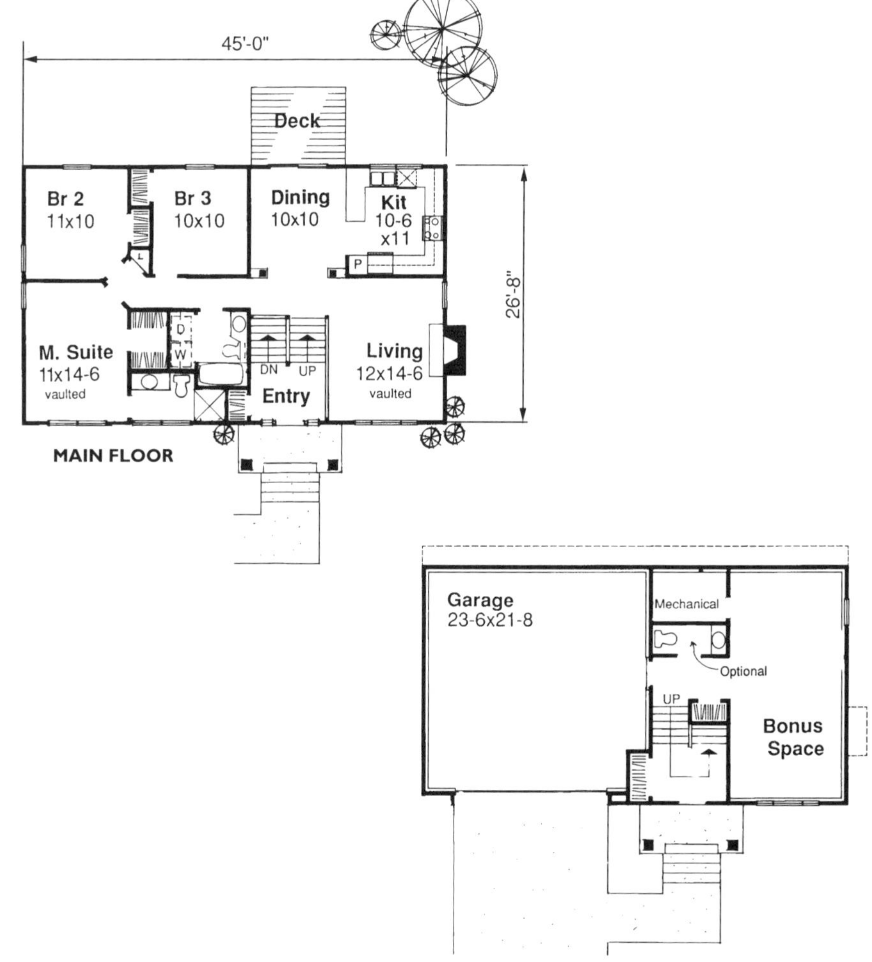

45'-0"
Deck
Br 2
11x10
Br 3
10x10
Dining
10x10
Kit
10-6
x11
P
M. Suite
11x14-6
vaulted
D
W
DN
UP
Entry
Living
12x14-6
vaulted
26'-8"
MAIN FLOOR
Garage
23-6x21-8
Mechanical
Optional
UP
Bonus
Space
LOWER FLOOR

PLAN NO. 9

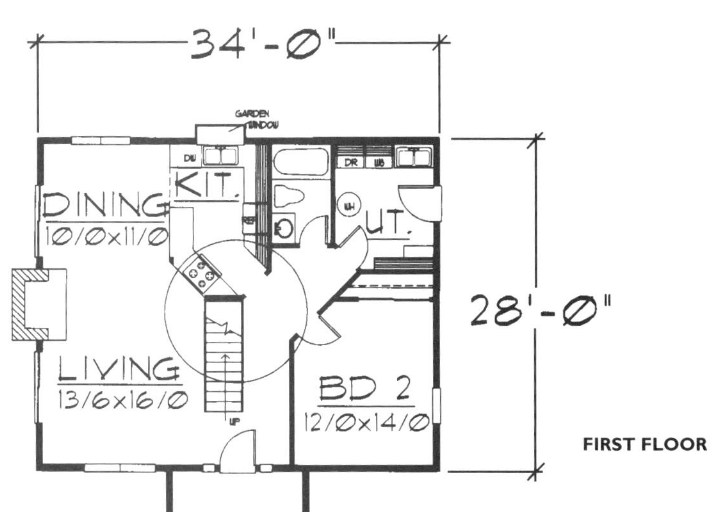
34'-0"
GARDEN WINDOW
DINING
10/0x11/0
KIT.
UT.
28'-0"
LIVING
13/6x16/0
BD 2
12/0x14/0
FIRST FLOOR

Neat and Tidy

Price Code: A

- This plan features:
  - Two bedrooms
  - Two full baths
- A two-story Living Room and Dining Room with a handsome stone fireplace
- A well-appointed Kitchen with a peninsula counter
- A Master Suite with a walk-in closet and private Master Bath
- A large Utility Room with Laundry facilities
- This home is designed with basement and crawlspace foundation options

FIRST FLOOR — 952 SQ. FT.
SECOND FLOOR — 297 SQ. FT.

Total living area:
1,249 sq. ft.

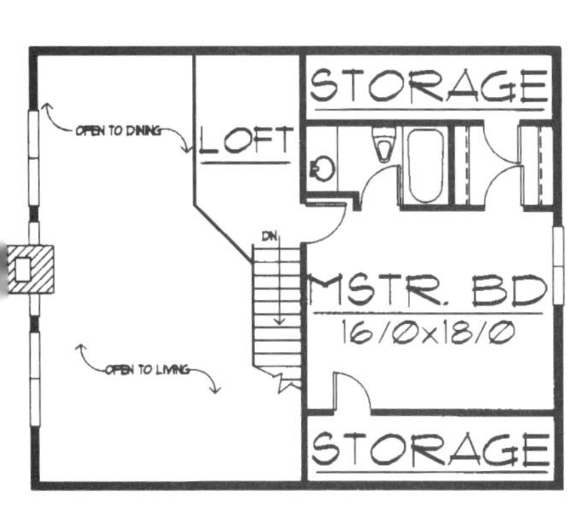
STORAGE
OPEN TO DINING
LOFT
MSTR. BD
16/0x18/0
OPEN TO LIVING
STORAGE
SECOND FLOOR

OPTIONAL BASEMENT OPTION

PLAN NO. 65

Appealing Farmhouse

Price Code: D

- This plan features:
- — Three bedrooms
- — Two full and one half baths
- Interior doors provide privacy options in the Study and Living Room
- Luxurious amenities in the Master Suite include a fireplace, large walk-in closet and Bath with separate tub and shower
- This home is designed with a basement foundation

FIRST FLOOR — 1,146 SQ. FT.
SECOND FLOOR — 943 SQ. FT.
BONUS — 313 SQ. FT.
BASEMENT — 483 SQ. FT.

Total living area:
2,089 sq. ft.

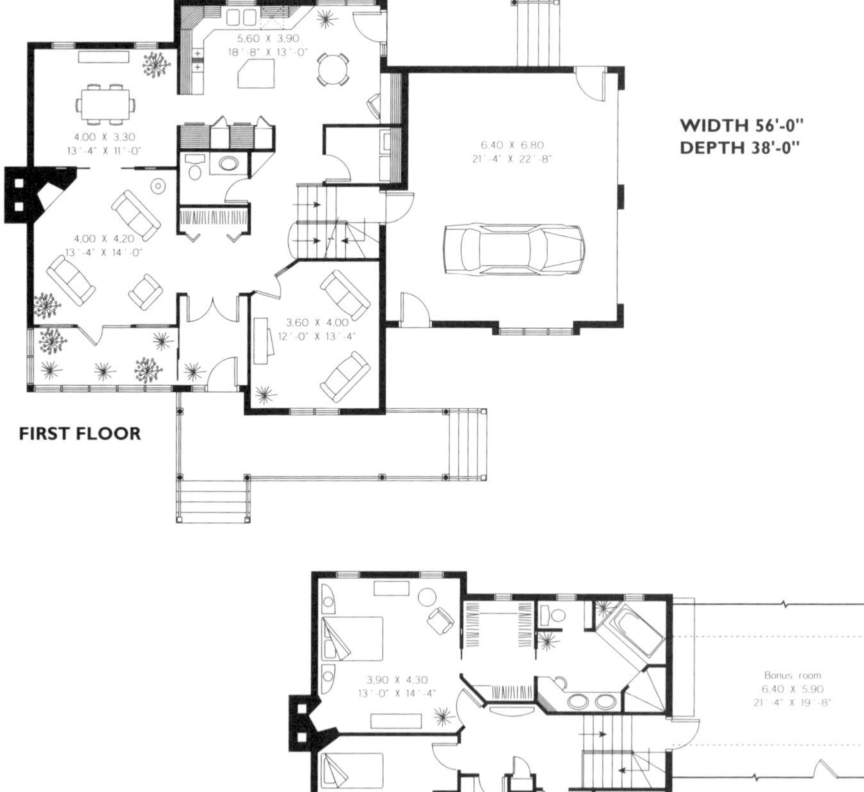
WIDTH 56'-0"
DEPTH 38'-0" 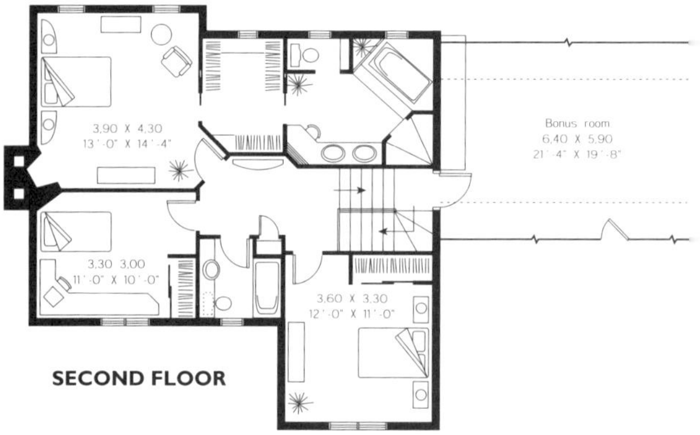
FIRST FLOOR
SECOND FLOOR

To order your Blueprints, call 1-800-235-5700

PLAN NO. 98912

Simply Cozy

Price Code: A

- This plan features:
- — Three bedrooms
- — Two full baths
- Quaint front Porch sheltering Entry into the Living Area showcased by a massive fireplace and built-ins below a vaulted ceiling
- Formal Dining Room accented by a bay of glass with Sun Deck access
- Secluded Master Bedroom offers a roomy walk-in closet and plush Bath with two vanities and a garden window tub
- This home is designed with a basement foundation

MAIN FLOOR — 1,325 SQ. FT.
LOWER — 20 SQ. FT.
BASEMENT — 556 SQ. FT.
MAIN FLOOR — 724 SQ. FT.

Sundeck 14-0 x 10-0

Brkfst. 8-2 x 8-2
Kit. 10-0 x 8-2
Dining 11-10 x 10-0
Bdrm.3 10-0 x 11-6
Bth.2
Master Bdrm. 10-8 x 16-10
M.Bath
Living Area 13-8 x 15-0
Flat Ceil. 12-9 High
Vaulted Ceil.
Bdrm.2 13-6 x 11-2
Front Porch

MAIN FLOOR

WIDTH 52'-0"
DEPTH 42'-0"

Total living area:
1,345 sq. ft.

PLAN NO. 92527

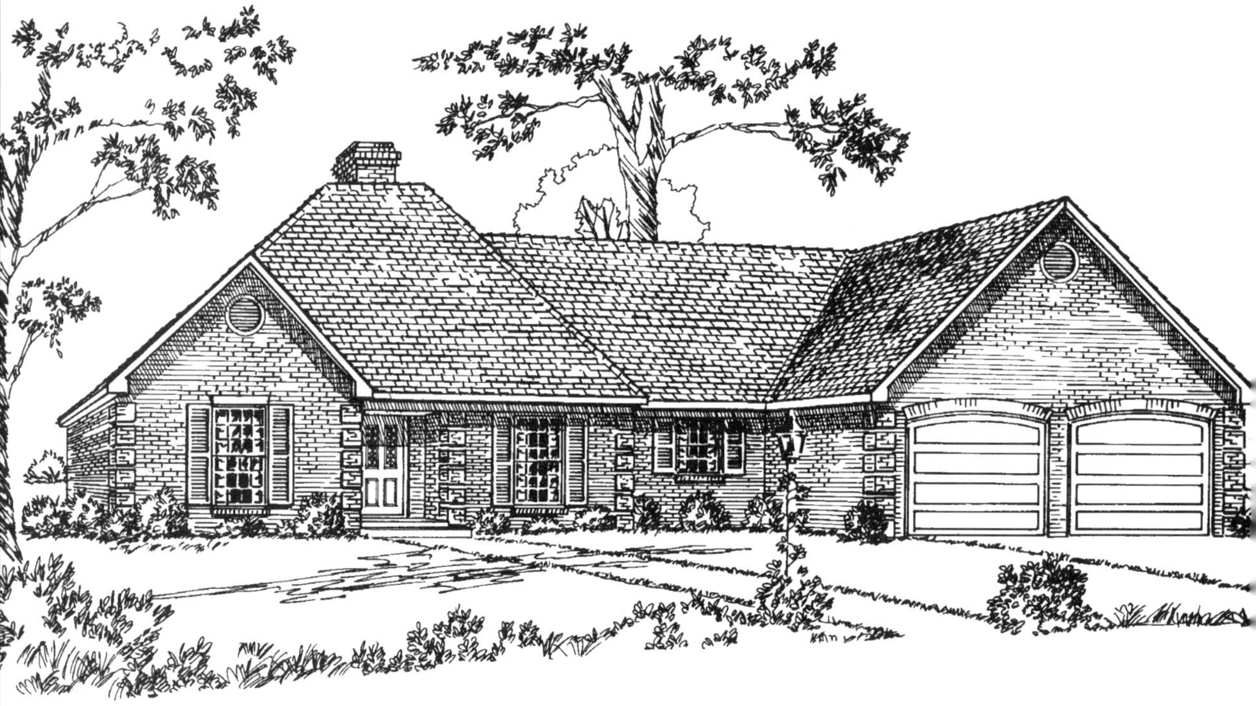

Secluded Master Suite

Price Code: B

- This plan features:
- — Three bedrooms
- — Two full baths
- A convenient one-level design with an open floor plan between the Kitchen, Breakfast Area and Great Room
- A vaulted ceiling and a cozy fireplace in the spacious Great Room
- A well-equipped Kitchen using a peninsula counter as an eating bar
- A Master Suite with a luxurious Master Bath
- Two additional Bedrooms having use of a full Bath
- This home is designed with crawlspace and slab foundation options

MAIN FLOOR — 1,680 SQ. FT.
GARAGE — 538 SQ. FT.

Total living area: 1,680 sq. ft.

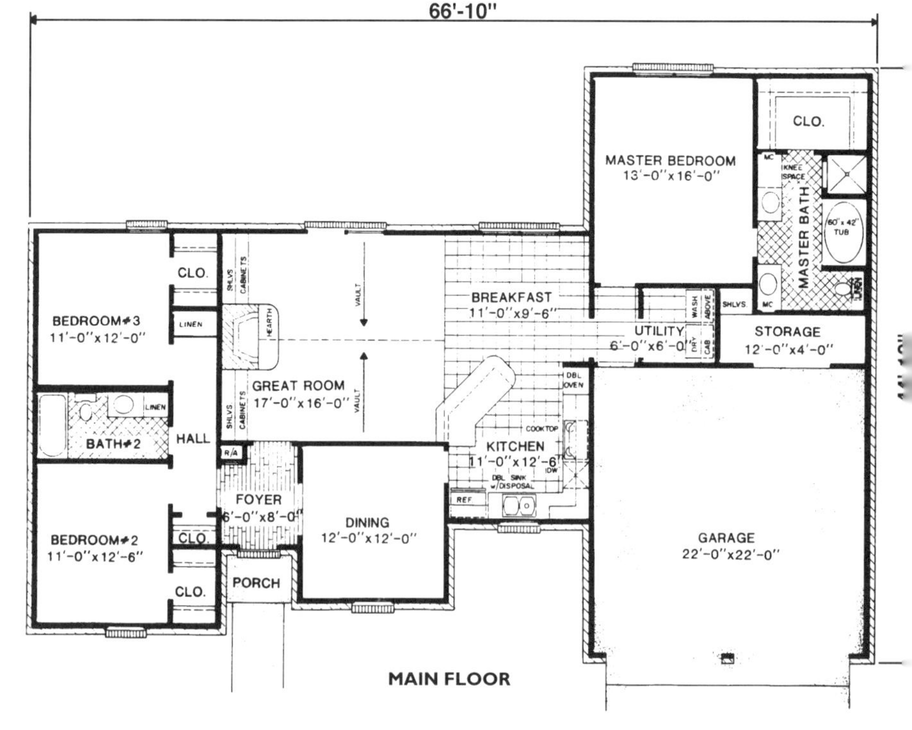

66'-10"
MASTER BEDROOM
13'-0"x16'-0"
CLO.
MASTER BATH
BEDROOM#3
11'-0"x12'-0"
CLO.
LINEN
BREAKFAST
11'-0"x9'-6"
UTILITY
6'-0"x6'-0"
STORAGE
12'-0"x4'-0"
GREAT ROOM
17'-0"x16'-0"
BATH#2
HALL
KITCHEN
11'-0"x12'-6"
FOYER
6'-0"x8'-0"
DINING
12'-0"x12'-0"
BEDROOM#2
11'-0"x12'-6"
CLO.
CLO.
PORCH
GARAGE
22'-0"x22'-0"
MAIN FLOOR

PLAN NO. 98460

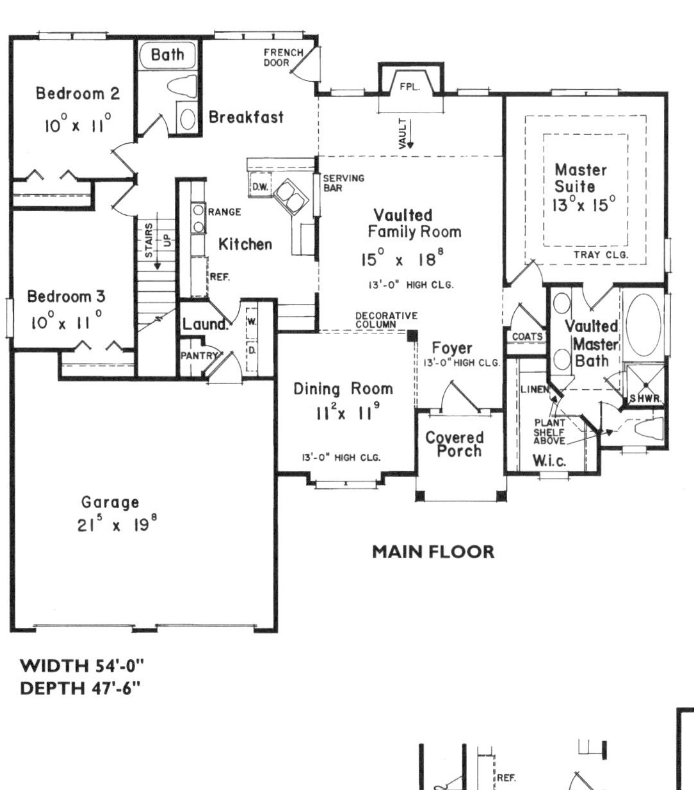

Bath
FRENCH DOOR
Bedroom 2
10⁰ x 11⁰
Breakfast
FPL.
VAULT
D.W.
SERVING BAR
Master Suite
13⁰x 15⁰
RANGE
Kitchen
STAIRS UP
Vaulted Family Room
15⁰ x 18⁸
13'-0" HIGH CLG.
TRAY CLG.
REF.
Bedroom 3
10⁰ x 11⁰
Laund.
W.
D.
PANTRY
DECORATIVE COLUMN
Foyer
13'-0" HIGH CLG.
COATS
Vaulted Master Bath
LINEN
SHWR.
Dining Room
11² x 11⁹
PLANT SHELF ABOVE
Covered Porch
W.i.c.
13'-0" HIGH CLG.
Garage
21⁵ x 19⁸
MAIN FLOOR
WIDTH 54'-0"
DEPTH 47'-6"

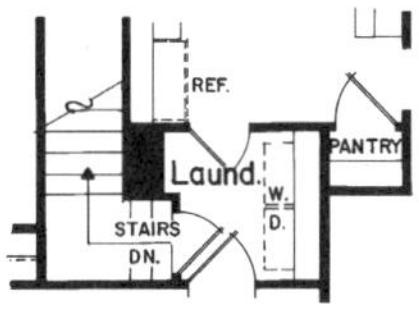

REF. PANTRY Laund. W. D. STAIRS DN.

OPTIONAL BASEMENT STAIR LOCATION

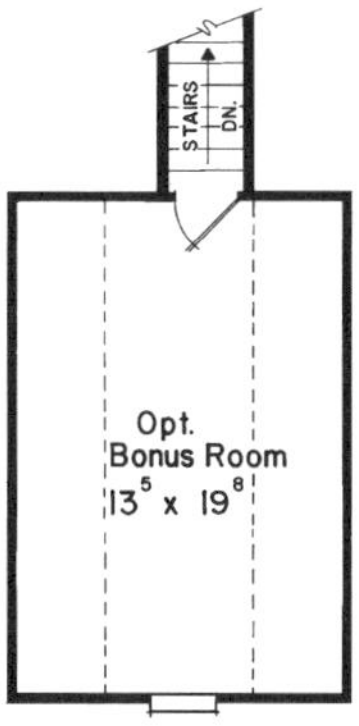

STAIRS DN.

Opt. Bonus Room 13⁵ x 19⁸

BONUS ROOM

European Flair

Price Code: B

- This plan features:
- — Three bedrooms
- — Two full baths
- Large fireplace serving as an attractive focal point for the vaulted Family Room
- Kitchen including a serving bar for the Family Room and a Breakfast area
- Master Suite topped by a tray ceiling over the Bedroom and a vaulted ceiling over the five-piece Master Bath
- This home is designed with basement and crawlspace foundation options

MAIN FLOOR — 1,544 SQ. FT.
BONUS ROOM — 284 SQ. FT.
GARAGE — 440 SQ. FT.

Total living area: 1,544 sq. ft.

PLAN NO.34077

Expandable Home

Price Code: C

- This plan features:
  - — Four bedrooms
  - — Three full baths
- The front Entry is open to the Living Room which is highlighted by a double window
- The bright Dining Area opens to the optional Patio with a sliding glass door
- The compact, efficient Kitchen has a peninsula serving/snack bar, Laundry c et and outdoor access
- Two first floor Bedrooms have ample cl et space and share a full Bath
- The second floor Master Bedroom and a additional Bedroom feature dormer wi dows, private Baths and walk-in closets
- This home is designed with basement, s and crawlspace foundation options.

FIRST FLOOR — 957 SQ. FT.
SECOND FLOOR — 800 SQ. FT.

Total living area:
1,757 sq. ft.

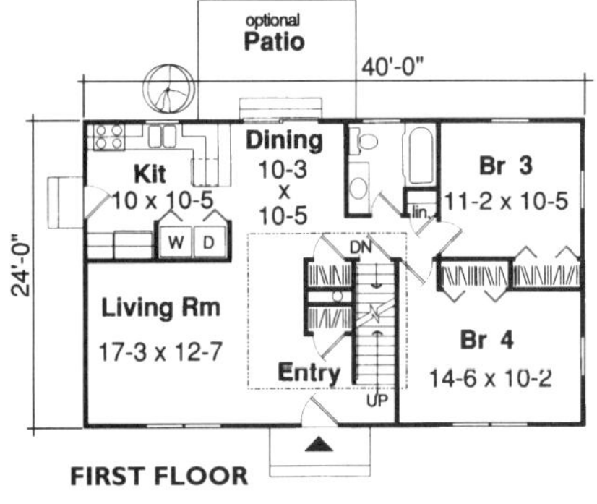

optional
Patio
40'-0"
Dining
10-3
x
10-5
Kit
10 x 10-5
Br 3
11-2 x 10-5
W D
lin.
DN
24'-0"
Living Rm
17-3 x 12-7
Entry
UP
Br 4
14-6 x 10-2

FIRST FLOOR

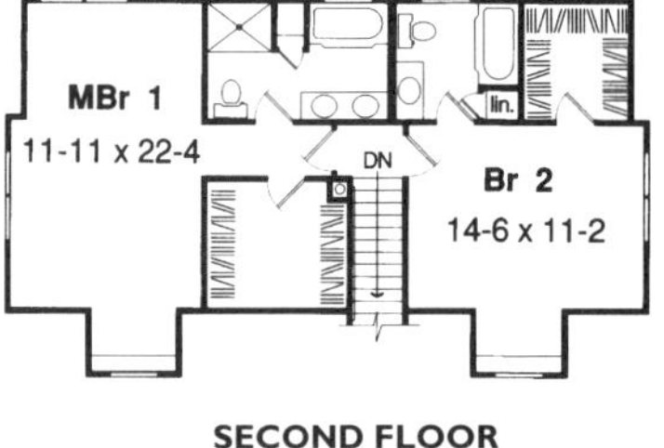

MBr 1
11-11 x 22-4
DN
Br 2
14-6 x 11-2
lin.

SECOND FLOOR

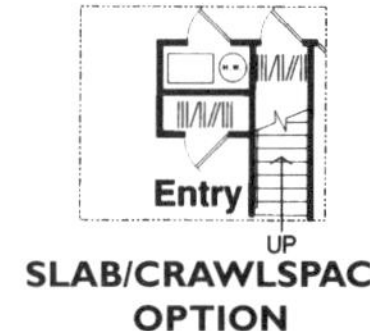

Entry
UP

SLAB/CRAWLSPACE OPTION

PLAN NO.99928

Convenient One-Floor Living

Price Code: A

- This plan features:
  - — Three bedrooms
  - — Two full baths
- One floor living offers step saving convenien with even the laundry room located on the ma floor
- The Master Bedroom includes a build in dres and a whirlpool Bath with a glass block wind
- The Great Room has a gas fireplace, build in bookcases and a vaulted ceiling
- The third Bedroom would make a terrific priv study or home office
- This home is designed with a basement foundation

MAIN FLOOR — 1,407 SQ. FT.

Total living area:
1,407 sq. ft.

Master Br
14-0 x 12-10
9'-0" ceiling
Built-in dresser
Great Room
14-0 x 16-0
vaulted clg.
Dining Room
10-0 x 11-6
9'-0" ceiling
Laundry
coats
Double Garage
22-0 x 21-0
raised bar
Pan
whirlpool
Shwr
glass blocks
Ens.
42" H. bookcase
Kitchen
10-0 x 13-0
Foyer
railing
9'-0" ceiling
Bath
Hall
Lin
coats
Fr doors
Porch
Br #2
10-8 x 10-2
Br #3/Study
10-2 x 10-10

WIDTH 64'-0"
DEPTH 39'-4"

MAIN FLOOR

PLAN NO. 91413

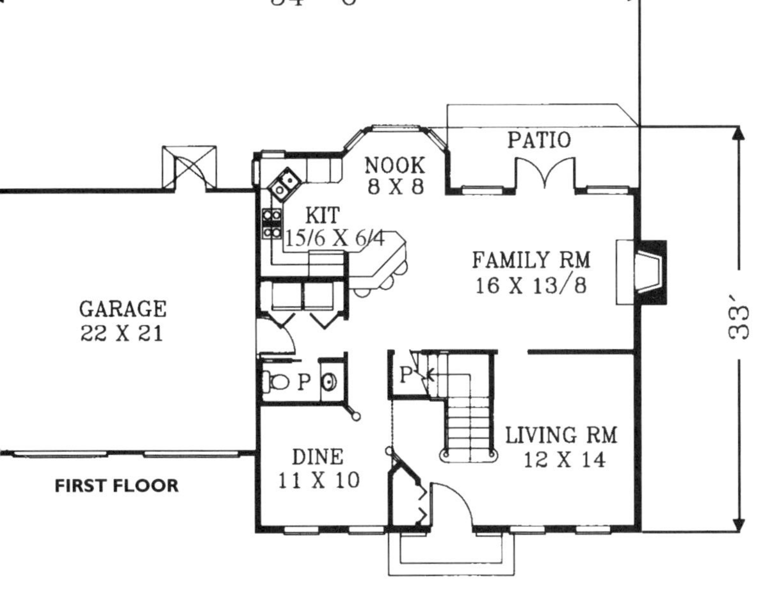

54′–6″
33′
PATIO
NOOK
8 X 8
KIT
15/6 X 6/4
FAMILY RM
16 X 13/8
GARAGE
22 X 21
P
P
LIVING RM
12 X 14
DINE
11 X 10

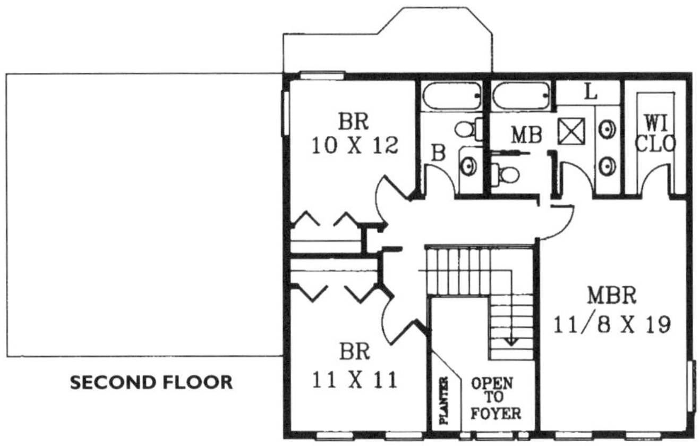

FIRST FLOOR

Compact Classic

Price Code: B

- This plan features:
  - — Three bedrooms
  - — Two full and one half baths
- A spacious Family Room with a cozy fireplace and direct access to the patio
- A well-appointed Kitchen with an eating bar peninsula, double sink and sunny eating Nook
- A formal Living Room and Dining Room located at the front of the home
- This home is designed with basement, slab and crawlspace foundation options

FIRST FLOOR — 963 SQ. FT.
SECOND FLOOR — 774 SQ. FT.

Total living area: 1,737 sq. ft.

SECOND FLOOR

PLAN NO.94307

Easy Entertaining

Price Code: A

- This plan features:
  - Two bedrooms
  - Two full baths
- This plan features a spacious Great Room runn front to back with an adjacent Galley Kitchen, featuring dramatic sloped ceilings
- The Great Room inlcudes a massive stone firep which adds depth and texture to this compact h
- Large windows flood the public spaces with natural light
- Two Bedrooms, one with private Bath, include ample closet space
- An expansive Deck extends the interior living space outdoors
- This home is designed with a crawlspace foundation

MAIN FLOOR — 786 SQ. FT.

Total living area:
786 sq. ft.

WIDTH 46'-0"
DEPTH 22'-0"

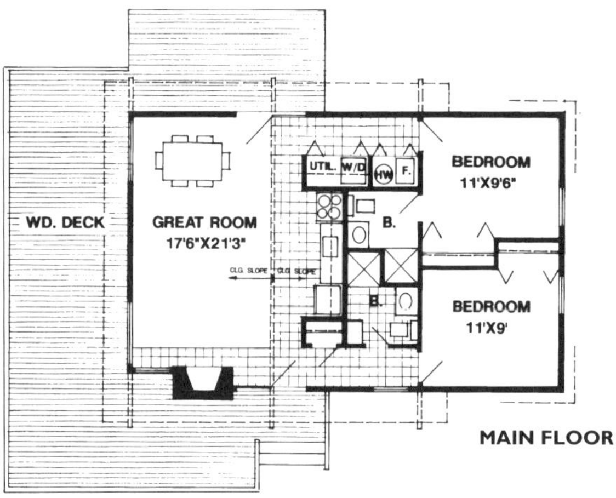

WD. DECK
GREAT ROOM
17'6"X21'3"
UTIL.
W/D
HW
F.
BEDROOM
11'X9'6"
B.
B.
BEDROOM
11'X9'
MAIN FLOOR

PLAN NO.92630

Charming Brick Ranch

Price Code: C

- This plan features:
  - Three bedrooms
  - Two full baths
- Sheltered entrance leads into open Foyer and Dining Room defined by columns
- Vaulted ceiling spans Foyer, Dining Room, an Great Room with corner fireplace and Atrium to rear yard
- Central Kitchen with separate Laundry and Pa easily serves Dining Room, Breakfast Area an Screened Porch
- Luxurious Master Bedroom offers tray ceiling French doors to double vanity, walk-in closet a whirlpool tub
- Two additional Bedrooms, one easily converte a Study, share a full Bath
- This home is designed with a basement founda

MAIN FLOOR —1,782 SQ. FT.
BASEMENT — 1,735 SQ. FT.
GARAGE — 407 SQ. FT.

Total living area:
1,782 sq. ft.

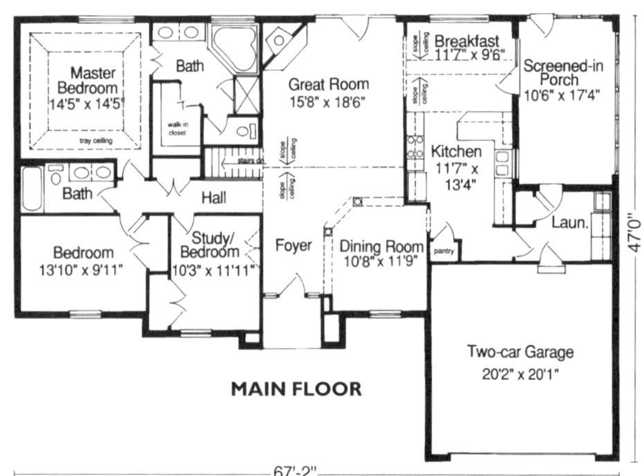

Master Bedroom
14'5" x 14'5"
tray ceiling
Bath
walk in closet
Great Room
15'8" x 18'6"
Breakfast
11'7" x 9'6"
Screened-in Porch
10'6" x 17'4"
Kitchen
11'7" x 13'4"
Bath
Hall
Laun.
Bedroom
13'10" x 9'11"
Study/ Bedroom
10'3" x 11'11"
Foyer
Dining Room
10'8" x 11'9"
pantry
47'0"
Two-car Garage
20'2" x 20'1"
MAIN FLOOR

67'-2"

To order your Blueprints, call 1-800-235-5700

PLAN NO. 68160

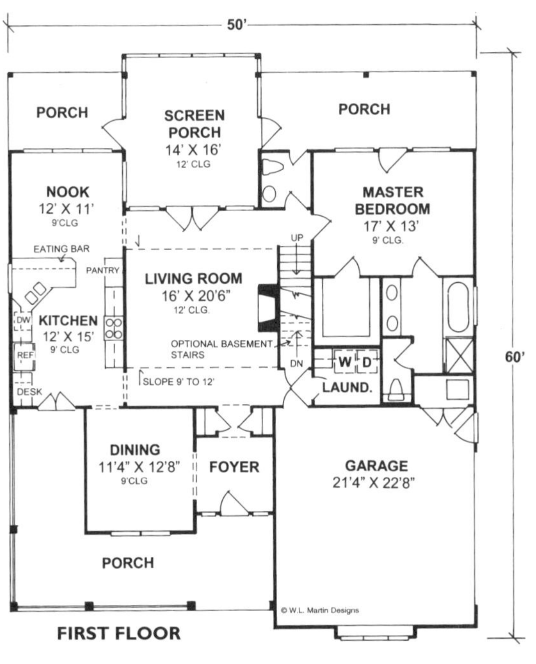
50'
60'
PORCH
SCREEN PORCH
14' X 16'
12' CLG
PORCH
NOOK
12' X 11'
9'CLG
MASTER BEDROOM
17' X 13'
9' CLG.
EATING BAR
PANTRY
UP
LIVING ROOM
16' X 20'6"
12' CLG.
DW
KITCHEN
12' X 15'
9' CLG
REF
OPTIONAL BASEMENT STAIRS
DN
W
D
LAUND.
DESK
SLOPE 9' TO 12'
DINING
11'4" X 12'8"
9'CLG
FOYER
GARAGE
21'4" X 22'8"
PORCH
© W.L. Martin Designs
FIRST FLOOR

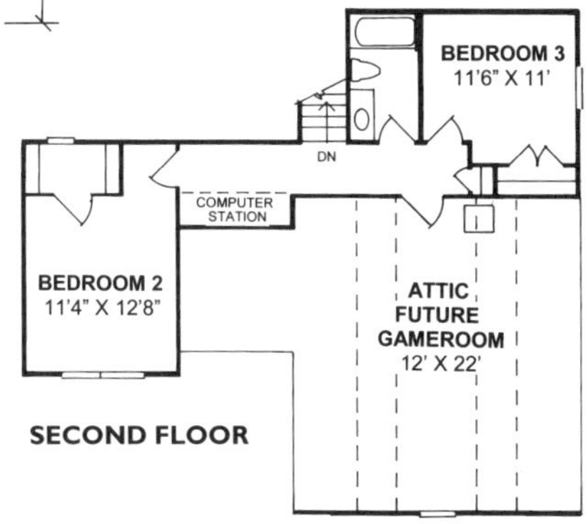

BEDROOM 3
11'6" X 11'
DN
COMPUTER STATION
BEDROOM 2
11'4" X 12'8"
ATTIC
FUTURE GAMEROOM
12' X 22'
SECOND FLOOR

Children's Retreat

Price Code: D

- This plan features:
- — Three bedrooms
- — Two full and one half baths
- Two Bedrooms share a computer station and a Bonus Room offering expansion options
- A large Screened Porch off the Living Room creates a protected outdoor living Area
- This home is designed with slab and crawlspace foundation options
- Alternate foundation options available at an additional charge. Please call 1-800-235-5700 for more information.

FIRST FLOOR — 1,486 SQ. FT.
SECOND FLOOR — 519 SQ. FT.
BONUS — 264 SQ. FT.

Total living area:
2,005 sq. ft.

PLAN NO. 98431

With Room to Expand

Price Code: B

- This plan features:
  - — Three bedrooms
  - — Two full and one half baths
- This plan is designed with an impressive two-story Foyer
- The spacious Family Room flows from the Breakfast Bay and is highlighted by a fireplace and a French door to the rear yard
- The Master Suite is topped by a tray ceiling and is enhanced by a vaulted, five-piece Master Bath
- This home is designed with basement, slab and crawlspace foundation options

FIRST FLOOR — 882 SQ. FT.
SECOND FLOOR — 793 SQ. FT.
BONUS — 416 SQ. FT.
BASEMENT — 882 SQ. FT.
GARAGE — 510 SQ. FT.

Total living area:
1,675 sq. ft.

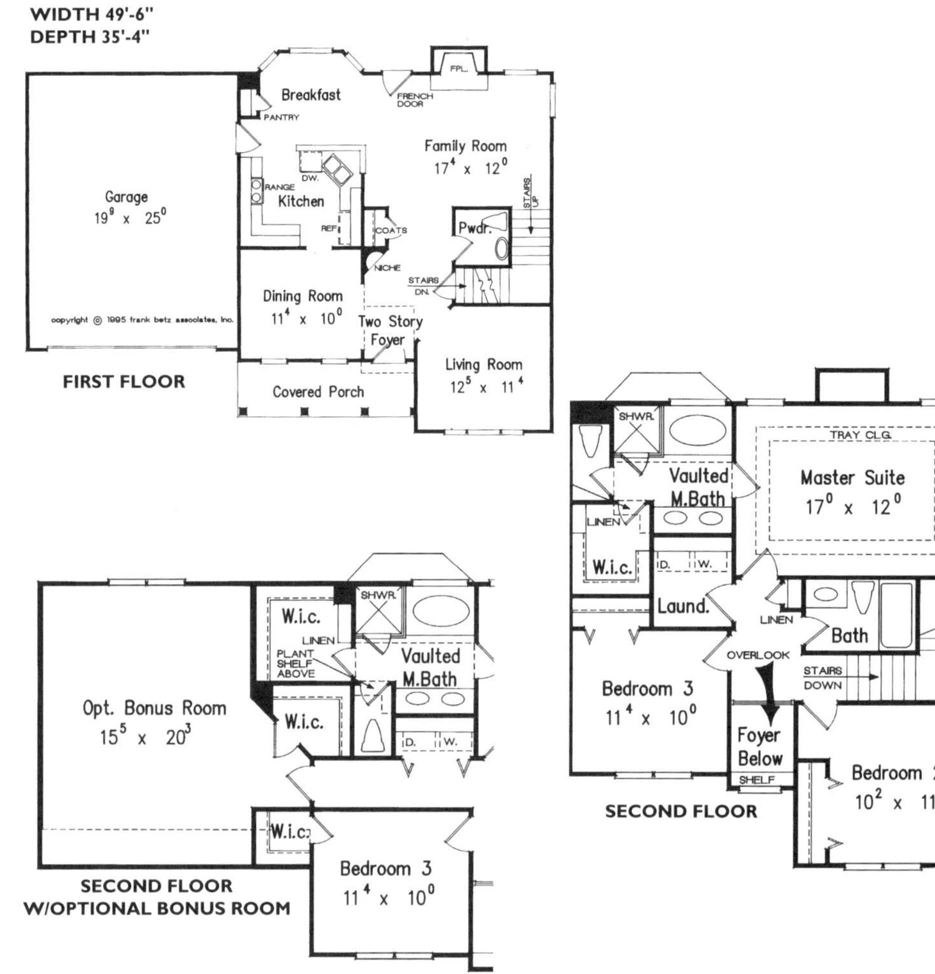

WIDTH 49'-6"
DEPTH 35'-4"
Breakfast
PANTRY
FRENCH DOOR
FPL.
Family Room
17⁴ x 12⁰
STAIRS UP
Garage
19⁹ x 25⁰
RANGE
DW.
Kitchen
REF.
COATS
Pwdr.
NICHE
STAIRS DN.
copyright © 1995 frank betz associates, inc.
Dining Room
11⁴ x 10⁰
Two Story Foyer
Living Room
12⁵ x 11⁴
Covered Porch
FIRST FLOOR
SHWR.
TRAY CLG.
Vaulted M.Bath
Master Suite
17⁰ x 12⁰
LINEN
W.i.c.
D.
W.
Laund.
LINEN
Bath
OVERLOOK
STAIRS DOWN
Bedroom 3
11⁴ x 10⁰
Foyer Below
SHELF
Bedroom 2
10² x 11⁴
SECOND FLOOR
SHWR.
W.i.c.
LINEN
PLANT SHELF ABOVE
Vaulted M.Bath
Opt. Bonus Room
15⁵ x 20³
W.i.c.
D.
W.
W.i.c.
Bedroom 3
11⁴ x 10⁰
SECOND FLOOR W/OPTIONAL BONUS ROOM

PLAN NO.99327

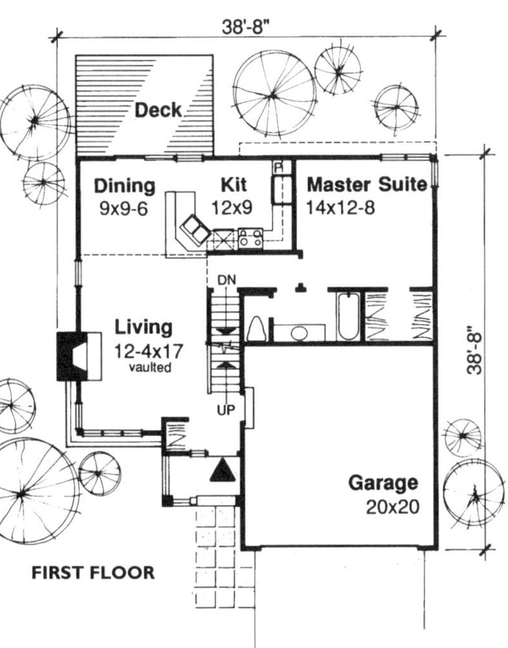

38'-8"
Deck
Dining
9x9-6
Kit
12x9
Master Suite
14x12-8
DN
Living
12-4x17
vaulted
UP
38'-8"
Garage
20x20
FIRST FLOOR

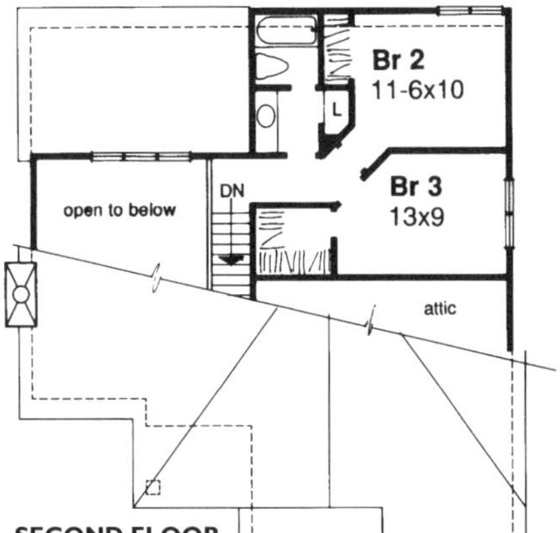

Br 2
11-6x10
Br 3
13x9
open to below
DN
attic

SECOND FLOOR

Contemporary Style

Price Code: A

- This plan features:
  - — Three bedrooms
  - — Two full baths
- The Entry has a vaulted ceiling
- The formal Living Room has a fireplace and a half-round transom window
- The Dining Room has sliders to the deck, and easy access to the Kitchen
- The main floor Master Suite has corner windows, a walk-in closet and private access to a full Bath
- This home is designed with a basement foundation

MAIN FLOOR — 858 SQ. FT.
UPPER FLOOR — 431 SQ. FT.
BASEMENT — 858 SQ. FT.
GARAGE — 400 SQ. FT.

Total living area:
1,289 sq. ft.

PLAN NO.93048

Perfect For First-Time Buyer

Price Code: A

- This plan features:
  - — Three bedrooms
  - — Two full baths
- The efficiently designed Kitchen includes a co ner sink, ample counter space and a peninsula counter
- Ten-foot ceilings in the public spaces and Ma Bedroom add to the feeling of spaciousness ir this compact home
- The sunny Breakfast Room has a convenient hide-away Laundry center
- The expansive Family Room includes a corne fireplace and offers direct access to the Patio
- The private Master Bedroom with slope ceilin includes a walk-in closet and a double vanity Bath
- Two additional Bedrooms, both with walk-in closets, share a full Bath
- This home is designed with crawlspace and sl foundation options

MAIN FLOOR — 1,310 SQ. FT.
GARAGE — 449 SQ. FT.

Total living area:
1,310 sq. ft.

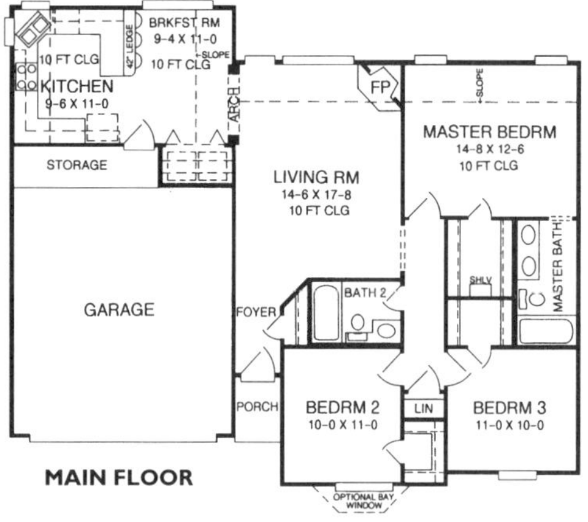

BRKFST RM
9-4 X 11-0
10 FT CLG
SLOPE
10 FT CLG
KITCHEN
9-6 X 11-0
ARCH
FP
STORAGE
LIVING RM
14-6 X 17-8
10 FT CLG
MASTER BEDRM
14-8 X 12-6
10 FT CLG
MASTER BATH
SHLV
GARAGE
FOYER
BATH 2
PORCH
BEDRM 2
10-0 X 11-0
LIN
BEDRM 3
11-0 X 10-0
OPTIONAL BAY WINDOW
MAIN FLOOR

WIDTH 49'-10"
DEPTH 40'-6"

PLAN NO.99639

One-Story Country Home

Price Code: A

- This plan features:
  - — Three bedrooms
  - — Two full baths
- The dramatic Living Room features an imposi high ceiling — topped with a skylight — that slopes down to a standard eight-feet height, focusing on the heat-circulating fireplace
- The efficient Kitchen adjoins the Dining Roor which has a triple set of windows opening on the front Porch
- The Dinette Area for informal eating in the Kitchen can comfortably seat six people and h sliding glass doors opening to a rear Terrace
- The Master Suite includes a large Dressing Ar with a walk-in closet plus two linear closets a space for a vanity
- Two family Bedrooms share a full Bath
- This home is designed with basement and slab foundation options

MAIN FLOOR — 1,367 SQ. FT.
BASEMENT — 1,267 SQ. FT.
GARAGE — 431 SQ. FT.

Total living area:
1,367 sq. ft.

WIDTH 71'-4"
DEPTH 33'-10"

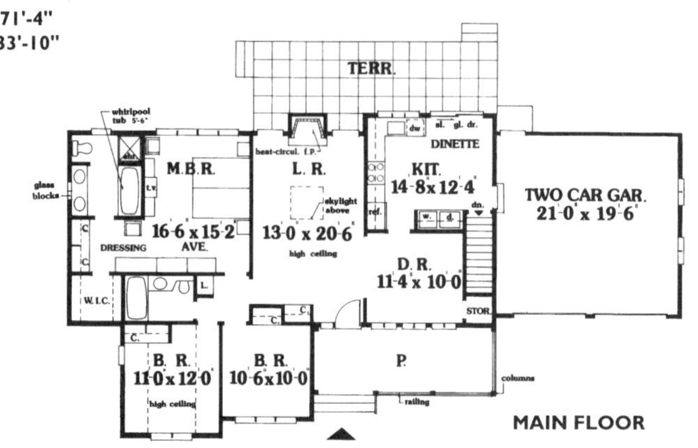

TERR.
whirlpool tub
glass blocks
M.B.R.
16-6 x 15-2
DRESSING AVE.
W.I.C.
heat-circul. f.p.
L. R.
skylight above
13-0 x 20-6
high ceiling
DINETTE
KIT.
14-8 x 12-4
D. R.
11-4 x 10-0
TWO CAR GAR.
21-0 x 19-6
STOR.
B. R.
11-0 x 12-0
high ceiling
B. R.
10-6 x 10-0
P.
columns
railing
MAIN FLOOR

PLAN NO. 65177

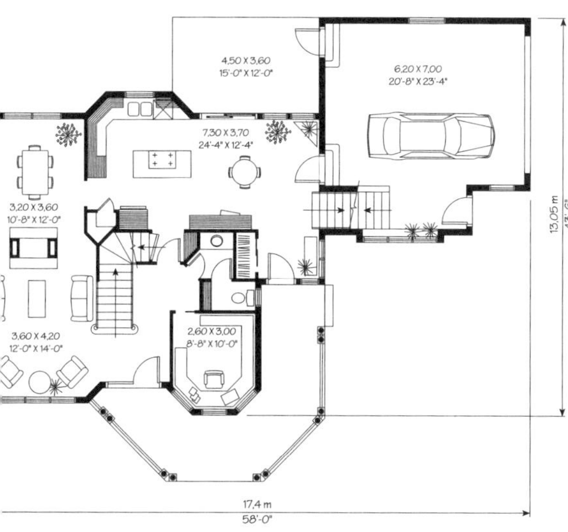

4,50 X 3,60
15'-0" X 12'-0"
6,20 X 7,00
20'-8" X 23'-4"
7,30 X 3,70
24'-4" X 12'-4"
3,20 X 3,60
10'-8" X 12'-0"
3,60 X 4,20
12'-0" X 14'-0"
2,60 X 3,00
8'-8" X 10'-0"
13,05 m
43'-6"
17,4 m
58'-0"

IRST FLOOR

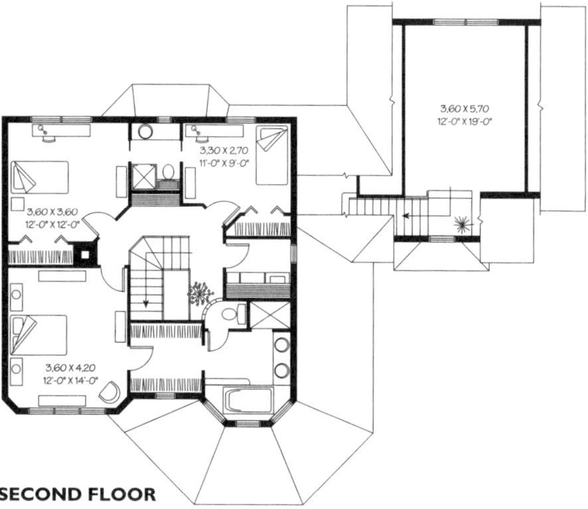

3,60 X 5,70
12'-0" X 19'-0"
3,30 X 2,70
11'-0" X 9'-0"
3,60 X 3,60
12'-0" X 12'-0"
3,60 X 4,20
12'-0" X 14'-0"

SECOND FLOOR

Welcoming Porch

Price Code: C

- This plan features:
  - — Three bedrooms
  - — Two full and one half baths
- Stone and siding accent this home along with the front curving Porch and double door Entry
- The active first floor Living Room, Dining Room and Kitchen with Breakfast area are designed for and easy traffic flow
- The two-sided fireplace warms the air and atmosphere in the Living Room and the Dining Room
- This home is designed with a basement foundation

FIRST FLOOR — 1,044 SQ. FT.
SECOND FLOOR — 894 SQ. FT.
GARAGE — 487 SQ. FT.

Total living area: 1,938 sq. ft.

PLAN NO.90412

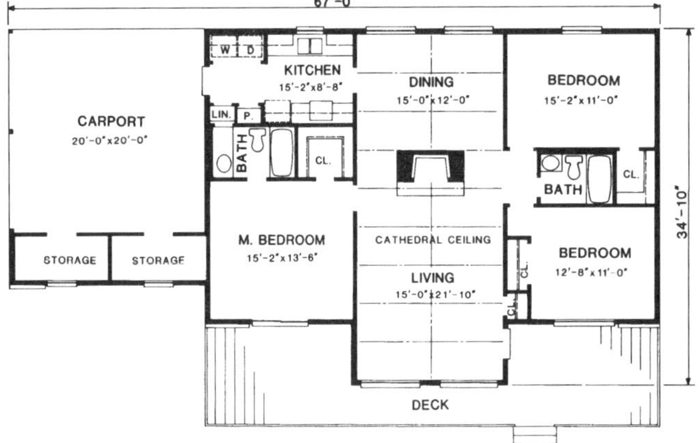

67'-0"
CARPORT
20'-0"x20'-0"
STORAGE
STORAGE
W D
KITCHEN
15'-2"x8'-8"
LIN.
P.
BATH
CL.
DINING
15'-0"x12'-0"
BEDROOM
15'-2"x11'-0"
BATH
CL.
M. BEDROOM
15'-2"x13'-6"
CATHEDRAL CEILING
LIVING
15'-0"x21'-10"
BEDROOM
12'-8"x11'-0"
CL.
CL.
34'-10"
DECK

MAIN FLOOR

No Wasted Space

Price Code: A

- This plan features:

— Three bedrooms

— Two full baths

- The centrally located Great Room features a cathedral ceiling, exposed wood beams, and large areas of fixd glass
- The Living Room and Dining Room are separated by a massive stone fireplace
- The secluded Master Bedroom has a walk-in closet and private Bath
- An efficient Kitchen with a convenient Laun Area
- The Carport offers two storage spaces for all your lawn and gardening equipment
- This home is designed with basement, slab a crawlspace foundation options

MAIN FLOOR — 1,454 SQ. FT.

Total living area:
1,454 sq. ft.

PLAN NO.20231

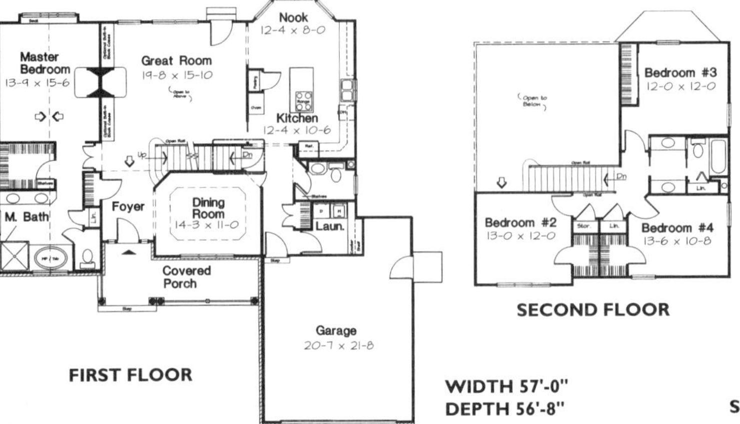

Master Bedroom
13-9 x 15-6
Great Room
19-8 x 15-10
Nook
12-4 x 8-0
Kitchen
12-4 x 10-6
M. Bath
Foyer
Dining Room
14-3 x 11-0
Laun.
Covered Porch
Garage
20-7 x 21-8
Bedroom #3
12-0 x 12-0
Bedroom #2
13-0 x 12-0
Bedroom #4
13-6 x 10-8

FIRST FLOOR

SECOND FLOOR

WIDTH 57'-0"
DEPTH 56'-8"

OPTIONAL SLAB/CRAWLSPACE

Hip-Roof and Gables

Price Code: E

- This plan features:

— Four bedrooms

— Two full and one half baths

- The covered Porch leads into the Foyer and two-story Great Room beyond, which featur fireplace and built-ins
- The Dining Room has a tray ceiling and ope both the Foyer and a short hall that leads to bright and efficient Kitchen
- The Master Bedroom has a cathedral ceiling continues into the amenity-laden Bath
- The Master Bedroom also has a fireplace w efficiently and cost-effectively uses the sam chimney as the one in the Living Room
- Three additional second floor Bedrooms sha full Bath and each has ample closet space
- This home is designed with a basement, cra space and slab foundation options

FIRST FLOOR — 1,540 SQ. FT.
SECOND FLOOR — 717 SQ. FT.
BASEMENT — 1,545 SQ. FT.
GARAGE — 503 SQ. FT.

Total living area:
2,257 sq. ft.

PLAN NO.99757

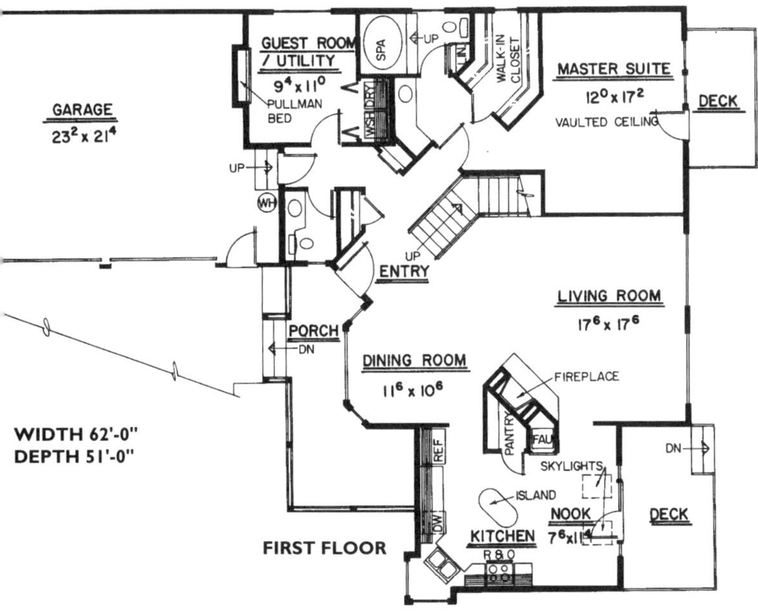

GUEST ROOM / UTILITY
9^4 x 11^0
PULLMAN BED
SPA
UP
WALK-IN CLOSET
MASTER SUITE
12^0 x 17^2
VAULTED CEILING
DECK
GARAGE
23^2 x 21^4
WSH DRY
UP
WH
UP
ENTRY
LIVING ROOM
17^6 x 17^6
PORCH
DN
DINING ROOM
11^6 x 10^6
FIREPLACE
PANTRY
FAU
REF
SKYLIGHTS
DN
ISLAND
NOOK
7^6x11^4
DECK
DW
KITCHEN
R&O
WIDTH 62'-0"
DEPTH 51'-0"
FIRST FLOOR

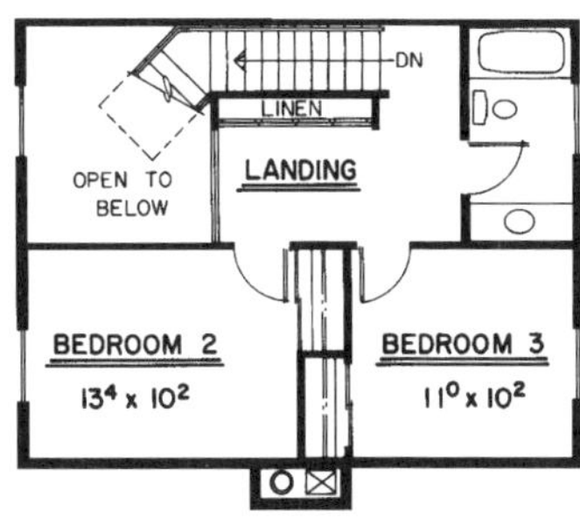

DN
LINEN
OPEN TO BELOW
LANDING
BEDROOM 2
13^4 x 10^2
BEDROOM 3
11^0 x 10^2
SECOND FLOOR

The Ultimate Kitchen

Price Code: C

- This plan features:
- — Three bedrooms
- — Two full and one half baths
- The front Porch invites visitors and leads into the open Entry which has an angled staircase
- The Living Room with a wall of windows and an island fireplace, opens to the Dining Room with a bright bay window
- The Guest/Utility Room has a pullman bed and a Laundry closet
- Two second floor Bedrooms with large closets share a full Bath
- This home is designed with a crawlspace foundation

FIRST FLOOR — 1,472 SQ. FT.
SECOND FLOOR — 478 SQ. FT.
GARAGE — 558 SQ. FT.

Total living area: 1,950 sq. ft.

PLAN NO. 90436

Modern Country Living

Price Code: D

- This plan features:
  — Three bedrooms
  — Two full and two half baths
- The expansive Family Room has a fireplace
- The Dining Room and Breakfast Area are lit by natural light from bay windows
- The first floor Master Suite has a deluxe Master Bath
- This home is designed with basement, slab and crawlspace foundation options

FIRST FLOOR — 1,477 SQ. FT.
SECOND FLOOR — 704 SQ. FT.
BASEMENT — 1,374 SQ. FT.
GARAGE — 528 SQ. FT.

Total living area: 2,181 sq. ft.

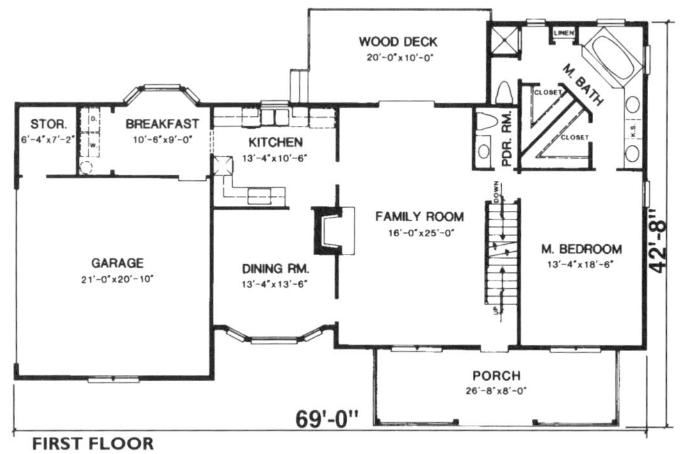
WOOD DECK
20'-0"x10'-0"
STOR.
6'-4"x7'-2"
BREAKFAST
10'-6"x9'-0"
KITCHEN
13'-4"x10'-6"
M. BATH
CLOSET
CLOSET
PDR. RM.
FAMILY ROOM
16'-0"x25'-0"
M. BEDROOM
13'-4"x18'-6"
GARAGE
21'-0"x20'-10"
DINING RM.
13'-4"x13'-6"
PORCH
26'-8"x8'-0"
69'-0"
42'-8"
FIRST FLOOR

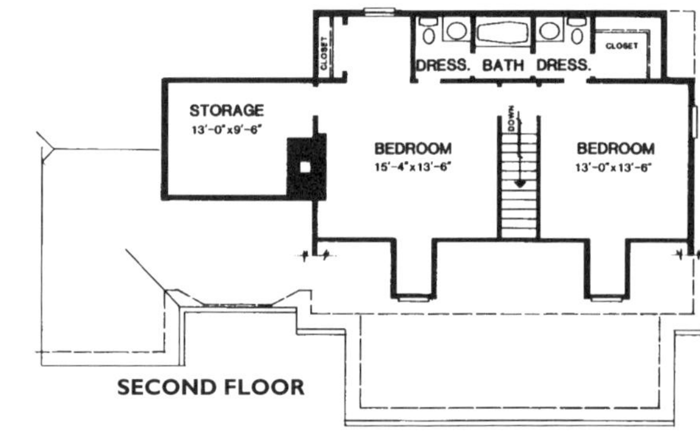
CLOSET
DRESS. BATH DRESS.
CLOSET
STORAGE
13'-0"x9'-6"
BEDROOM
15'-4"x13'-6"
BEDROOM
13'-0"x13'-6"
SECOND FLOOR

PLAN NO. 65012

Rear Elevation

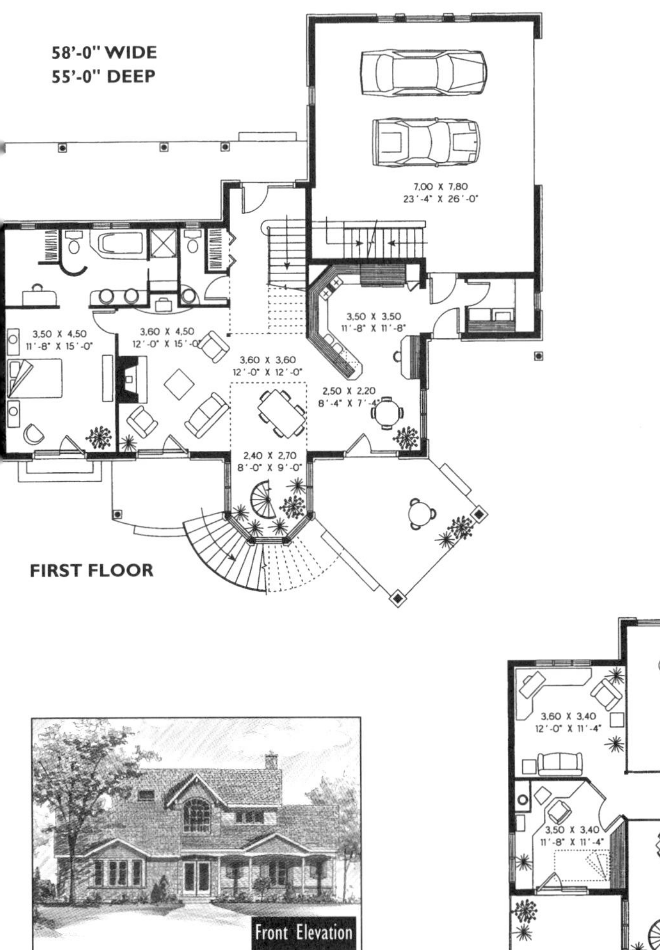
58'-0" WIDE
55'-0" DEEP
7,00 X 7,80
23'-4" X 26'-0"
3,50 X 4,50
11'-8" X 15'-0"
3,60 X 4,50
12'-0" X 15'-0"
3,50 X 3,50
11'-8" X 11'-8"
3,60 X 3,60
12'-0" X 12'-0"
2,50 X 2,20
8'-4" X 7'-4"
2,40 X 2,70
8'-0" X 9'-0"
FIRST FLOOR
Front Elevation

Outdoor Circular Stair

Price Code: C

- This plan features:
  - — Four bedrooms
  - — Two full and one half baths
- The spacious Kitchen offers ample cabinet space and has a built-in desk
- A turreted, two-story plant area has spiral stair access into the Basement
- This home is designed with a basement foundation

FIRST FLOOR — 1,293 SQ. FT.
SECOND FLOOR — 629 SQ. FT.
BASEMENT — 1,293 SQ. FT.
GARAGE — 606 SQ. FT.

Total living area:
1,922 sq. ft.

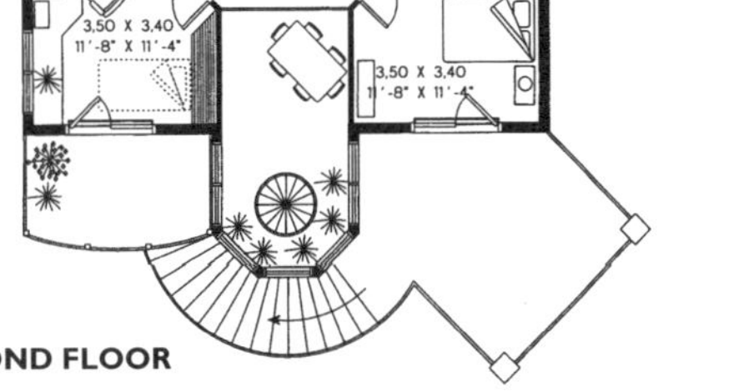

7,00 X 4,40
23'-4" X 14'-8"
3,60 X 3,40
12'-0" X 11'-4"
3,50 X 3,40
11'-8" X 11'-4"
3,50 X 3,40
11'-8" X 11'-4"

SECOND FLOOR

PLAN NO. 24302

Champagne Style on a Soda-Pop Budget

Price Code: A

- This plan features:
- — Three bedrooms
- — Two full baths
- Multiple gables, arched windows, and a unique exterior set this delightful Ranch apart in any neighborhood
- Living and Dining Rooms flow together to create very roomy feeling
- Sliding doors lead from the Dining Room to a covered patio
- The Master Bedroom includes a private Bath
- This home is designed with basement and crawlspace foundation options

MAIN FLOOR — 988 SQ. FT.
BASEMENT — 988 SQ. FT.
GARAGE — 280 SQ. FT
OPTIONAL 2-CAR GARAGE — 400 SQ.

Total living area:
988 sq. ft.

54'-0"
Mstr. Br.
13-7 x 11-6
Kitchen
8-6 x 8-3
Dining
8-10 x 11-6
Covered Patio
Ref.
W
D.
Furn
Linen
Crawl Access
28'-0"
Br 2
9-8 x 11-8
Br 3
11-0 x 10-2
Living Rm
15-8 x 11-7
Garage
13-4 x 19-5
Optional 2-Car Garage
Plant Box

MAIN FLOOR

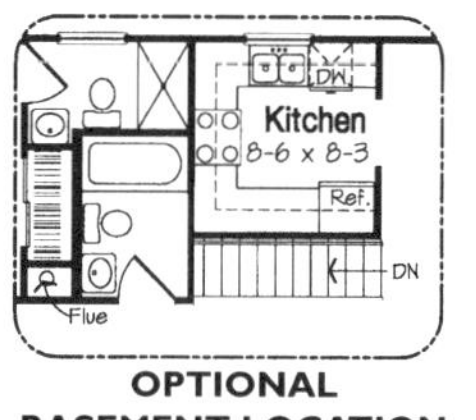

Kitchen
8-6 x 8-3
Ref.
DW
DN
Flue

OPTIONAL BASEMENT LOCATION

PLAN NO. 92503

Charming Southern Traditional

Price Code: A

- This plan features:
- — Three bedrooms
- — Two full baths
- The covered front Porch features striking columns, brick quoins, and dentil molding
- The spacious Living Room, with vaulted ceilings, a fireplace, and built-in cabinets, open to the formal Dining Rom
- The Utility Room adjacent to the efficient Kitchen leads to the two-car Garage and Storage Room
- The Master Bedroom includes a large walk-in closet and a compartmentalized Bathroom
- Two additional Bedrooms feature large closets with built-in shelves
- This home is designed with crawlspace and slab foundation options

MAIN FLOOR — 1,271 SQ. FT.
GARAGE — 506 SQ. FT.

Total living area:
1,271 sq. ft.

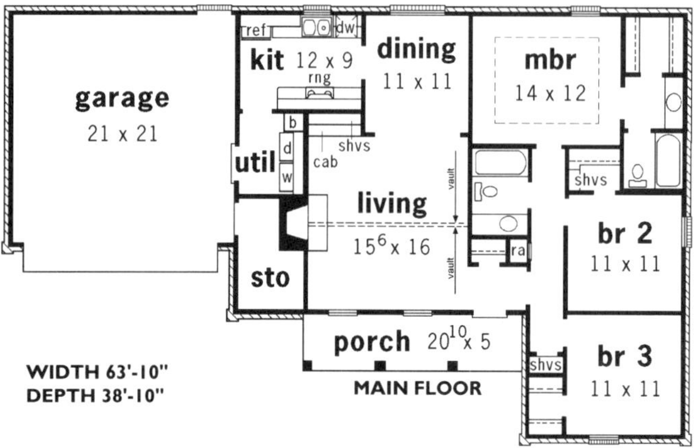

garage
21 x 21
ref
dw
kit 12 x 9
rng
dining
11 x 11
mbr
14 x 12
b
d
w
util
cab
shvs
living
15⁶ x 16
vault
vault
sto
shvs
br 2
11 x 11
ra
porch 20¹⁰ x 5
shvs
br 3
11 x 11

WIDTH 63'-10"
DEPTH 38'-10"

MAIN FLOOR

PLAN NO.24736

Attractive Covered Entry

Price Code: D

This plan features:

- Three bedrooms
- Two full and one half baths
- The angled, covered Porch welcomes everyone to this home
- The Great Room is accented by a vaulted ceiling and a fireplace
- The spacious Kitchen offers a Pantry and a Breakfast Bay
- The Master Bedroom wing has a bay window, a decorative ceiling, two walk-in closets and a plush Bathroom
- On the second floor, two additional Bedrooms share a full Bath, a Loft and a Computer Center
- This home is designed with basement, slab and crawlspace foundation options

IRST FLOOR — 1,403 SQ. FT.
ECOND FLOOR — 641 SQ. FT.
ASEMENT — 1,394 SQ. FT.
ARAGE — 680 SQ. FT.

Total living area: 2,044 sq. ft.

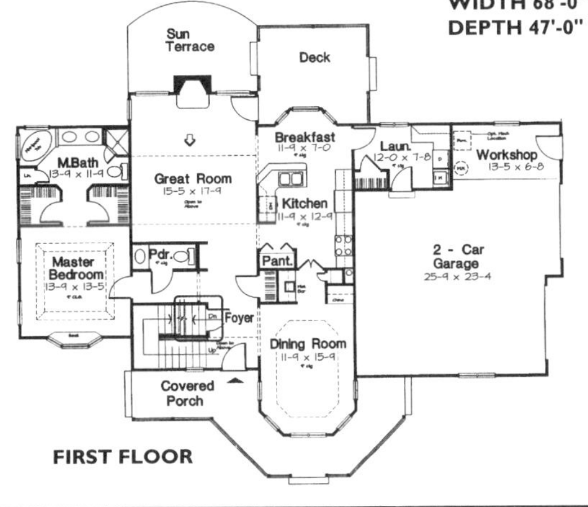
WIDTH 68'-0"
DEPTH 47'-0"
Sun Terrace
Deck
M.Bath 13-9 x 11-9
Great Room 15-5 x 17-9
Breakfast 11-9 x 7-0
Laun. 12-0 x 7-8
Workshop 13-5 x 6-8
Kitchen 11-4 x 12-9
Master Bedroom 13-9 x 13-5
Pdr.
Pant.
2 - Car Garage 25-9 x 23-4
Foyer
Dining Room 11-9 x 15-9
Covered Porch
FIRST FLOOR

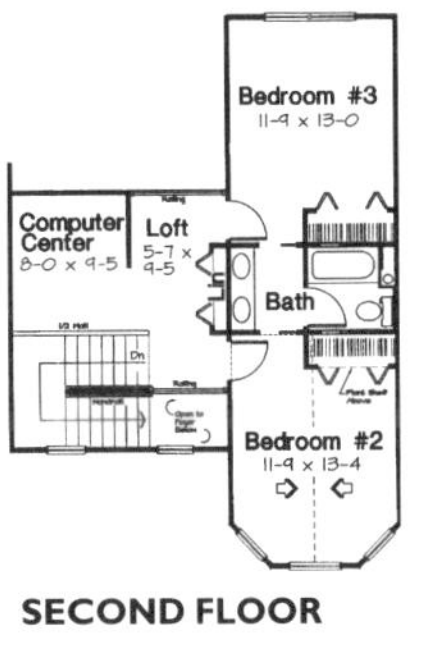
Bedroom #3 11-4 x 13-0
Computer Center 8-0 x 9-5
Loft 5-7 x 9-5
Bath
Bedroom #2 11-9 x 13-4
SECOND FLOOR

SLAB/CRAWLSPACE OPTION

PLAN NO.24964

Space Stretching Tricks

Price Code: D

This plan features:

- Three bedrooms
- Two full and one half baths
- The Foyer, with lovely open-rail staircase, is open to the Dining Room
- The Breakfast Room feels larger because of the two-story ceiling and bay window
- The large Great Room includes a fireplace and offers access to two different Decks
- The Master Suite is near the secondary Bedrooms so children can be supervised
- A Bonus Room will add more living space if finished
- This home is designed with basement, crawlspace and slab foundation options

IRST FLOOR — 1,195 SQ. FT.
ECOND FLOOR — 1,045 SQ. FT.
ASEMENT — 1,195 SQ. FT.
ONUS — 338 SQ. FT.
ARAGE — 635 SQ. FT.

Total living area: 2,240 sq. ft.

WIDTH 55'-8"
DEPTH 46'-0"

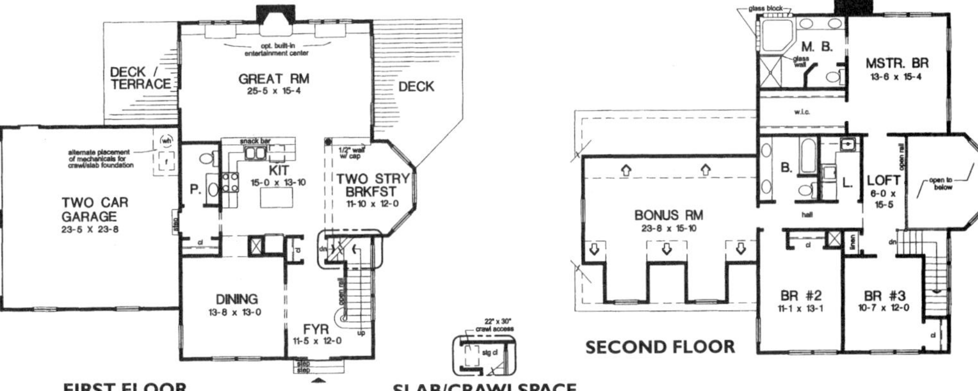
DECK / TERRACE
GREAT RM 25-5 x 15-4
DECK
TWO CAR GARAGE 23-5 X 23-8
KIT 15-0 x 13-10
P.
TWO STRY BRKFST 11-10 x 12-0
DINING 13-8 x 13-0
FYR 11-5 x 12-0
FIRST FLOOR
M. B.
MSTR. BR 13-6 x 15-4
B.
L.
LOFT 6-0 x 15-5
BONUS RM 23-8 x 15-10
BR #2 11-1 x 13-1
BR #3 10-7 x 12-0
SECOND FLOOR

SLAB/CRAWLSPACE OPTION

PLAN NO. 94904

Distinctive Design

Price Code: C

- This plan features:
- — Three bedrooms
- — Two full and one half baths
- The Living Room is distinguished by the warmth of a bay window and French doors leading to the Family Room
- This home is designed with a basement foundation
- Alternate foundation options available at an additional charge. Please call 1-800-235-5700 for more information.

FIRST FLOOR — 1,093 SQ. FT.
SECOND FLOOR — 905 SQ. FT.
BASEMENT — 1,093 SQ. FT.
GARAGE — 527 SQ. FT.

Total living area:
1,998 sq. ft.

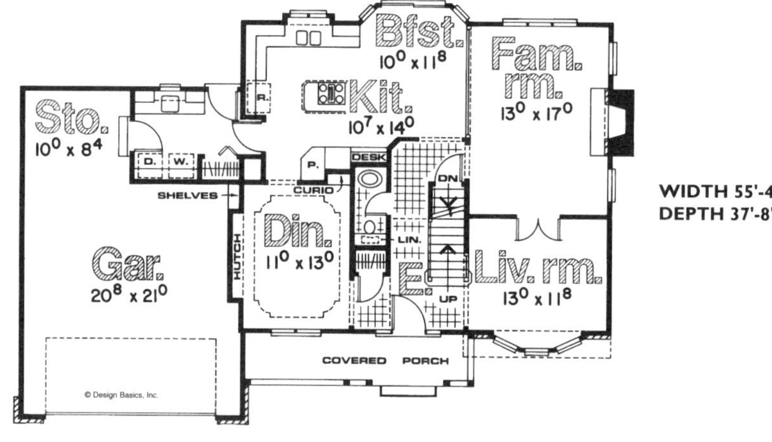

Bfst.
$10^{0} \times 11^{8}$
Fam. rm.
$13^{0} \times 17^{0}$
Sto.
$10^{0} \times 8^{4}$
Kit.
$10^{7} \times 14^{0}$
R.
D.
W.
P.
DESK
SHELVES
CURIO
DN
LIN.
HUTCH
Din.
$11^{0} \times 13^{0}$
Gar.
$20^{8} \times 21^{0}$
E.
UP
Liv. rm.
$13^{0} \times 11^{8}$
COVERED PORCH
© Design Basics, Inc.
WIDTH 55'-4"
DEPTH 37'-8"

FIRST FLOOR

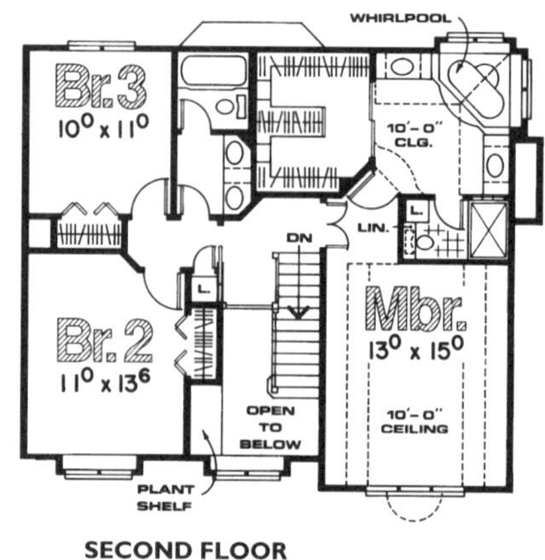

WHIRLPOOL
Br. 3
$10^{0} \times 11^{0}$
10'-0" CLG.
LIN.
L
DN
Br. 2
$11^{0} \times 13^{6}$
Mbr.
$13^{0} \times 15^{0}$
OPEN TO BELOW
10'-0" CEILING
PLANT SHELF

SECOND FLOOR

PLAN NO. 90356

Balcony Overlook

Price Code: A

'his plan features:

- Three bedrooms
- Two full and one half baths
- 'he Living Room has a vaulted ceiling, a balcony, nd a fireplace
- 'his design has an efficient, well-equipped ‹itchen with a cooktop work island
- 'he Deck is accessible from the Dining Room
- The luxurious Master Suite has a bay window seat, a walk-in closet, a Dressing Area, and a private shower
- 'he two additional Bedrooms share a full Bath
- This home is designed with a basement foundation

AIN FLOOR — 674 SQ. FT.
PER FLOOR — 677 SQ. FT.
SEMENT — 674 SQ. FT.

Total living area: 1,351 sq. ft.

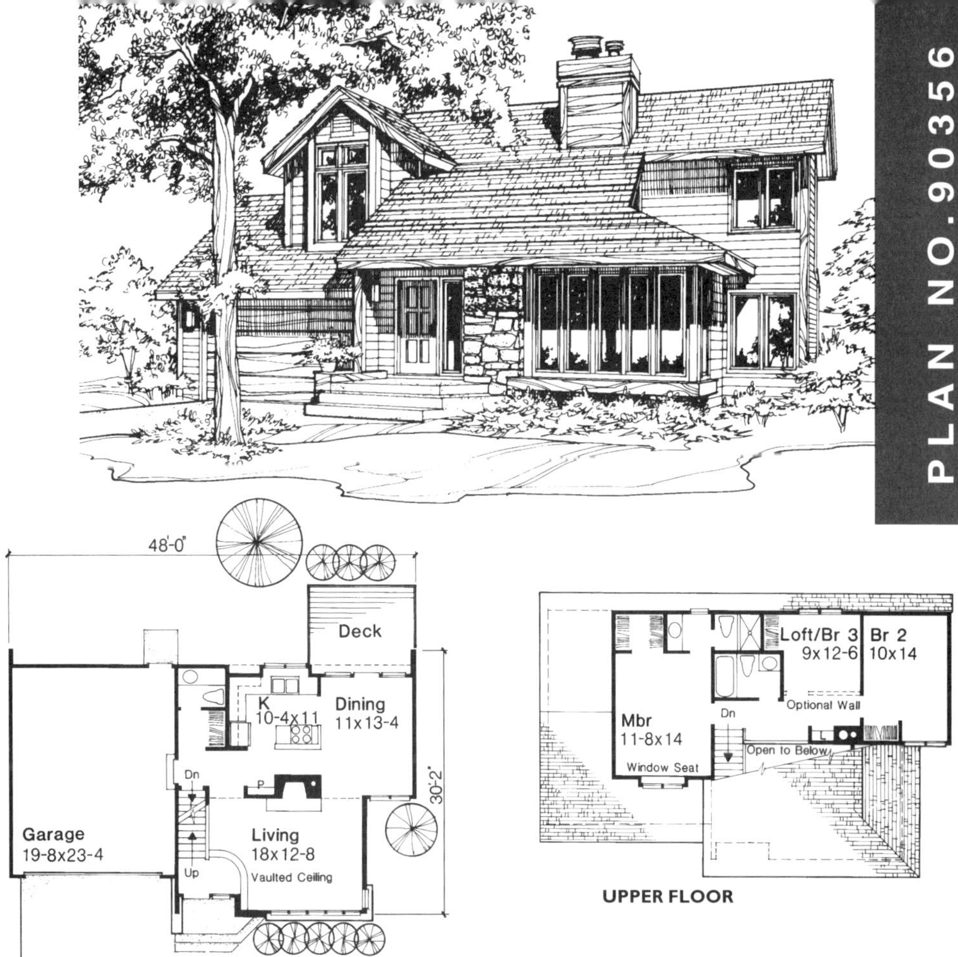

48'-0"
Deck
K
10-4x11
Dining
11x13-4
Dn
P
30'-2"
Garage
19-8x23-4
Living
18x12-8
Vaulted Ceiling
Up
MAIN FLOOR
Loft/Br 3
9x12-6
Br 2
10x14
Optional Wall
Dn
Mbr
11-8x14
Open to Below
Window Seat
UPPER FLOOR

PLAN NO. 24654

Country Influence

Price Code: B

'his plan features:

- Three bedrooms
- Two full and one half baths
- 'he Front Porch leads into a unique Sunroom vith a half bath and a coat closet
- 'he open Living Room is enhanced by a alladian window, a focal point fireplace and atrim doors to the Deck
- bay window brightens the formal Dining Room 'hich is conveniently located between the Living ;oom and the Kitchen
- 'he efficient L-shaped Kitchen has a bay window ating area, a Laundry closet and a handy Garage ntrance
- 'he plush Master Bedroom offers another bay 'indow crowned by tray ceiling and a private ath with double vanity
- 'wo additional Bedrooms, with arched windows nd ample closets, share a full Bath
- 'his home is designed with basement, slab and rawlspace foundation options

RST FLOOR — 806 SQ. FT.
COND FLOOR — 748 SQ. FT.
RAGE — 467 SQ. FT.

Total living area: 1,554 sq. ft.

50'-0"
40'-0"
Deck
Living
13-4 x 17-4
Dining
11-0 x 12-2
Kitchen
14-5 x 11-10
Sun
Rm
Garage
21-4 x 21-8
FIRST FLOOR

Master Br
16-0 x 11-11
Br 2
11-8 x 10-8
Br 3
11-4 x 10-7
SECOND FLOOR

PLAN NO. 93222

For an Established Neighborhood

Price Code: A

- This plan features:
  - — Three bedrooms
  - — Two full baths
- The welcoming covered entrance shelters your visitors
- The expansive Living Room features a vaulted ceiling and large front windows for plenty of natural light
- A bayed formal Dining Room offers direct acc to the Sun Deck and the Living Room for entertainment ease
- The large Master Suite is equipped with a walk closet and a full private Bath
- Two additional Bedrooms that share a full Bath
- This home is designed with a basement founda

MAIN FLOOR — 1,276 SQ. FT.
FINISHED STAIRCASE — 16 SQ. FT.
BASEMENT — 392 SQ. FT.
GARAGE — 728 SQ. FT.

Total living area: 1,292 sq. ft.

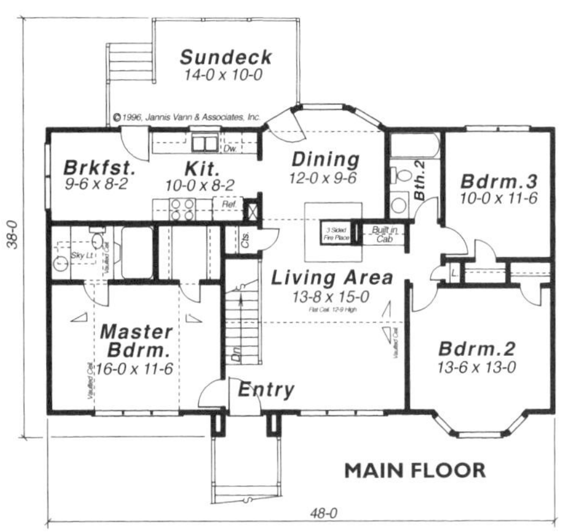
Sundeck
14-0 x 10-0
©1996, Jannis Vann & Associates, Inc.
Brkfst.
9-6 x 8-2
Kit.
10-0 x 8-2
Dining
12-0 x 9-6
Bth.2
Bdrm.3
10-0 x 11-6
Living Area
13-8 x 15-0
Master
Bdrm.
16-0 x 11-6
Bdrm.2
13-6 x 13-0
Entry
38-0
48-0
MAIN FLOOR

PLAN NO. 90601

Perfect Family Ranch

Price Code: B

- This plan features:
  - — Three bedrooms
  - — Two full and one half baths
- The spacious Family Room with a heat-circulating fireplace is visible from the Foyer
- The large Kitchen with cooktop island opens the bay-windowed Dinette, which includes a Pantry
- The Master Bedroom includes his-and-her closets and a private Bath
- Two additional Bedrooms share a full Bath
- The formal Dining and Living Rooms flow in each other for easy entertaining
- This home is designed with basement and sla foundation options

MAIN FLOOR — 1,613 SQ. FT.
BASEMENT — 1,060 SQ. FT.
GARAGE — 461 SQ. FT.

Total living area: 1,613 sq. ft.

PATIO
83'-8"
LAV
mud rm laund.
DINETTE
7'8" x 12'4"
KIT
8'6" x 13'
island cook top
sl.gl.dr.
fireplace
FAMILY RM
15'8" x 13'0"
BATH
MASTER BED RM
14'6" x 13'0"
TWO CAR GARAGE
22'0" x 20'0"
pantry
ref
HALL
DINING RM
11'0" x 12'0"
LIVING RM
17'6" x 13'4"
FOYER
BED RM
10'0" x 10'0"
BED RM
10'0" x 13'4"
27'-4"
MAIN FLOOR
COVERED PORCH

To order your Blueprints, call 1-800-235-5700

PLAN NO. 94105

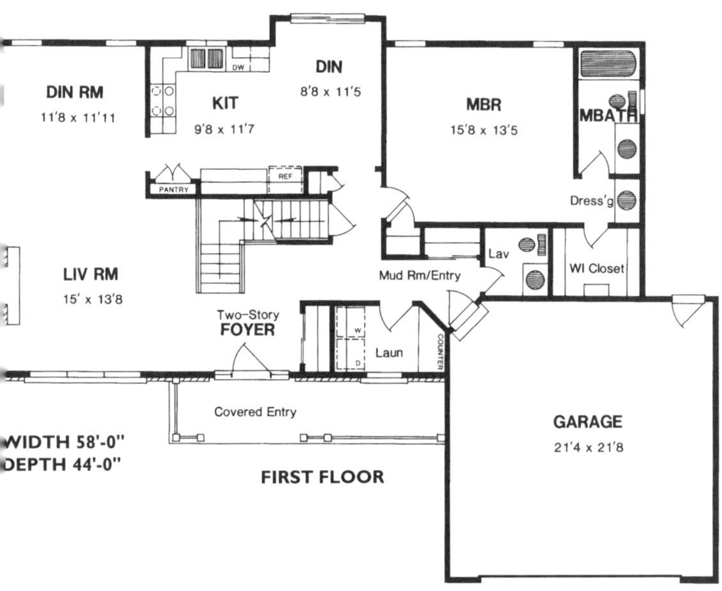
DIN RM
11'8 x 11'11
KIT
9'8 x 11'7
DIN
8'8 x 11'5
MBR
15'8 x 13'5
MBATH
Dress'g
WI Closet
Lav
PANTRY
REF
DW
LIV RM
15' x 13'8
Mud Rm/Entry
Two-Story
FOYER
Laun
COUNTER
Covered Entry
GARAGE
21'4 x 21'8
WIDTH 58'-0"
DEPTH 44'-0"
FIRST FLOOR

Classic Style and Comfort

Price Code: C

- This plan features:
  - — Three bedrooms
  - — Two full and one half baths
- The covered Entry into the two-story Foyer has a dramatic landing staircase brightened by a decorative window
- The spacious Living/Dining Room combination has a hearth fireplace and decorative windows
- The hub Kitchen has a built-in Pantry and informal Dining Area with sliding glass door to rear yard
- This home is designed with a basement foundation

FIRST FLOOR — 1,281 SQ. FT.
SECOND FLOOR — 511 SQ. FT.
GARAGE — 481 SQ. FT.

Total living area: 1,792 sq. ft.

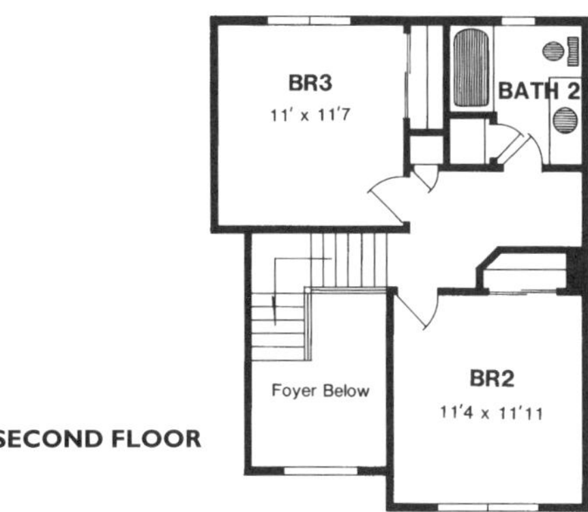
BR3
11' x 11'7
BATH 2
Foyer Below
BR2
11'4 x 11'11
SECOND FLOOR

PLAN NO.10690

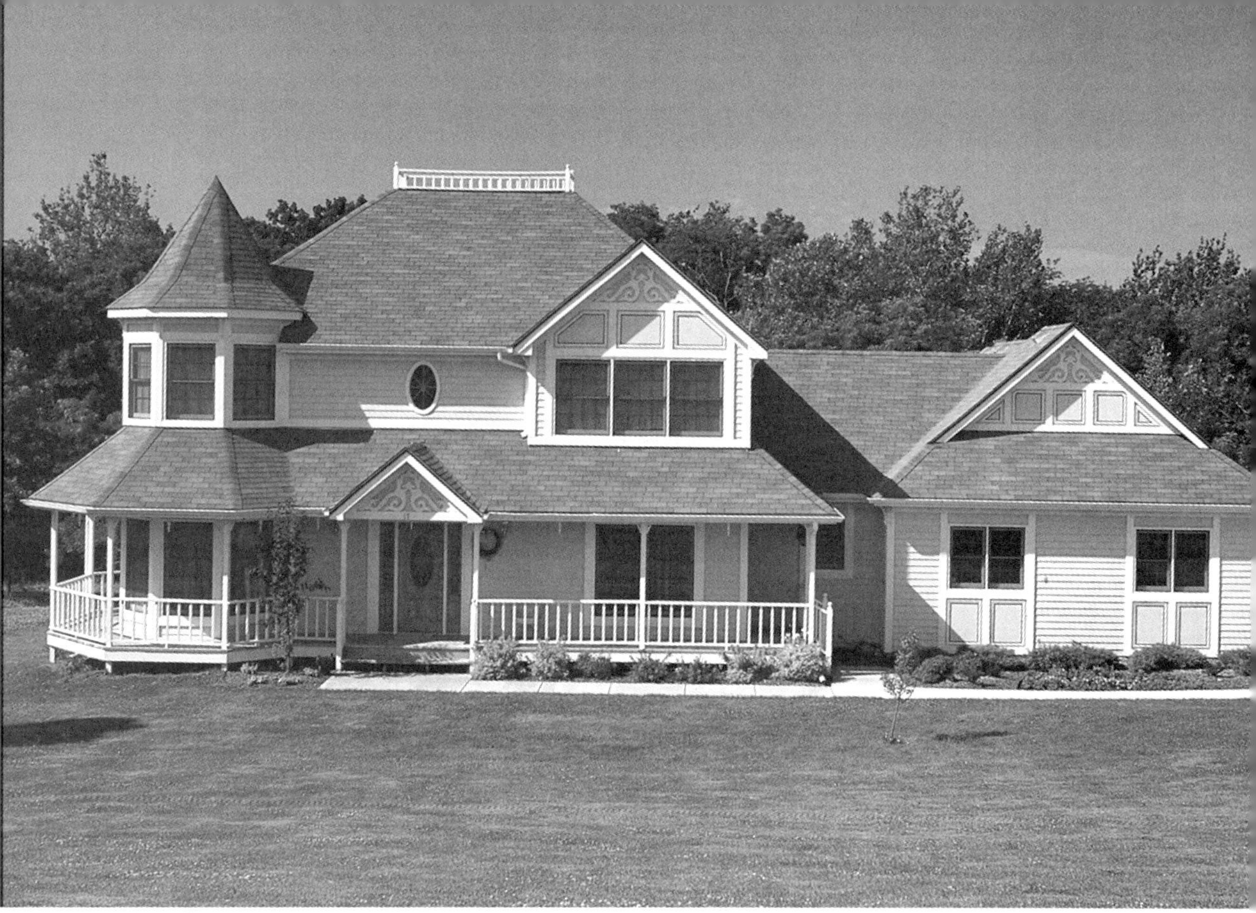

Photography supplied by John Ehrenclou

Gingerbread Charm

Price Code: E

- This plan features:
  - Three bedrooms
  - Two and one half baths
- A wrap-around Porch and rear Deck adding lots of outdoor living space
- A formal Parlor and Dining Room just off the central Entry
- A Family Room with a fireplace
- A Master Suite complete with a five-sided Sitting Nook, walk-in closets and a sunken tub
- This home is designed with basement, slab and crawlspace foundation options

FIRST FLOOR — 1,260 SQ. FT.
SECOND FLOOR — 1,021 SQ. FT.
BASEMENT — 1,186 SQ. FT.
GARAGE — 851 SQ. FT.

**Total living area:
2,281 sq. ft.**

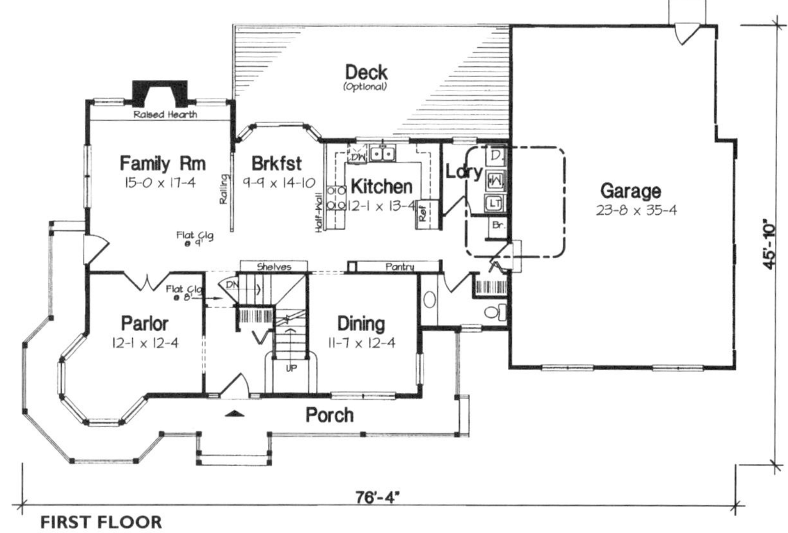

Deck
(Optional)
Raised Hearth
Family Rm
15-0 x 17-4
Brkfst
9-9 x 14-10
Kitchen
12-1 x 13-4
Ldry
Garage
23-8 x 35-4
Shelves
Pantry
Parlor
12-1 x 12-4
Dining
11-7 x 12-4
Porch
45'-10"
76'-4"

FIRST FLOOR

SLAB/CRAWLSPACE OPTION

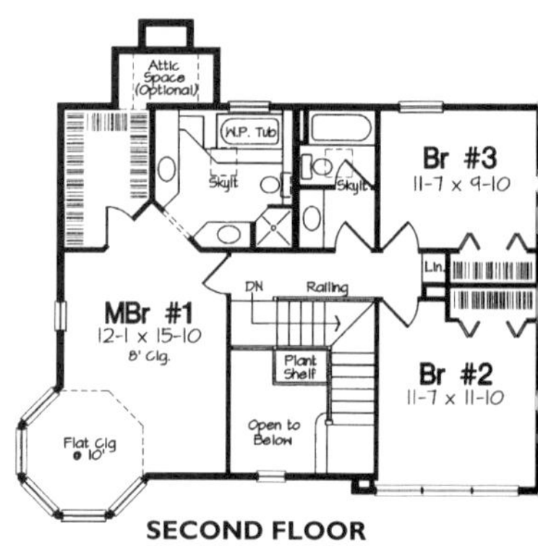

Attic Space (Optional)
Br #3
11-7 x 9-10
MBr #1
12-1 x 15-10
Br #2
11-7 x 11-10
Open to Below

SECOND FLOOR

Spacious and Bright

Price Code: C

'his plan features:

- Three bedrooms
- Two full and one half baths
- oaring ceilings in the two-story Family and)ining Rooms and a full-height stone fireplace urrounded by windows creates a spacious, sun-illed interior
- A circular snack bar and separate Dining Area ffers informal or formal dining options
- urrounded by angled balconies, the upper level oasts a private Computer Room and a spacious 3edroom with access to a large attic
- 'his home is designed with a basement foundation

RST FLOOR — 1,525 SQ. FT.
COND FLOOR — 470 SQ. FT.
SEMENT — 1,525 SQ. FT.
RAGE — 623 SQ. FT.

Total living area:
1,995 sq. ft.

PLAN NO.65368

FIRST FLOOR

SECOND FLOOR

Efficent Kitchen

Price Code: C

This plan features:

- Three bedrooms
- Two full baths
- The efficient island kitchen includes a pantry, easy access from the garage for unloading of groceries and a laundry room is close proximity
- A Morning Room for sit down meals, flows from the Kitchen
- A fireplace flanked by windows highlights the Great Room
- The master suite has a cozy Sitting Area and ample closet space
- Two additional bedrooms have easy access to a full bath
- This home is designed with a basement foundation
- Alternate foundation options available at an additional charge. Please call 1-800-235-5700 for more information.

AIN FLOOR —1,902 SQ. FT.
ARAGE — 540 SQ. FT.

Total living area:
1,902 sq. ft.

PLAN NO.68120

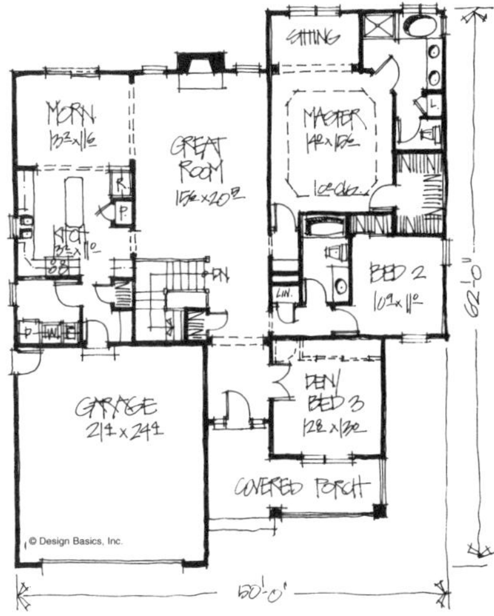

MAIN FLOOR

PLAN NO. 20205

Small, But Room to Grow

Price Code: B

- This plan features:
- — Three bedrooms
- — Two full baths
- A Master Suite with a vaulted ceiling and private skylit Bath
- A fireplaced Living Room with a sloped ceiling
- Efficient Kitchen with a Breakfast Nook
- Options for growth on the lower floor
- This home is designed with a basement foundation

MAIN FLOOR — 1,321 SQ. FT.
LOWER FLOOR — 286 SQ. FT.
GARAGE — 655 SQ. FT.

Total living area:
1,607 sq. ft.

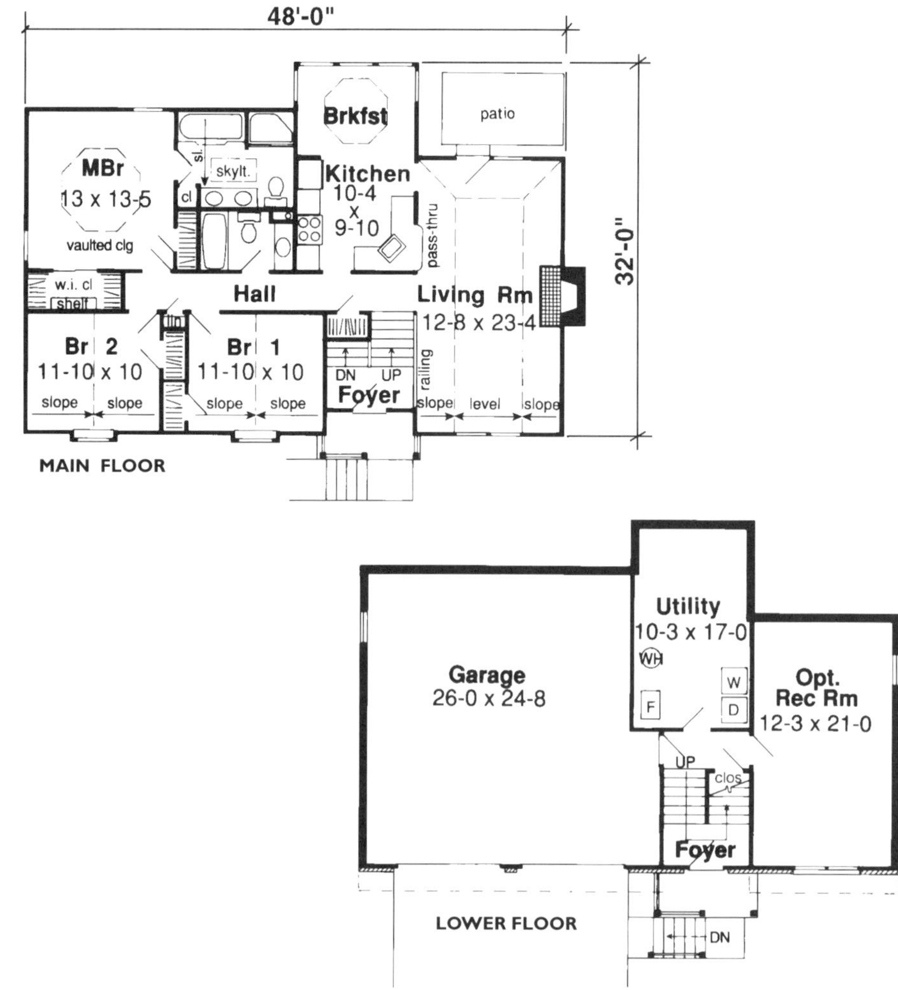

48'-0"
32'-0"
Brkfst
patio
MBr
13 x 13-5
vaulted clg
skylt.
sl.
cl
Kitchen
10-4
x
9-10
pass-thru
w.i. cl
shelf
Hall
Living Rm
12-8 x 23-4
Br 2
11-10 x 10
slope
slope
Br 1
11-10 x 10
slope
slope
DN
UP
Foyer
railing
slope
level
slope
MAIN FLOOR
Utility
10-3 x 17-0
WH
W
D
F
Garage
26-0 x 24-8
Opt.
Rec Rm
12-3 x 21-0
UP
clos
Foyer
LOWER FLOOR
DN

Fabulous Rear Deck

Price Code: A

'his plan features:

- 'wo bedrooms
- 'wo full baths
- terrific stone fireplace highlights the Great oom, which is crowned in a vaulted ceiling vith skylights
- 'rench doors lead to the rear Deck from the reat Room, perfect for entertaining or just njoying the outdoors
- 'he Master Suite includes double French doors o the deck, adding additional sunlight to the oom
- he Loft has a vaulted ceiling and a full bath vith a skylight
- 'his home is designed with a slab foundation

RST FLOOR — 862 SQ. FT.

COND FLOOR — 332 SQ. FT.

Total living area: 1,194 sq. ft.

PLAN NO.61004

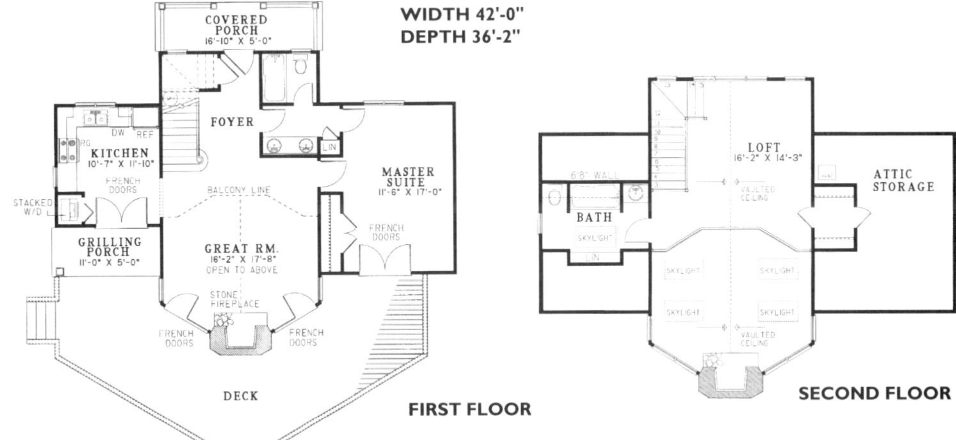

WIDTH 42'-0"
DEPTH 36'-2"
COVERED PORCH 16'-10" X 5'-0"
FOYER
KITCHEN 10'-7" X 11'-10"
DW
REF
FRENCH DOORS
STACKED W/D
GRILLING PORCH 11'-0" X 5'-0"
BALCONY LINE
GREAT RM. 16'-2" X 17'-8" OPEN TO ABOVE
STONE FIREPLACE
FRENCH DOORS
FRENCH DOORS
MASTER SUITE 11'-6" X 17'-0"
FRENCH DOORS
LIN
DECK
FIRST FLOOR
LOFT 16'-2" X 14'-3"
VAULTED CEILING
BATH
SKYLIGHT
SKYLIGHT
SKYLIGHT
SKYLIGHT
ATTIC STORAGE
VAULTED CEILING
SECOND FLOOR

Small and Stylish

Price Code: A

'his plan features:

- 'wo bedrooms
- 'wo full baths
- reat open living space between the Family oom, Kitchen and Nook
- 'he Dining Room is open to the Family Room nd directly accesses the Kitchen for ease in erving
- 'he Master Bedroom Suite is tuck into the right ear corner of the home for privacy
- 'he Den/Study is located off the main hall from he Entry with a half Bath close by
- green house is planned off the nook area next o the covered Patio
- 'his home is designed with a slab foundation

AIN FLOOR — 1,309 SQ. FT.

ARAGE — 383 SQ. FT.

Total living area: 1,309 sq. ft.

PLAN NO.63049

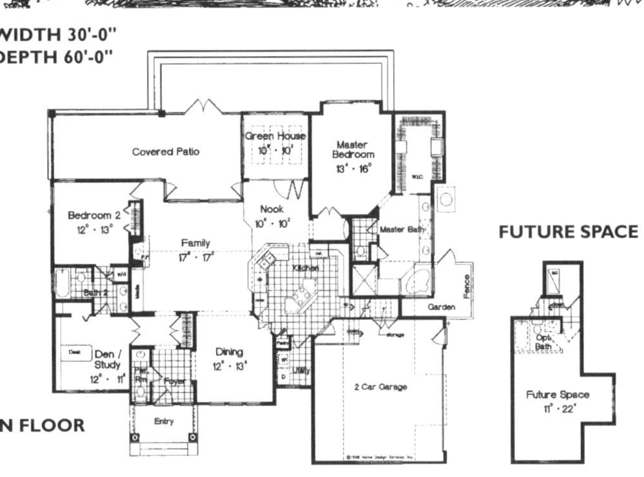

WIDTH 30'-0"
DEPTH 60'-0"
Covered Patio
Green House
Master Bedroom
Bedroom 2
Nook
Family
Master Bath
Kitchen
Bath 2
Garden
Fence
Den / Study
Dining
Utility
Foyer
Entry
2 Car Garage
MAIN FLOOR
FUTURE SPACE
Opt. Bath
Future Space

PLAN NO. 24326

Fireplace-Equipped Family Room

Price Code: B

- This plan features:
  - Four bedrooms
  - Two full and one half baths
- A lovely front Porch shading the entrance
- A spacious Living Room that opens into the Dining Area which flows into the efficient Kitchen
- A Family Room equipped with a cozy fireplace and sliding glass doors to a Patio
- This home is designed with basement, slab and crawlspace foundation options

FIRST FLOOR — 692 SQ. FT.
SECOND FLOOR — 813 SQ. FT.
BASEMENT — 699 SQ. FT.
GARAGE — 484 SQ. FT.

Total living area: 1,505 sq. ft.

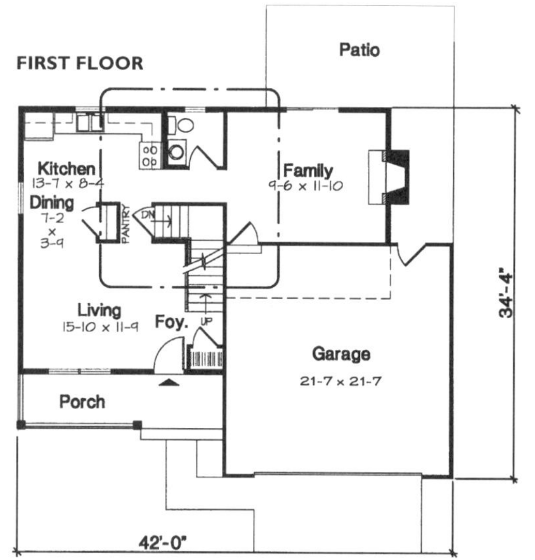
FIRST FLOOR
Patio
Kitchen
13-7 x 8-4
Dining
7-2 x 3-9
PANTRY
DN
Family
9-6 x 11-10
Living
15-10 x 11-9
Foy.
UP
Garage
21-7 x 21-7
Porch
34'-4"
42'-0"

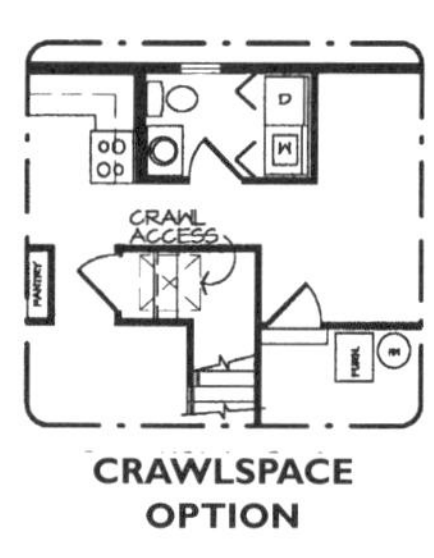
CRAWL ACCESS
CRAWLSPACE OPTION

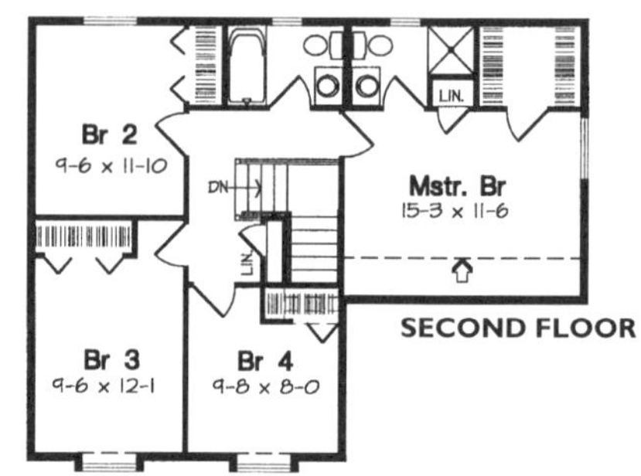
Br 2
9-6 x 11-10
DN
LIN.
Mstr. Br
15-3 x 11-6
Br 3
9-6 x 12-1
Br 4
9-8 x 8-0
SECOND FLOOR

Style and Convenience

Price Code: A

his plan features:

hree bedrooms

wo full baths

arge front windows, dormers and an old-fash-
oned Porch give a pleasing style to the home

vaulted ceiling tops the Foyer, which flows
nto the Family Room is highlighted by a fire-
lace

he formal Dining Room is open to the Family
oom, both of which are crowned in elegant
aulted ceilings

n efficient Kitchen is enhanced by a Pantry, a
ass-through to the Family Room and direct
ccess to the Dining Room and Breakfast Room

decorative tray ceiling, a five-piece private
ath and a walk-in closet are highlights of the
laster Suite

wo additional Bedrooms, roomy in size, sharing
ne full Bath in the hall

his home is designed with basement and crawl-
pace foundation options

AIN FLOOR — 1,373 SQ. FT.
SEMENT — 1,386 SQ. FT.

**Total living area:
1,373 sq. ft.**

PLAN NO.98411

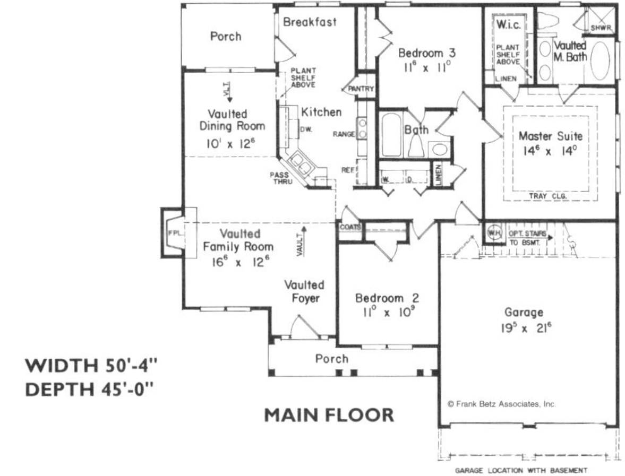

Porch
Breakfast
PLANT SHELF ABOVE
Bedroom 3
11⁶ x 11⁰
W.i.c.
PLANT SHELF ABOVE
SHWR.
Vaulted M. Bath
LINEN
PANTRY
Vaulted Dining Room
10' x 12⁶
Kitchen
D.W.
RANGE
Bath
Master Suite
14⁶ x 14⁰
PASS THRU
REF.
TRAY CLG.
COATS
OPT. STAIRS TO BSMT.
FPL.
Vaulted Family Room
16⁶ x 12⁶
VAULT
Vaulted Foyer
Bedroom 2
11⁰ x 10⁹
Garage
19⁵ x 21⁶
Porch
© Frank Betz Associates, Inc.
GARAGE LOCATION WITH BASEMENT

WIDTH 50'-4"
DEPTH 45'-0"

MAIN FLOOR

Easy Everyday Living

Price Code: B

his plan features:

hree bedrooms

wo full baths

he front entrance is accented by segmented
ches, sidelights and transom windows

pen Living Room features focal point fireplace,
et bar and access to Patio

ining Area opens to both the Living Room and
e Kitchen

fficient Kitchen has a cooktop island, walk-in
antry and access to a Utility Area with a Garage
ntry

arge walk-in closet, double vanity bath and
ccess to Patio are features of the Master
edroom suite

wo additional Bedrooms share a double-vanity
ath

his home is designed with basement, slab and
rawlspace foundation options

AIN FLOOR — 1,664 SQ. FT.
SEMENT — 1,600 SQ. FT.
RAGE — 440 SQ. FT

**Total living area:
1,664 sq. ft.**

PLAN NO.92238

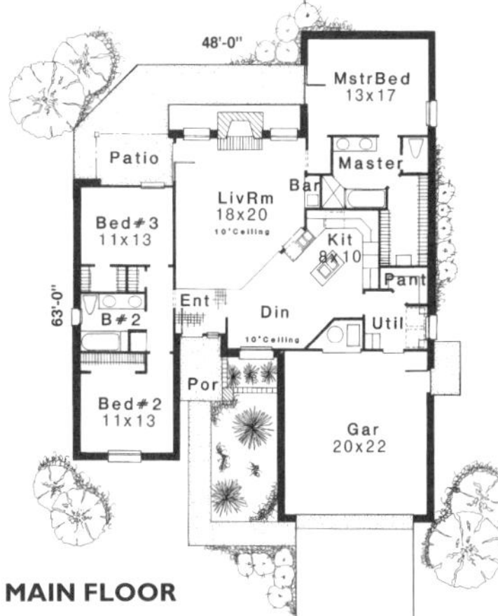

48'-0"
MstrBed
13x17
Patio
Master
Bar
LivRm
18x20
10' Ceiling
Bed#3
11x13
Kit
8x10
Pant
63'-0"
B#2
Ent
Din
10' Ceiling
Util
Por
Bed#2
11x13
Gar
20x22

MAIN FLOOR

PLAN NO. 99045

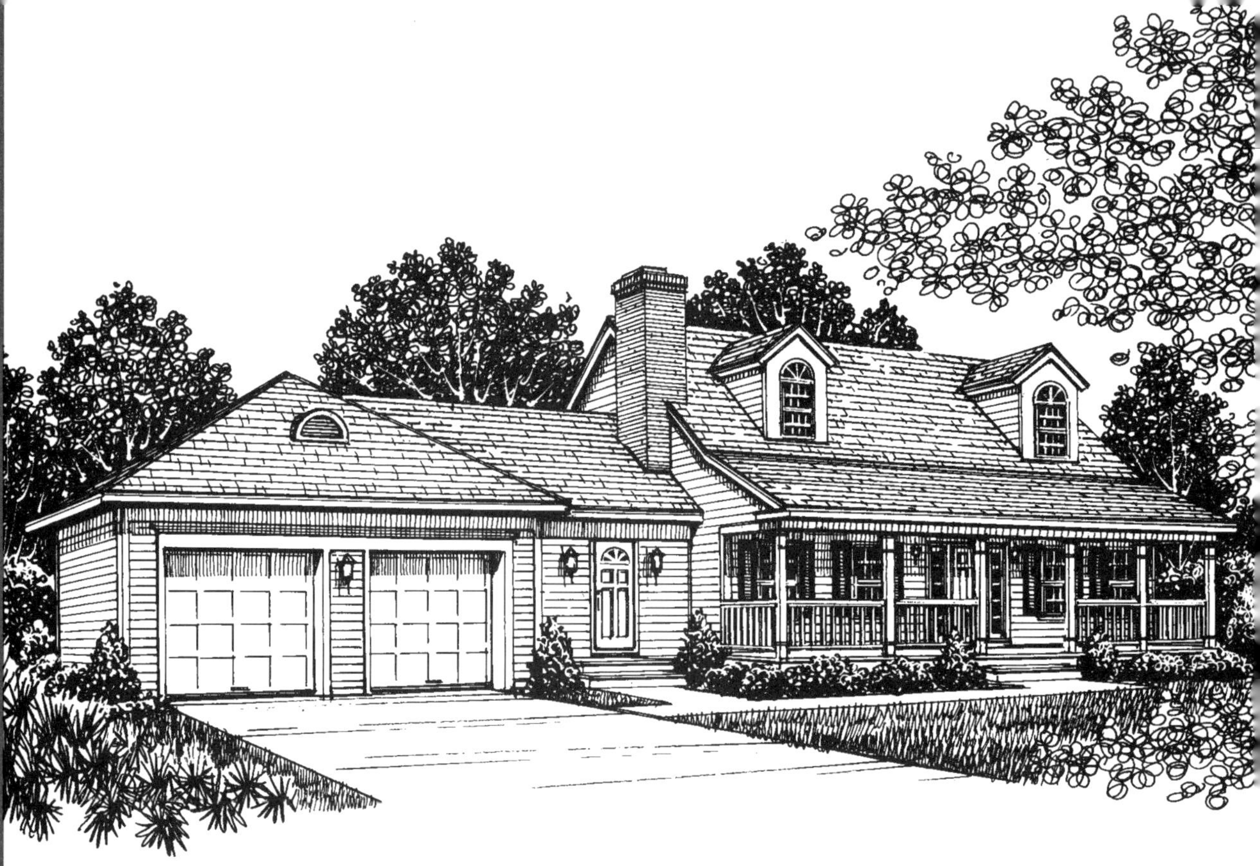

Country Convenience

Price Code: C

- This plan features:
  - — Three bedrooms
  - — Two full and one half baths
- The full front Porch provides comfortable visiting and a sheltered entrance
- The expansive Living Room with an inviting fireplace opens to the bright Dining Room and Kitchen
- The U-shaped Kitchen has a peninsula serving counter to the Dining Room, and nearby Pantry, Laundry and Garage Entry
- This home is designed with a basement foundation

FIRST FLOOR — 1,108 SQ. FT.
SECOND FLOOR — 659 SQ. FT.
BASEMENT — 875 SQ. FT.

Total living area: 1,767 sq. ft.

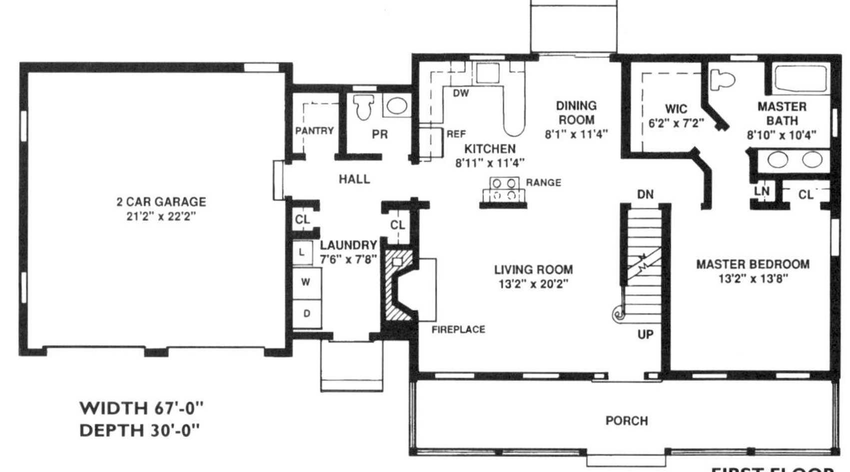
DW
DINING ROOM 8'1" x 11'4"
WIC 6'2" x 7'2"
MASTER BATH 8'10" x 10'4"
PANTRY
PR
REF
KITCHEN 8'11" x 11'4"
RANGE
HALL
2 CAR GARAGE 21'2" x 22'2"
DN
LN
CL
CL
CL
LAUNDRY 7'6" x 7'8"
L
W
D
LIVING ROOM 13'2" x 20'2"
MASTER BEDROOM 13'2" x 13'8"
FIREPLACE
UP
PORCH
WIDTH 67'-0"
DEPTH 30'-0"
FIRST FLOOR

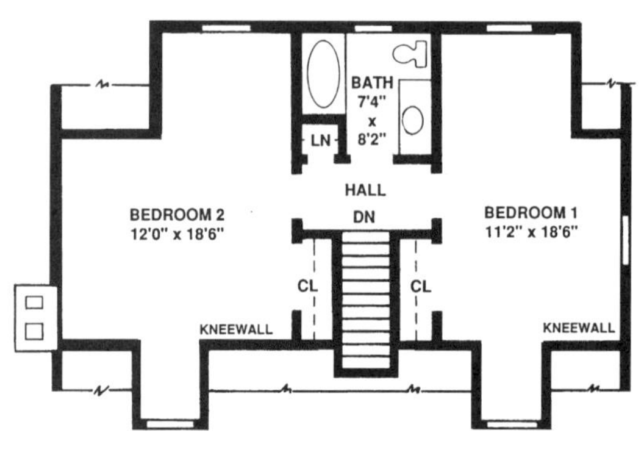
BATH 7'4" x 8'2"
LN
HALL
DN
BEDROOM 2 12'0" x 18'6"
BEDROOM 1 11'2" x 18'6"
CL
CL
KNEEWALL
KNEEWALL
SECOND FLOOR

PLAN NO.65004

Angled Front Porch

Price Code: E

his plan features:

- our bedrooms
- wo full and one half baths
- huge, angled front Porch provides a unique, outoor Foyer with access to the Living Room and ining Room
- reestanding and angled workspaces make it a onvenient and efficient Kitchen
- uxurious appointments in the Master Suite iclude a fireplace, and a private Bath featuring a olumned whirlpool tub
- he home is designed with a basement foundation

RST FLOOR — 1,067 SQ. FT.
COND FLOOR — 1,233 SQ. FT.
SEMENT — 1,067 SQ. FT.

Total living area: 2,300 sq. ft.

FIRST FLOOR

WIDTH 58'-0"
DEPTH 33'-0"

SECOND FLOOR

PLAN NO.65234

Classic Country Home

Price Code: E

his plan features:

- Three bedrooms
- Two full and one half baths
- o the left of the Entry is a small Office
- he Living Room, Dining Room and Kitchen all low seamlessly one to another in this surprisingly nodern plan with many of the built-in amenities ou expect from a larger home
- he first floor Master Bedroom has a large closet onveniently located within the private Bath
- This home is designed with a basement foundation

RST FLOOR — 1,620 SQ. FT.
COND FLOOR — 680 SQ. FT.
RAGE — 595 SQ. FT.

Total living area: 1,995 sq. ft.

Rear Elevation

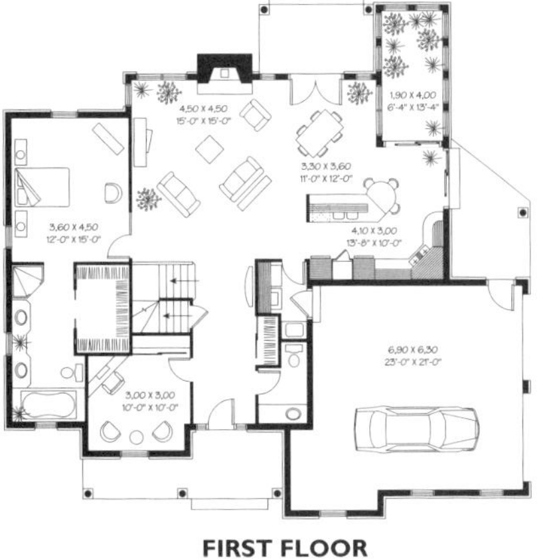

FIRST FLOOR

WIDTH 56'-0"
DEPTH 53'-2"

SECOND FLOOR

PLAN NO. 91002

Lovely Second Home

Price Code: A

- This plan features:
- — Two bedrooms
- — One full and one three-quarter baths
- A firedrum fireplace warms the whole house from its central location
- The Dining and Living Rooms, with loads of windows, open onto the Deck, which surrounds the home on three sides
- The convenient Kitchen opens to both the Dining and Living Rooms
- This home is designed with a crawlspace foundation

MAIN FLOOR — 808 SQ. FT.
UPPER FLOOR — 288 SQ. FT.

Total living area:
1,096 sq. ft.

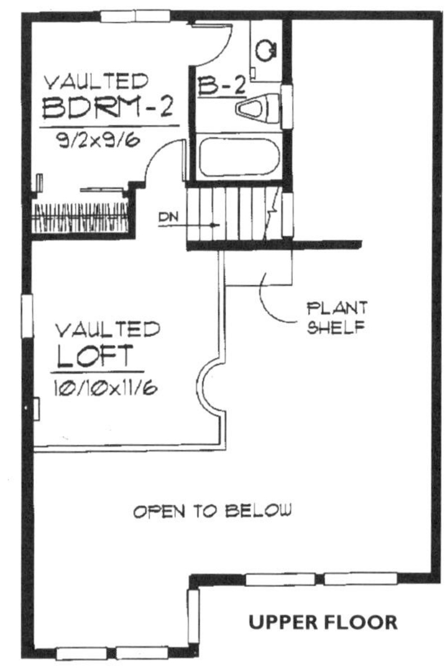
VAULTED
BDRM-2
9/2x9/6
B-2
DN
PLANT SHELF
VAULTED
LOFT
1Ø/1Øx11/6
OPEN TO BELOW
UPPER FLOOR

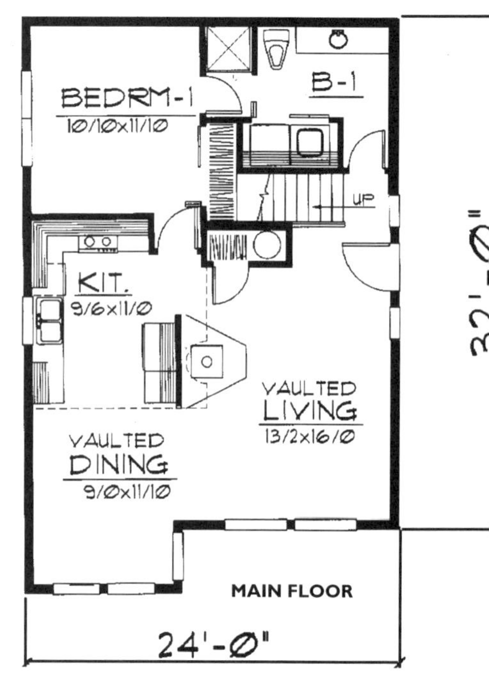
BEDRM-1
1Ø/1Øx11/1Ø
B-1
UP
KIT.
9/6x11/Ø
VAULTED
LIVING
13/2x16/Ø
VAULTED
DINING
9/Øx11/1Ø
MAIN FLOOR
24'-Ø"
32'-Ø"

Compact Home is Surprisingly Spacious

Price Code: A

This plan features:

- Three bedrooms
- Two full baths
- The spacious Living Room is warmed by a fire- place
- The Dining Room flows off the Living Room, with sliding glass doors to the Sun Deck
- An efficient, well-equipped Kitchen with a snack bar, double sink, and ample cabinet and counter space
- A Master Suite with a walk-in closet and private full Bath
- Two additional, roomy Bedrooms with ample clos- et space and protection from street noise thanks to the two-car Garage
- This home is designed with a basement foundation

AIN FLOOR — 1,314 SQ. FT.
ASEMENT — 1,488 SQ. FT.
ARAGE — 484 SQ. FT.

Total living area: 1,314 sq. ft.

PLAN NO.90905

MBR
12-0x14-0
3657x4267
BATH
KITCHEN
13-2x11-8
4013x3556
SUNDECK
DINING
10-0x11-0
3048x3352
WIC
Hall
BR 2
10-4x11-0
3149x3352
BR 3
10-4x11-0
3149x3352
Foyer
LIVINGROOM
18-6x15-0
5638x4572
Porch
DOUBLE GARAGE

MAIN FLOOR

WIDTH 50'-0"
DEPTH 54'-0"

Classic Styling

Price Code: E

This plan features:

- Four bedrooms
- Two full and one half baths
- A wrap-around Porch adding a cozy touch to this classic style
- The two-story Foyer is open to the formal Dining and Living Rooms
- The large Family Room is accentuated by columns and a fireplace
- A sunny Breakfast area provides direct access to the Sun Deck, Screened Porch and the Kitchen
- A convenient Kitchen is situated between the for- mal Dining Room and informal Breakfast Area has a Laundry Center and a Pantry
- A private Deck highlights the Master Suite which includes a luxurious Bath and a walk-in closet
- Three additional Bedrooms share a full Bath
- This home is designed with a basement foundation

RST FLOOR — 1,250 SQ. FT.
COND FLOOR — 1,166 SQ. FT.
NISHED STAIRS — 48 SQ. FT.
ASEMENT — 448 SQ. FT.
ARAGE — 706 SQ. FT.

Total living area: 2,464 sq. ft.

PLAN NO.93209

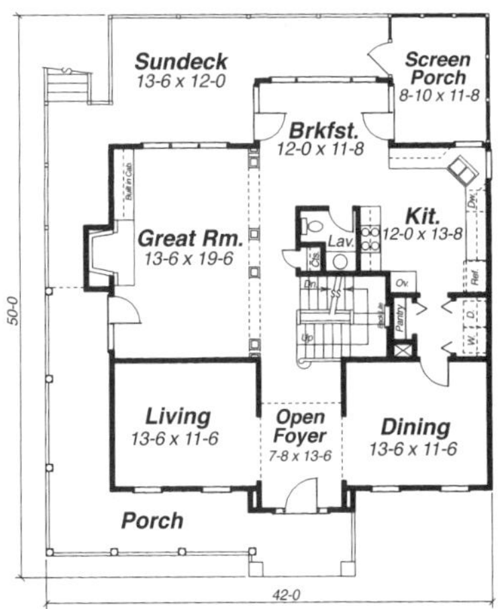

Sundeck
13-6 x 12-0
Screen Porch
8-10 x 11-8
Brkfst.
12-0 x 11-8
Great Rm.
13-6 x 19-6
Kit.
12-0 x 13-8
Lav.
Living
13-6 x 11-6
Open Foyer
7-8 x 13-6
Dining
13-6 x 11-6
Porch
50-0
42-0

FIRST FLOOR

SECOND FLOOR

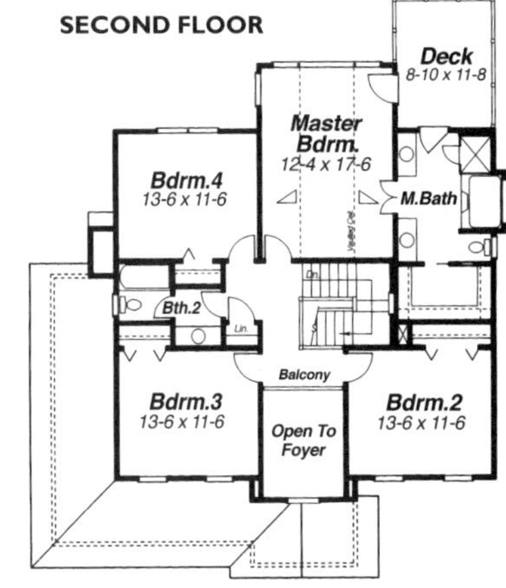

Deck
8-10 x 11-8
Master Bdrm.
12-4 x 17-6
Bdrm.4
13-6 x 11-6
M.Bath
Bth.2
Balcony
Bdrm.3
13-6 x 11-6
Open To Foyer
Bdrm.2
13-6 x 11-6

PLAN NO. 92631

Special Details

Price Code: D

- This plan features:
- — Four bedrooms
- — Two full and one half baths
- Front entrance into two-story Foyer with a plant shelf and lovely railing staircase
- Expansive Great Room with corner fireplace and access to rear yard topped by two-story ceiling
- Efficient Kitchen with peninsula counter, walk-in Pantry, Breakfast bay and access to Deck, Laundry, Garage and formal Dining Room

FIRST FLOOR — 1,511 SQ. FT.
SECOND FLOOR — 646 SQ. FT.
BASEMENT — 1,479 SQ. FT.
GARAGE — 475 SQ. FT.

Total living area:
2,157 sq. ft.

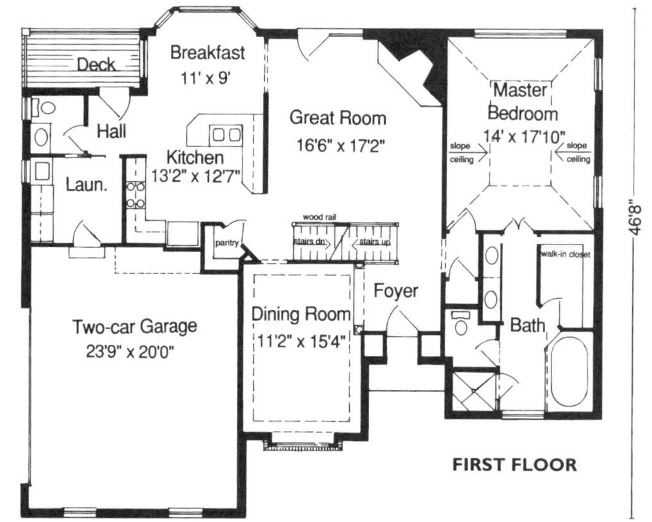

Deck
Breakfast
11' x 9'
Hall
Kitchen
13'2" x 12'7"
Laun.
Great Room
16'6" x 17'2"
Master
Bedroom
14' x 17'10"
slope ceiling
slope ceiling
wood rail
stairs dn
stairs up
pantry
walk-in closet
Two-car Garage
23'9" x 20'0"
Dining Room
11'2" x 15'4"
Foyer
Bath
46'8"
54'8"

FIRST FLOOR

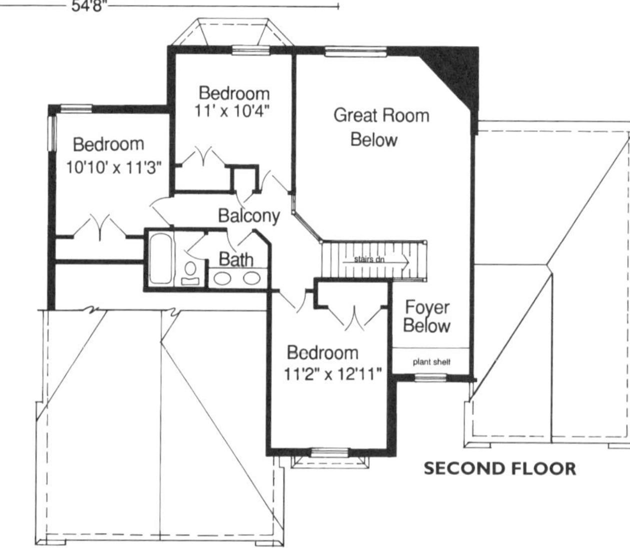

Bedroom
11' x 10'4"
Great Room
Below
Bedroom
10'10' x 11'3"
Balcony
Bath
stairs dn
Foyer
Below
Bedroom
11'2" x 12'11"
plant shelf

SECOND FLOOR

To order your Blueprints, call 1-800-235-5700

PLAN NO.19422

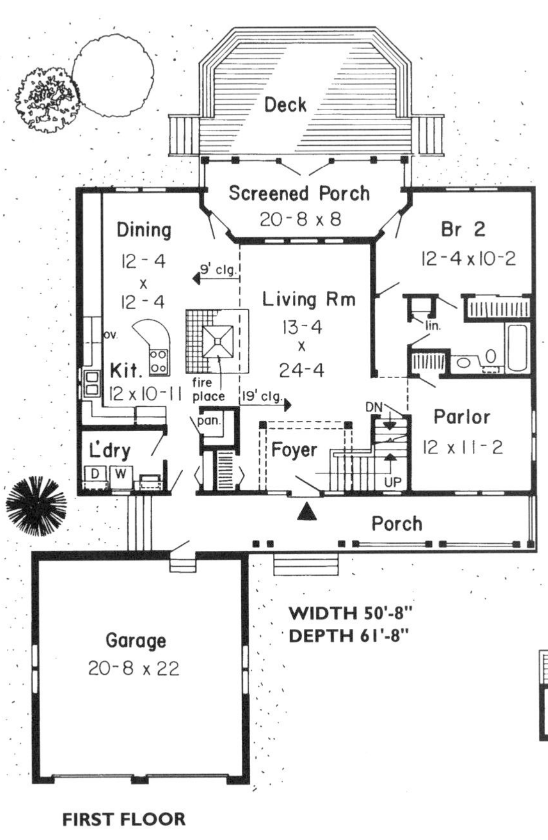

Deck
Screened Porch
20-8 x 8
Dining
12-4
x
12-4
9' clg.
Br 2
12-4 x 10-2
Living Rm
13-4
x
24-4
lin.
ov.
Kit.
12 x 10-11
fire
place
19' clg.
pan.
DN
Parlor
12 x 11-2
L'dry
D
W
Foyer
UP
Porch
Garage
20-8 x 22
WIDTH 50'-8"
DEPTH 61'-8"

FIRST FLOOR

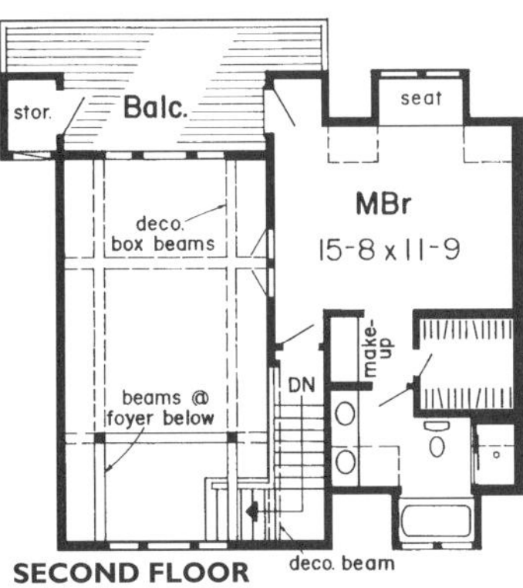

stor.
Balc.
seat
deco.
box beams
MBr
15-8 x 11-9
make-up
DN
beams @
foyer below
deco. beam

SECOND FLOOR

Master Retreat Crowns Home

Price Code: B

- This plan features:
  - — Two bedrooms
  - — Two full baths
- A unique four-sided fireplace separates the Living Room, Dining Area and Kitchen
- The well-equipped Kitchen features a cooktop island, a walk-in Pantry and easy access to the Dining Area and Laundry Room
- This home is designed with basement and crawlspace foundation options

FIRST FLOOR — 1,290 SQ. FT.
SECOND FLOOR — 405 SQ. FT.
SCREENED PORCH — 152 SQ. FT.
GARAGE — 513 SQ. FT.

Total living area:
1,695 sq. ft.

PLAN NO.65284

2.40 X 2.70
8'-0" X 9'-0"
3.30 X 5.70
11'-0" X 19'-0"
4.20 X 4.80
14'-0" X 16'-0"
FIRST FLOOR

WIDTH 26'-0"
DEPTH 33'-0"

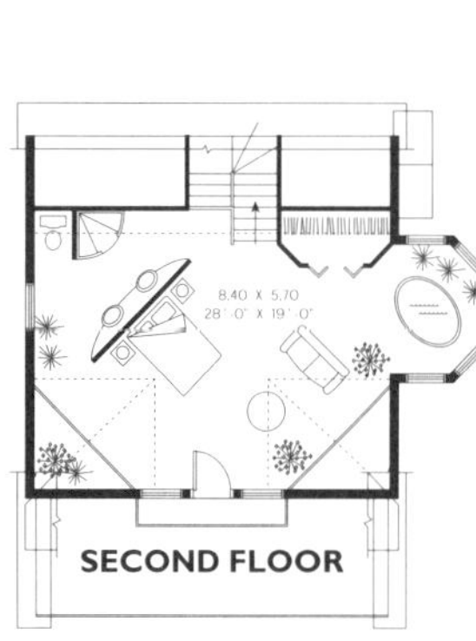

8.40 X 5.70
28'-0" X 19'-0"
SECOND FLOOR

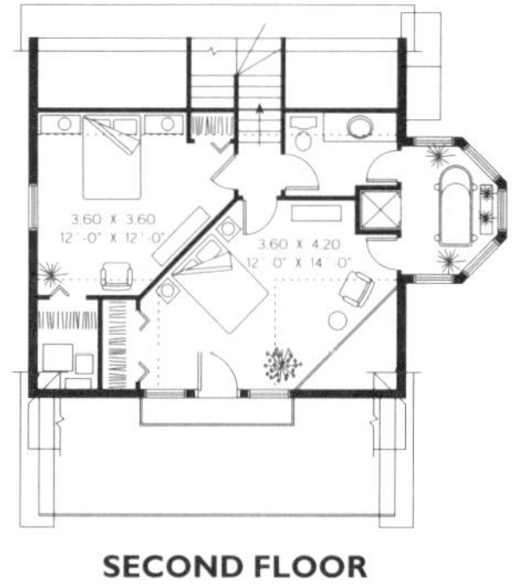

3.60 X 3.60
12'-0" X 12'-0"
3.60 X 4.20
12'-0" X 14'-0"

SECOND FLOOR
2-BED OPTION

Vacation Fun

Price Code: A

- This plan features:

— Two bedrooms

— One full and one half baths

- In good weather or bad, this fun-filled house w provide hours of entertainment
- The open floor plan and abundant windows flo this charming home with natural light
- Gabled Entry includes a large coat closet
- Efficient L-shaped Kitchen with center-island c top is open to the Living and Dining Areas, ensuring that the cook doesn't get left out of th family fun
- Expansion possibilities abound in the walk-out lower level
- This home is designed with a basement founda

FIRST FLOOR — 737 SQ. FT.
SECOND FLOOR — 587 SQ. FT.

**Total living area:
1,324 sq. ft.**

PLAN NO.69018

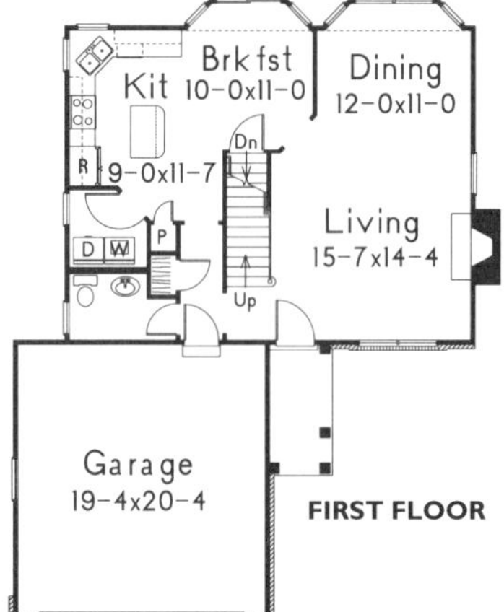

Brkfst
10-0x11-0
Kit
9-0x11-7
Dining
12-0x11-0
Dn
Living
15-7x14-4
Up
D
W
P
R
Garage
19-4x20-4

FIRST FLOOR

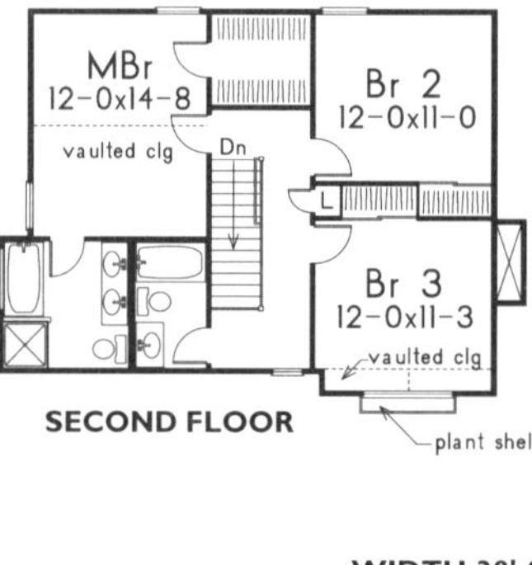

MBr
12-0x14-8
vaulted clg
Dn
Br 2
12-0x11-0
L
Br 3
12-0x11-3
vaulted clg
plant shelf

SECOND FLOOR

WIDTH 38'-0"
DEPTH 47'-0"

Bay Windows Let in the Light

Price Code: B

- This plan features:

— Three bedrooms

— Two full and one half baths

- The well-proportioned Living Room, with its fireplace and double windows, leads gracefully into the bay-windowed Dining Room at the rea the house
- The Breakfast Room features an additional bay window, allowing light to stream into the L-shaped, center-island Kitchen
- The second floor Master Bedroom has a vaulte ceiling, double-vanity Bath with separate show and large walk-in closet
- Two additional second floor Bedrooms have go sized closets and share a full Bath
- Bedroom three has a vaulted ceiling which dramatically increases the visual size of the roo
- This home is designed with a basement founda

FIRST FLOOR — 802 SQ. FT.
SECOND FLOOR — 773 SQ. FT.

**Total living area:
1,575 sq. ft.**

PLAN NO. 90847

WIDTH 27'-0"
DEPTH 32'-0"

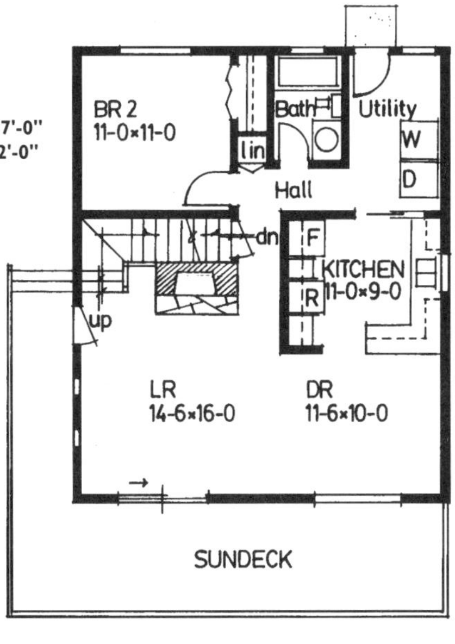

BR 2
11-0×11-0
Bath
Utility
lin
W
D
Hall
dn
F
KITCHEN
11-0×9-0
R
up
LR
14-6×16-0
DR
11-6×10-0
SUNDECK

FIRST FLOOR

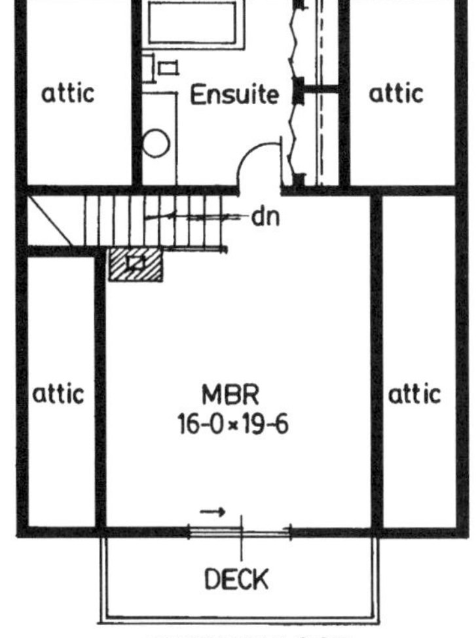

attic
Ensuite
attic
dn
attic
MBR
16-0×19-6
attic
DECK

SECOND FLOOR

Versatile Chalet

Price Code: A

- This plan features:
  - — Two bedrooms
  - — Two full baths
- There is a Deck Entry into a spacious Living Room/Dining Room which has a fieldstone fireplace, a large window and a sliding glass door
- The well-appointed Kitchen has extended counter space and easy access to the Dining Room and the Utility Area
- The spacious Master Bedroom has a private Deck, a Bath, and plenty of storage
- This home is designed with a basement foundation

FIRST FLOOR — 864 SQ. FT.
SECOND FLOOR — 496 SQ. FT.
BASEMENT — 864 SQ. FT.

Total living area:
1,360 sq. ft.

PLAN NO.82026

© Michael E. Nelson

Lovely Ranch

Price Code: A

- This plan features:
  - — Three bedrooms
  - — Two full baths
- Foyer opens to dramatic Great Room with bo: ceiling and corner fireplace
- The Kitchen features ample work space, an eating bar open to the Great Room, and a pan
- Breakfast Room with built-in computer desk opens to rear covered Porch
- Elegant octagonal Dining Room opens to Gre. Room
- The secluded Master Bedroom features a box ceiling, Bath with whirlpool tub and two large walk-in closets
- Two additional Bedrooms are located at the fr of the house
- This home is designed with slab and crawlspa foundation options

MAIN FLOOR — 1,485 SQ. FT.
GARAGE — 415 SQ. FT.

Total living area:
1,485 sq. ft.

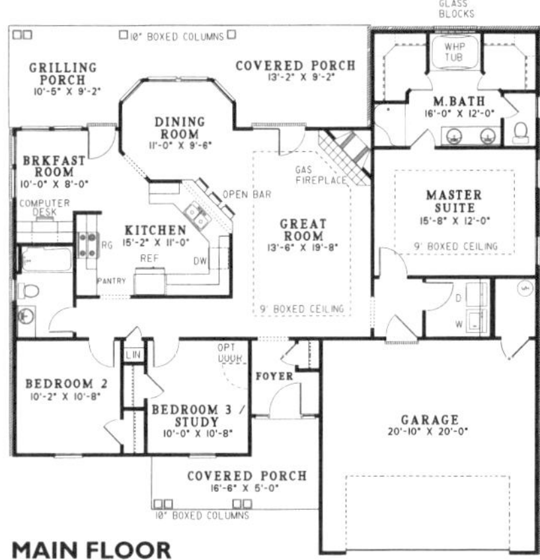
GRILLING PORCH
COVERED PORCH
DINING ROOM
BRKFAST ROOM
KITCHEN
GREAT ROOM
M.BATH
MASTER SUITE
BEDROOM 2
BEDROOM 3 / STUDY
FOYER
GARAGE
COVERED PORCH

WIDTH 51'-6"
DEPTH 49'-10"

MAIN FLOOR

PLAN NO.82028

Columns Outline Dining Roon

Price Code: C

- This plan features:
  - — Three bedrooms
  - — Two full and one half baths
- The entry to this charming home is enhanced the lovely front Porch with multiple columns
- The Master Bedroom includes a really large walk-in closet and a Bath with whirlpool tub a separate shower
- An island, computer desk, Pantry, and bay-windowed Breakfast Nook add to the functionality of the Kitchen
- The large storage closet in the Garage will hel keep clutter to a minimum — or entirely eliminate the need for an outside storage shed
- This home is designed with slab and crawlspa foundation options

MAIN FLOOR — 1,988 SQ. FT.
GARAGE — 598 SQ. FT.

Total living area:
1,988 sq. ft.

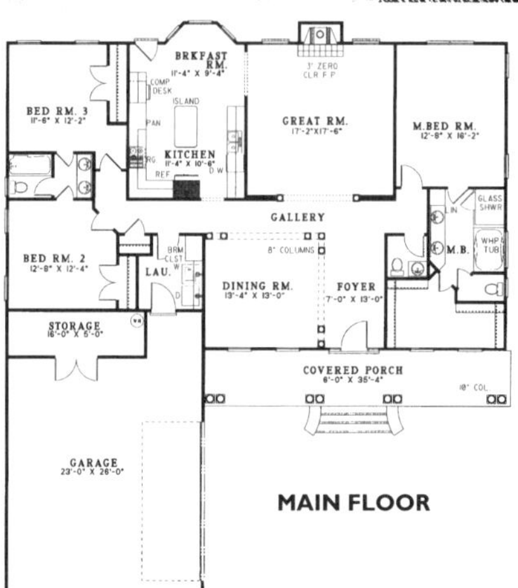
BRKFAST RM.
BED RM. 3
GREAT RM.
M.BED RM.
KITCHEN
GALLERY
BED RM. 2
LAU.
DINING RM.
FOYER
M.B.
STORAGE
COVERED PORCH
GARAGE

WIDTH 59'-0"
DEPTH 65'-4"

MAIN FLOOR

PLAN NO. 24400

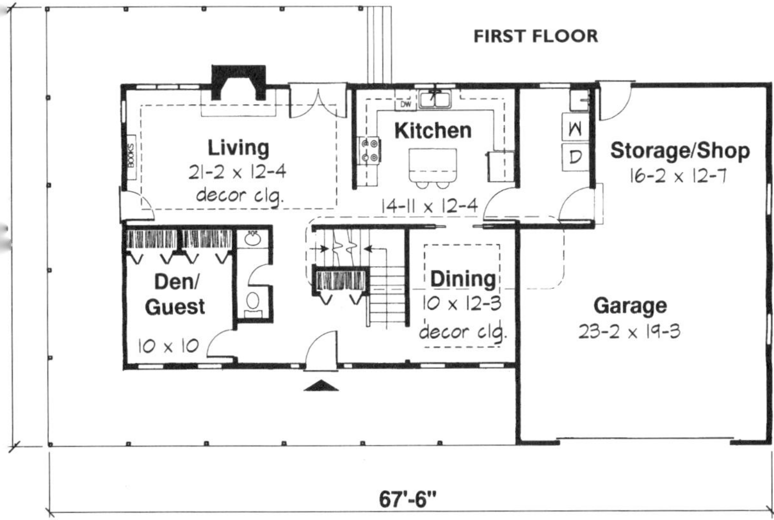
FIRST FLOOR
Living
21-2 x 12-4
decor clg.
Kitchen
14-11 x 12-4
Storage/Shop
16-2 x 12-7
Den/
Guest
10 x 10
Dining
10 x 12-3
decor clg.
Garage
23-2 x 19-3
67'-6"
awl access
Dining
furn. w/h

National Treasure

Price Code: C

- This plan features:
  - — Three bedrooms
  - — Two full and one half baths
- This design has a wrap-around covered Porch
- A decorative ceiling and fireplace is located are in the Living Room
- The large Kitchen has a central island/breakfast bar
- The handy Sitting Area is found on the second floor
- This home is designed with basement, slab and crawlspace foundation options

First floor — 1,034 sq. ft.
Second floor — 944 sq. ft.
Basement — 984 sq. ft.
Garage & storage — 675 sq. ft.

Total living area:
1,978 sq. ft.

SECOND FLOOR

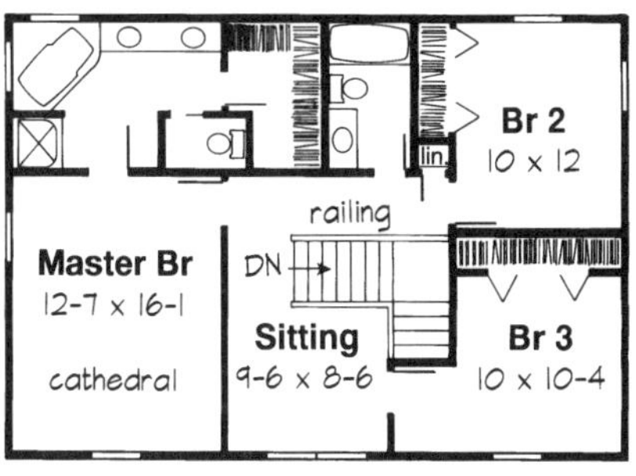
Br 2
10 x 12
lin.
railing
Master Br
12-7 x 16-1
cathedral
DN
Sitting
9-6 x 8-6
Br 3
10 x 10-4

PLAN NO. 20501

Home on a Hill

Price Code: C

- This plan features:
  - — Three bedrooms
  - — Two full baths
- Window walls combine with sliders to unite active areas with a huge Deck
- Interior spaces flow together for an open feeling that is accentuated by the sloping ceilings and a towering fireplace in the Living Room
- The Kitchen has an island counter and easy access to the Dining Room
- This home is designed with a basement, pier/post and basement/crawlspace foundation options

FIRST FLOOR — 1,316 SQ. FT.
SECOND FLOOR — 592 SQ. FT.

Total living area: 1,908 sq. ft.

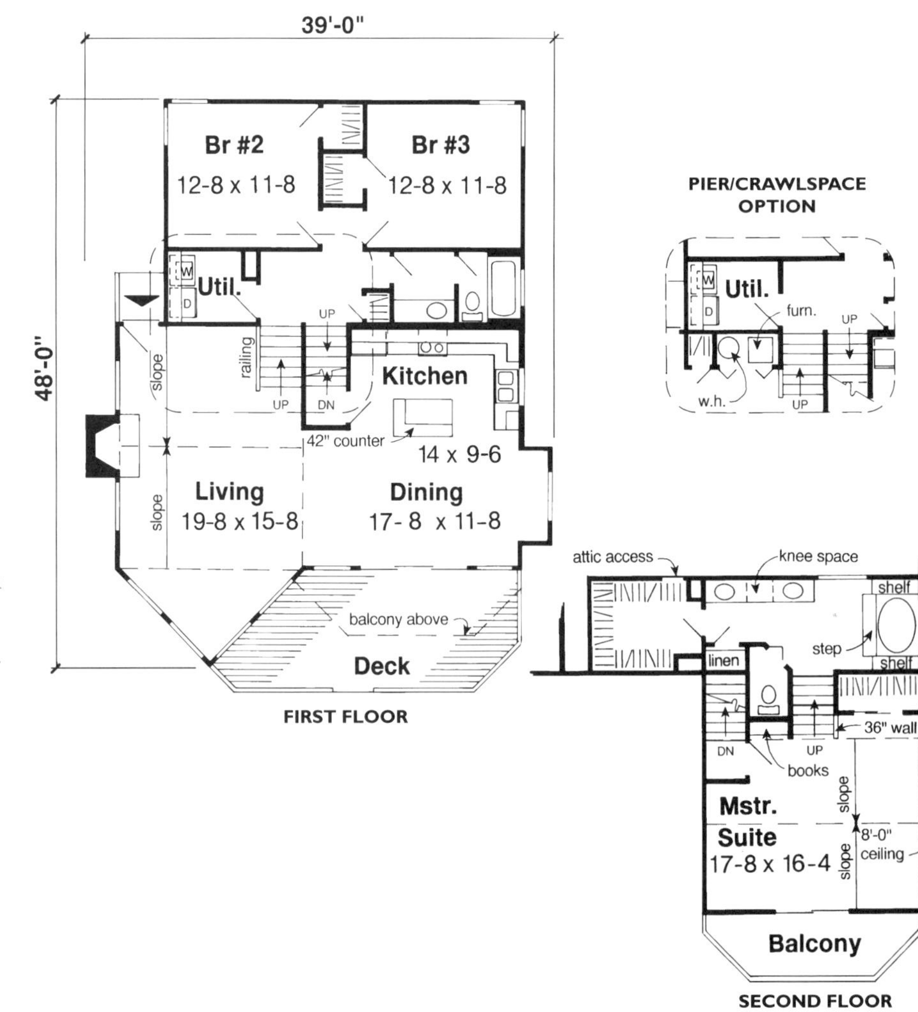
39'-0"
48'-0"
Br #2
12-8 x 11-8
Br #3
12-8 x 11-8
Util.
W
D
UP
railing
slope
UP
DN
Kitchen
42" counter
14 x 9-6
Living
19-8 x 15-8
Dining
17- 8 x 11-8
balcony above
Deck
FIRST FLOOR
PIER/CRAWLSPACE OPTION
Util.
furn.
UP
w.h.
UP
attic access
knee space
shelf
step
shelf
linen
36" wall
DN
UP
books
slope
Mstr.
Suite
17-8 x 16-4
8'-0" ceiling
slope
Balcony
SECOND FLOOR

PLAN NO.92559

Two-Car Garage

Price Code: A

'his plan features:

- Three bedrooms
- Two full baths
- 'he covered front Porch opens to the Foyer
- 'he Den has a sloped ceiling and a fireplace
- 'he Dining Room is adjacent to the Kitchen
- The galley Kitchen has access to the Garage and the Utility Room
- 'he Bedrooms are all on one side of the home
- 'his home is designed with crawlspace and slab oundation options

AIN FLOOR — 1,265 SQ. FT.
ARAGE — 523 SQ. FT.

Total living area:
1,265 sq. ft.

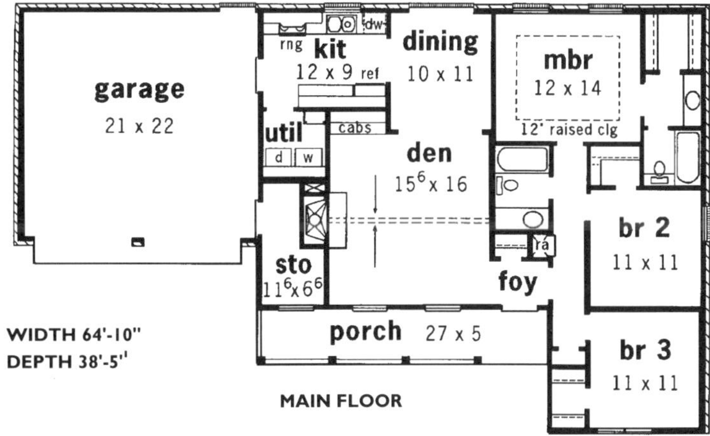

garage
21 x 22
rng
kit
12 x 9
ref
dw
dining
10 x 11
mbr
12 x 14
12' raised clg
util
d
w
cabs
den
15^6 x 16
br 2
11 x 11
sto
11^6x6^6
foy
porch
27 x 5
br 3
11 x 11
WIDTH 64'-10"
DEPTH 38'-5"
MAIN FLOOR

PLAN NO.98441

Fabulous Great Room

Price Code: B

'his plan features:

- Three bedrooms
- Two full and one half baths
- 'he open Foyer leads into the vaulted Great Room with fireplace
- 'he well-planned Kitchen opens to the sunny Breakfast Room to the rear of the house and to the legant Dining Room at the front
- 'he Master Suite with tray ceiling includes a 'aulted Sitting Room, compartmentalized Bath nd large walk-in closet
- 'wo additional Bedrooms have ample closet space
- 'he Garage features additional room for storage
- 'his home is designed with basement and crawl-pace foundation options

AIN FLOOR — 1,502 SQ. FT.
ASEMENT — 1,052 SQ. FT.
ARAGE — 448 SQ. FT.

Total living area:
1,502 sq. ft.

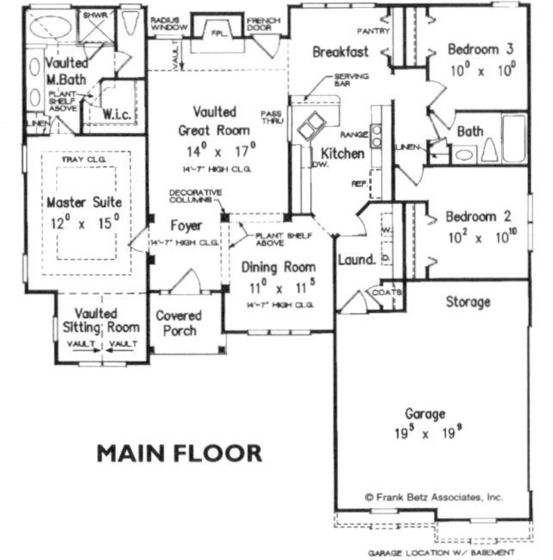

Vaulted M.Bath
W.i.c.
Master Suite
12^0 x 15^0
Vaulted Sitting Room
Vaulted Great Room
14^0 x 17^0
Foyer
Covered Porch
Dining Room
11^0 x 11^5
Breakfast
Kitchen
Bedroom 3
10^0 x 10^0
Bath
Bedroom 2
10^2 x 10^{10}
Laund.
Storage
Garage
19^5 x 19^9
© Frank Betz Associates, Inc.

MAIN FLOOR

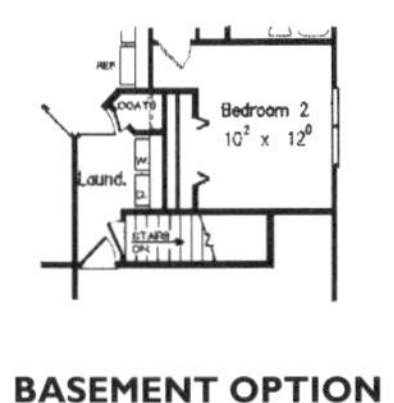

Bedroom 2
10^2 x 12^0
Laund.

BASEMENT OPTION

PLAN NO.20220

MAIN FLOOR

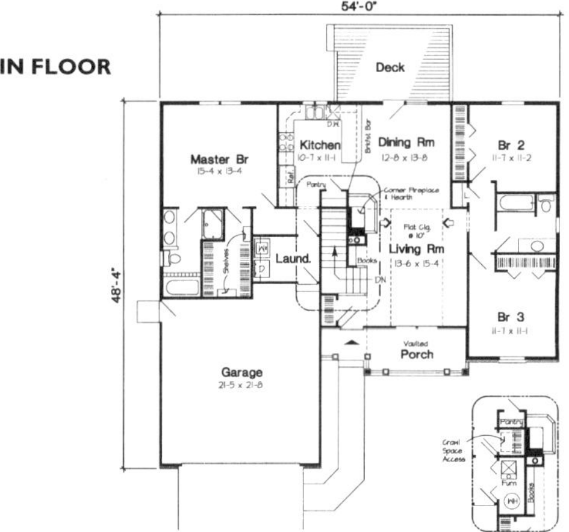
54'-0"
Deck
Master Br
15-4 x 13-4
Kitchen
10-7 x 11-1
Dining Rm
12-8 x 13-8
Br 2
11-7 x 11-2
Living Rm
13-6 x 15-4
Laund.
Br 3
11-7 x 11-1
Porch
Garage
21-5 x 21-8
48'-4"

Traditional Ranch

Price Code: B

- This plan features:
  - — Three bedrooms
  - — Two full baths
- A large front Palladian window gives this hom great curb appeal, and allows a view of the fro yard from the Living Room
- A vaulted ceiling in the Living Room adds to architectural interest and the spacious feel of room
- Sliding glass doors in the Dining Room lead t wood Deck
- A built-in Pantry, double sink and breakfast ba in the efficient Kitchen
- A Master Suite that includes a walk-in closet a private Bath with a double vanity
- Two additional Bedrooms that share a full Ba
- This home is designed with basement, slab an crawlspace foundation options

MAIN FLOOR — 1,568 SQ. FT.
BASEMENT — 1,568 SQ. FT.
GARAGE — 509 SQ. FT.

Total living area:
1,568 sq. ft.

PLAN NO.94923

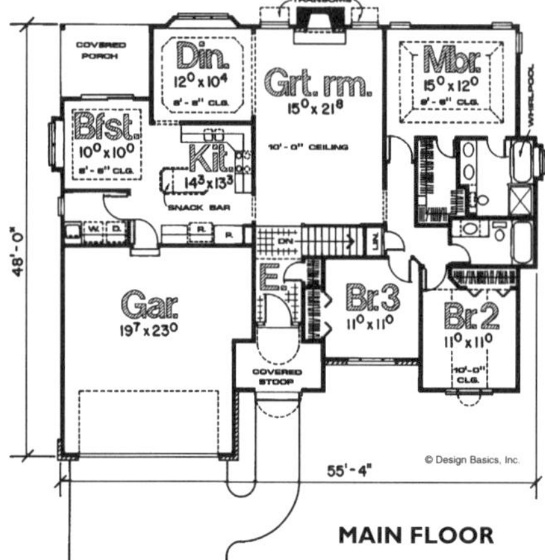
Din.
12⁰x10⁴
Grt. rm.
15⁰x21⁸
Mbr.
15⁰x12⁰
Bfst.
10⁰x10⁰
Kit.
14³x13³
Gar.
19⁷x23⁰
Br.3
11⁰x11⁰
Br.2
11⁰x11⁰
48'-0"
55'-4"
© Design Basics, Inc.

MAIN FLOOR

Keystone Arches and Decorative Windows

Price Code: B

- This plan features:
  - — Three bedrooms
  - — Two full baths
- Brick and stucco enhance the dramatic front el vation and volume entrance
- Inviting Entry leads into expansive Great Roo with hearth fireplace framed by transom windo
- Bay window Dining Room topped by decorati ceiling convenient to the Great Room and the Kitchen/Breakfast area
- Corner Master Suite enjoys a tray ceiling, roo walk-in closet and a plush Bath with a double vanity and whirlpool window tub
- Two additional Bedrooms with large closets share a full Bath
- This home is designed with basement, slab an crawlspace foundation options
- Alternate foundation options available at an ac tional charge. Please call 1-800-235-5700 for more information.

MAIN FLOOR — 1,666 SQ. FT.
BASEMENT — 1,666 SQ. FT.
GARAGE — 496 SQ. FT.

Total living area:
1,666 sq. ft.

PLAN NO. 92638

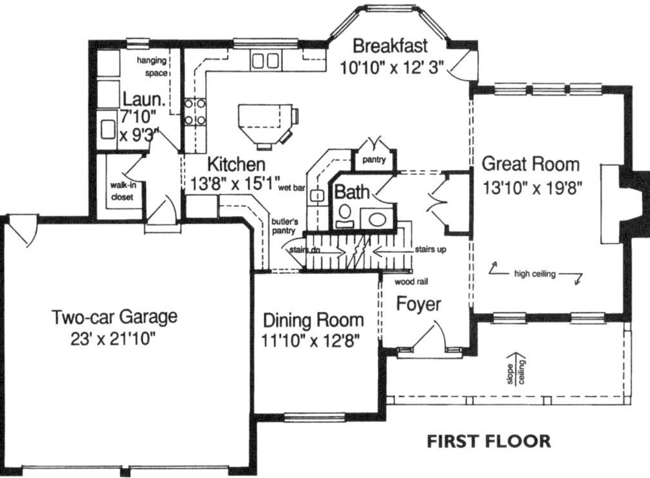
Breakfast
10'10" x 12' 3"
hanging space
Laun.
7'10" x 9'3"
Kitchen
13'8" x 15'1"
wet bar
pantry
Bath
Great Room
13'10" x 19'8"
walk-in closet
butler's pantry
stairs dn
stairs up
wood rail
high ceiling
Foyer
Two-car Garage
23' x 21'10"
Dining Room
11'10" x 12'8"
slope ceiling
FIRST FLOOR

WIDTH 61'-2"
DEPTH 41'-10"

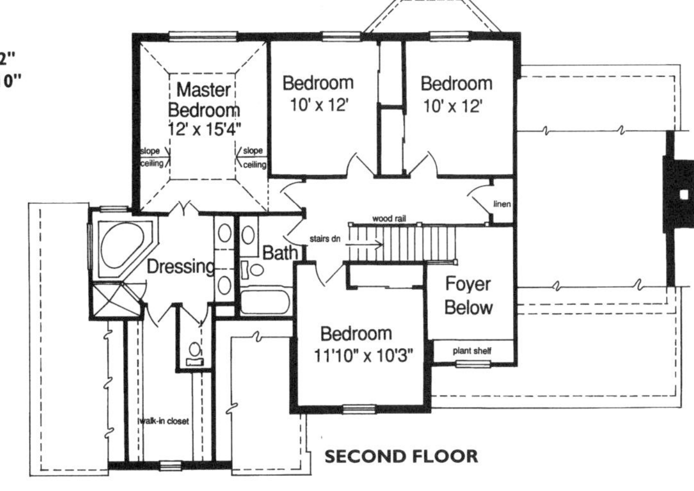
Master Bedroom
12' x 15'4"
slope ceiling
slope ceiling
Bedroom
10' x 12'
Bedroom
10' x 12'
linen
wood rail
stairs dn
Bath
Dressing
Foyer Below
Bedroom
11'10" x 10'3"
plant shelf
walk-in closet
SECOND FLOOR

Friendly Front Porch

Price Code: E

- This plan features:
- — Four bedrooms
- — Two full and one half baths
- Central Foyer with a graceful staircase, opens to formal Dining Room and expansive Great Room
- L-shaped Kitchen with work island/snack bar and butler's Pantry easily serves Dining Room and Breakfast Bay with outdoor access
- Nearby Laundry Room, walk-in closet and Garage entry add to Kitchen efficiency
- Corner Master Bedroom accented by a slope ceiling, Dressing Area and walk-in closet
- This home is designed with a basement foundation

FIRST FLOOR — 1,199 SQ. FT.
SECOND FLOOR — 1,060 SQ. FT.

**Total living area:
2,259 sq. ft.**

PLAN NO. 92688

Attention to Detail

Price Code: D

- This plan features:
  - — Three bedrooms
  - — Four full baths
- From the raised Foyer, a striking view is avai through the Great Room and beyond to the c ered Deck
- The Great Room features high ceilings, a fire flanked by built-ins, large windows and acce the rear Deck
- The spacious Kitchen offers an abundance of counter space plus an eating bar open to the Dining Room
- The lower-level Rec Room features its own f Kitchen, lots of lot and access to a Patio
- The Master Bedroom includes an octagonal S Area
- This home is designed with a basement foun

MAIN FLOOR — 2,041 SQ. FT.
BASEMENT — 1,911 SQ. FT.
GARAGE — 547 SQ. FT.

Total living area:
2,041 sq. ft.

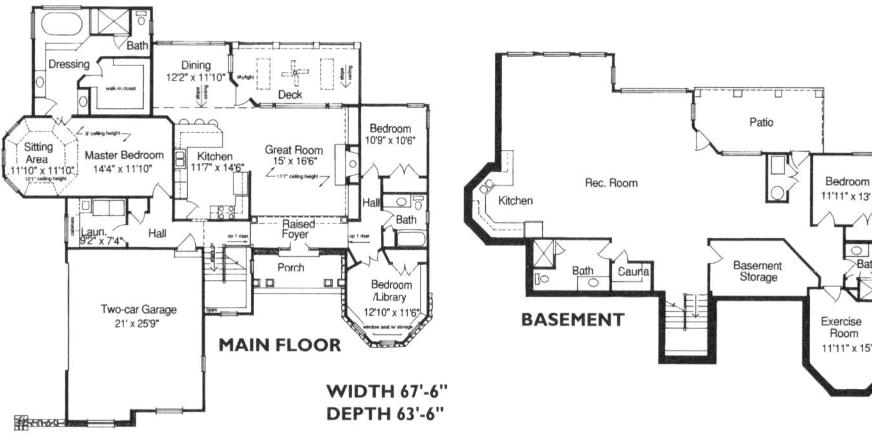

Bath
Dressing
Dining
12'2" x 11'10"
Deck
Sitting Area
11'10" x 11'10"
Master Bedroom
14'4" x 11'10"
Kitchen
11'7" x 14'6"
Great Room
15' x 16'6"
Bedroom
10'9" x 10'6"
Hall
Bath
Laun.
9'2" x 7'4"
Hall
Raised Foyer
Porch
Bedroom /Library
12'10" x 11'6"
Two-car Garage
21' x 25'9"
MAIN FLOOR
Patio
Kitchen
Rec. Room
Bedroom
11'11" x 13'
Bath
Sauna
Basement Storage
Bath
BASEMENT
Exercise Room
11'11" x 15'2"
WIDTH 67'-6"
DEPTH 63'-6"

PLAN NO. 93165

Brick Details Add Class

Price Code: A

- This plan features:
  - — Three bedrooms
  - — Two full baths
- Keystone entrance leads into easy-care tile Ent with plant ledge and convenient coat closet
- Expansive Great Room features cathedral ceili over triple window and a corner gas fireplace
- Hub Kitchen, accented by arches and columns, serves the Great Room and Dining Area, and is across the hall from the Laundry Area and Gar
- The Dining Area has large windows and access the rear yard and Screened Porch
- Private Master Bedroom suite includes a walk- closet and plush Bath with corner whirlpool tu
- Two additional Bedrooms share a full Bath
- This home is designed with a basement founda

MAIN FLOOR — 1,472 SQ. FT.
BASEMENT — 1,472 SQ. FT.
GARAGE — 424 SQ. FT.

Total living area:
1,472 sq. ft.

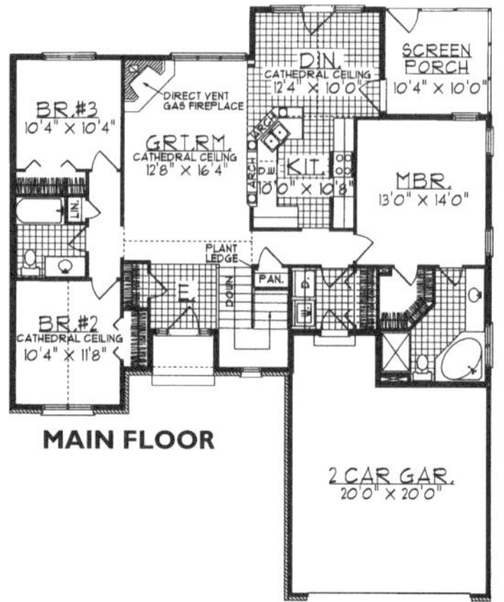

DIN.
CATHEDRAL CEILING
12'4" x 10'0"
SCREEN PORCH
10'4" x 10'0"
BR.#3
10'4" x 10'4"
DIRECT VENT GAS FIREPLACE
GRT.RM.
CATHEDRAL CEILING
12'8" x 16'4"
KIT.
10'0" x 10'8"
MBR.
13'0" x 14'0"
PLANT LEDGE
BR.#2
CATHEDRAL CEILING
10'4" x 11'8"
MAIN FLOOR
2 CAR GAR.
20'0" x 20'0"

WIDTH 48'-0"
DEPTH 56'-4"

Style and Convenience

Price Code: B

his plan features:

- 'hree bedrooms
- 'wo full baths
- . sheltered Porch leads into an easy-care tile ntry
- pacious Living Room offers a cozy fireplace, iple window and access to Patio
- .n efficient Kitchen with a skylight, work .land, Dining area, walk-in Pantry and 'tility/Garage entry
- ecluded Master Bedroom highlighted by a aulted ceiling, access to Patio and a lavish Bath
- 'wo additional Bedrooms, one with a cathedral eiling, share a full Bath
- his home is designed with a slab foundation

AIN FLOOR — 1,653 SQ. FT.
.RAGE — 420 SQ. FT.

Total living area: 1,653 sq. ft.

PLAN NO.92283

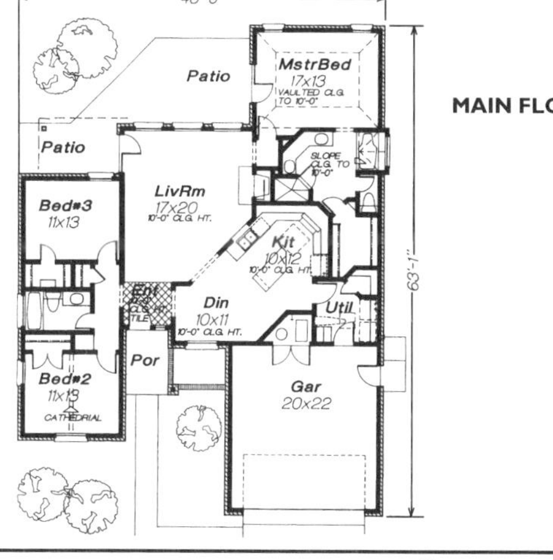

48'-0"
Patio
MstrBed
17x13
VAULTED CLG. TO 10'-0"
Patio
LivRm
17x20
Bed#3
11x13
Kit
10x12
Din
10x11
Util
Por
Bed#2
11x13
CATHEDRAL
Gar
20x22
63'-1"

MAIN FLOOR

Inviting Porch

Price Code: A

his plan features:

- 'hree bedrooms
- 'wo full baths
- large and spacious Living Room that adjoins e Dining Room for ease in entertaining
- private Bedroom wing offering a quiet mosphere
- Master Bedroom with his and her closets and a ivate Bathroom
- n efficient Kitchen with a walk-in Pantry
- iis home is designed with basement and slab undation options

.IN FLOOR — 1,160 SQ. FT.
3EMENT — 1,103 SQ. FT.
RAGE — 490 SQ. FT.

Total living area: 1,243 sq. ft.

PLAN NO.90682

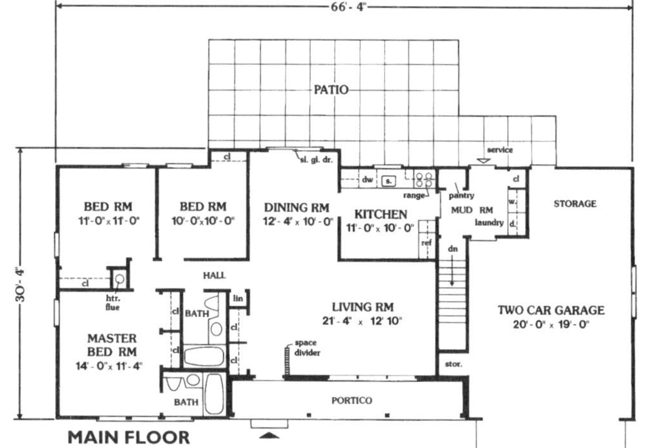

66'-4"
PATIO
BED RM
11'-0" x 11'-0"
BED RM
10'-0" x 10'-0"
DINING RM
12'-4" x 10'-0"
KITCHEN
11'-0" x 10'-0"
MUD RM
STORAGE
HALL
LIVING RM
21'-4" x 12'10"
TWO CAR GARAGE
20'-0" x 19'-0"
MASTER BED RM
14'-0" x 11'-4"
BATH
BATH
PORTICO
30'-4"

MAIN FLOOR

PLAN NO. 93183

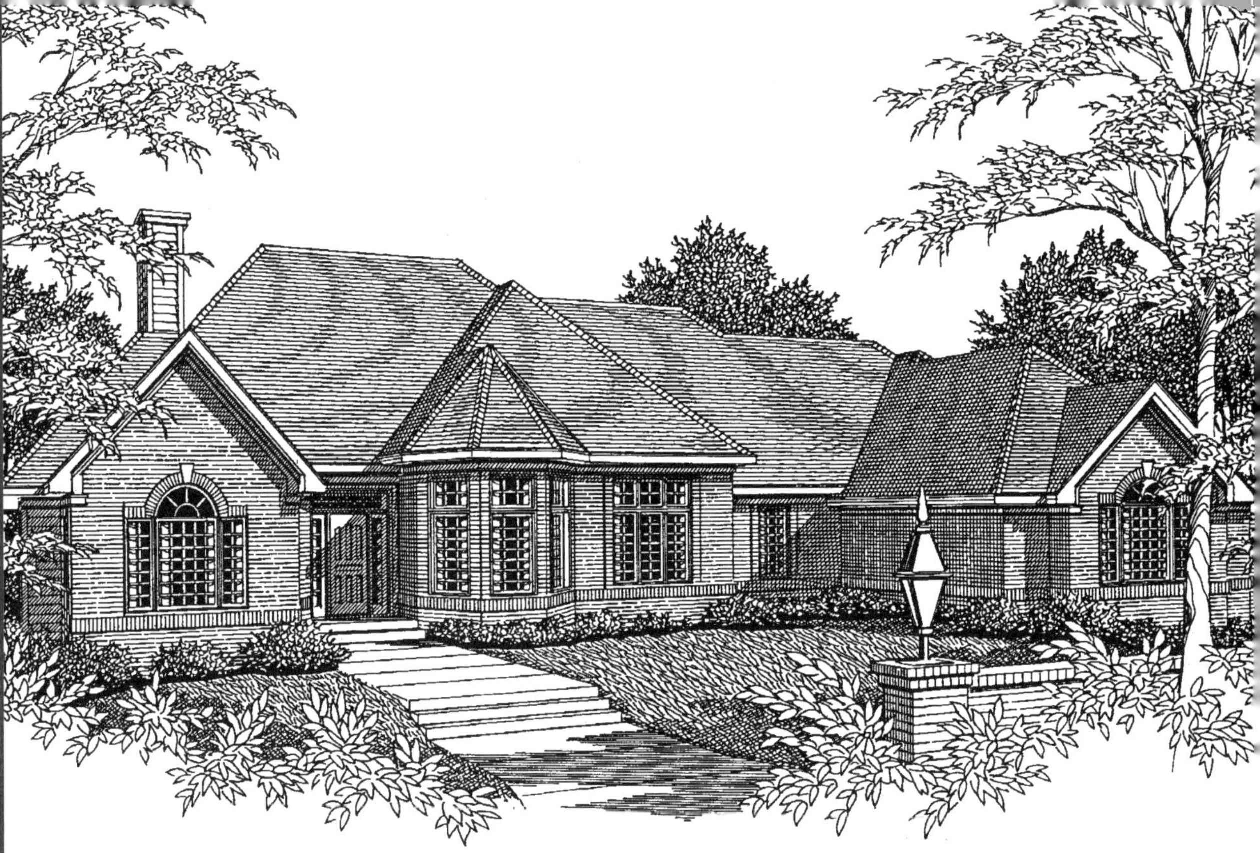

Gourmet's Dream

Price Code: F

- This plan features:
  - — Three bedrooms
  - — Two full and one half baths
- Formal Foyer invites guests into the comfort of the Great Room
- Formal Dining Room has arched entries and a large window
- Kitchen includes a center island and an abundance of cupboard space
- French doors open into the elegant Master Bedroom highlighted by a unique Sitting Area, two walk-in closets, and a private Master Bath
- This home is designed with a basement foundation

MAIN FLOOR — 2,600 SQ. FT.
BASEMENT — 2,600 SQ. FT.

Total living area:
2,600 sq. ft.

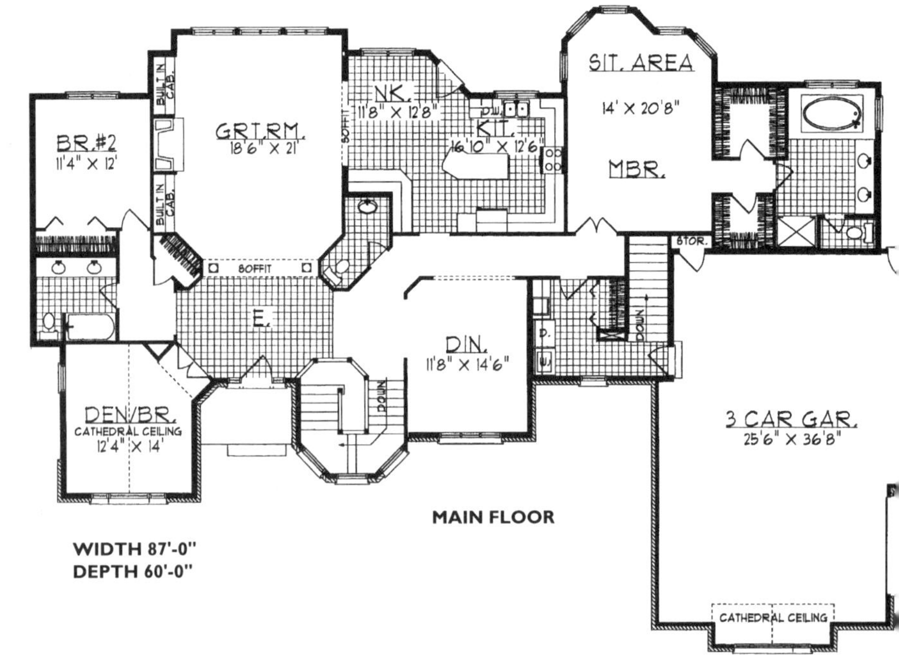
BR.#2
11'4" X 12'
BUILT IN CAB.
GRT.RM.
18'6" X 21'
NK.
11'8" X 12'8"
KIT.
16'10" X 12'6"
SIT. AREA
14' X 20'8"
MBR.
STOR.
BOFFIT
E.
DIN.
11'8" X 14'6"
DEN/BR.
CATHEDRAL CEILING
12'4" X 14'
DOWN
3 CAR GAR.
25'6" X 36'8"
MAIN FLOOR
WIDTH 87'-0"
DEPTH 60'-0"
CATHEDRAL CEILING

PLAN NO. 94907

WIDTH 40'-8"
DEPTH 46'-0"

Grt. rm. 14⁰ x 18⁴
Bfst. 11⁴ x 10⁰
COVERED PORCH
Kit. 13⁸ x 13⁸
PANT.
LIN.
SNACK BAR
R.
UP
DN
W.
D.
STORAGE
SEAT
E.
Din. 11⁰ x 12⁰
Gar. 20⁰ x 24⁸
COVERED PORCH
© Design Basics, Inc.

FIRST FLOOR

WHIRLPOOL
SEAT
Mbr. 13⁰ x 14⁴
CATHEDRAL CEILING
SKYLIGHT
LIN.
DN
Br. 2 10⁰ x 12⁰
Br. 3 11⁰ x 10⁰
10'-0" CLG.
SEAT

SECOND FLOOR

Victorian Accents

Price Code: C

- This plan features:
  - Three bedrooms
  - Two full and one half baths
- Covered Porch and double doors lead into Entry, accented by a window seat and curved banister staircase
- Decorative windows overlooking the backyard and a large fireplace highlight the Great Room
- This home is designed with a basement foundation
- Alternate foundation options available at an additional charge. Please call 1-800-235-5700 for more information.

FIRST FLOOR — 905 SQ. FT.
SECOND FLOOR — 863 SQ. FT.
BASEMENT — 905 SQ. FT.
GARAGE — 487 SQ. FT.

Total living area: 1,768 sq. ft.

PLAN NO. 98416

Bathed in Natural Light

Price Code: B

- This plan features:
- — Three bedrooms
- — Two full and one half baths
- A high, arched window illuminates the Foyer and adds style to the exterior of the home
- Vaulted ceilings in the the formal Dining Room, the Breakfast Room and the Great Room create elegance and volume
- The Master Suite is crowned with a decorative tray ceiling
- This home is designed with basement and crawlspace foundation options

FIRST FLOOR — 1,133 SQ. FT.
SECOND FLOOR — 486 SQ. FT.
BASEMENT — 1,133 SQ. FT.
BONUS — 134 SQ. FT.
GARAGE — 406 SQ. FT.

Total living area:
1,619 sq. ft.

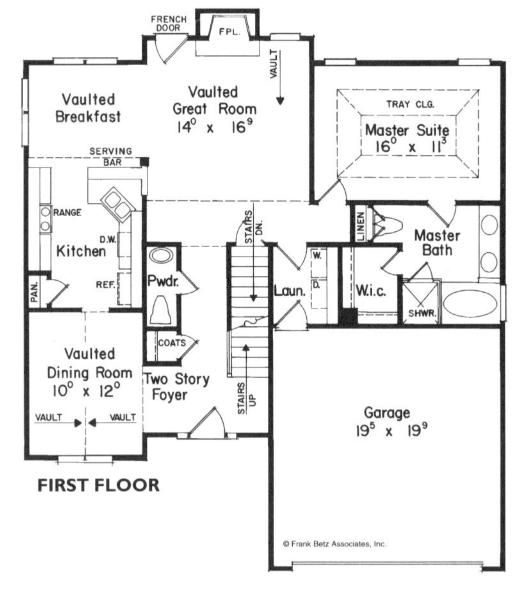

FRENCH DOOR
FPL.
VAULT
Vaulted Breakfast
Vaulted Great Room 14^{0} x 16^{9}
TRAY CLG.
Master Suite 16^{0} x 11^{3}
SERVING BAR
RANGE
D.W.
Kitchen
REF.
PAN.
Pwdr.
STAIRS DN.
LINEN
Master Bath
Laun.
W.
D.
W.i.c.
SHWR.
COATS
Vaulted Dining Room 10^{0} x 12^{0}
Two Story Foyer
VAULT
VAULT
STAIRS UP
Garage 19^{5} x 19^{9}
© Frank Betz Associates, Inc.

FIRST FLOOR

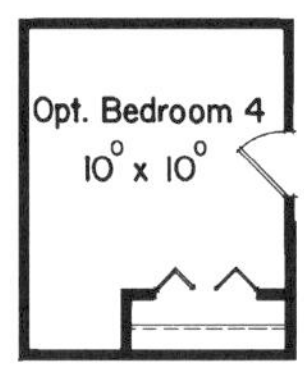

Opt. Bedroom 4 10^{0} x 10^{0}

OPTIONAL BEDROOM 4

WIDTH 41'-0"
DEPTH 46'-4"

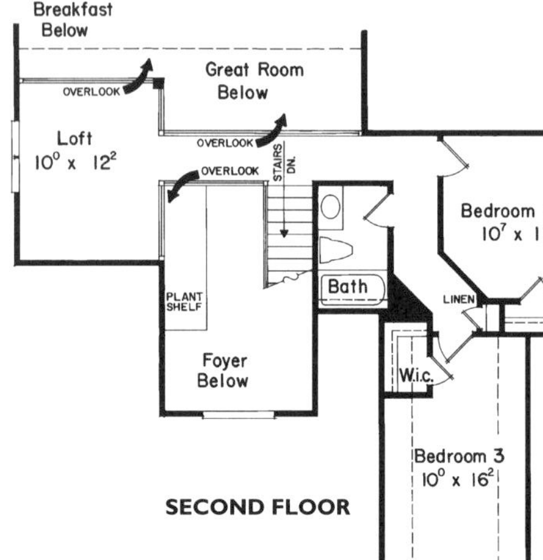

Breakfast Below
Great Room Below
OVERLOOK
OVERLOOK
OVERLOOK
Loft 10^{0} x 12^{2}
STAIRS DN.
Bedroom 2 10^{7} x 11^{2}
PLANT SHELF
Bath
LINEN
Foyer Below
W.i.c.
Bedroom 3 10^{0} x 16^{2}

SECOND FLOOR

PLAN NO. 24402

46'-1"
53'-1"
Mstr Br
13-9 x 11-10
cathedral
Br 2
9-11 x 11-7
Deck
linen
W
D
Br 3
9-11 x 11-4
Dining
7-11 x 10-8
Kitchen
11-8 x 10-8
furn. w/h
Living
24-1 x 14-4
cathedral
Garage
19-4 x 19-11
MAIN FLOOR

Cathedral Ceilings

Price Code: A

- This plan features:
- — Three bedrooms
- — Two full baths
- A spacious Living Room with a cathedral ceiling and elegant fireplace
- A Dining Room that adjoins both the Living Room and the Kitchen
- An efficient Kitchen with double sinks, ample cabinet space and peninsula counter that doubles as an eating bar
- A convenient hallway Laundry center
- This home is designed with crawl-space and slab foundation options

MAIN FLOOR — 1,346 SQ. FT.
GARAGE — 449 SQ. FT.

Total living area:
1,346 sq. ft.

PLAN NO. 20161

Delightful Doll House

Price Code: A

- This plan features:
- — Three bedrooms
- — Two full baths
- A sloped ceiling in the Living Room, which also has a focal point fireplace
- A decorative ceiling and sliding glass doors to the Deck in the Dining Room
- A Master Suite with a decorative ceiling, ample closet space and a private full Bath
- This home is designed with basement, crawlspace and slab foundation options

MAIN FLOOR — 1,307 SQ. FT.
BASEMENT — 1,298 SQ. FT.
GARAGE — 462 SQ. FT.

Total living area:
1,307 sq. ft.

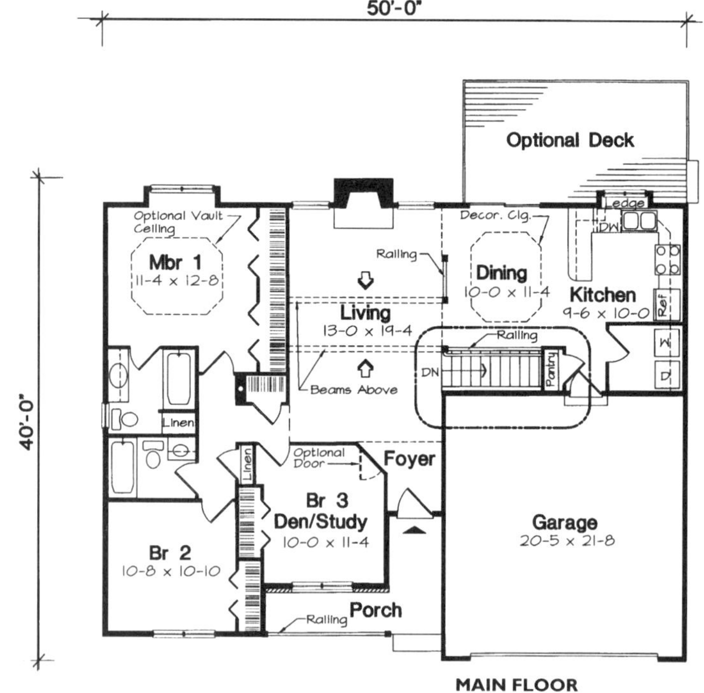
50'-0"
40'-0"
Optional Deck
Ledge
Optional Vault Ceiling
Mbr 1
11-4 x 12-8
Railing
Decor. Clg.
Dining
10-0 x 11-4
Kitchen
9-6 x 10-0
DW
Ref
Living
13-0 x 19-4
Railing
DN
Pantry
Beams Above
Linen
Linen
Optional Door
Foyer
Br 3
Den/Study
10-0 x 11-4
Garage
20-5 x 21-8
Br 2
10-8 x 10-10
Railing
Porch
MAIN FLOOR

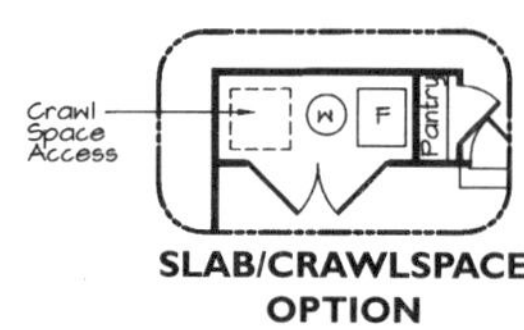
Crawl Space Access
W
F
Pantry

SLAB/CRAWLSPACE OPTION

Quaint Starter Home

Price Code: A

his plan features:

- hree bedrooms
- wo full baths
- vaulted ceiling gives an airy feeling to the ining and Living Rooms
- streamlined Kitchen includes a comfortable ork area, a double sink and ample cabinet pace
- cozy fireplace warms the Living Room
- Master Suite features a large closet, French oors leading to the Patio and a private Bath
- wo additional Bedrooms share a full Bathroom
- his home is designed with basement and slab oundation options

AIN FLOOR — 1,050 SQ. FT.
RAGE — 261 SQ. FT.

Total living area:
1,050 sq. ft.

PLAN NO. 92400

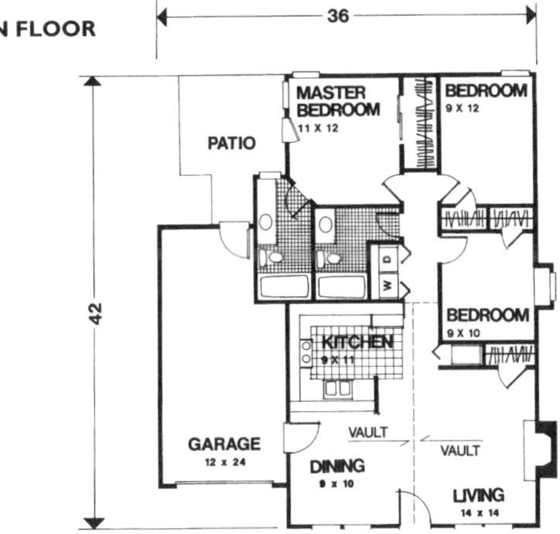
MAIN FLOOR
36
42
MASTER BEDROOM
11 X 12
BEDROOM
9 X 12
PATIO
BEDROOM
9 X 10
KITCHEN
9 X 11
GARAGE
12 x 24
VAULT
VAULT
DINING
9 x 10
LIVING
14 x 14

nposing and Practical Design

Price Code: D

his plan features:

- hree bedrooms
- wo full and one half baths
- wo-story keystone entrance with sidelights ads into Foyer with balcony above
- ay windows illuminate formal Dining and iving Rooms elegantly
- xpansive Family Room with cozy fireplace and wall of windows with access to Patio
- fficient, U-shaped Kitchen is convenient to both ormal and informal Dining Areas
- rivate Master Bedroom crowned by decorative eiling features a walk-in closet, two vanities and arden tub bath
- Two additional Bedrooms, full Bath and convenient Laundry closet complete the second floor
- his home is designed with basement and slab oundation options

RST FLOOR — 1,126 SQ. FT.
COND FLOOR — 959 SQ. FT.
ASEMENT — 458 SQ. FT.
ARAGE — 627 SQ. FT.

Total living area:
2,085 sq. ft.

PLAN NO. 93213

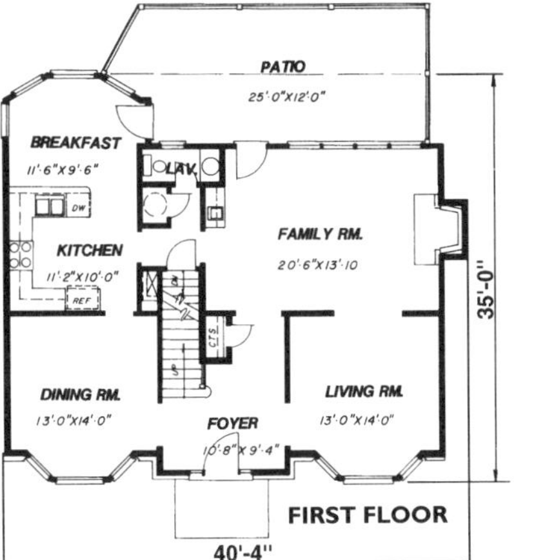
PATIO
25'0"X12'0"
BREAKFAST
11'6"X9'6"
LAV.
KITCHEN
11'2"X10'0"
FAMILY RM.
20'6"X13'10
DINING RM.
13'0"X14'0"
FOYER
10'8"X9'4"
LIVING RM.
13'0"X14'0"
35'-0"
FIRST FLOOR
40'-4"

BDRM.2
12'0"X11'0"
BATH
M.BATH
BALCONY
7'0"X9'0"
M.BDRM.
13'0"X17'0"
BDRM.3
13'0"X12'8
OPEN TO FOYER
SECOND FLOOR

PLAN NO. 34011

Windows Add Warmth

Price Code: B

- This plan features:
  - — Three bedrooms
  - — Two full baths
- A Master Suite with huge his and her walk-in closets and private Bath
- A second and third Bedroom with ample closet space
- A Kitchen equipped with an island counter, and flowing easily into the Dining and Family Rooms
- This home is designed with basement, slab and crawlspace foundation options

MAIN FLOOR— 1,672 SQ. FT.
OPTIONAL GARAGE — 566 SQ. FT.

Total living area:
1,672 sq. ft.

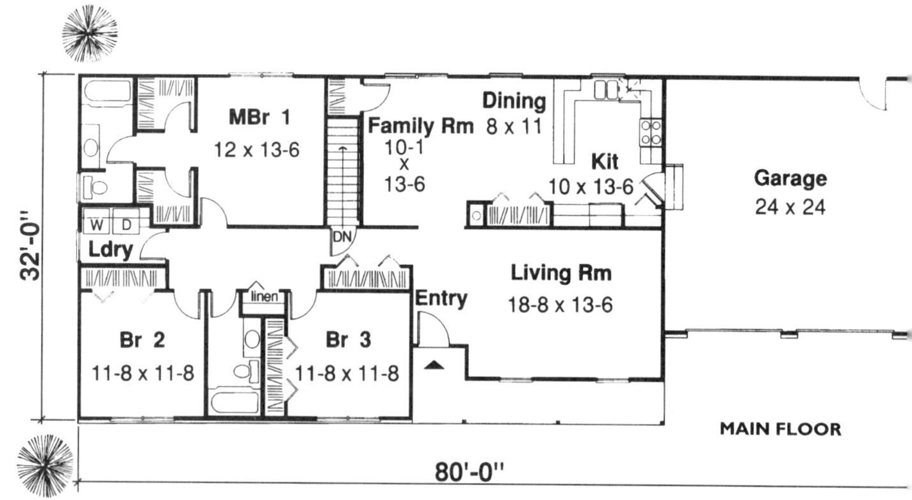
MBr 1
12 x 13-6
Family Rm
10-1
x
13-6
Dining
8 x 11
Kit
10 x 13-6
Garage
24 x 24
W
D
Ldry
DN
linen
Living Rm
18-8 x 13-6
Entry
Br 2
11-8 x 11-8
Br 3
11-8 x 11-8
32'-0"
80'-0"
MAIN FLOOR

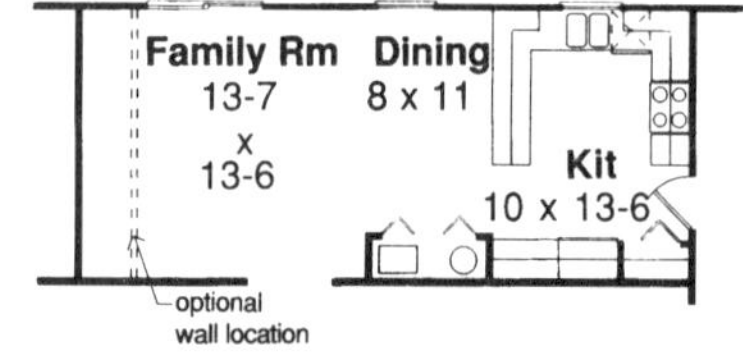
Family Rm
13-7
x
13-6
Dining
8 x 11
Kit
10 x 13-6
optional
wall location
OPTIONAL MAIN FLOOR

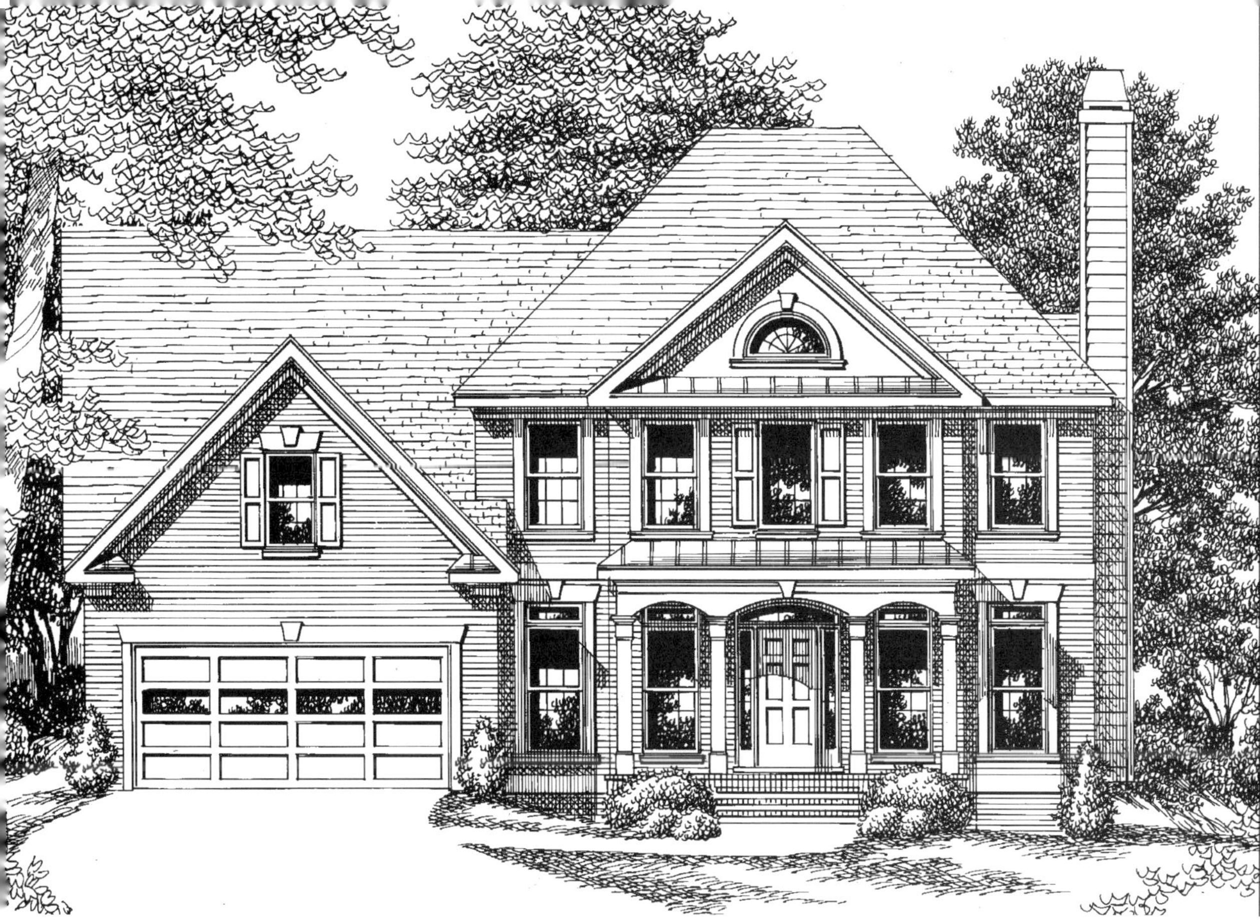

PLAN NO. 98407

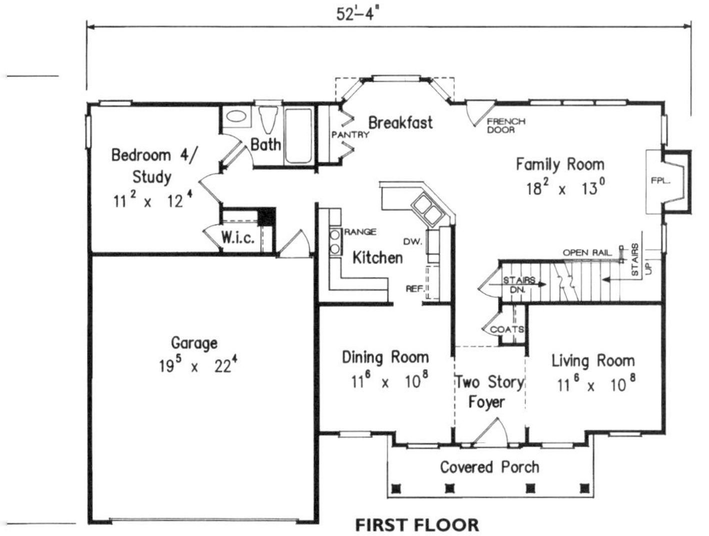

52'-4"

FIRST FLOOR

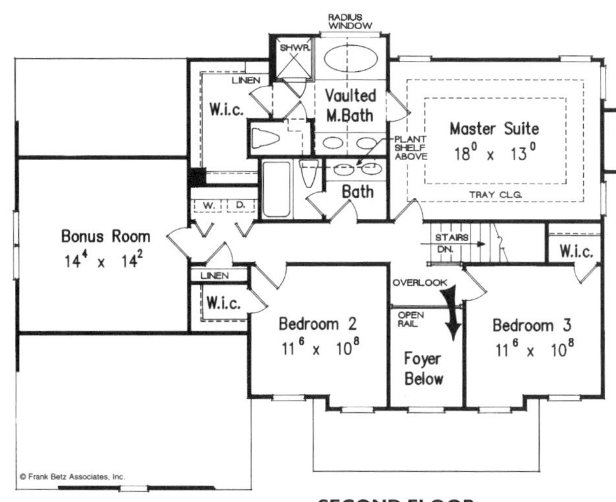
RADIUS WINDOW
SHWR.
LINEN
W.i.c.
Vaulted M.Bath
Master Suite
18^0 x 13^0
PLANT SHELF ABOVE
TRAY CLG.
Bath
W. D.
STAIRS DN.
W.i.c.
Bonus Room
14^4 x 14^2
LINEN
W.i.c.
OVERLOOK
OPEN RAIL
Bedroom 2
11^6 x 10^8
Foyer Below
Bedroom 3
11^6 x 10^8
© Frank Betz Associates, Inc.

SECOND FLOOR

Contemporary Interior

Price Code: D

- This plan features:
  - — Four bedrooms
  - — Three full baths
- The two-story Foyer is flanked by the Living Room and the Dining Room
- The Family Room features a fireplace and a French door
- The Master Suite, with a tray ceiling, has an attached Bath with a vaulted ceiling and a radius window
- This home is designed with basement, slab and crawlspace foundation options

FIRST FLOOR — 1,135 SQ. FT.
SECOND FLOOR — 917 SQ. FT.
BONUS — 216 SQ. FT.
BASEMENT — 1,135 SQ. FT.
GARAGE — 452 SQ. FT.

Total living area:
2,052 sq. ft.

PLAN NO. 99255

Compact Colonial

Price Code: A

- This plan features:
- — Three bedrooms
- — Two full and one half baths
- The traditional Entry has a landing staircase, a closet and a Powder Room
- The Living Room, with a focal point fireplace, opens to the formal Dining Room for ease in entertaining
- The efficient L-shaped Kitchen has a built-in Pantry, an eating Nook and a Garage entry
- The corner Master Bedroom has a private Bath
- This home is designed with a basement foundation

FIRST FLOOR — 624 SQ. FT.
SECOND FLOOR — 624 SQ. FT.
GARAGE — 510 SQ. FT.

Total living area: 1,248 sq. ft.

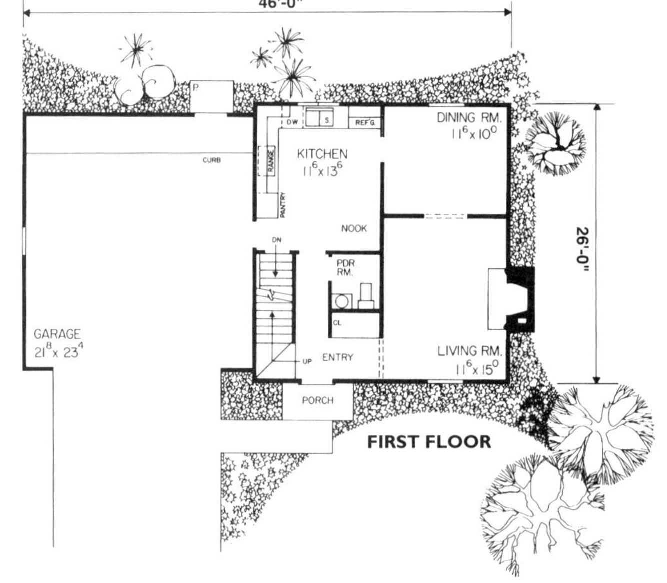

46'-0"
26'-0"
DINING RM. 11⁶x10⁰
KITCHEN 11⁶x13⁶
DW
S
REFG.
RANGE
PANTRY
CURB
NOOK
DN
PDR RM.
CL
GARAGE 21⁸x23⁴
UP
ENTRY
LIVING RM. 11⁶x15⁰
PORCH
P

FIRST FLOOR

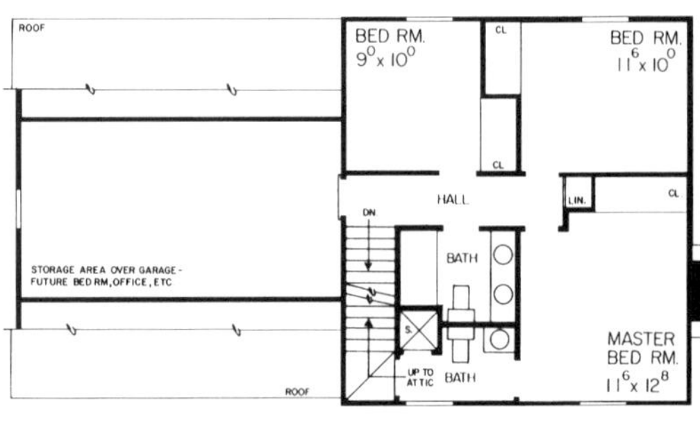

ROOF
BED RM. 9⁰x10⁰
BED RM. 11⁶x10⁰
CL
HALL
LIN.
DN
BATH
STORAGE AREA OVER GARAGE - FUTURE BED RM, OFFICE, ETC
UP TO ATTIC
BATH
MASTER BED RM. 11⁶x12⁸

SECOND FLOOR

PLAN NO.99238

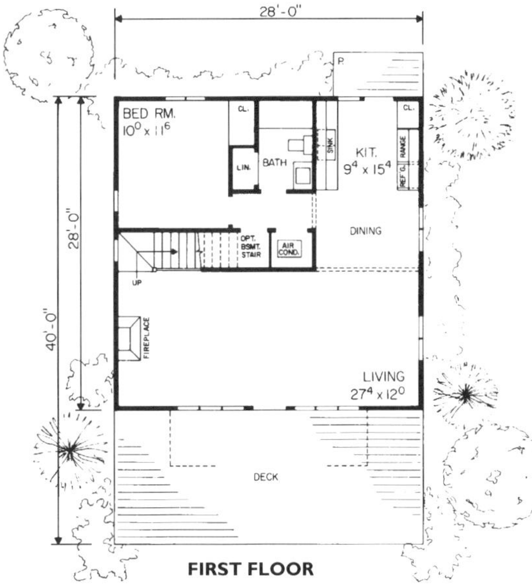

Economical, Vacation Home

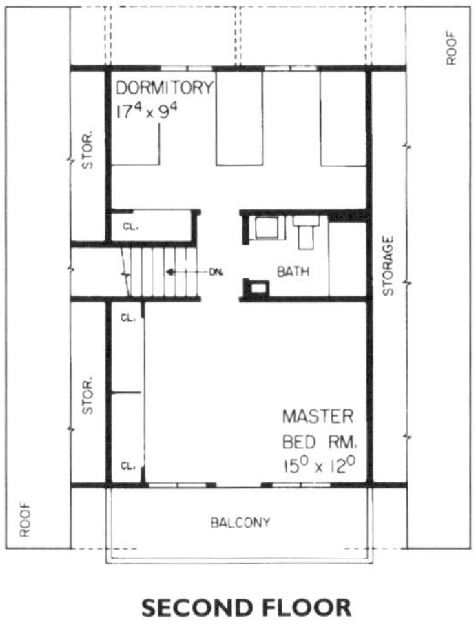

Price Code: A

- This plan features:
- — Three bedrooms
- — Two full baths
- The large bright Living Room has a fireplace at one end and plenty of room for separate activities
- The galley-style Kitchen adjoins the Dining area
- The second floor Master Bedroom has a children's Dormitory across the hall
- The balcony is located outside the Master Bedroom
- This home is designed with a basement foundation

FIRST FLOOR — 784 SQ. FT.
SECOND FLOOR — 504 SQ. FT.

Total living area:
1,288 sq. ft.

FIRST FLOOR

SECOND FLOOR

PLAN NO. 98473

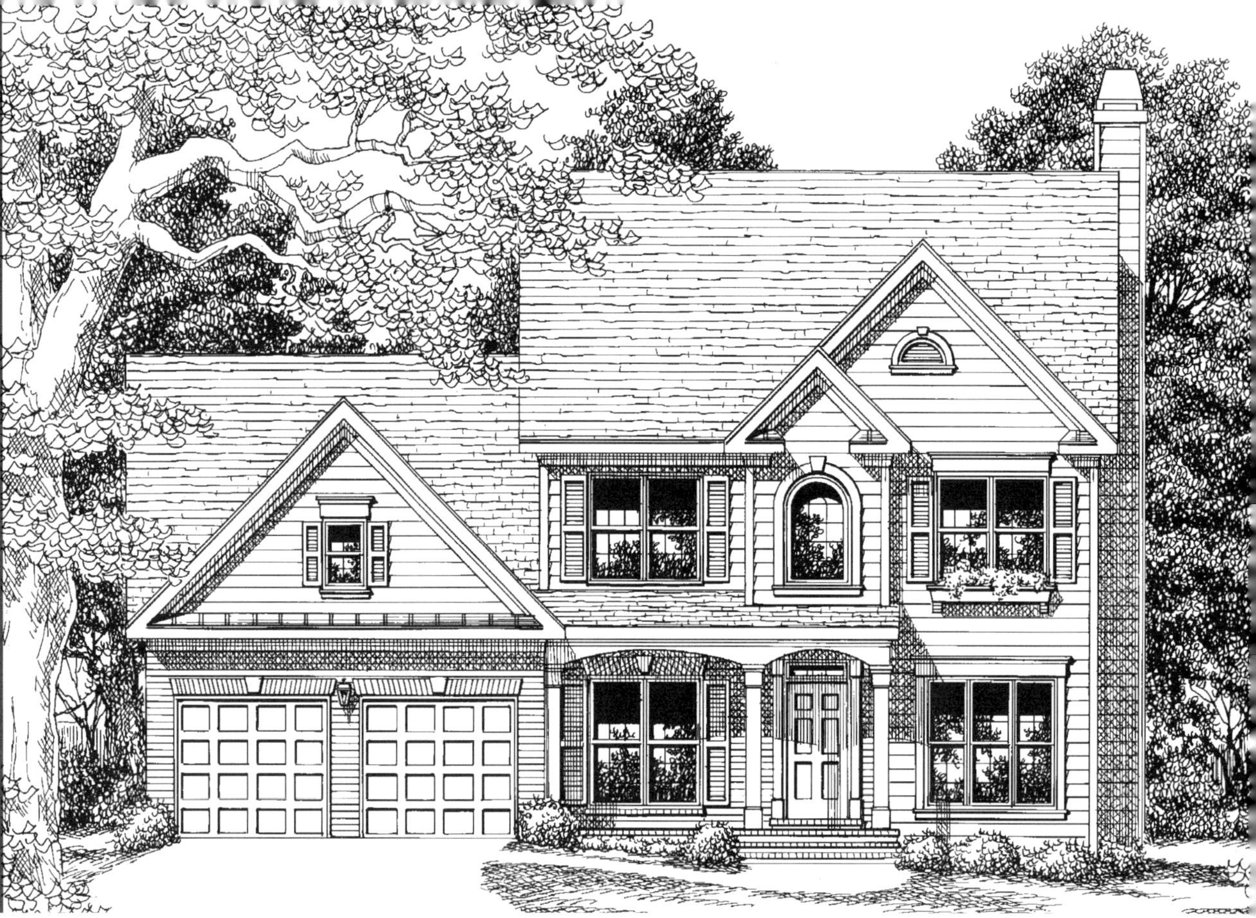

For the Growing Family

Price Code: C

- This plan features:
- — Four bedrooms
- — Three full baths
- There is an open rail staircase in the Living Room, and the Dining Room features easy access to the Kitchen
- The Kitchen is equipped with a corner double sink, a servicing bar and adjoins the Breakfast Area
- This home is designed with basement and crawlspace foundation options

FIRST FLOOR — 1,103 SQ. FT.
SECOND FLOOR — 759 SQ. FT.
BONUS — 342 SQ. FT.
BASEMENT — 1,103 SQ. FT.
GARAGE — 420 SQ. FT.

**Total living area:
1,862 sq. ft.**

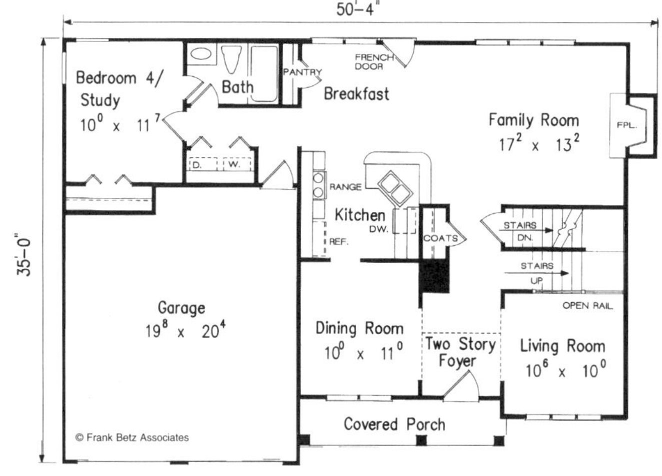

50'-4"
35'-0"
Bedroom 4/ Study
10^{0} x 11^{7}
Bath
PANTRY
FRENCH DOOR
Breakfast
Family Room
17^{2} x 13^{2}
FPL.
D. W.
RANGE
Kitchen
DW.
REF.
COATS
STAIRS DN.
STAIRS UP
OPEN RAIL
Garage
19^{8} x 20^{4}
Dining Room
10^{0} x 11^{0}
Two Story Foyer
Living Room
10^{6} x 10^{0}
© Frank Betz Associates
Covered Porch

FIRST FLOOR

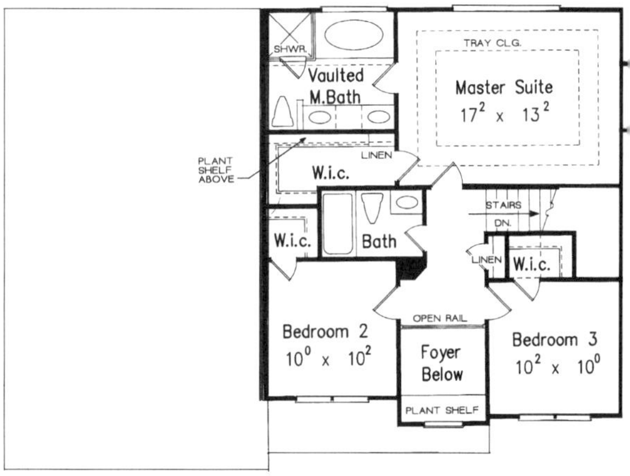

SECOND FLOOR

Center-Island Kitchen

Price Code: A

'his plan features:

- Three bedrooms
- Two full baths
- 'his efficient floor plan easily supports a busy amily's lifestyle
- ienerous center-island Kitchen facilitates quick ieal preparation
- 'amily Room features a distinctive corner fire- lace
- Bedroom wing contains three Bedrooms each vith abundant closet space
- Deck connects home to Garage
- 'his home is designed with crawlspace and slab oundation options

AIN FLOOR — 1,475 SQ. FT.
ARAGE & STORAGE — 455 SQ. FT

Total living area:
1,475 sq. ft.

PLAN NO. 93416

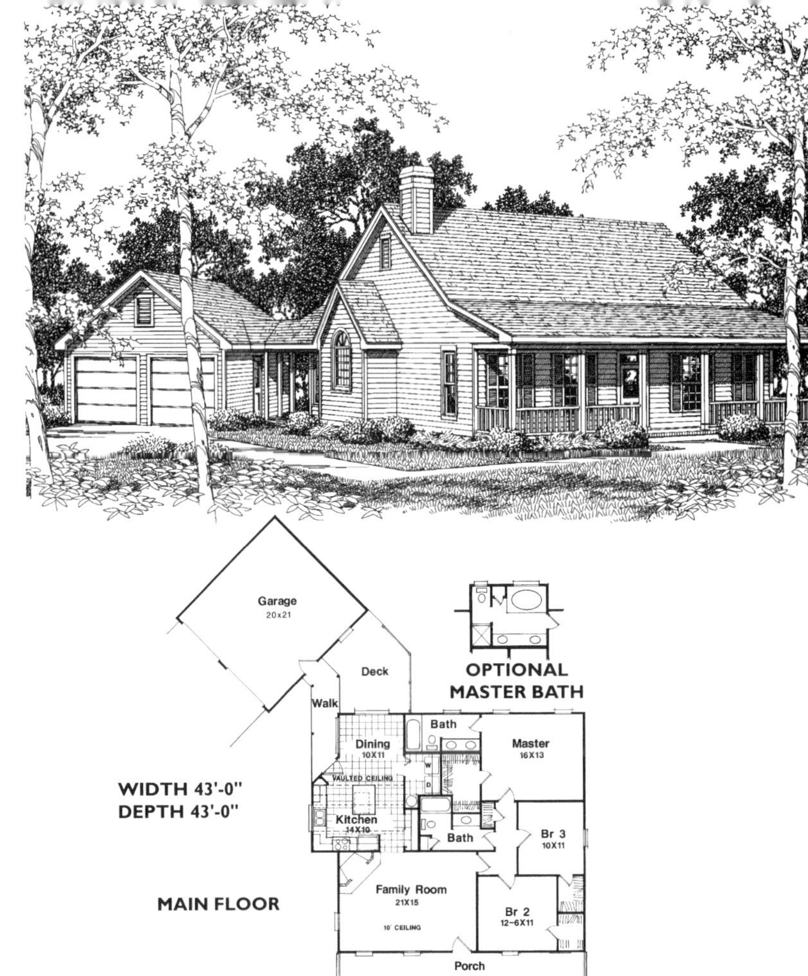

Garage
20x21
Deck
Walk
OPTIONAL
MASTER BATH
Dining
10X11
VAULTED CEILING
Bath
Master
16X13
Kitchen
14X10
Bath
Br 3
10X11
WIDTH 43'-0"
DEPTH 43'-0"
Family Room
21X15
10' CEILING
Br 2
12-6X11
MAIN FLOOR
Porch

Country Classic

Price Code: A

'his plan features:

- Three bedrooms
- Two full baths
- An efficient, U-shaped Kitchen with center land workspace makes meal preparation a snap
- 'he full-width Porch and covered Carport offers rotection from the elements
- pecial features in the Master Bedroom include a ecorative ceiling and private Bath with separate hower and tub
- 'his home is designed with crawlspace or slab oundation options

AIN FLOOR — 1,333 SQ. FT.

Total living area:
1,333 sq. ft.

PLAN NO. 93453

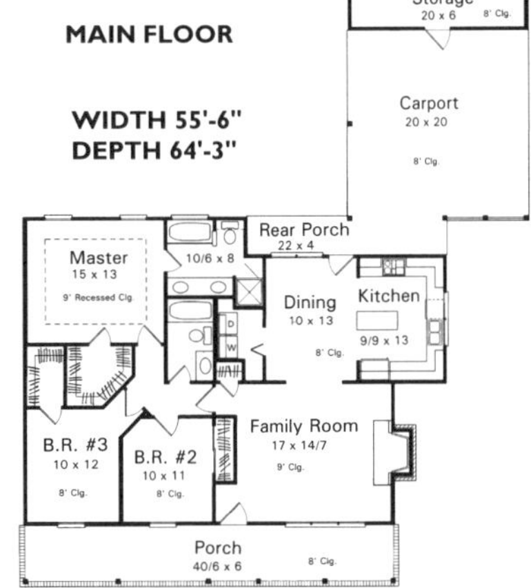

Storage
20 x 6
MAIN FLOOR
Carport
20 x 20
WIDTH 55'-6"
DEPTH 64'-3"
Rear Porch
22 x 4
Master
15 x 13
9' Recessed Clg.
10/6 x 8
Dining
10 x 13
Kitchen
9/9 x 13
Family Room
17 x 14/7
B.R. #3
10 x 12
B.R. #2
10 x 11
Porch
40/6 x 6

PLAN NO. 34003

Delightful, Compact Home

Price Code: A

- This plan features:
  - — Three bedrooms
  - — Two full baths
- A fireplaced Living Room brightened by a wonderful picture window
- A counter island featuring double sinks separating the Kitchen and Dining Areas
- A Master Bedroom that includes a private Master Bath and double closets
- This home is designed with basement, slab and crawlspace foundation options

MAIN FLOOR — 1,146 SQ. FT.

Total living area:
1,146 sq. ft.

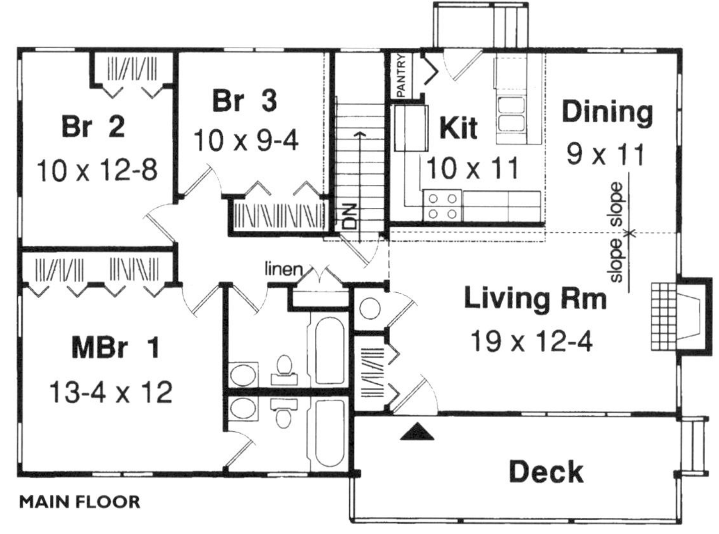

Br 2
10 x 12-8
Br 3
10 x 9-4
PANTRY
Kit
10 x 11
Dining
9 x 11
slope
slope
DN
linen
Living Rm
19 x 12-4
MBr 1
13-4 x 12
Deck

MAIN FLOOR

WIDTH 44'-0"
DEPTH 28'-0"

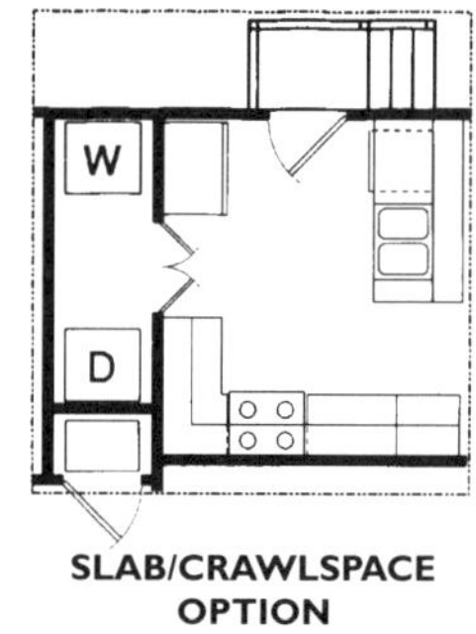

W
D

SLAB/CRAWLSPACE OPTION

Cul-de-Sac Favorite

Price Code: D

his plan features:

- 'our bedrooms
- 'wo full and one half baths
- he incredible efficiency of the design of this ome makes it seem much larger than it is
- triking gables and large Palladian windows contribute to this home's considerable curb appeal
- he large Parlor opens to the Dining Room
- he fireplaced Gathering Room is removed from e formal areas of the house to create a real mily retreat
- our Bedrooms on the second floor make this ome ideal for the growing family
- his home is designed with a basement foundaon
- dditional foundation options available at an lditional charge. Please call 1-800-235-5700 for ore information.

ST FLOOR — 1,113 SQ. FT.
'OND FLOOR — 965 SQ. FT.
SEMENT — 1,113 SQ. FT.
RAGE — 486 SQ. FT.

Total living area: 2,078 sq. ft.

PLAN NO.94936

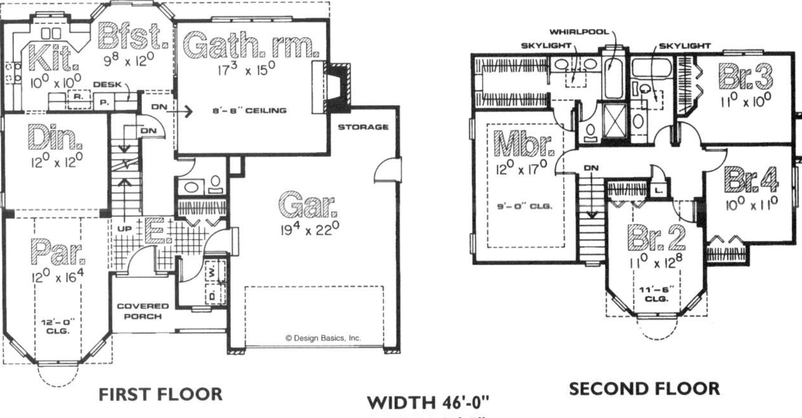

Kit.
10⁰ x 10⁰
Bfst.
9⁸ x 12⁰
Gath. rm.
17³ x 15⁰
8'-8" CEILING
DESK
DN
STORAGE
Din.
12⁰ x 12⁰
Gar.
19⁴ x 22⁰
UP
E.
Par.
12⁰ x 16⁴
12'-0" CLG.
COVERED PORCH
© Design Basics, Inc.
WHIRLPOOL
SKYLIGHT
SKYLIGHT
Br. 3
11⁰ x 10⁰
Mbr.
12⁰ x 17⁰
9'-0" CLG.
DN
Br. 4
10⁰ x 11⁰
Br. 2
11⁰ x 12⁸
11'-6" CLG.

FIRST FLOOR

WIDTH 46'-0"
DEPTH 41'-5"

SECOND FLOOR

osen Up in Your Whirlpool Tub

Price Code: B

'his plan features:

- Three bedrooms
- Two full and one half baths
- nviting wrap-around Porch leads into large 'oyer with big closet and views of the fireplaced Great Room
- 'he second floor Master Bedroom Suite offers he serenity of a whirlpool tub and ample closet pace
- 'his home is designed with a basement foundaon
- Additional foundation options available at an dditional charge. Please call 1-800-235-5700 for nore information.

RST FLOOR — 891 SQ. FT.
COND FLOOR — 759 SQ. FT.
SEMENT — 891 SQ. FT.
ARAGE — 484 SQ. FT.

Total living area: 1,650 sq. ft.

PLAN NO.94938

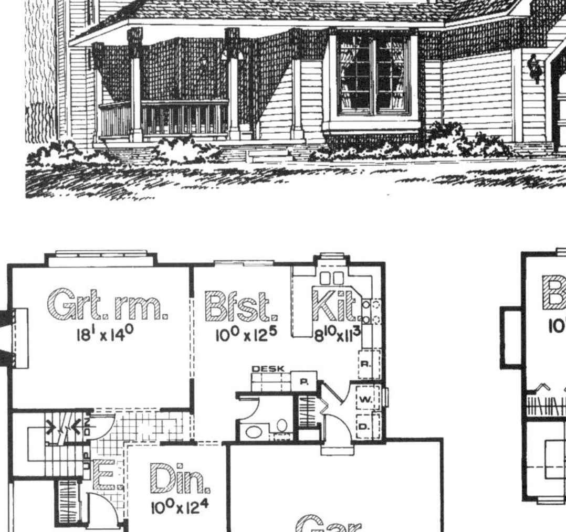

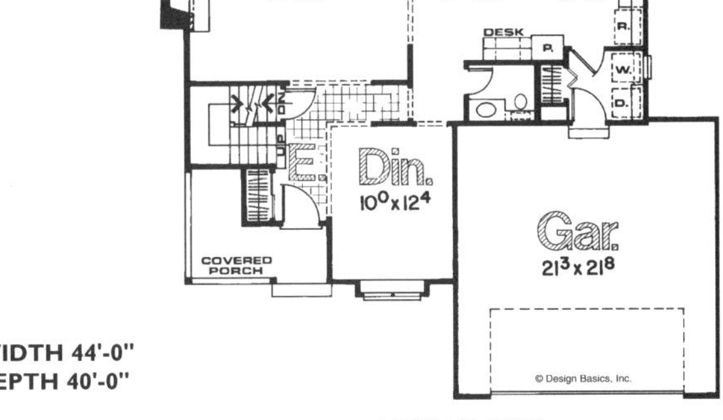

Grt. rm.
18¹ x 14⁰
Bfst.
10⁰ x 12⁵
Kit.
8¹⁰ x 11³
DESK
E.
Din.
10⁰ x 12⁴
Gar.
21³ x 21⁸
COVERED PORCH
© Design Basics, Inc.

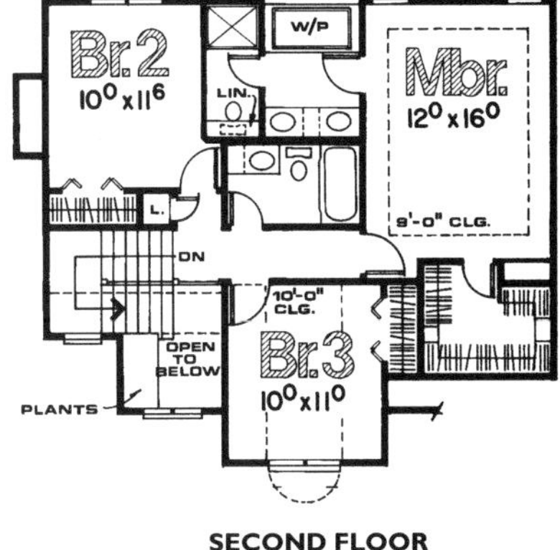

W/P
Br. 2
10⁰ x 11⁶
LIN.
Mbr.
12⁰ x 16⁰
9'-0" CLG.
DN
10'-0" CLG.
OPEN TO BELOW
Br. 3
10⁰ x 11⁰
PLANTS

WIDTH 44'-0"
DEPTH 40'-0"

SECOND FLOOR

FIRST FLOOR

PLAN NO.90689

Formal Balance

Price Code: A

- This plan features:
- — Three bedrooms
- — Two full baths
- The long Living Room has a cathedral ceilin and a heat-circulating fireplace as the focal p
- A bow window in the Dining Room adds ele- gance as well as natural light
- The well-equiped Kitchen efficiently serves b the Dinette and the formal Dining Room
- The Master Bedroom includes three closets a Bath with sliding glass doors to a private Dec which could be the perfect spot for a hot tub
- This home is designed with basement and sla foundation options

MAIN FLOOR — 1,374 SQ. FT.
MUDROOM/LAUNDRY — 102 SQ. FT
BASEMENT — 1,361 SQ. FT.
GARAGE — 548 SQ. FT.

Total living area:
1,476 sq. ft.

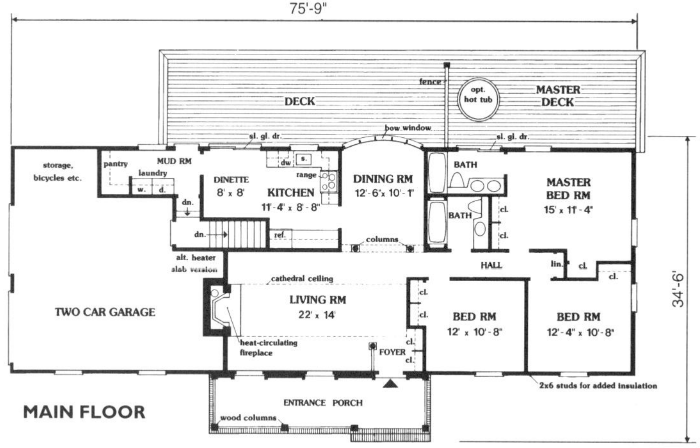
75'-9"
DECK
fence
opt. hot tub
MASTER DECK
sl. gl. dr.
bow window
storage, bicycles etc.
pantry
MUD RM
laundry
DINETTE 8' x 8'
KITCHEN 11'-4' x 8'-8"
DINING RM 12'-6"x 10'-1"
BATH
MASTER BED RM 15' x 11'-4"
columns
HALL
alt. heater slab version
cathedral ceiling
LIVING RM 22' x 14'
TWO CAR GARAGE
BED RM 12' x 10'-8"
BED RM 12'-4" x 10'-8"
heat-circulating fireplace
FOYER
ENTRANCE PORCH
wood columns
2x6 studs for added insulation
34'-6"
MAIN FLOOR

PLAN NO.93133

Tandem Garage

Price Code: C

- This plan features:
- — Three bedrooms
- — Two full baths
- Open Foyer leads into spacious Living Room highlighted by a wall of windows
- Country-size Kitchen with efficient, U-shaped counter, work island, and eating Nook offers access to the backyard
- French doors open to the pampering Master Bedroom with bay window alcove, walk-in clo and double-vanity Bath
- Two additional Bedrooms with large closets, sh a full Bath
- This home is designed with a basement founda

MAIN FLOOR —1,761 SQ. FT.
BASEMENT — 1,761 SQ. FT.
GARAGE — 658 SQ. FT.

Total living area:
1,761 sq. ft.

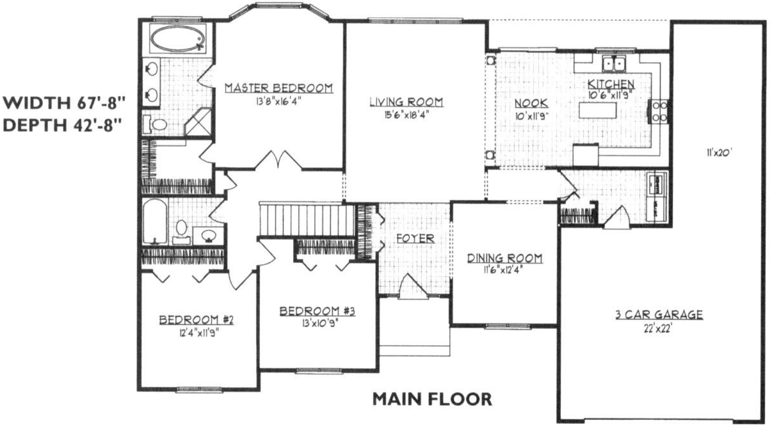
WIDTH 67'-8"
DEPTH 42'-8"
MASTER BEDROOM 13'8"x16'4"
LIVING ROOM 15'6"x18'4"
NOOK 10'x11'9"
KITCHEN 10'6"x11'9"
11'x20'
FOYER
DINING ROOM 11'6"x12'4"
BEDROOM #2 12'4"x11'9"
BEDROOM #3 13'x10'9"
3 CAR GARAGE 22'x22'
MAIN FLOOR

Private Master Suite

Price Code: D

his plan features:

- 'hree bedrooms
- 'wo full and one half bath
- ecluded Master Bedroom Suite tucked into the ear left corner of the home with a five-piece ath and two walk-in closets
- wo additional Bedrooms at the opposite side of e home sharing the full Bath in the hall
- xpansive Living Room highlighted by a corner replace and access to the rear Porch
- itchen is sandwiched between the bright, bayed ook and the formal Dining Room, providing ase in serving
- his home is designed with crawlspace and slab undation options

AIN FLOOR — 2,069 SQ. FT.
RAGE — 481 SQ. FT.

Total living area:
2,069 sq. ft.

PLAN NO.96505

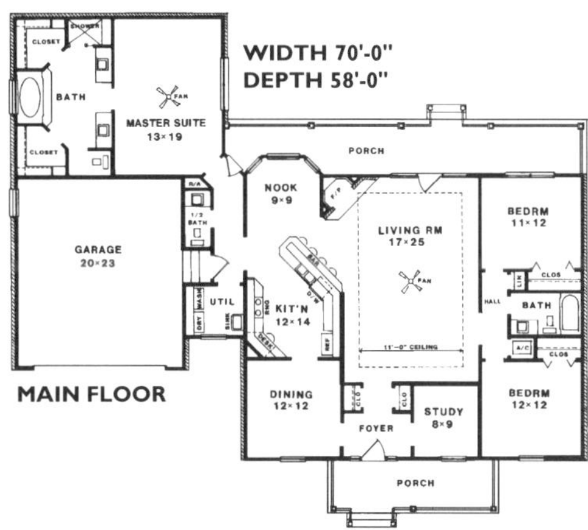
WIDTH 70'-0"
DEPTH 58'-0"
CLOSET
SHOWER
BATH
CLOSET
MASTER SUITE
13×19
PORCH
NOOK
9×9
LIVING RM
17×25
BEDRM
11×12
GARAGE
20×23
KIT'N
12×14
UTIL
BATH
DINING
12×12
FOYER
STUDY
8×9
BEDRM
12×12
PORCH
MAIN FLOOR

Farmhouse Favorite

Price Code: C

his plan features:

- 'our bedrooms
- 'wo full and one half baths
- eep wrap-around Porch contributes to the ountry appeal of this wonderful home
- ne Great Room has built-ins, a fireplace, access the Porch and a bay-windowed Nook
- ne formal Dining Room is separated from the -shaped Kitchen by a set of French doors
- ne second floor includes a vaulted Sitting Area the head of the stairs
- ne Master Bedroom has a large walk-in closet nd private Bath
- wo additional second floor Bedrooms share a ll Bath
- ne two-car Garage includes space for a Shop
- his home is designed with a basement, crawl-ace and slab foundation options

ST FLOOR — 1,014 SQ. FT.
COND FLOOR — 826 SQ. FT.
RAGE — 690 SQ. FT.

Total living area:
1,840 sq. ft.

PLAN NO.96819

WIDTH 62'-7"
DEPTH 45'-0"
8' WIDE COVERED PORCH
STEPS
NOOK
GREAT ROOM
22'-6"x14'-0"
(9' CLG)
BOOKS
F.P.
BOOKS
DW
KITCHEN
10'-9"x11'-8"
(9' CLG)
FRIG
LNDRY
COATS
9' CLG
PWDR
PANTRY
DESK
FRENCH DOORS
SHOP/STORAGE
11'-10"x15'-5"
(9'-6" CLG)
OFFICE/GUEST/
HOME SCHOOL
11'-8"x10'-1"
(9' CLG)
FOYER
(9' CLG)
UP
DN
FORMAL DINING
11'-8"x11'-0"
(9' CLG)
COATS
GARAGE
21'-0"x21'-10"
(9'-6" CLG)
9' OVERHEAD DOOR
8' WIDE COVERED PORCH
STEPS
FIRST FLOOR

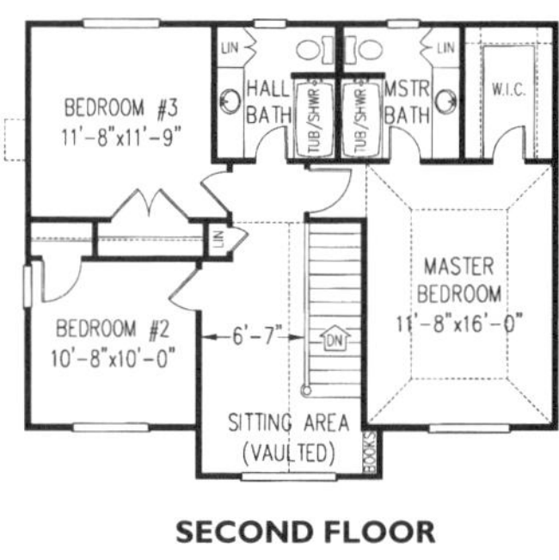
BEDROOM #3
11'-8"x11'-9"
LIN
HALL
BATH
TUB/SHWR
MSTR
BATH
LIN
W.I.C.
BEDROOM #2
10'-8"x10'-0"
6'-7"
DN
MASTER
BEDROOM
11'-8"x16'-0"
SITTING AREA
(VAULTED)
SECOND FLOOR

PLAN NO.96509

Country Charmer

Price Code: A

- This plan features:
  - —Three bedrooms
  - —Two full baths
- Quaint front Porch is perfect for sitting and rela:
- Great Room opens into Dining Area and Kitche
- Corner Deck in rear of home is accessible from Kitchen and Master Suite
- Master Suite features a private Bath, walk-in clc and built-in shelves
- Two large secondary Bedrooms in the front of t home share a Bath
- Two-car Garage is tucked away in the rear of th home
- This home is designed with crawlspace and slab foundation options

MAIN FLOOR — 1,438 SQ. FT.
GARAGE — 486 SQ. FT.

Total living area:
1,438 sq. ft.

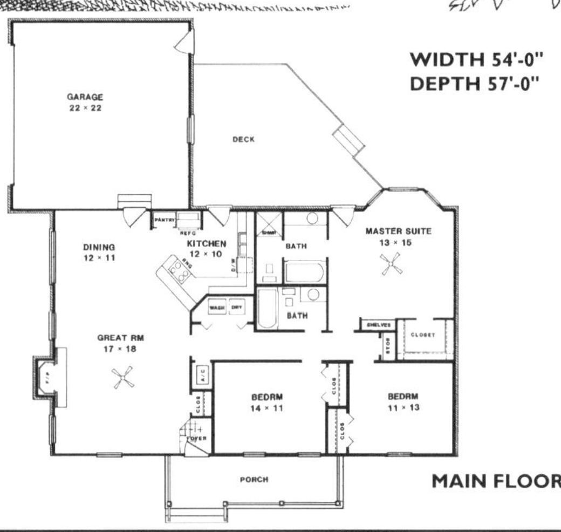
WIDTH 54'-0"
DEPTH 57'-0"
GARAGE 22 × 22
DECK
DINING 12 × 11
KITCHEN 12 × 10
BATH
MASTER SUITE 13 × 15
BATH
GREAT RM 17 × 18
BEDRM 14 × 11
BEDRM 11 × 13
PORCH

MAIN FLOOR

PLAN NO.26112

Contemporary Design

Price Code: A

- This plan features:
  - — Two bedrooms, with possible third bedroom/d
  - — One full and one half baths
- This plan features a solar design with Souther glass doors, windows, and an air-lock Entry
- R-26 insulation is used for floors and sloping ceilings
- The Deck rims the front of the home
- The Dining Room is separated from the Living Room by a half wall
- The efficient Kitchen has an eating bar
- This home is designed with a basement founda

FIRST FLOOR — 911 SQ. FT.
SECOND FLOOR — 576 SQ. FT.
BASEMENT — 911 SQ. FT.

Total living area:
1,487 sq. ft.

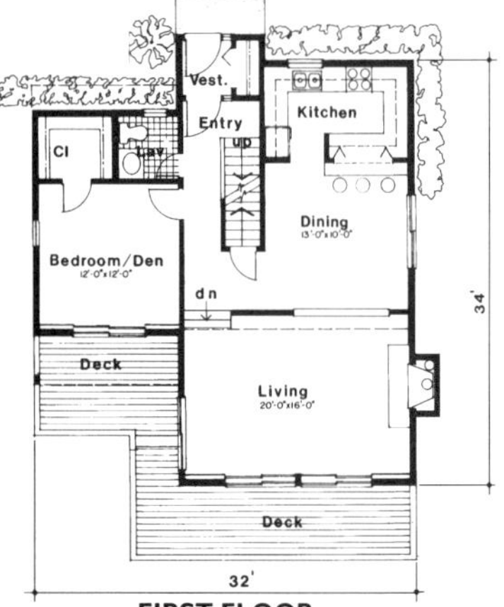
Vest.
Entry
Kitchen
Cl
Lav
Dining
Bedroom/Den
dn
Deck
Living
Deck
34'
32'

FIRST FLOOR

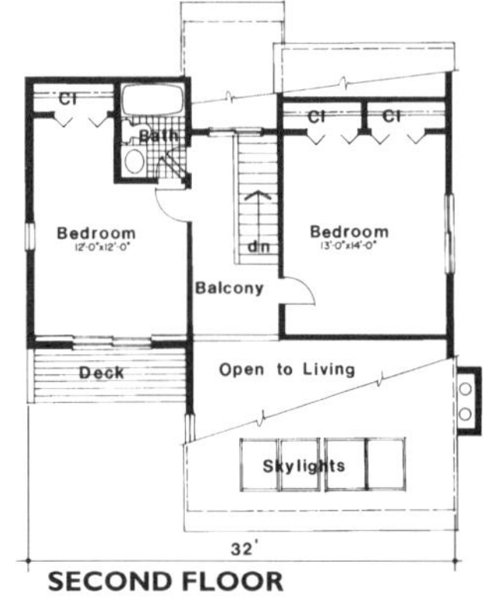
Cl
Bath
Cl
Cl
Bedroom
Bedroom
dn
Balcony
Deck
Open to Living
Skylights
32'

SECOND FLOOR

PLAN NO. 32109

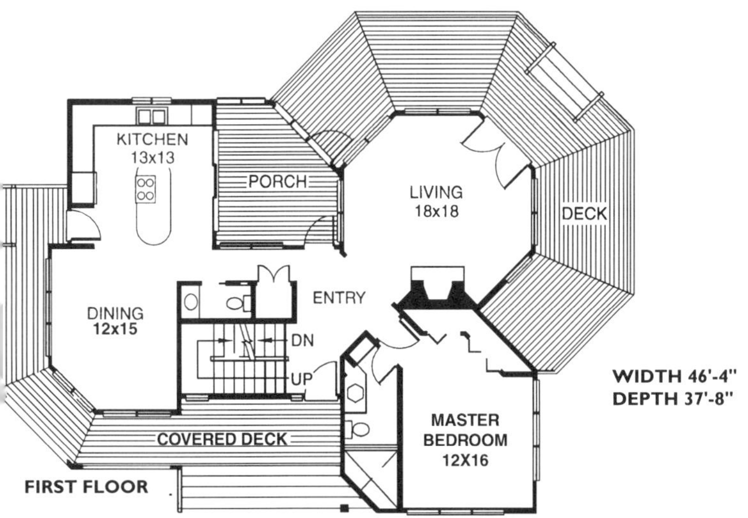
KITCHEN
13x13
PORCH
LIVING
18x18
DECK
DINING
12x15
ENTRY
DN
UP
MASTER
BEDROOM
12X16
COVERED DECK
FIRST FLOOR
WIDTH 46'-4"
DEPTH 37'-8"

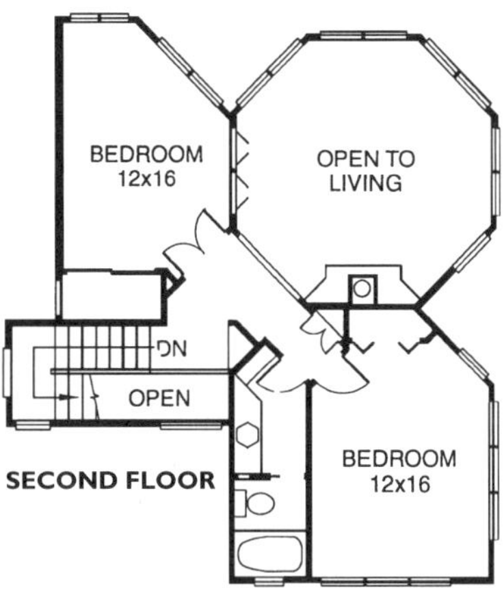
BEDROOM
12x16
OPEN TO
LIVING
DN
OPEN
BEDROOM
12x16
SECOND FLOOR

Prairie-Style Retreat

Price Code: D

- This plan features:
  - — Three bedrooms
  - — Two full and one half baths
- Shingle siding, tall expanses of glass and wrapping decks accent the exterior
- The octagonal Living Room has a two-story ceiling and French doors
- The first floor Master Suite offers a private Bath
- Two additional, second floor Bedrooms share a full Bath
- This home is designed with a basement foundation

FIRST FLOOR — 1,213 SQ. FT.
SECOND FLOOR — 825 SQ. FT.
BASEMENT — 1,213 SQ. FT.
PORCH — 144 SQ. FT.

Total living area:
2,038 sq. ft.

PLAN NO.97100

Family Faire

Price Code: D

- This plan features:
- — Four bedrooms
- — One full, one half and one three-quarter baths
- The two-story Entry, with large coat closet, op to the Study at the front of the house and the large, fireplaced Great Room at the rear of the house
- The eat-in Kitchen features a sunny bump-out, efficient L-shaped counter configuration and c ter-island work area
- The half Bath and Laundry Room are just off t Kitchen on either side of a short hall that leads the lovely bay-windowed Dining Room
- The second floor Master Bedroom has a cathec ceiling, large walk-in closet and three-quarter Bath
- Three additional second floor Bedrooms have ample closet space and share a full Bath
- This home is designed with a basement founda

FIRST FLOOR — 995 SQ. FT.
SECOND FLOOR — 1,125 SQ. FT.
BASEMENT — 995 SQ. FT.

Total living area: 2,120 sq. ft.

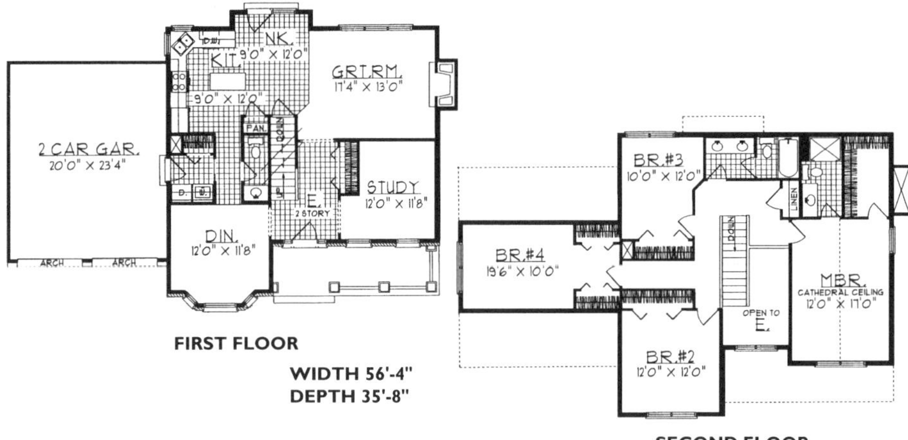

NK. 9'0" X 12'0"
KIT. 9'0" X 12'0"
GRT.RM. 17'4" X 13'0"
2 CAR GAR. 20'0" X 23'4"
STUDY 12'0" X 11'8"
E. 2 STORY
DIN. 12'0" X 11'8"
BR.#3 10'0" X 12'0"
BR.#4 13'6" X 10'0"
MBR. CATHEDRAL CEILING 12'0" X 17'0"
BR.#2 12'0" X 12'0"
OPEN TO E.

FIRST FLOOR

WIDTH 56'-4"
DEPTH 35'-8"

SECOND FLOOR

PLAN NO.97113

Perfectly Sized Home

Price Code: A

- This plan features:
- — Three bedrooms
- — Two full baths
- The Entry hallway is crowned in a vaulted ceil and views the Great Room
- A direct vent fireplace accents the Great Room while a large window views the backyard vista
- The split bedroom floor plan is designed for th utmost privacy in Master Bedroom
- The efficient Kitchen flows into the dining roo for ease in serving
- This home is designed with a basement founda

MAIN FLOOR — 1,416 SQ. FT.

Total living area: 1,416 sq. ft.

WIDTH 48'-0"
DEPTH 55'-4"

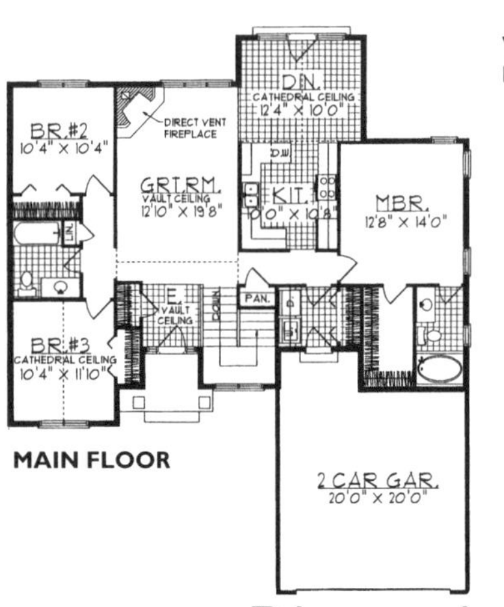

BR.#2 10'4" X 10'4"
DIRECT VENT FIREPLACE
GRT.RM. VAULT CEILING 12'10" X 19'8"
DIN. CATHEDRAL CEILING 12'4" X 10'0"
MBR. 12'8" X 14'0"
E. VAULT CEILING
PAN.
BR.#3 CATHEDRAL CEILING 10'4" X 11'10"
2 CAR GAR. 20'0" X 20'0"

MAIN FLOOR

PLAN NO. 24319

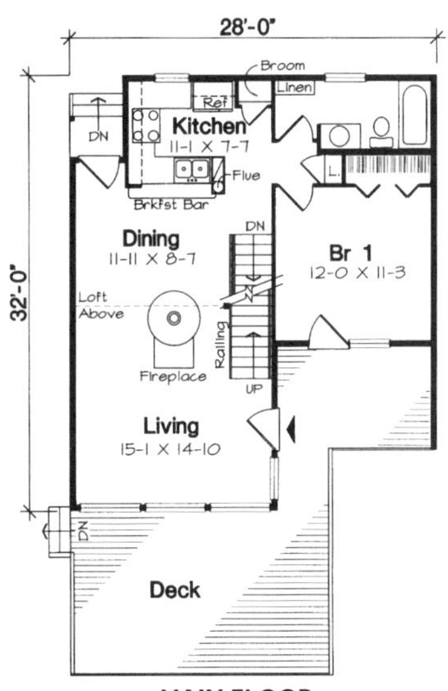

28'-0"
32'-0"
Broom
Linen
Ref
Kitchen
11-1 X 7-7
Flue
Brkfst Bar
DN
Dining
11-11 X 8-7
Br 1
12-0 X 11-3
Loft Above
Fireplace
Railing
UP
Living
15-1 X 14-10
DN
Deck

MAIN FLOOR

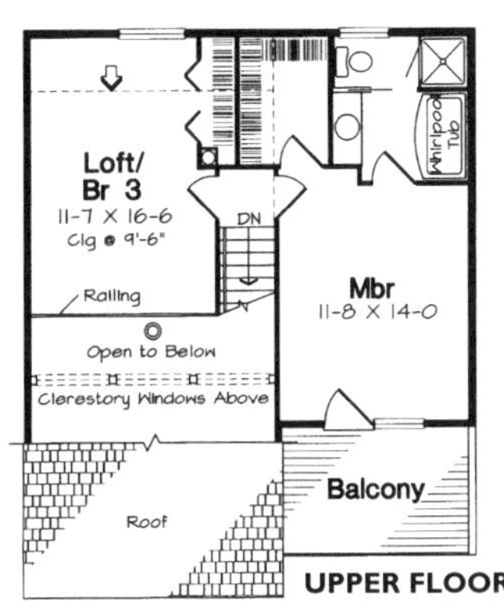

Loft/
Br 3
11-7 X 16-6
Clg @ 9'-6"
DN
Whirlpool Tub
Railing
Mbr
11-8 X 14-0
Open to Below
Clerestory Windows Above
Roof
Balcony

UPPER FLOOR

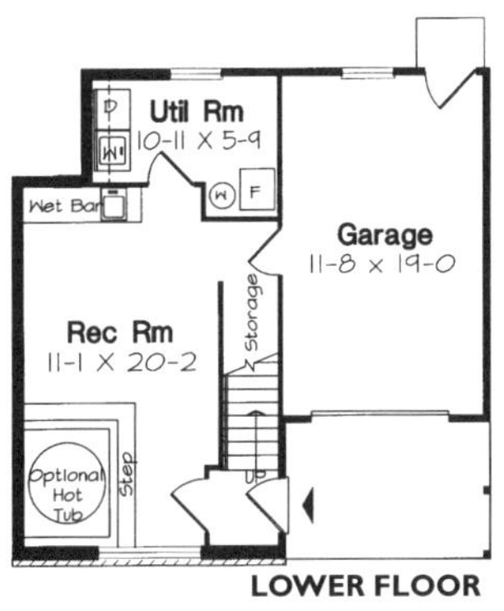

Util Rm
10-11 X 5-9
W
F
Wet Bar
Garage
11-8 x 19-0
Rec Rm
11-1 X 20-2
Storage
Optional Hot Tub
Step
UP

LOWER FLOOR

Home with Many Views

Price Code: B

- This plan features:
  - — Three bedrooms
  - — Two full baths
- Large Decks and windows take full advantage of the view
- The fireplace divides the Living Room and the Dining Room
- The Kitchen flows into the Dining Room
- The Master Bedroom features a full Master Bath
- The Recreation Room sports a whirlpool tub and a bar
- This home is designed with a basement foundation

MAIN FLOOR — 728 SQ. FT.
UPPER FLOOR — 573 SQ. FT.
LOWER FLOOR — 409 SQ. FT.
GARAGE — 244 SQ. FT.

Total living area:
1,710 sq. ft.

PLAN NO.97219

Secluded Study/Bedroom

Price Code: D

- This plan features:
- — Four bedrooms
- — Three full and one half baths
- The Kitchen includes a Pantry and easy acces the formal Dining Room
- The first floor Study, with nearby Bath, can b used as a fourth Bedroom
- This home is designed with basement and cra space foundation options

FIRST FLOOR — 1,257 SQ. FT.
SECOND FLOOR — 871 SQ. FT.
BASEMENT — 1,257 SQ. FT.
BONUS ROOM — 444 SQ. FT.
GARAGE — 462 SQ. FT.

Total living area:
2,128 sq. ft.

WIDTH 61'-0"
DEPTH 40'-6"

Study/ Bedroom 4 11⁰ x 12⁵ · Laund. · Breakfast · Family Room 20⁰ x 13⁰ · Bath · W.i.c. · Kitchen · Pwdr. · Garage 20⁰ x 21⁸ · Dining Room 11⁸ x 11⁰ · Living Room 12⁰ x 10⁰ · Two Story Foyer · Covered Porch

copyright © 1997 frank betz associates, inc.

FIRST FLOOR

Bedroom 2 11⁰ x 11⁸ · W.i.c. · Vaulted M.Bath · Bath · Master Suite 12⁰ x 18⁰ · Bedroom 3 11⁸ x 10⁰ · Foyer Below

SECOND FLOOR

Bath · Bedroom 2 11⁰ x 11⁸ · Opt. Bonus 15¹ x 23⁵ · W.i.c. · Bedroom 3 11⁸ x 10⁰

SECOND FLOOR W/ OPTIONAL BONUS ROOM

PLAN NO.97254

Elegant Ceiling Treatment

Price Code: B

- This plan features:
- — Three bedrooms
- — Two full baths
- A cozy wrapping front Porch sheltering entra
- Dining Room defined by columns at the entrances
- Kitchen highlighted by a peninsula counter/ serving bar
- Breakfast Room flowing from the Kitchen
- Vaulted ceiling highlighting the Great Room which also includes a fireplace
- Master Suite crowned in a tray ceiling over th Bedroom, a Sitting Room and plush Master E
- Two additional Bedrooms are located at the o side of the house
- This home is designed with basement and cra space foundation options

MAIN FLOOR — 1,692 SQ. FT.
BONUS ROOM — 358 SQ. FT.
BASEMENT — 1,705 SQ. FT.
GARAGE — 472 SQ. FT.

Total living area:
1,692 sq. ft.

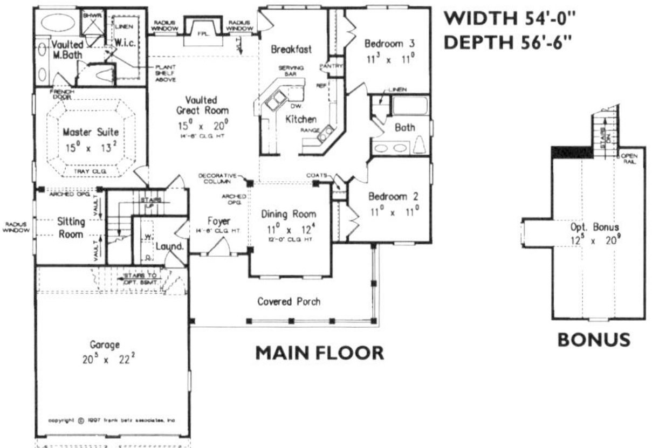
WIDTH 54'-0"
DEPTH 56'-6"
Vaulted M.Bath
W.i.c.
Breakfast
Bedroom 3 11³ x 11⁰
Vaulted Great Room 15⁰ x 20⁰
Master Suite 15⁰ x 13²
Kitchen
Bath
Bedroom 2 11⁰ x 11⁰
Sitting Room
Foyer
Laund.
Dining Room 11⁰ x 12⁴
Covered Porch
Garage 20⁵ x 22²
copyright © 1997 frank betz associates, inc.
MAIN FLOOR
Opt. Bonus 12⁵ x 20⁹
BONUS

To order your Blueprints, call 1-800-235-5700

PLAN NO. 98410

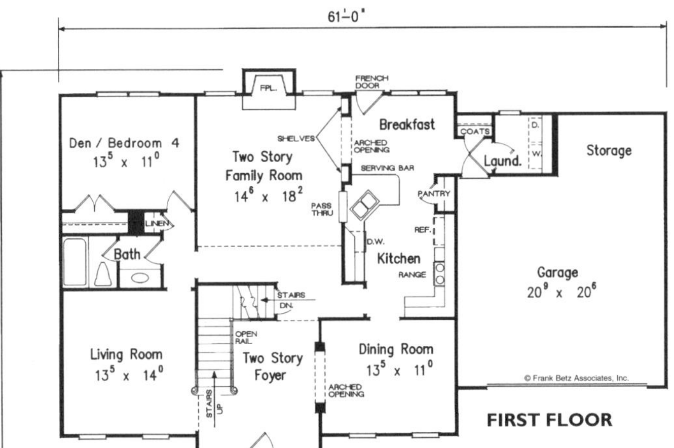
61'-0"
FPL.
FRENCH DOOR
Breakfast
COATS
Den / Bedroom 4
13^{5} x 11^{0}
SHELVES
ARCHED OPENING
Two Story Family Room
14^{6} x 18^{2}
SERVING BAR
Laund.
Storage
PANTRY
LINEN
PASS THRU
REF.
Bath
D.W.
Kitchen
RANGE
Garage
20^{9} x 20^{6}
STAIRS DN.
OPEN RAIL
Living Room
13^{5} x 14^{0}
Two Story Foyer
Dining Room
13^{5} x 11^{0}
ARCHED OPENING
STAIRS UP
© Frank Betz Associates, Inc.
FIRST FLOOR

Magnificent Manor

Price Code: E

- This plan features:
  - Four bedrooms
  - Three full baths
- The efficient Kitchen opens to the formal Dining Room and Breakfast Area
- The two-story Family Room is highlighted by a fireplace framed by windows
- A tray ceiling crowns the Master Bedroom
- This home is designed with basement and crawlspace foundation options

FIRST FLOOR — 1,428 SQ. FT.
SECOND FLOOR — 961 SQ. FT.
BONUS — 472 SQ. FT.
BASEMENT — 1,428 SQ. FT.
GARAGE — 507 SQ. FT.

Total living area:
2,389 sq. ft.

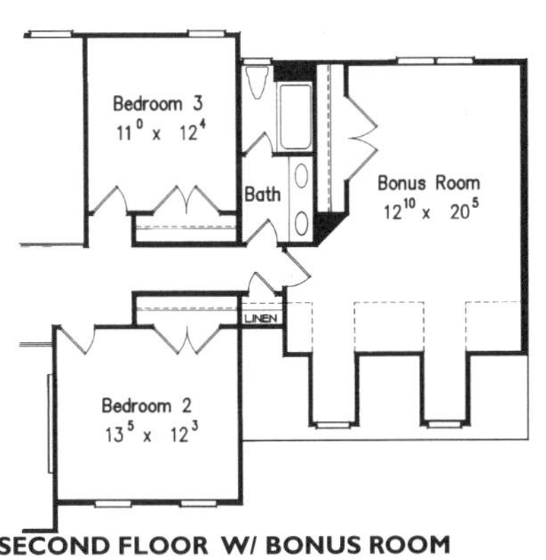
Bedroom 3
11^{0} x 12^{4}
Bath
Bonus Room
12^{10} x 20^{5}
LINEN
Bedroom 2
13^{5} x 12^{3}
SECOND FLOOR W/ BONUS ROOM

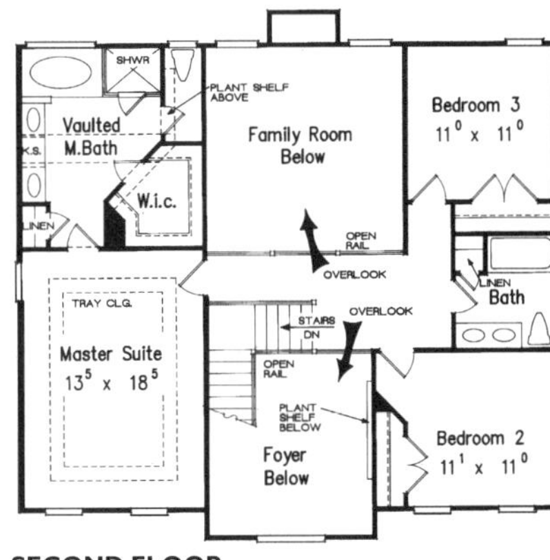
SHWR
PLANT SHELF ABOVE
Vaulted M.Bath
Family Room Below
Bedroom 3
11^{0} x 11^{0}
W.i.c.
LINEN
OPEN RAIL
OVERLOOK
Bath
TRAY CLG.
STAIRS DN
OPEN RAIL
Master Suite
13^{5} x 18^{5}
PLANT SHELF BELOW
Foyer Below
Bedroom 2
11^{1} x 11^{0}
SECOND FLOOR

PLAN NO. 92531

Enhanced by a Columned Porch

Price Code: C

- This plan features:
- — Three bedrooms
- — Two full baths
- A Great Room with a fireplace and decorative ceiling
- A large efficient Kitchen with Breakfast Area
- A Master Bedroom with a private Master Bath and walk-in closet
- A formal Dining Room conveniently located near the Kitchen
- This home is designed with crawlspace and slab foundation options

MAIN FLOOR — 1,754 SQ. FT.
GARAGE — 552 SQ. FT.

**Total living area:
1,754 sq. ft.**

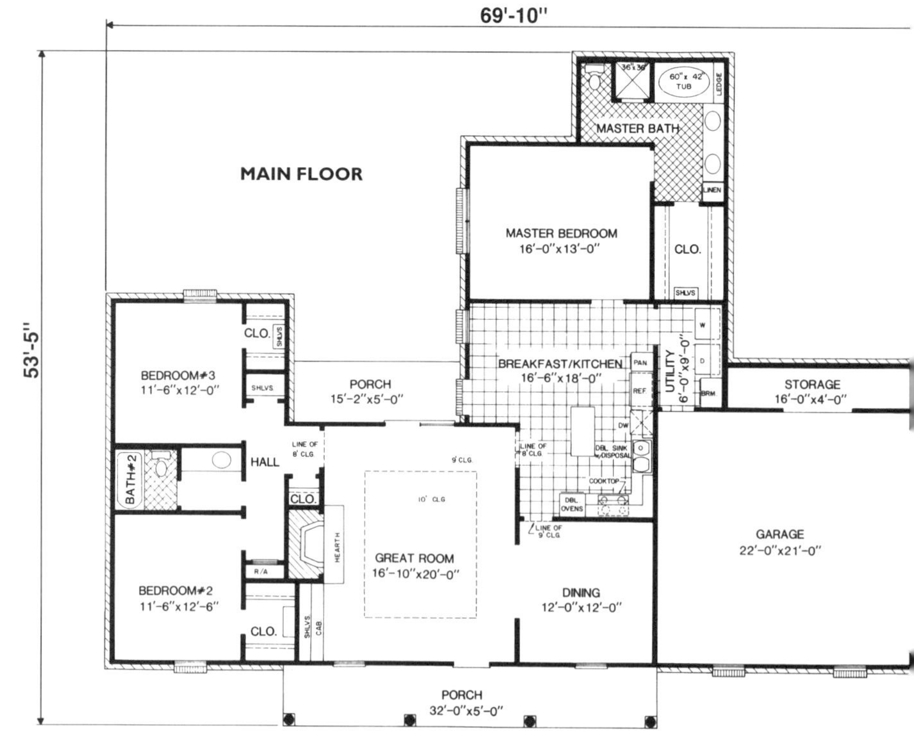
69'-10"
53'-5"
MAIN FLOOR
MASTER BATH
60" x 42" TUB
LEDGE
LINEN
MASTER BEDROOM
16'-0"x13'-0"
CLO.
SHLVS
BREAKFAST/KITCHEN
16'-6"x18'-0"
PAN
REF
UTILITY
6'-0"x9'-0"
STORAGE
16'-0"x4'-0"
DW
DBL SINK DISPOSAL
COOKTOP
DBL OVENS
LINE OF 8' CLG
LINE OF 9' CLG
BEDROOM#3
11'-6"x12'-0"
CLO.
SHLVS
PORCH
15'-2"x5'-0"
HALL
LINE OF 8' CLG
9' CLG
10' CLG
BATH#2
CLO.
HEARTH
GREAT ROOM
16'-10"x20'-0"
GARAGE
22'-0"x21'-0"
BEDROOM#2
11'-6"x12'-6"
CLO.
SHLVS
CAB
DINING
12'-0"x12'-0"
PORCH
32'-0"x5'-0"

To order your Blueprints, call 1-800-235-5700

Detailing with Keystones

Price Code: A

his plan features:

- ıree bedrooms
- full baths
- front window, the entry, and the two Garage ors feature detailing and keystones adding style the front elevation
- ne Foyer flows into the Great Room, which is cented by a fireplace flanked by windows
- ne Kitchen includes a Pantry, Laundry Center, d a serving bar to the Breakfast Area
- ne Master Suite, crowned in a tray ceiling, cludes a Sitting Room and a Bath with a ulted ceiling
- edroom four is situated for use as either a edroom or a Study.
- ne home is designed with a basement or crawl-ace foundation

N FLOOR — 1,354 SQ. FT.
EMENT — 1,390 SQ. FT.
RAGE — 434 SQ. FT.

Total living area: 1,354 sq. ft.

PLAN NO.97272

WIDTH 47'-0"
DEPTH 46'-0"

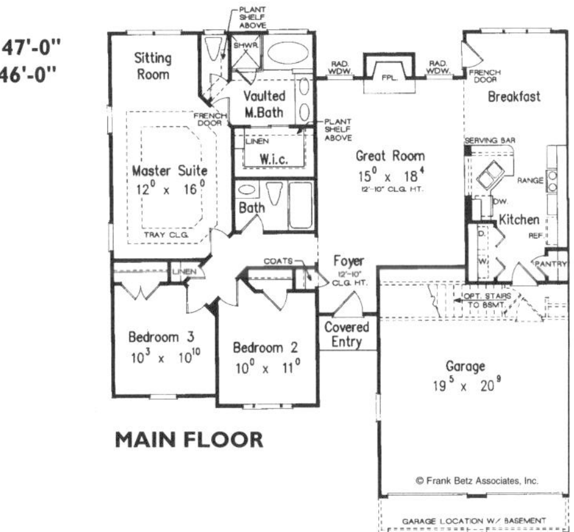

Sitting Room
Vaulted M.Bath
W.i.c.
Master Suite
12° x 16°
Bath
TRAY CLG.
Great Room
15° x 18⁴
Breakfast
Kitchen
Foyer
Covered Entry
Bedroom 3
10³ x 10¹⁰
Bedroom 2
10° x 11°
Garage
19⁵ x 20⁹
© Frank Betz Associates, Inc.
GARAGE LOCATION W/ BASEMENT

MAIN FLOOR

Family Haven

Price Code: C

his plan features:

- our bedrooms
- wo and one half full baths
- he bay window in the Living Room, the fire-ace in the Family Room, the bay-windowed eakfast Nook in the Kitchen, and the tray ceil-g in the Master Bedroom are just a few of the oughtful details that make this home special
- his home is designed with a basement and awlspace foundation options

ST FLOOR — 961 SQ. FT.
OND FLOOR — 889 SQ. FT.
NUS — 386 SQ. FT.
RAGE — 501 SQ. FT.

PLAN NO.97295

Total living area: 1,850 sq. ft.

WIDTH 53'-10"
DEPTH 34'-6"

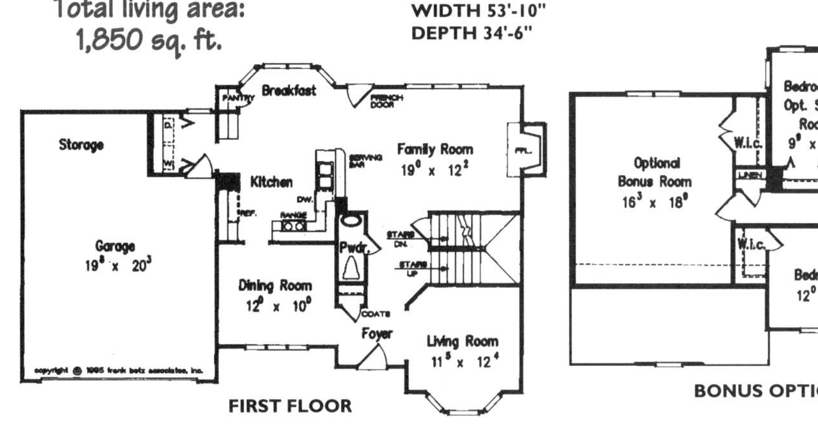

Breakfast
Storage
Family Room
19° x 12²
Kitchen
Garage
19⁸ x 20³
Pwdr.
Dining Room
12° x 10°
Foyer
Living Room
11⁵ x 12⁴
copyright © 1995 frank betz associates, inc.
Bedroom 4/ Opt. Sitting Room
9⁸ x 11⁴
Optional Bonus Room
16³ x 18⁸
Bedroom 3
12° x 10°

FIRST FLOOR

BONUS OPTION

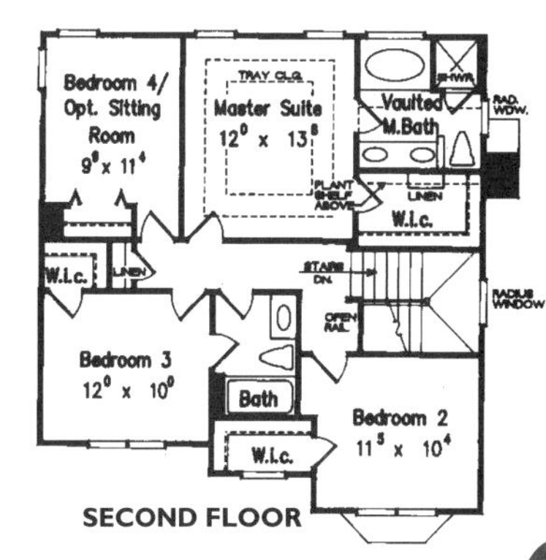

Bedroom 4/ Opt. Sitting Room
9⁸ x 11⁴
Master Suite
12° x 13⁸
Vaulted M.Bath
W.i.c.
Bedroom 3
12° x 10°
Bath
Bedroom 2
11⁵ x 10⁴

SECOND FLOOR

PLAN NO. 34029

Skylight Brightens Master Bedroom

Price Code: B

- This plan features:
- — Three bedrooms
- — Two full baths
- A covered Porch Entry
- A Foyer separating the Dining Room from the Breakfast Area and Kitchen
- A Master Bedroom with a decorative ceiling and a skylight in the private bath
- An optional Deck accessible through sliding doors off the Master Bedroom
- This home is designed with basement, slab and crawlspace foundation options

MAIN FLOOR — 1,686 SQ. FT.
BASEMENT — 1,676 SQ. FT.
GARAGE — 484 SQ. FT.

Total living area:
1,686 sq. ft.

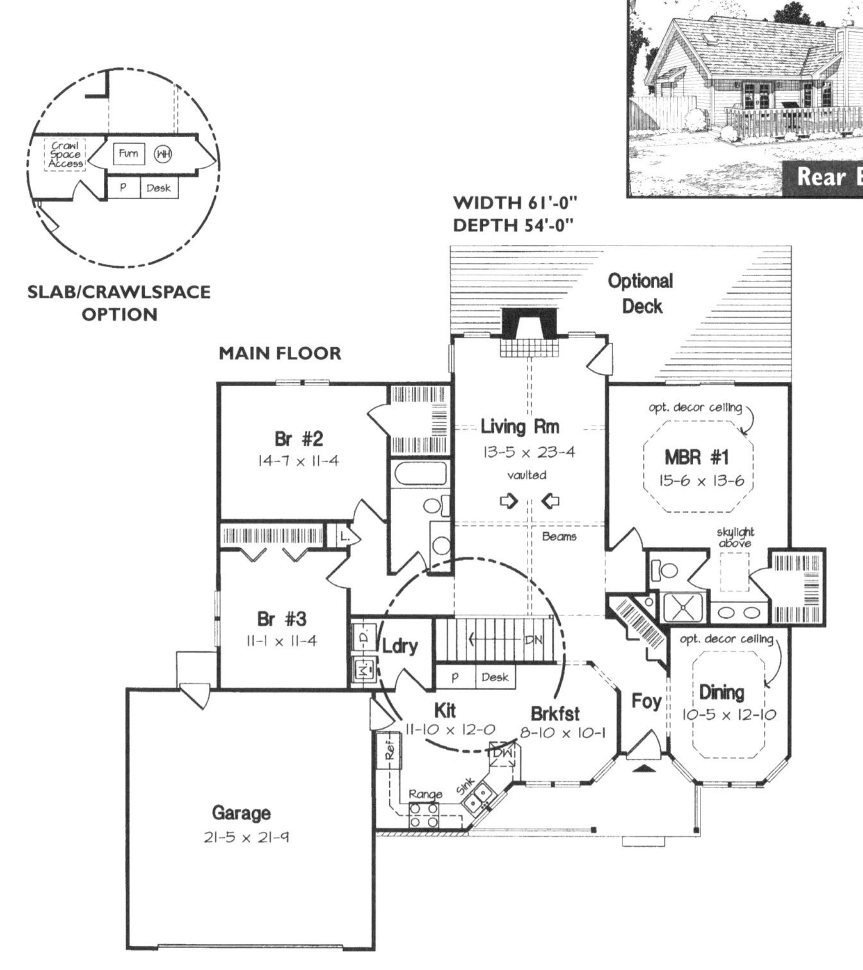

Crawl Space Access
Furn
WH
P
Desk
SLAB/CRAWLSPACE OPTION
WIDTH 61'-0"
DEPTH 54'-0"
Optional Deck
MAIN FLOOR
Br #2
14-7 x 11-4
Living Rm
13-5 x 23-4
vaulted
Beams
opt. decor ceiling
MBR #1
15-6 x 13-6
skylight above
Br #3
11-1 x 11-4
Ldry
DN
P
Desk
opt. decor ceiling
Dining
10-5 x 12-10
Foy
Kit
11-10 x 12-0
Brkfst
8-10 x 10-1
Ref
DW
Range
Sink
Garage
21-5 x 21-9

Rear Elevati

High Ceilings

Price Code: A

ıis plan features:

- ıree bedrooms
- vo full baths
- ıgh ceilings permeate the main living space
- n arched window in the Dining Room compli-ents the design of the Porch
- ıe large Pantry increases the Kitchen storage ace
- tray ceiling beautifies the Master Bedroom
- rear wall fireplace warms the Great Room
- ıis home is designed with basement and crawl-ace foundation options

N FLOOR — 1,459 SQ. FT.
EMENT — 1,466 SQ. FT.
ɹAGE — 390 SQ. FT.

Total living area: 1,459 sq. ft.

PLAN NO. 97601

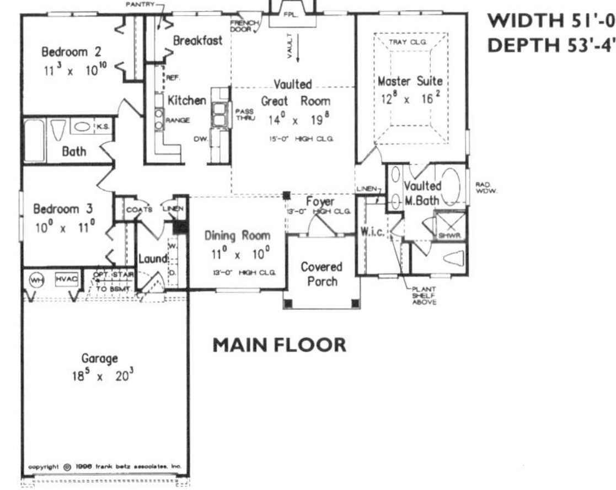
WIDTH 51'-0"
DEPTH 53'-4"
Bedroom 2
Breakfast
Kitchen
Vaulted Great Room
Master Suite
Bath
Bedroom 3
Dining Room
Foyer
Vaulted M.Bath
Laund.
Covered Porch
Garage
MAIN FLOOR

Stone and Siding

Price Code: B

his plan features:

- 'hree bedrooms
- 'wo full baths
- n arched opening with decorative columns ccenting the Dining Room
- mple cabinet and counter space with a built-in antry and serving bar in the Kitchen
- rench door to the outdoors or an optional bay indow in the Breakfast Room
- vaulted ceiling crowning the Great Room, ighlighted by a fireplace
- avish Master Suite topped by a tray ceiling and ampered by a plush Master Bath

AIN FLOOR — 1,571 SQ. FT.
NUS — 334 SQ. FT.
SEMENT — 1,642 SQ. FT.
RAGE — 483 SQ. FT.

Total living area: 1,571 sq. ft.

PLAN NO. 97615

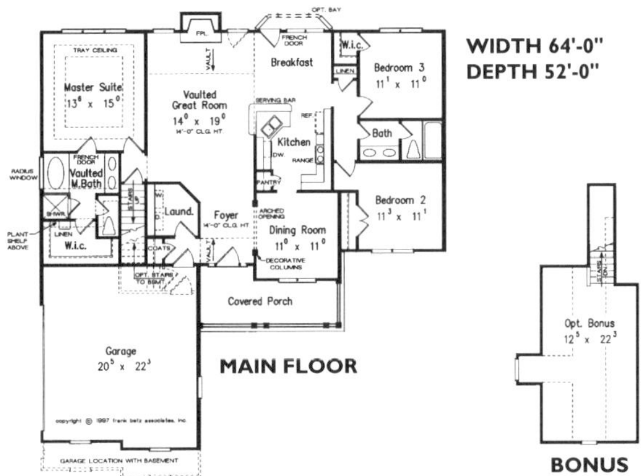
WIDTH 64'-0"
DEPTH 52'-0"
Master Suite
Vaulted Great Room
Breakfast
Bedroom 3
Kitchen
Bath
Vaulted M.Bath
Bedroom 2
Laund.
Foyer
Dining Room
Covered Porch
Garage
MAIN FLOOR
Opt. Bonus
BONUS

PLAN NO. 90441

Great Master Suite

Price Code: C

- This plan features:
- — Three bedrooms
- — Two full baths
- A large Great Room with a vaulted ceiling an stone fireplace with bookshelves on either sid
- A spacious Kitchen with ample cabinet space conveniently located next to the large Dining Room
- A Master Suite having a large Bath with a ga tub, double vanity and a walk-in closet
- Two other large Bedrooms, each with a walk- closet and access to the full Bath
- This home is designed with basement, slab ar crawlspace foundation options

MAIN FLOOR — 1,811 SQ. FT.
BASEMENT — 1,811 SQ. FT.
GARAGE — 484 SQ. FT.

Total living area: 1,811 sq. ft.

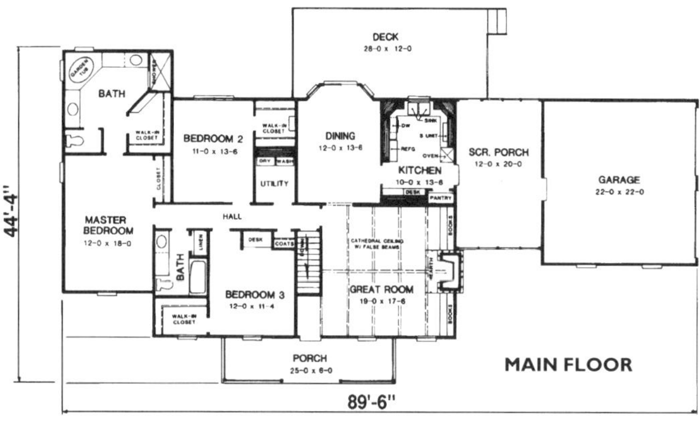
DECK
28-0 x 12-0
BATH
BEDROOM 2
11-0 x 13-6
DINING
12-0 x 13-6
UTILITY
KITCHEN
10-0 x 13-6
SCR. PORCH
12-0 x 20-0
GARAGE
22-0 x 22-0
MASTER
BEDROOM
12-0 x 18-0
HALL
BATH
BEDROOM 3
12-0 x 11-4
GREAT ROOM
19-0 x 17-6
PORCH
25-0 x 6-0
MAIN FLOOR
44'-4"
89'-6"

PLAN NO. 97108

Classic Ranch

Price Code: C

- This plan features:
- — Three bedrooms
- — Two full baths
- A fabulous Great Room with a step ceiling ar cozy fireplace
- An elegant arched soffit connects the Great Room to the Dining Room
- The Kitchen has wrap-around counters, a cen island and a Nook
- The Master Bedroom is completed with a wa in closet, and a private Bath
- Two additional Bedrooms with ample closet space share a full Bath
- This home is designed with a basement foundation

MAIN FLOOR — 1,794 SQ. FT.
BASEMENT — 1,794 SQ. FT.

Total living area: 1,794 sq. ft.

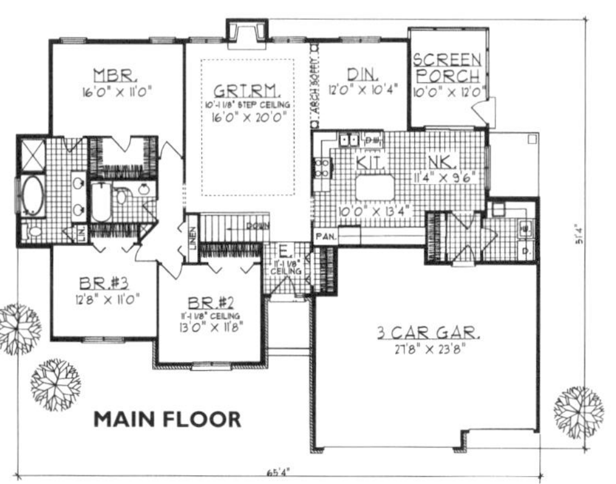
MBR.
16'0" x 11'0"
GRT.RM.
16'0" x 20'0"
DIN.
12'0" x 10'4"
SCREEN
PORCH
10'0" x 12'0"
KIT.
NK.
11'4" x 9'6"
10'0" x 13'4"
BR.#3
12'8" x 11'0"
BR.#2
13'0" x 11'8"
3 CAR GAR.
27'8" x 23'8"
MAIN FLOOR

PLAN NO. 24404

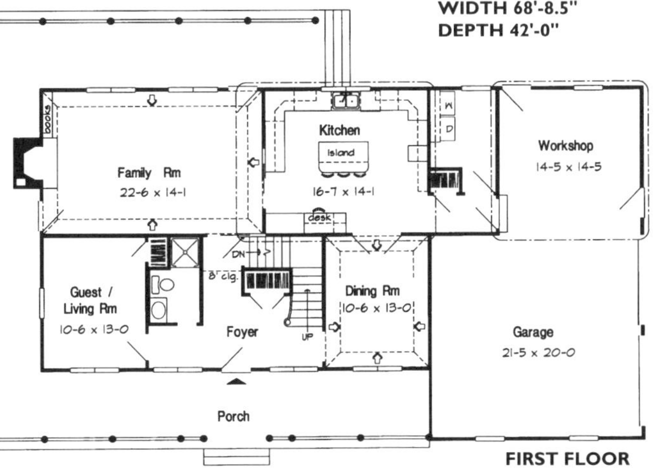

WIDTH 68'-8.5"
DEPTH 42'-0"
Family Rm
22-6 x 14-1
books
Kitchen
Island
16-7 x 14-1
desk
W
D
Workshop
14-5 x 14-5
Guest /
Living Rm
10-6 x 13-0
DN
8' clg.
Foyer
UP
Dining Rm
10-6 x 13-0
Garage
21-5 x 20-0
Porch

FIRST FLOOR

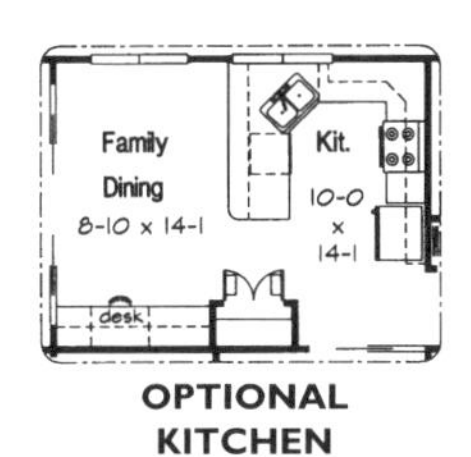

Family
Dining
8-10 x 14-1
Kit.
10-0
x
14-1
desk

OPTIONAL KITCHEN

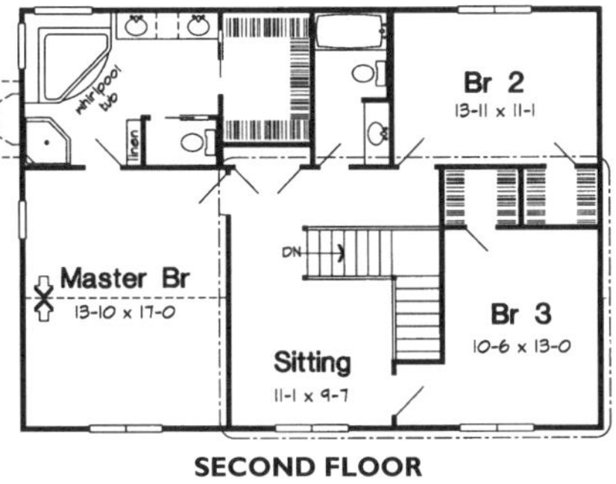

whirlpool tub
Br 2
13-11 x 11-1
Master Br
13-10 x 17-0
DN
Sitting
11-1 x 9-7
Br 3
10-6 x 13-0

SECOND FLOOR

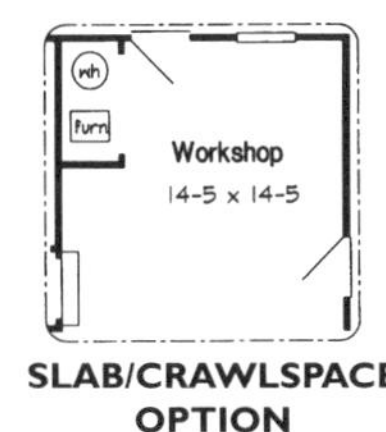

wh
furn
Workshop
14-5 x 14-5

SLAB/CRAWLSPACE OPTION

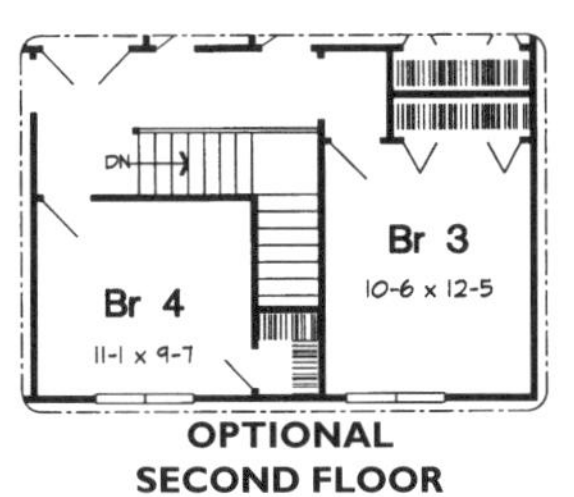

DN
Br 3
10-6 x 12-5
Br 4
11-1 x 9-7

OPTIONAL SECOND FLOOR

Flavor of Yesteryear

Price Code: E

- This plan features:
  - Three or four bedrooms
  - Two full and one three-quarter baths
- The formal Living Room could double as a Guest Room
- The huge Family Room is highlighted by a decorative ceiling, cozy fireplace, bookshelves and Porch access
- The Country-size Kitchen has an island snack bar, built-in desk and is near the Dining Room, Laundry/Workshop and Garage
- This home is designed with basement, slab, crawlspace foundation options

FIRST FLOOR — 1,236 SQ. FT.
SECOND FLOOR — 1,120 SQ. FT.

Total living area: 2,356 sq. ft.

PLAN NO. 90930

A-Frame for Year-Round Living

Price Code: B

- This plan features:
- — Three bedrooms
- — One full and one three-quarter baths
- A vaulted ceiling in the Living Room with a massive fireplace
- A wrap-around Sun Deck that gives you a lot of outdoor living space
- A luxurious Master Suite complete with a walk-in closet, full Bath and private Deck
- This home is designed with a basement foundation

MAIN FLOOR — 1,238 SQ. FT.
LOFT — 464 SQ. FT.
BASEMENT — 1,175 SQ. FT.

Total living area:
1,702 sq. ft.

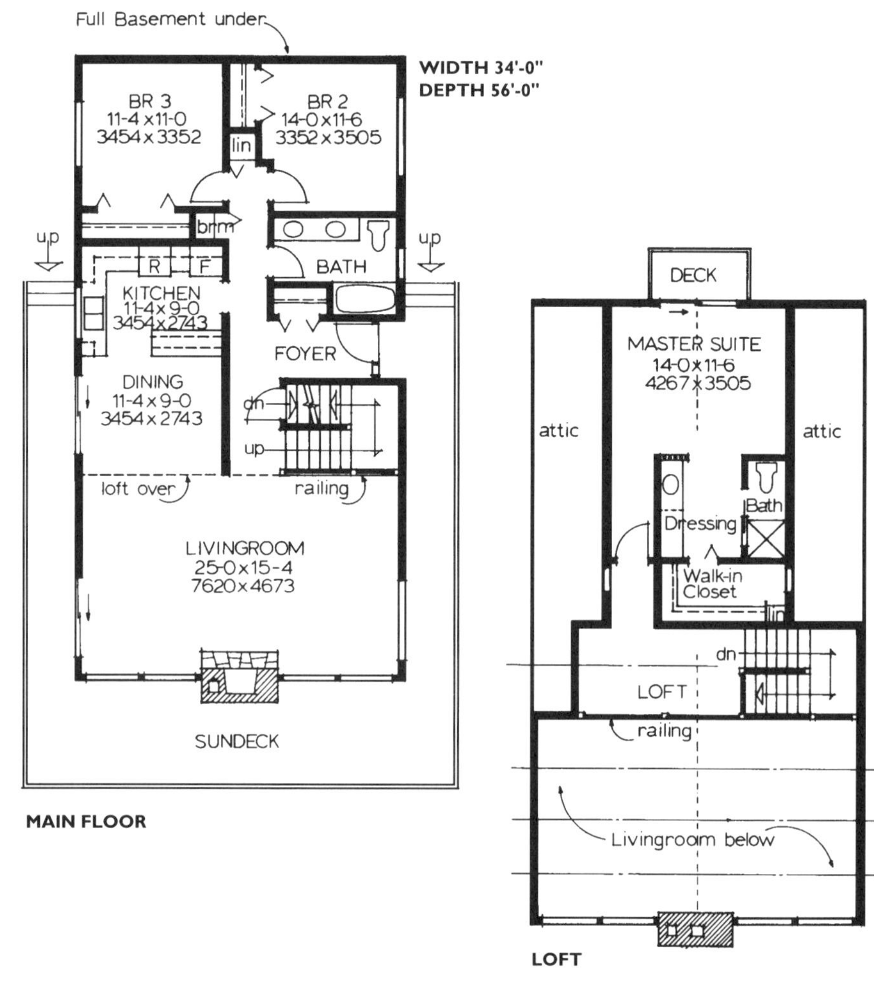

Full Basement under
WIDTH 34'-0"
DEPTH 56'-0"
BR 3
11-4 x 11-0
3454 x 3352
BR 2
14-0 x 11-6
3352 x 3505
lin
brm
up
up
R
F
KITCHEN
11-4 x 9-0
3454 x 2743
BATH
FOYER
DINING
11-4 x 9-0
3454 x 2743
dn
up
loft over
railing
LIVINGROOM
25-0 x 15-4
7620 x 4673
SUNDECK
MAIN FLOOR
DECK
MASTER SUITE
14-0 x 11-6
4267 x 3505
attic
attic
Bath
Dressing
Walk-in Closet
lin
dn
LOFT
railing
Livingroom below
LOFT

PLAN NO. 90606

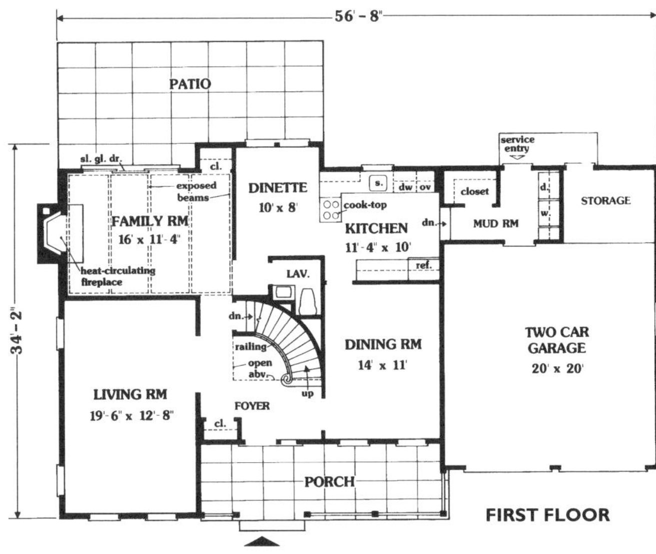

56' - 8"
PATIO
sl. gl. dr.
cl.
exposed beams
FAMILY RM
16' x 11' - 4"
heat-circulating fireplace
DINETTE
10' x 8'
s.
dw
ov
cook-top
KITCHEN
11' - 4" x 10'
ref.
dn.
closet
service entry
MUD RM
d.
w.
STORAGE
LAV.
dn.
railing
open abv.
up
DINING RM
14' x 11'
TWO CAR GARAGE
20' x 20'
34' - 2"
LIVING RM
19' - 6" x 12' - 8"
FOYER
cl.
PORCH

FIRST FLOOR

Friendly Colonial

Price Code: D

- This plan features:
  - — Four bedrooms
  - — Two and one half baths
- A beautiful circular stair ascending from the central Foyer and flanked by the formal Living Room and Dining Room
- Exposed beams, wood paneling, and a brick fireplace wall in the Family Room
- A separate Dinette opening to an efficient Kitchen
- This home is designed with a basement foundation

FIRST FLOOR — 1,099 SQ. FT.
SECOND FLOOR — 932 SQ. FT.
BASEMENT — 1,023 SQ. FT.
GARAGE — 467 SQ. FT.

Total living area:
2,031 sq. ft.

BED RM
12'- 8" x 11'- 4"
BED RM
11'- 4" x 10'- 4"
cl.
W.I.C.
BATH
H.
railing
planter
cl.
cl.
lin.
dn.
railing
open
MASTER BED RM
16' x 11'
BED RM
12'- 8" x 10'- 8"
BATH

SECOND FLOOR

PLAN NO.97622

Stately Front Porch with Columns

Price Code: D

- This plan features:
- — Three bedrooms
- — Two full baths
- Formal Living Room can be turned into an a tional Bedroom with ease
- Split-bedroom floor plan assuring Master Su of privacy
- Tray ceiling crowning Master Bedroom high lighted by a Sitting Room and French door t private Bath
- Arched openings accented by columns acces the formal Dining Room
- Efficient Kitchen with built-in Pantry and peninsula serving bar
- Expansive Family Room with fireplace flank by radius windows
- This home is designed with basement and cr space foundation options

MAIN FLOOR — 2,056 SQ. FT.
BONUS ROOM — 208 SQ. FT.
BASEMENT — 2,056 SQ. FT.
GARAGE — 454 SQ. FT.

Total living area:
2,056 sq. ft.

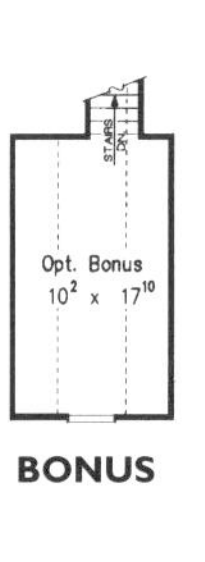

Opt. Bonus
10² x 17¹⁰

BONUS

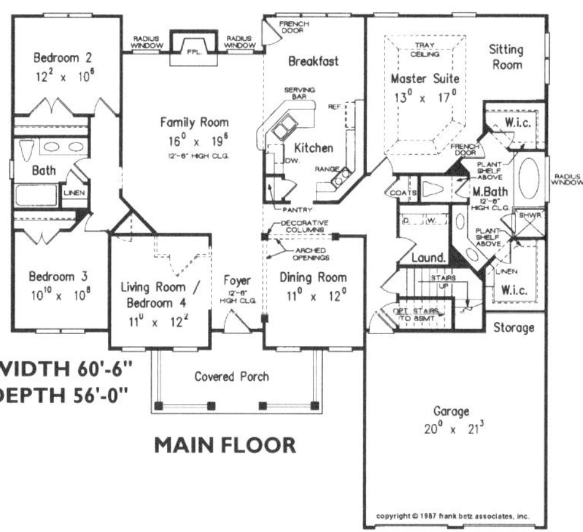

Bedroom 2
12² x 10⁶
Family Room
16⁰ x 19⁶
Breakfast
Kitchen
Master Suite
13⁰ x 17⁰
Sitting Room
W.i.c.
M.Bath
Bath
Bedroom 3
10¹⁰ x 10⁸
Living Room / Bedroom 4
11⁰ x 12²
Foyer
Dining Room
11⁰ x 12⁰
Laund.
W.i.c.
Storage
Covered Porch
Garage
20⁰ x 21³

WIDTH 60'-6"
DEPTH 56'-0"

MAIN FLOOR

PLAN NO.97707

Brick Beauty

Price Code: C

- This plan features:
- — Three bedrooms
- — Two full and one half baths
- The stylish Foyer is complimented by a well positioned, turned staircase
- The full-sized Great Room is enhanced by a large fireplace and oversized windows
- The Laundry Room is conveniently located j steps off the Kitchen and Garage
- The Formal Dining Room has a stepped ceili
- This home is designed with a slab foundatio

FIRST FLOOR — 980 SQ. FT.
SECOND FLOOR — 876 SQ. FT.
BONUS ROOM — 325 SQ. FT.
BASEMENT — 980 SQ. FT.
GARAGE — 577 SQ. FT.

Total living area:
1,856 sq. ft.

WIDTH 50'-6"
DEPTH 38'-0"

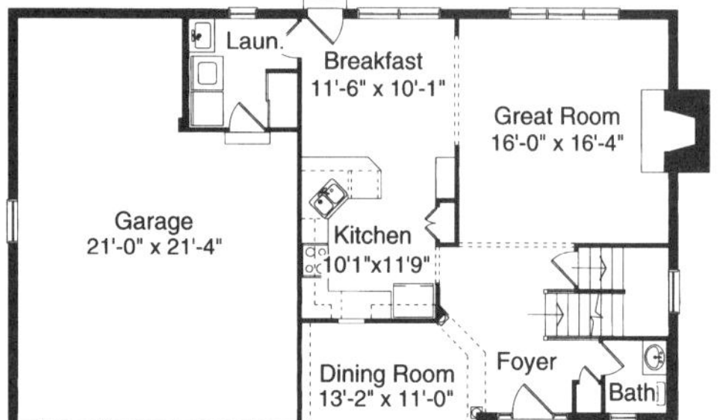

Laun.
Breakfast
11'-6" x 10'-1"
Great Room
16'-0" x 16'-4"
Garage
21'-0" x 21'-4"
Kitchen
10'1"x11'9"
Dining Room
13'-2" x 11'-0"
Foyer
Bath
Porch

FIRST FLOOR

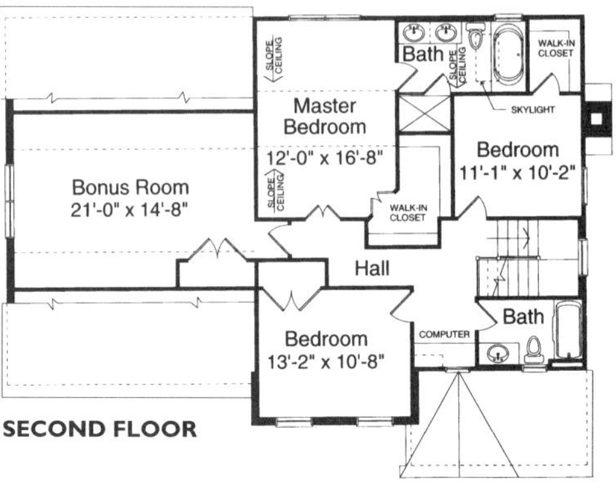

Bath
Master Bedroom
12'-0" x 16'-8"
Bedroom
11'-1" x 10'-2"
Bonus Room
21'-0" x 14'-8"
Hall
Bedroom
13'-2" x 10'-8"
Bath

SECOND FLOOR

PLAN NO. 99285

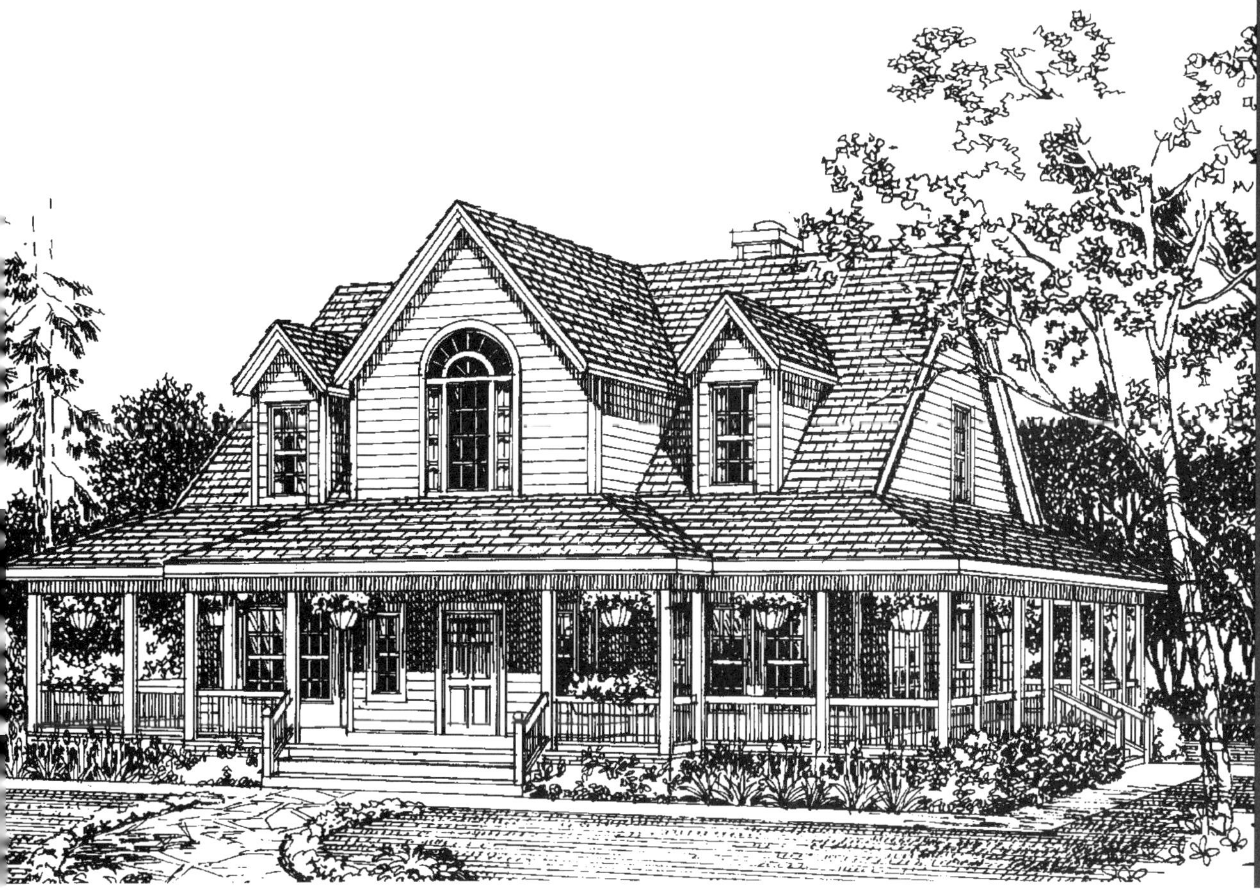

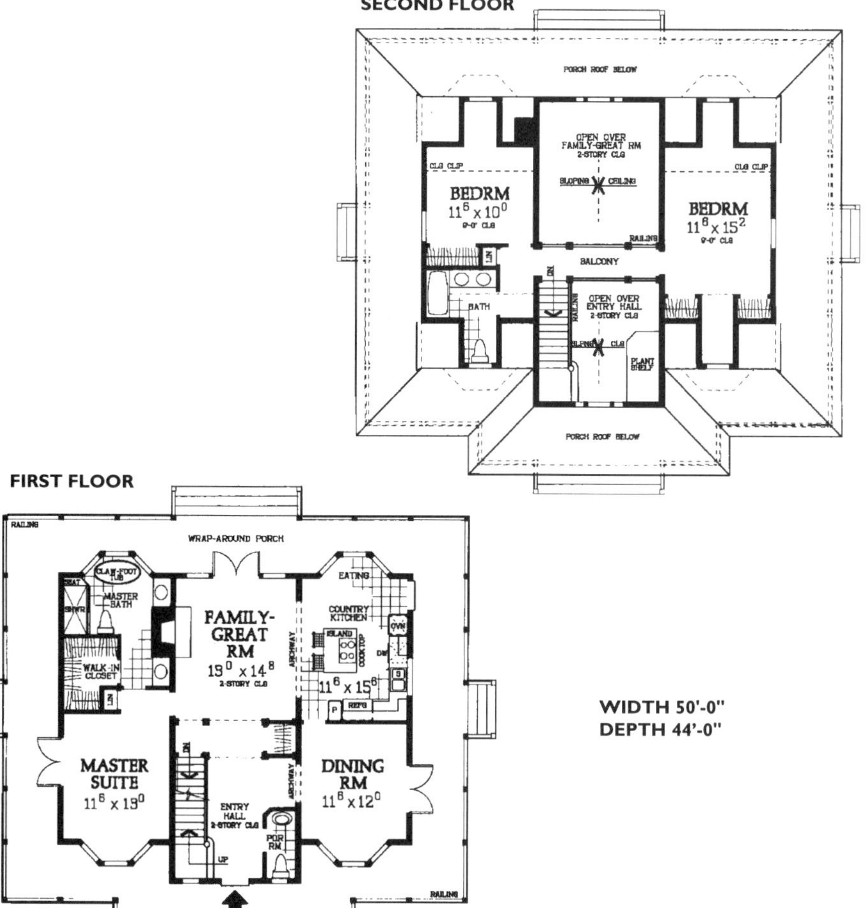
SECOND FLOOR
PORCH ROOF BELOW
OPEN OVER FAMILY-GREAT RM 2-STORY CLG
BEDRM 11⁶ x 10⁰
BEDRM 11⁶ x 15²
BALCONY
BATH
OPEN OVER ENTRY HALL 2-STORY CLG
PLANT SHELF
FIRST FLOOR
WRAP-AROUND PORCH
RAILING
CLAW-FOOT TUB
MASTER BATH
WALK-IN CLOSET
FAMILY-GREAT RM 13⁰ x 14⁸ 2-STORY CLG
EATING
COUNTRY KITCHEN
ISLAND
COOKTOP
ARCHWAY
11⁶ x 15⁶
REFG
MASTER SUITE 11⁶ x 13⁰
DINING RM 11⁶ x 12⁰
ENTRY HALL 2-STORY CLG
PDR RM
UP
WIDTH 50'-0"
DEPTH 44'-0"

Southern Hospitality

Price Code: C

- This plan features:
  - Three bedrooms
  - Two full and one half baths
- Double doors access to Porch from Family Great Room, Dining Room and Master Suite
- Country Kitchen with cooktop island / snack bar, Eating Alcove and archway to Family Room with cozy fireplace
- First floor Master Suite with bay window, walk-in closet and pampering Bath
- Two double dormer Bedrooms on second floor catch breezes and share a full Bath
- This home is designed with a basement foundation

First Floor — 1171 sq. ft.
Second Floor — 600 sq. ft.

Total living area: 1,771 sq. ft.

PLAN NO.91081

Letting The Light In

Price Code: B

- This plan features:
  - — Four bedrooms
  - — Two full baths
- Covered Porch leads into easy-care tiled Ent with angled staircase
- Vaulted ceiling tops, decorative corner windo and cozy wood stove in Living Room
- Sliding glass door to rear yard brightens Din Room and adjoining Living Room and Kitch
- Efficient Kitchen with built-in Pantry, pass-through counter and plant shelf window
- Two first floor Bedrooms with ample closets share a full Bath and Utility Area
- French doors lead into private Master Bedro with skylight Bath and walk-in closet
- Loft/Bedroom overlooking Living Room off many options
- This home is designed with a crawlspace foundation

FIRST FLOOR — 1076 SQ. FT.
SECOND FLOOR — 449 SQ. FT.
GARAGE — 495 SQ. FT.

Total living area:
1,525 sq. ft.

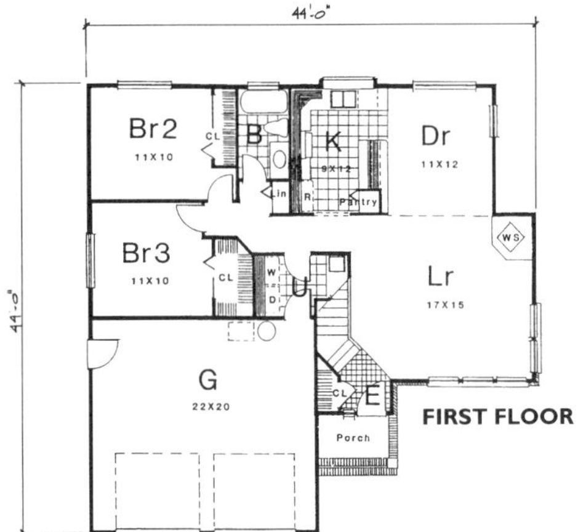
44'-0"
Br2
11X10
CL
B
K
9X12
Dr
11X12
Lin
R
Pantry
WS
Br3
11X10
CL
W
D
U
Lr
17X15
G
22X20
CL
E
Porch
FIRST FLOOR

SECOND FLOOR

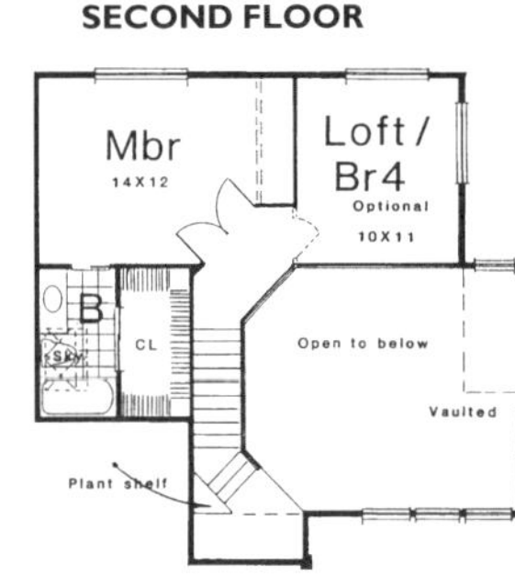
Mbr
14X12
Loft /
Br4
Optional
10X11
B
CL
Open to below
Vaulted
Plant shelf

PLAN NO.26740

Contemporary Ranch Desig

Price Code: B

- This plan features:
  - — Three bedrooms
  - — Two full baths
- Sloping cathedral ceilings
- An efficient, centrally located Kitchen
- A Daylight Room for dining pleasure
- A secluded Master Bedroom with Master B and access to private Deck
- A Great Hall with fireplace
- This home is designed with basement and c space foundation options

FIRST FLOOR — 1,512 SQ. FT.
GARAGE — 478 SQ. FT.

Total living area:
1,512 sq. ft.

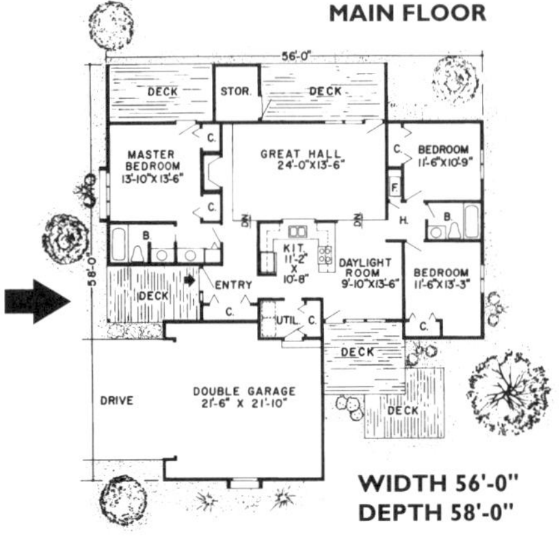
MAIN FLOOR
56'-0"
DECK
STOR.
DECK
MASTER BEDROOM 13'-10"X13'-6"
GREAT HALL 24'-0"X13'-6"
BEDROOM 11'-6"X10'-9"
KIT 11'-2" X 10'-8"
DAYLIGHT ROOM 9'-10"X13'-6"
BEDROOM 11'-6"X13'-3"
DECK
ENTRY
UTIL
DECK
DOUBLE GARAGE 21'-6" X 21'-10"
DRIVE
DECK
58'-0"
WIDTH 56'-0"
DEPTH 58'-0"

PLAN NO. 24610

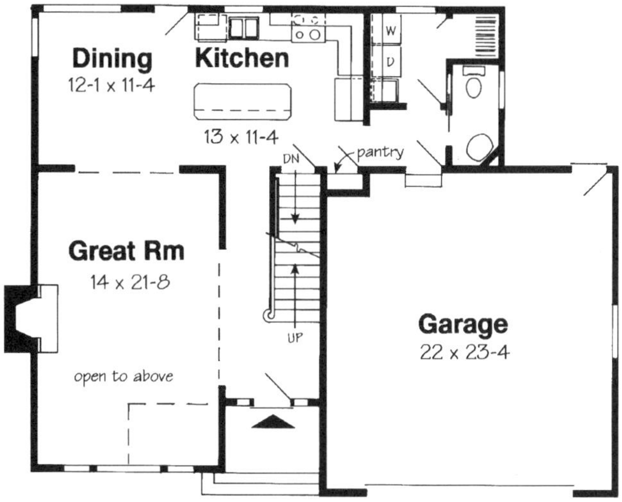

Dining
12-1 x 11-4
Kitchen
13 x 11-4
pantry
DN
UP
W
D
Great Rm
14 x 21-8
open to above
Garage
22 x 23-4
FIRST FLOOR

SECOND FLOOR

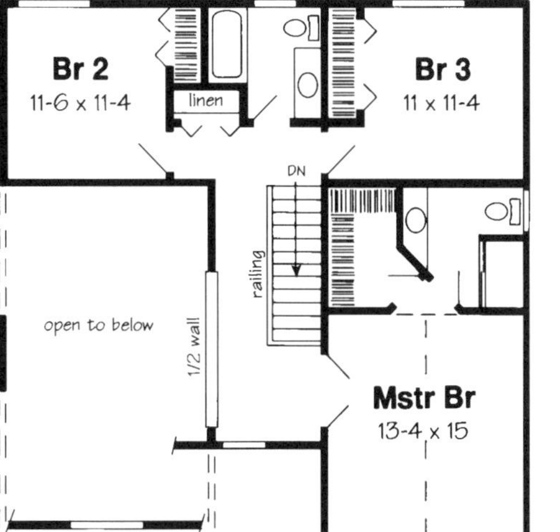

Br 2
11-6 x 11-4
linen
Br 3
11 x 11-4
DN
railing
open to below
1/2 wall
Mstr Br
13-4 x 15

WIDTH 46'-8"
DEPTH 35'-8"

Second Floor Balcony Overlooks Great Room

Price Code: C

- This plan features:
- — Three bedrooms
- — Two full and one half baths
- A Great Room with a focal point fireplace and a two-story ceiling
- An efficient Kitchen with an island, double sinks, built-in Pantry and ample storage and counter space
- A Master Suite with a private Master Bath and a walk-in closet
- This home is designed with basement, slab and crawlspace foundation options

FIRST FLOOR — 891 SQ. FT.
SECOND FLOOR — 894 SQ. FT.
BASEMENT — 891 SQ. FT.
GARAGE — 534 SQ. FT.

Total living area:
1,785 sq. ft.

PLAN NO. 98406

Easy Living Plan

Price Code: B

- This plan features:
- — Three bedrooms
- — Two full and one half baths
- Kitchen, Breakfast Bay, and Family Room blend into a spacious open Living Area
- Convenient Laundry Center is tucked into the rear of the Kitchen
- Luxurious Master Suite is topped by a tray ceiling while a vaulted ceiling is in the Bath
- This home is designed with basement, slab and crawlspace foundation options

FIRST FLOOR — 828 SQ. FT.
SECOND FLOOR — 772 SQ. FT.
BASEMENT — 828 SQ. FT.
GARAGE — 473 SQ. FT.

Total living area:
1,600 sq. ft.

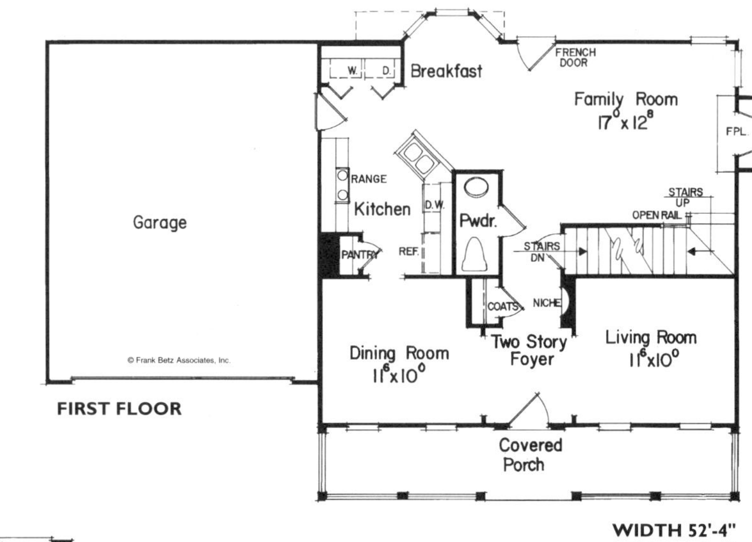

Breakfast
W.
D.
FRENCH DOOR
Family Room
17⁰ x 12⁸
FPL.
RANGE
Kitchen
D.W.
Pwdr.
STAIRS UP
OPEN RAIL
Garage
PANTRY
REF.
STAIRS DN
COATS
NICHE
© Frank Betz Associates, Inc.
Dining Room
11⁶x10⁰
Two Story Foyer
Living Room
11⁶x10⁰
Covered Porch

FIRST FLOOR

WIDTH 52'-4"
DEPTH 34'-0"

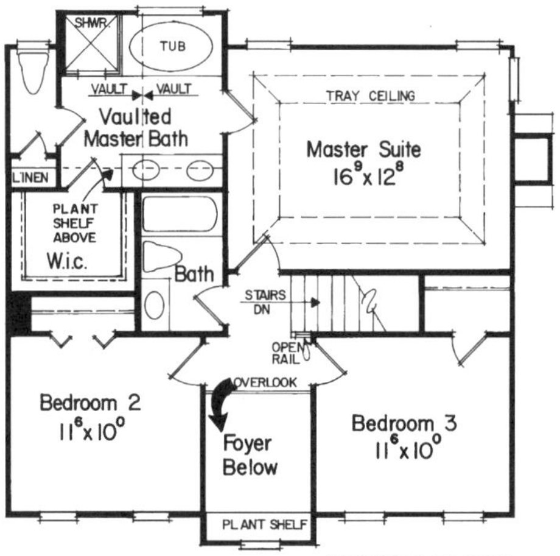

SHWR
TUB
VAULT
VAULT
Vaulted Master Bath
TRAY CEILING
Master Suite
16⁹x 12⁸
LINEN
PLANT SHELF ABOVE
W.i.c.
Bath
STAIRS DN
OPEN RAIL
OVERLOOK
Bedroom 2
11⁶x 10⁰
Foyer Below
Bedroom 3
11⁶x 10⁰
PLANT SHELF

SECOND FLOOR

Impeccable Style

Price Code: D

is plan features:

- ıree bedrooms
- vo full and one half baths
- ick, stone, and interesting rooflines showcase
- impeccable style of this home
- side a deluxe staircase highlights the Foyer
- e Dining Room has a bay window at one end d columns at the other
- e U-shaped Kitchen has an island in its center
- e two-story Great Room has a warm fireplace
- e shape of the Master Bedroom adds to its aracter
- ostairs find two Bedrooms and a full Bath
- ıis home is designed with a basement ındation

ST FLOOR — 1,706 SQ. FT.
OND FLOOR — 492 SQ. FT.
SEMENT — 1,706 SQ. FT.

Total living area:
2,198 sq. ft.

PLAN NO.97710

WIDTH 59'-4"
DEPTH 65'-0"
Breakfast
9' x 16'
Kitchen
8'4" x 15'4"
Great Room
16'10" x 21'
Dressing
walk in closet
Dining Room
13'8" x 11'8"
Hall
Foyer
Master Bedroom
14' x 17'4"
Bath
Porch
Laun.
Two-car Garage
21' x 29'8"
FIRST FLOOR

Bedroom
15' x 10'7"
Great Room
Below
Bath
Bedroom
13'10" x 10'7"
Foyer Below
SECOND FLOOR

Shake And Stone Accents

Price Code: A

his plan features:

- Three bedrooms
- Two full baths
- sloped ceiling unites the open Kitchen, Dining rea, Great Room and Foyer
- he Master Bedroom features a tray ceiling and ccess to the Deck
- he position of the Garage door allows this esign to fit a narrower lot
- his home is designed with a basement oundation

AIN FLOOR — 1,315 SQ. FT.
SEMENT — 1,315 SQ. FT.
RAGE — 488 SQ. FT.

Total living area:
1,315 sq. ft.

PLAN NO.97731

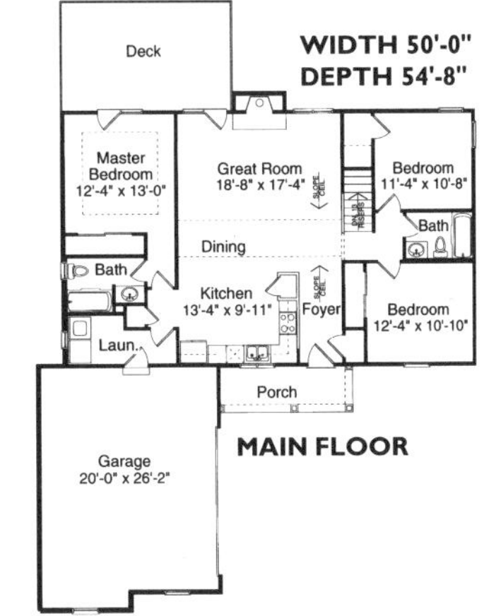

Deck
WIDTH 50'-0"
DEPTH 54'-8"
Master
Bedroom
12'-4" x 13'-0"
Great Room
18'-8" x 17'-4"
Bedroom
11'-4" x 10'-8"
Bath
Dining
Bath
Kitchen
13'-4" x 9'-11"
Foyer
Bedroom
12'-4" x 10'-10"
Laun.
Porch
Garage
20'-0" x 26'-2"
MAIN FLOOR

PLAN NO. 34601

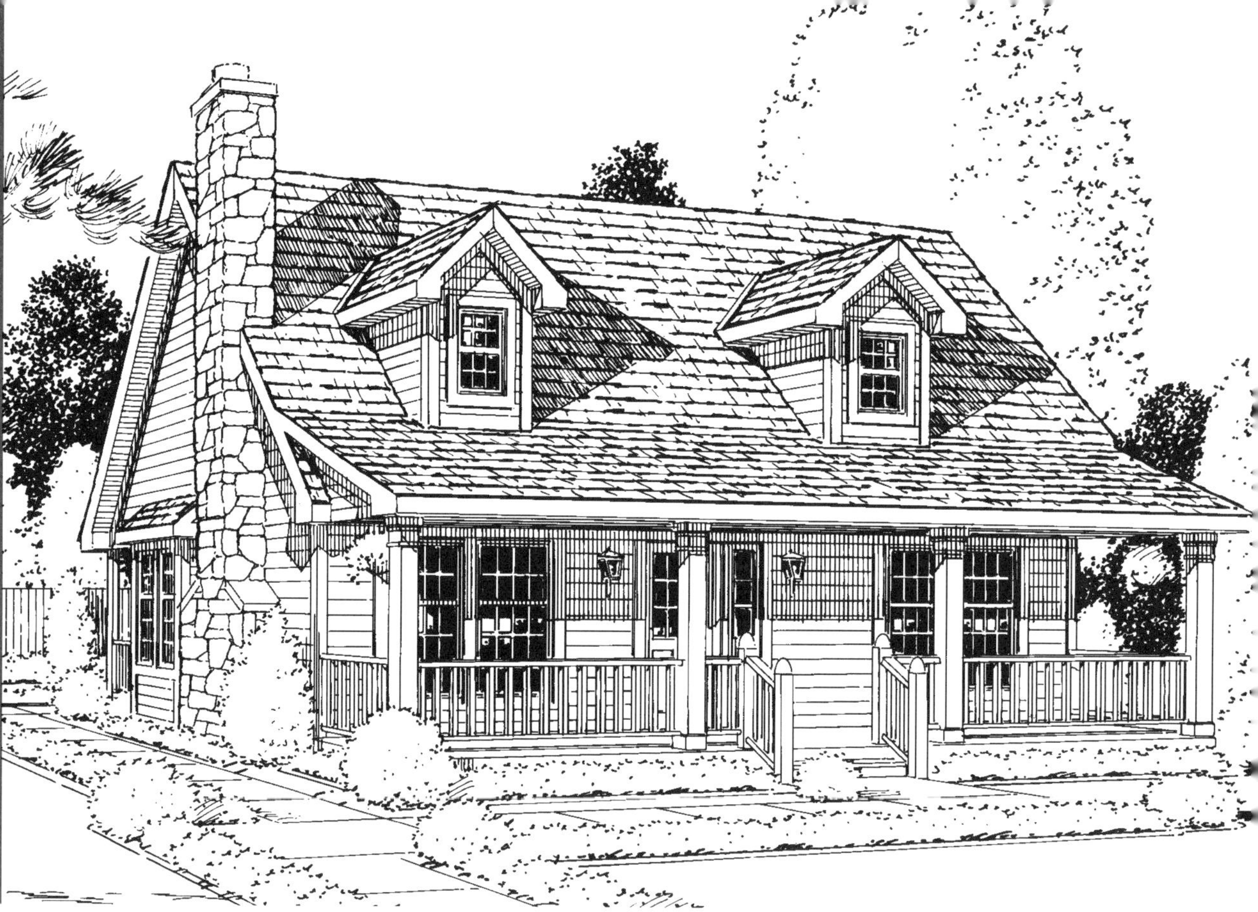

Large Front Porch Adds a Country Touch

Price Code: A

- This plan features:
- — Three bedrooms
- — Two full baths
- A country-styled front Porch
- Vaulted ceiling in the Living Room which includes a fireplace
- An efficient Kitchen with double sinks and peninsula counter that may double as an eating bar
- A second floor Master Suite with sloped ceiling, walk-in closet and private Master Bath
- This home is designed with basement, slab and crawlspace foundation options

FIRST FLOOR — 1,007 SQ. FT.
SECOND FLOOR — 408 SQ. FT.

Total living area:
1,415 sq. ft.

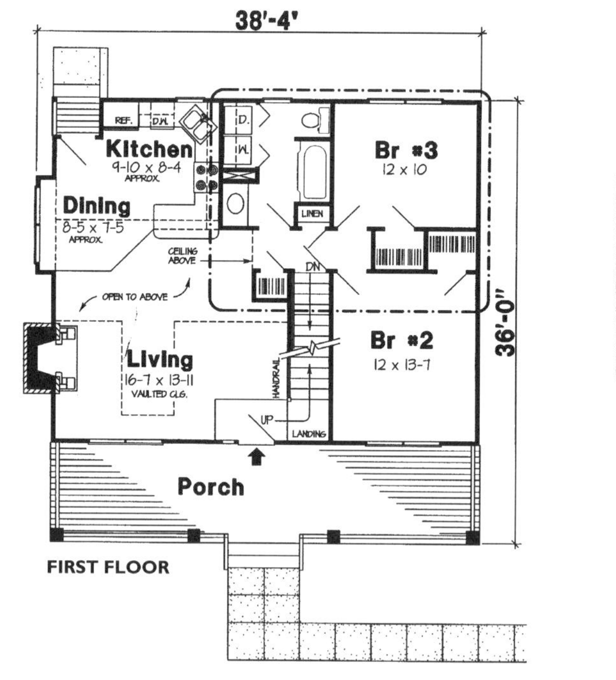

38'-4"
36'-0"
REF.
D.W.
Kitchen
9-10 x 8-4
APPROX.
Dining
8-5 x 7-5
APPROX.
CEILING ABOVE
OPEN TO ABOVE
Living
16-7 x 13-11
VAULTED CLG.
HANDRAIL
UP
DN
LANDING
LINEN
Br #3
12 x 10
Br #2
12 x 13-7
Porch

FIRST FLOOR

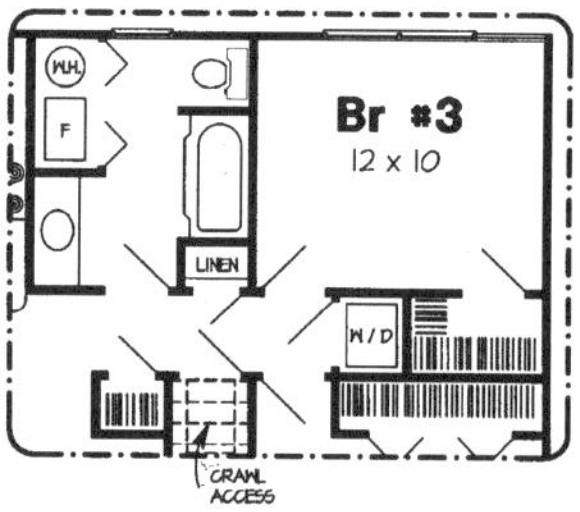

SLAB/CRAWLSPACE OPTION

SECOND FLOOR

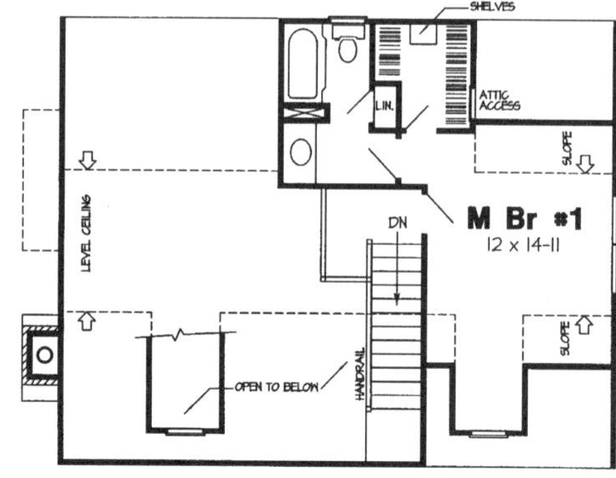

SHELVES
LIN.
ATTIC ACCESS
SLOPE
LEVEL CEILING
DN
M Br #1
12 x 14-11
OPEN TO BELOW
HANDRAIL

PLAN NO. 94911

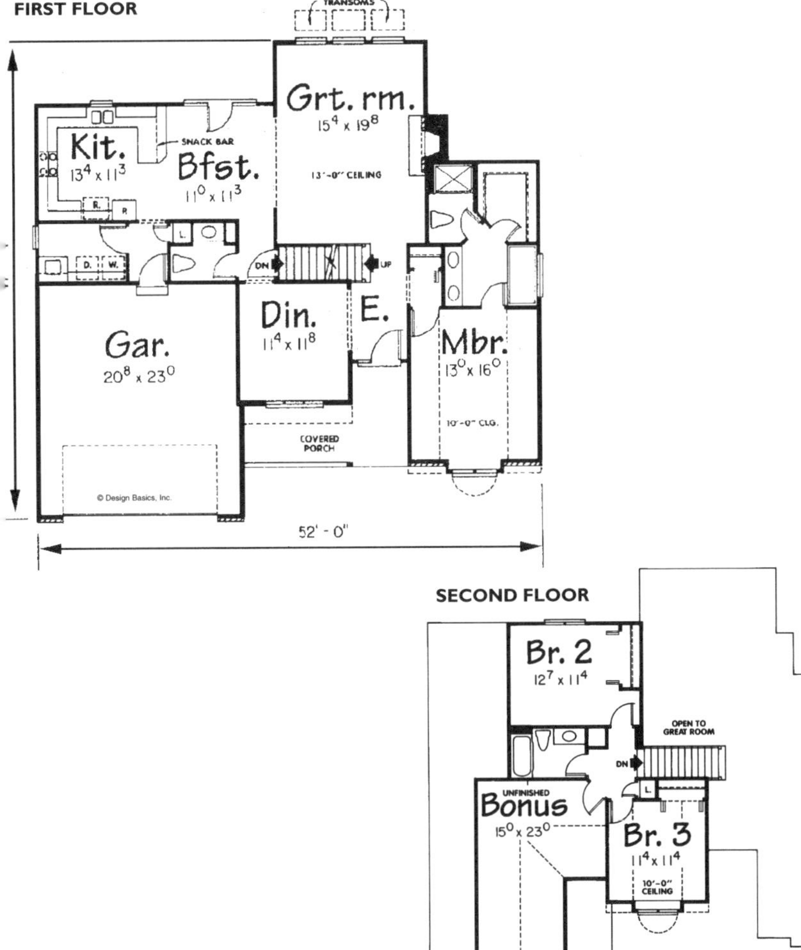

FIRST FLOOR
TRANSOMS
Grt. rm.
15⁴ x 19⁸
13'-0" CEILING
Kit.
13⁴ x 11³
SNACK BAR
Bfst.
11⁰ x 11³
D. W.
DN
UP
Din.
11⁴ x 11⁸
E.
Mbr.
13⁰ x 16⁰
10'-0" CLG.
Gar.
20⁸ x 23⁰
COVERED PORCH
© Design Basics, Inc.
52' - 0"
SECOND FLOOR
Br. 2
12⁷ x 11⁴
OPEN TO GREAT ROOM
DN
UNFINISHED
Bonus
15⁰ x 23⁰
Br. 3
11⁴ x 11⁴
10'-0" CEILING

Fieldstone Facade and Arched Windows

Price Code: C

- This plan features:
  - Three bedrooms
  - Two full and one half baths
- An efficient Kitchen includes counter snack bar and nearby Laundry and Garage Entry
- A first floor Master Bedroom suite features an arched window below a sloped ceiling and a double vanity Bath
- This home is designed with a basement foundation
- Alternate foundation options available at an additional charge. Please call 1-800-235-5700 for more information.

First floor — 1,405 sq. ft.
Second floor — 453 sq. ft.
Bonus room — 300 sq. ft.
Basement — 1,405 sq. ft.

Total living area: 1,858 sq. ft.

PLAN NO. 96513

A Modern Slant On a Country Theme

Price Code: B

- This plan features:

—Three bedrooms

—Two full baths

- Country-style front Porch highlighting exteri enhanced by dormer windows
- Modern open floor plan for a more spacious feeling
- Great Room accented by a quaint, corner fire place and a ceiling fan
- Dining Room flowing from the Great Room for easy entertaining
- Kitchen graced by natural light from attractiv bay window and a convenient snack bar for meals on the go
- Master suite secluded in separate wing for total privacy
- Two additional Bedrooms sharing full Bath
- This home is designed with a crawlspace and slab foundation options

FIRST FLOOR — 1,648 SQ. FT.
GARAGE — 479 SQ. FT.

Total living area:
1,648 sq. ft.

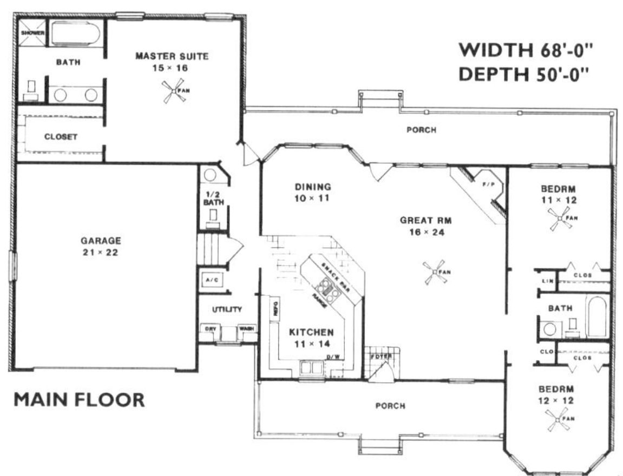
WIDTH 68'-0"
DEPTH 50'-0"
MASTER SUITE
15 × 16
BATH
CLOSET
GARAGE
21 × 22
1/2 BATH
UTILITY
PORCH
DINING
10 × 11
GREAT RM
16 × 24
KITCHEN
11 × 14
BEDRM
11 × 12
BATH
BEDRM
12 × 12
PORCH
MAIN FLOOR

PLAN NO. 90934

A Nest for Empy-Nesters

Price Code: A

- This plan features:

— Two bedrooms

— One full bath

- An economical design
- A covered Sun Deck adding outdoor living s
- A Mudroom/Laundry Area inside the side do trapping dirt before it can enter the house
- An open layout between the Living Room wi fireplace, Dining Room and Kitchen
- This home is designed with a slab foundation

MAIN FLOOR — 884 SQ. FT.

Total living area:
884 sq. ft.

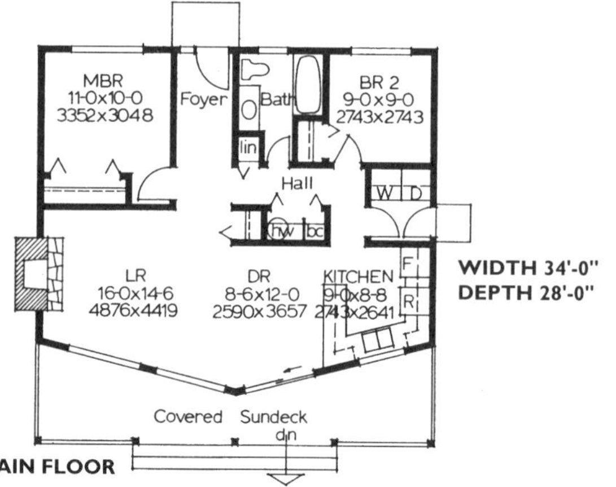
MBR
11-0x10-0
3352x3048
Foyer
Bath
BR 2
9-0x9-0
2743x2743
lin
Hall
W D
LR
16-0x14-6
4876x4419
DR
8-6x12-0
2590x3657
KITCHEN
9-0x8-8
2743x2641
Covered Sundeck
dn
WIDTH 34'-0"
DEPTH 28'-0"
MAIN FLOOR

PLAN NO. 94944

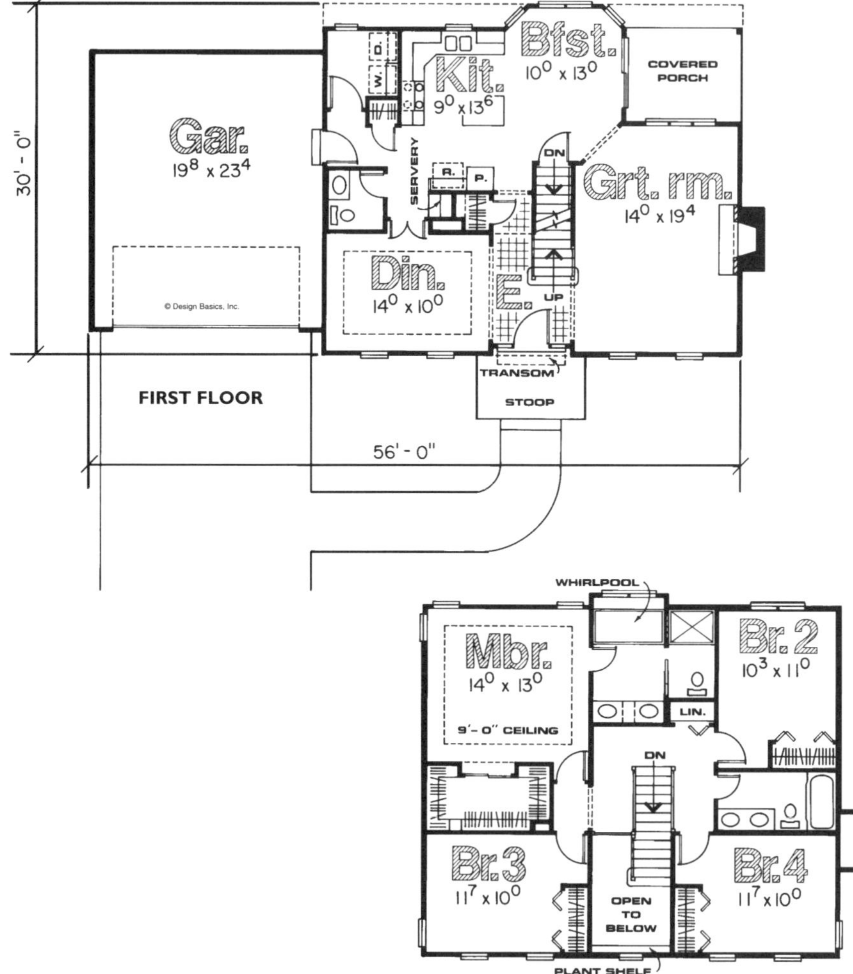

Gar.
19⁸ x 23⁴
Kit.
9⁰ x 13⁶
Bfst.
10⁰ x 13⁰
COVERED PORCH
SERVERY
Grt. rm.
14⁰ x 19⁴
Din.
14⁰ x 10⁰
E.
DN
UP
TRANSOM
STOOP
30' - 0"
56' - 0"
FIRST FLOOR
© Design Basics, Inc.
WHIRLPOOL
Mbr.
14⁰ x 13⁰
9'- 0" CEILING
Br. 2
10³ x 11⁰
LIN.
DN
Br. 3
11⁷ x 10⁰
Br. 4
11⁷ x 10⁰
OPEN TO BELOW
PLANT SHELF
SECOND FLOOR

Spectacular Sophistication

Price Code: C

- This plan features:
  - — Four bedrooms
  - — Two full and one half baths
- Great Room with an inviting fireplace and windows front and back
- Master Bedroom suite features a nine-foot boxed ceiling, a walk-in closet and whirlpool Bath
- This home is designed with basement and slab foundation options
- Alternate foundation options available at an additional charge. Please call 1-8--235-5700 for more information.

FIRST FLOOR — 941 SQ. FT.
SECOND FLOOR — 992 SQ. FT.
BASEMENT — 941 SQ. FT.
GARAGE — 480 SQ. FT.

Total living area: 1,933 sq. ft.

PLAN NO. 35007

Perfect for a Woodland Setting

Price Code: A

- This plan features:
- — Two bedrooms
- — One full bath
- The open public rooms at the front of the house feature slope ceilings
- A built-in entertainment center in the Living Room adding convenience
- The L-shaped Kitchen includes a double sink and Dining Area
- A Loft and Balcony overlooks the Living Room and the Dining Area
- This home is designed with basement, slab and crawlspace foundation options

FIRST FLOOR — 763 SQ. FT.
SECOND FLOOR — 264 SQ. FT.

Total living area: 1,027 sq. ft.

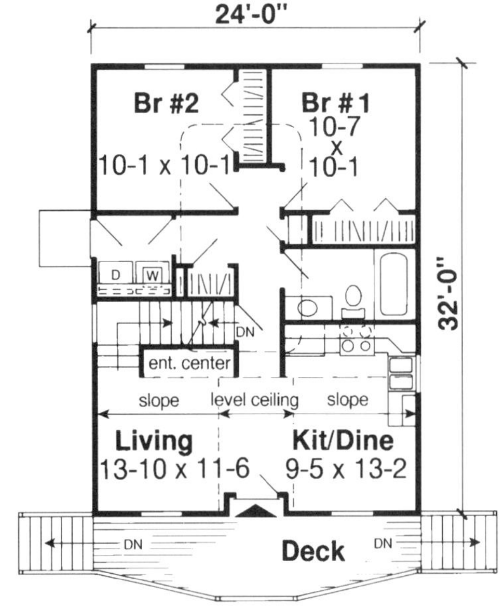

24'-0"
Br #2
10-1 x 10-1
Br #1
10-7
x
10-1
D
W
DN
ent. center
slope
level ceiling
slope
Living
13-10 x 11-6
Kit/Dine
9-5 x 13-2
32'-0"
DN
Deck
DN

FIRST FLOOR

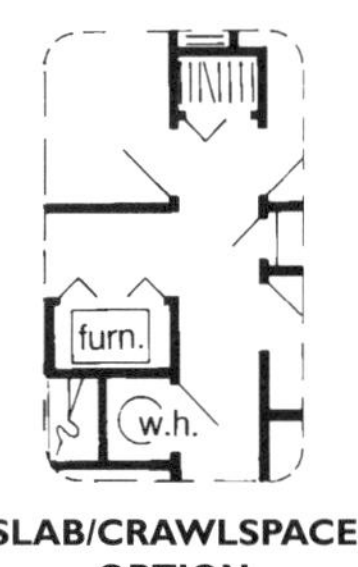

furn.
w.h.

SLAB/CRAWLSPACE OPTION

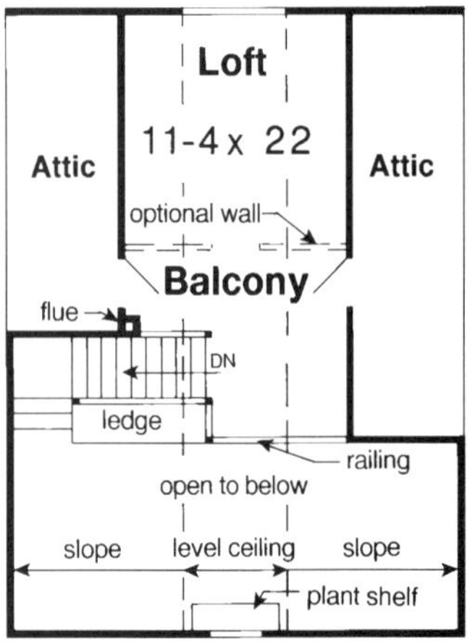

Loft
11-4 x 22
Attic
Attic
optional wall
Balcony
flue
DN
ledge
railing
open to below
slope
level ceiling
slope
plant shelf

SECOND FLOOR

PLAN NO.97757

Split Bedroom Privacy

Price Code: B

is plan features:

- ree bedrooms
- vo full baths
- ench doors flank the focal point fireplace in the eat Room and provide access to the backyard
- e well-equipped kitchen has a Pantry and large rving counter to the Dining Room
- third Garage bay offers ample storage and ace for a possible workshop
- is home is designed with a basement undation
- N FLOOR — 1,755 SQ. FT.
- EMENT — 1,755 SQ. FT.
- AGE — 796 SQ. FT.

Total living area: 1,755 sq. ft.

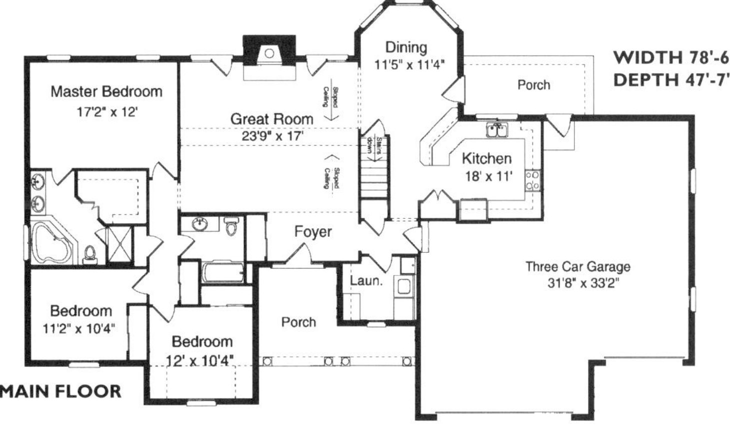

WIDTH 78'-6"
DEPTH 47'-7"
Dining
11'5" x 11'4"
Porch
Master Bedroom
17'2" x 12'
Great Room
23'9" x 17'
Kitchen
18' x 11'
Foyer
Laun.
Three Car Garage
31'8" x 33'2"
Bedroom
11'2" x 10'4"
Bedroom
12' x 10'4"
Porch
MAIN FLOOR

PLAN NO.97760

Screened Porch

Price Code: B

is plan features:

- ree bedrooms
- vo full baths
- ten-foot ceiling tops the Foyer
- olumns accent the Great Room and a fireplace ds a focal point to the room
- e Dining Area has a sunny bay window and cesses the Screened Porch through sliders
- e Kitchen includes a peninsula counter that n serve as a snack bar for after school snacks meals on the go
- e Master Suite has a ten-foot ceiling and a ısh Bath
- is home is designed with a basement undation
- N FLOOR — 1,611 SQ. FT.
- AGE — 430 SQ. FT.

Total living area: 1,611 sq. ft.

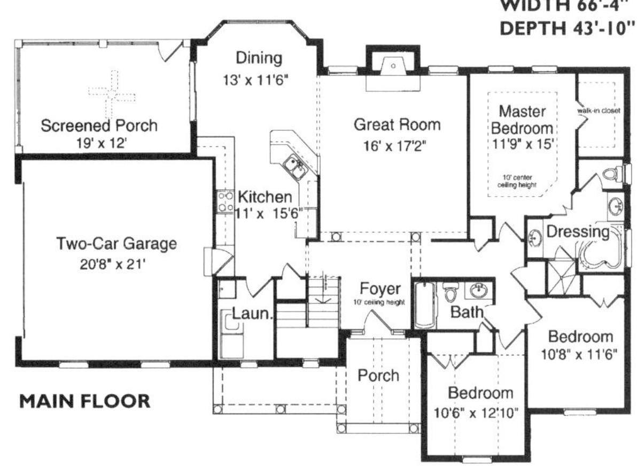

WIDTH 66'-4"
DEPTH 43'-10"
Dining
13' x 11'6"
Screened Porch
19' x 12'
Great Room
16' x 17'2"
Master Bedroom
11'9" x 15'
Kitchen
11' x 15'6"
Dressing
Two-Car Garage
20'8" x 21'
Foyer
Laun.
Bath
Bedroom
10'8" x 11'6"
Porch
Bedroom
10'6" x 12'10"
MAIN FLOOR

PLAN NO.92525

Amenity-Packed Affordabili

Price Code: A

- This plan features:
  - — Three bedrooms
  - — Two full baths
- A sheltered entrance inviting your guests on
- A fireplace in the Den offering a focal point, while the decorative ceiling adds definition to the room
- A well-equipped Kitchen flowing with ease the Breakfast Bay or Dining Room
- A Master Bedroom, having two closets and private Master Bath
- This home is designed with crawlspace and foundation options

MAIN FLOOR — 1,484 SQ. FT.
GARAGE — 544 SQ. FT.

Total living area:
1,484 sq. ft.

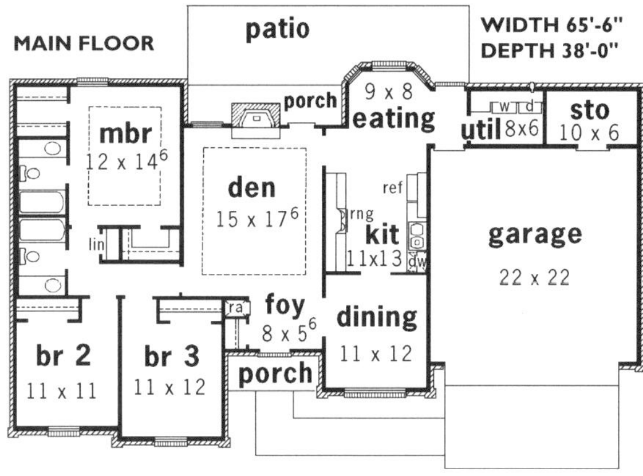

MAIN FLOOR
patio
WIDTH 65'-6"
DEPTH 38'-0"
porch
9 x 8
eating
util 8x6
sto
10 x 6
mbr
12 x 14⁶
den
15 x 17⁶
ref
rng
kit
11x13
dw
garage
22 x 22
lin
foy
8 x 5⁶
dining
11 x 12
br 2
11 x 11
br 3
11 x 12
porch

PLAN NO.96506

Attractive Ceiling Treatmen And Open Layout

Price Code: B

- This plan features:
  - — Three bedrooms
  - — Two full and one half baths
- Great Room and Master Suite with step-up ing treatments
- A cozy fireplace providing warm focal poin the Great Room
- Open layout between Kitchen, Dining and (Rooms lending a more spacious feeling
- Five-piece private Bath and walk-in closet pampering Master Suite
- This home is designed with a crawlspace ar slab foundation options

MAIN FLOOR — 1,654 SQ. FT.
GARAGE — 480 SQ. FT.

Total living area:
1,654 sq. ft.

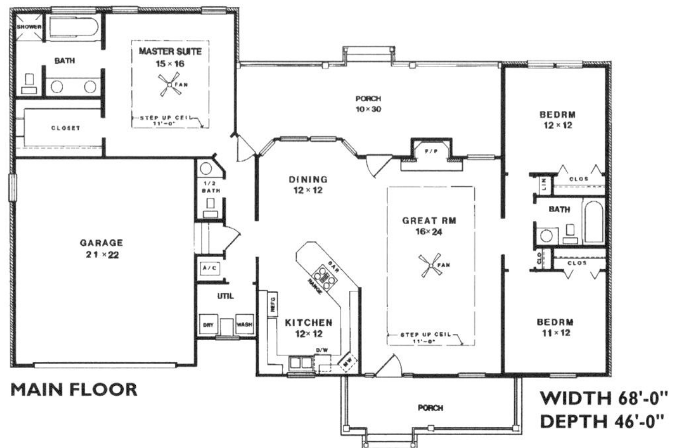

MASTER SUITE
15 × 16
BATH
CLOSET
PORCH
10 × 30
BEDRM
12 × 12
DINING
12 × 12
GREAT RM
16 × 24
GARAGE
21 × 22
UTIL
KITCHEN
12 × 12
BEDRM
11 × 12
PORCH
MAIN FLOOR
WIDTH 68'-0"
DEPTH 46'-0"

Library With Built-Ins

Price Code: B

'his plan features:

- Three bedrooms
- Two full baths
- 'he built-in bench in the Breakfast Area offers pace-saving seating for six
- Double doors open to the library, which features built-ins on two walls. This room can also be inished as a Bedroom
- 'he Great Room features a sloped ceiling and ireplace
- 'his home is designed with a basement oundation

AIN FLOOR 1,594 SQ. FT.
SEMENT— 1,594 SQ. FT.
ARAGE — 512 SQ. FT.

Total living area: 1,594 sq. ft.

PLAN NO.97762

WIDTH 52'-8"
DEPTH 55'-5"

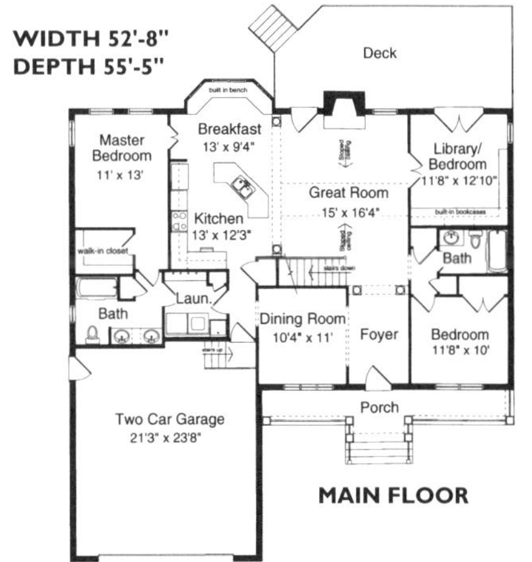

Deck
built in bench
Master Bedroom 11' x 13'
Breakfast 13' x 9'4"
Kitchen 13' x 12'3"
Great Room 15' x 16'4"
Library/ Bedroom 11'8" x 12'10"
walk-in closet
Bath
Laun.
Dining Room 10'4" x 11'
Foyer
Bedroom 11'8" x 10'
Two Car Garage 21'3" x 23'8"
Porch

MAIN FLOOR

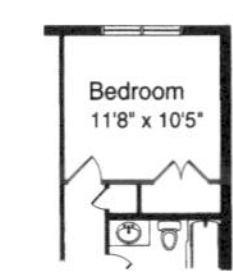

Bedroom 11'8" x 10'5"

OPTIONAL 3RD BEDROOM

Covered Porch With Columns

Price Code: C

'his plan features:

- Three bedrooms
- Two full baths
- 'he Foyer with 12-foot ceiling leads past decorative columns into the Family Room with a center ireplace
- 'he Living Room and Dining Room are linked y the Foyer and have windows overlooking the ront Porch
- 'he Kitchen has a serving bar and is adjacent to he Breakfast Nook, which has a French door that pens to the backyard
- 'he private Master Suite has a tray ceiling, a aulted Bath with a double vanity, and a walk-in loset
- 'he two other Bedrooms share a full Bath
- 'his home is designed with basement, slab and rawlspace foundation options

AIN FLOOR — 1,856 SQ. FT.
ARAGE — 429 SQ. FT.

Total living area: 1,856 sq. ft.

PLAN NO.98408

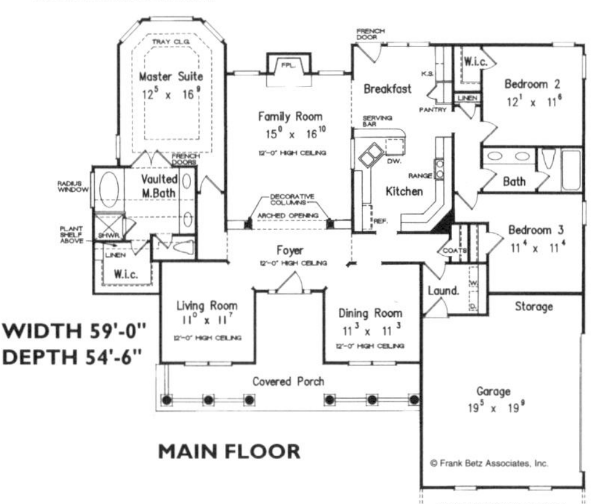

Master Suite
Family Room
Breakfast
Bedroom 2
Vaulted M.Bath
Kitchen
Bath
Foyer
Bedroom 3
W.i.c.
Living Room
Dining Room
Laund.
Storage
Covered Porch
Garage
© Frank Betz Associates, Inc.

WIDTH 59'-0"
DEPTH 54'-6"

MAIN FLOOR

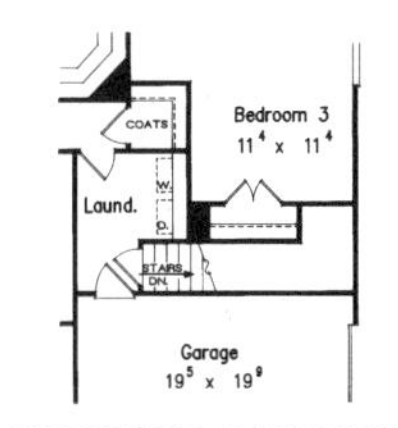

Bedroom 3
Laund.
Garage

OPTIONAL BASEMENT STAIR LOCATION

To order your Blueprints, call 1-800-235-5700

PLAN NO.93191

Perfect Plan for Busy Family

- This plan features:
  - — Three bedrooms
  - — Two full baths
- Covered Entry opens to vaulted Foyer and Family Room
- Spacious Family Room with a vaulted ceiling, central fireplace and expansive backyard views
- Angular and efficient Kitchen with an eating bar, built-in desk, Dining Area with outdoor access, and nearby Laundry and Garage Entry
- Secluded Master Bedroom with a large walk-in closet and double vanity Bath
- This home is designed with a basement foundation

MAIN FLOOR — 1,756 SQ. FT.

Total living area: 1,756 sq. ft.

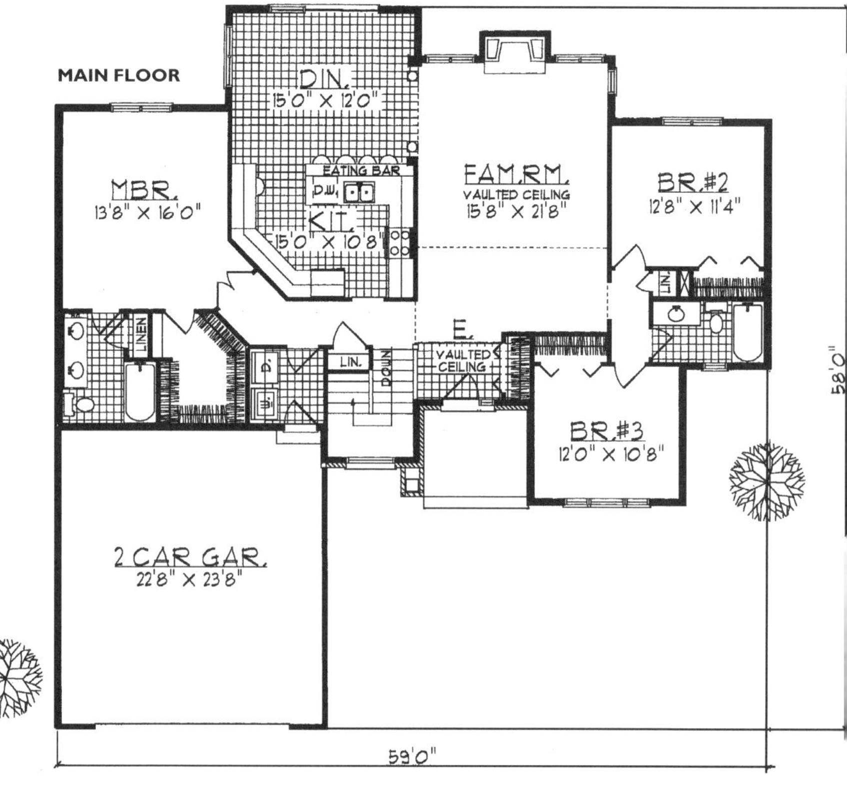
MAIN FLOOR
DIN.
15'0" X 12'0"
EATING BAR
KIT.
15'0" X 10'8"
MBR.
13'8" X 16'0"
FAM.RM.
VAULTED CEILING
15'8" X 21'8"
BR.#2
12'8" X 11'4"
LINEN
LIN.
DOWN
E.
VAULTED CEILING
BR.#3
12'0" X 10'8"
2 CAR GAR.
22'8" X 23'8"
59'0"
58'0"

PLAN NO. 24706

Country Porch Topped by Dormer

Price Code: A

- This plan features:
  - — Three bedrooms
  - — Two full baths
- Front Porch offers outdoor living and leads into tiled Entry and spacious Living Room with focal point fireplace
- Country-size Kitchen with cook-top island, bright Breakfast Area and access to Deck
- Second floor Master Bedroom offers lovely dormer window, vaulted ceiling, walk-in closet and double vanity Bath
- This home is designed with basement, slab and crawlspace foundation options

FIRST FLOOR — 1,036 SQ. FT.
SECOND FLOOR — 1,407 SQ. FT.
BASEMENT — 1,018 SQ. FT.

Total living area:
2,506 sq. ft.

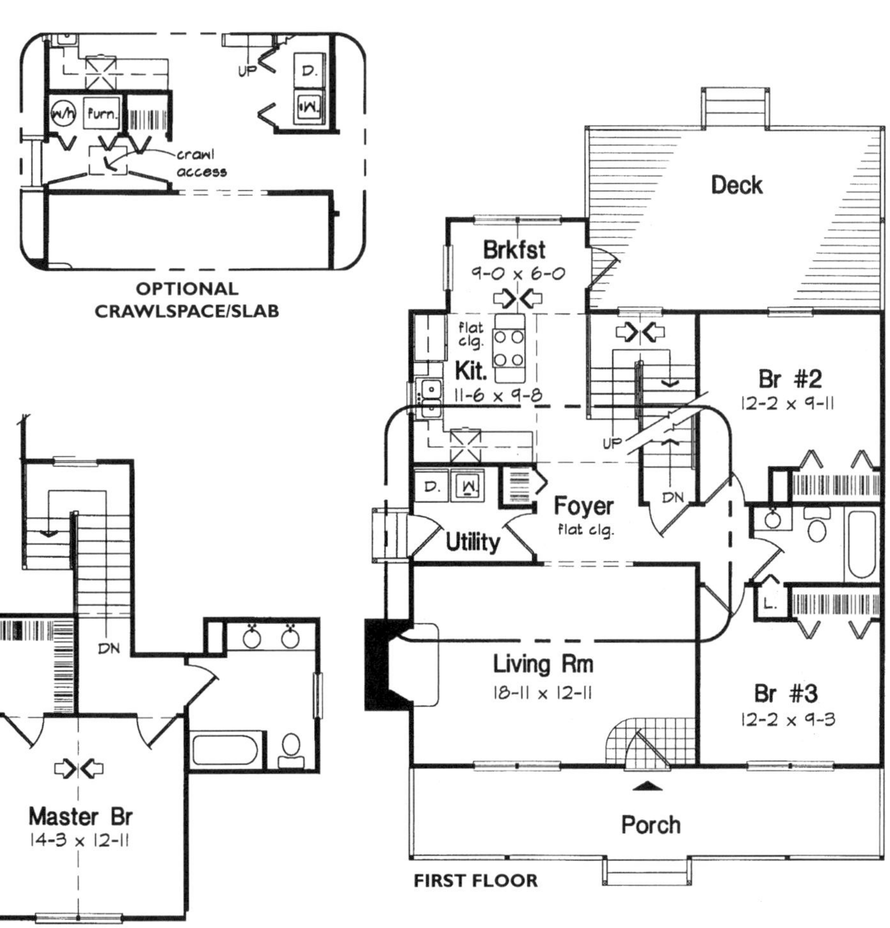

UP
D.
W.
W/H
Furn.
crawl access
OPTIONAL CRAWLSPACE/SLAB
Deck
Brkfst
9-0 x 6-0
Flat clg.
Kit.
11-6 x 9-8
Br #2
12-2 x 9-11
UP
DN
D.
W.
Foyer
Flat clg.
Utility
L.
Living Rm
18-11 x 12-11
Br #3
12-2 x 9-3
Porch
FIRST FLOOR
DN
Master Br
14-3 x 12-11
SECOND FLOOR

PLAN NO. 34602

Family Get-Away

Price Code: B

- This plan features:
  - — Three bedrooms
  - — Two full and one half baths
- A combination Dining/Kitchen with an island work area and Breakfast Bar opening to a Great Room and adjacent to the Laundry/Storage and Half-Bath Area
- A private two-story Master Bedroom with a dormer window, walk-in closet, double vanity Bath and optional Deck with hot tub
- This home is designed with basement, slab and crawlspace foundation options

FIRST FLOOR — 1,061 SQ. FT.
SECOND FLOOR — 499 SQ. FT.
BASEMENT — 1,061 SQ. FT.

Total living area:
1,560 sq. ft.

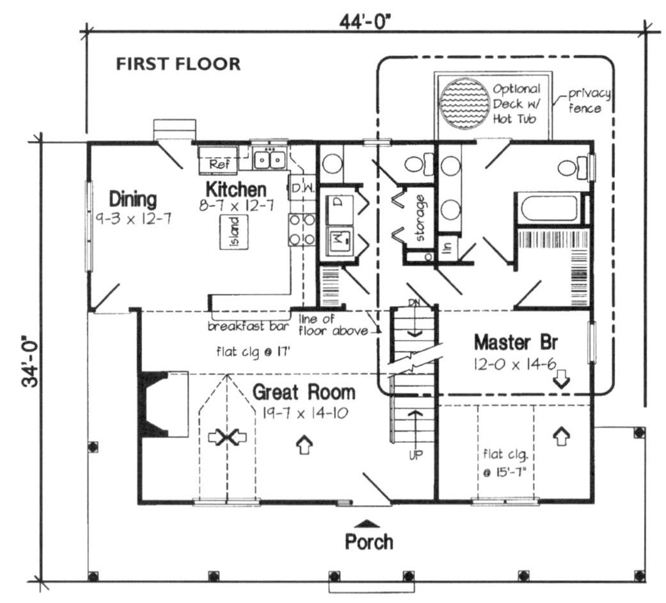
44'-0"
FIRST FLOOR
Optional Deck w/ Hot Tub
privacy fence
Ref
D.W.
Dining
9-3 x 12-7
Kitchen
8-7 x 12-7
island
storage
lin
breakfast bar
line of floor above
flat clg @ 17'
Master Br
12-0 x 14-6
34'-0"
Great Room
19-7 x 14-10
DN
UP
flat clg. @ 15'-7"
Porch

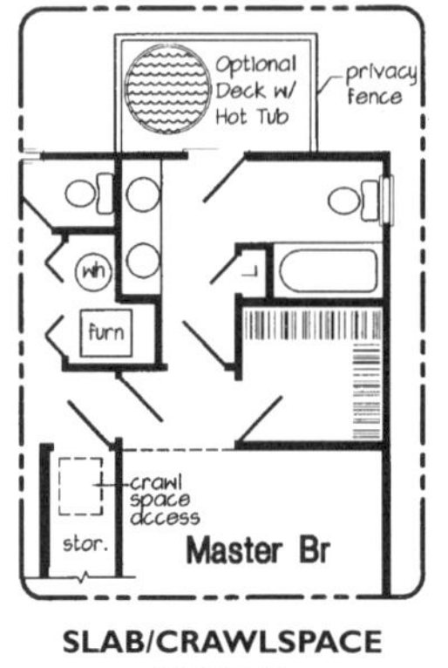
Optional Deck w/ Hot Tub
privacy fence
WH
furn
crawl space access
stor.
Master Br
SLAB/CRAWLSPACE OPTION

SECOND FLOOR

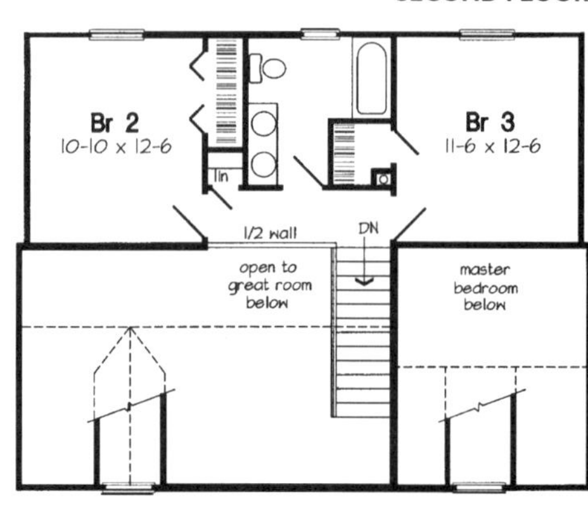
Br 2
10-10 x 12-6
Br 3
11-6 x 12-6
lin
1/2 wall
DN
open to great room below
master bedroom below

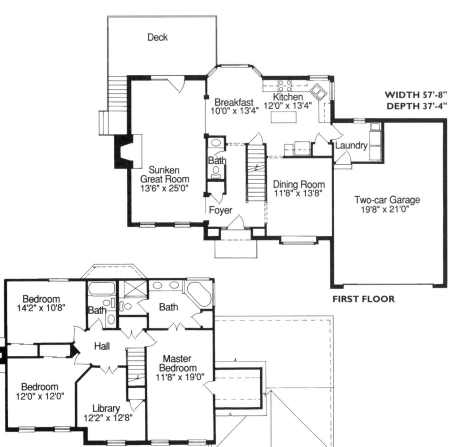

PLAN NO. 92622

Simple Elegance

Price Code: D

- This plan features:
- — Three bedrooms
- — Two full and one half baths
- A sunken Great Room, large enough for family gatherings, is enhanced by a fireplace
- A bay window in the Dining Room has direct access to the Kitchen
- A Master Bedroom Suite features a garden Bath and walk-in closet
- A second floor Library can double as a fourth Bedroom
- This home is designed with a basement foundation

FIRST FLOOR — 1,134 SQ. FT.
SECOND FLOOR — 1,083 SQ. FT.
BASEMENT — 931 SQ. FT.
GARAGE — 554 SQ. FT.

Total living area: 2,217 sq. ft.

Deck
Breakfast 10'0" x 13'4"
Kitchen 12'0" x 13'4"
WIDTH 57'-8"
DEPTH 37'-4"
Laundry
Bath
Sunken Great Room 13'6" x 25'0"
Dining Room 11'8" x 13'8"
Foyer
Two-car Garage 19'8" x 21'0"

FIRST FLOOR

Bedroom 14'2" x 10'8"
Bath
Bath
Hall
Master Bedroom 11'8" x 19'0"
Bedroom 12'0" x 12'0"
Library 12'2" x 12'8"

SECOND FLOOR

PLAN NO. 94956

Spacious Family Living

Price Code: E

- This plan features:
  - — Four bedrooms
  - — Two full and one half baths
- Entry opens to spacious Living Room with a tiered ceiling
- Hub Kitchen easily serves the Dining Room, the Breakfast Bay and the Family Room
- This home is designed with basement and slab foundation options
- Alternate foundation options available at an additional charge. Please call 1-800-235-5700 for more information.

FIRST FLOOR — 1,269 SQ. FT.
SECOND FLOOR — 1,034 SQ. FT.
BASEMENT — 1,269 SQ. FT.
GARAGE — 485 SQ. FT.

Total living area : 2,303 sq. ft.

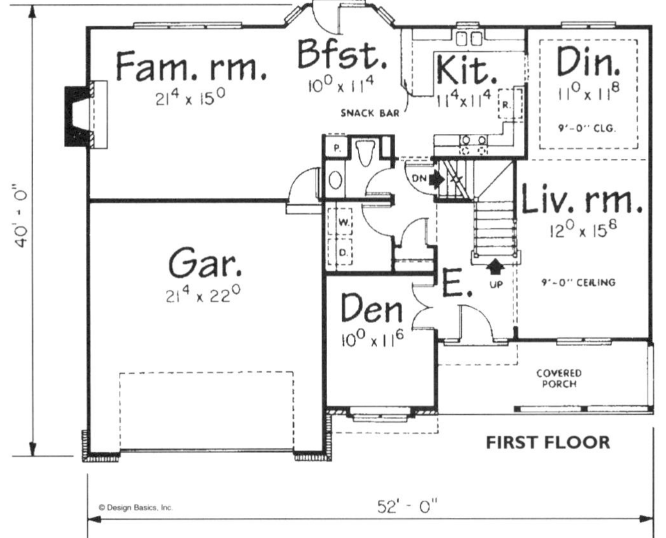
Fam. rm.
$21^{4} \times 15^{0}$
Bfst.
$10^{0} \times 11^{4}$
SNACK BAR
Kit.
$11^{4} \times 11^{4}$
Din.
$11^{0} \times 11^{8}$
9'-0'' CLG.
Liv. rm.
$12^{0} \times 15^{8}$
9'-0'' CEILING
Gar.
$21^{4} \times 22^{0}$
Den
$10^{0} \times 11^{6}$
E.
DN
UP
COVERED PORCH
40' - 0"
52' - 0"
© Design Basics, Inc.
FIRST FLOOR

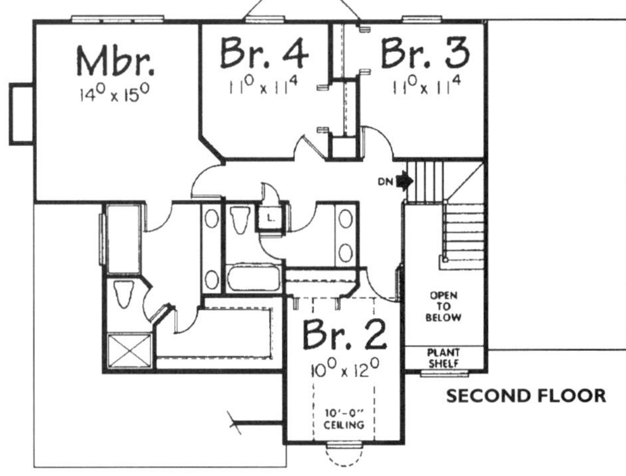
Mbr.
$14^{0} \times 15^{0}$
Br. 4
$11^{0} \times 11^{4}$
Br. 3
$11^{0} \times 11^{4}$
DN
OPEN TO BELOW
PLANT SHELF
Br. 2
$10^{0} \times 12^{0}$
10'-0'' CEILING
SECOND FLOOR

Split Bedroom Plan

Price Code: D

is plan features:

- ree bedrooms
- o full baths
- ing Room is crowned by a tray ceiling
- ing Room/Den privatized by double doors at entrance, and is enhanced by a bay window
- e Kitchen includes a walk-in Pantry and a ner double sink
- e vaulted Breakfast Room flows naturally m the Kitchen
- e Master Suite is topped by a tray ceiling, and ntains a compartmental Bath plus two walk-in sets
- o roomy additional Bedrooms share a full h in the hall
- is home is designed with basement, slab and wlspace foundation options

N FLOOR — 2,051 SQ. FT.
EMENT — 2,051 SQ. FT.
AGE — 441 SQ. FT.

Total living area:
2,051 sq. ft.

PLAN NO.98427

WIDTH 56'-0"
DEPTH 60'-6"

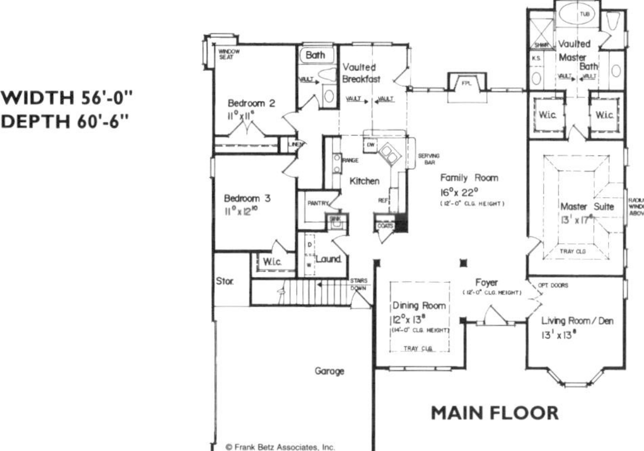

Bath
Vaulted Breakfast
Bedroom 2
Bedroom 3
Kitchen
Family Room
Vaulted Master Bath
W.i.c.
Master Suite
Laund.
Foyer
Dining Room
Living Room / Den
Stor.
Garage
© Frank Betz Associates, Inc.

MAIN FLOOR

With All the Amenities

Price Code: C

is plan features:

- ree bedrooms
- o full and one half baths
- sixteen-foot high ceiling over the Foyer
- ched openings highlight the hallway accessing Great Room, which is further enhanced by a eplace
- French door to the rear yard and decorative umns at its arched entrance
- other vaulted ceiling topping the Dining om, convenient to both the Living Room and Kitchen
- expansive Kitchen features a center work and, a built-in Pantry and a Breakfast Area fined by a tray ceiling
- Master Suite also has a tray ceiling treatment d includes a lavish private Bath and a huge lk-in closet
- condary Bedrooms have private access to a l Bath
- is home is designed with basement, slab and wlspace foundation options

N FLOOR — 1,884 SQ. FT.
EMENT — 1,908 SQ. FT.
AGE — 495 SQ. FT.

Total living area:
1,884 sq. ft.

PLAN NO.98430

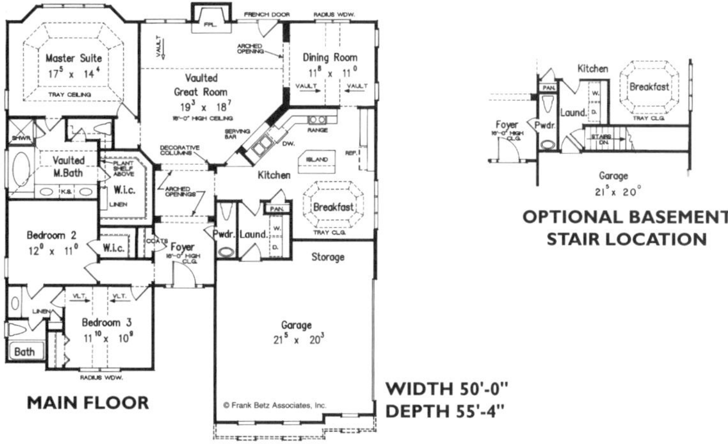

Master Suite
Vaulted Great Room
Dining Room
Vaulted M.Bath
W.i.c.
Kitchen
Breakfast
Bedroom 2
Foyer
Pwdr.
Laund.
Storage
Bedroom 3
Bath
Garage
© Frank Betz Associates, Inc.

MAIN FLOOR

WIDTH 50'-0"
DEPTH 55'-4"

OPTIONAL BASEMENT STAIR LOCATION

PLAN NO. 98463

Open Plan is Full of Air & Light

Price Code: B

- This plan features:
- —Three bedrooms
- —Two full and one half baths
- Foyer open to the Family Room and highlighted by a fireplace
- Dining Room with a sliding glass door to rear yard adjoins Family Room
- Second floor Master Suite topped by tray ceiling over the Bedroom and a vaulted ceiling over the lavish Bath
- This home is designed with basement and crawlspace foundation options

First floor — 767 sq. ft.
Second floor — 738 sq. ft.
Bonus room — 240 sq. ft.
Basement — 767 sq. ft.

Total living area: 1,505 sq. ft.

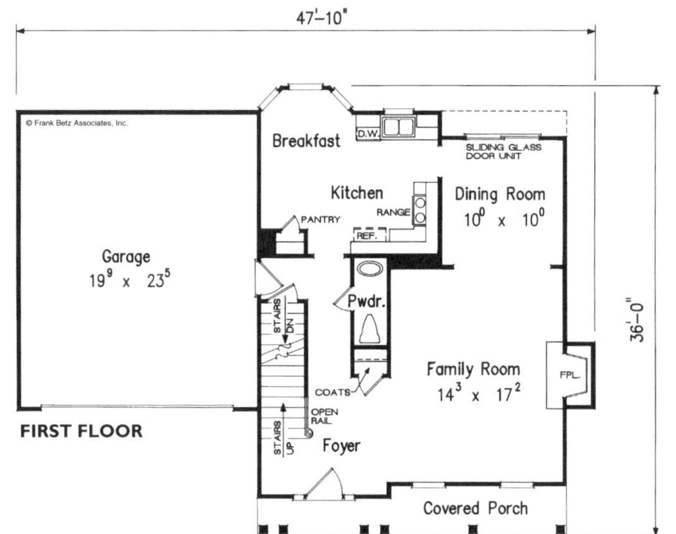

47'-10"
36'-0"
© Frank Betz Associates, Inc.
Breakfast
D.W.
SLIDING GLASS DOOR UNIT
Kitchen
PANTRY
RANGE
REF.
Dining Room
10⁰ x 10⁰
Garage
19⁹ x 23⁵
Pwdr.
STAIRS DN
Family Room
14³ x 17²
FPL.
COATS
OPEN RAIL
STAIRS UP
Foyer
Covered Porch
FIRST FLOOR

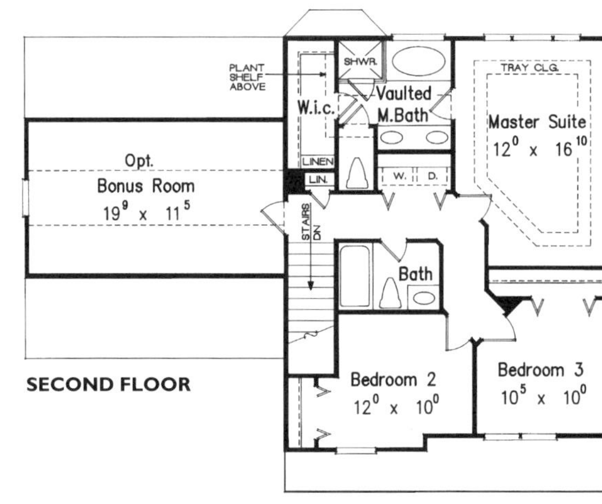

PLANT SHELF ABOVE
SHWR.
W.i.c.
Vaulted M.Bath
TRAY CLG.
Master Suite
12⁰ x 16¹⁰
LINEN
LIN.
W.
D.
Opt.
Bonus Room
19⁹ x 11⁵
STAIRS DN
Bath
Bedroom 2
12⁰ x 10⁰
Bedroom 3
10⁵ x 10⁰
SECOND FLOOR

PLAN NO. 90358

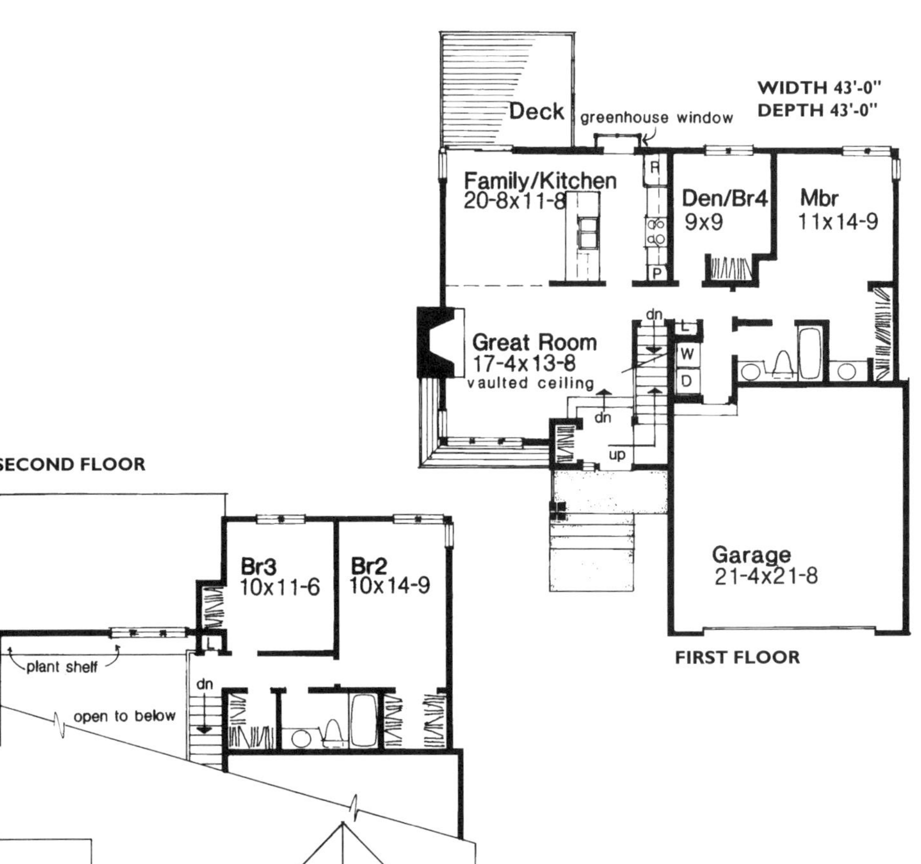
Deck
greenhouse window
WIDTH 43'-0"
DEPTH 43'-0"
Family/Kitchen
20-8x11-8
Den/Br4
9x9
Mbr
11x14-9
Great Room
17-4x13-8
vaulted ceiling
dn
up
Garage
21-4x21-8
FIRST FLOOR
SECOND FLOOR
Br3
10x11-6
Br2
10x14-9
plant shelf
open to below
dn

Three Bedroom
1½ Story Design

Price Code: B

- This plan features:
  - — Three bedrooms
  - — Two full baths
- An efficient Kitchen with a peninsula counter and double sink
- A Family Room with easy access to the wood Deck
- A Master Bedroom with private Bath entrance
- Convenient Laundry Facilities outside the Master Bedroom
- Two additional Bedrooms upstairs with walk-in closets and the use of the full hall Bath
- This home is designed with a basement foundation

FIRST FLOOR — 1,062 SQ. FT.
SECOND FLOOR — 469 SQ. FT.

Total living area:
1,531 sq. ft.

PLAN NO. 93219

Old-Fashioned Country Porc

Price Code: B

- This plan features:

— Three bedrooms

— Two full and one half baths

- A Traditional front Porch, with matching dorr above and a garage hidden below, leading int open, contemporary layout
- A Living Area with a cozy fireplace visible fr the Dining Room for warm entertaining
- A U-shaped, efficient Kitchen featuring a corner double sink and pass-through to the Dining Room
- A convenient half Bath with a Laundry Cente the first floor
- A spacious, first floor Master Suite with a lav Bath including a double vanity, walk-in closet and an oval, corner window tub
- Two large Bedrooms with dormer windows o the second floor sharing a full hall Bath
- This home is designed with a basement foundation

FIRST FLOOR — 1,057 SQ. FT.
SECOND FLOOR — 611 SQ. FT.
BASEMENT — 511 SQ. FT.
GARAGE — 546 SQ. FT.

Total living area:
1,668 sq. ft.

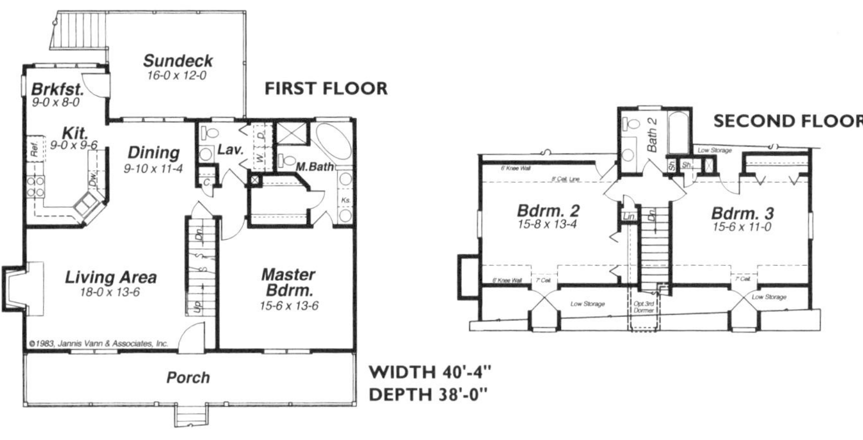

Sundeck
16-0 x 12-0
FIRST FLOOR
Brkfst.
9-0 x 8-0
Kit.
9-0 x 9-6
Dining
9-10 x 11-4
Lav.
M.Bath
Living Area
18-0 x 13-6
Master
Bdrm.
15-6 x 13-6
©1983, Jannis Vann & Associates, Inc.
Porch
WIDTH 40'-4"
DEPTH 38'-0"
SECOND FLOOR
Bath 2
Bdrm. 2
15-8 x 13-4
Bdrm. 3
15-6 x 11-0
Low Storage

PLAN NO. 94917

Attractive Gables and Arche

Price Code: C

- This plan features:

— Three bedrooms

— Two full baths

- Easy-care Entry opens to formal Dining Roo with arched window
- Angles and transom windows add interest to Great Room
- Bright Hearth Area expands Breakfast/Kitche Area and shares three-sided fireplace
- Efficient Kitchen offers an angled snack bar, large Pantry and nearby Laundry/Garage Ent
- Secluded Master Bedroom Suite crowned by decorative ceiling, a large walk-in closet and plush Bath with a whirlpool tub
- Two secondary Bedrooms in separate wing f Master Suite for added privacy
- This home is designed with basement and sla foundation options

MAIN FLOOR — 1,782 SQ. FT.
BASEMENT — 1,782 SQ. FT.
GARAGE — 466 SQ. FT.

Total living area:
1,782 sq. ft.

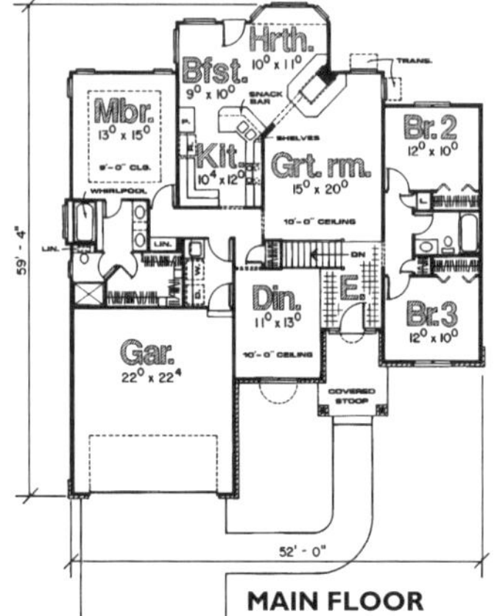

Hrth.
Bfst.
Mbr.
Kit.
Grt. rm.
Br. 2
Din.
E.
Br. 3
Gar.
59' - 4"
52' - 0"
MAIN FLOOR

Surrounded by Sunshine

Price Code: B

his plan features:

- hree bedrooms
- wo full baths
- n Italianate style, featuring columns and tile; riginally designed to sit on the edge of a golf ourse
- n open design with pananoramic vistas in every irection
- ile used from the Foyer, into the Kitchen and ook, as well as in the Utility Room
- whirlpool tub in the elaborate and spacious laster Bedroom Suite
- Great Room with a corner gas fireplace
- turreted Breakfast Nook and an efficient itchen with peninsula counter
- wo family Bedrooms that share a full Bath
- his home is designed with basement and crawl-pace foundation options

IN AREA — 1,731 SQ. FT.
SEMENT — 1,715 SQ. FT.
RAGE — 888 SQ. FT.

Total living area:
1,731 sq. ft.

PLAN NO. 90986

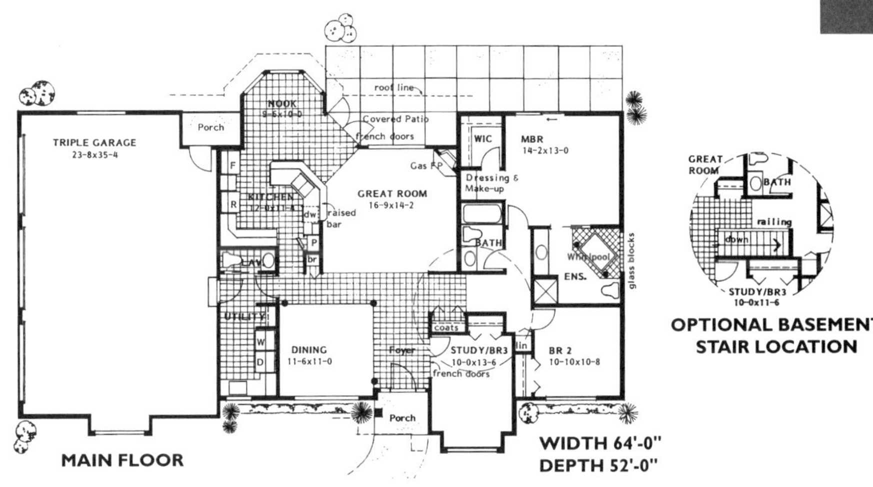
TRIPLE GARAGE
23-8x35-4
Porch
NOOK
9-6x10-0
roof line
Covered Patio
french doors
Gas FP
KITCHEN
12-0x11-8
raised bar
GREAT ROOM
16-9x14-2
WIC
MBR
14-2x13-0
Dressing & Make-up
BATH
Whirlpool
ENS.
glass blocks
UTILITY
DINING
11-6x11-0
Foyer
coats
STUDY/BR3
10-0x13-6
french doors
BR 2
10-10x10-8
Porch
MAIN FLOOR
WIDTH 64'-0"
DEPTH 52'-0"
GREAT ROOM
BATH
railing
down
STUDY/BR3
10-0x11-6
OPTIONAL BASEMENT
STAIR LOCATION

Cozy Three Bedroom

Price Code: B

his plan features:

- hree bedrooms
- wo full baths
- he triple arched front Porch adds to the curb ppeal of the home
- he expansive Great Room is accented by a cozy as fireplace
- he efficient Kitchen includes an eating bar that eparates it from the Great Room
- he Master Bedroom is highlighted by a walk-in loset and a whirlpool Bath
- wo secondary Bedrooms share use of a full athroom
- he rear Porch extends dining to the outdoors
- his home is designed with crawlspace and slab oundation options

AIN FLOOR — 1,515 SQ. FT.
ARAGE — 528 SQ. FT.

Total living area:
1,515 sq. ft.

PLAN NO. 96522

51'
GARAGE
22x24
MAIN FLOOR
60'
MASTER SUITE
15x13
WHIRLPOOL
UTILITY
KITCHEN
14x10
PORCH
BATH
BATH
EATING
CLOSET
BEDRM.
13x12
BEDRM./STUDY
13x12
GREAT ROOM
22x22
FOYER
9' CEILINGS
PORCH

PLAN NO.98435

Outstanding Four Bedroom

Price Code: C

- This plan features:
- — Four bedrooms
- — Two full baths
- Radius window highlighting the exterior and formal Dining Room
- High ceiling topping the Foyer for a grand fi impression
- Vaulted ceiling enhances the Great Room, accented by a fireplace framed by windows t either side
- Arched opening to the Kitchen from the Grea Room
- Breakfast Room topped by a vaulted ceiling a enhanced by elegant French door to the rear
- Tray ceiling and a five-piece compartmental gives luxurious presence to the Master Suite
- Three additional Bedrooms share a full, doub vanity Bath in the hall
- This home is designed with basement and cra space foundation options

MAIN FLOOR — 1,945 SQ. FT.

Total living area:
1,945 sq. ft.

WIDTH 56'-6"
DEPTH 52'-6"

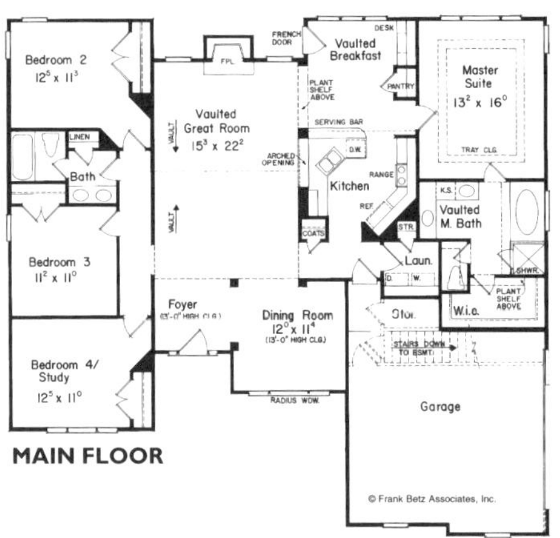
Bedroom 2
Vaulted Great Room
Vaulted Breakfast
Master Suite
Bath
Kitchen
Vaulted M. Bath
Bedroom 3
Foyer
Dining Room
Laun.
W.i.c.
Bedroom 4/ Study
Garage
MAIN FLOOR
© Frank Betz Associates, Inc.

PLAN NO.98549

Angled Elegance

Price Code: A

- This plan features:
- — Three bedrooms
- — Two full baths
- Cathedral and sloped ceilings characterize th family-friendly floor plan
- A fireplace with raised hearth and a built-in media cabinet enhance the Living Room
- The Dining Room and Master Bedroom ove the Patio and backyard
- This home is designed with a slab foundatio

MAIN FLOOR — 1,431 SQ. FT.

Total living area:
1,431 sq. ft.

WIDTH 44'-0"
DEPTH 57'-1"

Patio
MstrBed 12x15
Din 11x9
Kit 11x10
LivRm 19x17
Bed#3 11x11
Bed#2 12x11
Util
Por
Gar 19x21

MAIN FLOOR

PLAN NO. 98485

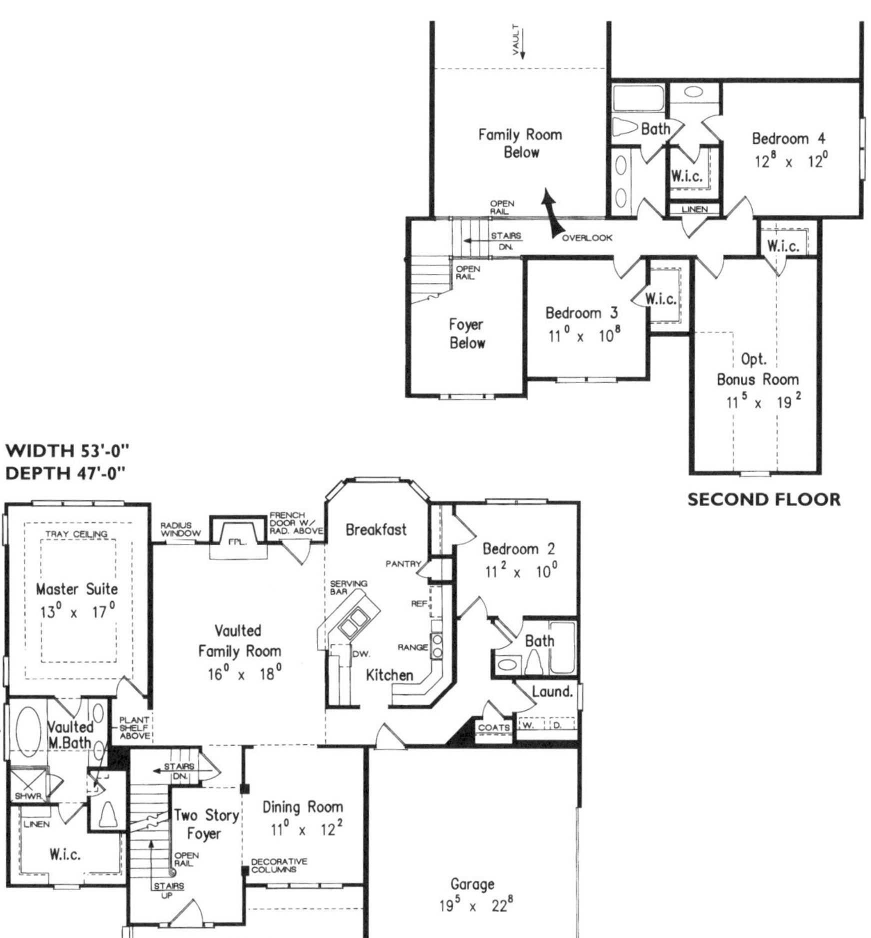

WIDTH 53'-0"
DEPTH 47'-0"
Family Room Below
VAULT
Bath
Bedroom 4
12⁸ x 12⁰
W.i.c.
LINEN
OPEN RAIL
STAIRS DN.
OVERLOOK
W.i.c.
Foyer Below
Bedroom 3
11⁰ x 10⁸
W.i.c.
Opt. Bonus Room
11⁵ x 19²
SECOND FLOOR
Master Suite
13⁰ x 17⁰
TRAY CEILING
RADIUS WINDOW
FPL.
FRENCH DOOR W/ RAD. ABOVE
Breakfast
Bedroom 2
11² x 10⁰
PANTRY
SERVING BAR
REF.
Vaulted Family Room
16⁰ x 18⁰
DW.
RANGE
Kitchen
Bath
Laund.
Vaulted M.Bath
PLANT SHELF ABOVE
COATS
W. D.
SHWR.
STAIRS DN.
Two Story Foyer
Dining Room
11⁰ x 12²
LINEN
W.i.c.
OPEN RAIL
DECORATIVE COLUMNS
STAIRS UP
Garage
19⁵ x 22⁸
Covered Porch
copyright © 1996 frank betz associates, inc.
FIRST FLOOR

Great Curb Appeal

Price Code: D

- This plan features:
  - Four bedrooms
  - Three full baths
- Covered Porch leads to two-story Foyer and striking angled staircase
- The vaulted Family Room has a fireplace and is open to the sunny, bay-windowed Breakfast Room
- The first floor Master Suite features a tray ceiling, plenty of windows, a vaulted Bath, and a large walk-in closet
- This home is designed with basement and crawlspace foundation options

FIRST FLOOR — 1,583 SQ. FT.
SECOND FLOOR — 543 SQ. FT.
BONUS — 251 SQ. FT.
BASEMENT — 1,583 SQ. FT.
GARAGE — 460 SQ. FT.

Total living area:
2,126 sq. ft.

PLAN NO.34603

Beckoning Country Porch

Price Code: B

- This plan features:
- — Three bedrooms
- — Two full and one half baths
- Country-styled exterior with dormer windows above friendly front Porch
- L-shaped Kitchen/Dining Room with work island and atrium door to backyard
- First floor Master Suite with vaulted ceiling, walk-in closet, private Bath and optional private Deck with hot tub
- This home is designed with basement, slab and crawlspace foundation options

FIRST FLOOR — 1,061 SQ. FT.
SECOND FLOOR — 499 SQ. FT.
BASEMENT — 1,061 SQ. FT.

Total living area:
1,560 sq. ft.

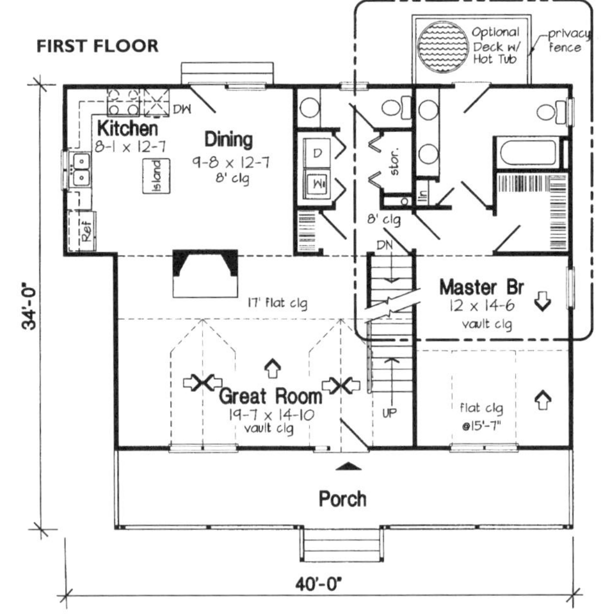
FIRST FLOOR
Optional Deck w/ Hot Tub
privacy fence
DW
Kitchen
8-1 x 12-7
Island
Ref
Dining
9-8 x 12-7
8' clg
D
W
stor.
lin
8' clg
DN
17' flat clg
Master Br
12 x 14-6
vault clg
Great Room
19-7 x 14-10
vault clg
UP
flat clg
@15'-7"
Porch
34'-0"
40'-0"

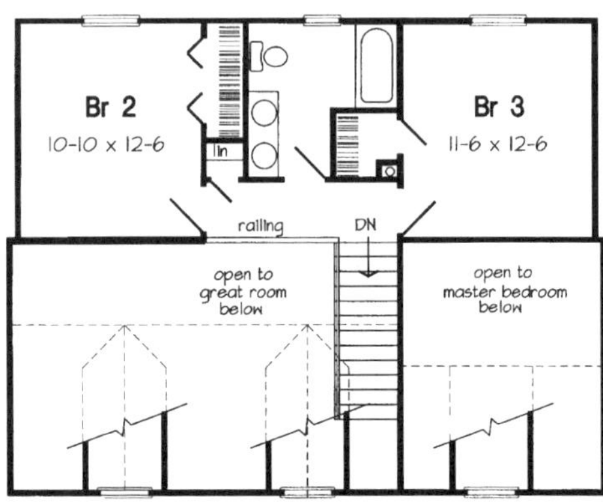
SECOND FLOOR
Br 2
10-10 x 12-6
lin
Br 3
11-6 x 12-6
railing
DN
open to great room below
open to master bedroom below

vered Front and Rear Porches

Price Code: B

nis plan features:

- hree bedrooms
- wo full baths
- aditional Country-styling with front and rear vered Porches
- eninsula counter/eating bar in Kitchen for meals the go
- formal Breakfast area and formal Dining Room th built-in cabinet
- ulted ceiling and cozy fireplace highlighting en
- aster Bedroom suite in private corner pampered five-piece Bath
- lit Bedroom plan with additional Bedrooms at e opposite of home sharing full Bath
- nis home is designed with a crawlspace and ab foundation

IN FLOOR — 1,660 SQ. FT.
RAGE — 544 SQ. FT.

Total living area:
1,660 sq. ft.

PLAN NO.92560

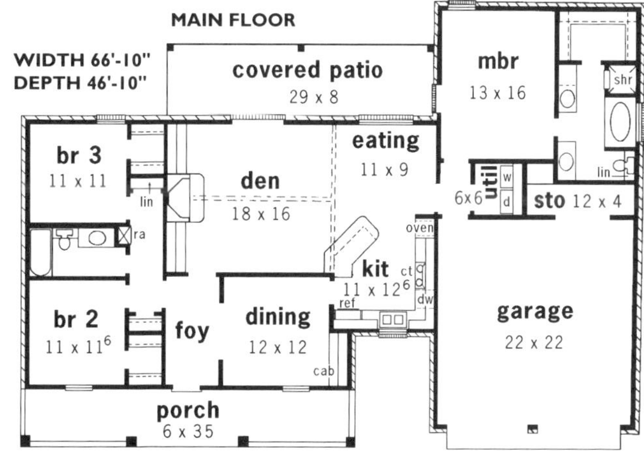
MAIN FLOOR
WIDTH 66'-10"
DEPTH 46'-10"
covered patio 29 x 8
mbr 13 x 16
shr
lin
br 3 11 x 11
lin
den 18 x 16
eating 11 x 9
util 6x6
w
d
sto 12 x 4
ra
oven
kit 11 x 12⁶
ct
dw
ref
br 2 11 x 11⁶
foy
dining 12 x 12
cab
garage 22 x 22
porch 6 x 35

Three Porches Offer Outdoor Charm

Price Code: A

nis plan features:

- hree bedrooms
- wo full baths
- n oversized log-burning fireplace in the acious Living/Dining Area which is two ories high
- nree Porches offering the maximum in outdoor ving space
- private Bedroom located on the second floor
- n efficient Kitchen including an eating bar and cess to the covered Dining Porch

ST FLOOR — 974 SQ. FT.
OND FLOOR — 300 SQ. FT.

Total living area:
1,274 sq. ft.

PLAN NO.90048

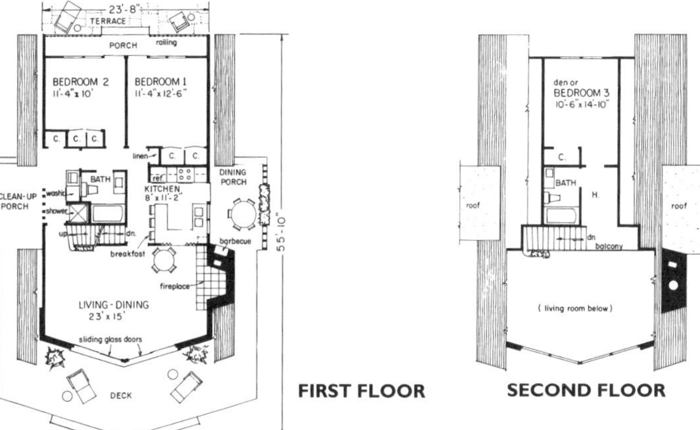
23'-8"
TERRACE
PORCH
railing
BEDROOM 2 11'-4" x 10'
BEDROOM 1 11'-4" x 12'-6"
linen
BATH
KITCHEN 8' x 11'-2"
DINING PORCH
CLEAN-UP PORCH
washer
shower
up
dn.
breakfast
barbecue
fireplace
55'-10"
LIVING - DINING 23' x 15'
sliding glass doors
DECK
FIRST FLOOR
den or BEDROOM 3 10'-6" x 14'-10"
BATH
roof
dn
balcony
(living room below)
SECOND FLOOR

PLAN NO. 98517

Massive Curb Appeal

Price Code: D

- This plan features:
- — Four bedrooms
- — Two full and one half baths
- An arched, two-story entrance starts a luxurious impression of this fine home
- The expansive Great Room boasts a large fireplace flanked by windows
- The angled Kitchen has a large pass-through to the Great Room
- This home is designed with a slab foundation

FIRST FLOOR — 1,472 SQ. FT.
SECOND FLOOR — 703 SQ. FT.
GARAGE — 540 SQ. FT.

Total living area: 2,175 sq. ft.

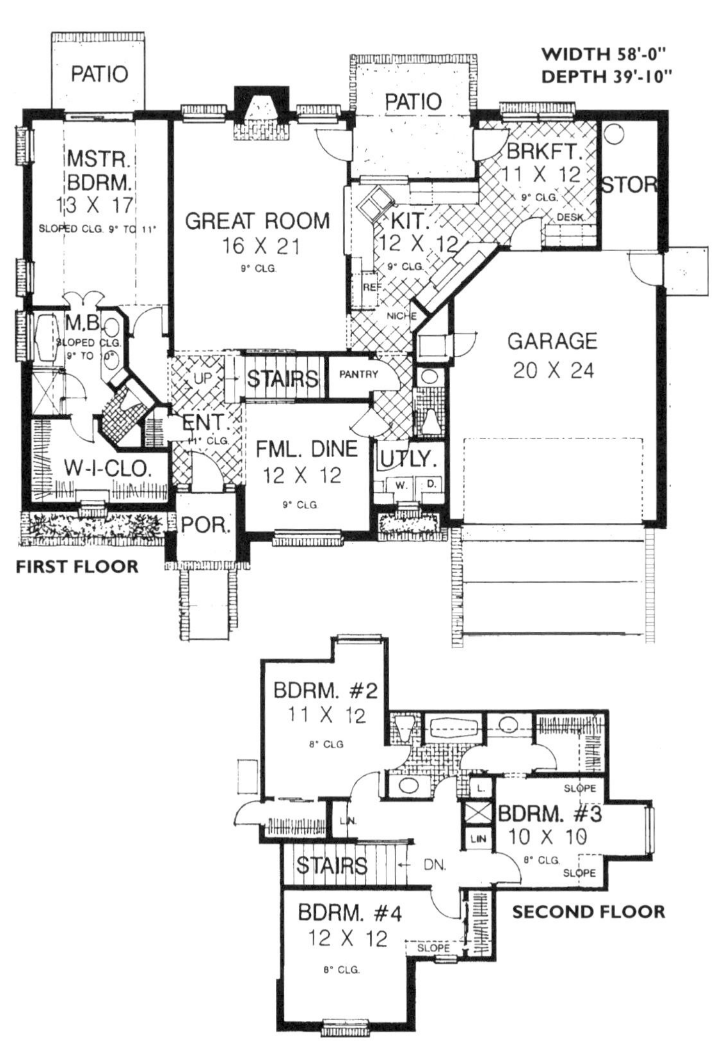

WIDTH 58'-0"
DEPTH 39'-10"
PATIO
PATIO
MSTR. BDRM. 13 X 17
SLOPED CLG. 9" TO 11"
GREAT ROOM 16 X 21
9" CLG.
BRKFT. 11 X 12
9" CLG.
STOR
DESK
KIT. 12 X 12
9" CLG.
REF
NICHE
M.B. SLOPED CLG. 9" TO 10"
UP
STAIRS
PANTRY
GARAGE 20 X 24
ENT.
FML. DINE 12 X 12
9" CLG.
UTLY.
W. D.
W-I-CLO.
POR.
FIRST FLOOR
BDRM. #2 11 X 12
8" CLG.
SLOPE
L.
LIN
BDRM. #3 10 X 10
8" CLG.
SLOPE
LIN
STAIRS
DN.
BDRM. #4 12 X 12
8" CLG.
SLOPE
SECOND FLOOR

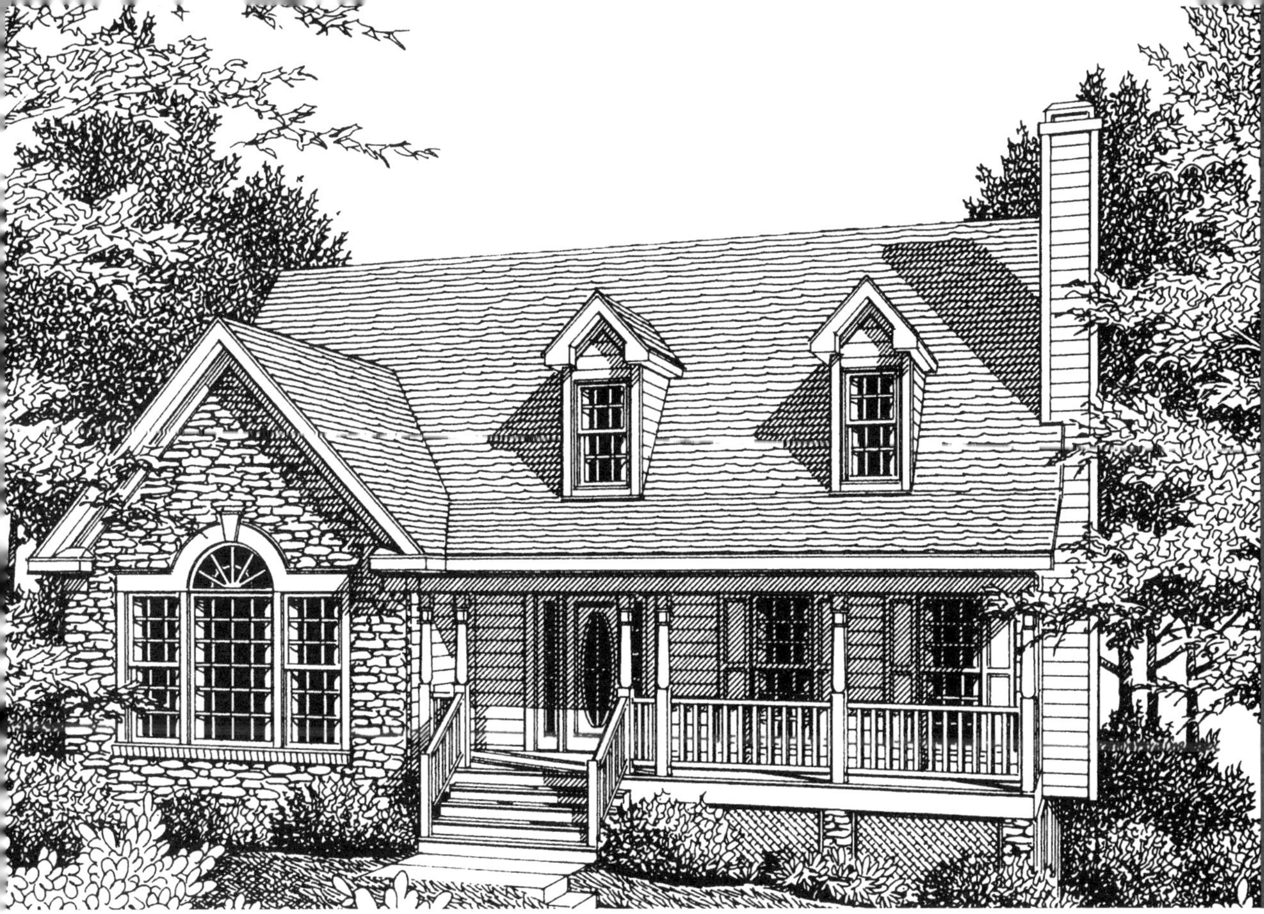

PLAN NO. 98931

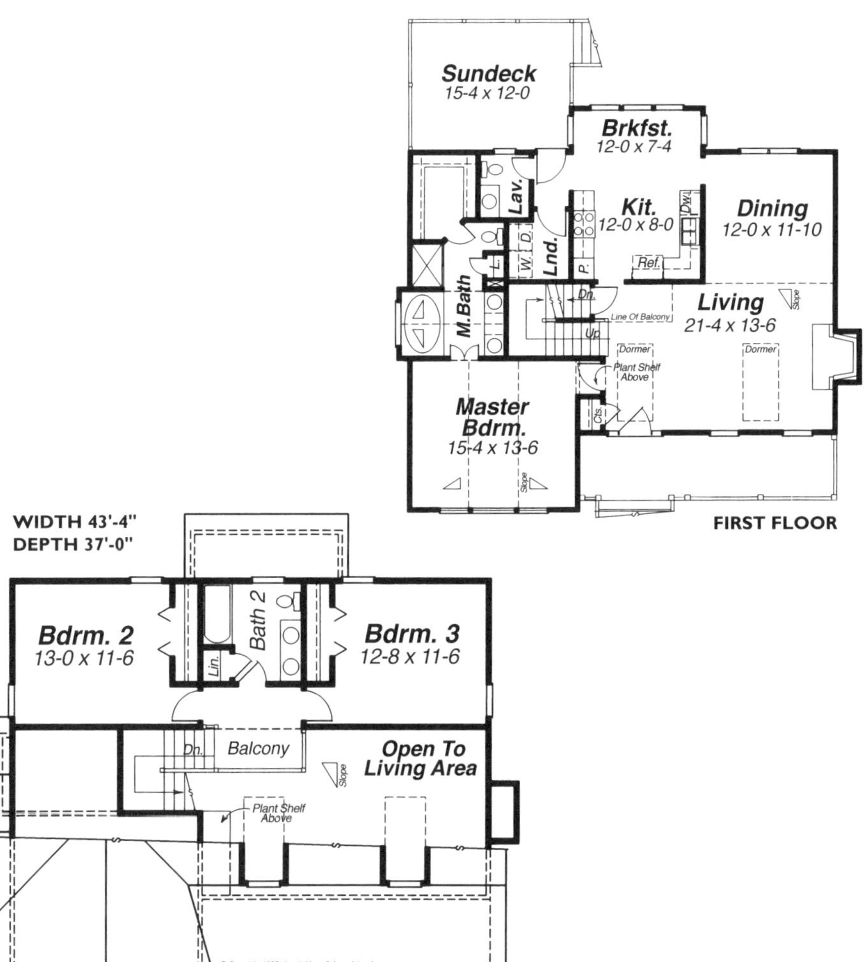
Sundeck
15-4 x 12-0
Brkfst.
12-0 x 7-4
Lav.
Kit.
12-0 x 8-0
Dining
12-0 x 11-10
W.
D.
Lnd.
P.
Ref.
Dw.
M.Bath
Dn.
Line Of Balcony
Up
Living
21-4 x 13-6
Slope
Dormer
Plant Shelf Above
Dormer
Master Bdrm.
15-4 x 13-6
Slope
Clo.
FIRST FLOOR
WIDTH 43'-4"
DEPTH 37'-0"
Bdrm. 2
13-0 x 11-6
Bath 2
Lin.
Bdrm. 3
12-8 x 11-6
Dn.
Balcony
Open To Living Area
Slope
Plant Shelf Above
SECOND FLOOR

Second-Floor Balcony

Price Code: C

- This plan features:
- — Three bedrooms
- — Two full and one baths
- The Living Room soars two full stories with pleasing architectural details like dormer windows and an overhead plant shelf
- The Master Bath has a sloped ceiling over the garden tub
- The open Breakfast Nook offers views of the Sun Deck and backyard
- This home is designed with a basement foundation

FIRST FLOOR — 1,210 SQ. FT.
SECOND FLOOR — 555 SQ. FT.
GARAGE — 612 SQ. FT.
PORCH — 144 SQ. FT.

Total living area:
1,765 sq. ft.

PLAN NO. 92539

Arches Add Ambiance

Price Code: D

- This plan features:
- — Four bedrooms
- — Two full and one half baths
- Arched two-story entrance highlighted by a lovely arched window
- Expansive Den offers hearth fireplace between book shelves, raised ceiling and access to rear yard
- Efficient Kitchen with peninsula counter, built-in Pantry, Breakfast Bay, Garage Entry, Laundry and adjoining Dining Room
- This home is designed with crawl-space and slab foundation options

FIRST FLOOR — 1,250 SQ. FT.
SECOND FLOOR — 783 SQ. FT
GARAGE AND STORAGE — 555 SQ. FT.

**Total living area:
2,033 sq. ft.**

57'-0"
40'-0"
BOOKS
DEN
18'-0" x 16'-0"
BREAKFAST
11'-0" x 10'-0"
WASH
DRY
STORAGE
12-0" x 6'-0"
UP
PANT
SINK
KITCHEN
RANGE
DW
REF
HVAC
M. BATH
LIN
GARAGE
22-0" x 22'-0"
DINING
11'-0" x 14'-0"
FOYER
MASTER BED
14'-0" x 12'-0"
PORCH
FIRST FLOOR
33'-0"
OPEN TO DEN
BEDROOM 2
11'-0" x 13'-0"
DOWN
LIN
HVAC
BEDROOM 3
11'-0" x 13'-0"
OPEN TO FOYER
BEDROOM 4
14'-0" x 12'-0"
SECOND FLOOR

PLAN NO. 98474

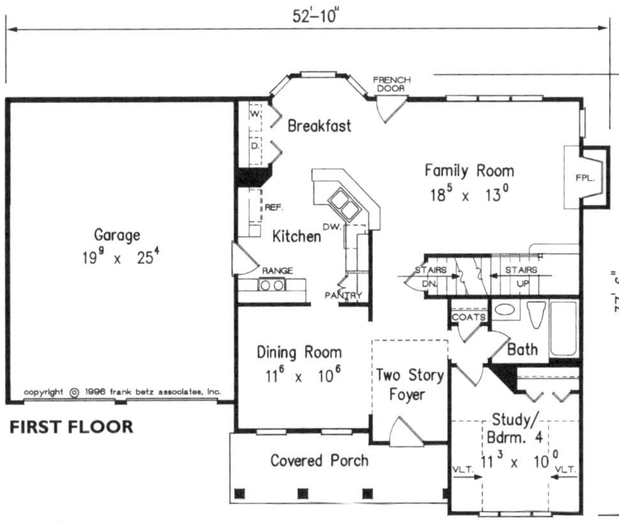

Triple Arched Porch

Price Code: B

- This plan features:
- — Four bedrooms
- — Three full baths
- A triple arched front Porch, segmented arched window keystones and shutters accent the exterior
- The Study/Bedroom Four is topped by a vaulted ceiling and is located close to a full Bath
- The Master Suite is topped by a tray ceiling while there is a vaulted ceiling over the Bath
- This home is designed with basement and crawlspace foundation options

FIRST FLOOR — 972 SQ. FT.
SECOND FLOOR — 772 SQ. FT.
BONUS ROOM — 358 SQ. FT.
BASEMENT — 972 SQ. FT.
GARAGE — 520 SQ. FT.

Total living area: 1,744 sq. ft.

52'-10"
37'-6"
Garage 19⁹ x 25⁴
Breakfast
Family Room 18⁵ x 13⁰
Kitchen
Dining Room 11⁶ x 10⁶
Two Story Foyer
Bath
Study/ Bdrm. 4 11³ x 10⁰
Covered Porch

FIRST FLOOR

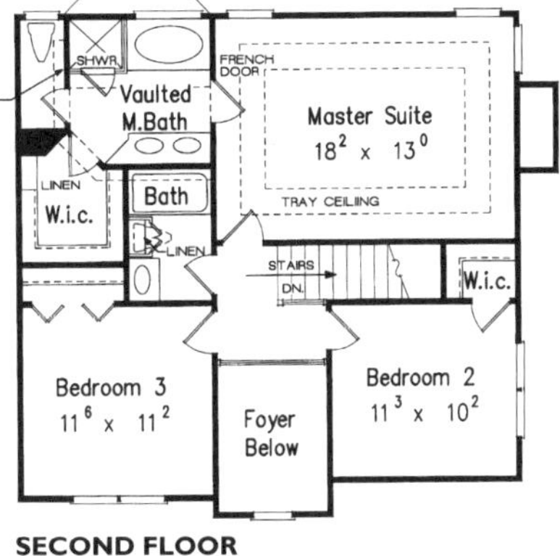
Vaulted M.Bath
Master Suite 18² x 13⁰
TRAY CEILING
W.i.c.
Bath
Bedroom 3 11⁶ x 11²
Foyer Below
Bedroom 2 11³ x 10²

SECOND FLOOR

BONUS

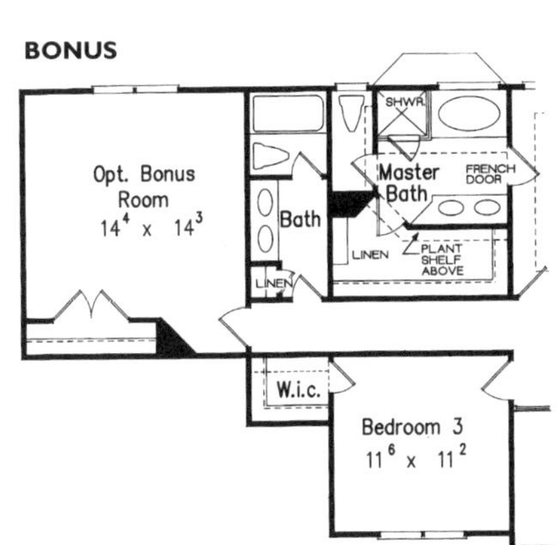
Opt. Bonus Room 14⁴ x 14³
Bath
Master Bath
W.i.c.
Bedroom 3 11⁶ x 11²

PLAN NO. 92655

Backyard Views

Price Code: B

- This plan features:
- — Three bedrooms
- — Two full baths
- Front Porch accesses open Foyer, and spacic Dining Room and Great Room with sloped ceilings
- Corner fireplace, windows and atrium door Patio enhance Great Room
- Convenient Kitchen with a Pantry, peninsula serving counter for bright Breakfast Area an nearby Laundry/Garage Entry
- Luxurious Bath, walk-in closet and backyard view offered in Master Bedroom
- Two additional Bedrooms, one with an arch window, share full Bath
- This home is designed with a basement foundation

MAIN FLOOR — 1,746 SQ. FT.
BASEMENT — 1,746 SQ. FT.
GARAGE — 480 SQ. FT.

Total living area:
1,746 sq. ft.

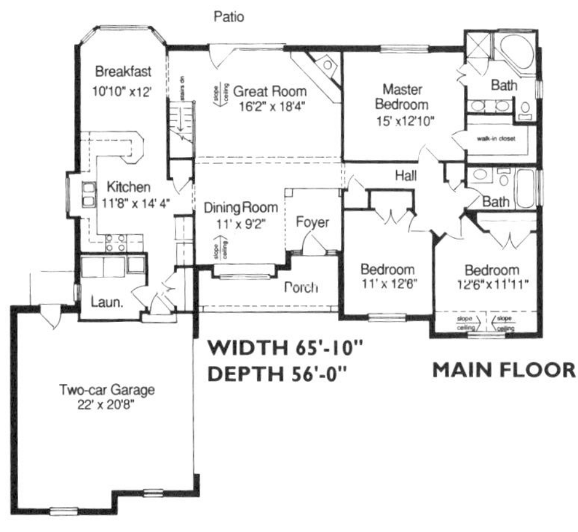
Patio
Breakfast
10'10" x12'
Great Room
16'2" x 18'4"
Master
Bedroom
15' x12'10"
Bath
walk-in closet
Hall
Kitchen
11'8" x 14' 4"
Dining Room
11' x 9'2"
Foyer
Bath
Bedroom
11' x 12'6"
Bedroom
12'6"x11'11"
Porch
Laun.
Two-car Garage
22' x 20'8"
WIDTH 65'-10"
DEPTH 56'-0"
MAIN FLOOR

PLAN NO. 93161

Hip Roof Ranch

Price Code: B

- This plan features:
- — Three bedrooms
- — Two full baths
- Cozy front Porch leads into Entry with vaul ceiling and sidelights
- Open Living Room enhanced by a cathedral ceiling, a wall of windows and corner firepl
- Large and efficient Kitchen with an extende counter and a bright Dining Area with acces to Screened Porch
- Convenient Utility Area with access to Gara and Storage Area
- Spacious Master Bedroom with a walk-in cl and private Bath
- Two additional Bedrooms with ample closet share a full Bath
- This home is designed with a basement foundation

MAIN FLOOR — 1,540 SQ. FT.
BASEMENT — 1,540 SQ. FT.

Total living area:
1,540 sq. ft.

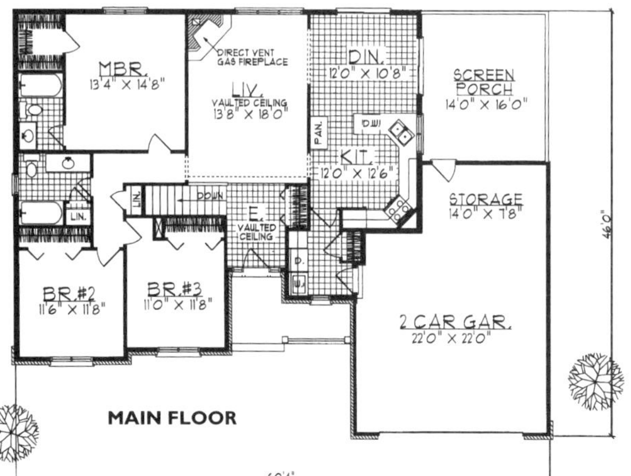
MBR.
13'4" X 14'8"
DIRECT VENT
GAS FIREPLACE
LIV.
VAULTED CEILING
13'8" X 18'0"
DIN.
12'0" X 10'8"
SCREEN
PORCH
14'0" X 16'0"
PAN.
KIT.
12'0" X 12'6"
LIN.
DOWN
E.
VAULTED
CEILING
STORAGE
14'0" X 7'8"
BR.#2
11'6" X 11'8"
BR.#3
11'0" X 11'8"
2 CAR GAR.
22'0" X 22'0"
46'0"
MAIN FLOOR
60'4"

PLAN NO. 20069

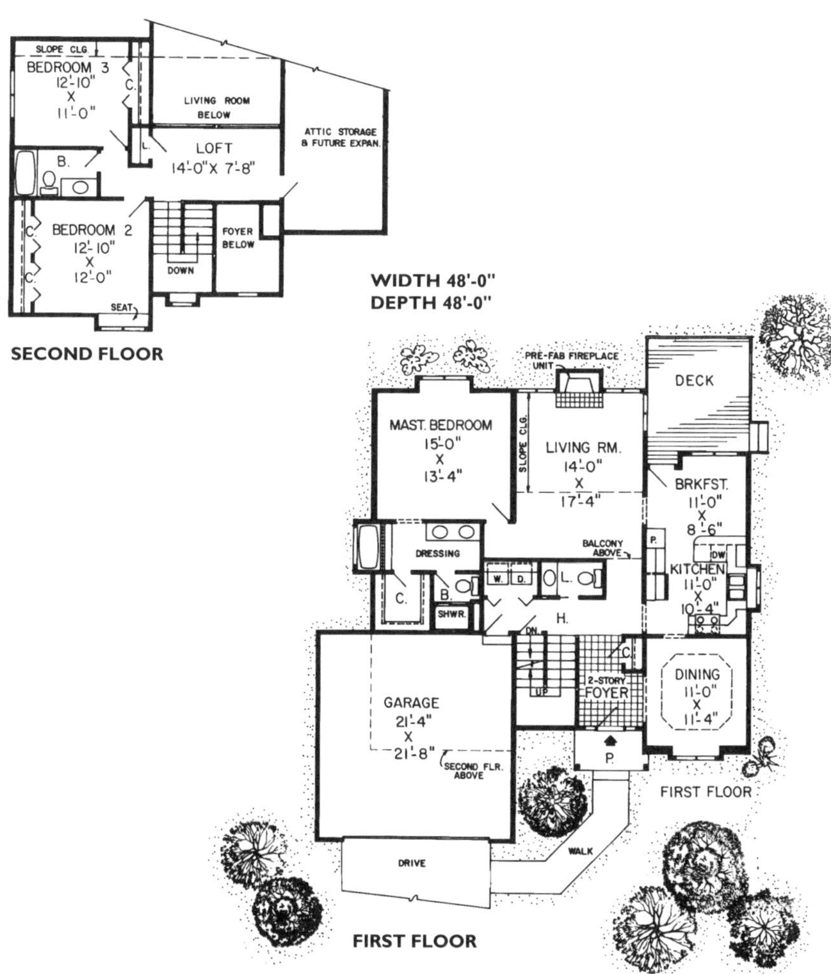
SLOPE CLG
BEDROOM 3
12'-10" X 11'-0"
C.
LIVING ROOM BELOW
ATTIC STORAGE & FUTURE EXPAN.
LOFT
14'-0" X 7'-8"
L.
B.
BEDROOM 2
12'-10" X 12'-0"
C.
FOYER BELOW
DOWN
SEAT
SECOND FLOOR
WIDTH 48'-0"
DEPTH 48'-0"
PRE-FAB FIREPLACE UNIT
DECK
MAST. BEDROOM
15'-0" X 13'-4"
SLOPE CLG.
LIVING RM.
14'-0" X 17'-4"
BRKFST.
11'-0" X 8'-6"
P.
DW
BALCONY ABOVE
KITCHEN
11'-0" X 10'-4"
DRESSING
C.
B.
SHWR.
W.
D.
L.
H.
DN
UP
2-STORY FOYER
DINING
11'-0" X 11'-4"
GARAGE
21'-4" X 21'-8"
SECOND FLR. ABOVE
P.
DRIVE
WALK
FIRST FLOOR
FIRST FLOOR

Stylish and Practical Plan

Price Code: D

- This plan features:
  - — Three bedrooms
  - — Two and one half baths
- A Kitchen with a Breakfast Area large enough for most informal meals
- A spacious Living Room with a fireplace
- A formal Dining Room with a decorative ceiling for comfortable entertaining
- A first floor Master Bedroom providing a private retreat and lavish Master Bath

FIRST FLOOR — 1,345 SQ. FT.
SECOND FLOOR — 662 SQ. FT.
BONUS — 122 SQ. FT.
BASEMENT — 1,304 SQ. FT.
GARAGE — 477 SQ. FT.

Total living area:
2,007 sq. ft.

PLAN NO. 99174

A Traditional Ranch

Price Code: C

- This plan features:
- — Three bedrooms
- — Two full and one half baths
- The two-car Garage offers the option of a third bay or extra storage space
- Columns and a lowered soffit define the separation of Kitchen from Living Room
- The Master Bedroom features a private Bath with separate shower and large walk-in closet
- Two additional Bedrooms offer ample closet space
- This home is designed with a basement foundation

MAIN FLOOR — 1,859 SQ. FT.
GARAGE — 750 SQ. FT.

Total living area:
1,859 sq. ft.

Rear Elevat

MAIN FLOOR

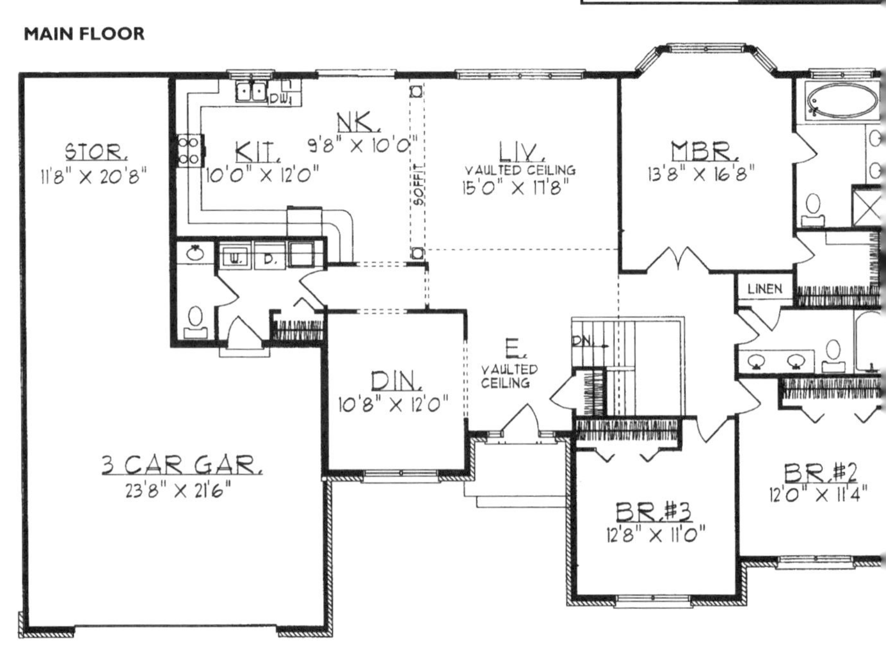

STOR.
11'8" X 20'8"
KIT.
10'0" X 12'0"
NK.
9'8" X 10'0"
DW
SOFFIT
LIV.
VAULTED CEILING
15'0" X 17'8"
MBR.
13'8" X 16'8"
W.
D.
LINEN
DN
E.
VAULTED CEILING
DIN.
10'8" X 12'0"
3 CAR GAR.
23'8" X 21'6"
BR.#3
12'8" X 11'0"
BR.#2
12'0" X 11'4"

PLAN NO. 93413

Open & Airy

Price Code: C

- This plan features:
  - — Three bedrooms
  - — Two full and one half baths
- The Foyer is naturally lit by a dormer window above
- Family Room is highlighted by two front windows and a fireplace
- Dining Area opens to the Kitchen, for a more spacious feeling
- The roomy Master Suite is located on the first floor and has a private five-piece Bath plus a walk-in closet
- Laundry Room doubles as a Mud Room from the side entrance
- This home is designed with a basement founation

FIRST FLOOR — 1,271 SQ. FT.
SECOND FLOOR — 537 SQ. FT.
BASEMENT — 1,271 SQ. FT.
GARAGE — 555 SQ. FT.

Total living area: 1,808 sq. ft.

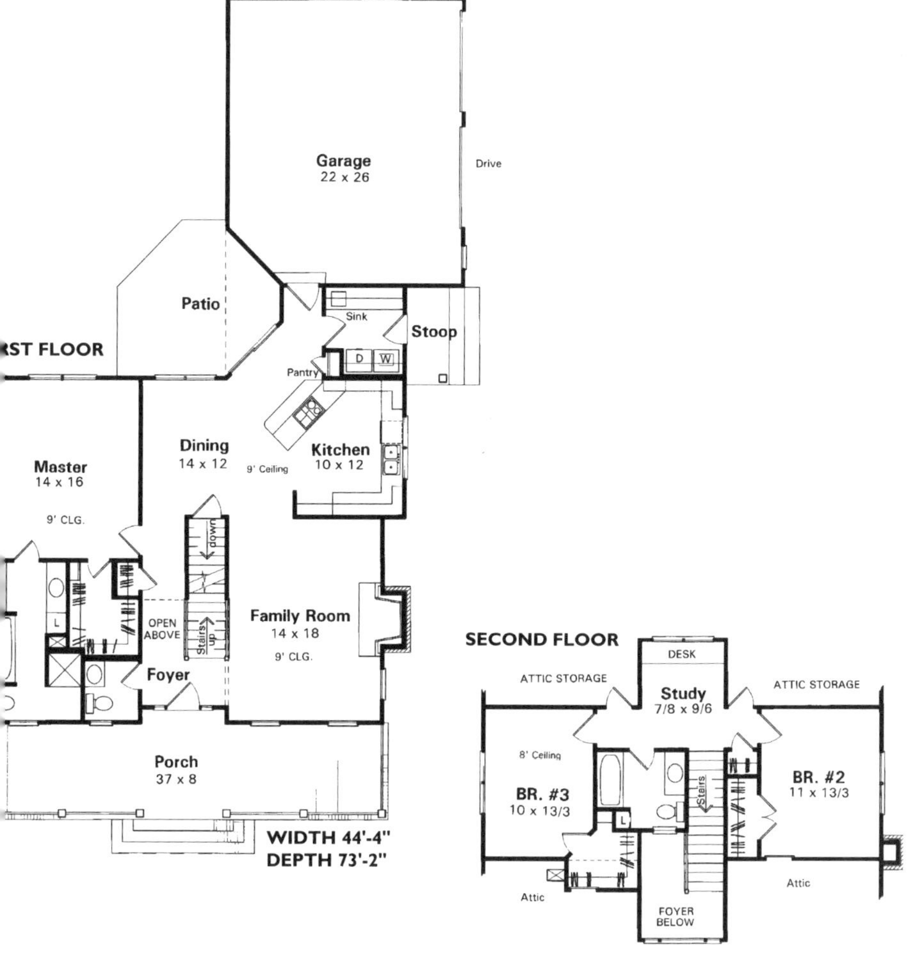
Garage
22 x 26
Drive
Patio
Stoop
Sink
D
W
Pantry
RST FLOOR
Dining
14 x 12
9' Ceiling
Kitchen
10 x 12
Master
14 x 16
9' CLG.
down
OPEN ABOVE
Stairs up
Family Room
14 x 18
9' CLG.
Foyer
Porch
37 x 8
WIDTH 44'-4"
DEPTH 73'-2"
SECOND FLOOR
DESK
ATTIC STORAGE
Study
7/8 x 9/6
ATTIC STORAGE
8' Ceiling
BR. #3
10 x 13/3
Stairs
BR. #2
11 x 13/3
Attic
Attic
FOYER BELOW

PLAN NO. 68161

Backyard Oasis

Price Code: C

- This plan features:
- — Three bedrooms
- — Two full baths
- Screened and covered Porches add to the living space in this gracious home
- The large fireplaced Living Room offers access to the Screened porch and opens to a sunny Nook
- Optional doors from the Foyer to the third Bedroom create a Study
- This home is designed with slab and crawlspace foundation options
- Alternate foundation options available at an additional charge. Please call 1-800-235-5700 for more information.

FIRST FLOOR — 1,995 SQ. FT.
GARAGE — 678 SQ. FT.

Total living area: 1,955 sq. ft.

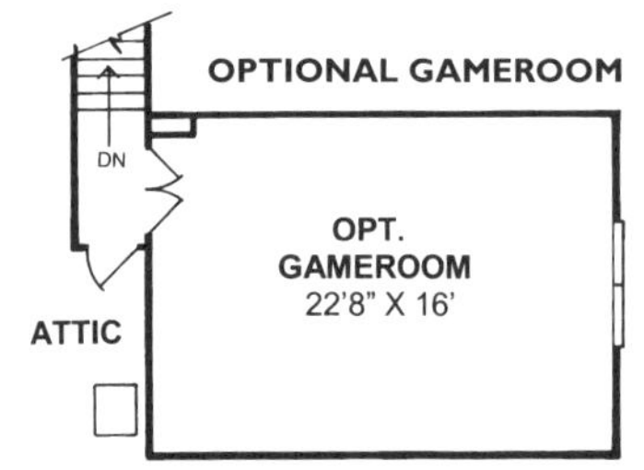
OPTIONAL GAMEROOM
DN
OPT. GAMEROOM
22'8" X 16'
ATTIC

Rear Elevat

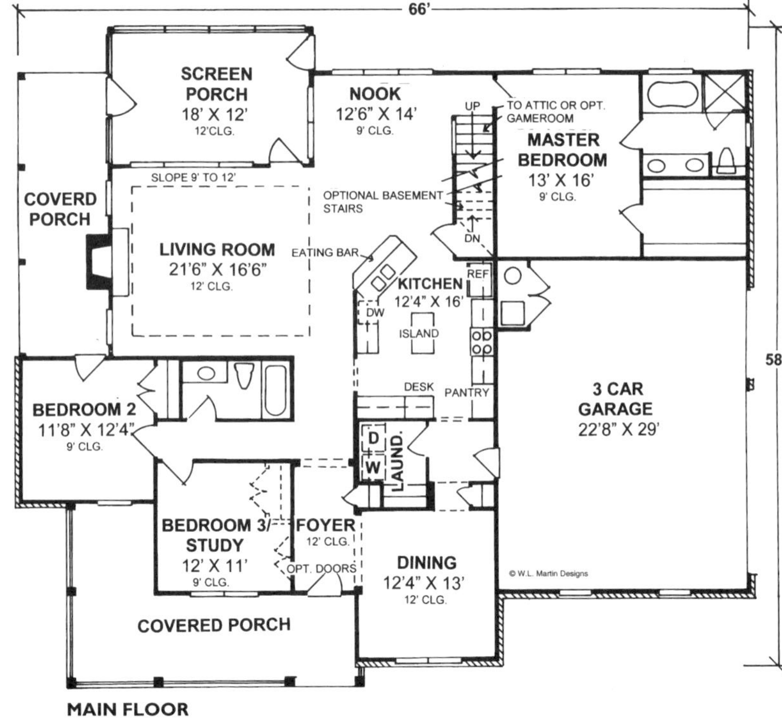
66'
58'
SCREEN PORCH
18' X 12'
12'CLG.
NOOK
12'6" X 14'
9' CLG.
UP
TO ATTIC OR OPT. GAMEROOM
MASTER BEDROOM
13' X 16'
9' CLG.
COVERD PORCH
SLOPE 9' TO 12'
OPTIONAL BASEMENT STAIRS
LIVING ROOM
21'6" X 16'6"
12' CLG.
EATING BAR
DN
KITCHEN
12'4" X 16'
REF
DW
ISLAND
DESK
PANTRY
3 CAR GARAGE
22'8" X 29'
BEDROOM 2
11'8" X 12'4"
9' CLG.
D
W
LAUND.
BEDROOM 3/ STUDY
12' X 11'
9' CLG.
FOYER
12' CLG.
OPT. DOORS
DINING
12'4" X 13'
12' CLG.
© W.L. Martin Designs
COVERED PORCH
MAIN FLOOR

PLAN NO. 94248

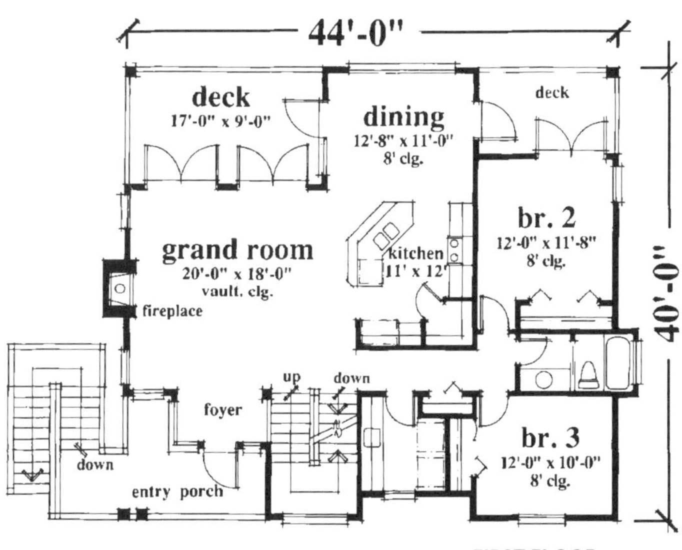

44'-0"
40'-0"
deck
17'-0" x 9'-0"
dining
12'-8" x 11'-0"
8' clg.
deck
br. 2
12'-0" x 11'-8"
8' clg.
grand room
20'-0" x 18'-0"
vault. clg.
kitchen
11' x 12'
fireplace
up
down
foyer
down
entry porch
br. 3
12'-0" x 10'-0"
8' clg.

FIRST FLOOR

SECOND FLOOR

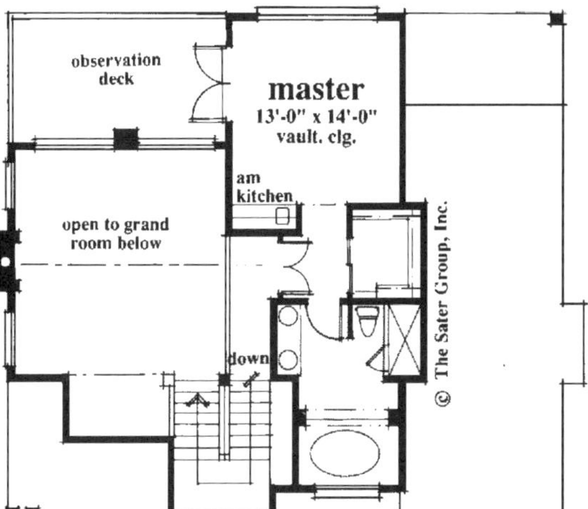

observation deck
master
13'-0" x 14'-0"
vault. clg.
am kitchen
open to grand room below
down
© The Sater Group, Inc.

Delightful Home

Price Code: D

- This plan features:
  - — Three bedrooms
  - — Two full baths
- Grand Room features a fireplace, vaulted ceiling and double French doors to the rear deck
- Kitchen has a large walk-in Pantry and island with a sink and dishwasher, creating a perfect triangular workspace
- Master Bedroom features a double door Entry, private Bath, and a morning Kitchen
- This home is designed with a pier/post foundation
- Alternate foundation options available at an additional charge. Please call 1-800-235-5700 for more information.

FIRST FLOOR — 1,342 SQ. FT.
SECOND FLOOR — 511 SQ. FT.

Total living area:
1,853 sq. ft.

PLAN NO. 20100

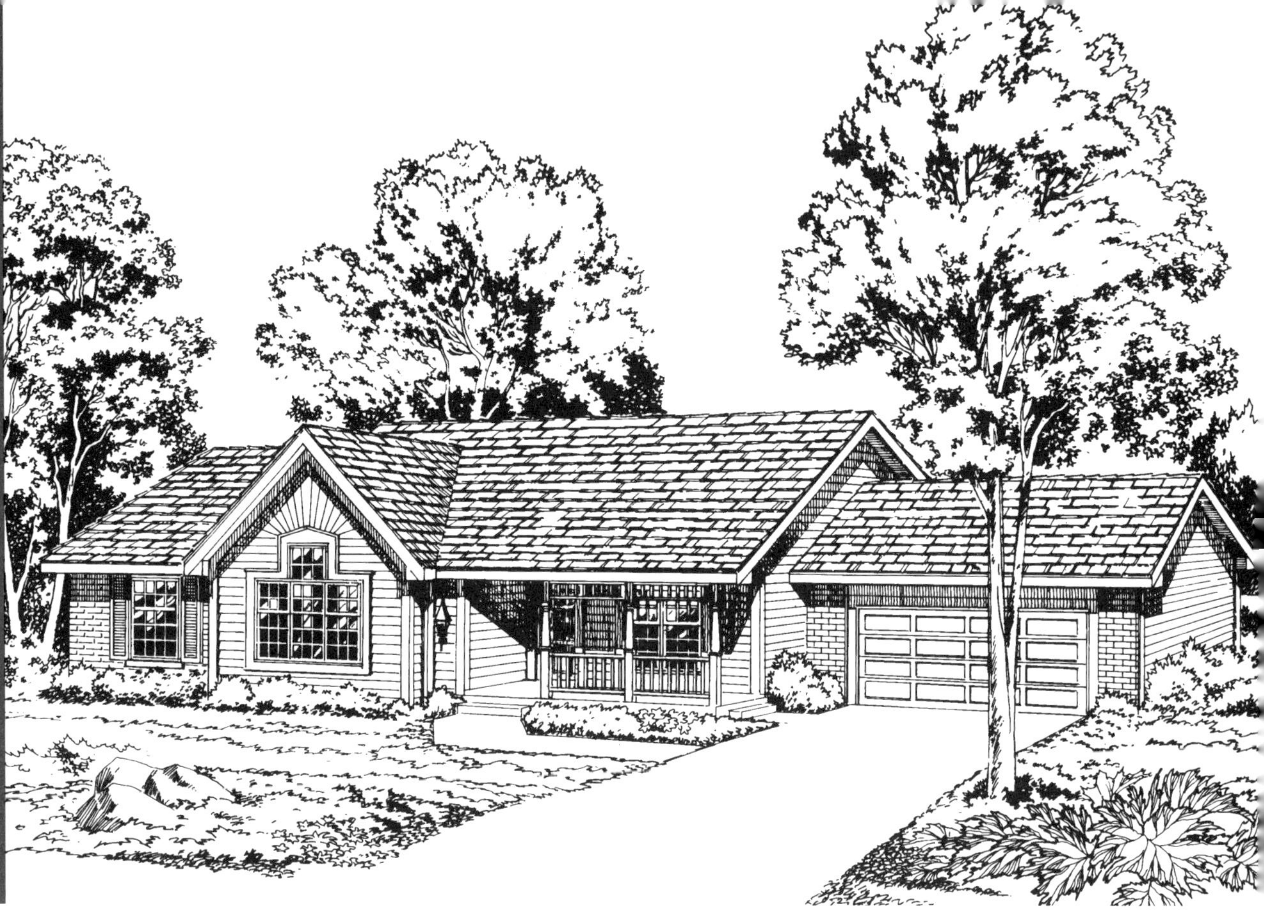

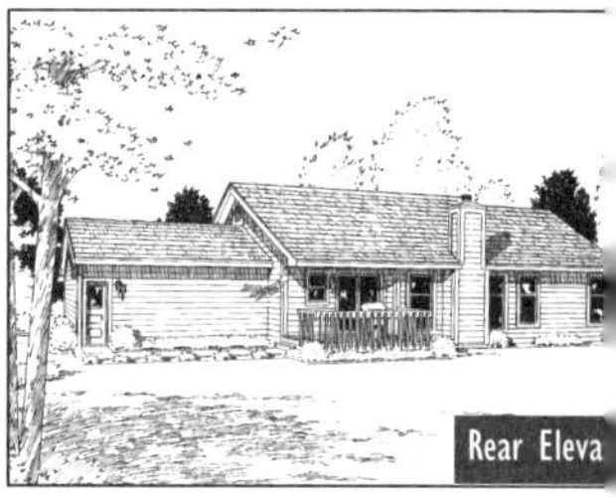

Rear Eleva

Wide Open and Convenient

- This plan features:
- — Three bedrooms
- — Two full baths
- Vaulted ceilings in the Dining Room and Master Bedroom
- A sloped ceiling in the fireplaced Living Room
- A skylight illuminating the Master Bath
- A large Master Bedroom with a walk-in closet
- This home is designed with basement, slab and crawlspace foundation options

MAIN FLOOR — 1,737 SQ. FT.
BASEMENT — 1,727 SQ. FT.
GARAGE — 484 SQ. FT.

Total living area: 1,737 sq. ft.

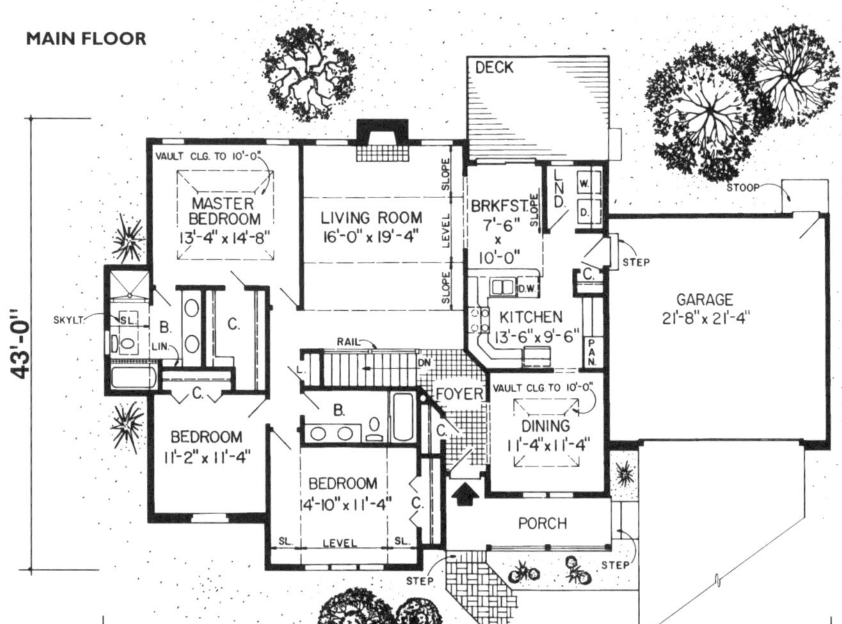

MAIN FLOOR
DECK
VAULT CLG. TO 10'-0"
MASTER BEDROOM 13'-4" x 14'-8"
LIVING ROOM 16'-0" x 19'-4"
BRKFST. 7'-6" x 10'-0"
LND.
STOOP
STEP
GARAGE 21'-8" x 21'-4"
KITCHEN 13'-6" x 9'-6"
SKYLT.
RAIL
FOYER
VAULT CLG TO 10'-0"
DINING 11'-4" x 11'-4"
BEDROOM 11'-2" x 11'-4"
BEDROOM 14'-10" x 11'-4"
PORCH
43'-0"
72'-4"

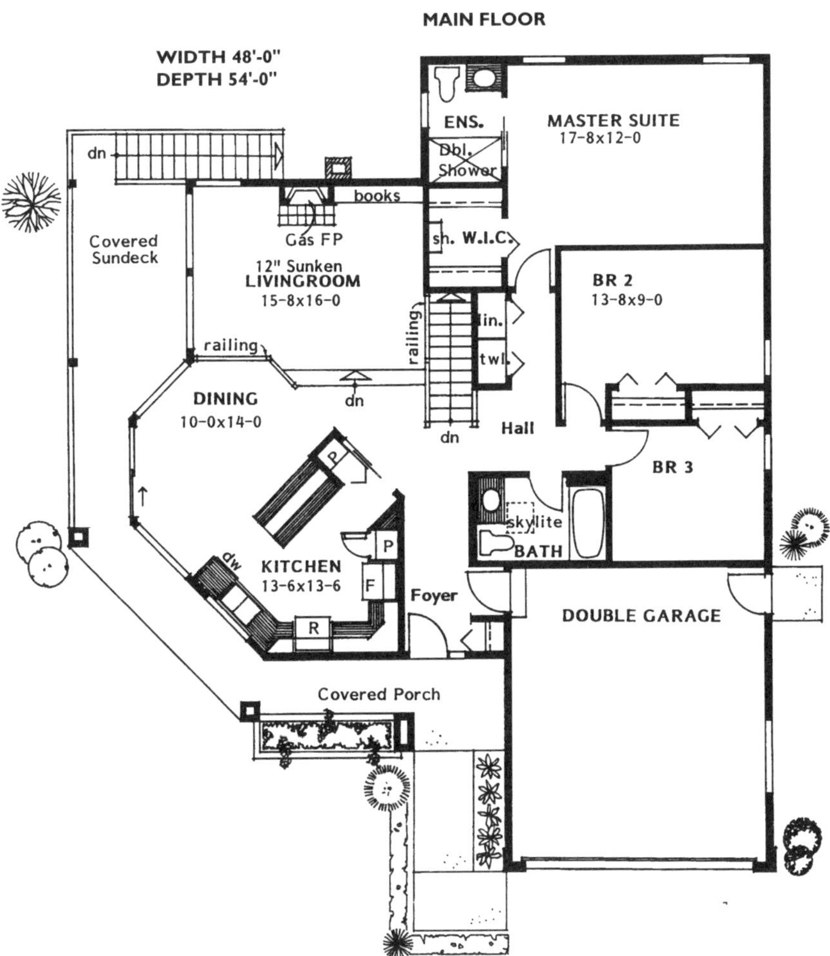
MAIN FLOOR
WIDTH 48'-0"
DEPTH 54'-0"
ENS.
Dbl. Shower
MASTER SUITE
17-8x12-0
dn
books
Gas FP
Covered Sundeck
12" Sunken
LIVINGROOM
15-8x16-0
sh. W.I.C.
BR 2
13-8x9-0
lin.
twl.
railing
railing
DINING
10-0x14-0
dn
dn
Hall
BR 3
P
skylite
BATH
dw
KITCHEN
13-6x13-6
P
F
R
Foyer
DOUBLE GARAGE
Covered Porch

Attractive Roof Lines

Price Code: A

- This plan features:
- — Three bedrooms
- — Two full baths
- A contemporary open floor plan is shared by the sunken Living Room, Dining and Kitchen Areas
- The unfinished daylight Basement could provide future Bedrooms, a Bathroom and Laundry facilities
- The Master Suite features a big walk-in closet and a private Bath featuring a double shower
- This home is designed with a basement foundation

MAIN FLOOR — 1,396 SQ. FT.
BASEMENT — 1,396 SQ. FT.
GARAGE — 389 SQ. FT.

Total living area:
1,396 sq. ft.

PLAN NO.92705

Plush Master Bedroom Win

Price Code: C

- This plan features:
- — Three bedrooms
- — Two full baths
- A raised, tile Foyer with a decorative window leading into an expansive Living Room, acce by a tiled fireplace and framed by French do
- An efficient Kitchen with a walk-in Pantry a serving bar adjoining the Breakfast and Utili Areas
- A private Master Bedroom, crowned by a ste ceiling, offering an atrium door to outside, a walk-in closet and a luxurious Bath
- Two additional Bedrooms with walk-in close share a full Bath
- This home is designed with a slab foundatio

MAIN FLOOR — 1,849 SQ. FT.
GARAGE — 437 SQ. FT.

Total living area:
1,849 sq. ft.

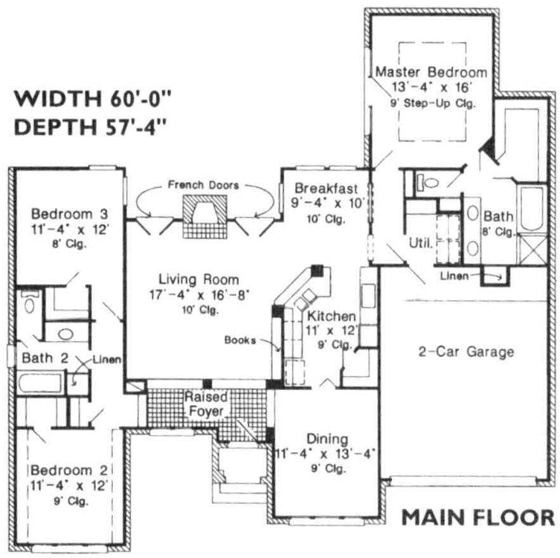
WIDTH 60'-0"
DEPTH 57'-4"
Master Bedroom
13'-4" x 16'
9' Step-Up Clg.
Bedroom 3
11'-4" x 12'
8' Clg.
French Doors
Breakfast
9'-4" x 10'
10' Clg.
Bath
8' Clg.
Util.
Linen
Living Room
17'-4" x 16'-8"
10' Clg.
Kitchen
11' x 12'
9' Clg.
Books
Bath 2
Linen
2-Car Garage
Raised
Foyer
Dining
11'-4" x 13'-4"
9' Clg.
Bedroom 2
11'-4" x 12'
9' Clg.
MAIN FLOOR

PLAN NO.93261

A Terrific Front Porch and Bay Windows

Price Code: C

- This plan features:
- — Three bedrooms
- — Two full baths
- A Country front Porch
- An expansive Living Area that includes a fireplace
- A Master Suite with a private Master Bath a walk-in closet, as well as a bay window view the front yard
- An efficient Kitchen that serves the sunny Breakfast Area and the Dining Room with ec ease
- A built-in Pantry and a desk add to the conve niences in the Breakfast Area
- Two additional Bedrooms that share a full B
- A convenient main floor Laundry Room
- This home is designed with a basement foundation

MAIN FLOOR — 1,778 SQ. FT.
BASEMENT — 1,008 SQ. FT.
GARAGE — 728 SQ. FT.

Total living area:
1,778 sq. ft.

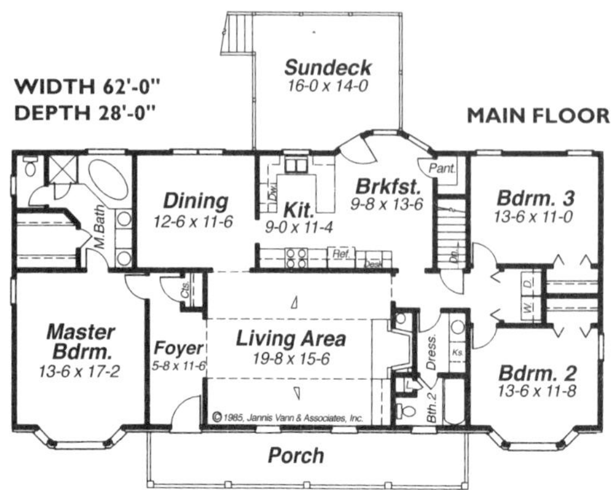
WIDTH 62'-0"
DEPTH 28'-0"
Sundeck
16-0 x 14-0
MAIN FLOOR
Dining
12-6 x 11-6
Kit.
9-0 x 11-4
Brkfst.
9-8 x 13-6
Pant.
Bdrm. 3
13-6 x 11-0
M.Bath
Master
Bdrm.
13-6 x 17-2
Foyer
5-8 x 11-6
Living Area
19-8 x 15-6
Dress.
Bdrm. 2
13-6 x 11-8
Bth.2
Porch
© 1985, Jannis Vann & Associates, Inc.

PLAN NO. 65378

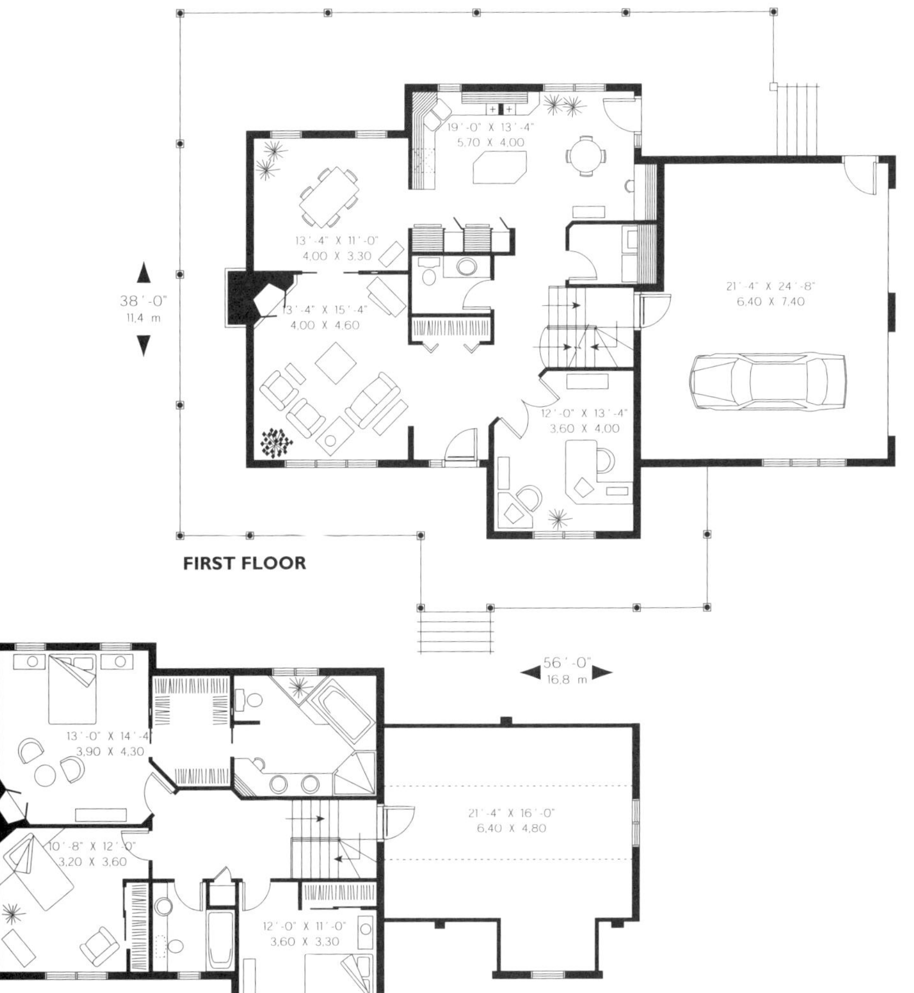
19'-0" X 13'-4"
5,70 X 4,00
13'-4" X 11'-0"
4,00 X 3,30
13'-4" X 15'-4"
4,00 X 4,60
38'-0"
11,4 m
21'-4" X 24'-8"
6,40 X 7,40
12'-0" X 13'-4"
3,60 X 4,00
FIRST FLOOR
56'-0"
16,8 m
13'-0" X 14'-4"
3,90 X 4,30
10'-8" X 12'-0"
3,20 X 3,60
21'-4" X 16'-0"
6,40 X 4,80
12'-0" X 11'-0"
3,60 X 3,30
SECOND FLOOR

Ready For The Future

Price Code: D

- This plan features:
- — Four bedrooms
- — Two full and one half baths
- A wrap-around Porch provides ample space for outdoor entertaining
- French doors off the Foyer provide privacy in the Computer Room
- The Media Room includes the warmth of a fireplace
- Pampering amenities in the Master Suite include a corner fireplace and a luxurious Bath with an angled tub
- The home is designed with a basement foundation

FIRST FLOOR — 1,132 SQ. FT.
SECOND FLOOR — 987 SQ. FT.
BASEMENT — 1,132 SQ. FT.
GARAGE — 556 SQ. FT.

Total living area:
2,119 sq. ft.

PLAN NO. 34901

Covered Porch Graces Farm-Style Traditional

Price Code: C

- This plan features:
- — Three bedrooms
- — Two and one half baths
- The Dining Room features a bay window and elegant octagonal tray ceiling
- The fireplaced Living Room offers access to a rear Deck, which may also be accessed from the sunny Breakfast Room
- Ample storage space is found throughout the home
- This home is designed with basement, slab and crawlspace foundation options

FIRST FLOOR — 909 SQ. FT
SECOND FLOOR — 854 SQ. FT.
BASEMENT — 899 SQ. FT.
GARAGE — 491 SQ. FT.

Total living area: 1,763 sq. ft.

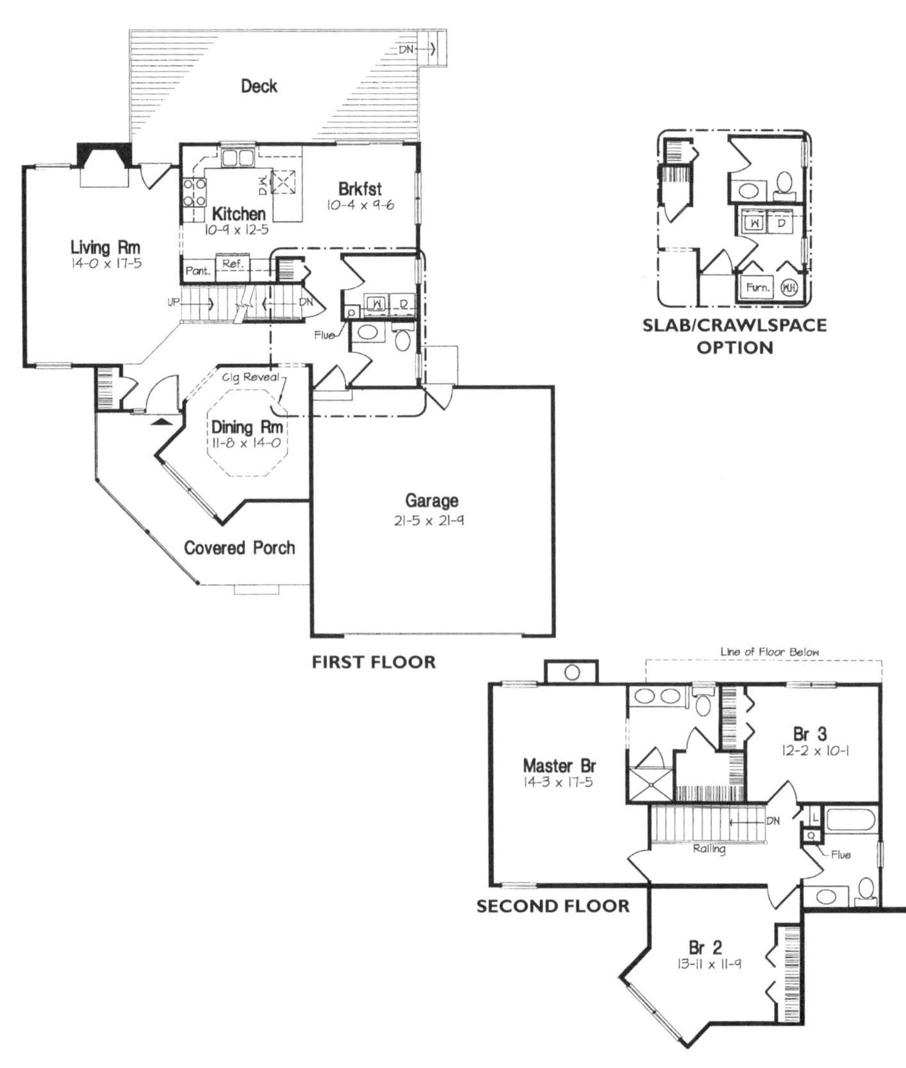

Deck
DN
Brkfst
10-4 x 9-6
Kitchen
10-9 x 12-5
DW
Living Rm
14-0 x 17-5
Pant.
Ref.
UP
DN
Flue
W
D
Clg Reveal
Dining Rm
11-8 x 14-0
Covered Porch
Garage
21-5 x 21-9
FIRST FLOOR
W
D
Furn.
WH
SLAB/CRAWLSPACE OPTION
Line of Floor Below
Master Br
14-3 x 17-5
Br 3
12-2 x 10-1
DN
Railing
Flue
SECOND FLOOR
Br 2
13-11 x 11-9

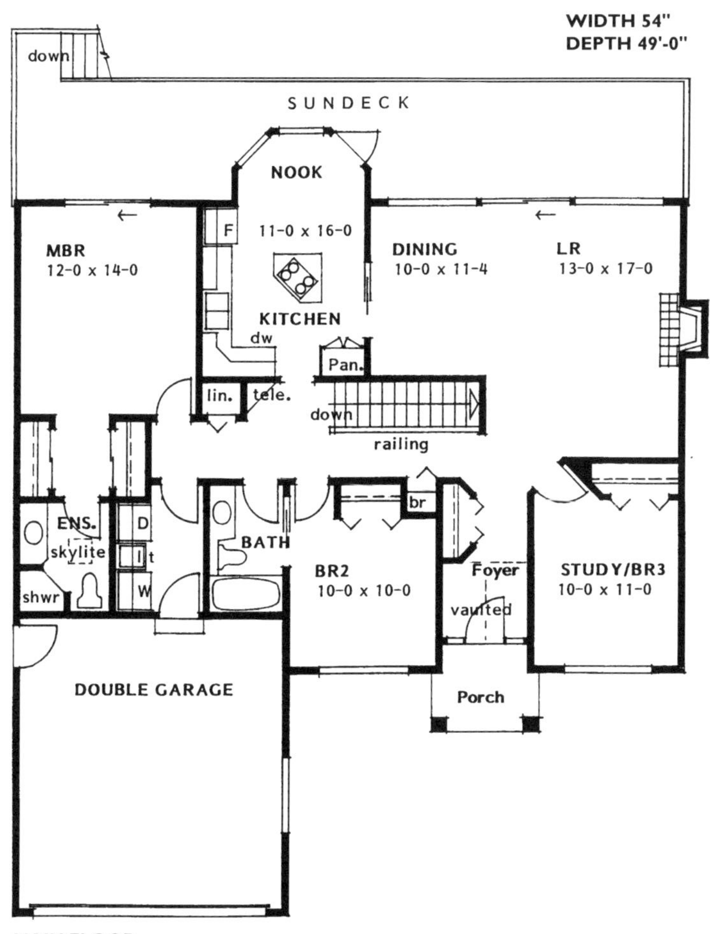
WIDTH 54"
DEPTH 49'-0"
down
SUNDECK
NOOK
11-0 x 16-0
F
MBR
12-0 x 14-0
DINING
10-0 x 11-4
LR
13-0 x 17-0
KITCHEN
dw
Pan.
lin.
tele.
down
railing
br
ENS.
skylite
shwr
D
W
BATH
BR2
10-0 x 10-0
Foyer
vaulted
STUDY/BR3
10-0 x 11-0
DOUBLE GARAGE
Porch
MAIN FLOOR

Comfort and Style

Price Code: A

- This plan features:
  - Two bedrooms with possible third bedroom/den
  - Two full baths
- An unfinished daylight basement provides possible space for family recreation
- A Master Suite is complete with private Bath and skylight
- A large Kitchen includes an Eating Nook
- The Sun Deck is easily accessible from the Master Suite, Nook and the Living/Dining Area
- This home is designed with a basement foundation

First floor — 1,423 sq. ft.
Basement — 1,423 sq. ft.
Garage — 399 sq. ft.

**Total living area:
1,423 sq. ft.**

PLAN NO. 98432

Keystones and Arched Windows

Price Code: B

- This plan features:
  - Three bedrooms
  - Two full baths
- A large arched window in the Dining Room offers eye-catching appeal
- A decorative column helps to define the Dining Room from the Great Room
- A fireplace and French door to the rear yard can be found in the Great Room
- An efficient Kitchen includes a serving bar, Pantry and pass through to the Great Room
- This home is designed with basement, slab and crawlspace foundation options

MAIN FLOOR — 1,670 SQ. FT.
GARAGE — 240 SQ. FT.

Total living area:
1,670 sq. ft.

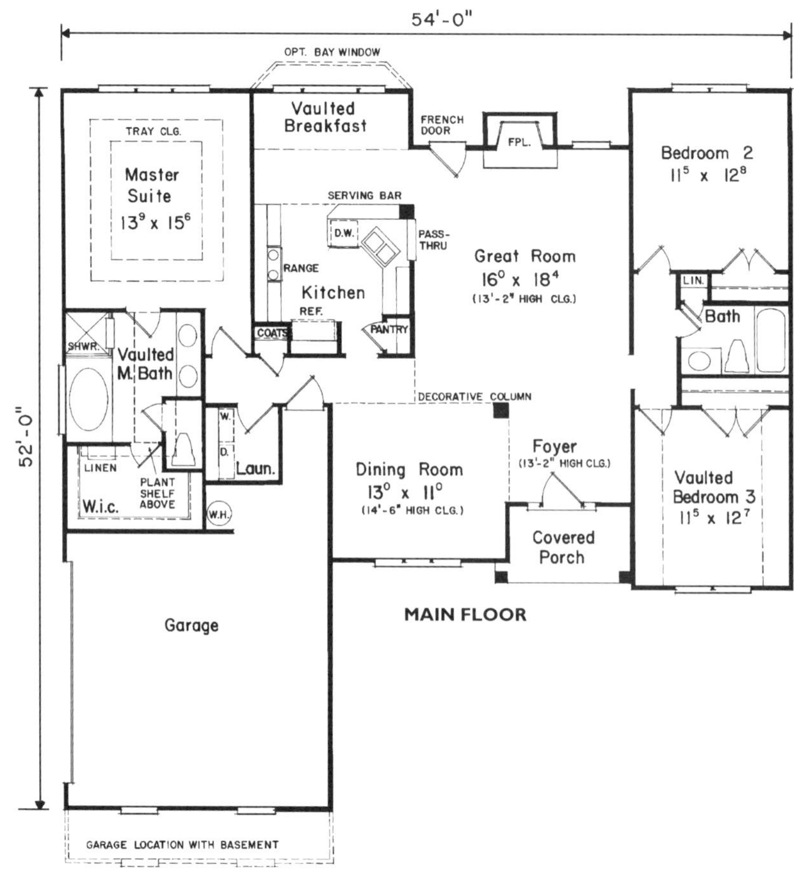

54'-0"
52'-0"
OPT. BAY WINDOW
Vaulted Breakfast
FRENCH DOOR
FPL.
TRAY CLG.
Master Suite
13^9 x 15^6
SERVING BAR
D.W.
PASS-THRU
RANGE
Kitchen
REF.
COATS
PANTRY
Great Room
16^0 x 18^4
(13'-2" HIGH CLG.)
Bedroom 2
11^5 x 12^8
LIN.
Bath
SHWR.
Vaulted M. Bath
DECORATIVE COLUMN
W.
D.
Laun.
LINEN
PLANT SHELF ABOVE
W.i.c.
W.H.
Dining Room
13^0 x 11^0
(14'-6" HIGH CLG.)
Foyer
(13'-2" HIGH CLG.)
Covered Porch
Vaulted Bedroom 3
11^5 x 12^7
Garage
MAIN FLOOR
GARAGE LOCATION WITH BASEMENT

PLAN NO. 9964

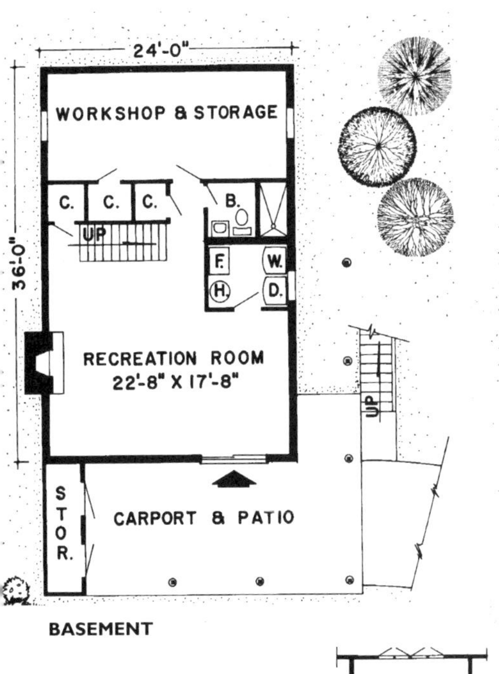
24'-0"
36'-0"
WORKSHOP & STORAGE
C.
C.
C.
B.
UP
F.
W.
H.
D.
RECREATION ROOM
22'-8" X 17'-8"
UP
S
T
O
R.
CARPORT & PATIO

BASEMENT

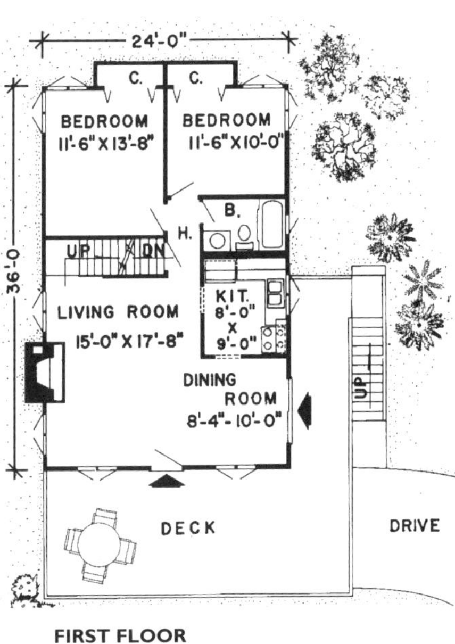
24'-0"
36'-0
C.
C.
BEDROOM
11'-6" X 13'-8"
BEDROOM
11'-6" X 10'-0"
B.
H.
UP
DN
LIVING ROOM
15'-0" X 17'-8"
KIT.
8'-0"
X
9'-0"
DINING
ROOM
8'-4"-10'-0"
UP
DECK
DRIVE

FIRST FLOOR

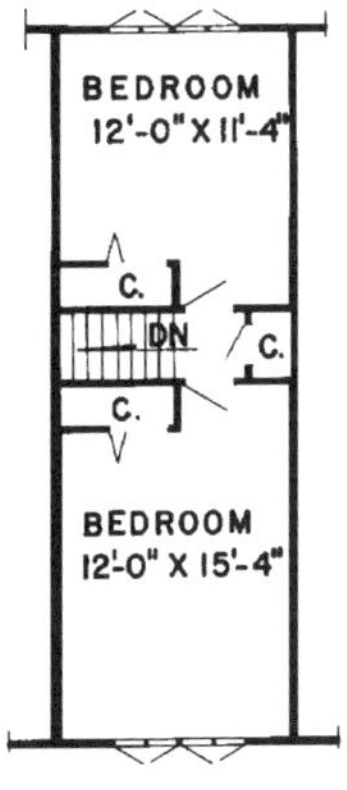

BEDROOM
12'-0" X 11'-4"
C.
DN
C.
C.
BEDROOM
12'-0" X 15'-4"

SECOND FLOOR

Recreation Room Houses Fireplace

Price Code: C

- This plan features:
  - — Four bedrooms
  - — Two full baths
- A wood-burning fireplace warms the Living/Dining Room, which is accessible to the large wooden Sun Deck
- Two first floor Bedrooms have access to a full Bath
- There are two ample-sized second floor Bedrooms
- A Recreation Room features a cozy fireplace and convenient half Bath
- This home is designed with a basement foundation

FIRST FLOOR — 906 SQ. FT.
SECOND FLOOR — 456 SQ. FT.
BASEMENT — 279 SQ. FT.

Total living area: 1,956 sq. ft.

PLAN NO. 94203

A Decorative Widows Walk

Price Code: F

- This plan features:
- — Two bedrooms
- — Two full baths
- Living area above the Carport and Storage/Bonus areas offering a "piling" design for coastal, waterfront or low-lying terrain
- A Great Room with a vaulted ceiling, cozy fireplace and double glass door to the screened Veranda
- An efficient, L-shaped Kitchen with a work island and Dining Area
- This home is designed with a pier/post foundation

FIRST FLOOR — 1,136 SQ. FT.
SECOND FLOOR — 636 SQ. FT.
GARAGE — 526 SQ. FT.

Total living area: 1,772 sq. ft.

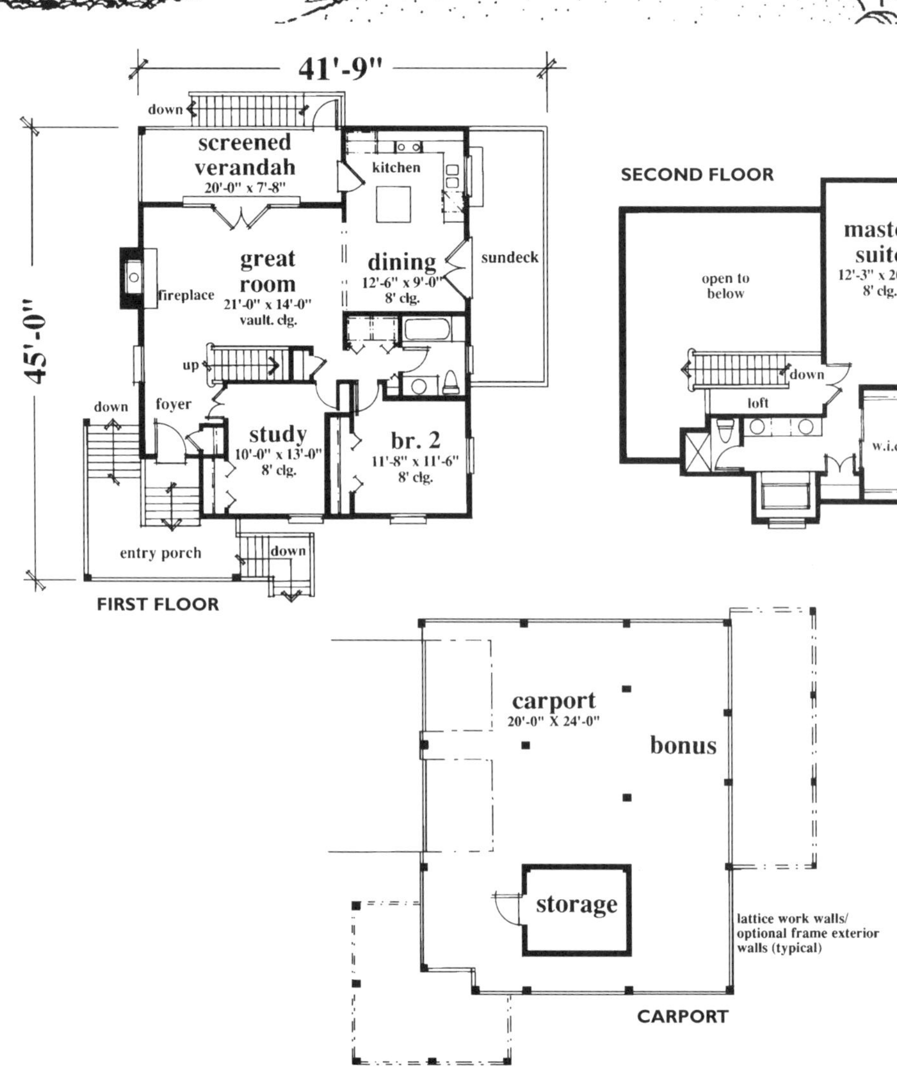

41'-9"
45'-0"
down
screened verandah
20'-0" x 7'-8"
kitchen
great room
21'-0" x 14'-0"
vault. clg.
fireplace
dining
12'-6" x 9'-0"
8' clg.
sundeck
up
foyer
down
study
10'-0" x 13'-0"
8' clg.
br. 2
11'-8" x 11'-6"
8' clg.
entry porch
down
FIRST FLOOR
SECOND FLOOR
open to below
maste
suite
12'-3" x 20
8' clg.
down
loft
w.i.c
carport
20'-0" X 24'-0"
bonus
storage
lattice work walls/
optional frame exterior
walls (typical)
CARPORT

PLAN NO. 20070

Sheltered Porch is an Inviting Entrance

Price Code: C

- This plan features:
- — Three bedrooms
- — Two and one half baths
- A dramatic two-story Entry
- A fireplaced Living Room
- A modern Kitchen flowing easily into a sunny Breakfast Nook
- A formal Dining Room with elegant decorative ceiling
- A Master Bedroom highlighted by a sky-lit Bath
- This home is designed with a basement foundation

FIRST FLOOR — 877 SQ. FT.
SECOND FLOOR — 910 SQ. FT.
BASEMENT — 877 SQ. FT.
GARAGE — 458 SQ. FT.

Total living area: 1,787 sq. ft.

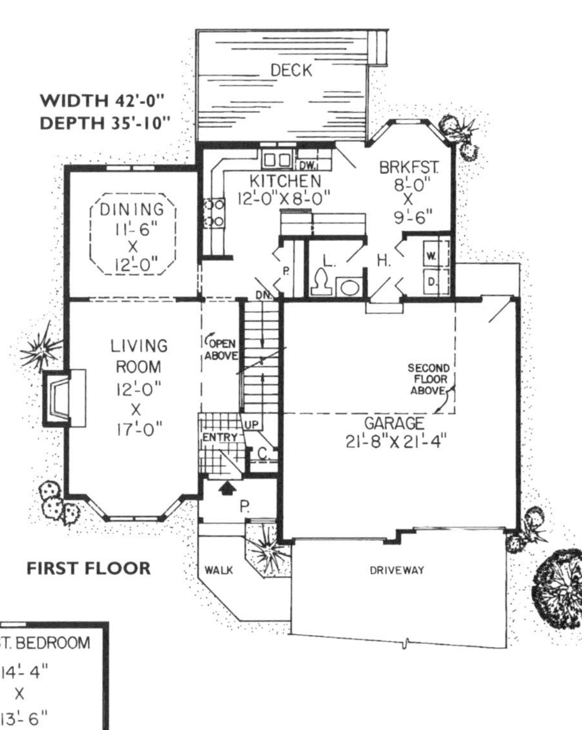
WIDTH 42'-0"
DEPTH 35'-10"
DECK
KITCHEN 12'-0" X 8'-0"
BRKFST. 8'-0" X 9'-6"
DINING 11'-6" X 12'-0"
LIVING ROOM 12'-0" X 17'-0"
OPEN ABOVE
SECOND FLOOR ABOVE
GARAGE 21'-8" X 21'-4"
ENTRY
WALK
DRIVEWAY

FIRST FLOOR

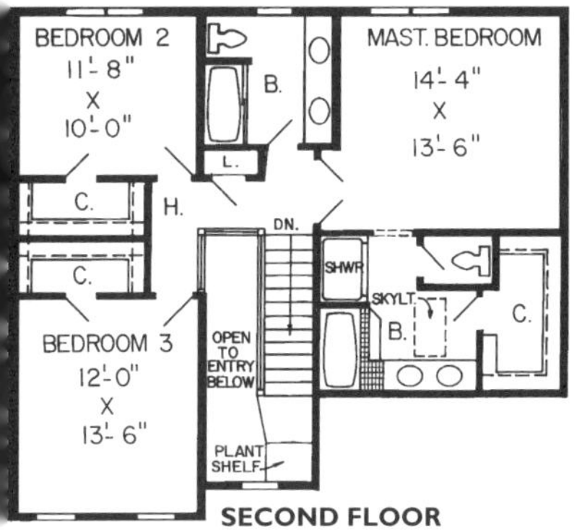

SECOND FLOOR

PLAN NO.99115

A Very Distinctive Ranch

Price Code: C

- This plan features:
  - — Three bedrooms
  - — Two full and one half baths
- The recessed entrance has sidelights which work to create a formal Entry
- The formal Dining Room has a butler's Pantry for added convenience
- The Master Suite includes a walk-in closet, private Bath and an elegant bay window
- A Laundry Room is on the main level between the three-car Garage and the Kitchen
- This home is designed with a basement foundation

MAIN FLOOR — 1,947 SQ. FT.
BASEMENT — 1,947 SQ. FT.

Total living area: 1,947 sq. ft.

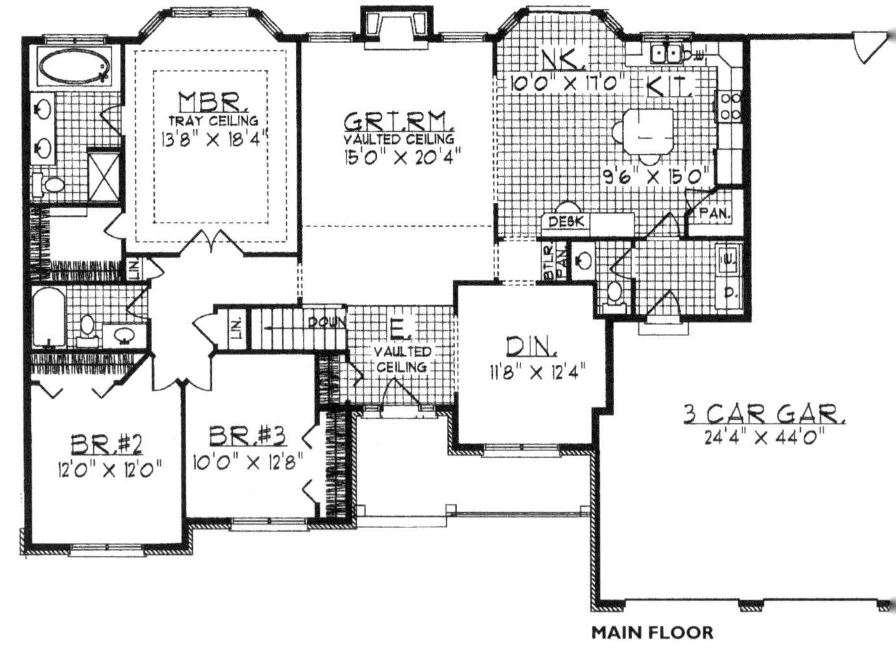
MBR.
TRAY CEILING
13'8" X 18'4"
GRT.RM.
VAULTED CEILING
15'0" X 20'4"
NK.
10'0" X 11'0"
KIT.
9'6" X 15'0"
DESK
PAN.
BTLR. PAN.
LIN.
LIN.
DOWN
E.
VAULTED CEILING
DIN.
11'8" X 12'4"
BR.#2
12'0" X 12'0"
BR.#3
10'0" X 12'8"
3 CAR GAR.
24'4" X 44'0"

MAIN FLOOR

PLAN NO. 94902

Abundance of Windows for Natural Lighting

Price Code: C

- This plan features:
- — Four bedrooms
- — Two and a half baths
- Ten-foot ceiling above transom windows and hearth fireplace accent the Great Room
- Kitchen conveniently accesses Laundry Area and Garage
- Four second floor Bedrooms have ample closet space
- This home is designed with a basement foundation
- Alternate foundation options available at an additional charge. Please call 1-800-235-5700 for more information.

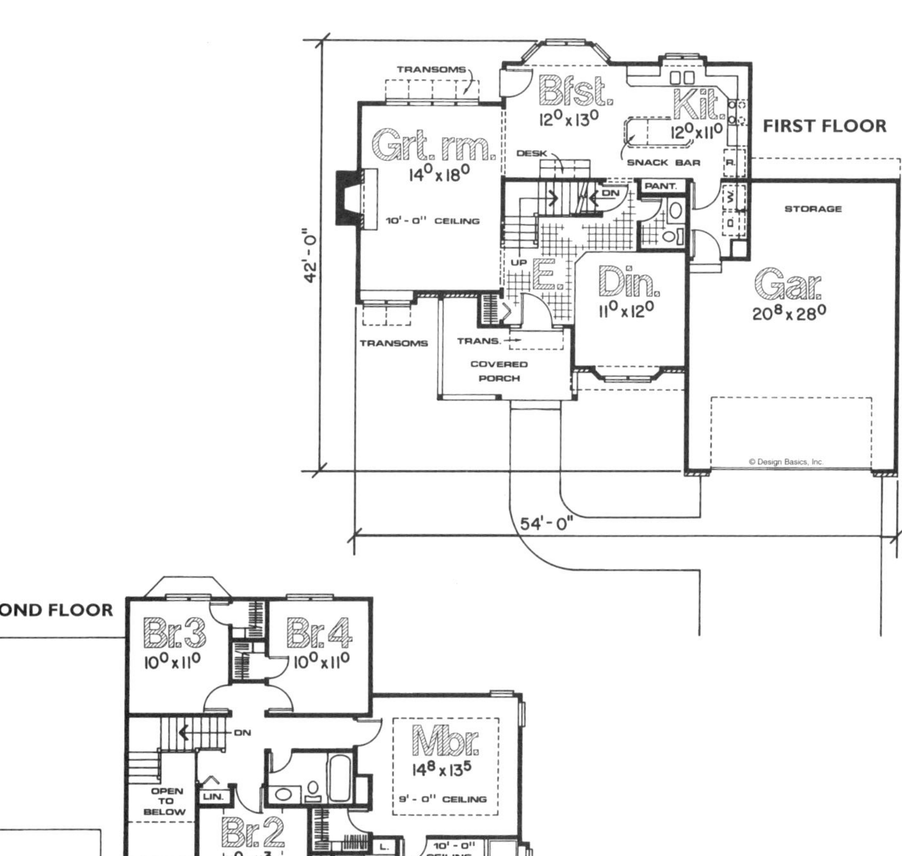

FIRST FLOOR
TRANSOMS
Bfst.
12^{0}x13^{0}
Kit.
12^{0}x11^{0}
Grt. rm.
14^{0}x18^{0}
DESK
SNACK BAR
R.
DN
PANT.
10'-0" CEILING
STORAGE
42'-0"
UP
E.
Din.
11^{0}x12^{0}
Gar.
20^{8}x28^{0}
TRANSOMS
TRANS.
COVERED PORCH
54'-0"
OND FLOOR
Br.3
10^{0}x11^{0}
Br.4
10^{0}x11^{0}
DN
Mbr.
14^{8}x13^{5}
9'-0" CEILING
OPEN TO BELOW
LIN.
Br.2
11^{0}x11^{3}
10'-0" CEILING
L.
10'-0" CEILING
W/P
TRANSOM

FIRST FLOOR — 944 SQ. FT.
SECOND FLOOR — 987 SQ. FT.
BASEMENT — 944 SQ. FT.
GARAGE — 557 SQ. FT.

Total living area: 1,931 sq. ft.

PLAN NO. 68138

Lovely Family Home

Price Code: C

- This plan features:
- — Three bedrooms
- — Two full and on half baths
- Lovely Entry opens to elegant Dining Room
- The two-story Family Room features a cathedral ceiling and corner fireplace
- The large, center-island Kitchen opens to the Breakfast Room
- This home is designed with a slab foundation
- Alternate foundation options available at an additional charge. Please call 1-800-235-5700 for more information.

FIRST FLOOR — 1,366 SQ. FT.
SECOND FLOOR — 453 SQ. FT.
BONUS — 217 SQ. FT.
BASEMENT — 1,366 SQ. FT.
GARAGE — 622 SQ. FT.

Total living area: 1,819 sq. ft.

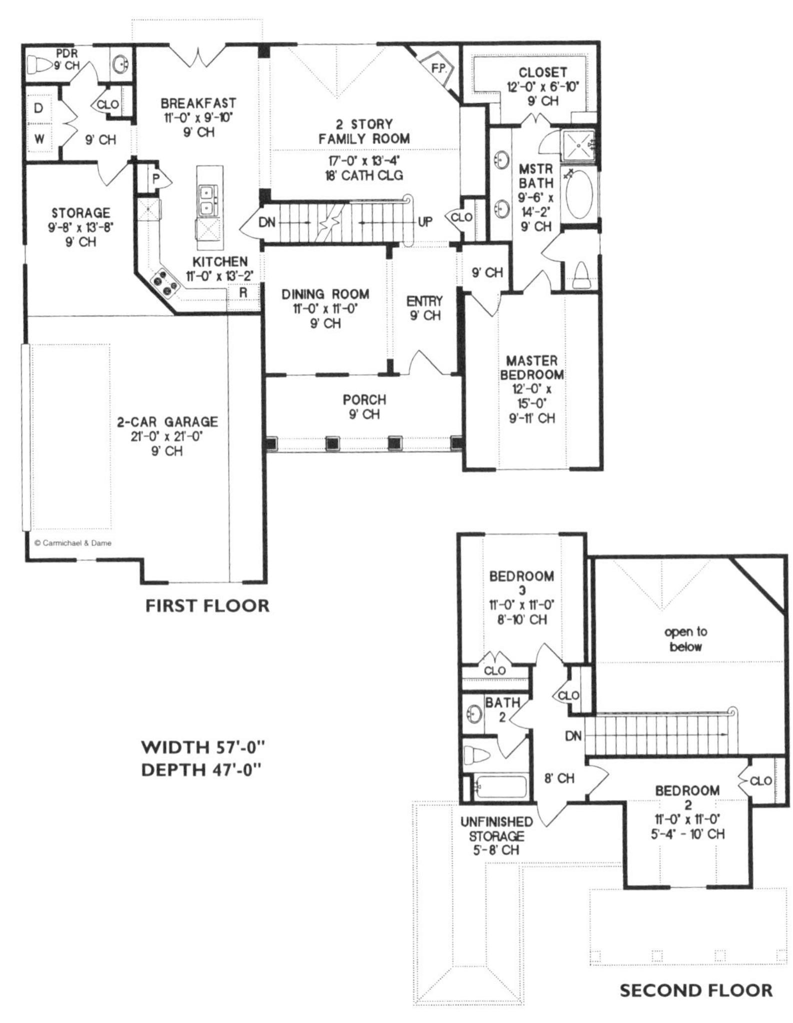

PDR 9' CH
D
W
CLO
9' CH
BREAKFAST 11'-0" x 9'-10" 9' CH
F.P.
2 STORY FAMILY ROOM 17'-0" x 13'-4" 18' CATH CLG
CLOSET 12'-0" x 6'-10" 9' CH
MSTR BATH 9'-6" x 14'-2" 9' CH
STORAGE 9'-8" x 13'-8" 9' CH
P
DN
UP
CLO
KITCHEN 11'-0" x 13'-2"
R
9' CH
DINING ROOM 11'-0" x 11'-0" 9' CH
ENTRY 9' CH
MASTER BEDROOM 12'-0" x 15'-0" 9'-11' CH
PORCH 9' CH
2-CAR GARAGE 21'-0" x 21'-0" 9' CH
© Carmichael & Dame
FIRST FLOOR
BEDROOM 3 11'-0" x 11'-0" 8'-10' CH
open to below
CLO
BATH 2
CLO
DN
WIDTH 57'-0"
DEPTH 47'-0"
8' CH
CLO
BEDROOM 2 11'-0" x 11'-0" 5'-4" - 10' CH
UNFINISHED STORAGE 5'-8' CH
SECOND FLOOR

Well-Planned Family Home

Price Code: C

his plan features:

- hree bedrooms
- wo full and one half baths
- plit Bedroom layout affords privacy to the laster Suite
- cathedral ceiling, bay window and double-door ntry highlight the Study at the front of this home
- he Master Suite includes a double-vanity and a alk-in closet
- he Family Room includes a corner fireplace and uilt-in shelves
- he cook top island with snack bar and the antry cupboards add efficiency to the Kitchen
- wo secondary Bedrooms include private access a full Bath
- his home is designed with a basement oundation
- lternate foundation options available at an additional charge. Please call 1-800-235-5700 for ore information.

IN FLOOR — 1,876 SQ. FT.
SEMENT — 1,876 SQ. FT.
RAGE — 567 SQ. FT.

Total living area: 1,876 sq. ft.

PLAN NO.68135

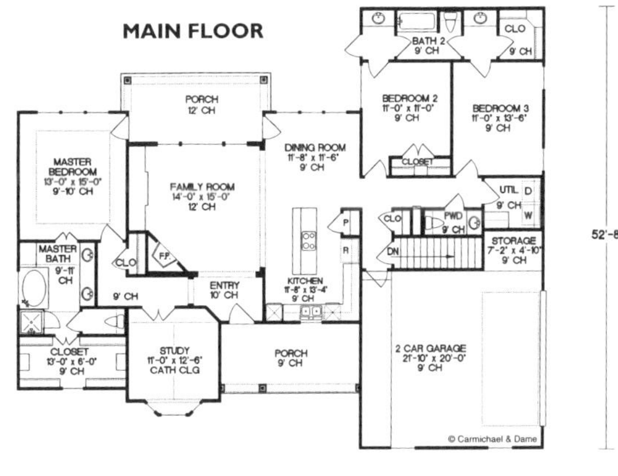
MAIN FLOOR
PORCH 12' CH
MASTER BEDROOM 13'-0" x 15'-0" 9'-10' CH
FAMILY ROOM 14'-0" x 15'-0" 12' CH
DINING ROOM 11'-8" x 11'-6" 9' CH
BATH 2 9' CH
CLO
BEDROOM 2 11'-0" x 11'-0" 9' CH
BEDROOM 3 11'-0" x 13'-6" 9' CH
CLOSET
UTIL
PWD 9' CH
STORAGE 7'-2" x 4'-10" 9' CH
MASTER BATH
FF
ENTRY 10' CH
KITCHEN 9' CH
DN
CLOSET 13'-0" x 6'-0" 9' CH
STUDY 11'-0" x 12'-6" CATH CLG
PORCH 9' CH
2 CAR GARAGE 21'-10" x 20'-0" 9' CH
© Carmichael & Dame
52'-8"
65'-0"

Master Suite Crowns Plan

Price Code: C

his plan features:

- ree bedrooms
- wo full baths
- he Master Bedroom occupies the entire second oor
- his home features and efficient passive solar esign
- he dramatic Living Room rises two stories in e front of the home and features large windows
- kylights in the sloping ceilings of the Kitchen nd Master Bath add to the light and spacious eling of this home
- wo additional Bedrooms are on the first floor
- his home is designed with a basement, crawlace and slab foundation options

ST FLOOR — 1,306 SQ. FT.
OND FLOOR — 472 SQ. FT.
RAGE — 576 SQ. FT.

Total living area: 1,778 sq. ft.

PLAN NO.10394

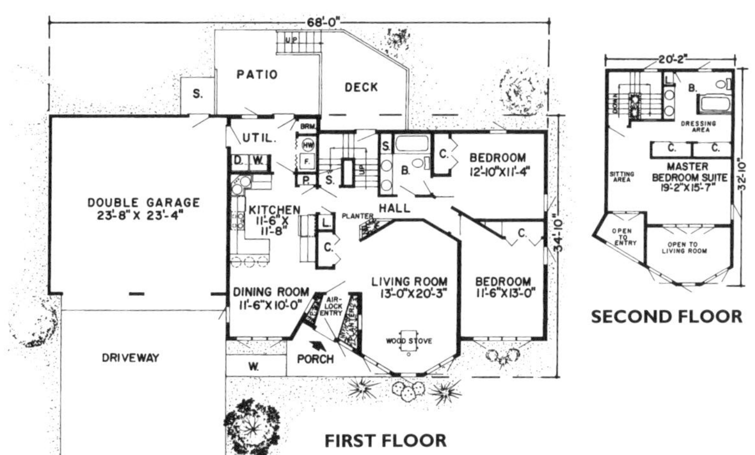
68'-0"
UP
PATIO
DECK
S.
UTIL.
D. W.
KITCHEN 11'-6" X 11'-8"
PLANTER
HALL
BEDROOM 12'-10"X11'-4"
DOUBLE GARAGE 23'-8" X 23'-4"
LIVING ROOM 13'-0"X20'-3"
BEDROOM 11'-6"X13'-0"
DINING ROOM 11'-6"X10'-0"
AIR-LOCK ENTRY
WOOD STOVE
PORCH
DRIVEWAY
W.
34'-10"
FIRST FLOOR
20'-2"
DRESSING AREA
MASTER BEDROOM SUITE 19'-2"X15'-7"
SITTING AREA
OPEN TO ENTRY
OPEN TO LIVING ROOM
32'-10"
SECOND FLOOR

PLAN NO. 91031

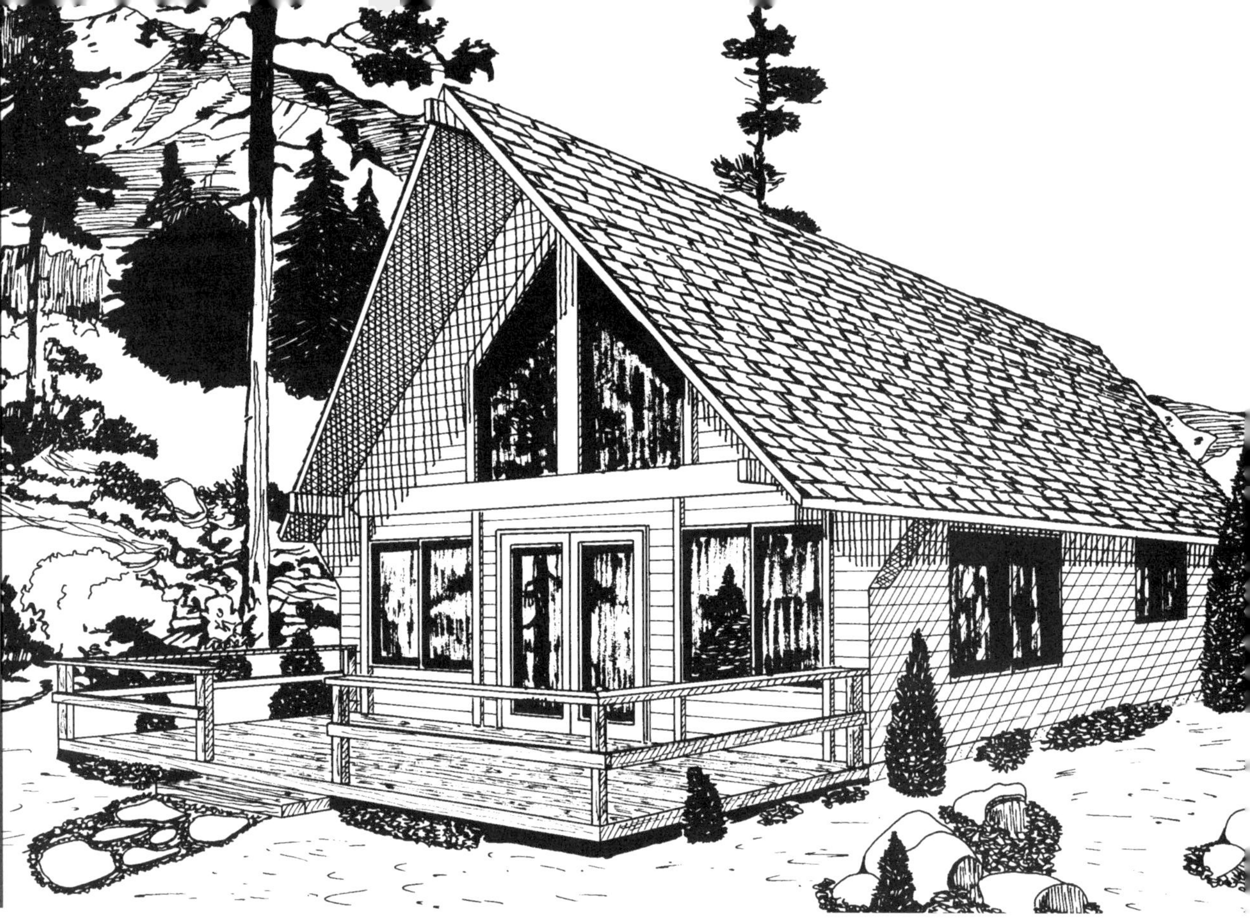

Snug Retreat With A View

Price Code: A

- This plan features:
  - — One bedroom plus loft
  - — One three-quarter bath
- A large front Deck providing views and an expansive entrance
- A two-story Living/Dining Area with double glass doors leading out to the Deck
- An efficient, U-shaped Kitchen with a pass through counter to the Dining Area
- A first floor Bedroom, with ample closet space, located near a full shower Bath
- A Loft/Bedroom on the second floor offering multiple uses

MAIN FLOOR — 572 SQ. FT.
LOFT — 308 SQ. FT.

Total living area: 880 sq. ft.

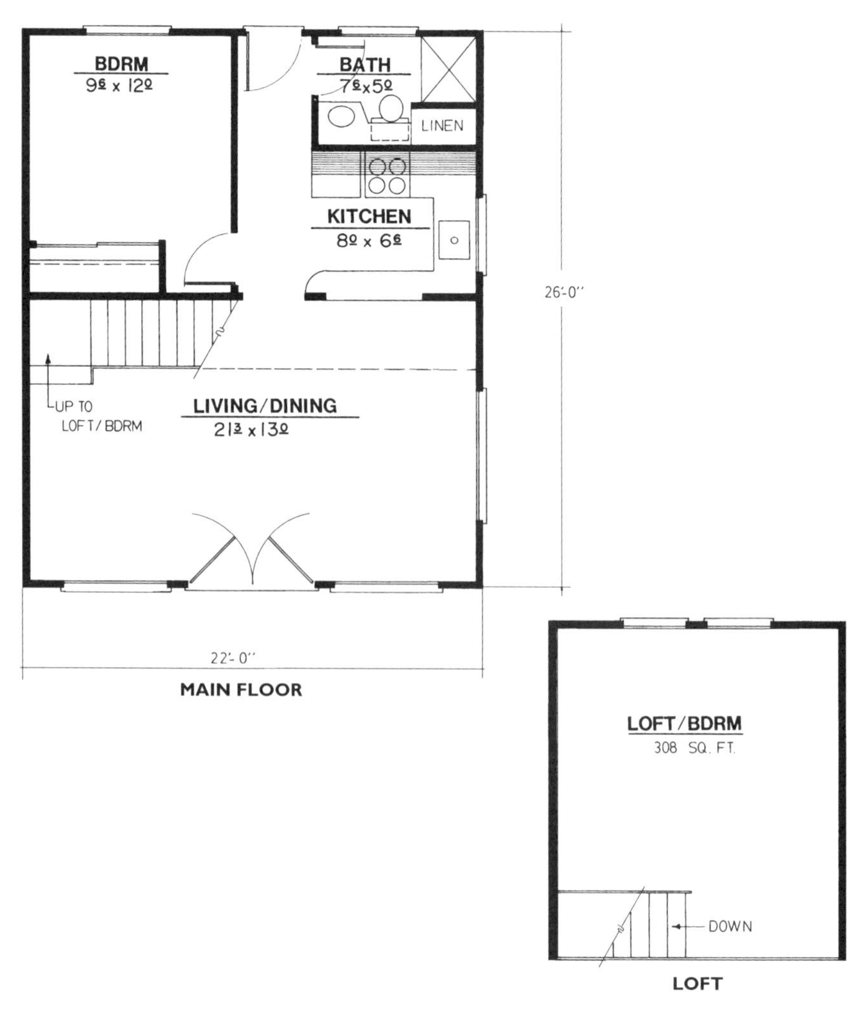

BDRM
9⁶ x 12⁰
BATH
7⁶x5⁰
LINEN
KITCHEN
8⁰ x 6⁶
26'-0"
UP TO LOFT/BDRM
LIVING/DINING
21³ x 13⁰
22'-0"
MAIN FLOOR
LOFT/BDRM
308 SQ. FT.
DOWN
LOFT

Expansive Living Room

Price Code: A

his plan features:

- hree bedrooms
- wo full baths
- aulted ceiling crowns spacious Living Room ghlighted by a fireplace
- uilt-in Pantry and direct access from the Garage dding to the conveniences of the Kitchen
- alk-in closet and a private five-piece Bath pped by a vaulted ceiling in the Master edroom Suite
- oximity to the full Bath in the hall from the condary Bedrooms
- is home is designed with basement, slab and awlspace foundation options

AIN FLOOR — 1,346 SQ. FT.

RAGE — 395 SQ. FT.

Total living area: 1,346 sq. ft.

PLAN NO.98434

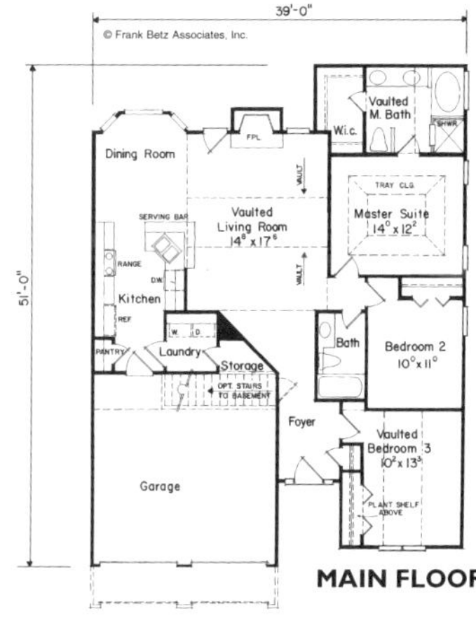

39'-0"
© Frank Betz Associates, Inc.
51'-0"
Dining Room
Vaulted Living Room
Vaulted M. Bath
W.i.c.
Master Suite
Kitchen
Pantry
Laundry
Storage
Bath
Bedroom 2
Foyer
Vaulted Bedroom 3
Garage
MAIN FLOOR

Elegant Brick Exterior

Price Code: A

his plan features:

- hree bedrooms
- wo full baths
- etailing and accenting columns highlighting the overed front Porch
- en is enhanced by a corner fireplace and djoins with Dining Room
- fficient Kitchen well-appointed and with easy ccess to the Utility/Laundry Room
- edroom topped by a vaulted ceiling and ampered by a private Bath and a walk-in closet
- wo secondary Bedrooms are located at the pposite end of home sharing a full Bath
- his home is designed with crawlspace and slab undation options

AIN FLOOR — 1,390 SQ. FT.

RAGE — 590 SQ. FT.

Total living area: 1,390 sq. ft.

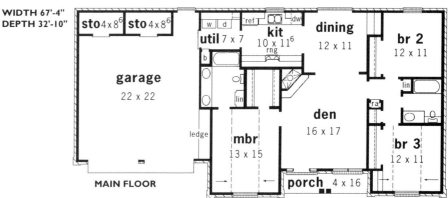

PLAN NO.92557

WIDTH 67'-4"
DEPTH 32'-10"

sto 4 x 8[6] sto 4 x 8[6]
util 7 x 7
kit 10 x 11[6]
dining 12 x 11
br 2 12 x 11
garage 22 x 22
den 16 x 17
mbr 13 x 15
br 3 12 x 11
porch 4 x 16
ledge

MAIN FLOOR

PLAN NO. 90671

Adapt this Colonial to Your Lifestyle

Price Code: B

- This plan features:
- — Four bedrooms
- — Two full baths
- A Living Room with a beam ceiling and a fireplace
- An eat-in Kitchen efficiently serving the formal Dining Room
- A Master Bedroom with his and her closets
- Two upstairs Bedrooms sharing a split Bath
- This home is designed with a basement foundation

FIRST FLOOR — 1,056 SQ. FT.
SECOND FLOOR — 531 SQ. FT.

**Total living area:
1,587 sq. ft.**

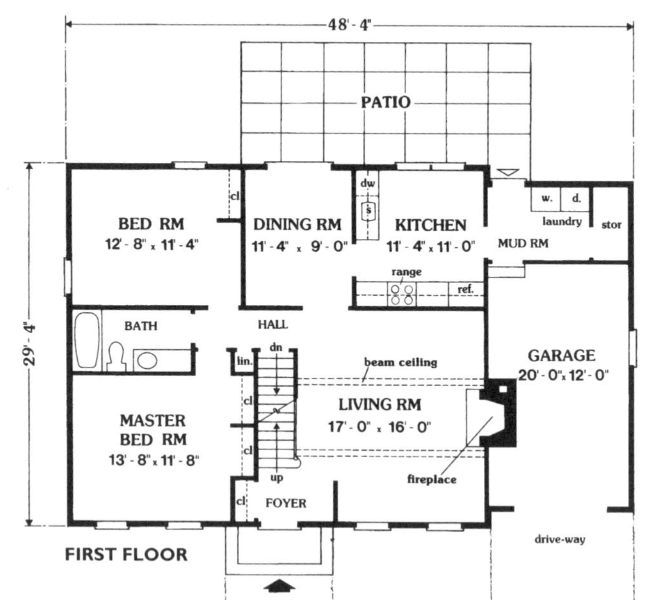

48'-4"
PATIO
29'-4"
BED RM
12'-8" x 11'-4"
DINING RM
11'-4" x 9'-0"
KITCHEN
11'-4" x 11'-0"
dw
range
ref.
w.
d.
laundry
stor
MUD RM
BATH
HALL
dn
lin.
cl
beam ceiling
GARAGE
20'-0" x 12'-0"
MASTER
BED RM
13'-8" x 11'-8"
LIVING RM
17'-0" x 16'-0"
up
fireplace
FOYER
drive-way
FIRST FLOOR

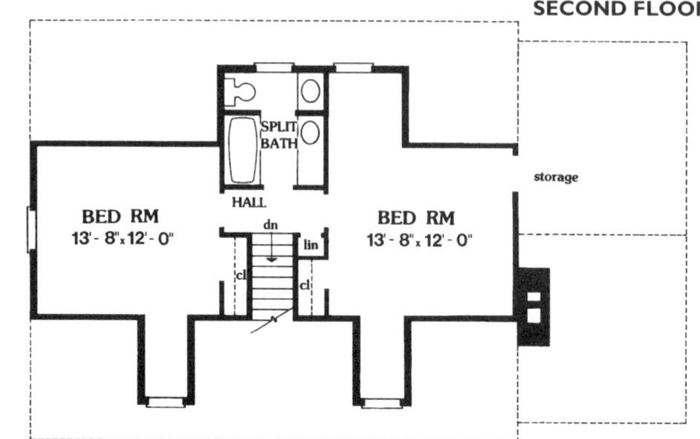

SECOND FLOOR
SPLIT
BATH
HALL
storage
BED RM
13'-8" x 12'-0"
dn
lin
cl
BED RM
13'-8" x 12'-0"

PLAN NO. 92647

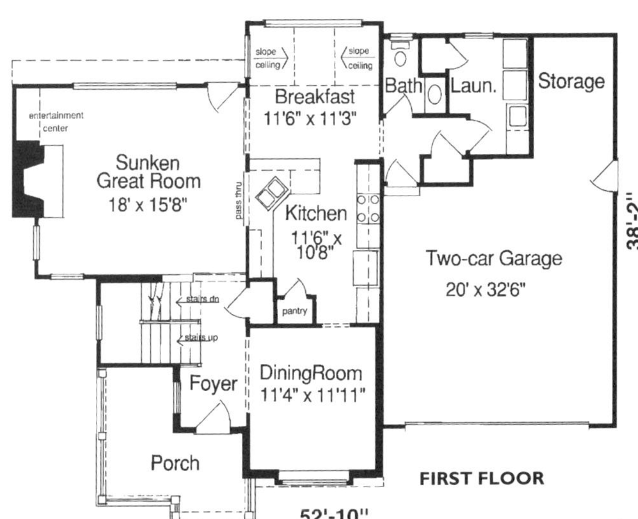

slope ceiling
slope ceiling
Breakfast
11'6" x 11'3"
Bath
Laun.
Storage
entertainment center
Sunken
Great Room
18' x 15'8"
pass thru
Kitchen
11'6" x
10'8"
Two-car Garage
20' x 32'6"
38'-2"
stairs dn
stairs up
pantry
Foyer
DiningRoom
11'4" x 11'11"
Porch
FIRST FLOOR
52'-10"

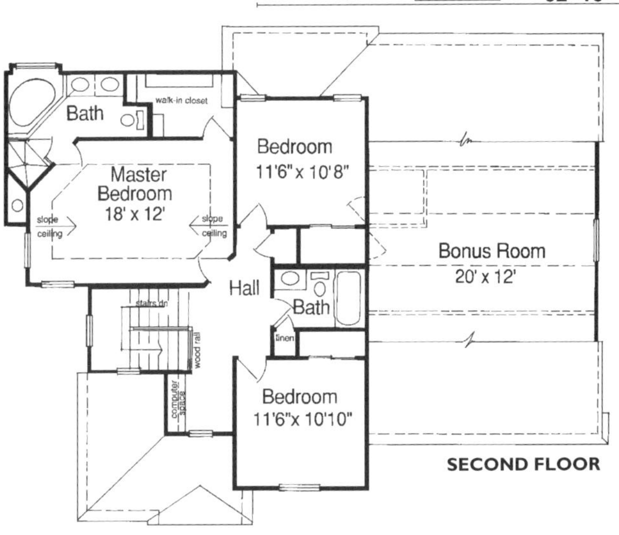

Bath
walk-in closet
Master
Bedroom
18' x 12'
slope ceiling
slope ceiling
Bedroom
11'6" x 10'8"
Hall
Bath
linen
Bonus Room
20' x 12'
stairs dn
wood rail
computer center
Bedroom
11'6" x 10'10"
SECOND FLOOR

Plenty of Room to Grow

Price Code: C

- This plan features:
  - — Three or four bedrooms
  - — Two full and one half baths
- Sunken Great Room features a large fireplace, built-in entertainment center and access to rear yard
- Hub Kitchen includes built-in Pantry, serving counter, bright Breakfast Area and adjoins Dining Room, Laundry and Garage Entry
- Corner Master Bedroom is topped by a sloped ceiling
- This home is designed with a basement foundation

FIRST FLOOR — 1,065 SQ. FT.
SECOND FLOOR — 833 SQ. FT.
BONUS ROOM — 254 SQ. FT.
GARAGE — 652 SQ. FT.

Total living area: 1,898 sq. ft.

PLAN NO. 35001

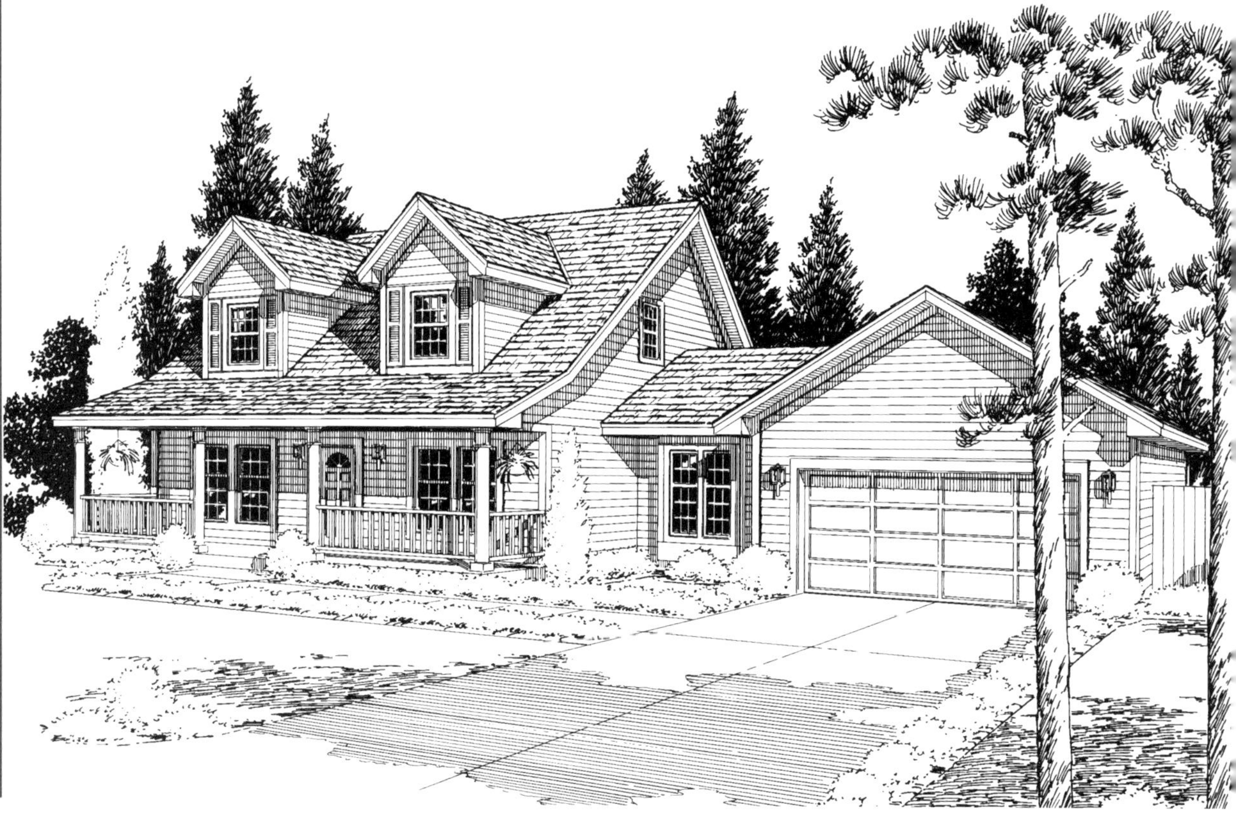

Family Living Made Easy

Price Code: B

- This plan features:
  - — Three bedrooms
  - — Two full and one half baths
- A large Living Room that flows into the Dining Room creating a great area for entertaining
- An efficient U-shaped Kitchen that includes an informal Breakfast Area and a Laundry Center
- A Den/Office with ample closet space, enabling it to double as a Guest Room
- This home is designed with basement, slab and crawlspace foundation options

FIRST FLOOR — 1,081 SQ. FT.
SECOND FLOOR — 528 SQ. FT.

Total living area:
1,609 sq. ft.

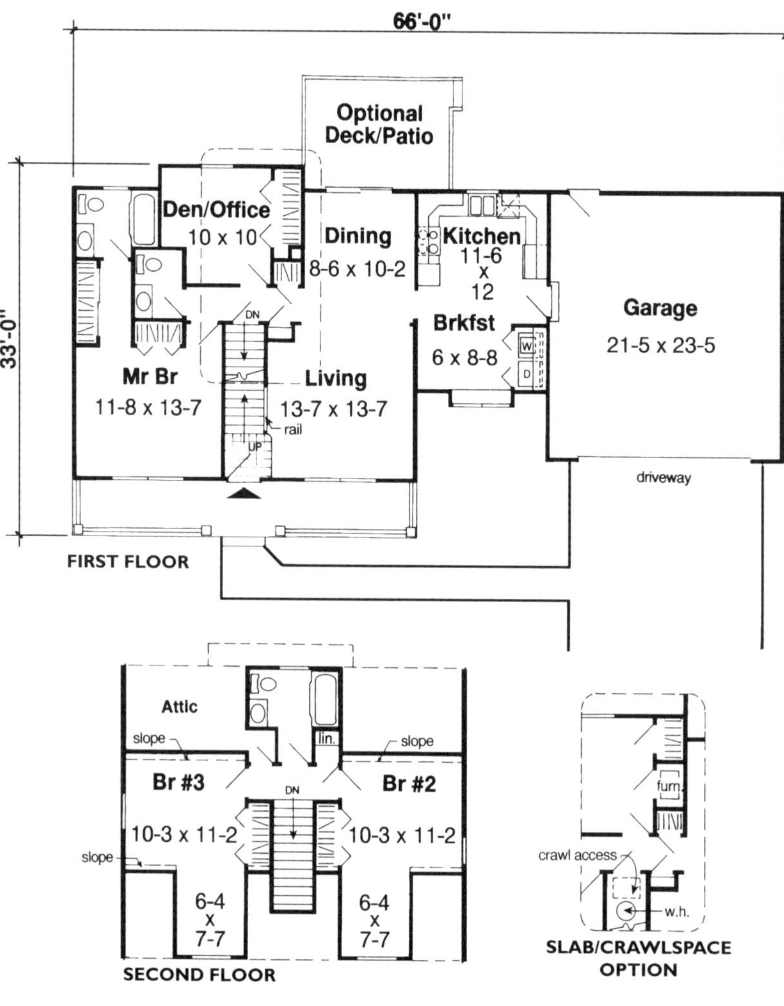

66'-0"
33'-0"
Optional Deck/Patio
Den/Office
10 x 10
Dining
8-6 x 10-2
Kitchen
11-6 x 12
Brkfst
6 x 8-8
Garage
21-5 x 23-5
Mr Br
11-8 x 13-7
Living
13-7 x 13-7
DN
UP
rail
W
D
driveway
FIRST FLOOR
Attic
slope
lin.
Br #3
10-3 x 11-2
Br #2
10-3 x 11-2
DN
6-4 x 7-7
6-4 x 7-7
SECOND FLOOR
furn.
crawl access
w.h.
SLAB/CRAWLSPACE OPTION

PLAN NO. 90680

Affordable Energy-Saver

Price Code: A

- This plan features:
  - Three bedrooms
  - Two full baths
- A covered Porch leads into an open Foyer and Living/Dining Room with skylights and front-to-back exposure
- The efficient Kitchen features a bay-windowed Dinette Area
- The private Master Bedroom leads to a private Deck
- Two additional Bedrooms have access to a full Bath
- This home is designed with basement and slab foundation options

MAIN FLOOR — 1,393 SQ. FT.
BASEMENT — 1,393 SQ. FT.
GARAGE — 542 SQ. FT.
PORCH — 195 SQ. FT.

Total living area:
1,393 sq. ft.

MAIN FLOOR

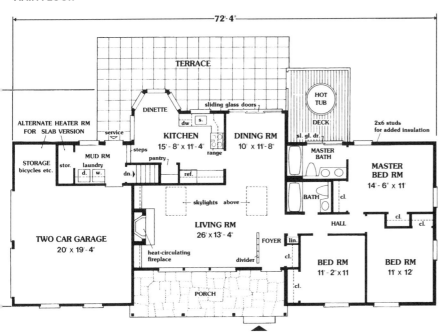

72'-4"
TERRACE
HOT TUB
DECK
sliding glass doors
DINETTE
dw s.
KITCHEN 15'-8" x 11'-4"
range
DINING RM 10' x 11'-8"
sl. gl. dr.
2x6 studs for added insulation
ALTERNATE HEATER RM FOR SLAB VERSION
service
STORAGE bicycles etc.
stor.
MUD RM laundry
d. w.
steps
pantry
dn.
ref.
MASTER BATH
MASTER BED RM 14'-6" x 11'
BATH
cl.
skylights above
TWO CAR GARAGE 20' x 19'-4"
LIVING RM 26' x 13'-4"
HALL
cl.
FOYER
lin.
heat-circulating fireplace
divider
BED RM 11'-2" x 11
BED RM 11' x 12'
PORCH

PLAN NO. 98454

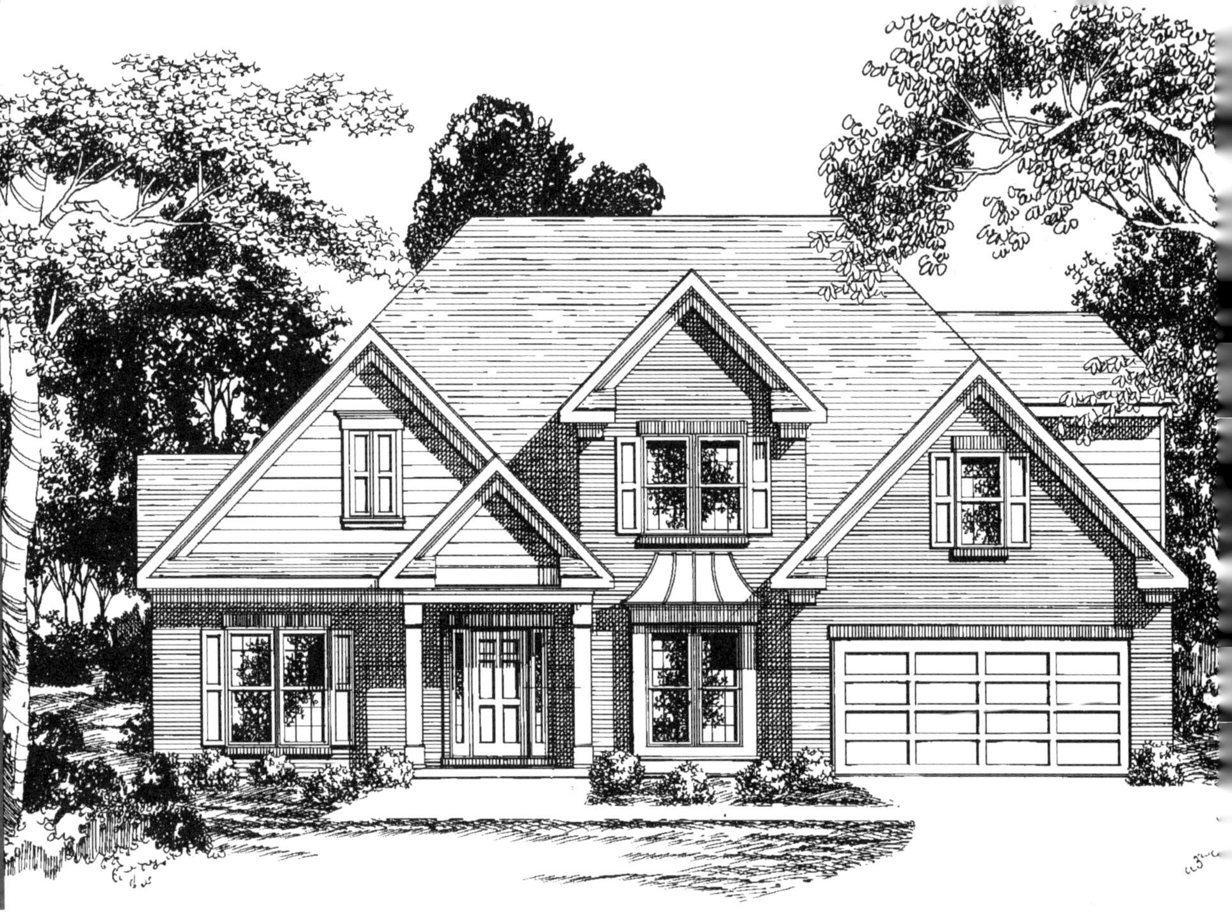

Family-Sized Accommodations

Price Code: C

- This plan features:
  - — Four bedrooms
  - — Two full and one half baths
- The Master Bedroom is accented by a tray ceiling, a lavish bath and a walk-in closet
- On second floor find three additional bedrooms that share a double vanity bath and an optional Bonus Room
- This home is designed with basement and crawlspace foundation options

FIRST FLOOR — 1,320 SQ. FT.
SECOND FLOOR — 554 SQ. FT.
BONUS ROOM — 155 SQ. FT.
GARAGE — 406 SQ. FT.

Total living area: 1,874 sq. ft.

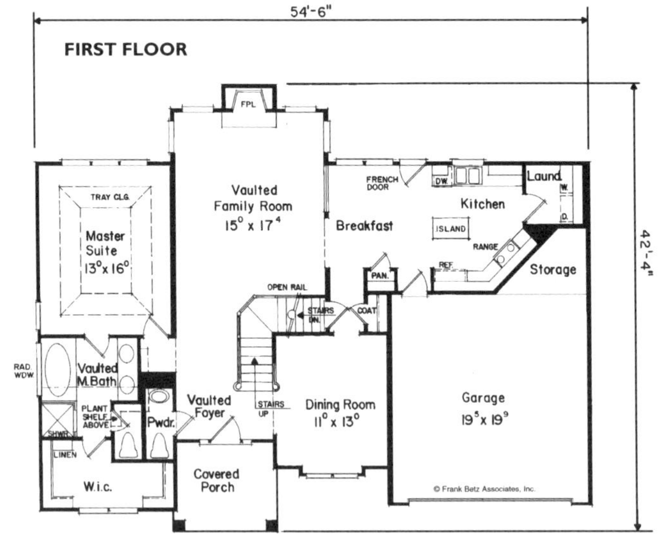
54'-6"
FIRST FLOOR
FPL
Vaulted Family Room 15⁰ x 17⁴
TRAY CLG.
Master Suite 13⁰x 16⁰
FRENCH DOOR
Breakfast
Kitchen
ISLAND
RANGE
Laund.
Storage
42'-4"
OPEN RAIL
PAN.
STAIRS DN.
COAT
RAD WDW
Vaulted M.Bath
PLANT SHELF ABOVE
Pwdr.
Vaulted Foyer
STAIRS UP
Dining Room 11⁰ x 13⁰
Garage 19⁵x 19⁹
LINEN
W.i.c.
Covered Porch
© Frank Betz Associates, Inc.

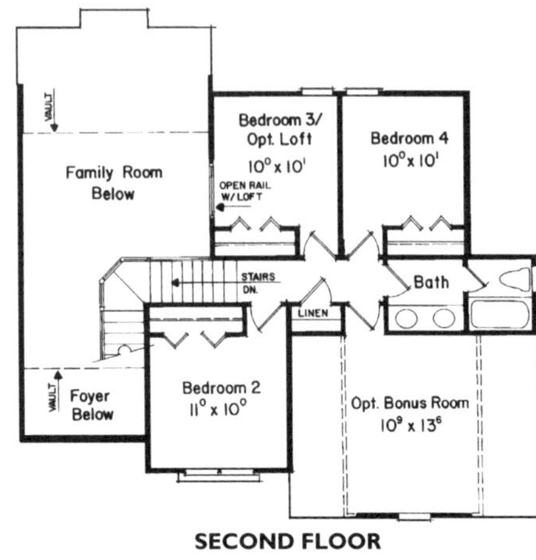
VAULT
Family Room Below
Bedroom 3/ Opt. Loft 10⁰ x 10¹
OPEN RAIL W/LOFT
Bedroom 4 10⁰x 10¹
STAIRS DN.
LINEN
Bath
Foyer Below
Bedroom 2 11⁰ x 10⁰
Opt. Bonus Room 10⁹ x 13⁶
SECOND FLOOR

PLAN NO. 98414

Three Bedroom Ranch

Price Code: B

- This plan features:
- — Three bedrooms
- — Two full baths
- Dining Room is enhanced by a plant shelf and a side window
- Wetbar is located between the Kitchen and the Dining Room
- Breakfast Room includes a radius window and a French door to the rear yard
- Master Suite features a vaulted ceiling over the Sitting Area, a Master Bath and a walk-in closet
- This home is designed with basement and crawlspace foundation options

MAIN FLOOR — 1,575 SQ. FT.
BASEMENT — 1,658 SQ. FT.
GARAGE — 459 SQ. FT.

Total living area:
1,575 sq. ft.

RADIUS WDW.
Vaulted Sitting Room
OPT. FRENCH DR.
Master Suite $13^{0} \times 15^{0}$
TRAY CLG.
Vaulted M. Bath
SHWR.
W.i.c.
LIN.
PLANT SHELF ABOVE
Bath
Bedroom 3 $11^{0} \times 11^{0}$
Bedroom 2 $11^{2} \times 11^{0}$
LIN.
COATS
Foyer
FPL.
Great Room $17^{0} \times 15^{10}$
16'-0" HIGH CLG.
SERVING BAR
PLANT SHELF ABOVE
WET BAR
RADIUS WDW.
Vaulted Breakfast
FRENCH DOOR
PLANT SHELF ABOVE
REF.
RANGE
Kitchen
D.W.
PAN.
Laun.
D. W.
Dining Room $11^{3} \times 10^{7}$
Storage
Garage $19^{5} \times 19^{8}$
© Frank Betz Associates, Inc.
GARAGE LOCATION W/ BASEMENT

MAIN FLOOR

WIDTH 50'-0"
DEPTH 52'-6"

WET BAR
W. D.
Laund.
STORAGE
Dining Room $11^{3} \times 10^{7}$
Storage
STAIRS DN.
Garage $19^{5} \times 19^{8}$

BASEMENT STAIR LOCATION OPTION

PLAN NO. 10521

Elegant Design Offers Special Living

Price Code: C

- This plan features:
- — Four bedrooms
- — Two and one half baths
- A Balcony overlooking the two-story Foyer
- A Master Suite including a five-piece Bath, an oversized walk-in closet, and a separate linen closet
- A Kitchen including a Breakfast Nook, Pantry and desk
- A formal Living Room with access to a rear Deck
- This home is designed with a basement foundation

FIRST FLOOR — 1,191 SQ. FT.
SECOND FLOOR — 699 SQ. FT.
BASEMENT — 1,191 SQ. FT.
GARAGE — 454 SQ. FT.

Total living area:
1,890 sq. ft.

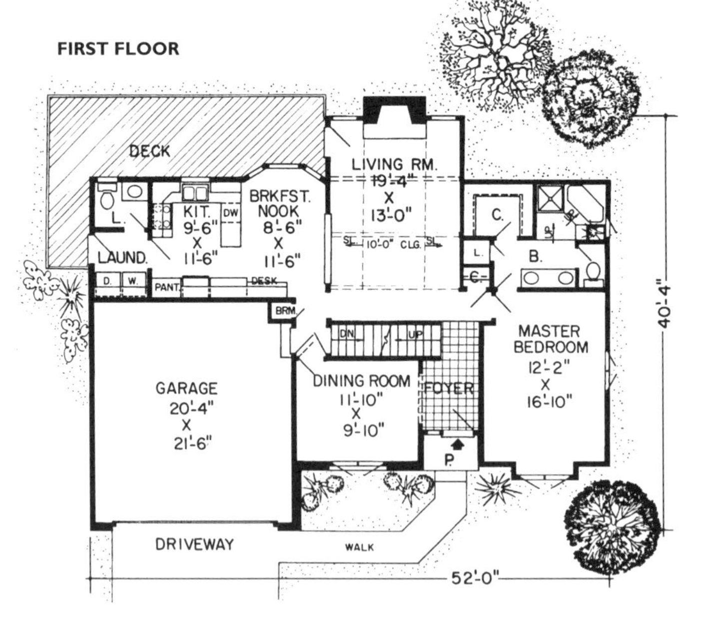
FIRST FLOOR
DECK
LIVING RM.
19'-4"
X
13'-0"
10'-0" CLG.
KIT.
9'-6"
X
11'-6"
DW
BRKFST.
NOOK
8'-6"
X
11'-6"
L.
LAUND.
D.
W.
PANT.
DESK
BRM.
C.
L.
B.
C.
MASTER
BEDROOM
12'-2"
X
16'-10"
DN
UP
GARAGE
20'-4"
X
21'-6"
DINING ROOM
11'-10"
X
9'-10"
FOYER
P.
40'-4"
DRIVEWAY
WALK
52'-0"

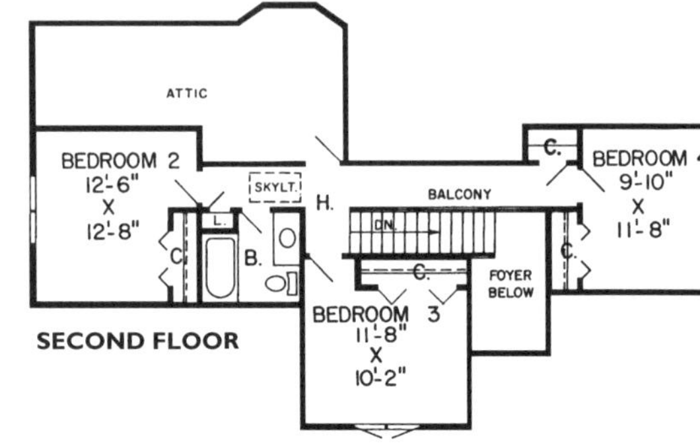
ATTIC
BEDROOM 2
12'-6"
X
12'-8"
SKYLT.
H.
BALCONY
C.
BEDROOM 4
9'-10"
X
11'-8"
C.
L.
B.
DN
C.
FOYER
BELOW
C.
BEDROOM 3
11'-8"
X
10'-2"
SECOND FLOOR

PLAN NO. 98357

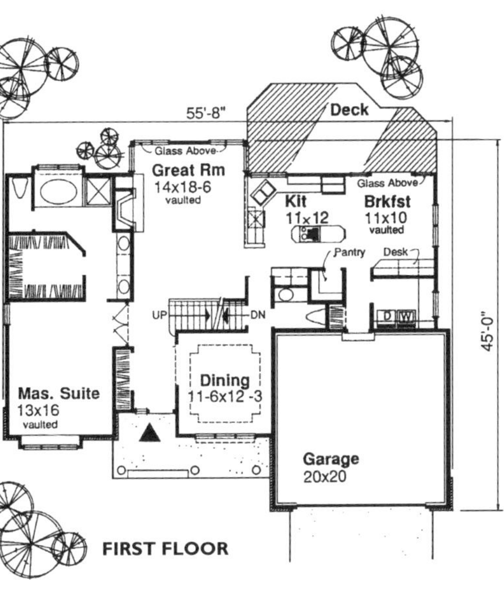

55'-8"
Deck
Glass Above
Great Rm
14x18-6
vaulted
Glass Above
Kit
11x12
Brkfst
11x10
vaulted
Pantry
Desk
UP
DN
45'-0"
Mas. Suite
13x16
vaulted
Dining
11-6x12-3
Garage
20x20
FIRST FLOOR

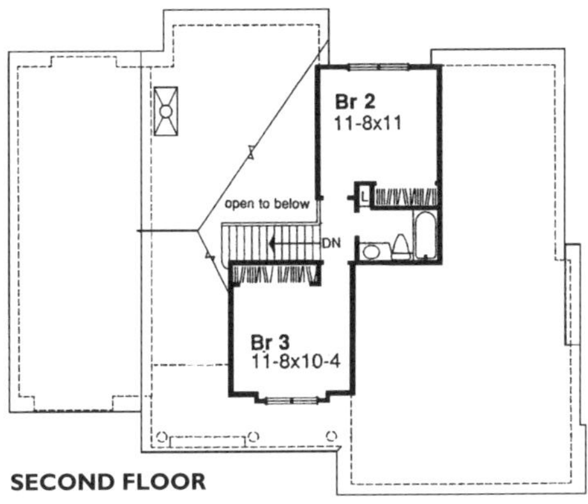

Br 2
11-8x11
open to below
DN
Br 3
11-8x10-4
SECOND FLOOR

First Floor Master Suite

Price Code: C

- This plan features:
  - — Three bedrooms
  - — Two full and one half baths
- The front Porch and dormer add to the Country appeal of this home
- The elegant Dining Room is topped by a decorative ceiling
- The Kitchen/Breakfast Room includes a cooktop island, a double corner sink, a walk-in Pantry, a built-in desk and a vaulted ceiling
- This home is designed with a basement foundation

FIRST FLOOR — 1,490 SQ. FT.
SECOND FLOIOR — 436 SQ. FT.
BASEMENT — 1,490 SQ. FT.
GARAGE — 400 SQ. FT.

Total living area:
1,926 sq. ft.

PLAN NO. 98456

High Ceilings Add Volume

Price Code: B

- This plan features:
- — Three bedrooms
- — Two full baths
- A covered entry gives way to a 14-foot high ceiling in the Foyer
- An arched opening greets you in the Great Room that also has a vaulted ceiling and a fireplace
- The Dining Room is brightened by triple windows with transoms above
- This home is designed with basement, slab and crawlspace foundation options

MAIN FLOOR — 1,715 SQ. FT.
BASEMENT — 1,715 SQ. FT.
GARAGE — 450 SQ. FT.

Total living area:
1,715 sq. ft.

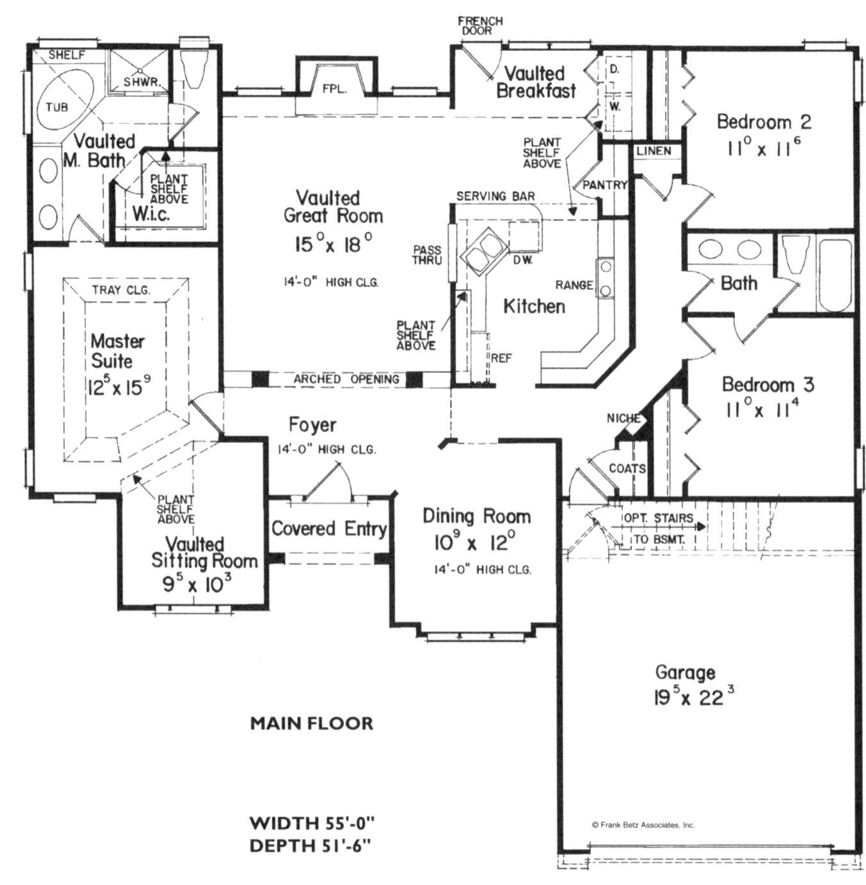
FRENCH DOOR
SHELF
SHWR.
TUB
Vaulted M. Bath
PLANT SHELF ABOVE
W.i.c.
FPL.
Vaulted Breakfast
D.
W.
Bedroom 2
11^0 x 11^6
LINEN
PANTRY
PLANT SHELF ABOVE
SERVING BAR
Vaulted Great Room
15^0 x 18^0
14'-0" HIGH CLG.
PASS THRU
D.W.
RANGE
Kitchen
PLANT SHELF ABOVE
REF
TRAY CLG.
Master Suite
12^5 x 15^9
ARCHED OPENING
Bath
Bedroom 3
11^0 x 11^4
NICHE
Foyer
14'-0" HIGH CLG.
COATS
PLANT SHELF ABOVE
Vaulted Sitting Room
9^5 x 10^3
Covered Entry
Dining Room
10^9 x 12^0
14'-0" HIGH CLG.
OPT. STAIRS TO BSMT.
Garage
19^5 x 22^3
MAIN FLOOR
WIDTH 55'-0"
DEPTH 51'-6"
© Frank Betz Associates, Inc.

·xterior Elevations

:aled drawings of the front, ar, sides of the home. ıformation pertaining to the xterior finish materials, roof tches and exterior height mensions.

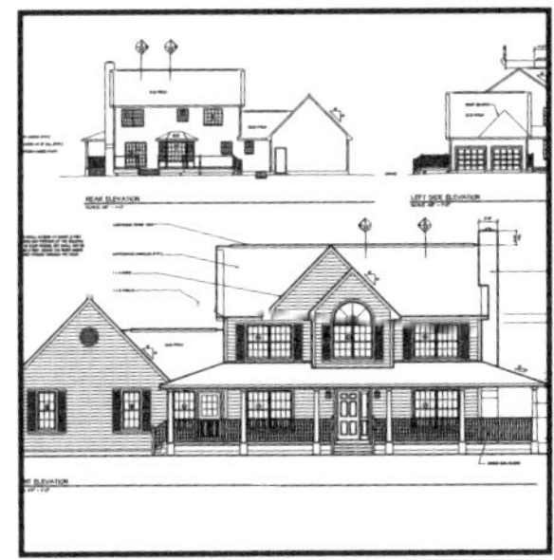

·abinet Plans

hese plans, or in some cases evations, will detail the lay-ıt of the kitchen and bath-om cabinets at a larger scale. vailable for most plans.

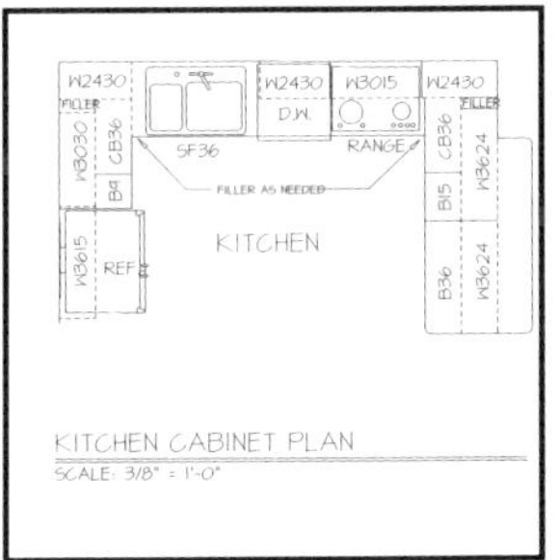
W2430
W2430
W3015
W2430
SF36
DW
RANGE
KITCHEN
KITCHEN CABINET PLAN
SCALE: 3/8" = 1'-0"

·ypical Wall Section

his section will address ısulation, roof components ıd interior and exterior wall nishes. Your plans will be esigned with either 2x4 or x6 exterior walls, but most ofessional contractors can ısily adapt the plans to the all thickness you require.

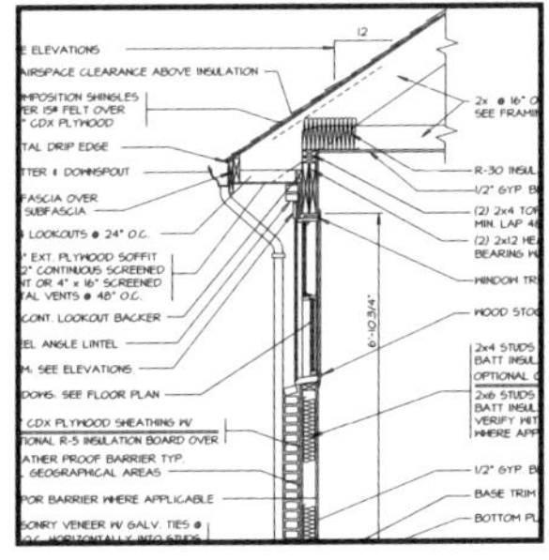

·ireplace Details

the home you have chosen ıcludes a fireplace, the fire-lace detail will show typical ethods to construct the fire-ox, hearth and flue chase for ıasonry units, or a wood ame chase for a zero-clear-ıce unit. Available for most lans.

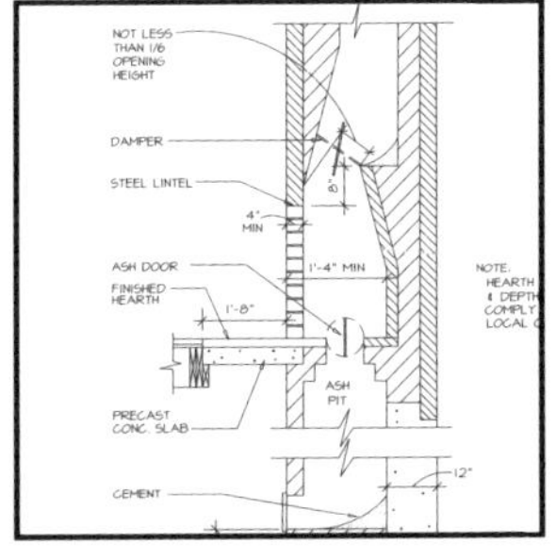

·oundation Plan

hese plans will accurately imension the footprint of our home including load earing points and beam lacement if applicable. The oundation style will vary from lan to plan.

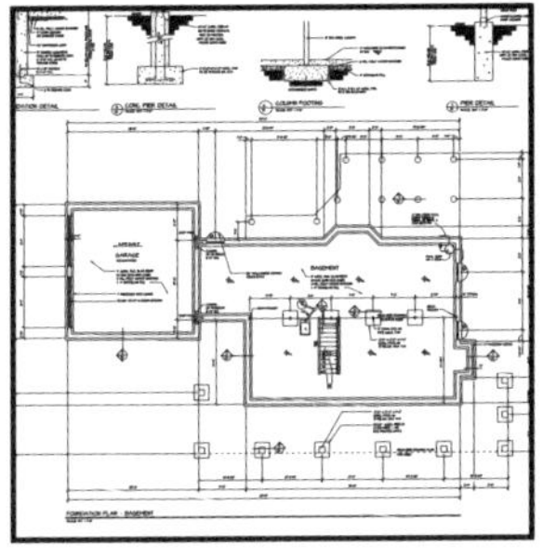

Roof Plan

The information necessary to construct the roof will be included with your home plans. Some plans will reference roof trusses, while many others contain schematic framing plans. These framing plans will indicate the lumber sizes necessary for the rafters and ridgeboards based on the designated roof loads.

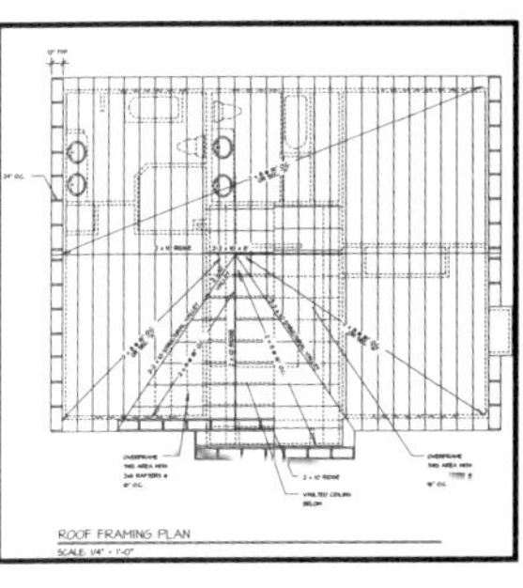

Typical Cross-Section

A cut-away cross-section through the entire home shows your building contractor the exact correlation of construction components at all levels of the house. It will help to clarify the load bearing points from the roof all the way down to the basement. Available for most plans.

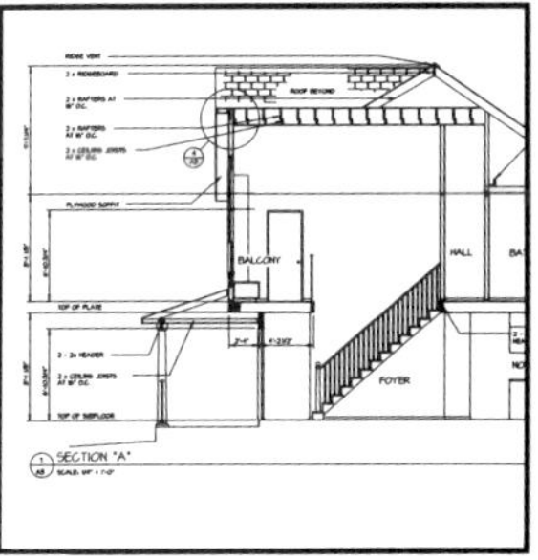

Detailed Floor Plans

The floor plans of your home accurately dimension the positioning of all walls, doors, windows, stairs and permanent fixtures. They will show you the relationship and dimensions of rooms, closets and traffic patterns. The schematic of the electrical layout may be included in the plan.

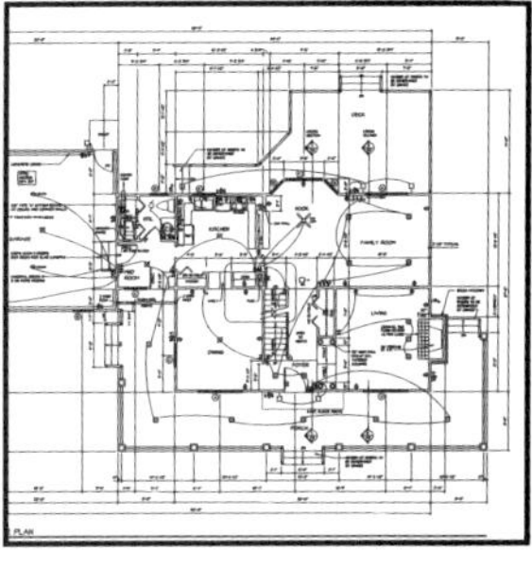

Stair Details

If stairs are an element of the design you have chosen, the plans will show the necessary information to build these, either through a stair cross-section or on the floor plans.

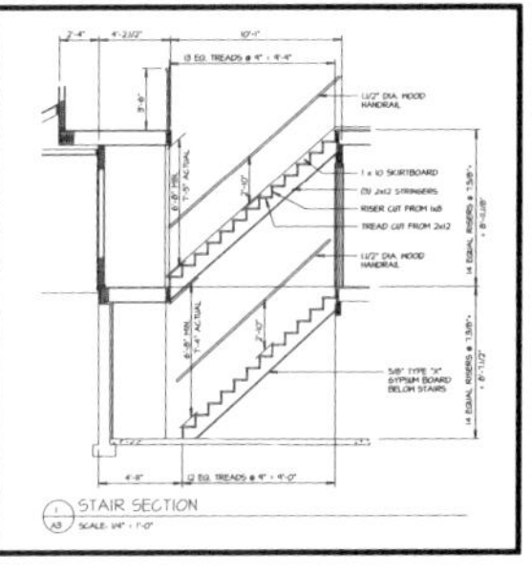
STAIR SECTION

Garlinghouse Options & Extras

Reversed Plans Can Make Your Dream Home Just Right!

You could have exactly the home you want by flipping it end-for-end. Simply order your plans "reversed." We'll send you one full set of mirror-image plans (with the writing backwards) as a master guide for you and your builder.

The remaining sets of your order will come as shown in this book so the dimensions and specifications are easily read on the job site...but most plans in our collection come stamped "reversed" so there is no confusion.

We can only send reversed plans with multiple-set orders. There is a $50 charge for this service.

Some plans in our collection are available in Right Reading Reverse. Right Reading Reverse plans will show your home in reverse, with the writing on the plan being readable. This easy-to-read format will save you valuable time and money. Please contact our Customer Service Department to check for Right Reading Reverse availability. There is a $135 charge for Right Reading Reverse. **RRR**

Remember To Order Your Materials List

Available at a modest additional charge, the Materials l gives the quantity, dimensions, and specifications for the major materials needed to build your home. You will get faster, more accurate bids from your contractors and building suppliers — and avoid paying for unused materials and waste. Materials Lists are available for all home plans except as otherwise indicated, but can only be ordered with a set of home plans. Due to differences in regional requirements and homeowner or builder preferences... electrical, plumbing and heating/air conditioning equipment specifications are not designed specifically for each plan. **ML**

What Garlinghouse Offers

Home Plan Blueprint Package

By purchasing a multiple set package of blueprints or a vellum from Garlinghouse, you not only receive the physical blueprint documents necessary for construction, but you are also granted a license to build one, and only one, home. You can also make simple modifications, including minor non-structural changes and material substitutions to our design, as long as these changes are made directly on the blueprints purchased from Garlinghouse and no additional copies are made.

Home Plan Vellums

By purchasing vellums for one of our home plans, you receive the same construction drawings found in the blueprints, but printed on vellum paper. Vellums can be erased and are perfect for making design changes. They are also semi-transparent making them easy to duplicate. But most importantly, the purchase of home plan vellums comes with a broader license that allows you to make changes to the design (ie, create a hand drawn or CAD derivative work), to make copies of the plan and to build one home from the plan.

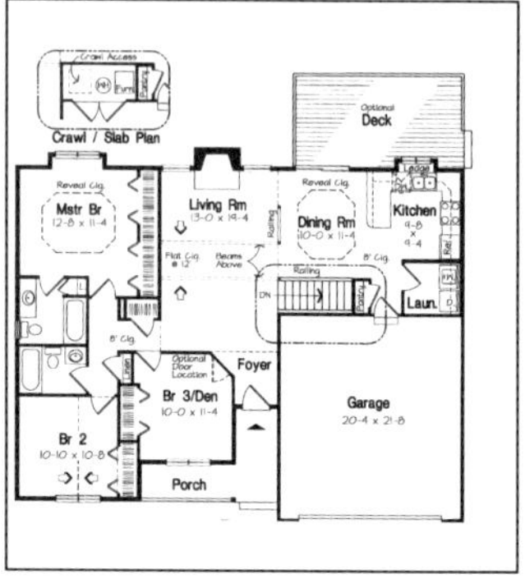
Crawl / Slab Plan
Optional Deck
Mstr Br
Living Rm
Dining Rm
Kitchen
Laun.
Foyer
Br 3/Den
Br 2
Porch
Garage

License To Build Additional Homes

With the purchase of a blueprint package or vellums you automatically receive a license to build one home and only one home, respectively. If you want to build more homes than you are licensed to build through your purchase of a plan, then additional licenses may be purchased at reasonable costs from Garlinghouse. Inquire for more information.

Modify Your Favorite Design, Made Easy

ODIFICATION PRICING GUIDE

'EGORIES	ESTIMATED
ST	
:hen Layout	
1 and Elevation	$175.00
hroom Layout	
1 and Elevation	$175.00
place Plan and Details	$200.00
rior Elevation	$125.00
erior Elevation	
:erial Change	$140.00
erior Elevation	
l Brick or Stone	$400.00
erior Elevation	
e Change	$450.00
1 Bearing Walls(interior)	$200.00
ring and/or	
erior Walls	$325.00
l Framing Change	
to 2x6 or 2x6 to 2x4	$240.00
l/Reduce Living Space	
are Footage	Quote Required
v Materials List	Quote Required
nge Trusses to Rafters	
Change Roof Pitch	$300.00
ming Plan Changes	$325.00
age Changes	$325.00
l a Foundation Option	$300.00
ndation Changes	$250.00
nt Reading Plan Reverse	$575.00
hitects Seal (available for most states)	$300.00
rgy Certificate	$150.00
it and Ventilation Schedule	$150.00

uestions?

our customer service department
.860.659.5667

#1 Modifying Your Garlinghouse Home Plan

Simple modifications to your dream home, including minor non-structural changes and material substitutions, can be made between you and your builder by marking the changes directly on your blueprints. However, if you are considering making significant changes to your chosen design, we recommend that you use the services of The Garlinghouse Design Staff. We will help take your ideas and turn them into a reality, just the way you want. Here's our procedure!

When you place your Vellum order, you may also request a free Garlinghouse Modification Kit. In this kit, you will receive a red marking pencil, furniture cut-out sheet, ruler, a self addressed mailing label and a form for specifying any additional notes or drawings that will help us understand your design ideas. Mark your desired changes directly on the Vellum drawings. NOTE: Please use only a ***red pencil*** to mark your desired changes on the Vellum. Then, return the redlined Vellum set in the original box to us.

Important: Please roll the Vellums for shipping, ***do not fold***.

We also offer modification estimates. We will provide you with an estimate to draft your changes based on your specific modifications before you purchase the vellums, for a $50 fee. After you receive your estimate, if you decide to have us do the changes, the $50 estimate fee will be deducted from the cost of your modifications. If, however, you choose to use a different service, the $50 estimate fee is non-refundable. (Note: Personal checks cannot be accepted for the estimate.)

Within 5 days of receipt of your plans, you will be contacted by a member of the design staff with an estimate for the design services to draw those changes. A 50% deposit is required before we begin making the actual modifications to your plans.

Once the design changes have been completed to your vellum plan, a representative will call to inform you that your modified Vellum plan is complete and will be shipped as soon as the final payment has been made. For additional information call us at 1-860-659-5667. Please refer to the Modification Pricing Guide for estimated modification costs.

#2 Reproducible Vellums for Local Modification Ease

If you decide not to use Garlinghouse for your modifications, we recommend that you follow our same procedure of purchasing Vellums. You then have the option of using the services of the original designer of the plan, a local professional designer, or architect to make the modifications.

With a Vellum copy of our plans, a design professional can alter the drawings just the way you want, then you can print as many copies of the modified plans as you need to build your house. And, since you have already started with our complete detailed plans, the cost of those expensive professional services will be significantly less than starting from scratch. Refer to the price schedule for Vellum costs.

gnoring Copyright Laws Can Be A $100,000 Mistake

ent changes in the US Copyright Laws allow for statutory penalties of up to $100,000 per incident for copyright infringement olving any of the copyrighted plans found in this publication. The law can be confusing. So, for your own protection, take the to understand what you can and cannot do when it comes to home plans.

What You Can't Do!

Cannot Duplicate Home Plans

chasing a set of blueprints and making additional sets by reproducing the original is illegal. If you need multiple sets of a partic- home plan, you must purchase them.

Cannot Copy Any Part of a Home Plan to Create Another

ating your own plan by copying even part of a home design found in this publication is called "creating a derivative work" and egal unless you have permission to do so.

Cannot Build a Home Without a License

must have specific permission or license to build a home from a copyrighted design, even if the finished home has been nged from the original plan. It is illegal to build one of the homes found in this publication without a license.

"How to obtain a construction cost calculation based on labor rates and building material costs in your Zip Code area!"

What will your dream home cost? ZIP QUOTE has the answer!

Why? Do you wish you could quickly find out the building cost for your new home without waiting for a contractor to compile hundreds of bids? Would you like to have a benchmark to compare your contractor(s) bids against? Well, Now You Can!, with Zip-Quote Home Cost Calculator. Zip-Quote is only available for zip code areas within the United States.

How? Our Zip-Quote Home Cost Calculator will enable you to obtain the calculated building cost to construct your new home, based on labor rates and building material costs within your zip code area without the normal delays or hassles usually associated with the bidding process. Zip-Quote can be purchased in two separate formats, an itemized or a bottom line format.

"How does Zip-Quote actually work?" When you call to order, you must choose from the options available for your specific home, in order for us to process your order. Once we receive your Zip-Quote order, we process your specific home plan building materials list through our Home Cost Calculator which contains up-to-date rates for all residential labor trades and building material costs in your zip code area. "The result?" A calculated cost to build your dream home in your zip code area. This calculation will help you (as a consumer or a builder) evaluate your building budget.

All database information for our calculations is furnished by Marshall & Swift L.P. For over 60 years, Marshall & Swift L.P. has been a leading provider of cost data to professionals in all aspects of the construction and remodeling industries.

Option 1- The **Itemized Zip-Quote** is a detailed building material list. Each building material list line item will separately state the labor cost, material cost and equipment cost (if applicable) for the use of that building material in the construction process. This building materials list will be summarized by the individual building categories and will have additional columns where you can enter data from your contractor's estimates for a cost comparison between the different suppliers and contractors who will actually quote you their products and services.

Option 2- The **Bottom Line Zip-Quote** is a one line summarized total cost for the home plan of your choice. This cost calculation is also based on the labor cost, material cost and equipment cost (if applicable) within your local zip code area. Bottom Line Zip-Quote is available for most plans. Please call for availability.

Cost The price of your Itemized Zip-Quote is based upon the pricing schedule of the plan you have selected, in addition to the price of the materials list. Please refer to the pricing schedule on our order form. The price of your initi Bottom Line Zip-Quote is $29.95. Each additional Bottom Line Zip-Quote ordered in conjunction with the initial ord is only $14.95. Bottom Line Zip-Quote may be purchased separately and does NOT have to be purchased in conjunction with a home plan order.

FYI An Itemized Zip-Quote Home Cost Calculation can ONLY be purchased in conjunction with a Home Plan orde The Itemized Zip-Quote can not be purchased separately. I you find within 60 days of your order date that you will be unable to build this home, you may then exchange the plar and the materials list towards the price of a new set of plans (see order info pages for plan exchange policy). The Itemiz Zip-Quote and the Bottom Line Zip-Quote are NOT return able. The price of the initial Bottom Line Zip-Quote order can be credited towards the purchase of an Itemized Zip-Quote order, only if available. Additional Bottom Line Zip Quote orders, within the same order can not be credited. Please call our Customer Service Department for more info mation.

An Itemized Zip-Quote is available for plans where you see this symbol. ZIP

A Bottom-line Zip-Quote is available for all plans under 4,000 sq. ft. or where you see this symbol. BL

Please call for current availability.

Some More Information The Itemized and Bottor Line Zip-Quotes give you approximated costs for constructi the particular house in your area. These costs are not exac and are only intended to be used as a preliminary estimate help determine the affordability of a new home and/or as a guide to evaluate the general competitiveness of actual pric quotes obtained through local suppliers and contractors. However, Zip-Quote cost figures should never be relied upo as the only source of information in either case. **Land, landscaping, sewer systems, site work, contractor overhead and profit and other expen es are not included in our building cost figures. Excluding land and landscaping, you may incur an additional 20% to 40% in cos from the original estimate.** Garlinghouse and Marshall & Swift L.P. can not guarantee any level of data accuracy or correctness in a Zip-Quote and disclaim all liab ity for loss with respect to the same, in excess of the origin purchase price of the Zip-Quote product. All Zip-Quote ca culations are based upon the actual blueprints and do not reflect any differences or options that may be shown on th published house renderings, floor plans or photographs.

the arlinghouse company

BEST PLAN VALUE IN THE INDUSTRY!

Order Code No. **H2AF5**

rder Form

Plan prices guaranteed until 4/1/03 After this date call for updated pricing

__________ foundation

_ set(s) of blueprints for plan #________	$_____
_ Vellum & Modification kit for plan #________	$_____
_ Additional set(s) @ $50 each for plan #________	$_____
_ Mirror Image Reverse @ $50 each	$_____
_ Right Reading Reverse @ $135 each	$_____
_ Materials list for plan #________	$_____
_ Detail Plans @ $19.95 each	
❑ Construction ❑ Plumbing ❑ Electrical	$_____
_ Bottom line ZIP Quote@$29.95 for plan #________	$_____
_ Additional Bottom Line Zip Quote	
@ $14.95 for plan(s) #________	$_____
Zip Code where building ________	
_ Itemized ZIP Quote for plan(s) #________	$_____
Shipping	$_____
Subtotal	$_____
Sales Tax (CT residents add 6% sales tax)	$_____
TOTAL AMOUNT ENCLOSED	**$_____**

Send your check, money order or credit card information to:
(No C.O.D.'s Please)

Please submit all United States & Other Nations orders to:
Garlinghouse Company
174 Oakwood Drive
Glastonbury, CT. 06033
CALL: (800) 235-5700 FAX: (860) 659-5692

Please Submit all Canadian plan orders to:
Garlinghouse Company
102 Ellis Street
Penticton, BC V2A 4L5
CALL: (800) 361-7526 FAX: (250) 493-7526

DDRESS INFORMATION:

ME: ____________________

REET: ____________________

Y: ____________________

TE: __________ ***ZIP:*** __________

TIME PHONE: ____________________

AIL ADDRESS: ____________________

Credit Card Information

arge To: ❑ Visa ❑ Mastercard

rd # |_|_|_|_|_|_|_|_|_|_|_|_|_|_|_|_|

nature ____________________ Exp. ____/____

ment must be made in U.S. funds. Foreign Mail Orders: Certified bank checks in U.S. funds only

MS OF SALE FOR HOME PLANS: *All home plans sold through this publication are copyright cted. Reproduction of these home plans, either in whole or in part, including any direct copying and/or aration of derivative works thereof, for any reason without the prior written permission of Garlinghouse, is strictly prohibited. The purchase of a set of home plans in no way transfers any copyright or other rship interest in it to the buyer except for a limited license to use that set of home plans for the truction of one, and only one, dwelling unit. The purchase of additional sets of that home plan at a ced price from the original set or as a part of a multiple set package does not entitle the buyer with a se to construct more than one dwelling unit.*

Privacy Statement (please read)

Dear Valued Garlinghouse Customer,

Your privacy is extremely important to us. We'd like to take a little of your time to explain our privacy policy.

As a service to you, we would like to provide your name to companies such as the following:

- Building material manufacturers that we are affiliated with. Who would like to keep you current with their product line and specials.
- Building material retailers who would like to offer you competitive prices to help you save money.
- Financing companies who would like to offer you competitive mortgage rates.

In addition, as our valued customer, we would like to send you newsletters to assist your building experience. *We* would appreciate your feedback with a customer service survey to improve our operations.

You have total control over the use of your contact information. You can let us know exactly how you want to be contacted. Please check all boxes that apply. Thank you.

☐ Don't mail
☐ Don't call
☐ Don't email
☐ Only send Garlinghouse newsletters and customer service surveys

In closing, Garlinghouse is committed to providing superior customer service and protection of your privacy. We thank you for your time and consideration.

Sincerely,

James D. McNair III
CEO

BEFORE ORDERING PLEASE READ ALL ORDERING INFORMATION

For Our **USA** Customers:
Order Toll Free — 1-800-235-5700
Monday-Friday 8:00 a.m. to 8:00 p.m. Eastern Time
or FAX your Credit Card order to 1-860-659-5692
All foreign residents call 1-860-659-5667

For Our **Canadian** Customers:
Order Toll Free — 1-800-361-7526
Monday-Friday 8:00 a.m. to 5:00 p.m. Pacific Time
or FAX your Credit Card order to 1-250-493-7526
Customer Service: 1-250-493-0942

Please have ready: 1. Your credit card number 2. The plan number 3. The order code number ⇨ **H2AF5**

Garlinghouse 2002 Blueprint Price Code Schedule

	1 Set	4 Sets	8 Sets	Vellums	ML	Itemized ZIP Quote
A	$345	$385	$435	$525	$60	$50
B	$375	$415	$465	$555	$60	$50
C	$410	$450	$500	$590	$60	$50
D	$450	$490	$540	$630	$60	$50
E	$495	$535	$585	$675	$70	$60
F	$545	$585	$635	$725	$70	$60
G	$595	$635	$685	$775	$70	$60
H	$640	$680	$730	$820	$70	$60
I	$685	$725	$775	$865	$80	$70
J	$725	$765	$815	$905	$80	$70
K	$765	$805	$855	$945	$80	$70
L	$800	$840	$890	$980	$80	$70

Shipping — (Plans 1-59999)	1-3 Sets	4-6 Sets	7+ & Vellum
Standard Delivery (UPS 2-Day)	$25.00	$30.00	$35.00
Overnight Delivery	$35.00	$40.00	$45.00

Shipping — (Plans 60000-99999)	1-3 Sets	4-6 Sets	7+ & Vellum
Ground Delivery (7-10 Days)	$15.00	$20.00	$25.00
Express Delivery (3-5 Days)	$20.00	$25.00	$30.00

International Shipping & Handling	1-3 Sets	4-6 Sets	7+ & Vellum
Regular Delivery Canada (7-10 Days)	$25.00	$30.00	$35.00
Express Delivery Canada (5-6 Days)	$40.00	$45.00	$50.00
Overseas Delivery Airmail (2-3 Weeks)	$50.00	$60.00	$65.00

Additional sets with original order $50

IMPORTANT INFORMATION TO READ BEFORE YOU PLACE YOUR ORDER

How Many Sets Of Plans Will You Need?

The Standard 8-Set Construction Package

*Our experience shows that you'll speed every step of construction and avoid costly building errors by ordering enough sets to go around. Each tradesperson wants a set — the general contractor and all subcontractors; foundation, electrical, plumbing, heating/air conditioning and framers. Don't forget your lending institution, building department and, of course, a set for yourself. * Recommended For Construction **

The Minimum 4-Set Construction Package

*If you're comfortable with arduous follow-up, this package can save you a few dollars by giving you the option of passing down plan sets as work progresses. You might have enough copies to go around if work goes exactly as scheduled and no plans are lost or damaged by subcontractors. But for only $60 more, the 8-set package eliminates these worries. *Recommended For Bidding **

The Single Study Set

We offer this set so you can study the blueprints to plan your dream home in detail. They are stamped "study set only-not for construction", and you cannot build a home from them. In pursuant to copyright laws, it is illegal to reproduce any blueprint.

Our Reorder and Exchange Policies:

If you find after your initial purchase that you require additional sets of plans you may purchase them from us at special reorder prices (please call for pricing details) provided that you reorder within 6 months of your original order date. There is a $28 reorder processing fee that is charged on all reorders. For more information on reordering plans please contact our Customer Service Department. Your plans are custom printed especially for you once you place your order. For that reason we cannot accept any returns. If for some reason you find that the plan you have purchased from us does not meet your needs, then you may exchange that plan for any other plan in our collection. We allow you sixty days from your original invoice date to make an exchange. At the time of the exchange you will be charged a processing fee of 20% the total amount of your original order plus the difference in price between the plans (if applicable) plus the cost to ship the new plans to you. Call our Customer Service Department for more information. Please Note: Reproducible vellums can only be exchanged if they are unopened.

Important Shipping Information

Please refer to the shipping charts on the order form for service availability for your specific plan number. Our delivery service must have a street address or Rural Route Box number — never a post office box. (PLEASE NOTE: Supplying a P.O. Box number only will delay the shipping of your order.) Use a work address if one is home during the day. Orders being shipped to APO or FPO must go via First Class Mail. Please include the proper postage.

For our International Customers, only Certified bank checks and money orders are accepted and must be payable in U.S. currency. For speed, we ship international orders Air Parcel Post. Please refer to the chart for the correct shipping cost.

Important Canadian Shipping Information

To our friends in Canada, we have a plan design affiliate in Penticton, BC. This relationship will help you avoid the delays and charges associated with shipments from the United States. Moreover, our affiliate is familiar with the building requirements in your community and country. We prefer payments in U.S. Currency. If you, however, are sending Canadian funds please add 45% to the prices of the plans and shipping fees.

An Important Note About Building Code Requirements:

All plans are drawn to conform to one or more of the industry's major national building standards. However, due to the variety of local building regulations, your plan may need to be modified to comply with local requirements — snow loads, energy loads, seismic zones, etc. Do check them fully and consult your local building officials.

A few states require that all building plans used be drawn by an architect registered in that state. While having your plans reviewed and stamped by such an architect may be prudent, laws requiring non-conforming plans like ours to be completely redrawn forces you to unnecessarily pay very large fees. If your state has such a law, we strongly recommend you contact your state representative to protest.

The rendering, floor plans and technical information contained within this publication are not guaranteed to be totally accurate. Consequently, no information from this publication should be used either as a guide to constructing a home or for estimating the cost of building a home. Complete blueprints must be purchased for such purposes.

Index

Option Key

BL Bottom-line Zip Quote **ML** Materials List Available **ZIP** Itemized Zip Quote **RRR** Right Reading Reverse **DUP** Duplex Plan

TOP SELLING GARAGE PLANS

Save money by Doing-It-Yourself using our Easy-To-Follow plans. Whether you intend to build your own garage or contract it out to a building professional, the Garlinghouse garage plans provide you with everything you need to price out your project and get started. Put our 90+ years of experience to work for you. Order now!!

No. 06016C $86.00

Apartment Garage With One Bedroom

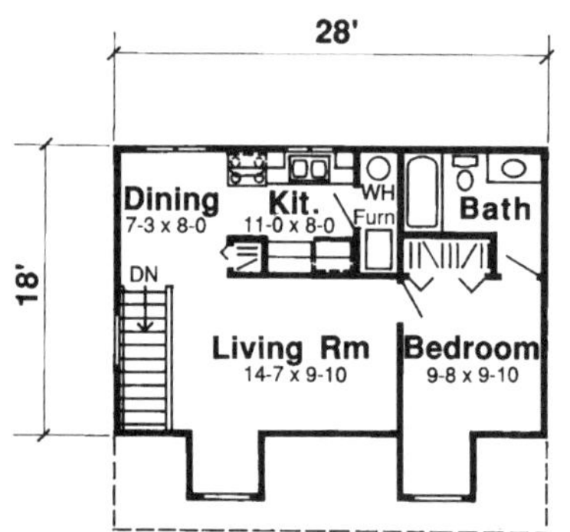

28'
18'
Dining
7-3 x 8-0
Kit.
11-0 x 8-0
WH
Furn
Bath
DN
Living Rm
14-7 x 9-10
Bedroom
9-8 x 9-10

- 24' x 28' Overall Dimensions
- 544 Square Foot Apartment
- 12/12 Gable Roof with Dormers
- Slab or Stem Wall Foundation Options

No. 06015C $86.00

Apartment Garage With Two Bedrooms

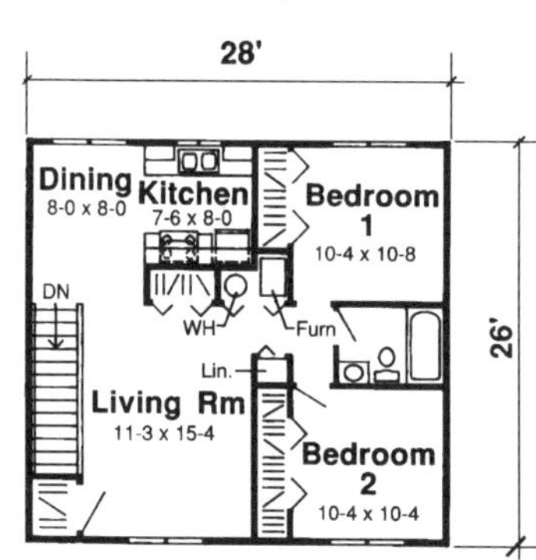

28'
26'
Dining
8-0 x 8-0
Kitchen
7-6 x 8-0
Bedroom
1
10-4 x 10-8
DN
WH
Furn
Lin.
Living Rm
11-3 x 15-4
Bedroom
2
10-4 x 10-4

- 26' x 28' Overall Dimensions
- 728 Square Foot Apartment
- 4/12 Pitch Gable Roof
- Slab or Stem Wall Foundation Options

No. 06012C $54.00

30' Deep Gable &/or Eave Jumbo Garages

- 4/12 Pitch Gable Roof
- Available Options for Extra Tall Walls, Garage & Personnel Doors, Foundation, Window, & Sidings
- Package contains 4 Different Sizes
- 30' x 28' • 30' x 32' • 30' x 36' • 30' x 40'

No. 06013C $68.00

Two-Car Garage With Mudroom/Breezeway

- Attaches to Any House
- 24' x 24' Eave Entry
- Available Options for Utility Room with Bath, Mudroom, Screened-In Breezeway, Roof, Foundation, Garage & Personnel Doors, Window, & Sidings

No. 06001C — $48.00

12', 14' & 16' Wide-Gable 1-Car Garages

- Available Options for Roof, Foundation, Window, Door, & Sidings
- Package contains 8 Different Sizes
- 12' x 20' Mini-Garage • 14' x 22' • 16' x 20' • 16' x 24'
- 14' x 20' • 14' x 24' • 16' x 22' • 16' x 26'

No. 06003C — $48.00

24' Wide-Gable 2-Car Garages

- Available Options for Side Shed, Roof, Foundation, Garage & Personnel Doors, Window, & Sidings
- Package contains 5 Different Sizes
- 24' x 22' • 24' x 24' • 24' x 26'
- 24' x 28' • 24' x 32'

No. 06007C — $60.00

Gable 2-Car Gambrel Roof Garages

- Interior Rear Stairs to Loft Workshop
- Front Loft Cargo Door With Pulley Lift
- Available Options for Foundation, Garage & Personnel Doors, Window, & Sidings
- Package contains 5 Different Sizes
- 22' x 26' • 22' x 28' • 24' x 28' • 24' x 30' • 24' x 32'

No. 06006C — $48.00

22' & 24' Deep Eave 2 & 3-Car Garages

- Can Be Built Stand-Alone or Attached to House
- Available Options for Roof, Foundation, Garage & Personnel Doors, Window, & Sidings
- Package contains 6 Different Sizes
- 22' x 28' • 22' x 32' • 24' x 32'
- 22' x 30' • 24' x 30' • 24' x 36'

No. 06002C — $48.00

20' & 22' Wide-Gable 2-Car Garages

- Available Options for Roof, Foundation, Garage & Personnel Doors, Window, & Sidings
- Package contains 7 Different Sizes
- 20' x 20' • 20' x 24' • 22' x 22' • 22' x 28'
- 20' x 22' • 20' x 28' • 22' x 24'

No. 06008C — $60.00

Eave 2 & 3-Car Clerestory Roof Garages

- Interior Side Stairs to Loft Workshop
- Available Options for Engine Lift, Foundation, Garage & Personnel Doors, Window, & Sidings
- Package contains 4 Different Sizes
- 24' x 26' • 24' x 28' • 24' x 32' • 24' x 36'

Order Code No: **G2AF5**

Garage Order Form

Please send me 3 complete sets of the following GARAGE PLANS:

Item no. & description	Price
Additional Sets	$ ______
(@ $10.00 EACH)	$ ______
Shipping Charges: UPS-$3.75, First Class-$4.50	$ ______
Subtotal:	$ ______
Resident sales tax: KS-6.15%, CT-6% (NOT REQUIRED FOR OTHER STATES)	$ ______
Total Enclosed:	$ ______

My Billing Address is:

Name: ______

Address: ______

City: ______

State: ______ Zip: ______

Daytime Phone No. ( ) ______

My Shipping Address is:

Name: ______

Address: ______

(UPS will not ship to P.O. Boxes)

City: ______

State: ______ Zip: ______

For Faster Service...Charge It!

U.S. & Canada Call
1(800)235-5700

All foreign residents call 1(860)343-5977

MASTERCARD, VISA

Card # ______

Signature ______ Exp. ___/___

If paying by credit card, to avoid delays:
billing address must be as it appears on credit card statement

or FAX us at (860) 343-5984

Here's What You Get

- Three complete sets of drawings for each plan ordered
- Detailed step-by-step instructions with eas to-follow diagrams on how to build your garage (not available with apartment garag
- For each garage style, a variety of size anc garage door configuration options
- Variety of roof styles and/or pitch options f most garages
- Complete materials list
- Choice between three foundation options: Monolithic Slab, Concrete Stem Wall or Concrete Block Stem Wall
- Full framing plans, elevations and cross-se tionals for each garage size and configurat

Build-It-Yourself PROJECT PLAN

Order Information For Garage Plans:
All garage plan orders contain three complete sets drawings with instructions and are priced as listed nex the illustration. Additional sets of plans may be obtair for $10.00 each with your original order. UPS shipping used unless otherwise requested. Please include proper amount for shipping.

the Garlinghouse company

Send your order to:

(With check or money order payable in U.S. funds only)

The Garlinghouse Company
174 Oakwood Drive
Glastonbury, CT 06033

No C.O.D. orders accepted; U.S. funds only. UPS will not ship to Pos Office boxes, FPO boxes, APO boxes, Alaska or Hawaii. Canadian orders must be shipped First Class.

Prices subject to change without notice.